Religion and Culture in Canada / Religion et Culture au Canada

Peter Slater

CCSR

RELIGION AND CULTURE IN CANADA/
RELIGION ET CULTURE AU CANADA

essays by members of the
Canadian Society for the Study of Religion/

recueil d'articles par des membres de
la Société Canadienne pour l'Etude de la Religion

edited by

sous la direction de

Peter Slater

Canadian Cataloguing in Publication Data

Main entry under title:

Religion and culture in Canada = Religion et
    culture au Canada

Text in English or French.
Includes index.
ISBN 0-919812-06-6 pa.

1. Religion and culture - Addresses, essays,
lectures. 2. Canada - Religion - Addresses,
essays, lectures. I. Slater, Peter, 1934-
II. Canadian Society for the Study of Religion.
III. Title: Religion et culture au Canada.

BL65.C8R45   200'.971   C77-001669-3E

Données de catalogage avant publication (Canada)

Vedette principale au titre:

Religion and culture in Canada = Religion et
    culture au Canada

Texte en anglais et en français.
Comprend un index.
ISBN 0-919812-06-6 br.

1. Religion et culture - Discours, essais,
conférences. 2. Canada - Religion - Discours,
essais, conférences. I. Slater, Peter, 1934-
II. Société canadienne pour l'étude de la
religion. III. Titre: Religion et culture au
Canada.

BL65.C8R45   200'.971   C77-001669-3F

©1977 Corporation Canadienne des Sciences Religieuses/
Canadian Corporation for Studies in Religion

ACKNOWLEDGEMENTS

We are pleased to be able to quote in the following
essays: in full from "A Theological Perspective on
Nationalism," by A.R. Gualtieri in the Anglo-Welsh
Review 1973, Vol. 22:49, by permission of the Editor;
from E.L.H. Taylor, "A Secular Revolution in Christian
Disguise," in the Canadian Bar Journal 1958, reprinted
by permission of the Editor of the Canadian Bar Review
and the author; from James W. Ortego, "The Halifax
North End Project," Dalhousie Law Review 3, 1977, by
permission of the Editor; from Death On The Ice copyright (c) 1972 by Cassie Brown and Harold Horwood,
reprinted by permission of Doubleday & Company, Inc.;
from Emile Nelligan, Poésies complètes 1896-1899, texte
établi et annoté par Luc Lacourcière, Montréal, Fides,
coll. du Nénuphar, 1952; un extrait de l'ouvrage La Plus
Grande Aventure du Monde par François Cali paru aux
Editions Arthaud, Paris/Grenoble; from Whatever Became
of Sin? C 1973 by Karl Menninger M.D., reprinted by
permission of Hawthorn Books, Inc.; from Report: Our
Criminal Law (1976), from Criminal Responsibility for
Group Action (1976), from Paul Weiler and John Hogarth,
Studies on Sentencing (1974), from Douglas Schmeiser,
The Native Offender and the Law (1974) and from John
Hogarth, Studies in Diversion (1975), all reprinted by
permission from the Law Reform Commission of Canada;
from l'église dans la cité de demain, Art Sacré #3, 1968,.
by G. Lercaro, by permission of Les Editions du Cerf;
from "Tous les palmiers" by permission of Les Productions
Géant Beaupré; from The Invisible Religion by Thomas
Luckmann, copyright (c) 1967 by MacMillan Publishing
Co., Inc.; from The Watch That Ends The Night (1975) by
Hugh MacLennan, by permission of Charles Scribner's Sons
(U.S. rights) and Macmillan Co. of Canada Ltd. (Canadian
rights); from Glengarry School Days (1902) by Ralph
Connor (pseudonym for Charles W. Gordon), from The
Scalpel, the Sword (1971) by Ted Allan and Sydney Gordon,
from The Pattern of Politics (1970) by Charles Taylor,
from Capital Punishment in Canada (1976) by David Chandler, and from Dying Hard (1975) by Elliot Leyton, all
reprinted by permission of The Canadian Publishers,
McClelland and Stewart Limited, Toronto; from an essay
by G. Wills published 4/3/75 reprinted with permission
from The New York Review of Books, copyright (c) 1975
Nyrev, Inc.; from The Persistence of Religion in Modern
Society, Concilium Volume #81, edited by Andrew Greeley
and Gregory Baum, copyright (c) 1973 by Herder and Herder and Stichting Concilium, used by permission of The

Seabury Press; from A Prophet in Politics (1959) by
Kenneth McNaught, reprinted by permission of the University of Toronto Press; from The Crime of Punishment
(1966) by Karl Menninger, reprinted by permission of the
Viking Press; from Power and Innocence (1972) by Rollo
May, reprinted by permission of W.W. Norton & Co.; from
Islam Observed: Religious Developments in Morocco and
Indonesia (1968) reprinted by permission of Yale University Press; and to reprint the articles (3 & 4) by
Keith Clifford and Louis Rousseau from Studies in
Religion/Sciences Religieuses Volumes 2.4 and 3.2 (1973)
respectively. Finally, the articles (10 and 11) by
Roger Hutchinson and Patrick Kerans were originally
commissioned by the Church Council on Justice and
Corrections/Le Conseil des Eglises pour la Justice et
la Criminologie, and are printed here for the first
time by arrangement with the Council (the Rev. David
McCord, Executive Director, Cowansville, Québec).

* See the note on page 219 for reference to E.L.H.
  Taylor's more recent work on this subject.

TABLE OF CONTENTS

Page

INTRODUCTION

by

Peter Slater

The authors of the essays collected in this volume
are, when we remember to pay our annual dues, members
of the Canadian Society for the Study of Religion/la
société canadienne pour l'étude de la religion. This
is the major learned society in Canada for university
teachers of religion, especially in departments of
Religious Studies as contrasted with theological
seminaries. There are more specialized societies,
particularly for biblical and oriental studies, and
those who belong to the CSSR/SCER typically represent
a more broadly based, multidisciplinary constituency.
Accordingly in this volume the reader will find a
number of essays whose disciplinary milieu is primarily
historical, others which are anthropological or sociological, others which are more ethical-philosophical
and still others which cross boundaries into literary
criticism. What gives to all a common point of view
is the fact that university departments are avowedly
secular and non-denominational. The other common
point of reference is that each essay in one way or
another applies the particular academic methods of the
author to some aspect of Canadian life or history. As
a result what this volume represents is a first report
on how we see ourselves when we turn our professional
attention to various facets of our own cultural
heritage. We are conscious as we do so that while our
assumptions and interests overlap they do not form a
single pattern or build up towards a single central
thesis or point of view. No doubt for this reason some
essays will have more appeal to particular readers than
others. Our hope is that by providing a reasonable
cross-section of religious studies approaches we shall
have included something for almost everyone. The
purpose of this introduction is to provide a brief
guide to the orientation of each contribution so that
readers may turn first to those essays which seem
likely to be of most interest to them.

Because religion is a subject without a single
disciplinary core and without a clearly definable
object for investigation, what the term 'religion'
means varies according to the emphasis of each author.
Some have given definitions as they go but readers are

best advised to see how the term is used in each
context as it comes up. For instance, with reference
to early Canadian history the term may denote primarily
church-related topics and concerns. By contrast, the
religious connotations of Hockey Night in Canada may
best be appreciated from a perspective which owes more
to cultural anthropology than to theology. In between
are studies which espouse the pivotal moral values of
particular traditions and point out their implications
for our critical appraisals of current social issues.
Here normative as well as descriptive tasks are undertaken, but in a way which does justice to both the
need for intelligent commitment on the part of
concerned individuals and for informed analysis in an
academic context. This return to normative questions
is, I think, one sign of the increasing impact of the
social sciences on the study of religion. For as I
read them the best of contemporary social scientists
are no longer dominated by the myth of "value-freedom"
in their investigations. In any case an eye for underlying values and interest in the contrasting symbol
systems which we use in articulating meaning in life
are characteristic concerns of studies in religion and
culture.

   En français le mot 'culture' indique peut-être une
espéce de dilettantisme. Mais en anglais l'expression
'religion et culture' évoque la dialectique caractéristique de la pensée occidentale entre l'immanence et la
transcendance. Notre tradition est pluraliste, grecque
et hébraïque, latine et indigène. Il n'y a pas de
perspective autoritaire pour juger des affaires
humaines. Au Canada l'Eglise catholique a exercé
longtemps cette autorité parmi les Québecois mais cela
est en train de changer. Au contraire, les sectes
protestantes ont toujours distingué entre les pouvoirs
temporels et la parole divine. Aujourd'hui pour beaucoup de gens l'Eglise n'est plus qu'une secte parmi
d'autres. L'interaction entre les idées de provenances
diverses ébranle tous les mondes fermés. C'est alors
que nous parlons de 'religion et culture' pour
représenter la juxtaposition du spirituel et du
temporel.

   'Religion and culture' is a code phrase among
students of western traditions for a range of interests
in the religious dimensions of ordinary practices and
in the extraordinary practices of religious denomina-

tions. On the theoretical side it includes what used
to be called apologetics -- a laying of theological
insights alongside secular philosophies. In history
it comprehends inquiries into cultural influences on
ecclesiastical developments. In literary studies it
signals less concern with infighting among old-new
critics and more attention to symbolic depths and
ultimate transformations. In short, it is a useful
umbrella phrase for referring to ways of studying
religion which leave aside questions of revelation and
doctrinal purity and concentrate instead on the
inevitable interpenetration in thought and practice
between weekday and week-end patterns of action and
concern.[1] In analyses of these patterns social anthropologists tend to focus on general culture whereas
"religiologists" focus on whatever seems sacred or of
highest value in the thought of those who set the pace
or seem to speak for their generation. Unfortunately,
in the highly specialized and compartmentalized milieu
of our universities the two groups of scholars do not
always keep in touch. Consequently, those who are
abreast of scholarship in social anthropology tend to
use outdated conceptual schemes for religious thought
and vice versa. The writers of the essays in this
volume do not claim to be particularly original in
their conceptions of Canadian culture. But we do
have some claim to expertise in the sifting of what is
and is not religiously significant in that cultural
complex.

Our collection begins with three essays whose disciplinary thrust is historical. The first is by the
"dean" of Canadian church historians, John Webster
Grant. His discussion of Canadian character in relation to questions of national unity is as topical today
as it was when he presented it as a public lecture in
1973. He sees the role of traditional churches as
formative for critical appraisals of religion in Canada.
Where Canada used to be regarded by politicians as a
colony to be exploited it was regarded by churchmen as
a challenge to missionary activity. The breakdown of
old patterns of expectation in the course of our history is delineated by Keith Clifford particularly with
reference to Christian reactions to successive waves of
immigration. His essay exemplifies the way in which in
the context of religious studies religious historians
look beyond the confines of particular denominational
prejudices to wider issues concerning the nature of man

in the specific setting of our part of North America.
In the third essay Louis Rousseau takes up parallel
developments in the French vision of Québec and
environs as a model Catholic colony. In the process he
draws on insights from structural analyses of myth in a
way that is only just beginning to command attention
among writers in English.

The ideological cast of early histories of Canada is
illustrated by Georges Tissot's studies of Christian
missionary attitudes to Amerindians. His paper
concerning an Iroquois creation myth reflects his
training in cultural anthropology and sensitivity to
values in a pluralistic setting. Cultural anthropology
also guides the analysis of a myth from the Yukon set
forth by Robert Florida, who illustrates for us the
contemporary approach to such data advocated by Claude
Lévi-Strauss.

The next two essays turn our attention to English-
speaking Catholics, particularly in the Maritimes, and
to problems specifically in social ethics. John Williams
confronts us with some hard data from the history of
industrial accidents in Newfoundland and the consequences
of a soul-centred ethic that neglects the body. Gregory
Baum recounts for us the more activist responses of
Catholics in Cape Breton who saw in the Co-operative
Movement a viable alternative to both capitalism and
communism. Following these Monique Dumais returns us to
Québec, but now with the feminist movement and more
contemporary sets of facts and values in mind.

The two major papers by Roger Hutchinson and Patrick
Kerans come from a series commissioned by the Church
Council on Justice and Corrections/le Conseil des
Eglises pour le Justice et la Criminologie, which
serves eleven major denominations in seeking a more
effective ministry in matters of legal and social
concern. Hutchinson considers several ways of viewing
the interplay of factual and symbolic issues raised in
the debate on capital punishment while Kerans seeks to
apply the Christian ideal of reconciliation to our
treatment of criminals.

The complex of religious and political issues
resulting from our varied background is further brought
out for us by William Klassen who comments on the
careers of Louis Riel and J. S. Woodsworth.

4

Biographical materials for religious studies are also discussed by Peter Slater, who illustrates some technical contrasts between myths and parables by reference to the story of Norman Bethune. This story served as a model for one of the major characters in the Hugh MacLennan novel discussed by William C. James. And with his paper we are fully into questions concerning religion and literature. For Francophones similar questions are raised by Yvon Desrosiers' study of the poetry of Emile Nelligan.

Michel Campbell's paper on a popular song from Québec serves as a bridge to various ways of assessing the religious dimensions of contemporary culture. He still draws on biblical themes. But Tom Sinclair-Faulkner goes directly to sociology for his critique of hockey in Canada, as does John Badertscher in his response. Yet both of these add ethical reflections to their more descriptive passages.

Missing so far from our essays on religion is any direct consideration of rituals and ritual settings. Norman Pagé considers the latter with reference to church architecture while Fred Bird analyses the former among religious groups which are relatively new on the Canadian scene. Both acknowledge briefly the presence of oriental patterns in our religious mélange. This presence also underlies Jordan Paper's account of a Toronto artist's work with children. The primary data on one oriental group in Canada is recorded for us by Leslie Kawamura, who gives us a chronicle of his roots in Alberta.

We end where we began with the issue of our national identity, discussed now in more theoretical terms. Antonio Gualtieri gives theological backing to the nationalist point of view while Michel Despland affirms a more internationalist vision on the basis of his reading of political philosophy. Except for this last paper, which was originally written and delivered in English, we have followed the practice in our society of using whichever official language is our mother tongue. However, to help those whose reading is unilingual I have included with the biographical note at the beginning of each paper a résumé in the other official language. These summaries are the work of Betty Lynn Viney. The index was done by Doris Hope.

Our membership has yet to produce papers on many minority groups important to the story of religion in Canada. Readers may fill some of the gaps by seeking out the new Journal of the Jewish Historical Society of Canada. Also they should look for reports on research and films currently being directed by members of the Department of Religious Studies at the University of Alberta. The idea for the present collection came to us at the Laval Conference in 1976 and we hope that this evidence of continuing work on religion in Canada will encourage many more to give it its due.[2] I hope also that those whose conception of religion is confined to traditionally theological and ecclesiastical preoccupations may gain from these papers more imaginative ways in which to open up the subject.

Finally a word is in order concerning the production of this volume and the series of which it is a part. There are aesthetically more pleasing modes of production. But our concern has been to publish without undue delay at a price that students can afford. I am especially grateful to two private donors and to the Deans of Arts and of Graduate Studies and Research at Carleton University for grants in aid of this publication and to Carolyn McGarvie and Jeannette Gomez-Morales for their careful secretarial work. We have tried to keep the English and French essays internally consistent in matters of style. I have interpreted my role as more that of a compiler than an arbiter of style or methodology, seeking to give readers some sense of the variety of approaches and topics of interest to our members rather than to produce a tightly knit set of essays on a single theme. I thank those writers who took time from other obligations to revise their papers for publication in this form. Without them it would not be as complete a collection as it is. None of the writers will receive royalties from this book.

NOTES

1. See the pioneering works by H. Richard Niebuhr, notably The Social Sources of Denominationalism (1929), The Kingdom of God in America (1937), Christ and Culture (1951) and Radical Monotheism and Western Culture (1943).

2. Readers should also consult Studies in Religion/ Sciences Religieuses Vol. 6, No. 4, 1976-77, which is devoted to Canadiana.

NATIONAL IDENTITY: THE BACKGROUND

JOHN WEBSTER GRANT's paper was first presented as a
public lecture at Carleton University in 1973. He is
the author of ten books, most notably for reader's of
this volume The Church in the Canadian Era (1972),
Volume 3 of A History of the Christian Church in
Canada. He is professor of Church History at Emmanuel
College, Toronto and has served as Managing Editor of
Studies in Religion/Sciences Religieuses.

RÉSUMÉ

Depuis la naissance des colonies de l'Amérique du Nord,
la question d'identité nationale se posait aux communautés religieuses. Cependant, ces communautés pren-
naient intérêt moins à l'existence du Canada qu'à l'
essence ou la formation du caractère canadien. Cet
intérêt passe par trois étapes.

La première est celle de l'établissement européen qui
envisageait leur but comme un transfert de la société
chrétienne à la nouvelle terre. Pour eux, l'église et
l'état étaient tous deux sacrés et dédiés à la mise en
oeuvre de la même entreprise. Catholique ou protestant,
la vision était, donc, d'une continuité. La deuxième
étape est celle du mouvement des missionnaires surtout
au 19e siècle. Ici, on voit une polarisation entre les
catholiques qui poursuivaient l'idéal d'une société stable autour du prêtre et les protestants qui étaient dédiés au jugement privé et au progrès économique. Mais
les deux étaient unis dans leur image du Canada comme
un pays en train de se faire, avec une vraie vocation
nationale vis-à-vis le monde.

La troisième étape est celle du 20e siècle, siècle
d'immigration, d'industrialisation et d'urbanisation.
Malgré leurs efforts, les églises perdent du terrain
à la sécularisation. Mais, depuis 1970, on voit un
renouvellement religieux, qui est peut-être une quatrième étape. Le Canada s'ouvre à toute religion qui peut
contribuer à la vie nationale. Avec quoi remplace-t-
on les anciennes visions? On ne le sait pas encore.
Cependant, il est fort possible qu'on verra dans sa
formation une bonne corrélation et une interaction active entre des concepts religieux et séculiers comme
auparavant.

JOHN WEBSTER GRANT

Religion and the Quest for a National Identity: The Background in Canadian History

National identity is an issue with which Canadian religious communities have had to wrestle ever since the
colonies of British North America first showed promise
of developing into a nation or nations. My first
thought when you asked me to speak was that I might
discuss specific occasions on which the churches have
cultivated national or at least ethnic awareness, and
I could easily find enough material to fill an hour by
talking about such things as the formative role of the
Roman Catholic Church in the emergence of a sense of
French-Canadian nationality, the infatuation of English-
speaking church leaders around the turn of this century
with the manifest destiny of the Anglo-Saxon peoples,
and the relatively unpublicized contributions of Roman
Catholic prelates and Protestant editors to the popular
acceptance of confederation among both language groups.

   As I tried to piece together a coherent presentation
along these lines, however, I was constantly troubled
by a suspicion that on the one hand the contribution of
the churches was somewhat peripheral to the development
of an awareness of being distinctively Canadian, and
that on the other the cultivation of a specifically
Canadian consciousness was always somewhat peripheral
to the interests of the churches. When Stewart Wallace
wrote his pioneer work The Growth of Canadian National
Feeling[1] he did not find it necessary to mention the
contribution of the churches, and those following him
have had little more to say on the subject. Similarly,
one can read through the minutes of many church assemblies without turning up any ringing assertions of
Canadian identity.

   What diverted me from my original intention was the
sudden reflection that by taking the liberty of replacing an 'in' word with a distinctly 'out' one I could
move the discussion into an area that has always been
of central concern to religious communities and to
which their contribution has always been admitted to be
considerable. If the churches have occupied themselves
only fitfully with the quest for a Canadian identity,
they have been deeply engaged from the beginning in an
attempt to shape a Canadian character. Their interest
has been less in the existence of Canada than in its
essence, their concern not so much that Canada should

8

be as <u>what</u> it should be. In thus redefining the
assigned topic I feel somewhat apologetic for disappoin-
ting your expectation but also fairly confident that
this indirect approach will in the end be more productive than a direct attack in illuminating the relation
between Canada's religious communities and its quest
for a national identity.

Although there has been tremendous variety both in
the ideals with which Canadian religious communities
have sought to impregnate the national character and
in the methods by which they have sought to inculcate
them, I think I can detect three distinct, though overlapping, stages in the interplay between the churches
and the Canadian character. I propose to discuss
these in turn and then to suggest in a postscript that
a fourth stage may be in process of emerging.

1. The Transplanting of Christendom

The first set of religious assumptions to be tried
out on Canadian soil were those of the old folk churches
of Christendom, churches which in Europe were typically
fortified with the status of official establishments
and naturally carried the assumptions of establishment
over into the new world. The church in New France, as
recent scholars emphasize, was organized along familiar
Gallican lines. In accordance with the mercantilist
thinking of the time it enjoyed a religious monopoly in
the colony - Protestants being excluded after the first
years in which they had been commercially useful - and
in return had to submit to a good deal of regulation
by the state. Although such exclusive privileges for
any denomination were unthinkable among the mixed popu-
lations of the succeeding British colonies, the colonial
office interpreted the American revolution as the result
of a failure to introduce the British system of aristo-
cracy complete with an established church and sought to
shut the stable door in the remaining colonies by providing the Church of England with an endowment and a
measure of official status.

The practice of religious establishment, which to
Canadians of 1973 evokes only a memory of what seems a
very distant past, rested on assumptions that had been
held by Europeans for centuries and were vigorously
propounded in nineteenth-century Canada by such churchmen as Bishop John Strachan of Toronto. Its basic

premise was that in Europe there already existed a
society in all important respects Christian, a society
of which one's own nation was undoubtedly the highest
and purest representative. The task of christianizing
new colonies essentially consisted, therefore, of
transferring to them the existing religious beliefs and
institutions of Christendom. This Christian society
was normally conceived as a unified entity within which
religious, social and political structures could be
distinguished but not separated. It was thought to be
both natural and legitimate, therefore, to introduce
Christianity to new colonies in conjunction with a
whole social and economic complex and as part of the
normal machinery of government. To us direct state
subsidies to a church would suggest an unnatural alliance between the sacred and the secular, and the
deliberate use of that church to promote loyalty to
the state would be even more offensive. In so reasoning, however, we are taking for granted a model of
society which supporters of establishment would not
for a moment have accepted as valid. To them church
and state were alike sacred, alike Christian, and their
interaction betokened not the interference of one with
the other but the harmonious operation of a single
enterprise.

The provision of a religious establishment, closely
allied with the state and thus with the whole standing
order, was not likely to touch off campaigns for the
radical renewal of church and society. Such was
scarcely its purpose, which was rather the more modest
one of ensuring that the beliefs and moral standards
of Christendom as then understood should set the tone
of colonial life. Individual clergy were expected, no
doubt, to encourage their people to strive towards
perfection. The function of an establishment as such
was to preserve an existing allegiance, not to bring
about a radical transformation in the character of
society.

The establishment idea was strongly opposed in English
Canada almost from the outset, and it is so foreign to
our usual way of thinking that such advocates as Bishop
Strachan seem to us not only undemocratic and élitist -
terms that would not have troubled them - but mere gras-
pers after undeserved privilege. Even such an admirer
as J.L.H. Henderson has written of Strachan, "He was not
always successful in getting what he wanted, and no one
would wish that he had been."[2] Yet it is important to

remember that for centuries the principle of establishment had been unquestioned in Europe and that even in
the nineteenth century it could be maintained without
embarrassment. Thus Strachan could argue unblushingly
that 'a Christian nation without a religious establishment is a contradiction'[3] or that 'the colonies of a
country have as good a right to receive moral and religious instruction from the parent state, as her laws
and government.'[4]

By Strachan's time, indeed, this view had become controversial, in Britain almost as much as in Upper
Canada and within the Church of England as well as
without. It still had influential support, however,
and it may be significant that one of Strachan's confi-
dants throughout his struggle was Dr. Thomas Chalmers,
an evangelical Presbyterian who became the acknowledged
leader of the Church of Scotland and eventually broke
from it because he insisted on its right to spiritual
independence from the state. Strachan's argument for
establishment in a letter written in 1830 would re-
appear in developed form, but with a recognizable
similarity in wording and order, in Chalmers' 1838
'Lectures on the Establishment and Extension of National
Churches'. Since Chalmers was not only a theologian
but a political economist of sufficient stature to draw
fire from Karl Marx, since he had been lecturing on
the subject for many years, and since the arguments are
better adapted to Scotland than to Upper Canada, it
seems reasonable for the moment to assume that Strachan
was borrowing from an earlier draft. This would account
for his use of an economic argument against the effectiveness of free enterprise for disseminating Christianity: 'Nature does not go forth in search of Christianity, but Christianity goes forth to knock at the door
of nature, and, if possible, to awaken her out of her
sluggishness.'[5] It is also suggestive that Strachan
shared with Chalmers an argument for which he has
frequently been subjected to ridicule, that a conscien-
tious and tactful clergyman of the establishment would
'soon win those, who were at first the most opposed to
him, over to his views', that he would 'be able to
remove their prejudices, to inform their ignorance, and
to infuse into them the spirit of the Gospel.'[6] It
appears, in any case, that Chalmers was consistent in
applying to Upper Canada the principles he espoused in
Scotland. Robert McGill, a Kirk missionary in the
province, complained in a letter to the Glasgow Colonial
Society that 'Dr. Chalmers, in an interview in London,

11

recommended that the Presbyterians should succumb to the
Church of England and allow her to seize upon all the
Clergy Reserves and to hold the ecclesiastical pre-
eminence within the province.'[7] And even Strachan's
most resolute opponents, of whom Egerton Ryerson is best
remembered, were sufficiently under the spell of the old
concept of a unified society to find it difficult to
resist when there was a possibility of state aid to
Indian missions or to denominational projects of education.

   Religious establishment ended officially in Québec
with the British conquest. In other provinces its
rejection became final when the clergy reserves were
secularized in 1854. Ever since that time there has
been a tendency to assume that the assumptions it
embodied were incompatible with the Canadian character.
Yet something of the attitude it represented survives
in the quasi-establishment of the Roman Catholic Church
in Québec, in an emphasis on old-world ties that is by
no means confined to the Anglican Church, in a conspicuous lack of religious innovation, and notably in what
the American church historian Robert T. Handy describes
as a tendency on the part of 'the several major
churches...to fulfil some of the functions of national
churches.'[8] Among its most conspicuous legacies are
the various provincial systems of confessional schools.

   The importance of the establishment tradition not
only in forming the Canadian character but in distin-
guishing the Canadian identity is made apparent by a
comparison with the situation in the United States.
American churches were affected in their formative
years both by the Puritan attempt to create a new
commonwealth of saints and by the enlightenment faith
in the possibilities inherent in human nature. The
two in combination inspired the American republic to
conceive itself as a new creation superior to the
static society of Europe precisely because of its
ability to innovate. In Canada, where both ingredients
were largely lacking, it was natural to think of the
newly emerging society as a replica, or even extension,
of England and France; or, by analogy, as a mosaic of
all the cultures imported into it. A sense of
continuity, rather than of novelty, was the establishment contribution to the Canadian quest for a national
identity.

12

2. The Building of a Christian Nation

More influential in the long run than the establishment principle in shaping the Canadian character, however, was the missionary drive that has been such a
conspicuous feature of the modern history of Christendom. This drive issued from the conviction that it was
possible, and therefore a matter of obligation for
Christians, to extend the sway of Christ over every part
of the world and over every segment of life both personal
and social. The missionary spirit was already evident
in New France early in the seventeenth century, alike
in the intrepid Jesuits who prepared their martyrdoms
in Huronia and in the circle of pious ladies around Marie
de l'Incarnation and Mme de la Peltrie who gave the
infant settlement of Québec a distinct air of exalted
religiosity. A striking expression of it was the
foundation of Montrëal as a holy outpost of the faith,
and one catches its authentic tone in the words of
Father Vimont on the occasion, 'You are a grain of
mustard-seed, that shall rise and grow till its branches
overshadow the earth. You are few, but your work is
the work of God.'[9] In the English-speaking colonies,
almost from the outset, most of the effective clergy
owed their appointment not to the state but to the initiative of missionary societies. But the main impact
of the missionary movement in Canada, like the peak of
the impulse elsewhere, was in the nineteenth century.
In English-speaking colonies Christian institutions
took root early in that century, mainly through the
efforts not of representatives of the established
churches of England, Scotland or even New England but
of upstart Methodist saddlebag preachers, intruding
Baptists and separatist Scottish Presbyterians. In
French Canada, where in earlier times missionary fervour
had largely been dedicated to the conversion of the
Indians, the habitants were roused from nominal to
fervent Catholicism during the same period by members
of expanding French orders or by native orators who
imbibed their zeal.

Thus the missionary impulse operated most conspicuous-
ly at the two ends of the ecclesiastical spectrum. At
the one end were the ultramontane or papally oriented
Roman Catholics of Québec, pursuing the ideal of a
stable society in which the faithful would be grouped
in orderly and submissive ranks about their priests,
their bishops, and ultimately the Holy Father in Rome.
At the other were several important denominations of

unequivocally Protestant conviction that magnified private judgment, welcomed economic progress, and regarded the Roman Catholic Church as a world-wide conspiracy to abridge hard-won freedoms. Since the missionary spirit nourished militancy both in attack and defence, this polarization in its expression involved Canada in religious controversy throughout most of the nineteenth century. Indeed, many people of the time would have ascribed the basic rift in the Canadian identity more to religious than to ethnic differences.

Now that the fires of controversy have burned low, however, it is the similarities between the two missionary forces that begin to stand out. Both were products of the primary missionary impulse to assert the lordship of Christ over every aspect of life. Both included the christianization of national life within this agenda, one group thinking expansively in terms of the whole of Canada, the other more often defensively of French Canada alone. Admittedly, there were striking differences in the content of the missionary vision. Ultramontanists sought to reconstruct society along traditional lines, finding their model in an idealized middle age. Protestants drew upon millennial concepts popular in the nineteenth century, organizing campaigns against such enemies as alcohol and Sunday recreation, each of which was seen in turn as the last barrier to the establishment of Christ's kingdom in Canada, and ultimately secularizing the expectation of Christ's return into the hope of a transformed social order. But both were animated by the conviction that society requires sanctification as much as the individuals composing it. Both envisaged the national righteousness they sought in highly moralistic terms, habitually stylizing its demands into readily identifiable taboos. Both, voluntarist Protestants as much as ultramontane Catholics, looked for the embodiment of their social vision in legislation and public institutions. Both considered churches, albeit different churches, to be the legitimate mentors of Canadian society.

The missionary task, as it related to the nation, was seen as essentially twofold. On the one hand, the winning of Canada itself was a major challenge, and the very difficulties imposed by vast distances and a sparse population made Canada seem a specially desirable prize. It could even seem practically the ultimate prize. A Congregational minister named Roat wrote from Toronto in 1838, 'Canada, be it remembered, is the extreme to

14

which the gospel has travelled from Bethlehem', showing
his ignorance of geography by adding that to go any
further would be to start back toward Bethlehem.[10] On
the other hand, Canada was regarded as important as a
base for further advance, whether through the extension
of the offices of the church to settlers in the west or
colonists in the Laurentians, through the conversion of
the native Indians and Eskimos, or through participation
in the enterprise of foreign missions.

Involvement in mission pushed the churches, during
the latter part of the nineteenth century, into a massive
programme of reorganization. Vigorous Sunday school
movements in Protestant churches sought to ensure the
Christian dedication of future Canadians, while both
Protestants and Roman Catholics undertook programmes
specifically directed toward women and youth. Women's
missionary societies, student volunteer groups and
mission bands enlisted the support of various segments
of the church for its total mission, while among Catholics an expansion of religious orders performed a
similar function. I used to regard missionary societies and young people's unions as innocuous organizations, but on closer examination I have been
impressed to discover the thorough mobilization of
missionary energy they made possible in their time.

The old-time missionary enthusiasm now seems almost
as extinct as the principle of religious establishment,
and historians tend to dismiss the nineteenth-century
missionary as a bumbling fanatic. I have no interest
in discussing here the merits of the missionary enterprise, but I suggest that it would be a serious mistake
to underestimate the significance of the missionary
spirit in the development of the Canadian consciousness.
It was probably never decisive in making Canadians what
they were, but it went a long way toward determining
what they thought they ought to be and accordingly
toward shaping their view of the significance of Canada's
existence as a nation.

Missionary crusaders shared with the defenders of establishment a concept of the Christian task in Canada
as one of strengthening known values rather than of
discovering new values. They believed, in the words of
Goldwin French, that 'the destiny of Canada was not to
figure as a great experiment, cut off from the history
of its peoples, but to prolong and blend its traditions
in a new context.'[11] Yet the missionary view was in at

15

least two respects more open to new possibilities than
the establishment principle and thus capable of contributing to the growth of a sense of distinctive identity.
On the one hand it conceived Canada as a society in the
making, not quite a 'lively experiment' as Sidney E.
Mead described the United States from a Christian perspective[12] but at least an unfinished task calling not
merely for the transplanting of extant structures into
a new environment but for the creation of a national
character through a deliberate programme of action. The
prevalence of this view in the late nineteenth century
can readily be illustrated and has been convincingly
demonstrated for one denomination by William H. Magney
in his article 'The Methodist Church and the National
Gospel, 1884-1914.'[13] I was struck, however, to find
the Presbyterian Robert McGill, in a letter I have
already quoted for its strictures on Chalmers, referring
almost casually in 1837 to a search for 'the best means
of building up a Christian nation.'[14] That was before
many secular politicians were thinking in such expansive
terms.

Another missionary contribution to Canadian identity
was the sense of a unique national vocation. This was
usually seen at first in terms of a special responsibility of the Anglo-Saxon peoples or of North America's
beleagured minority of French-speaking Catholics, but
it was capable of being transformed into the concept
of a special role for Canada either abroad in promoting
peace and mutual aid or at home in developing an alternative to the materialistic society of the United States.
Our very propensity for describing Canadian national
identity as the object of a 'quest' rather than as a
natural endowment reflects, more than we commonly realize,
the missionary impulse that could never be content to
leave well enough alone.

3. Secularization

The twentieth century initiated a further stage in
the relation between religion and Canadian nationhood
as new developments began to blunt the missionary thrust
just when it seemed to be on the verge of forging Canada
according to its varied convictions. A massive immigration from many lands introduced ways of living and thinking that had little in common with the Victorian and
papal ideals of most of the churches. The onset of
large-scale industrialization and urbanization made it

16

difficult for the churches to maintain their personal-
ized pastoral approach and easy for the promoters of
tabooed recreations to find a ready market. Constant
improvements in communication combined with this immigration and urbanization to make Canadians aware of
alternatives to their tidy, church-centred way of life.

The churches responded to these unwelcome changes in
the Canadian situation with considerable determination
and ingenuity, although perhaps without a great deal of
theological acumen. At first they sought to head off
the infection of novelty by opposing immigration and
upholding the virtues of rural life. When this strategy did not work, they set out energetically to establish
their presence in threatened areas: turning to informal
topical preaching and mounting ambitious social programmes to hold young people newly arrived in the cities;
setting up rescue missions in slum areas; sending
missionaries into immigrant communities to convert them,
if possible, but more urgently to convince them of the
virtues of solid Canadian ways. They pressed their
familiar moral campaigns more vigorously than ever,
some of the Québec bishops even endorsing the Protestants' favourite project of prohibition. A number of
leaders, deciding that such efforts were no more than
palliatives, began to work for political and economic
reforms that might remove the conditions that made so
many Canadians unresponsive to their appeal. Among
Protestants the social gospel had its heyday, while
Roman Catholics sought to apply the social encyclicals
of Leo XIII and later Pius XI. The churches also sought
to consolidate their forces for the war against un-
righteousness, and the United Church of Canada came
into being.

Although these efforts had many positive results, on
the whole they did not fulfil the purposes for which
they were designed. The minorities resisted attempts
to conform them to Victorian patterns of behaviour.
The moral campaigns, after some promising early
successes, began to collapse when Ontario repealed its
prohibition law in 1926. Church union, while fulfill-
ing many of the dreams of its promoters, did not bring
about the consensus on national goals that had been one
of their fondest hopes for it. The whole Christian
programme of nation-building had been based on the
values of a rural or semi-rural society, and the progress of the technological revolution made it seem more
and more anachronistic. In French Canada, where the

17

effects of twentieth-century pressures were so greatly
delayed that they seemed to have been successfully
resisted, the whole scenario would eventually unwind
with dazzling speed.

The collapse of the nineteenth-century Christian
programme for Canada is so recent that even now we are
too much under its shadow to be able to sift out what
is significant in the contemporary reaction to it. What
is certain, however, is that in a well-developed technological society we have been involved in a process of
disengagement from the hegemony of the churches that
took place in most other western countries at a much
earlier stage. One manifestation of this has been a
belated resentment of the taboos with which we have
long been encircled and of the intellectual and cultural narrowness that has characterized much Canadian
church life. This resentment, only too evident in the
carpings of television pundits who cannot quite escape
the repressions they deplore, has perhaps been given
its most adequate expression by Jean Le Moyne: 'Cursed
guilt, that voice heard from the first stirrings of
consciousness, thunder of unhappiness in the paradise
of childhood, venom of fear, mistrust, doubt and para-
lysis in beautiful youth, that filth over the world and
the sweetness of life, snuffer-out of light, wet blan-
ket, ice around the heart of love, irreconcilable
enemy of being - we breathed it like air, we always
heard it like the wind, we ate it like ashes with every
food, heavenly and earthly.'[15] It is scarcely surprising that many Canadians regard their religious heritage
as a brake upon the growth of the nation toward maturity
and that they are almost pathetically eager to demonstrate that they have emancipated themselves from the
tutelage of the churches.

More significant in the long run than these manifestations of adolescent rebellion, however, has been a
steady process of secularization that has detached from
the control of the churches important instruments
through which they once exerted their influence. Phil-
anthropy has long gone, taken over by big business and
the state. Politics has been almost completely secularized, despite the religious origins of the CCF and
Social Credit. Community life, once dominated by
religious societies and even church-sponsored athletic
clubs, now has its centre elsewhere. Most significantly of all, the transmission of culture through schools
and universities no longer rests on even implicitly

religious foundations.

The vision of a Christian society, whether conceived
as a replica of the old Christendom or as an anticipa-
tion of the promised millennium, has clearly lost its
power to inspire. What foundations of national identity have we put in its place? I confess myself hard
put to give a satisfying answer. The discovery of not
being British that once helped to define Canada for
many of us has been replaced by that of not being
American, and so long as the United States remains in
its present state of disarray this will have some capacity to sustain us. I also detect - although this may
be no more than a local view from Toronto - a desire to
project the swinging image of a country liberated for
sophisticated pleasure that will erase the old mission-
inspired concept of Canada as a true north strong and
free. We still conceive of national identity as something to be created rather than as something given, but
having drained the vision of its former content we have
not yet succeeded in putting very much in its place.

Postscript

On this uncertain note my historical survey really
comes to an end. I hesitate to go further and in any
case I suspect that the secular stance I have described
represents substantially where we are now. Yet I cannot see any possibility that we shall remain long in the
transitional phase of rebellion against an oppressive
religion that no longer oppresses, and one of the
clearest messages being received in the 1970s is that
the dimension of meaning once provided by the churches
is still very much in demand. Already I see signs
pointing to the emergence of a new phase in the relation of religion to the national life. Assuredly this
will not be the restoration of religious communities
to their former dominant role, despite current manifestations of conservative reaction. It is more likely to
be an open attitude that will welcome religion when it
can contribute to a search for meaning, and that will
welcome any form of religion that promises to contribute to that search.

Undoubtedly - to use an overworked term - we have
entered an era of religious pluralism. The future is
likely to belong, however, neither to a static pluralism of inherited denominational traditions nor to a

polarized pluralism of competing claims to religious
control, but rather to a dynamic pluralism of cells
acting as leaven in the lump of society. One of the
first signs of this emerging situation was the establishment of departments of religion in state universities, signalling the end of a period when religion
represented a heavyhanded pressure to be resisted and
the beginning of one when it offers an exciting field
to be explored. One can hope that the next step will
be a general recognition that ecclesiastical power has
ceased to threaten the state and that Canada can afford
to welcome whatever religion can contribute to the
national life.

Current trends point to a religious presence marked
by dynamic dialogue among religious traditions rather
than static division into exclusive religious communities.

FOOTNOTES

1.   Toronto, Macmillan, 1927.

2.   J.L.H. Henderson (ed.), John Strachan: Documents
     and Opinions (Toronto: McClelland and Stewart,
     Carleton Library No. 44, 1969), vif.

3.   Ibid., p. 91.

4.   Ibid., p. 88.

5.   Henderson, John Strachan: Documents 110; cf. Thomas
     Chalmers, Works (Glasgow: William Collins n.-.),
     XVII 227.

6.   Ibid., p. 111; cf. Chalmers, Works, XVII 322-32.

7.   Robert McGill to Robert Burns, 10 October 1837;
     reprinted in The Bulletin of the Committee of Ar-
     chives of The United Church of Canada 21 (1969-70),
     19.

8.   'The "Lively Experiment" in Canada,' unpublished
     paper delivered to the American Society of Church
     History, 1972.

9.   Francis Parkman, The Jesuits in North America
     (Toronto: Morang, 1910), II 25.

10. John Waddington, Congregational History: Continua-
     tion to 1850 (1878), 498.

11. 'The Evangelical Creed in Canada' in W.L. Morton
     (ed.), The Shield of Archilles: Aspects of Canada
     in the Victorian Age (Toronto: McClelland and
     Stewart, 1968), 29.

12. Sidney E. Mead, The Lively Experiment: The Shaping
     of Christianity in America (New York: Harper and
     Row, 1963).

13. Bulletin 20 (1968).

14. Bulletin 21 (1969-71), p. 20.

15. Jean Le Moyne, Convergence, translated by Philip
     Stratford (Toronto: Ryerson, 1966), p. 44.

16. Philip LeBlanc, op. and Arnold Edinborough (eds.),
     One Church, Two Nations? (Don Mills: Longmans,
     1966), p. 8.

A VISION IN CRISIS

N. KEITH CLIFFORD's article first appeared in Studies in
Religion/Sciences Religieuses 2:4 (1973). He is Associate Professor of Religious Studies in the University
of British Columbia and is currently writing on the
history of Canadian Protestant discussions concerning
church union.

RÉSUMÉ

La vision du Canada comme le Royaume de Dieu était la
vision des protestants pendant une soixantaine d'années
suivant la Confédération. Cette vision comprenait un
peuple homogène et un héritage démocratique et évangélique. Mais, l'immigration menaçait cette vision et le
résultat était une série de persécutions contre les
immigrants : d'abord, les chinois de la Colombie Britan-
nique, ensuite, les slaves, les mormons, les juifs et
d'autres groupes religieux. La littérature des plus
grandes sectes protestantes à cette époque révèle les
mêmes réactions : pour sauver la vision, il fallait
christianiser les immigrants, leur convaincre la vision
- l'église étant l'institution responsable de la transmission des valeurs sacrées de la nation.

A partir du 20e siècle, la vision commençait à faillir,
l'immigration continuait, l'industrialisation et l'urbanisation étaient en marche. La nature pluraliste du
peuple empêchait la communauté protestante d'articuler
une idéologie unie de leur vision, tandis que l'éloquen-
ce des solutions simplistes sonnait faux. Surtout, le
mouvement du libéralisme protestant, y compris la doctrine du progrès et du Darwinisme, avaient comme résultat l'abandon de la vision.

Quoique l'abandon soit irrésistible pour la plupart
des protestants, l'adoption aujourd'hui par d'autres
groupes plus conservateurs indique la puissance de la
vision. Ces groupes, cependant, l'adoptent avec certaines révisions: par exemple, l'appui sur le salut personnel plutôt que sur la justice sociale. Dans l'inter-
valle, les autres cherchent une nouvelle image et d'
autres symboles qui feront honneur à leur nouveau dis-
cernement de la communauté chrétienne dans la société
canadienne de nos jours.

N.K. CLIFFORD

His Dominion: A Vision in Crisis

The inner dynamic of Protestatism in Canada during the
first two thirds of the century following Confederation
was provided by a vision of the nation as 'His Dominion.'
This Canadian version of the Kingdom of God had significant nationalistic and millennial overtones, and sufficient symbolic power to provide the basis for the
formation of a broad Protestant consensus and coalition.
Not only the major Protestant denominations but also a
host of Protestant-oriented organizations such as
temperance societies, missionary societies, Bible
societies, the Lord's Day Alliance, the YMCA's and
YWCA's utilized this vision as a framework for defining
their task within the nation, for shaping their conceptions of the ideal society, and for determining those
elements which posed a threat to the realization of
their purposes.

Amongst the threats to this vision was the massive
immigration to Canada, between 1880 and World War II,
of people who did not share it. The Protestant reaction
to these newcomers reveals how the vision of Canada as
'His Dominion' helped not only to define the threat of
immigration but also to direct their response into a
crusade to Canadianize the immigrants by Christianizing
them into conformity with the ideals and standards of
Canadian white Anglo-Saxon Protestants. Ultimately this
vision proved to be an inadequate framework for thought
and action in a pluralistic society. Without an understanding of its symbolic and formative power, however,
it is difficult to assess the nature of Protestant
aspirations and their impact on Canadian society.

The vision of Canada as 'His Dominion' implied a homogeneous population which shared a heritage of political
democracy and evangelical Protestant Christianity.[1]
When western Canada began to be populated by groups who
did not share this heritage, therefore, Protestants saw
their presence as a threat to the realization of their
vision and reacted by demanding either that these newcomers conform to their way of life or that their entry
into Canada be severely restricted.

The first to feel the sting of this reaction were the
Chinese in British Columbia. The Chinese had begun to

A VISION IN CRISIS

enter British Columbia in the 1850s from California.
Attracted by the gold rush to the Fraser Valley, they
continued to arrive in ever greater numbers. Initially
they experienced no prejudice, but in the 1870s the
British Columbia legislature, responding to public
pressure, began to pass legislation designed to place
heavy penalties on this group. When much of this legislation was declared ultra vires, the pressure mounted
and in 1907 resulted in riots in Vancouver. By 1923 it
issued in legislation which virtually excluded the
immigration of the Chinese to Canada.[2]

In 1881, when Jasper H. Preston of Montreal published an
anti-Chinese article in Rose Belford's Canadian Monthly
and National Review, George Monro Grant of Queen's shot
back a stinging rebuttal. Grant thought the anti-
Chinese argument was based upon 'unreason and ignorance
of the facts,' that it was sustained by 'misrepresenta-
tion' and 'selfishness,' and that it appealed to 'mob
law and race prejudices.' He was especially contemp-
tuous of the suggestion that the Chinese would 'degrade
or destroy the Christian civilization of America, by
the substitution or admixture with it of their own
inferior civilization.' After pointing out that Christ
'came not to the west, but to the east' and loved 'black,
brown, red, yellow men, as well as white,' he held up
to ridicule those who, 'in the interests of His civilization,' would invoke the government's protection 'from
the companionship of the yellow men!'[3]

Twenty year later, however, the climate of opinion
had changed, for when J.R. Conn published an even more
vigorous anti-Chinese article in the Queen's Quarterly,
it went unchallenged.[4] In fact, the Reverend R. G.
MacBeth, in a series of lectures to a Presbyterian
ministers' summer school at Manitoba College, put forth
similar arguments for the restriction of Chinese immigration. Basing his case on 'the law of cosmic evolution in history' which 'justifies the superseding of a
lower civilization by a higher,' he concluded that the
unrestricted immigration of the Chinese into British
Columbia would not be in the interests of human advancement because 'the Chinese are a people of a lower
civilization.'[5]

The Protestant reaction to the 'yellow peril,' however, tended to be divided. By the turn of the century
several of the major Protestant denominations had
launched extensive foreign mission endeavours in China,

25

and for over twenty years the churches in Canada had
been carrying on home mission work among the Chinese in
Canada. Consequently, while there was a distinct fear
of the 'yellow peril' among the Protestant community,
particularly on the West Coast, there was also a fear
lest the treatment the Chinese were receiving in Canada
would create difficulties for Canadian Protestant
missionaries in China. These complementary fears led
to some interesting rationalizations. R.G. MacBeth,
for example, was convinced that the Chinese were unassi-
milable and that their 'Chinatowns' formed an undisges-
ted mass that would lower the moral and industrial
health of the country. This conviction led him to
conclude that 'the Chinese are most susceptible to
Christianity's influence in their own country.' 'Immigration,' he argued, 'proceeds largely from bad social
conditions, which in turn arise from wrong religious,
social, moral and ethical standards.' If Christian
missionaries removed these conditions by converting
China to Christianity, it seemed obvious to MacBeth,
'the Chinese would be more likely to remain at home to
develop their own country.'6

The second group to which the Canadian Protestants
turned their attention were the eastern and southern
Europeans. The first Ukrainian pioneers came in 1891,
but it was not until 1897 that they began to pour into
the Canadian west in significant numbers. No sooner
did they begin to appear than they became an object of
attack. By 1910, S.D. Chown, who was later to become
the General Superintendent of the Methodist Church, was
asking, 'How shall the foreigners govern us?' In an
article in The Christian Guardian he pointed out that
'in the province of Saskatchewan only thirty-three and
a third per cent of the population are British born.'
'What does that mean?' he asked, 'it means that one
third of the people have the unprecedented burden
thrust upon them of converting two-thirds of the population to high ideals of Canadian citizenship.' 'The
question of questions,' he continued, 'is which shall
prevail; the ideas of Southern Europe, or the noblest
conceptions of Anglo-Saxondom?' Then, in the homiletic
style of the period, he asked, 'Shall the hordes of
Southern Europe overrun our country as the Huns and
Vandals did the Roman Empire?' For Chown there was
'no disguising the fact that already in cities like
Toronto and Winnipeg the foreign vote is reaching for
control, if it has not already grasped it.' Therefore,
he concluded, 'the question that trembles in the

balance is "How shall the foreigners govern us?" That
they shall govern the West in a generation or two there
is no doubt.'7

It was in this sort of atmosphere that the Rev. C.W.
Gordon wrote his novel The Foreigner. The story is set
in Winnipeg, 'the cosmopolitan capital of the last of
the Anglo-Saxon Empires,' and particularly in the north
end of the city which had been overrun by the 'Polak
invasion.' Its plot reflects most of the characteristic reactions of the Anglo-Saxon community to these newcomers. Through the eyes of Mrs. Fitzpatrick, an Irish
charwoman, the housekeeping, the moral standards and
childrearing methods of 'slow-witted' Paulina Koval are
brought under review. When Anka Kusmirck does not share
Mrs. Fitzpatrick's horror of Paulina's moral condition,
Gordon comments: 'It was the East meeting the West,
the Slav facing the Anglo-Saxon. Between their points
of view stretched generations of moral development. It
was not a question of absolute moral character so much
as a question of standards.'8

Throughout the book Gordon continually makes comparisons between 'the good folk of Winnipeg' lying snug and
warm 'in their virtuous beds' and 'the steaming, sway-
ing, roaring dancers, both men and women, all reeking
with sweat and garlic,' at a Ukrainian wedding; between
British law and order as represented by Sergeant
Cameron and the attempts of a Russian nihilist, Michael
Koval, to balance the scales of justice in his own
manner. In this way the novel gives a vivid description
of the Anglo-Saxons' distaste for Slavic customs and
standards and their determination to show these newcomers that such practices would not be tolerated in
the Canadian west.

When Gordon's book appeared it was dubbed by his
critics as 'sensational, overdrawn, intensely exaggerated, a slander on the foreigners of the West.' Yet
many like The Christian Guardian's special correspondent
from 'The Prairie Provinces' were quick to point to
actual incidents in the Winnipeg police court which gave
credence to the conviction of many Anglo-Saxons that
Gordon's story was not a gross exaggeration.9 Gordon
was prepared to make no apoligies for the book. Commenting on the reception which it had received, he said,
'Yes, it has been severely criticized in many quarters,
but in its description of the prevailing conditions of
foreign settlements, I assert that it fails to be lurid

enough.'[10]

The Orientals and the Slavs were not the only groups which posed a threat to the Protestant vision, but merely the largest and most visible. Mormons, Jews, Mennonites, Hutterites, and Doukhobors, because of their religious, pacifist, or communal ideas, also offered threats to the vision. It is impossible here to deal with the attacks on all these groups but the Mormons provide a good example because they posed both a moral and political threat. R.G. MacBeth was convinced that they were a 'wholly undesirable class of settlers' who were basically antagonistic 'to the principles that make for a stable and righteous nation.'[11] MacBeth had three basic complaints against them which made them undesirables from his point of view. First of all, they claimed that the Book of Mormon was equal in authority to the Bible. Secondly, they practised polygamy and this made real home life an impossibility. 'If the home is the real heart of the nation,' he declared, 'then Mormonism is one of the spears that pierce the centre of the nation's life.' The third indictment was primarily political, for he argued that 'the Mormons have no conscience in the affairs of State apart from their leaders.' 'The Mormon vote,' he continued, 'is that most dangerous thing, a "solid" vote, and it is absolutely in the hands of the priesthood. This condition of things is ruinous to a free state ... We should give no place in Canada to a "Bossism" that seeks to control the State to the subversion of its highest ideals.'[12]

J.S. Woodsworth was convinced that 'their presence is a serious menace to our Western civilization,'[13] and to C.J. Cameron of the Baptist Church, Mormon was 'a name that carries bluebeardish horror.' More dangerous even than their polygamy, Cameron believed, was their surrender of personal liberty and the acknowledgment of the supreme authority of the priesthood, 'for it is the end of all free government - the confessed goal of Mormon effort.'[14]

The literature of all the major Protestant denominations contains similar nativist reactions to those immigrant groups which threatened their vision of Canada as 'His Dominion.' Some extremists advocated the exclusion of these groups and a few, especially after World War I, suggested massive deportations. The majority of Protestants, however, were more confident

28

of their ability to assimilate these newcomers into conformity with the values and standards of Anglo-Saxon Protestantism. They therefore launched a crusade to Canadianize the immigrants by Christianizing them.

If Canada were to become 'His Dominion' as Protestants had defined it, the new foreign elements which had been introduced into their society would have to become like them and share their values and standards. C.J. Cameron, the assistant superintendent of the Baptist Home Mission Board of Ontario and Québec, stated the problem clearly in his book Foreigners or Canadians?[15] For Cameron, it was a matter of 'How shall we mould the heterogeneous mass of immigration, formed of one hundred foreign elements, into one people making them moral and intelligent citizens, loyal to our free institutions and capable of self-government?[16] His solution was as follows:

We must endeavour to assimilate the foreigner. If the mixing process fails we must strictly prohibit from entering our country all elements that are non-assimilable. It is contrary to the Creator's law for white, black or yellow races to mix together. If the Canadian civilization fails to assimilate the great mass of foreigners admitted to our country the result will be destruction to the ideals of a free and nominally Christian nation which will be supplanted by a lower order of habits, customs and institutions.[17]

The basic threat of the immigrant for Cameron, however, was political. 'The millions of aliens admitted to Canada,' he argued, 'have transported to our soil political notions which we cannot tolerate. The continental ideas of the Sabbath, the nihilist's ideas of government, the communist's ideas of property and the pagan's ideas of religion.'[18] Therefore assimilation was the greatest problem, and, as far as Cameron was concerned, 'there is but one all-sufficient method by which this goal is reached: we shall Canadianize the foreigner by Christianizing him. Here is our greatest opportunity and our gravest responsibility, for if we do not Christianize him he will paganize us, and if we do not instill into him the highest ideals, the saloon-keeper and the ward politician will fill him with the lowest ideals.'[19]

29

Hugh Dobson, the field secretary for the Board of
Temperance and Moral Reform of the Methodist Church,
tried in 1920 to define what Canadianization meant. In
an article in Social Welfare he wrote, 'the purpose of
Canadianization is to secure on the part of Canada's
total population such an attitude to this country as
would prompt every citizen to live, and if necessary
die for its welfare.' The process of Canadianization,
he believed, involved 'three closely related processes,
(1) the development of individual citizens, (2) their
socialization, (3) the inculcation of loyalty to such
essential groups as the family, the community, the
nation and humanity as a whole.'[20]

Dobson acknowledged the work of a number of agencies
but felt that it was not being carried out on a broad
enough scale or in a systematic fashion. 'Various
Canadian groups,' he said, 'have made more or less
earnest and intelligent efforts directed toward Canadianization. Some of the Churches, certain school
groups and Boards, the Young Men's and Young Women's
Christian Associations, a few industrial and commercial
organizations and some governments have formulated
programmes and attempted work, but their efforts have
been spasmodic. Comprehensiveness and continuity have
been lacking.'[21] Among the methods which he suggested
for a comprehensive, nationwide, intensive, and continuous program of Canadianization was the turning of
schools and churches into community and educational
centres. He was also concerned that they utilize the
latest forms of communication technology in the process.
'The gramophone, stereopticon, and the movie or pathes-
cope,' he argued, 'ought to be commandeered for patriotic purposes.' He was also convinced that 'choral
singing of our great English folk and patriotic songs
is a wonderful instrument of socialization and breeds
loyalty.'[22]

Kate A. Foster, in Our Canadian Mosaic,[23] makes it
clear that Canadianization and assimilation into an
Anglo-Saxon monocultural system is her basic concern in
spite of the title of her book. Noting the shift in
the type of immigrants from northern Europeans to south-
eastern Europeans, she argued that the latter 'are less
readily assimilated.' The basic problem, she argued,
was that in the prairier provinces they had settled in
'solid blocks' and in the cities had gravitated to
congested areas thereby greatly intensifying 'the problem of Canadianization.'[24] She was convinced that

'the public school must be ranked as the greatest force
in moulding the new Canadian.'[25] But Protestant churchmen, like Cameron, were anxious to point to the church
and its home mission facilities as equally important
instruments in the process of assimilation and acculturation.

In the United Church of Canada's recently launched
paper, The New Outlook, the editor, W.B. Creighton, emphasized this point. An editorial entitled 'The Church
as Melting Pot' set forth the following position:

Large sections of our Dominion are being filled with
a polyglot people. . . . And the problem which confronts our statesmen and all who have at heart the
true welfare of our nation in the future is how to
fuse these diverse elements in our population so as
to form one great and homogeneous community committed
to the highest ideals of what is best in our modern
Christian civilization. The school has a great function to perform in this direction. . . . But neither
the school nor the workshop, nor the mart, go down to
the deepest springs of life. Our religious feelings
and interests reach down to what is deepest in our
common manhood, and it is on this sacred ground that
we are drawn most closely and sympathetically together.[26]

After pointing out that the church might well appeal
for support in her campaign for maintenance and extension on this ground alone, Creighton quoted with
approval an editorial from the Vancouver Sun entitled
'The Moral Energy of British Columbia.' The editorial
argued that the church was the country's real 'melting
pot' because while 'an alien may speak our language,
wear our clothes and buy our wares,' he does not really
become a Canadian until 'his moral standards and ideals
become our moral standards and ideals.'[27] This was the
essence of the problem for most liberal Protestant
churchmen in Canada, who saw the church as the institution responsible for the maintenance and transmission
of the nation's most sacred ideals and values. It
seemed obvious to them that only through the Canadian
church could the immigrant be introduced to what it
finally meant to be a true Canadian.

Whether the newcomer has been called upon to conform
as much in Canada as in the United States may be a
debatable question, but there is certainly no question
that the leadership of the Anglo-Saxon Protestant

31

community had this goal in mind and were prepared to
see the church playing a significant role in the assimilation process. From the inside it appeared like
God's work, but from the outside it looked like something else. Louis Rosenberg, from a Jewish perspective,
saw it as a denial of true religion. He wrote:

> Strangely enough religion is also dragged in as a
> motivating factor in prejudice. Among the most pro-
> minent opponents of 'foreign' immigration are
> ministers of religion of various denominations who
> are so absorbed in their desire for the supremacy of
> their particular denomination and their self-righteous
> belief in the superiority of their particular brand
> of salvation that they forget all about the common
> fatherhood of God and brotherhood of mankind.[28]

There were few Protestants at this time, however, who
could accept such a judgment because they had succeeded
in welding together their millennial hopes for the establishment of Christ's kingdom in Canada with their
deep desire to serve their nation and to save it from
racial and ideological contamination.[29]

By the 1930s, however, doubts began to appear concerning the attitude of the Protestant community toward
the immigrant and especially about the whole program
of 'Canadianization.' E.L. Chicanot, writing in the
Dalhousie Review in 1929, pointed out that because of
their 'nordic complex' and their attitude of superiority it occurs to few Canadians that the immigrant might
have 'something to add to the spiritual and cultural
side of Canadian life.' Chicanot was optimistic, however, because he believed that 'it is gradually being
realized that the welding of the cultural contributions
of these various nationalities may develop the process
of Canadianization on a higher plane than has yet been
conceived.' Moreover, he also believed that the 'very
heterogeneity which has often been deplored as Western
Canada's problem may be turned into the most valuable
of attributes.'[30]

This was a new and positive note in regard to the
contribution of immigrants to Canadian society which
began to be picked up by a number of writers both
inside and outside the churches. The Reverend J.C.
Cochrane, Superintendent of United Church Missions in
Northern Ontario, for example, put his finger on the

point when he wrote: 'The churches in Canada have been
represented as "Canadianizing" agencies concerned primarily with making people Canadian rather than Christian
- an impression which some of our unstudied utterances
may have unintentionally strengthened.'[31] This was not
exactly a confession of guilt but it was an indication
that some of the more perceptive churchmen were beginning to backpedal themselves out of the deadend street
into which enthusiasts for an alliance between Christianity and culture had led them.

Even the ideal of a homogeneous Canadian society was
abandoned by some churchmen in the 1930s. For example,
Dr. E.H. Oliver, after observing that the Greek and
English peoples were 'mixed peoples,' quoted with
approval Professor W.P. Thompson of the University of
Saskatchewan, who had argued that according to Mendel's
laws of heredity the results of the rapid intercrossing
of the many races would be much different from those
implied in the 'melting pot' conception. 'There will
be,' Thompson declared, 'no homogeneous fused mass in
the pot with extremes cancelling each other.' 'A
better comparison,' he concluded, 'would be with the
kaleidoscope if we could imagine all possible configu-
rations to exist simultaneously.'[32] The kaleidoscope
was a less stable image for Canadian society than a
'mosaic,' but it pointed in the same direction and
indicated an awareness that Canadian churchmen, if they
were to deal with the reality of Canadian experience,
would have to face the fact of heterogeneity and aban
don their former ideal of a homogeneous Canadian
society.

Others, such as the Baptist layman Watson Kirkconnell,
played a significant role in making Canadians aware of
the cultural contributions which the immigrants could
make to Canada. Arriving at Wesley College, Winnipeg,
in 1922, fresh from Oxford, he began his long career
of translating 'Canada's unseen literatures.'[33] As a
result of his efforts, interested Canadians were able
to discover in his twenty volumes of translated verse
and numerous articles the richness of the immigrant
tradition and experience which had entered Canada.
Such efforts raised doubts about the nativistic elements
which had entered into the justification of the Protestant mission to the new Canadians.

It was not until the end of the Second World War,
however, that such ideas began to penetrate into the

33

home mission enterprises of the Protestant churches.
Dr. R.B. Cochrane, the secretary of the United Church's
Board of Home Missions, is an interesting example of
how this change took place. Throughout the 1930s he
was defining the home missionary enterprise as an 'endeavour of idealists to produce through the religion of
Jesus Christ a Canadian Christian citizenshp out of
many varied and mutually contributing cultures.'[34] By
1941 he was predicting that 'when the history of
Canada's war effort comes to be written in the future,
writers will account it a matter of tremendous significance for Canadian unity that in the non-Anglo-Saxon
communities throughout Canada, there existed All Peoples
Missions and Churches of All Nations, to be rallying
centres for the development of the democratic spirit
and for the transformation into deeds of this spirit.'[35]

By the end of the war, however, his attitude dramatically changed. After observing closely what had
happened to the Japanese and other immigrant groups
during the war, Dr. Cochrane had become disturbed by
the hatred and bigotry which he had observed in the
Canadian Protestant community. The church was suffering
from a serious shortage of ministers and he knew it must
make an effort to recruit men returning from overseas if
it was going to move forward in the post-war period.
Thus shortly before his death on 17 July 1945, he wrote:

If our church is to appeal to these men who have, because of their experiences, become world citizens,
and who know little of narrowness and bigotry in their
relationship in the forces, the United Church must get
rid of a great deal of her racial and national prejudices and much of her formalism and half-heartedness,
and must develop a spirit of real Christian fellowship
which is anxious to share Christ with all men everywhere.[36]

Unfortunately, not all were able to change their minds
like Dr. Cochrane. The changes brought about by immigration, industrialization, and urbanization seemed to
threaten the most cherished traditions of the Protestant community and to put in question the realization of
their dream of making Canada 'His Dominion.' Faced with
such a dilemma, they tended to affirm the possibilities
of diversity for themselves but to deny it for those
who did not share their standards, values, and traditions. The nature and scope of these rapid social
changes, which they correctly identified, would not,

however, permit the maintenance of such an ambivalent
solution. Therefore, the Protestant vision of Canada
as 'His Dominion,' in the terms in which they had
defined it, collapsed.

It collapsed for several reasons. First of all, the
Protestant community was unable to articulate an ideology of Canadianism which was acceptable to those who
did not share their Anglo-Saxon Protestant heritage.[37]
The failure of their missions in French Canada, the
failure of much of their prohibitory legislation, and
the legacy of tension, bitterness, and hatred which
their bid for Protestant cultural hegemony in Canada
had created in the educational system and in the relations between Anglo-Saxons and other ethnic groups,
especially during the two world wars of the twentieth
century, indicated that whatever shape the Kingdom of
God might take in the Canadian context, it was not
going to be realized in the terms elaborated by those
who had fashioned the broad Protestant coalition and
consensus in the period following disestablishment in
the 1850s. The pluralistic nature of the political,
social, and religious dimensions of Canadian society
were such that the millennial dreams of any particular
group were an inadequate basis for the elaboration of
an ideology which would be acceptable to all.

Secondly, the Evangelical Protestant mind has never
relished complexity. Indeed its crusading genius,
whether in religion or politics, has always tended
toward an oversimplification of issues and the substitution of inspiration and zeal for critical analysis
and serious reflection. The limitations of such a
mind-set were less apparent in the relative simplicity
of a rural frontier society. By the 1920s, however,
more than half of Canada's population lived in urban
centres and industrialization was rapidly changing
Canadian society; by the end of World War II, Canada
was moving quickly in the direction of the welfare
state. In this new social order the rhetoric of
simplistic solutions to social problems and crusades
for righteousness and private charity began to have a
hollow ring. Protestant churches found themselves
entering a post-Protestant era in which they would be
unceremoniously relegated to the periphery of power.
Diplomacy, strategy, and expertise replaced charisma,
prophecy, and zeal as the necessary qualities of
leadership and various secularized utopias were sub-
stituted for the vision of Canada as 'His Dominion.'

35

Protestants, however, were not simply overtaken by
the complexity and secularization of modern urban and
industrialized society, or by their inability to articulate a viable ideology of Canadianism. Internal transformations in Protestant thought provided a third reason
for the abandonment of the vision. With the establishment of theological liberalism in Canada and the gradual
acceptance of biblical criticism and Darwinism in the
1880s and 90s, the pre-millennialism of the older
evangelical orthodoxy was abandoned in favour of a post-
millennialism which depended less upon the exegesis of
scriptural prophecy and more on the nineteenth-century
doctrine of progress. In this transition Protestantism
tended to identify closely with the progress of culture
and to lose all critical distance in relation to it.
The millennium, by being identified with the progressive
tendencies of history itself, became completely histo-
ricized, and Protestantism entered into a series of
easy alliances with Social Darwinist racial theories,
industrial capitalism, and middle class culture to the
point where it became almost indistinguishable from
these commitments.

The Social Gospellers who reacted against social injustice and the alliance of cultural Protestantism with
industrial capitalism failed on the whole to react with
equal vigour against Protestantism's other cultural
alliances. It was not until the 1930s, when Neo-
Orthodoxy began to dissect Protestantism's identification with the idea of progress, middle-class culture,
and nationalistic pretensions as a whole, that the
theological framework supporting the vision of Canada
as 'His Dominion' began to dissolve completely.

Although in retrospect these were extremely compel-
ling reasons for the abandonment of the vision, not all
Canadian Protestants could accept the rejection of the
vision. In fact, at the very point when most of the
mainline Protestant denominations were in the process
of exorcizing the remnants of the vision from their
programs and pronouncements, other groups as diverse as
the Anglo-Catholics and Conservative Evengelicals
picked up the image of 'His Dominion' for their own
purposes.[38]

The continued use of this image by conservative Protestant groups is a clear indication of its power to
reflect a certain type of Protestant self-understanding.
The fact, however, that it has been picked up by groups

who are opposed to church union, who are essentially
premillennarian in their outlook and more committed to
personal salvation than to the establishment of social
justice or national righteousness, also indicates that
it has been stripped of many of its original overtones.
That it is no longer being used in ecumenical discussions within the Protestant community or between Protestants and Roman Catholics shows that it has lost its
viability not only for the majority of Christians in
Canada but also for those who have perceived the inherent diversity and pluralism of Canadian society and
are searching for images and symbols which will more
accurately reflect the new dynamics and self-understanding of the Christian community within such a society.

FOOTNOTES

1. For a discussion of the climate of opinion at the
    time when the Protestant vision of Canada as 'His
    Dominion' began to take shape, cf. Carl Berger,
    'The True North Strong and Free' Nationalism in
    Canada Peter Russell (ed.) (Toronto: McGraw-Hill
    1966) 3-26; Edward N. Saveth American Historians
    and European Immigrants 1875-1925 (New York:
    Columbia University Press 1948); Richard Hofstader
    Social Darwinism in American Thought (Philadelphia:
    University of Pennsylvania Press 1944); Thomas F.
    Gossett Race: The History of an Idea in America
    (Dallas: Southern Methodist University Press 1963)
    187. Also R. Sutherland, 'The Body-Odour of Race'
    Canadian Literature 37:46-67; and C.C. Berger, 'Race
    and Liberty: The Historical Ideas of Sir John George
    Bourinot' Canadian Historical Association Report
    (1965) 87-104.

2. Cf. Cheng Tien-Fang Oriental Immigration in Canada
    (Shanghai 1931); S.S. Osterhout Orientals in Canada
    (Toronto: Ryerson Press 1929); and Stuart C. Miller
    The Unwelcome Immigrant: The American Image of the
    Chinese 1785-1882 (Berkeley: University of Califor-
    nia Press 1969).

3. Cf. J.H. Preston 'The Chinese Question' Rose Bel-
    ford's Canadian Monthly and National Review 7
    (1881) 81-83 and George M. Grant 'The Chinese
    Question' Ibid., 207-11.

4. J.R. Conn 'Immigration' Queen's Quarterly (October
    1900) 119.

5. R.G. MacBeth Our Task in Canada (Toronto: The
    Westminster Co. 1912) 80.

6. Ibid., 82; cf. N.L. Ward Oriental Missions in British
    Columbia (London 1925); Elmer C. Sandmeyer The Anti-
    Chinese Movement in California (1930); Jules Karlin
    'The Anti-Chinese Outbreaks in Seattle, 1885-1886'
    Pacific Northwest Quarterly 395 (1948) 103-30;
    Robert Seager II 'Some Denominational Reactions to
    Chinese Immigration to California 1856-1892' Pacific
    Historical Review 28 (1959) 40-66; Paul H. Clements
    'Canada and the Chinese: A Comparison with the
    United States' Annals of the American Academy of
    Political and Social Science 45 (January 1913) 99-130;

Henry Forbes Angus 'Legal Discrimination on Racial
Grounds in British Columbia' Pacific Affairs 22
(1949). The clearest picture of how rabid the
attack on the Orientals in Canada could become is
given in Thom MacInnes Oriental Occupation of
British Columbia (Vancouver: The Sun Publishing
Co. 1927).

7. S.D. Chown 'How Shall the Foreigners Govern Us? The
Christian Guardian (23 February 1910) 8.

8. C.W. Gordon (Ralph Connor) The Foreigner (New York:
Hodder and Stoughton 1909) 24.

9. Cf. The Christian Guardian (2 March 1910) 13.

10. C.W. Gordon 'The Church and Problems of Empire' The
Christian Guardian (21 September 1910) 10-11.

11. R.G. MacBeth Our Task in Canada 45-46.

12. Ibid., 47-48.

13. J.S. Woodsworth Strangers Within Our Gates (1909,
reprinted University of Toronto Press 1972).

14. C.J. Cameron Foreigners or Canadians? (Toronto:
Baptist Home Mission Board of Ontario and Quebec
1913). Cf. Lawrence B. Lee 'The Mormons Come to
Canada 1887-1902' Pacific Northwest Quarterly 59
(January 1968) for further material on the Mormons.

15. C.J. Cameron Foreigners or Canadians? More of the
same arguments were put forth in the post-war
period in C.H. Shutt and C.J. Cameron The Call of
Our Own Land (Toronto: The Home Mission Board of
the Baptist Convention of Ontario and Quebec 1922).

16. Ibid., 14.

17. Ibid., 14, cf. Rev. (Captain) Wellington Bridgeman,
who was prepared to go beyond restriction and to
send all the Huns home so that returning veterans
could have their lands and homesteads (Breaking
Prairie Sod (Toronto: The Musson Book Co. Ltd.
1920, 184ff.).

18. Ibid., 15.

19. _Ibid._, 17.

20. Hugh Dobson 'Canadianization and Our Immigrants'
    Social Welfare (1 January 1920) 95. In 1913 Hugh
    Dobson became a field secretary for the Methodist
    Board of Temperance and Moral Reform at thirty-four
    years of age. In 1925 he became an associate
    secretary of the Board of Evangelism and Social
    Service in the United Church of Canada and he re-
    tired as West Coast Secretary in 1949. Cf. Hugh
    Dobson 'My Thirty-Six Years' _Annual Report of the_
    Board of Evangelism and Service, The United Church
    of Canada (1949) 44-47.

21. _Ibid._, 96.

22. _Ibid._, 96.

23. Kate A. Foster _Our Canadian Mosaic_ (Toronto: The
    Commission Council of the YWCA 1926).

24. _Ibid._, 9.

25. _Ibid._, 80.

26. Editorial 'The Church as Melting Pot _The New Out-_
    look (2 December 1925) 4.

27. _Ibid._, 4.

28. Louis Rosenberg _Canada's Jews: A Social and Eco-_
    nomic Study of Jews in Canada (Montreal: Canadian
    Jewish Congress 1939) 123.

29. No studies of millennialism in Canadian Protestant
    thought have been made, but the millennial overtones
    in the vision of Canada as 'His Dominion' are obvious
    in the following: W.T. Gunn _His Dominion_ (Toronto:
    The Canada Council of the Missionary Education Move-
    ment 1917); Daniel Varmorman Lucas _Canaan and Canada_
    (Toronto: William Briggs 1904); C.H. Schutt and
    C.J. Cameron _The Call of Our Own Land_ 1944.

30. E.L. Chicanot 'Moulding a Nation' _Dalhousie Review_
    9 (1929-30) 232-37.

31. J.C. Cochrane _Trails and Tales of the North Land_
    (Toronto: The Committee on Young People's Mission-
    ary Education 1934) 129.

32. E.H. Oliver His Dominion of Canada (Toronto: The Board of Home Missions and the Woman's Missionary Society of the United Church of Canada 1932) 29-30.

33. Cf. W. Kirkconnell A Slice of Canada: Memoirs (Toronto: University of Toronto Press 1967).

34. United Church Year Book (1933) 134. For further material on Dr. R.B. Cochrane, see my article 'The Religion of WASPS' Christian Outlook 19 (April 1964) 3-7.

35. Ibid., (1941) 119-20.

36. Ibid., (1945) 137.

37. Cf. Allan Smith 'Metaphor and Nationality in North America' Canadian Historical Review 51 (September 1970) 247-75.

38. The continued use of this image among Anglo-Catholics and conservative Protestant groups can be traced through the following references: I.C. McCausland ssje His Dominion 6 (1 August 1957) 4; and 11 (1 November 1962) 5; Leslie K. Tarr This Dominion His Dominion: The Story of Evangelical Baptist Endeavour in Canada (Toronto: Fellowship of Evangelical Baptist Churches in Canada 1965) 172; T. Johnstone 'Our Spiritual Heritage' Canada's Centennial E.N.O. Kulbeck (ed.) (Toronto: Pentecostal Assemblies of Canada 1967) 10-11.

RÉCIT MYTHIQUE DES ORIGINES QUÉBÉCOISES

LOUIS ROUSSEAU : article paru dans Studies in Religion/
Sciences Religieuses 3: 2 (1973). Président de la SCER/
CSSR, directeur du départment des Sciences Religieuses
de l'Université du Québec à Montréal et auteur de La
Prédication à Montréal 1800-1830 : Approche religiologi-
que (1976).

RÉSUMÉ

Study of Québec historiography and other literary genres
of the 19th Century reveals a corpus whose purpose is to
establish a sacred foundation for the people of Québec
questioning themselves then about their future. Analysis
of this corpus as myth offers a new approach to the corpus which until recently was examined from a purely social
or ideological point of view.

Using the methods of R. Barthes, Rousseau distinguishes
in Faillon's Histoire de la colonie française en Canada
certain narrative aspects according to characters, code
of action and levels of narration. This Histoire is
written in such a way, then, that the Reality under the
surface of events may be seen as a living force moving
the new nation towards its sacred destiny.

Faillon's Histoire may be classified as myth because
it satisfies four essential elements of any mythic writing: its narrative form concerns events relating to
festive ritual; its characters are presented as supernatural heros or saints; their action involves the creation of a new reality; this reality points to the underlying, invariable and eternal World Order, History.
Providence reveals itself in history, promising blessings
and success to those who seek the salvation of man, instead of economic advances doomed to failure in the new
colony.

It remains now for religious studies to determine
whether Faillon's Histoire is alone in its mythical
interpretations of Québec history or whether it is part
of a whole tradition in which a dynamic set of symbols
are used to explain the force behind French Canadian
nationalism.

LOUIS ROUSSEAU

LA NAISSANCE DU RÉCIT MYTHIQUE DES ORIGINES QUÉBÉCOISES[1]

Le Québec connaît depuis la fin des années cinquante
un renouveau considérable de son historiographie[2].
Cette transformation du regard et de l'écriture historique s'est accompagnée d'une analyse de l'entreprise
des devanciers. Des "fondateurs" du dix-neuvième siècle,
seul Garneau et spécialement le premier Garneau,
nationaliste libéral, surnage. Les tenants d'une interprétation "providentialiste" du devenir collectif,
Faillon, Ferland et Casgrain, voient par exemple leur
cas réglé en deux pages par Serge Gagnon dans son essai
d'historiographie canadienne[3] : "auteurs d'une 'biographie' nationale empreinte d'héroisme" . Les études
sur l'idéologie ultramontaine au Québec dans les années
1840-90 s'attardent davantage à la version conserva-
trice et religieuse de l'histoire nationale.[4] Mais
jusqu'ici, personne, semble-t-il, ne s'est avisé de
considérer cette production historique dépassée sous
l'angle d'une production religieuse et de l'analyser
comme telle. Lorsque l'on y remarque la présence
d'une explication théologique de l'histoire, cela suffit
pour disqualifier l'oeuvre ou la refiler à l'historien
des mentalités.

La recherche dont cet article fournit un premier
exemple fait l'hypothèse qu'il existe, dans l'historiographie québécoise et dans d'autres genres littéraires
de la deuxième moitié du dix-neuvième siècle, un corpus
dont le propos est de fournir un fondement absolu à la
destinée d'une collectivité en crise qui s'interroge
publiquement et passionnément sur son avenir. Ce
corpus contiendrait les éléments quelque fois épars,
d'autres fois organisés, d'un récit des origines du
groupe canadien-français en Amérique du Nord, récit
possédant les éléments constitutifs du mythe et jouant
la fonction sociale de texte fondateur d'une collectivité qui, lorsqu'elle s'y reconnaît, est amenée à
dépasser la contingence de son destin particulier pour
s'intégrer dans un vouloir éternel à validité absolue
et à y trouver les ressorts profonds d'une action
conforme au code élaboré par le mythe. Sous cet aspect
cette recherche propose donc une relecture religiologique d'un moment de la production québécoise qui est
à l'origine d'une tradition et qui n'a reçu jusqu'ici
qu'une attention sociale et idéologique.

44

RÉCIT MYTHIQUE DES ORIGINES QUÉBÉCOISES

Historiens, sociologues et théologiens américains ont remarqué depuis quelques années déjà l'existence chez eux d'une véritable religion nationale dont les hiérophanies constitutrices sont faites des principaux événements de l'histoire américaine et qui se transmet dans le cadre de l'école et des principaux rites civiques.[5] Au Québec, depuis le célèbre essai de Michel Brunet sur les Trois dominantes de la pensée canadienne-française : l'agriculturisme, l'anti-étatisme et le messianisme (1957),[6] on ne cesse de parler de providentialisme et de messianisme en prenant ces traits pour acquis, sans chercher jusqu'à maintenant à situer exactement l'émergence de ces thèmes et leur rapports précis avec la vie religieuse collective. Notre hypothèse suppose qu'au Québec, comme aux États-Unis, il s'est constitué une véritable religion nationale à l'abri de la religion dominante, non pour faire l'unité de groupes ethniques divers,[7] mais pour résoudre la crise interne d'une collectivité qui se retrouve sans direction à la suite des crises politiques qui ont entraîné l'Union, et des crises économiques et démographiques qui provoquent l'émigration en masse vers les États-Unis. A son origine cette religion joue un rôle intégrateur ou réintégrateur. Elle se donne un rituel, les fêtes nationales du 24 juin. Elle articule aussi un récit mythique des origines et conscrit à cette fin l'historiographie. Le messianisme québécois d'antan provient de cette tradition religieuse nationale.

Pour faire apparaître l'existence d'une religion nationale québecoise il est nécessaire de déployer une perspective particulière sur des faits et documents qui n'ont pas jusqu'ici été interprété dans ce sens. On commencera par étudier celui qui semble le père de ce récit mythique des origines québécoises, Étienne-Michel Faillon, p.s.s., auteur de l'Histoire de la colonie française en Canada parue à Paris et à Montréal en 1865-66. Puis on soumettra ce texte aux critères de repérage d'un récit mythique afin d'en vérifier la teneur. Cette opération permettra d'évaluer finalement l'appartenance d'un certain nombre d'autres productions de la décennie 1860-70 à un corpus mythique et de tracer ainsi un premier tableau du moment d'apparition du récit mythique des origines québécoises.

RÉCIT MYTHIQUE DES ORIGINES QUÉBÉCOISES

1. ANALYSE DE l'Histoire DE FAILLON

Pour étudier l'ouvrage de Faillon nous allons nous
inspirer d'une méthode de description proposée par
R. Barthes pour l'analyse structurale des récits,[8]
genre littéraire auquel appartient l'oeuvre qui nous
intéresse. Cette méthode permet de faire apparaître
divers niveaux d'organisation du texte ayant entre eux
une relation intégrative. Dans les limites de cet article nous ferons l'analyse des séquences larges qui
intègrent les unités fonctionnelles plus petites, celle
des actions par lesquelles se définissent les personnages, et finalement celle du niveau narratif. Avant
d'aborder l'analyse elle-même, il sera utile d'indiquer
certains éléments du dossier bio-bibliographique pour
mieux situer notre texte.

1.1. Le narrateur de premier degré : Étienne-Michel Faillon, p.s.s. (1799-1870)

Né le 29 décembre 1799 à Tarascon, E.M. Faillon fréquen-
te le lycée d'Avignon et le séminaire d'Aix-en-Provence
(1818-21) avant de poursuivre ses études théologiques
chez les sulpiciens à Paris (1821-24). Entré dans la
Compagnie de Saint-Sulpice (1825), il fut professeur
au grand séminaire de Lyon (1826-29), de Paris (1829-37)
et directeur du noviciat sulpicien, la Solitude (1837-
1857). Entre-temps il effectua la visite des séminaires
d'Amérique, dont celui de Montréal (1849-50; 1854-55).
Son état de santé l'obligea alors à se retirer à Montréal (nov. 1857 - juin 1862), puis à Aix-en-Provence (1862-
64). Il partit ensuite pour Rome (1864) en qualité de
procureur général de la Compagnie de Saint-Sulpice et
s'occupa activement des intérêts du Séminaire de Montréal alors en brouille avec Mgr Bourget. En 1867, il re-
vint au Séminaire de Paris où, après deux voyages à
Rome (1868, 1869), il mourut le 25 octobre 1870.[9]

De 1829 à 1870 M. Faillon a publié 47 volumes dont
quelques biographies à intention hagiographique, des
documents catéchistiques reliés à la fonction éducative
de la Compagnie, des monuments sur les origines apostoliques de sa Provence natale et finalement quelque 4000
pages de Canadiana liés à ses séjours au Séminaire Saint-
Sulpice de Montréal (près de six ans au total).[10]

L'intérêt d'une lecture des ouvrages consacrés à
l'histoire canadienne et précédant la parution des trois

tomes de son Histoire, tient au fait que l'on assiste
ainsi à la naissance des thèmes principaux qui fourni-
ront la clef de l'interprétation présentée dans l'ouvrage majeur, au terme de quatorze ans de publications
"canadiennes".11 Le thème de base que l'on retrouve à
la fois dans la Vie de Madame d'Youville et dans la
Vie de la soeur Bourgeoys est celui d'un dessein particulier de Dieu dans la fondation de la colonie de Montréal : offrir dans cette colonie une image de l'Eglise
primitive par la sainteté de ses premiers colons. Ce
dessein est d'abord révélé à M. Olier, fondateur de la
Compagnie de Saint-Sulpice et l'un des principaux insti-
gateurs de la Compagnie de Notre-Dame responsable du
projet de colonisation de Montréal. Un second motif
théologique apparaît aussi dès ce moment et s'articule
au premier. Comme Dieu veut paraître en tout l'auteur
de son ouvrage et agir pour ainsi dire en transparence,
il fait éclater le succès de sa colonie au travers des
pires obstacles que l'on puisse imaginer. Sa Vie de
Mademoiselle Mance complète le tableau des premiers
acteurs du dessein providentiel en s'arrêtant au rôle
et à la mission de La Dauversière et de Mlle Mance.
Avec la Vie de Mademoiselle Le Ber le cadre théologique
achève d'être élaboré. Bien avant l'établissement de
Villemarie, les Rois de France, François 1er, Henri IV
et Louis XIII, en envoyant des navigateurs en Canada,
eurent pour motif principal d'étendre, dans ce pays,
les limites de l'Eglise catholique par l'établissement
d'une colonie française. Ce motif de zèle apostolique
guidant l'initiative royale, fut le même qui, un siècle
plus tard, fit s'établir dans l'Île de Montréal une
colonie catholique. Un seul dessein providentiel anime
toute l'Histoire de la colonie française au Canada.
Faillon peut se mettre à l'écrire.

1.2 Dégagement des séquences larges du récit total

La description de l'enchaînement des séquences larges
qui constituent l'Histoire de la colonie va permettre
de saisir d'un seul coup d'oeil l'architecture fonctionnelle générale du récit, la liaison entre les grands
blocs du texte. Pour ce faire, il faut tirer partie
des indications (raccord et coupures) évidentes dans
sa construction : chapitres, parties, qui constituent
autant de systèmes d'ouvertures-fermetures.

Les séquences larges du récit sont au nombre de
quatre et forment le plan de l'oeuvre : (a) une séquence

d'introduction : le religieux et noble dessein de
François 1er d'établir une colonie catholique en Canada
et des tentatives infructueuses; (b) une séquence des
marchands : diverses compagnies sont chargées de l'exé-
cution de ce religieux dessein et le font presqu'avorter;
(c) une séquence d'hommes religieux : une pieuse Société,
par le pur motif du zèle de la religion, entreprend de
réaliser le dessein de François 1er; (d) une séquence
royale : s'inspirant du modèle montréalais, Louis XIV
se met à la tête de l'entreprise pour réaliser le voeux
de François 1er (pp xii et xiii); cette dernière séquence est inachevée.

La première séquence large (introduction) regroupe
quatre sous-séquences dont la première a pour fonction
de donner l'intention fondamentale qui va guider les
sous-séquences qui suivent, ainsi que l'ensemble du récit
(fonction générale de l'Introduction dans la structure
générale du récit) : "désir de porter en Canada la connaissance du Rédempteur et d'y étendre les limites de
l'Église catholique" par le moyen de la colonisation (3).
Les trois autres sous-séquences présentent les 3 premiers
voyages de Cartier comme autant de moment d'une prise de
possession du territoire par des actions fondatrices
s'inscrivant dans le propos général missionnaire (spécialement le 2e voyage). D'une certaine manière il n'y
a pas échec mais suspension, puisque c'est la conjoncture européenne qui suspend l'activité colonisatrice.
Ces trois sous-séquences servent à montrer l'intention
fondamentale, en oeuvre d'une façon exemplaire dans la
prise de possession du territoire par Cartier, bon second
des intentions missionnaires de François 1er (52).

La deuxième séquence large (Les marchands) regroupe deux
sous-séquences (livre 1er et 2e), elles-mêmes regroupant
chacune plusieurs séquences d'extension moindre (la
première et la seconde:5 chapitres). Cette deuxième
séquence a pour fonction générale de montrer comment les
marchands, ne se conformant pas au dessein royal de colonisation à visée missionnaire, échouent. La première
sous-séquence lie des tentatives de colonisations en
Acadie et à Québec qui échouent de par la présence de
marchands huguenots qui empêchent à la fois la colonisation qui nuirait à leur commerce et la mission qui profi-
terait à l'Église catholique. Cette sous-séquence se
termine par la ruine totale de la colonie française de
Québec par les frères Kerke (226). La seconde sous-

séquence décrit une seconde colonie française, "toute
composée de catholiques" celle-là, et dépendante du
cardinal Richelieu. On voit donc rapidement la nouvelle
colonie se pourvoir des éléments les plus propres à
assurer son développement et à procurer la conversion
des nations sauvages (331). Mais le zèle des fondateurs
pour la colonie et la mission est mis en échec par la
Compagnie des Cent Associés qui ne s'occupe que du développement de son commerce et agit sans motifs surnaturels. La colonie est à la veille d'être détruite par
les Iroquois.

La troisième séquence large (les hommes religieux) a
pour fonction de renouer avec le motif de la première
séquence : enfin un projet colonisateur à visée strictement missionnaire et d'inspiration providentielle.
Après une sous-séquence (chap. 1-4) initiale qui pose
Montréal comme l'oeuvre même de Dieu, l'image de la
primitive Église, tout le reste ressortit aux guerres
avec les sauvages, avec ça et là des séquences isolées
qui concernent l'organisation de Villemarie et des événements politiques et religieux à Québec. Ces sous-
séquences d'hostilité indienne font ressortir l'héroïcité
toute surnaturelle de la communauté montréalaise, la
pureté de ses intentions colonisatrices et la protection
évidente de la Providence.

La quatrième séquence large (le roi colonisateur) se
rattache à la première directement : enfin le roi se
résoud à remplir lui-même sa mission de colonisation à
visée missionnaire. La première sous-séquence (livre I)
groupe des séquences qui décrivent la mise en oeuvre
presque systématique d'un programme de colonisation
adapté à la situation, non sans laisser apparaître les
tristes effets moraux de l'établissement des troupes
(ce qui menace le programme missionnaire);le 2e sous-
ensemble (livre 2e) expose la dégradation générale de
la situation sous Frontenanc (1672-82), alors que le
lucre domine dans la vente d'alcool aux Indiens. Et
c'est là que s'interrompt un récit qui devait continuer
beaucoup plus loin.

1.3 Les actions qui englobent les personnages

La brève description de l'organisation fonctionnelle
des séquences qui composent la trame du récit commence
à nous en faire voir le sens. Mais il est possible
d'aller plus loin et de découvrir en quelque sorte la

structure intemporelle qui se module au niveau des séquences temporelles. Et pour ce faire, gagnons le niveau
des actions auxquelles participent les personnages du
récit.

Le récit de Faillon est structuré par le conflit entre
deux désirs ou deux volontés : le désir du salut des
hommes vs l'intérêt personnel. Et comme le premier
désir est posé comme principal (et par conséquent normatif) les personnages peuvent être regroupés dans la
classe des adjuvants et celle des opposants. Nous n'écri-
rons pas ces listes pour le moment. Peut-être serait-il
plus intéressant de reprendre le récit dans ses séquences
larges sous une forme schématique, qui fait apparaître le
rôle structural de la lutte entre les deux désirs dans
l'organisation de l'action des personnages (voir 51-52).

Le système du récit obéit à un code des actions dans
lequel entrent tous les personnages. Ce code appartient
à une histoire de salut et détermine un champ de nécessité, une régulation à l'intérieur de laquelle les personnages futurs (les contemporains du narrateurs) comme les
personnages du récit sont condamnés à agir. La mémoire
réglée révèle la règle de l'imaginaire à venir.

1.4   Le narrateur de second degré et son destinataire

La description du récit débouche sur un dernier niveau
d'intégration du texte, la présence du narrateur et de
son destinataire.   Comment la communication narrative
est-elle signifiée tout au long du récit?

Le donateur du récit annonce dès le début qu'il va se
cacher derrière la facticité des documents qu'il utilise
et organise : Notre dessein est seulement de faciliter
le travail à d'autres, en mettant sous leurs yeux les
documents que nous avons recueillis, et en leur signa-
lant les sources où ils puissent recourir eux-mêmes
(iv). Faire un récit historique consiste à montrer
"la dépendance et l'enchaînement des événements entre
eux" (xi), à laisser s'organiser une pure séquence
factuelle identifiée au Réel. Les intentions surnaturelles et providentielles ne proviennent pas de "pré-
tendues vues générales (-) qu'on se plaît à décorer du
vain titre de philosophie de l'histoire" (x), mais des
faits documentaires eux-mêmes articulés en texte par le
récit. Le narrateur se cache pour que le Réel se manifeste lui-même.

SCHÉMA DES ACTIONS

	1ère séquence		2e séquence	
Adjuvants				
DIEU				
JÉSUS Ordre d'enseigner toutes les nations. S'applique particulièrement aux rois chrétiens.	FRANCOIS Ier Volonté surnaturelle : mission via colonisation.	J. CARTIER Inscrit l'intention missionnaire dans l'espace et le temps primitif.	RICHELIEU Renoue le projet missionnaire et colonisateur.	
opposants				
CONCUPISCENCE Volonté de gloire profane ou d'intérêt propre.		MARCHANDS HUGUENOTS Ne se conforment pas au dessein religieux. Échouent.		CENT ASSOCIÉS Faible appui à la mission, pas de colonisation. Échec.

51

SCHÉMA DES ACTIONS

3e séquence	4e séquence	Code fondamental du système historique
Nouvelle révélation de la vocation missionnaire.		
LES HOMMES RELIGIEUX Les Montréalais reprennent le projet colonisation-missionnaire dans toute sa pureté.	LOUIS XIV Le roi assume directement la réalisation de l'intention missionnaire via la colonisation.	Seul le désir du salut des hommes peut justifier les entreprises terrestres et attirer sur elles la bénédiction divine et le succès.
		Lutte entre les deux désirs.
	Domination du lucre et immoralité menacent la colonie d'un nouvel échec.	Le désir tourné vers la satisfaction de son bien propre pourrit les entreprises terrestres et entraîne leur échec.

RÉCIT MYTHIQUE DES ORIGINES QUÉBÉCOISES

Le destinataire du récit appartient à "la jeunesse
canadienne (qui) tourne (aujourd'hui) ses vues sur son
histoire nationale et se plaît à l'étudier" (ix).
Grâce au récit elle pourra "se former à elle-même une
juste idée du passé, et s'affranchir ainsi de la nécessité de s'en rapporter aveuglément à des écrivains
hardis et superficiels, qui osent donner comme le résumé
de l'histoire les idées qu'ils ont préconçues, sans
prendre la peine de l'étudier" (x). Grâce à la narration, le destinataire pourra donc entrer directement
en contact avec le Réel national, sans nécessité d'in-
termédiaires qui brouillent la communication. L'effet
d'immédiateté est rendu possible. L'absent (le passé
national) accède à la présence directe. Et c'est une
présence profonde qui transmet autant le principe providentiel créateur que la surface des événements. Le
récit est une révélation du Réel national faite à une
jeunesse menacée au moyen d'un narrateur qui se déclare
invisible.

Voilà donc décrite l'architecture de l'Histoire de
la colonie française en Canada à ses divers niveaux
d'intégration textuelle. Il est maintenant possible
de répondre correctement à la question de savoir si nous
sommes en présence d'un récit mythique. Et s'il est
permis de répondre par l'affirmative à cette question,
s'agit-il là du début d'un cycle mythique national?

2. LA NAISSANCE D'UN CYCLE MYTHIQUE NATIONAL

2.1 Les composantes d'un récit mythique

Tant de définitions du mythe circulent dans la littérature scientifique comme dans l'usage courant qu'il faut
préciser à chaque fois la compréhension attribuée à ce
concept de base en religiologie. Pour ce faire il est
utile de distinguer entre ce que l'on peut nommer les
composantes du mythe et ses fonctions (psychiques,
sociales, ontologiques). Comme il s'agit d'abord de
savoir, ici, si l'Histoire de Faillon appartient au
récit mythique, il faut commencer par établir des
critères de repérage.

Nous reconnaissons l'existence d'un récit mythique à
la présence dans une unité textuelle des quatre éléments
suivant :

1. Une forme narrative qui articule ensemble un certain
nombre d'événements. Le mythe doit être repérable au
niveau de la forme littéraire. Si tous les récits ne
sont pas des mythes, tous les mythes apparaissent, eux,
sous une forme narrative qui présente en surface la ré-
gularité d'un avant et d'un après qui lie entre eux
les événements. Si, comme le suppose Gaster,[12] les
récits mythiques les plus primitifs étaient destinés à
présenter les étapes d'un rituel particulier dans leur
contexte idéal éternel, il suffit, selon nous, qu'un récit
conserve ou acquière une relation quelconque avec un
rituel festif ("script" d'un drame, récitatif d'une
cérémonie, "histoire" rappelée à l'occasion d'une fête)
pour qu'on le distingue du pur conte et qu'on l'assigne
à la catégorie du mythe.

2. Les acteurs de ces événements sont présentés comme
des personnages hors de l'ordinaire. Les modes de représentation de cette exceptionnalité, de cette "différence" d'avec le commun des mortels, peuvent varier
énormément selon les systèmes culturels. On peut décrire ces acteurs comme des êtres surnaturels,[13] des
héros[14] des modèles ou des saints. Les héros ne sont
pas rares dans les récits. Aussi ne s'agit-il ici que
d'un élément qui doit coexister avec d'autres.

3. Les acteurs hors de l'ordinaire doivent faire apparaître une réalité nouvelle. Ils sont associés à une
action créatrice (mythes cosmogoniques) ou fondatrice
(la naissance d'un territoire, d'une ville, d'un nouveau mode d'être, etc...). Ils sont reliés à ce qui
est décrit comme une origine, une novation (qui peut
d'ailleurs être une recréation).

4. La réalité nouvelle mise à jour par les acteurs
exceptionnels doit manifester une idéalité ou une forme
éternelle (sacré). Ou, pour tenter de décrire autre-
ment cet élément du récit mythique, la réalité posée
doit être décrite comme porteuse de l'Ordre du monde
ou de l'Histoire. Elle manifeste la Réalité, ce qui
se doit d'apparaître parce que correspondant à la
structure invariable du monde, à la Pensée du monde ou
à sa Volonté.

Pris ensemble, ces éléments fournissent un outil de
repérage du récit mythique tel qu'il est compris le
plus souvent dans le travail religiologique. A ce stade
de développement sa valeur discriminante semble suffi-

sante pour l'interprétation des documents assignables
au dossier d'un mythe des origines québécoises.

2.2 L'Histoire de Faillon est un récit mythique

L'analyse précédante du texte de Faillon permet de voir
immédiatement que l'Histoire peut entrer dans la classe
des récits mythiques. Contentons-nous d'illustrer cette
conclusion.

Aucun doute à entretenir quand à la forme littéraire :
il s'agit bien d'une forme narrative qui articule des
événements selon la règle de l'avant et de l'après. Le
contexte rituel de ce récit n'apparaît pas. Il n'est
pas impossible que les fêtes de la Saint-Jean, organi-
sées par la Société Saint-Jean-Baptiste et indicatrices
d'un sentiment nationaliste assez fort dans la petite
bourgeoisie professionnelle et marchande à laquelle
Faillon destine son oeuvre, ait joué un certain rôle
d'incitation à l'origine de l'Histoire. Mais c'est
beaucoup plus du côté d'une relation conséquente à la
production de l'oeuvre qu'il faudra chercher.

Même réponse affirmative du côté du statut "héroïque"
des acteurs impliqués dans la naissance de la colonie
française en Canada. On a vu comment le récit structure
l'action dans un conflit entre deux types opposés d'ac-
tants, les adjuvants et les opposants. Les adjuvants
se caractérisent tout au long du texte par la force
active en eux des "motifs surnaturels" qui leurs permettent de développer la vertu héroïque nécessaire pour
participer au religieux dessein de François Ier. Les
héros singuliers qui se détachent sont François Ier,
Jacques Cartier, Champlain, Maisonneuve, Dollard et ses
compagnons, pour ne nommer que les principaux. Mais
tous les adjuvants, en bloc, participent au statut
d'exceptionnelle surnaturalité dans leur motivation et
leur conduite.

Faillon souligne dès le début de l'Introduction à
son Histoire que l'étude des toutes premières origines
de la colonie n'a pas encore été faite (il cite quand
même Ferland) et que ce sujet revêt,selon lui, un intérêt bien spécial pour les Canadiens. Il ne nous dit pas
pourquoi "l'histoire de la colonie, le motif de son
établissement, son origine, ses progrès, les obstacles
persévérants qu'elle a rencontrés, les moyens qui ont

triomphé de ces obstacles : tous ces détails (sont)
d'un intérêt particulier pour les Canadiens". (i).   Il
suffit qu'il ait effectivement décrit une fondation,
l'apparition d'une nouveauté radicale en terre américaine : une colonisation française destinée à étendre
"les limites de l'Eglise catholique" . Pour les Canadiens ce récit devenait celui de la genèse d'une nation.

   Le dernier élément caractéristique du récit mythique,
ce que nous avons décrit comme sa fonction hiérophanique,
transparaît clairement dans l'architecture des actions
schématisée plus haut.   La structure conflictuelle du
récit reproduit le code fondamental du système historique tel qu'établit par Dieu, la loi de l'économie sal-
vifique. "L'Histoire" révèle la Providence à l'oeuvre
pour réaliser en nouvelle France son dessein éternel
de rédemption et triomphant d'autant plus glorieusement
du mal que les héros se trouvent les plus démunis devant
les obstacles.   Dans le texte, la Réalité apparaît,
faisant oublier tous les processus des médiations (dont
l'auteur du texte).   Le Présent éternel parle, et ce
qu'il donne à espérer c'est que la bénédiction divine
et le succès attendent ceux qui justifient leurs entreprises terrestres par le seul désir du salut des hommes
tandis que l'échec est promis à ceux dont le désir n'est
tourné que vers la satisfaction de leur bien propre.

2.3 L'Histoire, texte unique ou début d'une tradition?

Dès lors que l'interprétation de l'oeuvre de Faillon qui
en fait un récit mythique des origines semble s'imposer,
deux types de questions apparaissent.   Le premier concerne la genèse et la structure d'un type spécifique de
discours (accompagnant possiblement un rituel), destiné
à former le noyau d'une "religion civile" canadienne
puis québécoise.   Le second concerne le ou les sens
fonctionnels à donner à ce discours : à quelle sorte de
besoin historiquement déterminé répond-il?   Nous vou-
drions consacrer les dernières pages de cet article à
un essai d'éclaircissement préliminaire de ces questions,
essai qui ne se présente qu'à titre d'orientations pour
des recherches ultérieures.

   Explorer la genèse d'un récit mythique des origines
devrait conduire non seulement à identifier un point
d'émergence à partir duquel une certaine structure de
récit se constitue, mais aussi éclaircir les processus
de production, notamment l'inscription du texte parti-

culier dans les conflits qui opposent des groupes en
lutte pour la domination de la société.[15] L'ambition de
la présente étude étant plus modeste, nous avons réduit
la question de la genèse à l'exploration d'un certain
nombre de productions susceptibles d'avoir participé
à la naissance du mythe national entre 1860 et 1870.

En 1859, un Français, François-Edme Rameau de Saint-
Père, fait paraître à Paris un ouvrage intitulé La
France aux colonies.[16] Inspiré par plusieurs correspondants canadiens au nombre desquels on retrouve l'historien F.X. Garneau,[17] et aussi par ses propres théories
sur la francophonie, l'ouvrage retient l'attention du
fait qu'il esquisse des propositions concernant l'avenir
des Français d'Amérique à partir d'un "tableau du développement progressif de la population et des faits qui
s'y rattachent" . Une analyse schématique de cet ouvrage qui connut une assez large diffusion au Canada, fait
apparaître une référence fondatrice à un passé, une
origine archaïque. Mais ce passé qui oriente le présent,
c'est l'idéal gréco-latin fait de modestie des moeurs
et de culture de l'esprit, idéal qui forme en quelque
sorte la "destinée naturelle" du peuple canadien, le
creuset de sa vraie puissance. S'il veut accomplir sa
vocation, le Canada français doit continuer dans la
ligne de l'agriculture et de la culture des valeurs
plus gratuites de l'esprit, ce qui le distingue des
États-Unis et lui confère la supériorité incontestable
du spiritualisme sur le matérialisme. Voilà un idéal
appelé à une grande fortune chez les définisseurs de
la vocation française en Amérique. Mais Rameau de Saint-
Père n'entreprend nulle part de conférer aux événements
fondateurs de l'histoire nationale une fonction hiérophanique et pour cette raison ne peut s'inscrire dans
la structure générale du récit mythique dont Faillon
fournit le modèle.

J.B.A. Ferland fit paraître à Québec en 1861 et 1865
les deux volumes de ses Cours d'histoire du Canada
d'abord livrés sous forme orale à l'Université Laval.
Il s'agit d'un cycle narratif, limité à la période
française, mais affecté d'une sorte de rigueur positi-
viste qui enlève aux séquences et aux actions toute
portée sursignifiante. Ferland fait l'histoire d'une
colonie catholique et estime que le peuple actuel gran-
dira s'il demeure fidèle à la religion qui l'a formé.
Mais ses convictions ne le conduisent pas à manifester,
dans le récit de fondation, l'oeuvre d'un dessein éter-

nel. On comprend que Faillon, qui l'a connu, ait estimé pouvoir apporter une nouvelle interprétation.

Le sondage peut être étendu du côté de la production littéraire qui baigne alors en plein romantisme, ce qui favorise une mise en forme d'un passé héroïque et normatif.[18] Nous nous arrêtons à un manifeste qui entend définir les voies d'avenir d'une littérature national, Le mouvement littéraire en Canada, de l'abbé H.R. Casgrain.[19] L'originalité de l'auteur tient dans sa position de deux stades dans l'histoire nationale. Le premier stade est marqué par la présence et l'action de trois types de figures à grandeur mythique : la France - mère patrie, le Défricheur et l'Évangélisateur. Ce premier stade détermine les caractères nécessaires pour l'entrée dans le deuxième stade qui est celui du récit littéraire sous les formes de l'histoire (F.X. Garneau) de la poésie (O. Crémazie) et du roman (F.A. de Gaspé) : "Notre littérature sera grave, méditative, spiritualiste comme nos missionnaires, généreuse comme nos martyrs, énergique et persévérante comme nos pionniers d'autrefois" (25). "Mais surtout elle sera essentiellement croyante, religieuse; telle sera sa forme caractéristique, son expression; sinon elle se tuera elle-même. C'est sa seule condition d'être; elle n'a pas d'autre raison d'existence; pas plus que notre peuple n'a de principe de vie sans religion" (26). Ces conditions se retrouvent dans la production littéraire récente. C'est pourquoi le critique Casgrain fait de ces pionniers de l'esprit le sujet d'un nouveau récit mythique : en eux se manifeste la vocation providentielle de notre peuple en Amérique, opposer au positivisme anglo-américain, à ses instincts matérialistes, à son égoïsme grossier, les tendances d'un ordre plus élevé qui sont l'appanage des races latines, une supériorité incontestée dans l'ordre moral et intellectuel, dans le domaine de la pensée (27). Inspirée par Rameau de Saint-Père dans son image de la vocation nationale, l'abbé Casgrain fonde mythiquement la destinée nouvelle de la nation en Amérique sur l'action des figures originelles de la Nouvelle France. A ce titre il apporte une contribution capitale dans la naissance et la structure d'un récit mythique national.

Le discours pastoral à contenu plus doctrinal pourrait-il témoigner lui-aussi de l'apparition d'un mythe des origines nationales. Un sondage de ce côté permet sinon de conclure du moins de situer les Quelques considérations sur les rapports de la société civile avec la religion et la famille[20] de ce champion de l'ultra-montanisme que fut Mgr L.-F. Laflèche, évêque des Trois-Rivières. Il ne s'agit pas d'un récit, bien que le texte enchasse ça et là des fragments narratifs. Lorsque l'auteur fait appel à l'histoire, c'est pour en dégager la structure de fond, qui est théologique. En ce sens il fournit un cadre providentialiste universel à ce fragment qu'est l'histoire nationale. La religion est à l'origine de tous les peuples. Il en est de même pour le Canada avec les figures de Cartier, Champlain, Brébeuf et Laval. Dans la mesure où une nation est fidèle à sa vocation originelle qui est d'origine divine, dans la même mesure elle encourt la bénédiction et le succès. Le discours doctrinal de Laflèche cadre bien avec la structure du monde révélée par le mythe des origines nationales, même s'il n'en reprend pas la forme narrative.

3. CONCLUSION

Ce premier sondage effectué dans la production de 1860-70 ne permet pas d'identifier un auteur unique comme la source ponctuelle d'un récit mythique des origines québécoises. L'Histoire de Faillon s'impose comme un texte singulier par la clarté de son appartenance aux critères du mythe. Il est le premier producteur reconnaissable. Mais il reste à établir s'il a été le fondateur d'une tradition. Le survol décennal que nous avons effectué ne permet pas de le dire. Il faudrait pousser plus avant la recherche.

L'enquête devrait se porter en priorité du côté des fêtes nationales et tout spécialement celle de la Saint-Jean-Baptiste.[21] Il faudrait conjuguer l'interprétation religiologique de leurs rituels assez complexes avec l'analyse des discours de circonstance qu'y prononçaient notables laïcs et clercs. Un début de sondage de ce côté révèle la présence d'une sacralisation des origines tout à fait dans la ligne de notre hypothèse. En plus des fêtes de la Saint-Jean-Baptiste, il faudrait être attentif aux dévoilements de monuments commémoratifs, aux grands congrès nationaux, aux tricentenaires, etc.

On est en droit d'attendre beaucoup d'une étude de ces sources. Elle permettra probablement d'identifier une tradition mythique qui a joué un rôle dans la constitution d'un stock dynamique de symboles qui expliquent la force étonnante du nationalisme canadien-français puis québécois à travers des conjonctures bien différentes. Elle a joué un rôle important aussi dans l'orientation de l'action collective, servant bien souvent de texte fondateur à nos courants idéologiques et permettant leur diffusion populaire. Plus profondément encore on peut dire que cette tradition a répondu au besoin fondamental qu'éprouve toute collectivité de sortir de la pure contingence où s'effrite sa valonté de vivre ensemble. Un "nous" collectif n'est vraiment assuré que lorsqu'il parvient à se donner une origine absolue. Et c'est là une tâche que seul le théologien - mythologue peut assurer. Seule la parole croyante peut franchir la rupture entre la contingence radicale d'une destinée nationale et la Parole qui assure du triomphe de la vie. Le religiologue ne peut qu'indiquer le lieu et la fonction d'une interprétation qu'il n'est pas à même d'exercer dans les limites qu'il assigne à son discours. Peut-être son travail aidera-t-il à mesurer l'urgence d'une intervention théologique dans la conjoncture québécoise actuelle. En d'autres temps ce service de l'espérance nationale a déjà été assumé.

60

NOTES

1. Elaboré dans le cadre d'un séminaire de maîtrise en religiologie à l'UQAM, ce texte doit beaucoup aux travaux de ses participants : Mlle Gabrielle D'Amour, M. Gaétan Bourdages, Fernand De Guise, Maurice Locat et Jean Rochon.

2. Pour un survol général du territoire occupé par l'histoire culturelle québécoise au cours des derniers quinze ans, avec insistance sur le réseau interdisciplinaire qui l'a rendue possible, on lira avec profit la note critique de Yvan Lamonde <Histoire, sciences humaines et culture au Québec (1955-70)> dans RHAF 25, 1 (1971) 106-13.

3. Dans A. Beaulieu, J. Hamelin, et B. Bernier Guide d'histoire du Canada, Les cahiers de l'Institut d'histoire 13 (Québec : PUL 1969) 27-8. L'auteur reprend actuellement en profondeur sa critique historiographique dans sa thèse doctorale.

4. Fernand Dumont s'est tout particulièrement interrogé sur la fonction sociale de cette historiographie : "Idéologie et savoir historique" Cahiers internationaux de sociologie 35 (1963) 43-60; "Idéologie et conscience historique dans la société canadienne-française du XIXe siècle" dans France et Canada-français du XVIe au XXe siècle (Québec : PUL 1966) 269-90.

5. Ces recherches ainsi que les principales sources documentaires se trouvent réunies dans Conrad Cherry, God's New Israel, Religious Interpretation of American Destiny (Englewood Cliffs, NJ : Prentice-Hall 1971).

6. Edition la plus récente dans La présence anglaise et les Canadiens (Montréal : Beauchemin 1968) 113-66. M. Dussault effectue présentement une recherche doctorale sur le messianisme québécois sous la direction d'Henri Desroches.

7. S.F. Wise, "God's Peculiar People" dans Le Bouclier d'Achille, éd. W.L. Morton (Toronto, Montréal : McClelland and Stewart 1968) a déjà souligné la fonction différentielle des théologies providentialistes au Canada. A l'inverse du cas américain,

chaque théologie est embrigadée au service d'un
groupe particulier. M. Despland a déjà soutenu une
hypothèse assez opposée à la nôtre, "Traditions
religieuses en Amérique du Nord" dans Religion,
Cahiers de Cité libre 3 (Montréal 1967) 27-52.

8. "Introduction à l'analyse structurale des récits"
    Communications 8 (1966), 1-27. Pour une présentation
    plus détaillée d'une technique d'analyse des unités
    fonctionnelles d'un récit qui dégage les types élé-
    mentaires qui structurent toute narration, on lira
    avec profit, Cl. BREMONT, "La logique des possibles
    narratifs", idem, 60-76.

9. S. Gagnon, art "FAILLON", E.-M." dans Dict. biogr.
    du Canada, IX, PUL, 1977, 271-274. Voir aussi
    O. Maurault, "M. Etienne Faillon" (1799-1870)",
    Cahiers des dix, 24 (1959), 151-65, avec portrait
    de Faillon.

10. On trouve une bibliographie partielle de Faillon
    dans C. Desmazures M. Faillon, prêtre de Saint-Sulpice
    (Montréal : Bibliothèque paroissiale 1879) II-IV.

11. Vie de Madame d'Youville, fondatrice des Soeurs de
    la Charité, de Villemarie, dans l'île de Montréal,
    en Canada, Villemarie, chez les Soeurs de la Charité,
    Hôpital Général, 1852, XXIX, 491 p; Vie de la soeur
    Bourgeoys, fondatrice de la Congrégation de Notre-
    Dame de Villemarie en Canada, suivie de l'histoire
    de cet Institut jusqu'à nos jours, Villemarie, Soeurs
    de la Congrégation, 1853, 2v; Vie de Mademoiselle
    Mance et histoire de l'Hôtel Dieu de Villemarie, en
    Canada, Villemarie, chez les Soeurs de l'Hôtel Dieu,
    1854, 2v; L'héroïne chrétienne du Canada ou Vie de
    Mlle Le Ber, Villemarie, chez les Soeurs de la Con-
    grégation de Notre-Dame, 1860, xix, 404 p.

12. Th.H. Gaster, "Myth and Story" Numen 1 (1954) 184-212.

13. Selon l'expression de M. Eliade, Aspects du mythe
    (Paris : Gallimard 1963) 30.

14. J. Campbell, The Hero with a Thousand Faces.

15. Dans le cas de Faillon on doit parler d'une double
    appartenance. En tant que membre du clergé de France
    son texte renvoie à la situation de la fraction clé-
    ricale de la bourgeoisie française qui tente d'ori-

enter l'impérialisme français des années 1850-70
du côté d'un appui réciproque des entreprises mar-
chandes et missionnaires en terre étrangère. En
tant qu'auxiliaire du clergé québécois et plus particulièrement les sulpiciens de Montréal, Faillon travaille d'autre part à confirmer la position dominante de l'appareil religieux dans la structure du
pouvoir et, plus largement, du discours religieux
au sein de l'instance idéologique. Pour situer ce
problème de la genèse du mythe des origines québécoises dans la perspective de l'analyse marxiste on
lira avec profit Gilles Bourque et Nicole Frenette,
"La structure nationale québécoise," Socialisme québécois, 1971, 109-155.

16. La France aux colonies: études sur le développements
de la race française hors de l'Europe. Les Français
en Amérique: Acadiens et Canadiens (Paris: A. Jouby
1859) xxxix, 160, 355 p.

17. J. Bruchesi, "Les correspondants canadiens de Rameau
de Saint-Père" Cahiers des Dix 14 (1949) 82ss.

18. Cf. l'étude de L. Lamontage, "Les courants idéologiques dans la littérature canadienne-française du
19e siècle" Recherche Sociographique 5, 1-2 (1964)
101-19.

19. Dans Le Foyer canadien, IV (1963), 1-31.

20. Parues d'abord sous forme d'articles dans le Journal
des Trois-Rivières, elles furent publiées en volume
à Montréal, 1866.

21. Une thèse de maîtrise en histoire portant sur la
fête de la Saint-Jean-Baptiste à Montréal de 1842
à 1908 vient d'être présentée au département d'Histoire de l'Université d'Ottawa.

DE LA CHUTE D'ATÉ au DRAGON VOLANT

GEORGES TISSOT : article écrit spécialement pour ce
volume. Etudes supérieures sous la direction de
Mircea Eliade à Chicago (Départment d'Histoire des
Religions). Il est auteur d'un volume de poèmes, En
Passant, avec Serge Fuertes et Pierre Pelletier (1975),
et a publié des articles dans SR sur les religions
amérindiennes. Il est professeur adjoint de sciences
religieuses à l'Université d'Ottawa.

RÉSUMÉ

From the early 18th Century comes Joseph-François Lafitau's
analysis of an Iroquois creation myth, a story of the
creation of three Indian tribes: the Wolf, the Bear and
the Tortoise. Lafitau compares this myth to other similar stories of creation, such as those of ancient
Greece and the Hebrew Bible. Despite what appears at
first as fortuitous similarities, Lafitau analyses the
stories' plots, themes and symbols and shows how the
Greeks and the Indians were expressing the same mythology. From further comparisons, Lafitau concludes that
within the Iroquois myth lies proof for the argument
that the American Indians originally came from far
Asiatic lands.

The purpose of the article, however, goes beyond the
presentation of Lafitau's analysis. Its concern centres
on the underlying presuppositions built into Lafitau's
analysis, presuppositions that reflect his own times
and the then current attitudes towards native literature.
These presuppositions include the supremacy of Christianity as the source of truth, the superiority of the
written form of a tradition over the oral, and the priority given to history and reason over myth. For the
readers of the 20th Century, then, this study of the
Iroquois story is an encounter with Lafitau's times and,
by reflection, with our own times. For, to disentangle
such presuppositions means to disentangle oneself: our
own cultural and religious norms begin to emerge and to
challenge our own approaches to other religions.

GEORGES TISSOT

DE LA CHUTE D'ATÉ au DRAGON VOLANT
Un mythe Iroquois au XVIIIe siècle

Je choisis un texte[1] du début du XVIIIe siècle. Dans cet
ensemble, un sous-ensemble : il s'agit d'un mythe iroquois
d'origine. Ce sous-ensemble est situé. Voici sa situation. Chez J.-F. Lafitau la connaissance passe par les
voies de la genèse. Elle suit aussi des tracés dans
l'escape. Ici, l'Amérique et ses habitants, là, l'Europe
et le monde connu de la Méditerranée à la Chine. Comment
les espaces et les habitants se rejoignent? Lafitau pose-
ra une conjecture à la suite d'Acosta : "L'opinion la plus
universellement suivie et la plus probable est celle qui
fait passer toutes ces Nations dans l'Amérique par les
terres de l'Asie"[2]. C'est vraiment par la découverte même que cette opinion peut être éclaircie[3]. Les conjectures touchent à une plus ou moins grande probabilité.
Lafitau affirme au début que de son travail de comparaison
des "Moeurs des Amériquains avec celles des Asiatiques
et des Nations comprises sous les noms des Peuples de la
Thrace et de la Scythie, il résultera dans la suite de
cet Ouvrage comme une espèce d'évidence, que l'Amérique
a été peuplée par les Terres les plus Orientales de la
Tartarie"[4]. Existent des différences de conviction, de
preuve, d'adhésion, d'appui, disons des niveaux de science. Il s'agit de cerner la question de l'origine des
nations qui habitent l'Amérique. Avec nuance, circons-
pection et mesure; la science ne fait pas fi de la découverte, reconnaîtra Lafitau, même si elle use de la comparaison.

Au sujet de la période de peuplement de l'Amérique on
trouve de semblables approximations. L'Ecriture Sainte
sera constamment une référence. Lafitau y regarde des
faits. Sur la manière du peuplement : "Le passage qu'ont
fait en Amerique les différentes Nations qui y ont péné-
tré, s'est fait probablement en divers temps. Les plus
recentes ont poussé les autres devant elles, les con-
traignant de leur céder la place"[5].

Quels peuples et pourquoi?[6] L'origine des Hurons et
des Iroquois?[7] Le sentiment de l'auteur?[8] L'enquête
n'est pas terminée; elle a exploré l'espace, le temps,
les moeurs, la langue, les ethnies. Que disent les sauvages eux-mêmes sur leur origine? Voilà la question.
Lafitau l'exprime. Le sauvage pourra lui aussi circuler
dans l'encyclopédie. Il prendra place à la bibliothèque
européenne. Il témoigne dans un discours fabriqué, conçu
et livré par un autre. La tradition orale sera traduite

en Lettres. Un passage de l'oralité à l'écriture par
la traduction. Le texte à scruter est ainsi situé :
Il est découpé d'un ensemble, les "Moeurs des Sauvages
Amériquains comparées aux moeurs des premiers temps"
et d'un sous-ensemble sur l'Origine des Peuples d'Amérique. Il suppose chez son auteur des choix, il renvoie
à toutes sortes de chemins. Il s'agit ici d'en dégager
la loi. De préciser comment fonctionne la démarche de
J.-F. Lafitau.

Passons aux éléments en jeu dans ce témoignage du
Sauvage traduit par Joseph-François Lafitau. Donnons le
texte ici même :

> "Voici comment les Iroquois racontent l'ori-
> gine de la Terre & la leur. Dans le commence-
> ment il y avoit disent-ils, fix hommes; (les
> Peuples du Pérou & du Bréfil conviennent d'un
> pareil nombre.) D'où étoient venus ces hom-
> mes? C'eft ce qu'ils ne fçavent pas. Il n'y
> avoit point encore de terre, ils erroient au
> gré du vent, ils n'avoient point non plus de
> femmes, & ils fentoient bien que leur race
> alloit périr avec eux. Enfin ils apprirent,
> je ne fçais où, qu'il y en avoit une dans le
> Ciel. Ayant tenu confeil enfemble, il fut ré-
> folu que l'un d'eux, nommé Hogouaho ou le Loup,
> s'y tranfporteroit. L'entreprife paroiffoit
> impoffible, mais les oifeaux du Ciel de concert
> enfemble, l'y éleverent, en lui faifant un
> fiége de leur corps, & fe foûtenant les uns
> les autres. Lorfqu'il y fut arrivé, il atten-
> dit au pied d'un arbre que cette femme fortit
> à fon ordinaire pour aller puifer de l'eau
> à une fontaine voifine du lieu où il s'étoit
> arrêté. La femme ne manqua point de venir
> felon fa coûtume. L'homme qui l'attendoit,
> lia converfation avec elle, & il lui fit un
> préfent de graiffe d'Ours, dont il lui donna
> à manger: Femme curieufe qui aime à caufer,
> & qui reçoit des préfens, ne difpute pas long-
> temps la victoire. Celle-ci étoit foible
> dans le Ciel même, elle fe laiffa féduire.
> Le maître du Ciel s'en apperçût, & dans fa
> colere il la chaffa & la précipita: mais dans
> fa chûte la Tortûe" la reçût fur fon dos, fur
> lequel la Loutre & les poiffons puifant de
> l'argile au fonds des eaux, formerent une

petite Ifle qui s'accrut peu à peu, & s'é-
tendit dans la forme où nous voyons la terre
aujourd'hui. Cette femme eut deux enfans
qui fe battirent enfemble; ils avoient des
armes inégales dont ils ne connoiffoient
point la force, celles de l'un étoient offen-
fives, & celles de l'autre n'étoient point
capables de nuire, de forte que celui-la
fut tué fans peine.

De cette femme font defcendus tous les autres
hommes par une longue fuite de generations,
& c'eft un évenement auffi fingulier qui a
fervi, difent-ils, de fondement à la dif-
tinction des trois familles Iroquoifes &
Huronnes, du Loup, de l'Ours, & de la
Tortue   lefquelles dans leurs noms font
comme une tradition vivante, qui leur remet
devant les yeux leur histoire des premiers
temps."9

Le Sauvage parle. L'Iroquois plutôt. Lafitau introduit ce texte. "On ne peut rien tirer des Sauvages en
general touchant leur origine."10 Le Sauvage parle et
ne parle pas. Pourtant dans leur nom de clan, le Loup,
l'Ours, et la Tortue, est inscrit "une Tradition vivante,
qui leur remet devant les yeux leur histoire des premiers
temps."11 Leur nom social parle d'un événement "aussi
singulier qui a servi, (...), de fondement à la distinction des trois familles Iroquoises et Huronnes"12. Même
si on ne peut rien tirer d'eux quand à leur origine, ils
conservent en mémoire "leur histoire des premiers temps".

Existe bien chez eux une inscription sociale de l'histoire, une mémoire liée à un type particulier d'écritu-
re13, une "espèce de Tradition sacrée qu'ils ont soin
d'entretenir"14. Histoire sociale, histoire religieuse
et histoire naturelle.

Cette histoire-mémoire est au régime de l'oralité.
L'événement tôt ou tard se dissémine, se disperse, fuit,
se perd, change. Il devient trace, vestige. Déguisé,
obscurci. Ne correspondant plus, ou le sait-on vraiment, comment le savoir? De bouche à bouche, la Tradition "reçoit dans toutes quelques altérations". L'original "dégenere en fables si absurdes".15 C'est la loi
de la rumeur : méfiance, incertitude, absurdité, dégradation. Sans contrôle, la vérité se transforme jusqu'au

68

méconnaissable. Les méditations sont indéfinies, à la
limite elles produiront le non-sens.

"N'ayant point de Lettres, ils n'ont point aussi de
fastes et d'Annales sur lesquelles on **puisse** compter."16
L'Ecriture est garante de la mémoire, de la conservation,
de l'histoire, de l'ordre, de la confiance. L'Ecriture
reçoit la confiance. Elle porte le sens parce qu'elle
demeure, parce qu'elle restreint au minimum les médiations. Tradition orale, médiations maximales, traditions
écrites, médiations minimales.

Ici, tradition et écriture s'opposent. Cette "Tradition sacrée" des Sauvages "ne peut point caractériser
aucun Peuple particulier pour les rapporter à une origine connue"17. Comment récupérer le récit? Est-il pure
absurdité, pur non-sens? Et alors, comment l'interpréter?

Et le texte enchaîne : "si ce n'est la premiere origine
de tous les hommes, qui étant de tous les faits historiques le plus frappant, a laissé de plus profondes traces
qu'on peut voir presque sans exception chez toutes les
Nations incultes"18. Une autre référence interfère :
le commencement, l'origine. La limite de l'histoire
comprend tous les hommes, toutes les origines et toutes
les traces. Elle comprend aussi toutes les Nations incultes presque sans exception. Ce qui est premier, l'est
à tous les plans. La profondeur première, horizon-
tale ou verticale, devient ineffaçable et donc normative
en tous sens. Origine, profondeur, référence, continuité et permanence.

Envers et contre toute altération, toute méfiance, tout
obscurcissement, toute absurdité, toute dégradation,
l'événement premier s'inscrit telle une trace inoubliable.
L'on sait que l'Ecriture Sainte en conserve la référence.
La mémoire peut être évaluée; l'oralité possède une mesure. L'écriture devient ici lieu de conservation, lieu de
continuité, mesure et référence. L'origine est une limite, elle définit l'histoire, elle détermine les traces.
Elle commande l'interprétation.

Le mythe-fable. Le résumé par Lafitau du mythe iroquois
est très succint.19 Par sa forme aussi, il indique une
différence d'espace mythique. Voyez les comparaisons,
les court-circuits, les questions, la schématisation, les
équivalences, la morale, l'économie des détails, l'essen-

tiel : la charpente du récit. L'oral devient l'écrit.
L'écrit est déjà dans l'oral.

Autre approche du récit par une allusion : Prométhée
et Deucalion. La fable des Sauvages et celle des Grecs
partagent l'absurde et le ridicule. Voilà que Lafitau
opère le partage du raisonnable et du fabuleux. Les
Grecs "qui étaient des gens si spirituels"[20] ont inventé
Prométhée et Deucalion. Fable du vol du feu, fable de
la réparation du monde, de l'humanité sauvée. A première vue on ne peut voir ici que des associations for-
tuites. Prométhée dérobant le feu, sauve les humains,
Hogouaho dans le mythe iroquois fait un voyage au ciel,
"dérobe" la femme et assure une descendance humaine.
Deucalion et Pyrrha peuple le monde, le mythe iroquois
fait allusion à la descendance humaine. Pourquoi évoquer
ces deux 'fables'? Voyez. La fable iroquoise raconte
un voyage au ciel et la chute de la femme, le peuplement
du monde après la formation de la terre sur les eaux.
Un parallèle possible : Prométhée, le voyage et le vol
du feu, Deucalion, le peuplement de la terre. Il y a
plus. Lafitau après son commentaire du mythe iroquois
rappelle : "Les Sauvages en general ont aussi tous quelque connaissance du Déluge (...); mais la maniere diffe-
rente dont ils racontent qu'en ont été préservez les
Réparateurs du Genre Humain, est aussi mêlée de fables
que celle des Déluges de Deucalion et d'Ogyges".[21] Il
rappelle plus loin que selon d'autres peuples une autre
"créance très-ancienne, (existe) par laquelle ils sont
persuadés (...) (que le monde) doit aussi périr à la fin
des temps par le feu qui doit le consumer entièrement"[22].
Indication brève. Certes. L'auteur laisse entendre des
parallèles possibles. Les Grecs et les Sauvages expriment la même mythologie et la même théologie. Voyage
au ciel, femme, feu, terre, eau, descendance, à l'origine
et à la fin. La construction est claire, les évocations
ne se font pas au hazard. Prométhée et Deucalion, voyez
le début et la fin du récit Iroquois. Considérez
l'allusion au déluge et celle ici au feu. Deucalion,
Prométhée, eau, feu, réparation, destruction. Ce premier
parallèle posé n'est qu'une indication de certaines simili-
tudes. Poursuivons.

Genèse. Trois appuis, trois fondements, trois lectures
passent "au travers de cette fable". Approfondir, démê-
ler, découvrir[23], creuser[24]. Dévoiler ou rejoindre le
"temps de la premiere invention de cette Theologie symbolique",[25] "la Religion ancienne que les peuples ont

travestie quand ils ont cessé de l'entendre"[26], enfin
l'origine première. Refaire le parcours et montrer le
système. Donc, dans cette fable "on croit entrevoir la
verité malgré les ténèbres épaisses qui l'enveloppent".[27]
La vérité se démêle : "la femme dans le Paradis terrestre, l'Arbre de la science du bien et du mal, la tentation où elle eut le malheur de succomber, (...) la colère
du Dieu chassant nos premiers Pères du lieu de délices"
au lieu de ronces et d'épines, et "le meurtre d'Abel par
son frère Caïn".[28] Premier appui, première lecture,
premier fondement : s'y dégage la charpente du récit.
Elle est claire. Le mythe iroquois est le miroir du récit
de la genèse. Seul la connaissance de l'origine première permet cette lecture. Déjà dit par l'auteur, l'origine première est ineffacable. D'où le déchiffrement du
mythe-fable iroquois. Il passe alors au deuxième fondement.

La chute d'Até. Le deuxième fondement est la "Mythologie des Anciens". La genèse déguisée. Doublement. La
vérité est plutôt déguisée "que tout-à-fait ignorée(s)".[29]
La fable iroquoise, c'est Homère qui raconte la chute
d'Até. Até et Eve sont inter-changeables. De même,
Ata-entsic, un nom huron, "c'est un nom composé d'Ata,
qui désigne la personne, et de Entsi, qui, dans la composition, signifie un excès de longueur, ou d'éloignement
de temps et de lieu, ou qui est un superlatif en matière
de bien ou de mal."[30] Ata, Até, d'Homère, Atté de l'Evasme des Bacchantes, formation d'Atté, Athene, Athena, Athre-
na, Atheronia (Minerve), d'Atergatis, d'Adargatis, Athar-
gatis, Athara, Athyr, Astur, Astarté.[31] "Des mots dé-
rivés de la même racine (Acte, Attis, Actea, Attica), et
se rapportent tous au temps de Cecrops l'époux de Pandore,
c'est-à-dire, au temps de nos premiers Pères, au temps
d'Adam, dont le nom signifiant l'Homme, convenait à
l'Epoux et à l'Epouse, et a pû être appliqué à des hommes
et à des femmes".[32] Au delà du détail, entendez le processus, un engendrement par similitude de nom, d'état,
d'action, de temps, un retour à l'origine, un déchiffrement des traces, une archéologie des espaces vers le fondement, un dévoilement de la lumière. Ce que la Religion
enseigne, "Cette fable a aussi son fondement dans la Mythologie des Anciens, ou bien des choses que la Religion
nous enseigne sont plûtôt déguisées que tout-à-fait igno-
rées".[33]

Homère "a voulu représenter la Concupiscence" ou bien
"le Peché même".[34] St. Justin Martyr, lui, "prétend

qu'Homère a décrit par Até le peché des Anges Rebelles, et le juste châtiment dont Dieu les punit".[35] Dégageons le trajet. Até égale Evohé, une acclamation des Baccha- nales. L'"Evasme des Bacchantes se rapportait à Eve", selon saint Clément d'Alexandrie.[36] Dans les Fêtes des Barbares Até sera aussi un nom par lequel Eve était dé- guisée. Et Homère a pris cette fable des Barbares, avoue l'auteur. Voilà, dans le temps, de l'origine aux Barba- res à Homère; dans la désignation, de Eve à Até à Ata- entsic;dans le récit, de la genèse aux Barbares à Homère et aux Iroquois; les événements, du Paradis au Péché à la chute; dans l'interprétation, d'Homère à St.-Clément d'Alexandrie à Lafitau. La ligne est tracée; le même se retrouve sous ses vêtements divers ou sous ses mouvements semblables.

Autre exemple. L'Ile flottante dans le récit Iroquois "a encore beaucoup de rapport à la fable de Latone". L'on sait qu'il s'agit de la naissance d'Apollon et de Diane (Artémis). Lafitau se permet une autre allusion historique. Déjà il a souligné qu'Homère a pris la fable d'Até chez les Barbares. Ici une autre note s'ajoute à la conjecture. Les Lyciens honoraient d'un culte parti- culier le Dieu Apollon. La fable de sa naissance pouvait avoir crédit chez eux. "Si les Iroquois sont originaires de ces Peuples barbares dont j'ai parlé,[38] les Grecs au- ront emprunté d'eux le fonds de cette fable qui pouvait avoir du crédit parmi les Lyciens".[39]

La mythologie des anciens dévoile un autre fondement. Fable de la femme et de la chute, fable de la Terre et de la naissance. L'indication vers les origines suggère qu'un fond vient de "ces Peuples Barbares". Lafitau prati- que ce qu'il nomme une Théologie symbolique. Elle a "com- me deux parties; l'une Physique, et l'autre Historique".[40] Déjà s'esquisse un vague croquis d'une dégradation de l'origine et d'une continuité par les traces. Des premiers temps à ceux des Barbares, de ceux-ci à une multitude de peuples dont les Grecs et les Amériquains.[41] D'une Re- ligion pure à une Religion ancienne, puis de celle-ci à celles qui en sont le travestissement. Le deuxième fonde- ment, "la Mythologie des Anciens", propose des parallèles entre les fables et suggère des repères 'historiques'. Conjectures. L'application d'un récit à un autre se rattache à la partie historique de la Théologie symboli- que.

L'auteur passe alors à un autre plan archéologique :

DE LA CHUTE D'ATÉ au DRAGON VOLANT

"Peut-être qu'en creusant encore d'avantage, on trouve-
rait que cette fable est fondée sur un autre symbole de
la Théologie Payenne".[42] Plus haut l'accent est placé
sur la correspondance entre des fables, maintenant on
introduit une correspondance entre symboles.

De la Tortue. Elle est le symbole de l'harmonie du
monde, de la génération, "de la Terre et de son Elément".
"Vichnou métamorphosé en Tortüe" a sauvé le monde de
l'abîme où il s'enfonçait.[43] Le Dieu sauveur. Le dragon
volant des Chinois "peint dans leur Temple couvert d'une
écaille Tortüe est le soutien du monde.[44] Le Dieu sauveur, source de vie, providence. "On voit dans les anciens monuments une Tortüe" aux pieds d'Harpocrate".[45]
Voir Venus Uranie dont les pieds portent sur le dos d'une
Tortue. Signification : Dieu est auteur de l'harmonie
du monde.[46] La symbolique de la théologie païenne montre
un Dieu créateur, sauveur et soutien du monde. La tortüe a conduit au Dragon volant.

Des sauvages à l'Ecriture Sainte (genèse), des sauvages
à la mythologie des anciens, des sauvages à la théologie
symbolique païenne, trois parcours à la recherche des
fondements sur l'unique fond. "Le fonds de cette fable,
qui est par-tout la même, prouve que la Tortüe était un
Symbole de cette Religion ancienne que les Peuples ont
travestie quand ils ont cessé de l'entendre".[47]

Suivons ces tracés. Le premier indique la charpente
du récit : la femme au ciel, l'Arbre, la faute, la chute
et le fratricide. Cette charpente est telle une trace
dans le récit iroquois. Première référence : la genèse.
Le deuxième tracé : la femme, le mal, péché ou concupiscence, la chute et le banissement; la terre, l'île
flottante, le salut possible, la suite des générations.
Le troisième : la tortue, symbole de l'harmonie ou de
l'auteur du monde, de la génération et du salut, de la
terre et du soutien du monde. Ici, le voyage passe chez
les anciens, en Inde et en Chine.

Tout l'espace est parcouru, de l'Amérique à la Chine.
Et l'espace mythologique, de même : de la création du
monde, de sa réparation, de son soutien ou de sa pré-
servation (Genèse, Chute d'Até, Ile flottante, Prométhée
et Deucalion, Vichnou, Dragon volant). Le trajet symbolique parcourt aussi trois noeuds : la tortue, symbole
de l'Auteur, du Sauveur et du soutien du monde. Hazard?
Non pas. Correspondances. La conjecture de fond n'est-
elle pas que les peuples d'Amérique sont venus de la

Tartarie orientale, et ces derniers seraient issus de ces peuples barbares d'avant les peuples de la Grèce?

La mythologie des anciens tout, comme les symbols de la théologie des paiens des modes de la genèse. Généralisons. Les traditions des peuples se rattachent à l'Ecriture Sainte, l'oral à l'écrit.[48] La théologie symbolique tant dans "sa physique" que dans "sa partie historique" est une. Existe donc une systématique symbolique. Quelles que soient les régions, l'espace mythique est "par-tout" le même. Il se rattache à une même origine qui, en tant que trace, est identique partout. L'Ecriture en est l'expression. Les fables et les symboles, qu'ils soient de Grèce, de l'Inde, de Chine ou de l'Amérique, possèdent déjà leur lecture. La loi de cette lecture : "par-tout le même". La loi du texte ici découpé : le même est partout. A comparer, on trouve le semblable; à descendre, à creuser, on trouve le fondement. La loi de la méthode, le même, partout le même. D'où la méthode, le texte et le réel religieux sont ici homologues.

Il resterait à montrer comment ce texte choisi et découpé comme un sous-ensemble, dit la loi d'un autre ensemble, le chapitre sur la religion, et celle du grand ensemble : les "Moeurs des Sauvages amériquains comparées aux moeurs des premiers temps".[49]

NOTES

1.   Joseph-François Lafitau, Moeurs des Sauvages
      Amériquains, comparées aux moeurs des premiers
      temps, Paris, Saugrain et Hochereau, 1724 (deux
      tomes, 610 p. avec une Préface, un Frontispice,
      19 planches et figures et explications (19 p.);
      490 p. avec 22 planches et figures et 7 pages
      d'explication, et table alphabétique des princi-
      pales matières (39 p.)). Je me réfère à cet ou-
      vrage : I, 39 ou II, 49. Sur Lafitau, voir ré-
      férences dans : Customs of the Americans Indians
      Compared with the Customs of Primitive Times,
      edited and translated by William N. Fenton and
      Elizabeth L. Moore, in two volumes, vol. 1,
      Toronto, The Champlain Society, 1974 (voir In-
      troduction, p. xxix-cxix; p.81-86 et note 1,
      p.82, sur le mythe iroquois de création).

      Georges Tissot, "Jean-François Lafitau : Figures
      anthropologiques", Sciences Religieuses, 4:2
      (1974/5), p.93-107 (corriger le titre à Joseph-
      François Lafitau); ajouter William N. Fenton,
      "J.-F. Lafitau (1681-1746), Precursor of Scien-
      tific Anthropology", South-western Journal of
      Anthropology, 25 (1969), p.173-187; Idem, arti-
      cle "Lafitau, Joseph-François", Dictionnaire
      biographique du Canada, t. III, 360-365; Pierre
      Vidal-Naquet, "Les jeunes. Le cru, l'enfant grec
      et le cuit", ds Faire de l'histoire sous la di-
      rection de Jacques le Goff et Pierre Nora, Paris,
      Gallimard, 1974, tome III, p. 137-168.

          Au début du XVIIIe siècle, la France comme
      d'autres pays continue de constituer son escape mythi-
      que ou l'espace de ses mythes. C'est une formation
      culturelle liée aux autres formations culturelles et
      aux formations en général : économiques, sociales,
      politiques... (M. Serres, "Les sciences" ds Faire
      de l'histoire, op. cit., p.203). Circulent dans
      cet espace mythique des mythes qui appartiennent
      à d'autres cultures. L'étude de ces mythes est
      une partie intégrante de cet espace si l'on tient
      l'hypothèse de Lévi-Strauss à savoir que l'étude du
      mythe recrée le mythe ou propage l'expansion du my-
      thique. Donc, trois éléments généraux permettent
      de circonscrire notre espace mythique : les mythes
      que l'on dit nous appartenir, les mythes appartenant
      à d'autres et qui circulent en travers de notre cul-

ture et l'étude de ceux-ci et de ceux-là. Le nous
utilisé ici est variable à souhait selon les limites que l'on désire choisir : France, Europe-
ouest, Occident-ouest, Indo-européen, Amérique du
nord, etc. D'où un problème : comment s'articule
le rapport entre nous et les autres, entre le même
et l'autre, dans cet espace mythique. Question de
coexistence, de la libre circulation des symboles,
des mythèmes, question des amalgames, des transformations, des interférences, des osmoses entre les
les mythes, etc. Ce problème est au centre des
préoccupations reliées à la rencontre des cultures,
à l'oecuménisme des religions, à la libre circulation des idées, des hommes et de toutes les formations, sciences, religions, arts, etc.

Toute étude des mythes d'une société donnée
soulève maintenant ces questions et contribue à
examiner les voies possibles de solution. C'est
à fonder : le mythe est lui-même un récit qui constitue des réseaux de communication, discours plein
de parcours connectés; la communication des mythes
favorise la communication entre les hommes; le mythe
émerge du lieu de l'être religieux, du lieu du devenir de l'homme, de ce lieu des communications
(M. Eliade, L'histoire des croyances et des idées
religieuses, tome 1, Paris, Payot, 1976, p.7-8);
s'y exprime la puissance créatrice et épiphanique
de l'homme, l'imaginaire, lui-même non délimité
par les frontières (G. Durand, L'imagination symbolique, Paris, P.U.F., 1968; Science de l'homme
et Tradition, Paris, Tête de feuilles, 1975, chap.
2e et conclusion; R. Alleau, La science des symboles, Paris, Payot, 1976); le mythe est lié à un
dispositif symbolique autonome et unique qui résout
les antinomies (D. Sperber, Le symbolisme en général,
Paris, Hermann, 1974, p.127-160; Le structuralisme
en anthropologie, Paris, Seuil (coll. Points),
1973); il parcourt tous les espaces, sa dynamique
transformatrice recèle un langage pourvu d'une
grammaire qui règle les questions d'échange (Lévi-
Strauss); bref, le mythe est peut-être le discours
de la coexistence ou de la co-incidence des opposés
-- penser à 'des différences'. L'histoire de la
rencontre des mythes montrerait, je suppose, que
l'espace des uns était exclusif, le même qui demeure le même contre l'autre, que l'espace d'autres
mythes était inclusif, le même-autre mais

ramené au même, ou que l'espace était inclusif-exclusif, il produit de la différence (cf. la problématique de l'ethnocide, R. Jaulin, De l'ethnocide, Paris, U.G.E., 1974).

Je remonte ici à une origine de ce processus de la circulation des mythes dans un même espace social donné. Cette origine est le début du XVIIIe siècle. Etudier un mythe iroquois tel que situé par J.-F. Lafitau, c'est choisir un moment de la problématique évoquée plus haut et d'en dégager la loi.

2.   I,34 Cf. Margaret T. Hodgen, Early Anthropology in the Sixteenth and Seventeenth Centuries, Philadelphia, University of Pennsylvania Press, 1964, p.313.

3.   Ibid.
4.   Ibid.
5.   I, 41.
6.   Ibid.
7.   I, 69-89.

8.   I, 89-91. Cf. "Les Sauvages en general n'ignorent point aussi qu'ils sont étrangers aux païs qu'ils habitent présentement. Ils disent qu'ils sont venus de loin du côté de l'Ouest, c'est-à-dire de l'Asie." I, 101.

9.   I, 93-95.
10.   I, 92-93.
11.   I, 94-95.
12.   I, 94.

13.   "(...) il me suffit de dire en general que tous ces Peuples ont entr'eux une très-grande quantité de symboles et de figures de toutes espèces, qu'on peut regarder comme un langage particulier, lequel est assez étendu, et supplée en beaucoup de choses au défaut de l'écriture, d'une manière même qui a quelque chose de plus commode qu'une lettre." II, 47.

14.   I, 93.
15.   Ibid.
16.   Ibid.
17.   Ibid.

18. Ibid.

19. Cf. Hewith, J.N.B., <u>Iroquoian Cosmology</u>, first part.
     Bureau of American Ethnology Annual Report,
     1899-1900. Washington, D.C., Government Prin-
     ting Office, 1903, p.133-339. <u>Iroquoian Cosmo-
     logy</u>, second part. Bureau of American Ethnology
     Annual Report, 1925-1926. Washington, D.C.,
     Government Printing Office, 1928, p.453-819.
     Le terme fable est employé par Lafitau. Nous
     le reprenons sans pour autant vouloir discuter
     tout le problème du statut du mythe et de la
     fable. W.N. Fenton, "This Island, The World on
     the turtle's back", <u>Journal of American Folklore</u>,
     75 (1962), p.283-300.

20. I, 95.
21. I, 100-101
22. I, 101.
23. I, 95.
24. I, 98.
25. I, 98.
26. I, 100.
27. I, 95.
28. Ibid.
29. I, 95-96.
30. I, 244.
31. I, 245-246.
32. I, 246.
33. I, 95-96.
34. I, 96.
35. I, 97.
36. Ibid.
37. I, 97. cf. Latone - Léto.
38. cf. I, 81-89, 89-91.
39. I, 98.

40. "La Théologie symbolique avait comme deux parties;
     l'une Physique, et l'autre Historique. La
     première regardait la Divinité dans son essen-
     ce, dans ses attributs, et dans ses effets, par
     où sa toute-puissance se manifeste aux hommes.
     La seconde renfermait, comme dans un corps
     d'histoire ou de fables, certain évenements,
     certains faits importants où la Religion avait
     part, et qui concernaient, ou la manifestation
     des Dieux aux hommes, ou l'histoire des hommes
     qui s'étaient le plus signales par leur piété

envers les Dieux, au nombre desquels ils
avaient mérité d'être mis." I, 224.

41. "Ces Barbares bien que confondus dans les Histoires
par une multitude de noms particuliers à chaque
petit Canton, sont neanmoins assez universellement compris sous les noms génériques de Pelagiens et d'Helleniens, qui, de quelques Peuples
particuliers, avaient passé à toute la Nation."
I, 90-91. "Ceux qui connaîtront suffisamment
les Peuples barbares de l'Amerique Septentrio-
nale, y trouveront le caractère de ces Helleniens et de ces Pelagiens; les uns compris sous
la Langue Huronne, cultivent des champs, bâtis-
sent des cabanes, et sont assez stables dans un
même lieu. Au contraire la plupart des Algon-
quins et des Sauvages du Nord font profession
d'une vie vagabonde, et ne vivent que du bene-
fice du hazard. C'est à peu près la même distinction de Peuples dans l'Amerique Méridiona-
le." I, 91.

42. I, 98.
43. I, 99.
44. I, 100.
45. I, 98.
46. I, 99.
47. I, 100.

48. Sur ce problème : J. Derrida, De la grammatologie,
Paris, éd. de Minuit, 1967; "Sémiologie et
grammatologie" dans Informations sur les Scien-
ces Sociales, V II, 3 (1968), p.135-148;
G. Granel, recension dans la revue Critique,
(1967), p.887-905; Luce Fontaine - De Visscher,
"Des privilèges d'une grammatologie", Revue
Philosophique de Louvain, (1969), p.461-475;
C. Macarin, "Jacques Derrida's Theory of Wri-
ting and the Concept of Trace", Journal of the
British Society for Phenomenology, 3, 2 (1972),
p.197-200; Michel de Certeau, L'écriture de
l'histoire, Paris, Gallimard, 1975 (3ᵉ partie,
Systèmes de sens : l'écrit et l'oral).

49. J'exprime ma gratitude au Dr. John Hare du Département des Lettres françaises de l'Université
d'Ottawa qui m'a prêté si gracieusement l'ouvrage de J.-F. Lafitau, les Moeurs des sauvages
amériquains (...).

THE GIRL WHO MARRIED THE BEAR

ROBERT E. FLORIDA is Associate Professor of Religion at
Brandon University and author of <u>Voltaire and the Soci-
nians</u> (1974). His current research is on John Locke's
religion. The present paper was presented in earlier
versions at the CSSR/SCER meetings in Toronto (1974)
and the International Association for the History of
Religions Congress in Lancaster, U.K. (1975).

RÉSUMÉ

Un mythe des indiens du Yukon nous raconte l'histoire
d'une fille qui a épousé l'ours. En faisant l'analyse
de ce mythe selon la méthode de Lévi-Strauss, on se
rend compte à la fois de la validité et des dangers de
cette méthode.

On découvre, par exemple, que le mythe comporte deux
niveau; d'une part, l'intrigue chronologique révèle le
niveau diachronique, de l'autre, les thèmes ou la
moralité du mythe présente le niveau synchronique, un
niveau qui se situe hors du temps. On découvre aussi
que le mythe est composé d'unités constitutives, que
Lévi-Strauss appelle "mythèmes". Ces mythèmes se
rangent selon les relations d'opposition binaire. De
plus, ces relations se déploient dans de séries de
triades entrecroisantes, par lesquelles un médiateur
devient un des points opposant d'une nouvelle triade.
De cette façon, le développement du mythe se poursuit
en spirale jusqu'à ce que le mouvement intellectuel
soit épuisé.

A chaque étape dans l'analyse, les résultats prévus
par Lévi-Strauss se réalisent et le mythe devient une
expression complexe de la vie sociale et intellectuelle
des indiens. Cependant, le danger du structuralisme
reste dans la prétention que la structure du mythe est
l'unique chose importante. Par contre, la structure
n'est que la grammaire. La signification du mythe devient même plus profonde si l'on incorpore le contenu de
l'analyse dans la forme du mythe.

Claude Lévi-Strauss Meets The Girl Who Married the Bear:
A Structural Analysis of a Canadian Indian Myth[1]

The work of Claude Lévi-Strauss on the structural study
of myth often has an unsettling effect on scholars. As
Edmund Leach put it, 'Lévi-Strauss often manages to give
me ideas even when I don't really know what he is saying.'[2] At times it seems that the structures found by
Lévi-Strauss in the myths he analyzes are not really
there and that he manipulates relationships beyond
credibility. Similar reservations sometimes apply to
the work of his followers: for example, the structural
analyses in Leach's book Genesis as Myth.[3]

In the 1972-73 academic year I had a chance to resolve
my apprehensions about Lévi-Strauss's methods when I
participated in a joint Anthropology and Religion course
at Brandon University on the study of myth. There Dr.
Samuel Corrigan, an anthropologist, formally introduced
me to structuralism. In the course of the course we
taught together, I became convinced of the general
validity of the structural approach to myth by applying
it to a Canadian Indian myth - The Girl Who Married the
Bear.[4] However, certain dangers inherent in this
methodology also became apparent.

In 'The Structural Study of Myth,'[5] Lévi-Strauss
argues that myth operates on two scales: the diachronic and the synchronic.[6] On the diachronic scale the
narrative forges along from event to event in chronological sequence whilst on the synchronic scale time
stands still or collapses upon itself, as it were. 'On
the one hand, a myth always refers to events alleged to
have taken place long ago. But what gives the myth an
operational value is that the specific pattern described
is timeless; it explains the present and the past as
well as the future. . . . [Thus myth has a] double structure, altogether historical and ahistorical.'[7]

To the specialist in religious studies the above
statement will likely evoke Eliade's repeated observation that myth has the quality of arresting time by
homologizing the present to sacral patterns from the
primal times. Whilst Eliade's formulations on the
nature of myth have always seemed or 'felt' right, I
do not think he has demonstrated just how myth functions
on both a chronological and timeless scale. Lévi-
Strauss's method, however, does demonstrate the way that

myth is simultaneously diachronic and synchronic. In short, the story line of the myth is diachronic, and the structure conveys the synchronic or timeless meaning.

Lévi-Strauss's structural anthropology borrows much from structural linguistics, and in his treatment of myth the debt to linguistics is particularly clear: '(1) If there is a meaning to be found in mythology, it cannot reside in the isolated elements which enter into the composition of a myth, but only in the way those elements are combined. (2) Although myth belongs to the same category as language, being, as a matter of fact, only part of it, language in myth exhibits specific properties. (3) Those properties are only to be found above the ordinary linguistic level, that is, they exhibit more complex features than those which are to be found in any other kind of linguistic expression'.8 Or again, 'Myth is language, functioning on an especially high level where meaning succeeds practically at 'taking off' from the linguistic ground on which it keeps rolling'.9

This leads directly to his three hypotheses that determine the practical details of his method. First, 'Myth like the rest of language is made up of constituent units'.10 Second, the constituent unit of myth is the sentence which presupposes the lower units of language: phoneme (the smallest unit of speech that can introduce a change in meaning, mat), morpheme (the smallest unit of stable meaning, mat), and sememe (the unit of meaning in the context of a sentence, definition of mat). Thus the sentence, or 'mytheme' as Lévi-Strauss calls it, is the gross constituent unit in mythology. It is the unit of meaning in the context of a myth.11

Using the first two hypotheses when analyzing a myth, one first isolates the mythemes and writes each one on a card, numbering the cards according to the sequence of mythemes in the story. This series of cards is the diachronic order of the myth. The next part of the exercise, to uncover the synchronic structure of the myth, is technically and intellectually the most difficult. It is here that Lévi-Strauss has made his most significant contribution to the study of myth.

His third hypothesis is that it is the relationships among the mythemes that unfold the ahistorical meaning

of a myth; more specifically, it is the relations among
the 'bundles of such relations' that are significant.[12]
To build on the linguistic analogy, the grammar that
governs the relationships among the mythemes is the a-
historical structure.

To discover this grammar of bundles of relationships,
he specifies that the mytheme cards be arranged in a
rectilinear grid-work pattern in which the horizontal
lines can be read for the historical or diachronic meaning of the myth whilst the relationships among the
vertical columns establish the ahistorical structures.
Again applying the theories of structural linguistics
to the study of myth, Lévi-Strauss postulates that the
grammar of the myth will reveal itself as relations
between binary pairs of contraries or contradictories.
These will be mediated by some character, or thing, or
activity in the myth that lies somewhere in between the
original contraries. This helps explain the often
bizarre forms that appear in mythology. However, when
the real contraries cannot be reconciled, the mediator
in them becomes one of a binary pair that needs mediating itself. Thus a myth structures itself dialectically.[13]

Does the theory work? It was not until I applied the
methodology to The Girl Who Married the Bear that I was
fully convinced that it was more than a beautiful con-
jurer's trick.

The Girl Who Married the Bear is one of 'the favourite
stories of the Tlingit- and Athabascan-speaking Indians
of the southern Yukon Territory.'[14] Catherine McClellan,
an American anthropologist, collected the myth in
English and published eleven variants of the story in
1970. That the myth is available in several versions
makes it more interesting as a test for structural analysis as one of the claims of the structural method is
that all the variants of a myth together constitute the
myth.[15]

One of the features of the analysis of myth is the
necessity for the scholar to present his version of the
myth in question. Because of the limitation of time
and space, it is nearly always necessary to condense
the story. However, in editing the myth, may not the
scholar be consciously or unconsciously shaping the
material to fit his analysis? I do not have a good
solution to this problem; I merely offer my simplified

composite outline[16] of The Girl Who Married the Bear and recommend consulting the complete versions.

A young unmarried girl while berrying by the river shows disrespect for grizzly bears by stepping over their excrement. A handsome man appears and she goes off to live with him. She spends a summer with him eating berries and gophers he catches and cooks, and she discovers that he really is a bear.

When they make a den in the fall, she betrays its position so that her brothers will find them. During the winter she has children who are part bear and part human. She is now also part bear and part human; both she and her children are partly furry.

In the spring the bear dreams that his wife's brothers will hunt and kill him. When they find the den with the aid of dogs, the bear allows them to kill him. Before his death, the bear instructs his wife in the proper rituals and gives her and his children his teeth (bear powers).

When the brothers discover their sister in the den, the younger brother communicates with her. [These people traditionally practised avoidance between brothers and sisters. Only the youngest brother could speak to his sister.][17] Her mother prepares human clothing for the girl and her children, and she lives in a half-way camp as she could not stand the odor of humans.

Next spring she returns to fully human habitation and helps her brothers by pointing out the smoke from bear camps which only she can see. They tease her by making her and her children wear bear skins. [This is a doubly bad act as it shows disrespect to bears and breaks the brother-sister avoidance rule.] Thereupon, she turns into a bear permanently, kills her human family, and she and her bear children go up into the mountains forever.

In analysing this myth, I first isolated the mythemes, a total of 583 in the eleven variants, and wrote them on index cards as Lévi-Strauss recommended. After puzzling for some time trying to find a grid-work that revealed the structure, I arbitrarily decided to concentrate on version 10 of The Girl Who Married the Bear and came upon an arrangement with only five vertical

columns. Although this later proved inadequate, it
unlocked the major structural relations. Then I turned
to version 1a, which with 94 mythemes is the richest
variant; this led to expanding the number of columns to
about ten. After that I worked with all eleven versions
simultaneously and ended up with fifteen columns, including one labeled extraneous. That only five out of
583 mythemes were classified extraneous encouraged me
to think that my categories were not hopelessly off
base. Something like a novice tinker who had taken
apart a clock and reassembled it, I was pleased to find
only five parts left over.

   In pondering the relationships between the vertical
columns, I noted that many of them were concerned with
mediating between the world of man (culture) and the
animal world (nature). This I believe constitutes the
major timeless structure of The Girl Who Married the
Bear. The story begins with a great tension or gulf
between animal and man, temporarily resolves the conflict by means of various mediators, and ends precisely
where it started. This is the sort of pattern that
Lévi-Strauss identifies as typical: To put it into the
type of algebric formulae he dotes upon:

```
culture : nature  ::  girl : bear
girl : bear       ::  girl-bear : bear-man
girl : bear       ::  camp : den
camp : den        ::  half-way camp : marital den
```

and so on.

   In all these algebraic transformations the original
conflict is lessened by substituting mediators that are
less contrary. But the resolution can only be temporary as the contraries are not reconcilable in reality.
Therefore, the story ends with the same gulf between
culture and nature, man and beast as it began with, but
nearly all of the situations are reversed:

Beginning state	Final State
girl	bear
unmarried with male	with children but no
siblings	siblings
low (river)	high (mountains)
food gathering	hunting
camp	den
clothes	fur

This sort of inversion is again precisely what Lévi-Strauss predicts.[18]

A convenient way to express the structure of the story is through a series of interlocked triads consisting of binary opposites and their mediators (figure 1).[19] Each mediator becomes one of the pairs of oppositions in a new triad until the story ends with the final separation. When specific material and social factors are singled out, they too fall into similar structures (figure 2). This, of course, confirms Lévi-Strauss's statement in his programmatic essay of 1955: 'Since the purpose of myth is to provide a logical model capable of overcoming a contradiction (an impossible achievement if, as it happens, the contradiction is real) a theoretically infinite number of slates will be generated, each one slightly different from the others. Thus, myth grows spiral-wise until the intellectual impulse which produced it is exhausted.'[20]

A final graphic rendition of the myth reveals something more of the structure. This time the tabu and social norm violations are stressed. After each one, there is a mythological transformation.

Tabu violations

Bear	Transformation	Family
1. girl violates bear feces tabu		
	girl-bear bear-man	
2. brothers kill bear		2. girl betrays husband and brothers kill brothers-in-law
	girl returns to human state (more or less)	

3. brothers show
   disrespect to
   bear by teasing
   sister with skin

3. brothers tease
   sister and her
   children

girl and cubs
become bears

4. girl kills
   brothers

girl is
permanently
bear

Note that stages two and three involve violations of both family and bear tabus.

On one level then, I have found structural analysis to be a very illuminating tool. Through it I was able to see much in The Girl Who Married the Bear that escaped me when first studying it. Indeed, now I take it very seriously as a complex expression of the material, social, and intellectual life of the Athabascan people, when at first it seemed little more than a vigorous, rough-hewn tale interesting mainly for its drama.

Furthermore, in every point, the basic methodology gave the results predicted by Lévi-Strauss. Since very little ethnographic data was used, this analysis even tends to confirm one of the more controversial claims of structuralism - that myth can be understood in its own context, that structure rather than content is the important thing.[21]

However, Lévi-Strauss's most successful analyses, his study of 'The Story of Asdiwal' and the Mythologiques, do rely heavily on ethnographic data, even though he claims that cultural correlations are structurally unimportant. Along with many other critics,[22] I believe Lévi-Strauss's practice is better than his theory on this point. A structural analysis is much richer, much more illuminating when it incorporates the content as well as the form of the myth.

For example, the basic structure identified in The Girl Who Married the Bear ties in very well with

FIGURE I

Most General Structure

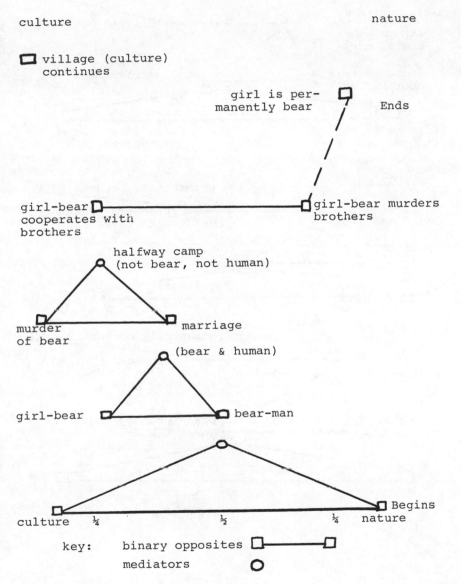

culture   nature

□ village (culture)
  continues

girl is per-
manently bear   □   Ends

girl-bear□————————————□girl-bear murders
cooperates with   brothers
brothers

halfway camp
(not bear, not human)

murder   marriage
of bear

(bear & human)

girl-bear   bear-man

□Begins
culture   ¼   ½   ¼ nature

key: binary opposites □————□
        mediators   O

89

FIGURE 2

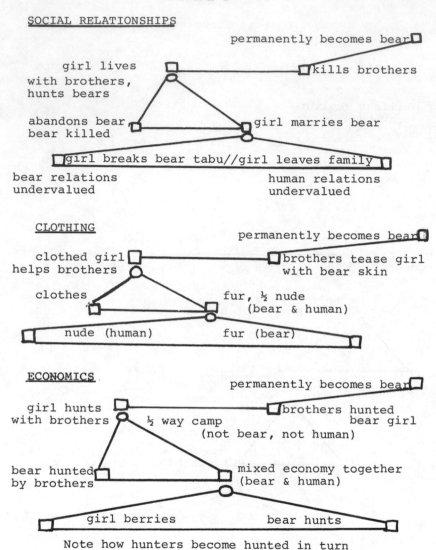

SOCIAL RELATIONSHIPS

permanently becomes bear

girl lives
with brothers,
hunts bears

kills brothers

abandons bear
bear killed

girl marries bear

girl breaks bear tabu//girl leaves family

bear relations
undervalued

human relations
undervalued

CLOTHING

permanently becomes bear

clothed girl
helps brothers

brothers tease girl
with bear skin

clothes

fur, ½ nude
(bear & human)

nude (human)

fur (bear)

ECONOMICS

permanently becomes bear

girl hunts
with brothers

½ way camp

brothers hunted
bear girl
(not bear, not human)

bear hunted
by brothers

mixed economy together
(bear & human)

girl berries

bear hunts

Note how hunters become hunted in turn

90

McClellan's ethnographic observation: 'Indeed, the major philosophical concern of all the Yukon Indians is how they may best live in harmony with the animals who basically have so much more power than do humans, especially since the Indians continually have to confront and kill the animals if they are to stay alive themselves.'[23] Furthermore, when we note that the Athabascans have very negative reactions to nudity,[24] the concern with clothing takes more significance. Similarly in order to comprehend the enormity of the social offenses committed in the story, it is useful to know that the brother-in-law is 'obligated to aid and defend his reciprocal in all ways'[25] and that the brother should always treat his sister with great respect.[26]

Perhaps enough has been said to give some idea of the strength of this methodology, and I would like to conclude with a serious reservation about structuralism. Lévi-Strauss denies that religion has any truth value. Whilst he consistently argues that the structure of mythological thought is no less complex or rational than scientific thought, the content is worthless.[27] Edmund Leach, one of his major followers in the study of myth, occasionally seems to delight in scorning the material he treats. In spite of that, much of Leach's work on the Bible, especially the essay 'The Legitimacy of Solomon' in Genesis as Myth, is brilliant. His structural analysis of the Arian controversy, 'Melchisedech and the Emperor: Icons of Subversion and Orthodoxy,' which relates the theology, social context, and art of the time, is one of the most interesting things I have ever read on the history of the early church.[28]

The most dangerous thing about the structural approach is that it tends to claim that the structure is the only important thing, that content is irrelevant. By its very nature structure is formal, abstract, even at times trivial. As Mary Douglas puts it, 'Instead of more and richer depths of meaning, we get a surprise, a totally new theme, and often a paltry one at that.... It seems that whenever anthropologists apply structural analysis to myth they extract not only a different but a lesser meaning.'[29] Douglas overstates her case[30] - the structural analysis of The Girl Who Married the Bear reveals deeper and more significant meanings than the surface of the story would suggest - but surely Leach goes too far in his 'The Legitimacy of Solomon' when he tries to reduce the entire Old Testament to a coded set of marriage rules.31

After all, the structure is only the grammar of the myth. No one would ever claim that a formal grammatical analysis exhausts the meaning and significance of a Shakespearean sonnet - even less in the case of religious literature. If the historian of religion continues to treat his data with respect and does not lose sight of the content and meaning, then structural analysis can unlock complexities and depths otherwise unsuspected.32 At the very least, a full scale structural analysis demands that every sentence of every variant of a myth be carefully considered and that all inconsistencies and repetitions be accounted for.

FOOTNOTES

1. Earlier versions of this paper were presented at the CSSR meeting of 1974 and the IAHR congress of 1975.

2. Edmund Leach (ed.), The Structural Study of Myth and Totemism (London: Tavistock, 1967), xvii.

3. Edmund Leach, Genesis as Myth and Other Essays (London: Jonathan Cape, 1969).

4. Catherine McClellan, The Girl Who Married the Bear (Ottawa: National Museum of Canada, 1970).

5. Claude Lévi-Strauss, Structural Anthropology (Garden City, N.Y.: Anchor, 1967), 202-228.

6. Ibid., 205 ff; see also Claude Lévi-Strauss, The Savage Mind (Chicago: University of Chicago Press, 1966), 205 ff and 231 ff.

7. Lévi-Strauss, Structural Anthropology, 205.

8. Ibid., 206.

9. Ibid., 206.

10. Ibid., 206.

11. Ibid., 207. The identification of the sentence as the mytheme has been criticized by Mary Douglas, 'The Meaning of Myth, in the Special Reference to "La Geste d'Asdiwal",' in Leach (ed.), Structural Study, 50. Douglas, I think, has confused mytheme with mediator here. For a similar critique, see K.O.L. Burridge, 'Lévi-Strauss and Myth', in Leach (ed.), Structural Study, 97 and 102.

12. Ibid., 207.

13. Ibid., 212, 226, and passim.

14. McClellan, Bear, 1.

15. Lévi-Strauss, Structural Anthropology, 213. This claim is vigorously challenged by G.S. Kirk, Myth: Its Meaning and Functions in Ancient and Other Cultures (Cambridge: Cambridge University Press, 1970), 75.

16. Based on a collation of all eleven versions in McClellan, Bear, and on McClellan's 'Summary', ibid., ix, and 'The Basic Plot', ibid., 5.

17. Ibid., 6.

18. Claude Lévi-Strauss, 'The Story of Asdiwal', in Leach (ed.), Structural Study, 21, for example.

19. This graphic form was suggested by the chart in Morris Freilich, 'Myth, Method, and Madness', Current Anthropology, 16 (1975), 218.

20. Lévi-Strauss, Structural Anthropology, 226.

21. Ibid.,206 and passim.

22. For example, Burridge, 'Lévi-Strauss', 111, and above all G.S. Kirk, Myth, ch. 2.

23. McClellan, Bear, 6.

24. Ibid., 8.

25. Ibid., 6.

26. Ibid., 7.

27. Lévi-Strauss, Savage Mind, 95 and passim.

28. Edmund Leach, 'Melchisedech and the Emperor: Icons of Subversion and Orthodoxy' in Proceedings of the Royal Anthropological Institute of Great Britain and Ireland for 1972. It is not quite so original, however, as Leach seems to think. 'In what sense was early Christian doctrine intermeshed with its social context? It is astonishing to find how little attention has been paid to this rather obvious problem.' (Ibid., 5). His bibliography fails to note the work of Ernst Troeltsch and Charles N. Cochrane.

29. Douglas, 'Meaning', 62-63.

30. Kirk, Myth, 58, points out that the paltriness of the meaning may rather be in the scholar's than the native's understanding.

31. In Leach, Genesis, 54 f and passim.

32. Kirk, Myth, ch. 2, one of the best treatments of Lévi-Strauss on myth, comes to a similar conclusion.

RELIGION IN NEWFOUNDLAND

JOHN R. WILLIAMS is Associate Professor of Religion at
Memorial University of Newfoundland. He has published
Martin Heidegger's Philosophy of Religion (1977) and is
currently doing research for an ethical analysis of
Canadian foreign aid policy.

RÉSUMÉ

Chaque analyse de la religion au Canada doit tenir compte
du régionalisme qui est un trait essentiel de la réalité
canadienne. Terre-Neuve est une des régions les plus
uniques du Canada anglophone. Et, un aspect important
de son identité est le grand rôle joué par des sectes
religieuses. Plus de 80 pour cent de la population est
catholique, anglicane ou de l'Eglise Unie, ces proportions datant de la naissance même de cette province.
Depuis le 19e siècle et jusqu'à 1974, le développement
des partis politiques et la répartition des sièges lé-
gislatifs dépendaient du "principe confessionnel". Presque tout l'enseignement dans la province est encore sous
l'autorité des églises. Ainsi, on voit que dans les
secteurs les plus importants, les églises à Terre-Neuve
ont une influence énorme. En quoi consiste plus précisément cette influence?

On nous donne deux exemples : la chasse au phoque qui
en 1913 a vu la mort de 253 chasseurs; et, plus récemment,
la mort des mineurs au village St. Lawrence. Les deux
exemples confirment l'argument que la religion institu-
tionnelle maintient l'ordre social, le status quo, même
en face de la souffrance et de la mort, causées par l'
irresponsabilité humaine. Dans le dernier exemple, un
anthropologue donne la réponse religieuse en dénonçant
les maux sociaux de nos jours. Auparavant, le silence
des églises s'expliquait par leur indifférence au nom
du salut des âmes. Lutter contre les autorités, c'était
lutter contre la Volonté de Dieu. Aujourd'hui, cette
théologie est rejetée par la plupart du monde. Les
injustices sociales demandent encore plus la participation des religions. Qu'attendent alors les églises
à Terre-Neuve?

JOHN R. WILLIAMS

Religion in Newfoundland: The Churches and Social Ethics

The impossibility of lumping together English-speaking and
French-speaking Canadians in any discussion of religion in
Canada has long been recognized. What is not so familiar,
however, is the great diversity among English-speaking
areas of the country. Over-zealous centralists in
Toronto and Ottawa tend to dismiss any concern for the
preservation of this diversity as "petty regionalism,"
but the diversity continues to exist nonetheless.
Whatever its value, regionalism is an essential feature
of the Canadian reality, and any serious attempt to
describe and analyse religion in Canada must take it
into account.

In many ways the province of Newfoundland is the most
unique region of English-speaking Canada. This is to be
expected, since Newfoundland has been a part of Canada
only since 1949. But even since then, its ethnic
homogeneity (affected hardly at all by immigration), its
speech, its culture and (unhappily) its economy have all
contributed to the maintenance of its distinctive identity. An important feature of that identity is the role
played by denominational religion, and the purpose of
this paper is to describe and analyse this role, with
particular reference to the involvement of the Newfoundland Churches in matters relating to social justice.
It is hoped that this discussion of religion in Newfoundland will contribute to a more complete understanding of religion in Canada.

The most notable feature of religion in Newfoundland
is the virtual monopoly exercised by five Christian
denominations, which together claim the affiliation of
no less than 97.2% of the population (all figures are
from the 1971 census). These five denominations are
the Roman Catholic Church, with 36.6% of the people, the
Anglican Church, with 27.7%, the United Church of Canada,
with 19.5%, the Salvation Army, with 7.9% and the Pentecostal Assemblies of Newfoundland, with 5.5%. These
figures in themselves would perhaps not be so remarkable
were it not for the significance they have been given
in the operation of the province's political and educational systems.

Although Newfoundland was settled by the British as
long ago as the 17th century, it was not granted any
measure of representative government until 1832. Even

96

then the legislature was controlled by a small group of wealthy St. John's merchants, most of whom were Anglican. Although the widely held view that the first political parties were based exclusively on sectarian differences, with the Conservatives being the Anglican party and the Liberals Catholic, is now being called into question, it is clear that one important result of the development of party politics was considerable antagonism between the adherents of the major Christian denominations, Anglicans, Methodists and Roman Catholics. When, in 1861, the Conservatives replaced the Liberals as the governing party, those Catholics who had identified their political fortunes with the Liberals were threatened with the loss of government patronage. Their response was to riot in front of the Legislative Building, and this gesture so affected the ruling Conservatives that they agreed to give a generous share of the spoils of office to the Catholics. According to this "denominational principle," as it was called, positions in the cabinet, the civil service, and all other patronage posts were awarded on a roughly proportional basis among the adherents of the various religious faiths.[1]

Although the denominational principle had been established at a time when there was a Protestant political party and a Catholic party, thus requiring a degree of coalition to be effective, in later times both parties ran candidates of different religious affiliation, although there was strict agreement between the parties that only Catholics would run in one district, only Anglicans in another, etc. In 1904 the makeup of the Legislature was fixed at 13 Catholic seats, 12 Anglican and 11 Methodist. This balance was relatively easy to maintain then, since in most districts the adherents of one denomination were in a definite majority. Since then the sectarian balance has changed significantly, especially in urban areas such as St. John's, Grand Falls and Corner Brook, but also in certain rural areas where the Salvation Army and the Pentecostal Assemblies have increased their membership (usually at the expense of the United Church). Despite these changes, the denominational principle was a major factor in every redistribution of legislative seats up to and including that of 1962. This often necessitated extraordinary measures in regulating district boundaries and/or the number of seats a district might have. It was only in 1974 that the legislative districts were revised in accordance with the principle of representation by population (modified somewhat by the interests of the

governing party at that time) rather than the denominational principle.

The other area in which the denominational allegiance
of Newfoundlanders is of major significance is education.
Primary and secondary education is today, as it has
been for more than a century, under the control of the
Churches. There are no secular or nondenominational
schools funded by the government; rather, public funds
are passed over to the denominational school boards who
own and operate almost all the schools in the province.

The origins of this system are relatively easy to
explain. The colonial administrators of Newfoundland
took no interest in providing educational services for
the residents of the Island, and it was only after the
establishment of the Legislature in 1832 that an Education Act was passed (in 1836) allocating public funds
to this activity. By this time the educational system
of Newfoundland, such as it was, was already operating
to a large extent along denominational lines. The
first schools in the colony had been founded in the 18th
century by the British-based Society for the Propagation
of the Gospel in Foreign Parts. The pioneering work of
this organization was limited to a few settlements, and
it was only with the coming of the 19th century that
schools began to multiply to an appreciable degree.
Although two of the first schools in St. John's, the
St. John's Charity School (1805) and the Benevolent
Irish Society School (1826), were nondenominational,
the trend from the beginning was towards denominational
schools, and eventually both of these schools were
incorporated into the denominational systems. Another
British-based organization, the Newfoundland School
Society (which changed its name several times), established over 40 schools throughout the Island from 1823
to 1845. Although theoretically nondenominational, it
employed only Anglican teachers, and eventually its
schools were included in the Anglican system. The
Methodist Church had also been active in educational
work from the beginning of the 19th century, although it
was not particularly committed to separate denominational
schools. But the opposition of the Anglicans to their
sharing the "Protestant" educational government grant
with the Methodists eventually led to complete separation between the two in 1874. The Salvation Army was
given separate status in 1892, and the Pentecostal
Assemblies in 1954. Both of these established their
own school systems.

98

RELIGION IN NEWFOUNDLAND

When the government of Newfoundland did finally begin
to take an interest in education, therefore, a network
of Church-related schools was already established.
Right from the beginning, the government decided against
the creation of a public school system, and the first
Education Act (of 1836) gave formal recognition to the
existing system by allocating public funds to the Church
related schools. During the 19th century, the ownership
and management of the schools was gradually consolidated
under the control of the denominational authorities, and
despite several attempts by subsequent governments to
modify the system, it still exists today, formally en-
shrined in the Terms of Union (Article 17) of Newfoundland with Canada. Two Royal Commissions, in 1933 and
1967, recommended major changes in the system, but
vigorous protests by the Anglicans (earlier on), the
Pentecostals, and especially the Roman Catholics have
deterred the government from making any drastic revisions.
The only significant development that has taken place in
recent times was the integration of the Anglican, United
Church and Salvation Army schools in 1968. The schools
are still owned and operated by these denominations,
however, so the system remains intact.

It is evident, therefore, that in these two important
sectors of society, politics and education, denominational Christianity has enjoyed considerable influence
in Newfoundland. But how has it used that influence?
This question will be answered here by first making some
general remarks about the social posture of the Newfoundland Churches and then by illustrating these remarks with reference to two specific cases.

Despite their differences with one another, the
Christian Churches of Newfoundland have all contributed
to the maintenance of the prevailing social order.
Church leaders have been most reluctant to agitate for
social change, no matter how obvious the need for such
change. A brief discussion of the social roles of the
three major denominations, Anglican, Roman Catholic,
and Methodist/United Church, will illustrate this
general principle.

Although the Church of England had enjoyed a quasi-
official ecclesiastical status in the colony since the
time of Sir Humphrey Gilbert in 1583, it was not until
the mid-19th century that it established an effective
organization in the colony. The Bishop of London,
under whose jurisdiction the Newfoundland Church fell,

99

left the colony without a minister from 1628 until 1699.
(This was probably the result of the British government's
attempt to discourage permanent residency in Newfoundland
--i.e., by denying the comforts of religion to the
settlers.) In 1787 the Newfoundland Church was incorporated into the diocese of Nova Scotia, but the bishops
of this diocese paid little more attention to the
Island's ecclesiastical affairs than had the bishops
of London. In 1839, when Newfoundland finally got its
own bishop, there were only eight ordained Anglican
ministers in the colony.

As the religion of the dominant merchant class, the
Church of England adopted a conservative stance on most
social issues. (There were many poor Anglican fishermen as well, but their influence on Church policy was
minimal compared to that of the merchants.) The outstanding Anglican churchman of 19th century Newfoundland,
Bishop Edward Feild (bishop from 1844 to 1876), was both
a Tory and a High-Churchman (Tractarian), and he led
the Anglican Church against social change. His attitude
towards the introduction of responsible government has
been described by one writer in this way: "Feild
believed responsible government to be not a religious
but a class issue, a battle of ignorant and uneducated
have-nots against able and educated haves."[2] Although
his feelings on that subject proved to be ineffective,
his attempts to establish a separate Anglican school
system did ultimately prove successful. In arguing for
sub-division of the Protestant educational grant, he
contributed greatly to the enmity between Anglicans
and Methodists, whose ordination and sacraments he
regarded as invalid. Thus, both in politics and in
education the Anglican Church under Feild's leadership
inclined toward a conservative rather than a progressive
standpoint. This attitude has been maintained down to
the present time, as both Church leaders and politicians
have been careful not to incur the disfavour of one
another. Thus, in 1960 the Anglican Bishop John Alfred
Meaden could say, "I am satisfied that everything that
lies within the power of both the Church and the State
is being done to improve education in Newfoundland..."[3]
If there are any areas in which the State is not doing
its best to improve the lot of Newfoundlanders, the
Church of England does not publicize them.

In contrast to the status of Anglicanism, Roman
Catholicism was officially illegal in Newfoundland until
the 19th century. But the large Catholic proportion of

the population, especially in the St. John's area, meant
that the restrictions against the practice of this religion could not be fully enforced. Indeed, Newfoundland
Catholics had their own bishop long before the Anglicans
did, and as this Church's organization developed, it
enabled Catholics not only to rid themselves of their
civil disabilities but even to assume dominant political
power in the 1850's. Having achieved this goal, however,
the Catholic Church turned into just as strong a defender
of the status quo in Newfoundland as the Anglican Church.

The conservative stance of the Catholic Church was in
evidence as far back as 1799 when Bishop O'Donel helped
the government of the colony put down an insurrection by
followers of Wolfe Tone's United Irishmen that could
easily have grown into a revolution against the British
Crown. As a reward, the Bishop received from the Crown
a pension of 50 pounds (Sterling) per year and a grant
of land.[4] Later bishops were to receive similar favours
from the Crown, such as the large tract of land on
which the St. John's Basilica Church and adjacent ecclesiastical buildings now stand. It is true that both
Bishop Fleming (1830-1850) and Bishop Mullock (1850-
1870) sometimes spoke out against the Conservative Party
when the civil rights and access to government patronage
of Catholics were threatened, but once the goals of
Church control of education and a just Catholic share
of patronage were achieved, the Church officials tended
to avoid pronouncements on social and political matters.

Apart from strong interventions against those who
would do away with denominational control of education,
the major political involvement of the Roman Catholic
Church in this century took place during the Confederation debate (1946-48). Under the direction of the
elderly Archbishop Roche, the Catholics waged an intensive campaign against Confederation, preferring instead
a return to responsible government (which had been suspended in 1933 because of the impending bankruptcy of
Newfoundland). The church leaders feared contamination
by the North American value system (including, perhaps,
loss of their control over education and marriage), but
their intervention in the campaign served only to alienate the Protestant majority, and the solid Catholic
vote against Confederation was not sufficient to determine the issue. Although Archbishop Roche did not take
this defeat lightly, refusing to grant Prime Minister
Louis St. Laurent an audience during his 1949 visit to
St. John's,[5] the Catholic Church lost none of its

101

privileges with Confederation. Since then, its leaders have maintained very cordial relations with the government, and, like the Anglicans, Catholic Church officials seldom if ever voice any criticism of government policies or actions or of the social order in general.

The social stance of the Methodist Church is well expressed in this excerpt from a letter of the Methodist missionaries in Newfoundland dated July 22, 1818, welcoming Sir Charles Hamilton as governor of the colony:

...of the Society to which we are connected it is a fundamental rule, that in conformity to the Apostolic injunction we should submit ourselves to every ordinance of man for the Lord's sake....We are expressly prohibited from interfering in political disputes, and it is from principle that we carefully avoid them, striving to be quiet and to mind our own business.[6]

This principle was not always adhered to, since the Methodists did lobby the government in favour of educational grants for their schools and against abuses of the Lord's Day and the consumption of alcohol. In general, though, the Methodists of Newfoundland were interested in the personal salvation of their adherents and not the rectification of social injustices.

Despite the fact that the Newfoundland Methodists were joined to the Eastern British America Methodist Church in 1855 and became part of the United Church of Canada in 1925, they seem to have been untouched by the Social Gospel movement so prominent in both Canada and the United States in the early 20th century. One explanation for this is the relative isolation of Newfoundland from mainland North America, as well as the isolation within Newfoundland of the outports where the strength of Methodism lay. In a paper entitled, "The Influence of Isolation on the Theology of Methodism in Newfoundland 1874-1924," Arthur Kewley states, "Because the Methodist accepted the material universe as God's handiwork, he did not rebel or ask why, nor did he blame God or nature when disaster occurred. His fervent prayer was not that the physical condition or situation should be changed to suit his needs, but that he and his family might be saved."[7] It would seem that the Methodists' acceptance of the world as it is extended not only to the natural order but to the social order as well. For they too have been most reluctant to agitate for social change, and continue to submit themselves to every ordinance of man, no matter how unjust these appear to be.

RELIGION IN NEWFOUNDLAND

An assessment of the Churches' role in social issues, with particular reference to political life, was given in the report of the Royal Commission appointed in 1933 to examine into the future of Newfoundland:

> It might have been expected that the influence of the Churches, so strong in Newfoundland, would have acted as a check to political malpractices. It is clear from our investigations that this is not the case, and we have reluctantly come to the conclusion that the denominational divisions, of which the people are daily reminded, so far from exercising a beneficent influence in the direction of cleaner politics, have failed to check, if indeed they have not contributed to the general demoralization, for members of successive administrations have been led consciously, or sub-consciously, to place the interests of particular sections of the church before the good of the country as a whole. . . .[8]

Despite the many shortcomings of this report, including its lack of objectivity, it is hard to deny the accuracy of this particular passage. And it can be argued that this indictment is just as valid today as it was in 1933, since the conduct of politics is qualitatively little different now than fifty or one hundred years ago, and the Churches' response to this conduct has not changed. To illustrate this continuity we shall now examine two particular social issues, both of which are described in detail in book form, and shall determine the type of response (or lack of response) which the Churches made in each case.

The first issue to be dealt with is the great Newfoundland sealing disaster of 1914, as described by Cassie Brown in her book, Death on the Ice.[9] The second issue also involves a disaster – the death of over one hundred miners from St. Lawrence, Newfoundland due to "occupational diseases." Their story is told in the book, Dying Hard, by Elliot Leyton.[10] Both books provide graphic illustrations of social injustice in Newfoundland society, and they present the ethical issues in such a way that a religious response of one kind or another cannot be avoided. The efforts by the Newfoundland Churches to ignore these issues only serve to confirm the analysis of their position as supporters of the status quo in society.

The Newfoundland seal hunt has received wide publicity
in recent years due to the efforts of certain conservation groups to have it stopped. The violent opposition
which these groups have encountered from Newfoundlanders,
including many who have never even seen a baby seal,
indicates to some extent the important role which the
hunt plays in Newfoundland culture (its once significant
economic role has vastly diminished). Thus, the death
of 253 sealers in 1914 was truly a national tragedy for
the Island, and the unethical practices which contributed to this loss of life were a matter of great public
controversy at the time.

The working conditions endured by the sealers are
described by Harold Horwood in these words:

> The hardships they endured were compounded by the
> greed of the shipowners, who refused to provide cloth-
> ing or safety equipment. The men had no meals to
> cook or any way to cook them: for weeks and months
> they lived on sea biscuit and tea. Even their drink-
> ing water was polluted with blood and seal fat until
> it stank. They slept like cattle in ships' holds
> without bedding. As the pelts and fat piled up, they
> simply lived on top of the cargo in utter filth.
> Injured men recovered as best they could, or died
> without medical help.[11]

In 1913, the leader of the newly formed Fishermen's
Party, several of whom had won election to the House of
Assembly earlier that year, introduced a Sealing Bill
calling for decent food, full-time cooks and other
improvements on board the sealing vessels. In order not
to alienate the fishermen's vote, the government reluc-
tantly allowed the bill to go through the following
year, but only after some of the ships had already left
for the hunt.[12] The government's approach to this
matter was simple and straightforward: the shipowners
(i.e., the wealthy merchants of St. John's) should be
allowed to maximize their profit from the hunt, even if
this meant the neglect of the sealers' safety and comfort. Indeed, the owners of one vessel, the Newfoundland,
even removed the wireless set from the ship because "it
was not giving returns for the money invested."[13] This
particular action was responsible for the death of 79 men.

The official day for seal killing to begin in 1914
was March 15. But by March 26 the crew of the Newfoundland had managed to take a mere few hundred pelts, since

the old ship had been stuck in the heavy ice far from
the main pack of seals. The other ships in the fleet
were doing better, but none of them had encountered the
main pack either. On Monday, March 30, the Newfoundland
met up with the rest of the fleet, and almost immediately the main pack was sighted close by. As the Newfoundland was still stuck in the ice, several miles from the
seals, the captain, Wes Kean, decided to send his men
across the ice to one of the ships closer to the seals
and hunt from there, spending the night on the other
ship if necessary. The other ship was the Stephano, a
new, modern vessel captained by Wes' father, Abram Kean,
the acknowledged master of the sealing captains.

At 7 a.m. on Tuesday, March 31, the Newfoundland's
crew set off. A storm was brewing and the walk across
the ice was difficult. After three hours, the men
still had not reached the Stephano, and 34 of them
decided to turn back. Despite the reprimand they received from their captain for disobeying orders, later
events were to prove the wisdom of their decision.
The other sealers continued on, and finally reached the
Stephano at 11:20 a.m. Snow was beginning to fall, and
the men expected either to remain on board the Stephano
until the storm was over or be taken back to the Newfoundland. Much to their surprise and consternation,
however, after a short lunch break they were ordered
back onto the ice by Abram Kean towards a patch of
seals some two miles farther on.

The Newfoundland crew did encounter some seals, but
after arguing among themselves they decided to abandon
the hunt for the day and return to their ship. By this
time it was 12:45 p.m. and the weather was worsening.
Visibility was down to zero, and the men could only
guess at the position of the Newfoundland. By 2 o'clock
they found the trail they had followed in the morning,
but they were still four hours' walk from their ship.
As the snow deepened, travelling became more and more
difficult, and eventually the path was lost altogether.
The only possible course of action was to prepare for
a night in the open, and the exhausted men set about
building ice shelters.

Meanwhile the crew of the Stephano were certain that
the Newfoundland sealers were in danger. Abram Kean,
however, was equally certain that they had reached their
ship safely, and he refused all suggestions that an attempt be made to find them. The lack of wireless on the
Newfoundland made communication with it impossible.

105

By nightfall a full-scale blizzard was raging. At
midnight the snow turned into rain, a torrential down-
pour. Then suddenly the wind turned around and the
temperature dropped to 16 degrees Fahrenheit, with a
wind-chill factor of minus 20. Some of the men tried
to move around; others, too exhausted, lay down to sleep.
The next morning many were dead. The weather was still
too bad for the survivors to set off again, and they
waited in their now useless shelters for rescue. One
by one the weakest passed away, while the others continued the struggle for survival. The storm was so
fierce that even Abram Kean did not put his men on the
ice to get seals.

Around mid-afternoon the skies began to clear and one
of the survivors spotted the vessel Bellaventure, about
two miles off. Several of the men started towards the
ship, which was approaching them. Two of them got
within a quarter mile of it, but then it turned around
and sailed away, apparently oblivious of the Newfoundland men. They now realized that nobody was looking
for them, nobody even knew that they were lost.

About four miles off in another direction was the
Newfoundland, and twelve of the sealers, having spotted
it, set out towards it. But just as they were getting
close, the Newfoundland finally freed itself from the
ice and started moving away in the opposite direction.
As night fell, the wind picked up and the men were no
closer to being rescued. By 11 p.m. the temperature
was 9 degrees and the wind chill factor was minus 30.
That same night another sealing vessel, the Southern
Cross, was reported lost near Cape Race on the south-
east tip of Newfoundland. No trace of it or its crew
of 173 was ever found.

The second night on the ice proved fatal for more of
the Newfoundland's crew. The next morning was clear,
and those survivors who could still walk once again set
off across the ice towards the two closest ships, the
Newfoundland and the Bellaventure. This time they were
sighted, much to the horror of those on board. A rescue operation was mounted immediately, and first the
survivors, then the corpses were brought to the ships.
It was not until the next day that the survivors were
all on board the Newfoundland and the roll call was
taken. Somehow, forty-seven men had managed to survive
their ordeal; sixty-nine corpses were found, and eight

106

were missing and presumed lost. The <u>Bellaventure</u>
started back to St. John's with the corpses, followed
by the <u>Newfoundland</u> with the survivors, many of whom
were in desperate need of medical treatment. The
<u>Stephano</u>, however, returned to the hunt. For Abram
Kean, the death of 77 men was no reason to stop catch-
ing seals.

On Tuesday, April 7, a magisterial inquiry into the
disaster opened in St. John's. The survivors all
blamed Abram Kean for what had happened. Kean himself
refused to accept responsibility for the loss of life.
He claimed to have been acting in the best interests of
the <u>Newfoundland</u>'s crew by putting them close to a patch
of seals, not far (he thought) from their own ship.
The magisterial inquiry ended inconclusively, and the
only significant result of it was an amendment to the
Sealing Law requiring all ships to carry wireless. A
"Permanent Marine Disaster Fund" was launched, but out
of it crippled survivors and widows and orphans were
paid next to nothing. According to Cassie Brown, "Not
a single cent of damages or other liability was ever
assessed against the companies that sent the men to
their deaths without proper clothing, a decent survival
outfit, the food needed to keep them going under stress,
or signalling equipment on their ships."[14] Later that
year, a public commission of enquiry was established to
reexamine the causes of the <u>Newfoundland</u> tragedy and to
investigate the loss of the <u>Southern Cross</u> and the conditions of the seal hunt in general. Two of the three
commissioners found Abram Kean guilty of a grave error
of judgment by putting the men on the ice at the beginning of a blizzard. However, Kean continued to participate in the seal hunt, and was later awarded the Order
of the British Empire for having killed more seals than
any other man in history.

Like most Newfoundlanders, the sealers were religious
men. They would not hunt seals on Sundays, but spent
the day singing hymns instead. Abram Kean was described
as "a tower of righteousness in a world constantly going
to the devil. . . a strict Methodist (who) campaigned
against liquor and advocated prohibition."[15] It was to
be expected, therefore, that church leaders would take
a significant part in the public reaction to the <u>New-
foundland</u> disaster. As the news of the tragedy reached
St. John's, civic and religious leaders issued messages
of condolance to the suffering and bereaved. The
Anglican Bishop, Llewelyn Jones, in his statement

emphasized the hope of eternal life: "The footsteps of
the merciful God were hard to trace. Yet through the
deep waters He led them, we may humbly hope, to the
haven where there shall be no more parting, and where
the former things are passed away."[16] The Catholic
Bishop, too, limited his comments to words of sympathy
and consolation. Only the Methodist minister, Rev. L.
Curtis, raised the question of responsibility for the
disaster when he asked, "Were we placing too high an
estimate on the value of seals, and too low an estimate
on the value of man?"[17] but he subordinated this concern
to the need for acceptance of whatever happens as an
expression of God's will: "Ours is rather to bow in
the spirit of submissiveness to the decree of the
eternal, and learn such lessons as the awful disaster
is calculated to teach."[18]

The arrival of the dead sealers in St. John's occa-
sioned a number of funeral and memorial services in the
city's churches. Accounts of these were given in The
Daily Mail of April 7, 1914. In all cases the sermons
were similar, emphasizing acceptance of the divine will
and hope of eternal life. At George Street Methodist
Church,

> The preacher advanced facts and arguments to prove
> God's beneficence in the agency of sea. The ocean
> sustains, purifies, unites and inspires. He narrated
> several touching incidents given him by the survivors
> to illustrate the truths advanced. Emphasis was laid
> upon the glorious certainty, that those who sleep
> shall awake.

At Queen Street Congregational Church the message was
even more straightforward:

> The essential thing is the spiritual life. Men do
> not perish by the murdering hand of Pilate, by the
> crushing of Siloma's Tower, or by the long exposure
> on the ice pans. The accidental manner of the physi-
> cal ending of a life is nothing, the supreme and
> essential fact and matter of urgency in every life
> is the relation of that life to God.

By thus ignoring the element of human responsibility
for the disaster, the Churches helped exonerate the
ship owners and captains and their government representatives whose greed for profit from the seal hunt was
the basic underlying cause of the sealers' deaths. With

the beginning of the First World War later that year,
the Churches proved themselves more interested in promoting the war effort among Newfoundlanders than in
advocating improved working conditions for them. Thus,
the Newfoundland Sealing Disaster of 1914 confirms the
view that the role of institutional religion in Newfoundland has been to provide a strong support for the prevailing social order, even when that order results in
the cruel loss of many human lives.

A more recent instance of Church neglect of social
issues can be seen in connection with the devastation
of the town of St. Lawrence Nfld. through industrial
diseases, as described by the anthropologist Elliot
Leyton in his book, Dying Hard. This book consists of
ten autobiographical accounts by miners afflicted with
silicosis, lung cancer, and other related diseases, and
by widows of deceased miners. Together with the
author's introduction and conclusion they document an
almost incredible story of human suffering and neglect,
all in the name of maximum profits for the companies
involved. Once again the Newfoundland Churches have
had little or nothing to say about the patent violation
of ethical principles evident in this case.

Once a fishing village, St. Lawrence turned into a
mining town after an earthquake off the Grand Banks in
1929 destroyed the local fishery. After three years on
government welfare (at six cents per day per person),
the men jumped at the opportunity presented by a New
York mining promoter, Walter Siebert, to help him exploit the area's fluorspar deposits. Using second-hand
equipment and the most primitive (and unsafe) mining
methods, the men of St. Lawrence turned Siebert's mine
into a very profitable operation. During the 1940's,
however, the miners began to experience an abnormally
high mortality rate. For many years these deaths were
attributed to tuberculosis, but unlike the inhabitants
of other villages, the miners of St. Lawrence and the
adjacent communities never recovered from their illnesses. In 1947 it was suspected that silicosis might
be the fatal disease rather than tuberculosis, and in
1950 the local medical health officer requested a dust
survey to be carried out in the mines. This was not
done until 1956, four years after the first case of
silicosis was definitely confirmed.[19]

Meanwhile, the miners continued getting sick and
dying. It was not until 1960 that the new owners of

the mines, Alcan, installed ventilating equipment in
the older mines. That same year, however, a new hazard
was discovered in the mines - radioactive radon gas.
This was felt to be the cause of the lung cancer
suffered by many of the miners. Between 1960 and 1967,
twenty-nine miners died of lung cancer and twelve
others of silicosis and related diseases. During this
period the miners and widows were subjected to every
sort of bureaucratic harassment in their attempts to
get Workmen's Compensation benefits, and when these
benefits did finally arrive they were pitifully inadequate. The situation of the miners finally received
widespread publicity in 1967, and the government
appointed a Royal Commission to study radiation, compensation and safety in the mines. Its report, submitted in 1969, treated only the medical and, to a
lesser extent, the economic issues, completely ignoring
the social and political implications of the miners'
plight. Although the report blamed the Provincial
Department of Health for their tardiness in responding
to the situation at St. Lawrence, it completely exono-
rated the Workmen's Compensation Board and made no
criticism at all of the mining companies.

The task of describing the social consequences of the
exploitation of the miners was taken up by Elliot Leyton. His interviews with the miners bring out the extent
to which the companies and the government have devalued
the lives of the workers. With regard to safe working
conditions, one miner had this to say:

Safety? All I ever heard when I was there was there
an Inspector or anything coming, start cleaning up
and barring off crossways, manways and everything.
About a month before they were coming, the Company
knows they were coming. And everybody was working
and cleaning it up and having it right for them to
look at. The Government gives the Company a chance
I suppose.[20]

In the early days the drilling of the fluorspar ore was
done exclusively with dry hammers which continually
spew dust in the miner's face. One miner described the
operation in these words:

The hammer was hung on the shoulder which brought the
drill hole directly opposite the driller's mouth. He
at times used curtain scrim or cheese cloth over his
mouth but this clogged in seconds and had to be

discarded. Every few minutes he would have to shut off the machine to clear his eyes and nostrils of dust.[21]

Although the dangers to health of this type of mining were widely known even in the 1930's, there were no government regulations dealing with the matter, and the companies were not inclined to introduce any safety features which might cost them some money.

Even after the illnesses of the miners had been confirmed, both the companies and the government agencies seemed to do everything possible to forestall the payment of compensation. One miner who was receiving $30 a week sick benefits from Alcan in 1969 wrote the Company asking for $50 for Christmas. They sent the $50, and then proceeded to deduct $10 from the sick benefits for the next five weeks.[22] Sick miners were often pressured into having lung operations by Workmen's Compensation Board doctors in order to receive benefits, even though it was their experience that all those who underwent such operations died soon afterwards. Even when they did finally receive back payments from Workmen's Compensation, the government often confiscated the money in order to offset welfare payments given previously. People were compensated at different rates, with some miners judged to be 100% disabled, some 80%, some 25%, etc. However, there was no alternative employment available for those less than 100% disabled, so to survive some of them had to go back working in the mine, thus hastening their deaths. Despite the increased payments from Workmen's Compensation to the St. Lawrence miners in the 1960's, Alcan's assessment to the Fund actually decreased during the period 1961-68.[23]

Elliot Leyton gives this assessment of Workmen's Compensation:

Compensation is normally geared either to comparable Welfare benefits or to some arbitrary proportion of the workman's former wage: the former is an affront to the dignity of men and women who have worked all their lives; the latter is unacceptable under the best of circumstances (the full salary was rarely enough) and is now made laughable by the process of inflation. Whatever the principle a country may use in the calculation of compensation, the normal consequence is that the dying or disabled workman finds

himself and his family reduced to the stature of
those who cling to Welfare. When he dies, his family
will enter that endless Welfare cycle of dependence
and humiliation which continues for generations.
   The stunning inadequacy of international systems
of Compensation is particularly apparent in communities such as St. Lawrence which have been devastated
by large-scale disasters. When the barest humanity
demands massive transfusions of public monies for
social, psychiatric and medical facilities, there is
only a meagre individual allotment.[24]

Leyton speaks harshly of what the Association of Trial
Lawyers of America has called the "total callousness,
stupidity and deceit of the medical-industrial complex
consisting of company doctors, industry consultants,
and key occupational-health officials."[25] His anger at
the situation of the St. Lawrence miners and their co-
sufferers from industrial diseases and accidents
throughout the world extends far beyond the normal
"scientific" evaluation of an anthropologist's subject
of investigation. His response is truly a religious
one, reminiscent of the Old Testament prophets' denunciation of social evils. That he, an anthropologist,
should be the one to give the religious response to
this situation is indeed indicative of the social posture of the Newfoundland Churches in this case as in
the one discussed earlier.

The role of the Churches in St. Lawrence, whose population is approximately two-thirds Catholic and one-
third Anglican, is described by one miner in these
words:

The ministers and the priest, they never helped or
hindered. They just stayed out of it. They had the
very least to say as any of the rest of them.
There's only one thing you can make out of it; they
get their wages, their living, and that's all they
care. All they wants is a great big money plate,
that's the way I got them sized up.[26]

Although one may dispute this miner's assessment of the
reason why the Churches have not become involved in the
social and political issues raised by the miners'
plight, his assertion of the non-involvement is corro-
borated by all available evidence. During the period
1967-1970 when the issue was receiving widespread publicity because of the activity of the Royal Commission,

neither the Roman Catholic diocesan newspaper, The Monitor, nor its Anglican counterpart, The Newfoundland Churchman, made a single reference to the St. Lawrence situation. In dealing with local news, both these papers studiously avoided commenting on social, economic or political issues (other than education), concentrating rather on internal Church matters such as finances, liturgy and parish organizations. No doubt the clergy of St. Lawrence have made references to the causes of death when conducting the miners' funerals, but it is likely that, like their counterparts in 1914, they stress the inscrutable Will of God and the joys of the afterlife in their orations rather than attempting to assign any blame for the deaths of the miners to company and government officials. But whatever their private statements on this issue may contain, it is evident that there has been no concerted attempt on the part of the Churches to denounce the miners' treatment by the companies and government agencies as immoral and contrary to Christian ethics or to otherwise bring about any change in this treatment.

The reluctance of the Christian Churches in Newfoundland to combat social injustices is as pronounced today as any time in the past. However, the theological justification of this position has lost much of its force, and the Church leaders must now rely on more mundane reasons for their non-involvement in social issues. In the past, there was general agreement among Christians that the New Testament required them to reject the values of this world in order to be worthy of heaven. Christians were obviously in the world, but were not to be of the world. This dichotomy between heaven and earth was closely related to the dichotomy between man's soul and body. The needs of the soul were paramount, while bodily needs, such as food, clothing, shelter, sexual pleasure, etc., were relatively unimportant. In addition to this antiworldliness, traditional Christian morality has another distinctive characteristic - its authoritarianism. Obedience to the Will of God is considered the highest virtue, and the Will of God is manifested in the Bible, the natural law, the laws of the Church and of society, and the commands of Church leaders, political leaders, bosses and parents. Any questioning of these authorities, no matter how outrageous their orders, is generally considered to be a rejection of God's will.

This view of Christian morality has been modified

greatly during the 20th century. The Social Gospel
Movement was a major factor in this development. Today
most Christian denominations are examining very closely
their involvement in the social, political and economic
structures of society, and are coming to the conclusion
that the massive social injustices which exist in the
world call for outspoken criticism from Church leaders
speaking on behalf of Christian moral principles. In
Canada, some of the Churches have established groups
such as the Task Force on Churches and Corporate Responsibility, Project North and Gatt-Fly to do action-
oriented research and public education on social,
economic and political issues. All this activity represents a decisive rejection of the view that Christianity is concerned solely with the salvation of souls.

In Newfoundland, though, this revaluation of traditional Christian morality has not occurred. The Church
leaders in this province have shown no inclination to
challenge the rich and powerful who are responsible
for many of the social injustices which exist here.
But Newfoundland is not so isolated from the rest of
the country that the Church leaders could not have
heard about what their counterparts on the mainland are
doing with regard to social problems. No, their continued support of the status quo must be the result of
a conscious decision to act in this way. Given the
questionable theological justification of this approach,
it would appear that other reasons are present - perhaps
the fear of losing control of education in the province;
perhaps the reluctance to risk alienating the wealthy
members of the Churches; perhaps the general conservatism of the Newfoundland people. But whatever the
reasons, it is obvious that the nature of denominational
Christianity in Newfoundland today renders the religious
situation of this province significantly different from
other parts of Canada. And any attempt to describe the
state of religion in Canada today must take this difference into account.

FOOTNOTES

1. S.J.R. Noel, Politics in Newfoundland, Toronto, University of Toronto Press, 1971, p. 24.

2. Frederick Jones, Bishop Feild, A Study in Politics and Religion in 19th Century Newfoundland, Ph.D. thesis, University of Cambridge, 1971, p. 190.

3. John Alfred Meaden, "The Anglican Church in New-foundland," The Canadian Church Historical Society Occasional Publication, No. 5, July, 1960, p. 8.

4. Paul O'Neill, The Early Church History of St. John's (unpublished lecture), 1972, p. 5.

5. Richard Gwyn, Smallwood: The Unlikely Revolutionary, Toronto, McClelland & Stewart, 1968, p. 110.

6. H.A. Batstone, Methodism in Newfoundland: A Study of its Social Impact, S.T.M. thesis, McGill University, 1967, pp. 65f.

7. Arthur E. Kewley, op. cit., paper presented to the Canadian Society of Church History, 1971, p. 16.

8. Quoted in H.A. Batstone, op. cit., pp. 163f.

9. Toronto, Doubleday Canada Ltd., 1974.

10. Toronto, McClelland & Stewart, 1975.

11. Harold Horwood, "Forward" to Cassie Brown, Death on the Ice, p. ix.

12. Death on the Ice, pp. 25f.

13. Ibid., p. 261.

14. Ibid., p. 259.

15. Ibid., p. 4.

16. The Daily Mail, St. John's, April 4, 1914.

17. Ibid.

18. Ibid.

19. Report of Royal Commission Respecting Radiation, Compensation and Safety at the Fluorspar Mines, St. Lawrence, Newfoundland, 1969, p. 190.

20. Dying Hard, p. 25.

21. Ibid., p. 14.

22. Ibid., p. 109.

23. Report of Royal Commission..., p. 252.

24. Dying Hard, p. 139.

25. Ibid., p. 138.

26. Ibid., p. 63.

SOCIAL CATHOLICISM IN NOVA SCOTIA

GREGORY BAUM's many published volumes include <u>Religion and Alienation</u> (1975). He is Professor of Religious Studies at St. Michael's College, Toronto.

RÉSUMÉ

Comme système symbolique et comme communauté, la religion a une influence importante sur la culture et sur la société en général. Les grands maîtres de cette influence sont les 'sociologues': Weber, Durkheim, Marx. Mais, pour évaluer les contradictions entre les maîtres, il faut un point de vue en dehors de la sociologie. En plus, il faut comprendre la religion comme une réalité ambigue et multiforme. C'est un mouvement vital, créateur, capable de produire de nouvelles réponses qui font de la critique même des structures dominantes de la société.

Le Mouvement Antigonish de la Nouvelle-Ecosse était une des répliques positives à la Grande Dépression. Au nom du Catholicisme Social, les pères fondateurs voyaient l'éducation du peuple fondée sur leur besoins économiques, comme l'idée maîtresse de la coopération qui engendrait une nouvelle société au delà du capitalisme.

Après une longue période de répression, de lutte et de conflit, le mouvement travailliste a atteint de l'unité et de la puissance au Cap-Breton par son affiliation au CCF. Des catholiques ont participé à la lutte travailliste et le Mouvement Antigonish a préparé la base pour l'association avec le CCF, dont l'appui était largement répandu. Pendant que l'hiérarchie catholique dans le reste du pays mettait les catholiques en garde contre le mouvement socialiste canadien, au Cap-Breton, des mineurs et des aciériste catholiques s'y identifiaient beaucoup. Le Cap-Breton industriel est le seul endroit au Canada d'une grande population catholique qui a élu des candidats socialistes aux parlements provinciaux et fédéraux.

GREGORY BAUM

Social Catholicism in Nova Scotia: The Thirties

The aspect of religion that has concerned me over the
last years is its social impact. What interests me is
what religion does. I have found that the great
teachers in this inquiry are the sociologists. They
were the scholars who first looked at the influence of
religious organizations on the people who belonged to
them and, through these, on the making of culture and
society. They were the first to discover that the
religious symbols and the religious vision of life,
which dominate the imagination of a people, determine
the manner in which they perceive their social reality
and in turn respond to it. Symbols have power. Especially important was the work of Max Weber on the
affinity between the aspirations of the ascending
bourgeoisie and the Protestant ethic. He demonstrated
that a certain religious consciousness accounted for
the rapid spread and extraordinary success of bourgeois
culture, at least at one time. He also suggested,
even though he never studied the matter in detail, that
the Catholic ethic, a prolongation of the religious
ethic of the middle ages, legitimated the more static,
aristocratic societies of Europe, hostile to industrial
development and democratic egalitarianism, expressing
a more organic understanding of the human community.

It is generally recognized that religious symbols and
religious organizations not only affect but also reflect the patterns of culture and society. Religion is,
in part at least, a mirror of the material conditions
of life. Emile Durkheim tried to demonstrate that
religion embodies in ritual and symbolic form the substance of the social order. Religion, he thought, was
society writ large. Prior to Durkheim, Karl Marx had
been equally unwilling to look upon religion as an
independent variable. For him religion was also a
reflection of the social order, albeit an inverted
reflection, an ideology, a projection onto the cosmos
of symbols designed to promote and protect the existing
power relations in society. Not the substance of
society but the sum total of its injustices and domination finds expression in religion. The student of
religion, I have become convinced, must listen to both
Durkheim and Marx. But more than sociology is needed
to evaluate whether such social elements as the family
are building blocks of a humane society and hence deserve to be protected, or whether they are structures

118

of domination that for the sake of justice should be
dismantled. For Durkheim, the family was the cradle of
the social order, for Marx it was the matrix of all
social oppression. We can resolve this dilemma only
from a vantage point beyond sociology.

At this point it is sufficient to say that both
Durkheim and Marx deserve to be heard. Since society
and religion are complex, many-levelled historical
phenomena it is unlikely that a uni-causal theory can
render an account of the inter-relationship between the
two. After due attention has been paid to the dependence of religion on society, it is important not to
forget that religion, at certain moments at least, is
also an independent variable. There is creative, innovative religion. Other sociologists besides Weber have
studied the innovative character of religion. Friedrich Engels appreciated the revolutionary intent of
some 16th century Anabaptists but interpreted their
religious language as a cloak for secular, political
purposes.[1] Against this, Ernst Bloch, a contemporary
Marxist, has demonstrated that radical Anabaptism while
indeed revolutionary was truly religious: the preaching
of Thomas Munzer was not a hidden language to express
purely political intentions but the articulation of
authentic religious passion and surrender to God's will
which had radical social consequences.[2]

How is it possible that religion, the same religion,
can be a dependent variable and, at another time or
another level, an independent variable? How can it be
that the Christian religion is conservative at Witten-
berg, and radical at Geneva? The answer is very simple.
Religion is a complex, many-levelled phenomenon. Religion is made up of many trends and movements differing
from one segment of society to the next and capable of
responding in new ways to different historical challenges. It produces symbols that protect the dominant
social structures while at another level generating a
critical spirituality that undermines the dominant
structures. This enormous ambiguity of religion has
been overlooked by scholars of more than one discipline.
Christian theologians tend to think of Christianity as
self-identical and hence often remain insensitive to
the various religious trends and meanings within the
same church. Similarly sociologists who look upon religion as a definable system often produce studies that
encourage a reified understanding of a particular religion. After Weber, we easily forget that Protestantism

has also produced movements of religious socialism that questioned the individualistic and competitive nature of modern society.[3] And the considerable strength of Catholic Marxists in the Latin countries in our day puzzles the scholar who has studied the Catholic religion in terms of a single ideal-type. What is necessary, I contend, is to study religion as a multi-leveled reality.

It is my personal conviction, based in part on historical evidence and in part, I think, on my faith in God's presence in the world, that the world religions are vital, creative movements, capable of generating new responses to new social situations and producing significant minority trends critical of the dominant structures. There seems to be an auto-regenerative power in the world religions. They should be studied accordingly.

In recent years, I have become increasingly interested in critical social movements in Canada and the contribution made to them by innovative Christian religion. I have been greatly impressed by historical studies of the Protestant Social Gospel in Canada which made considerable impact on the progressive political movements in the twenties and the formation of the new socialist party, the CCF, in the early thirties.[4] While the Anglican and Protestant churches on the whole regarded themselves as the upholders of traditional society, significant movements in these churches, represented even on ecclesiastical boards, favoured the radical reconstruction of the social order and produced sophisticated theologies of Christian socialism.

What was the reaction of Catholics to the spread of Canadian socialism? The public reaction of the hierarchy is well known: they warned the Catholic people against the new party as a form of socialism repudiated by papal teaching.[5] The bishops of Saskatchewan cautioned the people against the CCF without mentioning its name. Several bishops of Québec repudiated the new party by name. Archbishop Gauthier of Montréal published a long sermon in which he first analysed the reasons why Pope Pius XI had rejected moderate socialism - even moderate socialism promoted implicit atheism, war between classes and contempt for private property - and then showed how these reasons were verified in the Canadian version of socialism defined by the Calgary Program. On the other hand, the

120

Catholic hierarchy in England took a very different position in regard to British Socialism.[6] They upheld the view that Pope Pius XI's condemnation of non-revolutionary socialism did not apply to the British form of socialism and that Catholics were free to vote for the Labour Party. It was only in 1943 that the Canadian Catholic bishops changed their mind - by that time, we recall, the CCF too had modified its programme - and declared that Catholics were free to vote for the new party.[7] But since again they did not mention the party by name, several Catholic newspapers claimed that the CCF was still out of bounds for the Catholic people. On the whole, then, Catholics were suspicious of Canadian socialism. This was true of French Canadians, for a variety of reasons that deserve careful analysis, and this was true of the English-speaking Catholics largely, I think, because of the warnings from on high.

However, Catholicism, like other great religions, is a complex phenomenon. We must inquire, therefore, whether there were minority movements among Canadian Catholics that understood the Christian message as a summons to social criticism and social involvement, supported the CCF or favoured in some form the reconstruction of the social order. This question has not often been asked. I suppose one could deal with it on three levels, 1) Were there Catholics in leadership positions in the CCF or other critical social movements? 2) Did Catholic activists promote religious ideas that were critical of the economic order and demanded radical social change? and finally 3) Does a study of Canadian voting patterns reveal that, in some areas at least, Catholics voted for the CCF in significant numbers? In this paper I propose to deal with the first and second questions with reference to Catholic reaction to the Great Depression in Nova Scotia. It is a study of what is often called Social Catholicism.[8]

The notion of Social Catholicism first referred to Catholic movements in the European countries of the 19th century, which reacted against the spread of industrialization and the accompanying exploitation of the workers. Catholic leaders arose who, basing themselves on traditional values, objected to the emerging society defined by industrial competition and the free market and characterized by the waning of handcraft and home production. These Catholic leaders, following the ideals of medieval society, defended the view that the

121

task of government was to promote the common good, and
hence to restrain the power of the rich and protect the
poor from exploitation. Governments like the rest of
society were to serve the norms of justice. While
Social Catholicism was formulated against nineteenth
century socialism, Marxist or otherwise, which promoted
class antagonism and sought the elimination of private
ownership of all productive goods, Social Catholicism
also defined itself in opposition to the liberalism of
the more successful industrialized nations and
conservatism of the nations opposed to industrialization
that tried to prolong the hegemony of the old aristocratic families. This Social Catholicism later found
expression in papal teaching on the social order, beginning in 1891 with Leo XIII's famous encyclical <u>Rerum</u>
<u>novarum</u>.

Rejecting socialism, liberalism and conservatism, Pope
Leo XIII had blessed the formation of labour unions, but
asked that they function as industrial guilds represented in the councils of industry and government, not as
fighting units in a class war. Papal teaching expressed
the dream of a harmonious society, in which the various
social classes were proud of their role and proud of
their difference, each attempting to transcend its own
class interest to serve and build up the common good,
which included beyond the material needs the substance
of the spirit. Subsequent popes confirmed and developed
this Social Catholicism.

Since these papal teachings were offered not as
social policy in concrete historical situations but as
overall social principles intended for all the Western
nations, their social impact was fairly limited.[9] While
Catholic social doctrine fitted no actually existing
situation and hence could not be applied as such,
Catholic groups singled out certain principles that
seemed urgent and important to them. Thus Catholics
committed to Social Catholicism put great emphasis on
the papal teaching that defended trade unions, recommended government planning of economic life, rejected
the ideas of liberalism, advocated the theory of the
just wage and the just price, and demanded legislation
protecting the poor and helpless, while Catholics,
consciously or unconsciously identified with the existing order, stressed the papal repudiation of socialism,
the defense of private property, and the condemnation of
class war, and explained that Catholic social doctrine

122

condemns only abuses of capitalism, not capitalism as
such. Still, for the Catholics in various parts of the
world who struggled against social ills the papal social
teaching represented an authoritative Catholic perspective which allowed them to unite their religious aspirations with their social activism. This is the perspective of Social Catholicism.

In the thirties, Social Catholicism expressed itself
in an interesting and original way in Nova Scotia.
Eastern Nova Scotia is the home of a homogeneous group
of Catholics, mainly Highland Scots with a minority of
Irishmen blended in, who make up a substantial part of
the total population and constitute a cohesive, popular
Catholic culture, for which there is no parallel in
other English-speaking parts of Canada. In the rest of
the country, English-speaking Catholics are ethnically
more heterogeneous and represent minorities. The
Catholic immigrants arriving from continental European
countries prior to and after the turn of the century
did not settle in Eastern Nova Scotia, with the exception of the industrial area of Cape Breton; and even
there the influx was small. Eastern Nova Scotia
remained essentially Scottish, Catholic and Protestant.
Consulting the Canadian Almanac of 1931 we learn that
of the 6 counties of Eastern Nova Scotia, 4 had a
Catholic population of over 50%: on the mainland
Antigonish, and on Cape Breton Island Cape Breton
County, Inverness and Richmond. There was a strong
Catholic presence in the industrialized area of Cape
Breton County, the cluster of towns around Sydney.[10]

The counties of Eastern Nova Scotia were largely
populated by farmers and fishermen, with the exception
of Cape Breton County with its miners and steelworkers.
The people worked in primary production and the extrac-
tive industries. There was no production of goods to
speak of. The people depended for their survival on
the land and the sea, unless they worked at the mines and
steelworks of the industrialized part. There was no
local bourgeoisie of small industrialists or successful
merchants. The large companies that owned and directed
the coal mines and steel production were British, and
they made their decisions regarding their branches in
Cape Breton County in reliance on their wider, international concerns. The rulers, the powerful, the men
on whom the well-being of the people depended were all
'foreigners.' The result of this common dependency was
an extraordinary sense of solidarity, grounded in

kinship loyalty and religious sentiment, and strengthened by the growing poverty and a general feeling of
impotence. In these parts the Depression had already
begun in the twenties.

The élite in Eastern Nova Scotia was made up of
lawyers, doctors and priests, but they remained closely
tied to the people: they were in no sense a ruling
class. The kinship cohesion and religious sentiment
the Scottish settlers had brought with them and developed over more than a century never gave way, as they
do in most modern societies, to the emergence of distinct classes. Lawyers and doctors remained in solidarity with the people and their children were often
quite willing to leave the élite and marry farmers and
miners. Priests found it natural to exercise secular
leadership in the name of the people.

We conclude then that thanks to a combination of
three factors, the Catholics of Eastern Nova Scotia
formed a community for which there was no parallel in
the English-speaking parts of Canada: they constituted
a largely homogeneous group, they made up a substantial
section of the population, and they were linked by an
altogether unusual sense of solidarity. Under the
pressure of prolonged poverty inflicted by the powerful
outside the province, they reacted to the Depression in
a unique way. We shall examine two distinct but related
forms of Catholic social action, the Antigonish movement
operative among the farmers and fishermen and the identification of the Catholic miners with the Canadian
socialism of the thirties.

The Antigonish Movement was a cooperative movement,
based on a special kind of adult education, that sought
to enlighten farmers and fishermen in regard to their
economic helplessness and organize them as co-owners of
new enterprises for the distribution and, in some cases,
the production of goods. The creators of the movement
were largely priests, and the system of communication
used in promoting the cause was the network of Catholic
institutions. While the movement understood itself as
an expression of Social Catholicism, it assumed from the
very beginning a non-denominational character. It was
ecumenical before the word became current in its present
meaning. The movement wanted to transform the conditions of people's lives and in this way their consciousness, whatever their religious affiliation. Still,

124

given the division between Catholic and Protestant areas
in rural Eastern Nova Scotia, it was above all in the
strongly Catholic counties that the movement spread
rapidly. Many Protestants were suspicious of it. Its
success among Protestants came later and was more restricted. In the long run, the movement reached beyond
Nova Scotia to the other Maritime provinces.

The Antigonish Movement was created by two imaginative
and powerful personalities, Father J.J. Tompkins and
Father M.M. Coady. They are usually spoken of as Dr.
Tompkins and Dr. Coady since in that part of Nova Scotia
priests with a doctorate were addressed as 'doctor.'
Already before and during the twenties, Tompkins,
greatly disturbed by the growing depression and powerlessness of the region, devised a new philosophy of
adult education, based in part on English and Scandinavian models, which envisaged a movement from the
university to the people. He believed that people are
intelligent enough, even when they have little formal
education, to analyse the reasons for their poverty
and organize for co-operative action. In a pamphlet
written in 1920, entitled Knowledge for the People, he
described a process which came close to what today,
through the influence of radical educators such as Paolo
Freire, has been called consciousness-raising, and he
designated St. Francis Xavier University at Antigonish
as the institution which should and could bring this
education to the people.

According to Tompkins, the farmers and fishermen of
Nova Scotia were exploited largely by commercial enterprises which bought the primary products at a low price
and sold them dearly in the cities and who demanded high
prices for feed, fertilizer and equipment necessary
for the primary producers. The farmers and fishermen
lost at both ends. Co-operative ownership of trading
companies would enable farmers and fishermen to sell
their products on their own terms and to purchase the
goods they needed directly from the producers at more
advantageous prices. For the time being, the attempt
to create an Extension Department to propagate these
ideas remained unsuccessful. However, Tompkins was
able to promote his programme with the help of the
Carnegie Foundation, which regarded his movement as a
way of promoting self-help among the poor, without
discerning its critical, subversive edge.

It was only in 1928 and in effective terms only in

1930 that the Extension Department of St. Francis Xavier
University was founded, curiously enough with funds
coming from the conservative Catholic Scottish Society
which was interested less in social justice than in
staying the flow of emigration to other parts of North
America. Dr. M.M. Coady was appointed as director.
It was he who was most responsible for the rapid spread
of the Antigonish movement in Eastern Nova Scotia.
With the help of his co-workers he organized study-
clubs among the farmers and fishermen to teach them how
to set up stores for the buying and selling of goods,
co-operatively owned factories and mills and, eventually,
when greater numbers were involved, credit unions or
co-operative banks. Dr. Coady knew how to give people
the confidence to make a new start and inspired them
to organize their own study-clubs and cooperative ven-
tures. Each cooperative undertaking remained part of
the movement, kept abreast of new ideas through the
Bulletin of the Extension Department, and made financial
contributions from its modest resources to help the
Extension Department promote its educational task.

The Antigonish Movement is remarkable from several
points of view. We are particularly interested
in its ideology. The movement transformed people's
lives, their economic situation and, more especially,
their sense of self-worth and power, and initiated the
participants into a new, more social self-understanding,
thus laying the foundation of large-scale social reconstruction. Still, the movement has not been studied
a great deal.[11] At this time two doctoral dissertations
have been written on the movement, with a third one
still in progress, setting forth careful analyses of the
empirical data.[12] There is no article on the movement
in the collection, Prophecy and Protest: Social Movements in Twentieth-Century Canada, edited by Clark,
Grayson and Grayson. Yet it is of particular interest
to students of Canadian religion since it represents an
original form of the Social Gospel, Catholic-style.

The originators of the movement were, in the Weberian
sense of the term, charismatic personalities. They
articulated the misery in which Nova Scotians lived,
analysing the economy in simple language, and offering
a new vision of social organization that promised a
good and abundant life. Their success was grounded in
the oppressive conditions under which people lived and
the contradictions of the economic system that had produced them. The Antigonish Movement gave voice to a

126

to a radical criticism of contemporary capitalism. The
strong leadership knew how to create a grassroots movement, made up of the economically underprivileged, that
expressed an ethos at odds with dominant North American
culture, at odds even with the dominant Catholicism
which understood religion as a source of consolation
rather than a call to action.

In time, however, the Antigonish Movement lost its
radical character. Frank Mifflin defends the view that
already in the early forties the movement ceased to
challenge the social order.13 Why? He gives several
reasons. In part it was because the movement had been
successful in changing the conditions of life for a
great many people and in part because the leaders had
been willing, for the sake of greater institutional
support, to soften their critical stance. The war
removed some of the dire social need from the province.
Also the growth of the stores and credit unions demanded
ever greater commercial and technical expertise which
tended to exclude the ordinary people from directing
their own enterprises. When it became necessary to hire
salaried managers to run the cooperatives, the different
social conditions under which the managers lived kept
them from seeing themselves as participants in a radical
social movement. Mifflin also mentions that at that time
the various cooperatives ceased to reserve a certain
amount of money for the ongoing social mission of the
Extension Department. The Antigonish Movement, according
to Mifflin's study, became very largely a social service
organization. It no longer initiated people into a new
way of perceiving the social reality. While some students
of the movement may wish to argue about the relatively
early date that Mifflin assigns to the decline, all agree
that such a change has in fact taken place.

Of continuing interest to the student of religion and
society is the ideology of the Antigonish Movement,
especially in Coady's persuasive formulation. In Masters
of Their Own Destiny, he offers an analysis of the ills
of contemporary capitalism and presents the cooperative
movement as one of the principal levers for the reconstruction of society. What went wrong, according to
Coady, with the inherited capitalist system? The people
lost power over their economic life!14 Prior to the
industrial revolution, production took place in the
home and in small establishments. While there was a
trend away from a domestic economy, the shops in which
people made money by serving the interests of their

owners, were small establishments, responsible for small-scale production. What happened through the industrial revolution was the creation of large factories in which vast numbers of people were employed in large-scale production. The power of production slipped altogether out of the hands of the people. Still, distribution and consumption were left to them. But the organization of business enterprises, eventually on a large scale, took even that power away from them. The people became impotent participants in the economic order, subject to a minority of owners of industry and business that were ultimately to reduce them to total misery. Dr. Coady interpreted the Great Depression as the visible proof of the unworkability of the inherited economic order.

What had happened, according to Coady, was not due to bad will on the part of the owning classes. Rather, "an error had crept into the foundation of our economic structure."[15] To illustrate what an error is to ordinary people, Coady gives the example of a smoke stack 150 feet high that had been built by careless workers who constructed the foundation out of plumb and thus introduced an error at the base, scarcely visible to the naked eye, that would eventually be responsible for creating a leaning tower. Such a smoke stack, Coady continues, can be held up by props and wires for a time, but eventually it must be rebuilt. After 150 years of industrial capitalism, we have come to the moment when the economic system must be reconstructed.

What is the origin of Coady's theory? Neither he nor his older colleague, Tompkins, cite their sources. They mention the Rochdale Foundation of the mid-19th century in England and sometimes refer to Scandinavian cooperatives, but the reader has the impression that Tompkins and Coady read more widely than they are willing to admit. The theory of alienation which Coady proposed, even without mentioning the term, certainly recalls Marx's early formulation of it in his little work, On the **Jewish** Question. In this work, Marx recognizes the possibility of an alienating process in all spheres of human life, the economic system as well as the social and cultural orders. He gives us a cooperative vision of society: society can be truly humane only if people collectively, by direct participation, assume responsibility for the conditions of their lives. It is such a cooperative engagement alone that can transform the consciousness of the people.

Coady presented his own ideas in the context of Catholic social teaching, yet went considerably beyond it. Papal social teaching, as mentioned above, clearly recognized that modern industrial capitalism and the business civilization derived from it permitted the economic interests of a limited class to determine the policies of government. "Free enterprise," writes Pius XI in 1931 "has given way to economic dictatorship."[16] The papal teaching here repudiates the abuses of capitalism, the formation of trusts and the conglomeration of companies into economic empires, but these ills are not seen as flowing from an initial error in the system. In the view of Pope Pius XI, they were due to the greed of the rich and powerful. Coady and the Antigonish Movement differed here from the papal teaching since they associated the ills of the system with private ownership of the means of production and consumption.

Yet how much in line with the Catholic tradition the movement remained appears when we look at the solution Coady proposes to the chaos and misery of the economic order. People must regain their power over the means of production and consumption, acquire a new kind of consciousness in this process, and then reconstruct the entire social order. Coady was convinced however - and this put him plainly in the cooperative tradition - that people must begin the struggle by regaining the means of distribution and exchange, that is to say by acquiring cooperative ownership of stores, businesses, banks, service agencies, and so forth. "The (cooperative) ownership of such institutions is the natural means of eventually bringing back the control of the production to the people...The ills of the social order must be attacked from the consumers' end."[17] The cooperative movement is the main lever for the reconstruction of society.

Following this directive, the Antigonish Movement sought to protect those who still owned their means of production, however small their piece of land or fishing boats might be, from becoming propertyless wage earners in larger farming companies or fisheries and thus joining the rural proletariat. Capitalism destroys such ordinary people in more ways than one. The present economic system, Coady writes, by encouraging the ambitious to leave for the cities, constantly robs the rural people of their natural leaders.[18] At the same time, Coady did not recommend socialism. He was committed to

129

the principle that 'small is beautiful.'[19]   He was not
greatly interested in the labour movement since the
unions did not lay claim to the co-ownership of industries.   The unions, in Coady's view, perpetuated the
competitive nature of society; and when the workers
eventually succeeded in getting higher wages, they did
not actually increase their buying power.   Why?   Because
the institutions of consumption, over which they had no
control, and which were often in collaboration with the
owners of industry, would simply raise their prices and
the extra money spent by the owners on wages would return as increased profit on the consumption side.

The Antigonish Movement, it is important to note,
presented itself as politically neutral.   This was a
fundamental principle of cooperatism, even though in
the nineteen-thirties the cooperative movement in
England, after a long period of negotiation, joined the
Labour Party and identified itself with British socialism.[20] Coady was very insistent on the political neutrality of the Antigonish Movement.   The leaders were allowed
to vote but they were forbidden to support any party in
public.[21]   What were the reasons for this insistence on
political neutrality?   In the first place, the Extension
Department still received financial help from the Carnegie Foundation in New York City.   The movement was
also helped by government grants.   To guard neutrality
here seemed important.   Since the critical ideology of
the movement regarded capitalism as harbouring inner contradictions and favoured the social reconstruction of
society, the movement was constantly accused of being
socialist.   Coady again and again denied this, fearing
any links to the democratic socialism of the CCF could
undermine the movement's effectiveness.[22]

Coady went out of his way to show how his political
philosophy differed from the socialism repudiated by
papal teaching.   In the recent Depression encyclical of
Piux XI, both radical and moderate socialism had been
condemned because they were, in fact or by implication,
1) atheist, 2) promoting class war, and 3) opposed to
private proverty.   Of course, nobody accused the Antigonish Movement of being atheist; still the Movement's
insistence on the centrality of the economic factor
and their willingness to cooperate with other people,
be they religious or not, made them vulnerable to the
criticism offered by mainstream Catholics.   Coady contended that adult education based on economic cooopera-
tion did not promote class strife: what the Movement

aimed at was a society of universal cooperation. Nor
was the Movement opposed to all private ownership of
industry and business. While some cooperatists envisage
the transformation of society into a cooperative commonwealth, there are others - and Coady belonged to them -
who regarded cooperatives as such a powerful instrument
that they believe that as soon as a significant section
of consumption is cooperatively owned and a significant
number of large corporations are publicly owned, the
nature of society will radically change.[23] Even without removing private property and private enterprise
altogether, a significant cooperative sector of the
economy will produce a new social order. A difference
in quantity is here perceived as creating a difference
in quality.

Even though he never talked about it in public, Coady
himself was a political liberal. The vision of society
that appears in his writings is based on a balance of
powers, which he regarded as a Catholic principle,
between various sections of society, the cooperatively
owned sector, the privately owned sector, and the
publicly owned sector. Coady favoured the nationaliza-
tion of the main natural resources and the main service
agencies in the country. He advocated intelligent
political activity on the part of the government to
plan and promote the economy in the three spheres, and,
if I understand him correctly, to monitor the control
of the means of communication, press and radio, which
are presently in the hands of the economically powerful.[24] The cooperatively owned sector, Coady held,
was the foundation of newness; it created a new consciousness among the participants, and it would be
able to hold in check the other, more individualistic
and self-seeking forces in society.

What is curious is that the CCF, which in the early
thirties proposed a programme that sounded more radical,
by the end of the thirties, in the hope of winning elec-
toral victories and becoming the national alternative to
the established order, had modified its programme so
that it actually came very close to proposing the
mixed economy ruled by strong government that we find
in Coady's writings.[25] The CCF at that time shared the
same hope that these quantitative differences - significant enlargements of cooperative and public ownership
- would lead to a qualitative difference in the whole
of society. Yet Coady did not support the CCF.

Let me say one more word about the radical nature of
the Antigonish Movement. There can be no doubt that the
movement was inspired by an alternative vision of
society. Its leaders were well aware that the dominant
culture, promoted by the major institutions of society,
especially the economic institutions, made people feel
ignorant and passive, preoccupied them with trivia,
destroyed their self-confidence, and generated dependency on experts, expensive experts. The Antigonish
Movement was at odds with contemporary culture and
called upon religion, the Christian religion to be
more precise, as an ally in the creation of a new
cultural perception.

The critique of the economic system, proposed by the
Antigonish Movement, had implications for the understanding of all institutional life. For people become es-
tranged from their own resources and cease to be
masters of their own destiny whenever they are deprived
from direct participation in the operation of their
collective existence. Institutions are only sound if
they retain their grassroots character. Dr. Tompkins
used to express his distrust of institutions in formulations that had an anarchist ring. "Beware of institutionalization," he used to say. "When a thing
becomes over-institutionalized, it tends to become
sterile."26 What he meant, and what his friends and
followers meant after him, was that institutions almost
inevitably produce a full-time staff responsible for
its operation, a bureaucracy in other words, which becomes removed from the concerns of the people, defines
itself along organizational lines, and makes decisions
that foster the good of the institution rather than the
good of the people for the sake of which the institution
was created. The hesitation of the Antigonish Movement
(and all cooperative movements) in regard to socialism
was due to distrust of the party bureaucracy.

E.J. Garland, a Western progressive MP and a Catholic,
later elected as a CCF representative, wrote to Dr.
Tompkins concerning political parties, "The trouble is
not so much with parties or the party system, as with
the electorate. We are unorganized. We are not mobi-
lizing our collective intelligence...Everything under
the party system will remain much the same after the
first bloom is spent for the simple reason that a party,
created without intelligent organization, permanent in
the character, of the people who vote, will require
money and more money to win elections: the party

inevitably believes its existence to be so necessary
that it compromises - accepts money, donations, bribes,
presents, etc. Then the old masters are in the saddle
again."27 Garland here expresses the wish for a new
progressive party open to the participation of all members in policy making, which is promoted and financed
by ordinary people sharing the same vision of society.
The CCF, founded in 1932, tried to put this ideal into
practice.28 The critical principle implicit in the
cooperative movement retains an abiding validity. It
reveals what is wrong with political parties and even
with cooperative enterprises, and it points the way
toward their radical reorganization.

It seems to me the Antigonish Movement stood for a kind
of social reform that in the terminology of contemporary
political science is called 'system-transcending
reform.' Since the movement tried to insert new principles into the present social and economic order, it
was reformist; but since these principles were based
on an alternate vision of society, they in some significant way transcended the present order, undermined
it, and prepared people for a more radical reconstruction of society.

One may well question, however, how consistently the
leaders wanted to apply their institutional critique.
They did not apply it to the organization of the church.
Here they were conservatives. While Marx in the little
work mentioned above gives as an example of alienation
the institution of priesthood which removes from the
ordinary people responsibility for worship and makes
them dependent on the mediation of an élite, Coady
never applies his cooperative principle to the life of
the church. He was so deeply rooted in the Catholic
tradition that the idea probably never came to him.
The priest was for him the natural leader in the community to help free the people from the false imagination
created by the dominant culture.

One may furthermore ask the question whether there is
not an inner contradiction between the movement's cooperative ideal and its refusal to endorse a socialist
society, at least in principle. As remarked above, as
soon as credit unions and cooperative stores were
successful, they became practically indistinguishable
from other large business or banking enterprises. A
cooperatively-owned company can remain true to its
founding principles only in a non-competitive economic

133

system where production is for use, not for profit.
Hence to promote a cooperative movement while at the
same time refusing to identify with the socialist party
may well be a basic contradiction.[29]

Let me add that Coady had no illusions regarding the
capitalism of his day nor of the type of democracy it
created. "It should be abundantly clear by this time,"
he writes, "that the old methods of finance capitalism
- now monopoly capitalism - are not capable of doing the
job (overcoming poverty and distributing wealth). It
is a stupid rationalization on the part of the economically privileged to think that what has evolved in the
Western world, especially in America, is democracy. To
identify democracy with the ability of a man or a small
group of men to set up economic kingdoms which necessi-
tate the subservience and, I might add, the slavery of
the masses, is to indulge in a pure myth."[30]

The reader of Coady's writings is often puzzled by
the contrasting emphases. Coady rejected the modern
economic system and advocated a new economic order bent
not on profit but on service. He was able to talk about
this in terms which were Christian, in fact in keeping
with the great Catholic medieval tradition. At the same
time, when Coady spoke of what he called "the big picture," he promoted a reformist, not a radical stance
toward the present order. He reconciled the radical
and the reformist emphases through the idea that society
must be reconstructed beginning "from the fringes."[31]
He thought that the critical movements in Western Canada
and Nova Scotia were the beginning, or at least could be
the beginning, of a more universal transformation of
Canadian society. He held that when these fringes became significantly wide and represented more power, the
centre of society would undergo not only quantitative
but also qualitative changes. With such a cautious approach, Coady and the other leaders were able to create
a critical movement among basically conservative farmers and fishermen and promote a radical spirit that
was reminiscent not of socialism or communism but of
Christian philosophy.

The question has been asked whether the Antigonish
Movement was the church's response to communism. Such
a question can have two quite distinct meanings. It
is possible to ask whether a particular Catholic social
trend represents a church-sponsored attempt to gather
radical and reform-minded Catholics in a movement that

in fact acts as a defender of the status quo. Or it is
possible to ask whether a Catholic social trend is a
church-sponsored creative response to communism or
socialism which gathers radical and reform-minded Catholics in a movement that opposes communism and socialism
and at the same time rejects the inherited order.
European Social Catholicism, mentioned earlier, which
produced what was later called the church's social
teaching, can be classified as a response to socialism
in the second sense. For when the 19th century socialist movement made Catholic groups aware of the systematic oppression of the working class in the capitalist
system, these groups produced a social philosophy that
opposed - though usually quite ineffectively - both
socialism and monopoly capitalism.

However the Antigonish Movement was largely a much-
needed response to the helplessness and lack of organization of the impoverished farmers and fishermen of Nova
Scotia.[32] Since the decline of United Farmers organization in the early twenties, the cooperatives supported
by them had almost disappeared. It was in this situation
that individual Catholic priests like Jimmy Tompkins
adopted the philosophy of cooperatism from England and
Scandinavia and adapted it to the Catholic social tradition.
This, as I see it, is the origin of the Antigonish movement.

At the same time, when we study the creation of the
movement's organizational centre, the Extension Department of St. Francis Xavier University, the story becomes
more complex. Jimmy Tompkins had not met with early
success. He had in fact been removed, though for different reasons, from his association with the university
and placed as a parish priest in a small fishing village.
The friends of the cooperative movement were unable to
move the university to adopt the new adult education
programme. It was only at the end of the twenties that
the Catholic Scottish Society, strongly organized on
Cape Breton, provided the necessary funds for its
inauguration. To retain the cohesion of Scottish culture, the Society advocated economic development in
Nova Scotia and hoped that the educational facilities
of St. Francis Xavier University reaching out to
ordinary people - and here it specifically included
farmers, fishermen and miners - would help them to
improve the economic conditions of their lives.[33]
Politically the Society was conservation.[34] It expressed the concern of many Catholics in Eastern Nova Scotia

over the radicalism of the miners in the industrialized
part of Cape Breton. Some of the funds used in the
creation of the Antigonish Movement, then, coming from
the Catholic Scottish Society and also, as mentioned
above, from the Carnegie Foundation, represented an
intention of helping farmers and workingmen in order to
make more secure the present social order. This pressure, in my reading of the documents, did not greatly
influence the philosophy of the Antigonish Movement.

But as soon as we leave the rural world of farmers
and fishermen and turn to the industrialized part of
Cape Breton, we notice that the Antigonish Movement
encountered and reacted to radical unionism and began
to define itself as 'the middle way' between liberal
democracy and revolutionary communism. The St. Francis
Xavier Extension Department opened an office in Glace
Bay in 1932 in the hope of helping the labour movement
there to remain non-revolutionary, democratic and con-
genial to religion. This takes us to the next topic to
be discussed in this paper, Social Catholicism in industrialized Cape Breton in the thirties.

Prior to Paul MacEwan's recent Miners and Steelworkers[35] there was no book available on the labour movement in Cape Breton County, even though its history is
one of the most troubled of North America. Six times,
from 1882 to 1925, the government sent in federal
troops to smash the labour movement struggling for
unionization and political power.[36] The first attempts
to organize labour, MacEwan reports, united craftsmen
and industrial workers, until the more radical miners
of Cape Breton working under inhuman conditions,
succeeded after many attempts in creating an industrial
union allied to a political programme. These labour
struggles took place in the years 1909 to 1917. The
new, more political unionism was less interested in
consumers' cooperatives, favoured by the craft
unions as an important means of wrestling against
exploitation of the workers.[37] The industrial union
was more socialist in orientation. Following the
British model, its leaders favoured the creation of a
labour party to act as the political arm of the labour
movement.

For a brief time, in the early twenties, the politi-
cization of workers as well as farmers led to a joint
farmer-labour party, which was able to elect several
members to the Provincial House and constitute the

136

official opposition. Yet this union of farmers and
workers was not to last. The United Farmers declined
in Nova Scotia as they did in the rest of the country.
The farmers, moreover, were frightened by the outright
socialist language of the labour leaders. The dis-
appearance of the farmers as an organized force led to
the decline of the cooperatives they had sponsored.
This breakdown of organization among the farmers, as
mentioned earlier, belongs to the background of the
Antigonish Movement.

The labour movement in Cape Breton, after temporary
political success, came under brutal pressure from the
companies, aided by the government. The workers were
divided between radicals and moderates. The radicals
advocated an all-out opposition to the present system,
sometimes though by no means always expressed in
communist terms, and the moderates favoured more conventional collective bargaining and hoped that a more
just and more generous government would force management to settle for better terms. The radicals were
often able to win support among the workers but in
every case the government smashed their movement with
violent repression. After 1925, the last invasion of
Cape Breton County by the federal troops, the labour
movement was unable to produce significant results.
Between 1925 and 1936, the rift between radicals and
moderates within the unions absorbed the attention of
leaders and workers. There was much agitation and
strife among the workers, many of whom adopted a
revolutionary rhetoric, idealized the events that had
taken place in Russia and were happy to call themselves
communists.

It was during this time that the Catholic Rural Life
Conference extended its interest to the industrial
workers and began to call itself the Rural and Industrial Life Conference. This yearly Conference,
sponsored by the diocese of Antigonish since 1924, was
primarily concerned with the plight of the farmers.
After 1930, the newly founded Extension Department was
asked to plan and organize the Conferences. In order
to convince the 1932 Conference in Sydney that the
church should adopt a more open and sympathetic approach
to the labour struggle, a priest had invited Alex
MacIntyre, a former communist labour leader, blacklisted
by the company and now unemployed, to address the
assembly on the labour movement in Cape Breton.[38] His
speech has become famous among the men and women

associated with the Antigonish movement. He told the
audience that the clergy were on the whole identified
with the interests of the owners of industry and hence
with the powers that exploited the workers and their
families. He told them that the widely-spread Catholic
prejudice against the radical miners as materialists,
communists and atheists, was largely based on ignorance,
for it was the so-called materialist workers, communists
included, who were moved to compassion by the misery of
the workers and were ready to give their lives for the
well-being of others. He suggested that the church, by
its indifference to the well-being of the workers -
despite the papal encyclicals - was in fact driving the
workers into communism and contempt for religion. Mac-
Intyre exhorted the Conference to change its attitude
toward the labour movement.

The actual relationship of the Catholic Church to the
labour movement in Cape Breton has not been studied in
detail. It is true, of course, that the Catholics of
the rural areas, and especially Antigonish, the seat
of the diocese, on the mainland, were frightened by the
radicalism of the labour movement. Yet they were
united to the labourers by family ties and kinship
loyalty and hence in the hour of dire need, the church
organized help for the hungry strikers and their families. In 1925, the longest and most painful strike of
the miners, ending in violent repression and humiliation
of the workers, Bishop James Morrison of Antigonish
asked the Catholic parishes in his diocese to send them
food and money.[39] Still, on the whole the church in
rural areas was cautious. When the workers in the early
twenties created an Independent Labour Party and later
joined with the United Farmers, The Casket, the diocesan weekly of Antigonish, warned Catholics against the
third party.[40] The church appeared as the defender of
the traditional parties. Still, in the industrialized
area of Cape Breton, there was always a minority of
priests who identified with labour and its struggle
against oppression. Their story has yet to be written.

When in 1936, at a time when the steel workers were
not yet fully organized, Father 'Mickey' MacDonald
used his leadership position in the parish to help the
workers organize and, he defended their action from the
pulpit with papal citations. Mr. Kelley, then managing
director of the Steel Plant, complained to Bishop
Morrison about the priest and claimed that he had
interfered in the business of the company beyond the

scope of the church's authority. Yet Bishop Morrison,
despite his cautious style, did not interfere with
Father MacDonald's activity. While it may well be true,
as Alex MacIntyre had asserted, that the church as a
whole identified itself with the established order, there
was a minority of priests who identified with the workers and were accepted by them as brothers in the common
struggle.

   The Rural and Industrial Life Conference of 1932,
profoundly touched by MacIntyre's speech, resolved to
support the labourers of Cape Breton in their struggle
for social justice. Alex MacIntyre himself was hired
as a full-time organizer. Besides the usual pattern of
study-clubs and cooperative stores the Extension Department decided to open a labour school in Cape Breton.
They prepared workers to become labour leaders and play
an active role in the union. They wanted to introduce
them to the principles of modern economics, existing
labour legislation, and the principles of social justice. Here the anti-communist trend of Catholic teaching was a significant element. The Extension Department wanted to steer the workers, especially the
Catholics, away from revolutionary politics which,
because of their utter frustration, seemed attractive
to them. The labour school promoted an evolutionary
approach to the labour struggle. Following the principles of Social Catholicism, it taught the workers not
to regard the quest for their own class-interest as the
lever for the reconstruction of society but rather to
understand their struggle as a quest for social justice
that the government ought to honour and the owning
classes should accept. In the Catholic tradition of
that time, the labour struggle did not aim at the conquest of the exploiters by the exploited but at sub-
mission to the demands of justice of all sections of
society. Behind the labour struggle, in the Catholic
tradition, stands the vision of a corporate society,
based on the cooperation of the classes, united by a
common set of values.

   How influential was the Extension Department in Cape
Breton County? This is a difficult question. It is
easy to show that it was very influential in organizing
cooperative stores and credit unions. But what about
the effect on the workers' movement? From my own conversations with old-timers in Cape Breton who remember
the struggle of the thirties, I have the impression
that the labour school helped many to gain greater

139

self-confidence at public meetings, but that it had no
definable influence on the labour movement. The positions the workers took in the labour movement were
determined by the conditions of their lives and forces
within their own ranks.

It should be said at this point that religious affiliation did not play a significant role in the labour
movement of Cape Breton. Labour solidarity was stronger
than religious ties. While in the rural areas of
Eastern Nova Scotia the Scots were divided from one
another, in Cape Breton County, which was equally divided, in some towns with a Protestant and in others with
a Catholic majority, there was unity in the common
cause. This at least is how Cape Bretoners describe it
(detailed studies have not yet been undertaken). There
were tensions in the mines over job opportunities and
promotion, but these apparently never affected their
common opposition to the bosses. The conflict within
the labour movement was between militants and moderates,
especially during the years 1909 to 1917 and later
again between 1925 and 1936.[41] It was in no way a
division involving a religious factor, aligning Protestants against Catholics, or Christians against
atheists. The Scottish workers of Cape Breton remained
so linked to the country people that they rarely
adopted a hostile attitude toward their churches.
Even when they called themselves communists, they were
not usually committed to atheism in an ideological
sense. And while the churches as a whole, be they
Protestant or Catholic, did not join the struggle of
the labourers and sided, as churches usually do, with
the government and the ruling groups, there was always
a significant number of Presbyterian ministers and
Catholic priests in Cape Breton County that passionately
endorsed the cause of labour. In this social context,
therefore, the Extension Department did not exert any
specifically 'Catholic' influence on the labour movement.

What was the condition of labour in Cape Breton in
the early thirties? After 1925, the union which 15
years earlier had spearheaded the more radical movement
and with whom the mining companies had later come to an
agreement, was now regarded as soft and too obliging
to management. It seemed that when a miner left the
pit as a union leader and sat at his desk in shirt and
tie, he became a gentleman, polite and yielding to
company pressure. The frustrated workers formed a new

union but the companies, aided by government, supported
the old and refused to deal with them. This set the
stage for a profound division of the labour movement
with dire consequences for collective bargaining and
for the political influence of labour in the community.
For years since the early twenties, the workers had
been unable to elect representatives to the provincial
legislature.

By 1936 the miners were exhausted. They decided to
bury their old conflict, become reconciled in the old,
legitimate union, and present a more united political
force in the area.[42] We recall that prior to this, in
1932, the CCF had been founded in Calgary. It represented a Canadian form of socialism that regarded British
constitutionalism as an instrument for the radical
reconstruction of society. The party was still generally unknown in the East. The Regina Manifesto (1933) had
been read by Nova Scotian labour leaders, and some had even
endorsed it as their personal platform.[43] But the CCF
was not organized anywhere East of the Ottawa Valley.
The newly reconciled miners of District 26 decided to
found CCF clubs, to invite CCF leaders to visit Cape
Breton, and eventually in 1938, to organize and fund
the party in Nova Scotia. District 26 was the first
labour union to join the CCF, and since no statutory
provisions had been made for such affiliations, the
party decided to follow the rules of the British Labour
Party. Not all workers were behind the move. Some locals
did not pay their membership dues. The communists fought
the CCF as a counter-revolutionary force. Still, with
the arrival of the CCF, Cape Breton labour presented a
more united front than it had done since the early
twenties and was able to elect representatives to the
Provincial Parliament and to the House of Commons in
Ottawa.

Was the reconciliation of the workers and the creation of a democratic socialist movement in Cape Breton
in any way due to the influence of the Antigonish
Movement? I think not. From my conversations, I
gather that the Extension Department was associated by
the workers mainly with the cooperative stores and
credit unions. To Catholics the Extension also symbolized the church's concern for labour and allowed them to
link their political struggle with their religious
aspirations. But it had no direct influence on political developments.

Since our interest here is in Social Catholicism, we note the Catholic participation in the labour movement of Cape Breton from the beginning and in particular, the strong Catholic presence in the newly founded CCF party of Nova Scotia. This is unique in Canada. Cape Breton County is the only strongly Catholic area that has elected socialist representatives to parliament, beginning with the miner, Clarie Gillis, labour leader steeped in the Social Catholicism of Nova Scotia. The CCF members elected to the provincial legislature, Donald MacDonald in 1939 and Michael MacDonald in 1945, were Catholics of the same tradition. This ready identification of the Catholic workers with Canadian socialism deserves special mention because, as noted earlier, in the rest of Canada the Catholic Church had publicly warned against supporting the CCF. The bishop of Antigonish did not repeat the general ecclesiastical caveat but followed instead the example of the British Catholic hierarchy in dissociating the labour party from the kind of socialism condemned by papal teaching. The Catholic supporters of the CCF in Cape Breton, contrary to its usage in Saskatchewan, did not use the term 'socialist' and Cape Bretoners, even when they were linked to revolutionary politics, were not interested in ideology. They were culturally conservative, remaining close to the customs and the religion of their kinfolk. Their identification with socialism, whether democratic or revolutionary, was an act of class protest against a system that made them and their wives and children suffer.

In the strongly Catholic areas of Nova Scotia, the CCF leaders tried to show that Canadian socialism, more than the traditional parties, corresponded to the ideals outlined in Catholic social teaching. In a volume on the church's social doctrine published in Québec, which carefully analysed the repudiation of the CCF on the part of the Canadian bishops, the author complained that in Nova Scotia Clarence Gillis, the Catholic MP, sought the support of his people by brandishing the papal encyclicals.[44] In a letter to Dr. Coady - which might contain a touch of flattery - Gillis wrote: "Most of my ideas and principles were formed on the basis of the cooperative movement, and all my thinking is in this direction....I think you can be quite proud of the many young people who got their start through you and the cooperative movement."[45] After his election to the House of Commons in 1940, Gillis wrote an article entitled 'Miners Stand United' for

The New Commonwealth, the CCF weekly at Regina, Saskatchewan. There he made this observation: "In addition
to the political and industrial movements, the miners of
Nova Scotia recognized the value of education and when
St. Francis Xavier Extension Department inaugurated
their movement to bring the university to the people
and laid down the programme of adult education in the
establishments of credit unions and cooperative stores,
the miners of Nova Scotia became part of that organization, and today are marching forward and are practically
taking over, under the guidance of the Extension Department, the economic resources of the province."[46] In the
House, in his first speech on unemployment, on June 4,
1940, Gillis affirmed the value of the cooperative movement, saying: "The people of Nova Scotia are making a
wonderful effort to solve their own economic problems by
cooperative efforts. They have already established 180
credit unions, 43 stores, 17 lobster factories, 7 fish
plants, 8 community industries and some 10 other cooperatives. The total number of cooperative organizations in the Maritimes is 422."

In the memory of the old CCFers, today often NDPers,
those early years after the foundation of the party in
Nova Scotia were a period of victorious struggle and
unity among the workers. They recall that the workers
participated in three parallel movements, the political
movement of the CCF through identification with the party, the labour movement through the support of their
union, and the cooperative movement through credit
unions and cooperative stores. This is how Gillis described it. This is how David Lewis understood it in his
book, Make This Your Canada (1943).[47] This is how it has
remained in the memory of Donald MacDonald, labour leader
of the late thirties, elected as member of the legislature in 1939, who later became president of the Canadian
Labour Congress. This is how it appeared to other labour
leaders I have interviewed. Paul MacEwan, NDP member of
the legislature and historian of Nova Scotia, received as
the result of his studies the same impression of the early
years of the CCF. This memory of unity may have been a
little exaggerated. Many workers remained committed
to revolutionary politics. Some union locals did not
pay their dues to the CCF. The cooperative movement
did not publicly support the CCF at all. Still, at
the end of the thirties and the beginning of the forties, when in the whole of Canada the CCF made considerable strides and appeared, following the British and
Continental European pattern, to become the recognized
alternative to the government and possibly even form a

democratic socialist government of Canada, the workers of Cape Breton experienced more hope and less impotence than they ever had and backed a common politics to re-construct the social order. The Social Catholicism of Nova Scotia enabled Catholics to take part in this as an expression of their genuine religious aspirations.

FOOTNOTES

1. Friedrich Engels, Marx and Engels on Religion, intr. by R. Niebuhr, New York, 1964, p. 103.

2. Ernst Bloch, Thomas Münzer als Theologe der Revolution, rev. ed., Frankfurt a. M., 1968, p. 99.

3. Max Weber's three essays on the relation of religion and social class (The Sociology of Religion, transl. by E. Fischoff, Boston, 1968, pp. 80-137) remain the classical text on the many meanings present in the same religion.

4. Cf Richard Allen, The Social Passion: Religion and Social Reform in Canada, 1914-1928, Toronto, 1973; Roger Hutchinson, "The Fellowship for a Christian Social Order;" Th.D. thesis, Toronto School of Theology, 1975.

5. For documentation, see Jean Hulliger, L'enseigne-ment social des évêques canadiens, 1801-1950, Montréal, 1957, pp. 189-201.

6. For the view of Card. Bourne, Archbishop of West-minster, see The Tablet, June 20, 1931.

7. M.G. Ballantyne, "The Church and the CCF," Common-weal, March 3, 1944.

8. For useful introduction see Alec R. Vidler, A Cen-tury of Social Catholicism, 1820-1920, London, 1964.

9. For a brief discussion of the inapplicability of papal teaching in North America, see David O'Brien American Catholics and Social Reform, New York, 1972, pp. 182-83.

10.

Counties	Population	Catholics
Antigonish	10,073	8,736
Cape Breton C.	92,419	49,558
Inverness	21,005	14,949
Richmond	11,098	8,801

Cities & Towns	Population	Catholics
Sydney	23,089	11,360
Dominion	2,846	2,134
Glace Bay	20,706	10,705
New Waterford	7,745	5,553
North Sydney	6,139	2,420
Sydney Mines	7,769	3,744

11. There are books and articles written by Dr. Coady himself, e.g., Masters of Their Own Destiny, New York, 1939, and "The Social Significance of the Cooperative Movement," pamphlet, 1961. A very useful collection of Father Coady's thought, gathered from his many speeches and articles, is Alex Laidlaw's The Man from Margaree: Writings and Speeches of M.M. Coady, Toronto, 1971.

There are histories of the movement, written in an uncritical and admiring fashion that fail to communicate the radical nature of these men's thought and actions. Literature on the Antigonish Movement: M.E. Arnold, The Story of Tompkinsville, New York, 1940; George Boyle, Father Tompkins of Nova Scotia, New York, 1953; B.B. Fowler, The Lord Helps Those..., New York, 1938; A.F. Laidlaw, The Campus and the Community, Montreal, 1961; Jim Lotz, "The Antigonish Movement: A Critical Analysis," Studies in Adult Education, 5 (Oct. 1973), pp. 97-122.

12. Frank Mifflin, "The Antigonish Movement: A Revitalization Movement in Eastern Nova Scotia," Ph.D. thesis in sociology, Boston College, 1974; Robert Sacouman, "Social Origins of the Antigonish Movement," Ph.D. thesis in sociology, University of Toronto, 1976; Daniel McGinnis, "Clerics, Farmers, Fishermen and Workers: Religion and Collectivity in the Antigonish Movement," Ph.D. thesis in sociology (almost completed), McMaster University.

13. Mifflin's Ph.D. thesis (note 12 above), p. 120 and following.

14. M.M. Coady, Masters of Their Own Destiny, ch. ii, "The Great Default of the People," pp. 17-29.

15. Ibid., p. 20.

16. Quadragesimo anno, n. 109.

17. M.M. Coady, op. cit., p. 70.

18. Ibid., p. 122.

19. The title of E.F. Schuhmacher's celebrated book (1973), "Small is Beautiful," characterizes the Catholic social tradition in general and the Antigonish Movement in particular. The technical phrase for 'small is beautiful' in Catholic social thought is 'the principle of subsidiarity.'

20. G.D.H. Cole, A Century of Cooperation, London, 1944, pp. 103-19.

21. Mifflin's Ph.D. thesis (note 12 above), p. 95. In the early forties, Mifflin reports a liberal politician accused Alex MacIntyre of the Extension Department of promoting the CCF. Coady reacted vehemently. He investigated the charge, found it based on rumour, and only then notified his co-worker.

22. Ibid., p. 96.

23. M.M. Coady, Masters of Their Own Destiny, ch. ix, "Cooperation in our Social Blue Print," pp. 120-138.

24. Ibid., p. 134.

25. The growing moderation of CCF policy during the late thirties and early forties has been well documented. See, for instance, S.M. Lipset, Agrarian Socialism, updated edit., Berkeley, Cal., 1971, ch. 7, "Ideology and Program," pp. 160-194.

26. See the paragraph entitled 'Beware of Institutionalizing,' in Tompkins' pamphlet, "The Future of the Antigonish Movement," quoted in George Boyle's Father Tompkins of Nova Scotia, New York, 1953,

pp. 227-228. Tompkins' suspicion of institutions is a topic developed in McGinnes' Ph.D. thesis (note 12 above).

27. Quoted in George Boyle, op. cit., pp. 155-156.

28. F. Engelmann, "Membership Participation in Policy Making in the CCF," Canadian Journal of Economics and Political Science, 22 (May 1956), pp. 161-173.

29. This view is defended in Gary Webster, "Tignish and Antigonish: A Critique of the Antigonish Movement as a Cadre for Cooperation," The Abegweit Review, 2 (September 1975), pp. 94-102.

30. A.F. Laidlaw, ed., The Man from Margaree, p. 28.

31. Cf. ibid., pp. 25-26.

32. G.A. Rawlyk has suggested that the promotion of co-operatives on the part of the priests of Antigonish was largely due to the advances made by the radical farmers during the brief period in the early twenties when the Farmer-Labour party was able to elect representatives to the provincial legislature ("The Farmer Labour Movement and the Failure of Socialism in Nova Scotia," Essays on the Left, ed. L. LaPierre, Toronto, 1971, p. 36). Yet Rawlyk proposes this view as a conjecture rather than a conclusion. It is my impression that the priests involved in the cooperatives were moved by the plight of their people with whom they so strongly identified. By the time the movement became organized in the early thirties the radical farmers had long disappeared. It was, moreover, a policy of the young Antigonish Movement never to engage in red-baiting.

33. A letter written by the Catholic Scottish Society to St. Francis Xavier University, expressing their wish that 'extension work' be established among the miners, is quoted in P.A. Nearing, He Loved the Church: The Biography of Bishop John R. MacDonald, Antigonish, Nova Scotia, 1975, p. 36.

34. This is a topic treated in McGinnis' Ph.D. thesis (note 12 above).

35. Paul MacEwan, Miners and Steelworkers, Toronto, 1976.

36. _Ibid._, p. 142.

37. The relation of the labour movement to cooperatives is a topic studied in Sacouman's Ph.D. thesis (note 12 above).

38. P.A. Nearing, _op. cit._, p. 46. The impact of Alex MacIntyre on the Antigonish Movement is examined in McGinnis' Ph.D. thesis (note 12 above).

39. P.A. Nearing, _op. cit._, p. 27.

40. The topic is examined in McGinnis' Ph.D. thesis (note 12 above).

41. Paul MacEwan, _op. cit._, pp. 151-169.

42. _Ibid._, pp. 195-205.

43. _Ibid._, p. 173.

44. Jean Hulliger, _L'enseignement social des eveques canadiens_, 1891-1950, Montreal, 1957, p. 196.

45. Letter of March 25, 1955.

46. _The Commonwealth_, September 20, 1940, p. 3.

47. "The first major union to affiliate (with the CCF) was District 26 of the United Mine-Workers of America in the fall of 1938. The miners of Nova Scotia had benefitted greatly from the cooperative and credit union movement in that province. They had obtained an insight into the workings of the economic system through the educational work conducted by the Extension Department of St. Francis Xavier University. Political action through the CCF followed naturally." D. Lewis and Frank Scott, _Make This Your Canada_, Ottawa, 1943, p. 128.

FÉMINISME ET RELIGION AU QUÉBEC DEPUIS 1960

MONIQUE DUMAIS : membre du Département des Sciences
Religieuses de l'Université du Québec à Rimouski.
Thèse de doctorat: "l'Eglise de Rimouski et un Plan
de développement 1963-1972", présentée à Union Theological Seminary, New York (1977). Communication
donnée   en premier lieu aux Conférences de la SCER/
CSSR à Fredericton en 1977.

RÉSUMÉ

Any attempt to understand the relation between the
feminist movement and religion in Québec raises two
questions: that of the influence of religion on the
feminist movement and that of the movement's effect on
attitudes within the Churches.

A survey of events, studies, new organizations, maga-
zine articles, theses titles, and books published, over
the period from 1960 to 1977, indicates that there is a
real equality yet to be "conquered" by Québec women.
In the Church, a theoretical equality exists based on
Galatians 3:28. Yet, in actual practice, the Church
would seem to fear women abusing their rights and even
to exploit sexism in order to reconcile capitalist interests. Teaching that woman's primary role is that of
support to her husband and educator of children, the
Church nevertheless continues to see its own role as
one pertaining to matters such as family planning and
abortion. Such a posture is not without effect on
society at large. There, the images and stereotypes
of women have evolved very little and Québec women do
not seem yet decided to struggle concertedly for their
rights. Apart from some exceptional voices, Québec
women are only beginning to become aware of themselves
and of their role in society. In this respect, while
new forms of creative participation are slowly emerging,
Québec women still have areas of responsibility in secular and church societies, which they have yet to
assume. This is especially evident when the feminist
movement in Québec is compared with that movement in
other countries such as the United States and Latin
American nations or in other provinces such as Ontario.

MONIQUE DUMAIS

FÉMINISME ET RELIGION AU QUÉBEC DEPUIS 1960

> Sous le nom de féminisme, un mouvement pervers,
> une ambition fallacieuse entraîne hors de sa voie
> la plus élégante moitié de notre espèce, et me-
> nace les bases mêmes de la famille et de la so-
> ciété. On n'a pas cru d'abord au danger, tant le
> succès d'une telle anomalie semblait invraisem-
> blable. L'évidence est venue prouver que rien
> n'est à l'abri des emballements de l'esprit sé-
> duit par le prisme des théories captieuses.[1]

Ces propos de Mgr Louis-Adolphe Paquet, datés de 1919,
nous montrent que le mot "féminisme" a été utilisé au
Québec avant le milieu du XXe siècle, que des ecclésiastiques s'en sont servi pour dénoncer un mal. On peut
se demander si le féminisme est encore considéré comme
un danger public dans les milieux religieux. De fait,
on peut se poser les questions suivantes : quelle est
actuellement l'influence de la religion sur le féminisme?
Encourage-t-elle les aspirations des femmes visant à
s'affirmer dans la société, dans l'Eglise ou leur dresse-
t-elle des obstacles? D'autre part, le mouvement féministe exerce-t-il des pressions sur l'attitude des Eglises au Québec? Existe-t-il des féministes qui militent
dans les institutions religieuses?

Par féminisme, je veux désigner la détermination des
femmes de parvenir à une égalité réelle avec les hommes
dans les différentes sphères de la société y compris
l'Eglise. Deux grandes tâches s'imposent immédiatement
aux femmes : une tâche positive, consistant dans l'affirmation de leur propre identité et l'épanouissement de
leurs capacités; l'autre négative, tendant à s'opposer
à tout ce qui va à l'encontre de ce vouloir-être et
vouloir-vivre des femmes. Pour remplir ces tâches, les
femmes ont besoin de se regrouper, car nous sommes des
personnes isolées, que ce soit au foyer, ou dans les
divers milieux de travail, peu habituées à s'organiser
pour défendre nos droits, pour se faire une idée commune.
Il s'agit d'une égalité réelle à conquérir, non pas
d'une recherche d'identité avec les hommes, ce qui serait
renier une bonne partie de ce que nous sommes en tant
que femmes. J'insiste sur une égalité réelle et non pas
fictive : on a beaucoup parlé de matriarcat au Québec,
beaucoup de clercs "encensant" les femmes, de la Vierge
Marie à nos fondatrices canadiennes, à l'humble fermière,
à la ménagère dévouée, pour mieux nous faire taire et
nous rendre contentes de notre sort.

150

FÉMINISME ET RELIGION AU QUÉBEC DEPUIS 1960

Je traiterai du féminisme vis-à-vis la religion au Québec; je signalerai presque exclusivement l'attitude de l'Eglise catholique qui regroupe 86,7 pour cent de la population québécoise. Je ne possède pas suffisamment d'informations sur les trois autres groupes religieux plus importants au Québec : l'Eglise anglicane, 3 pour cent, l'Eglise Unie, 2.9 pour cent, la religion juive, 1,8 pour cent.[2] L'étude portera sur la période de 1960 à 1977, vu que la plupart des analystes s'accordent à dire que le mouvement féministe connaît un nouveau départ avec la deuxième moitié des années soixante. Juliet Mitchell a montré comment la montée féministe s'inscrit à l'intérieur des mouvements révolutionnaires des années soixante : les Noirs, les étudiants, et les jeunes (Hippies, Yippies et les Insoumis).

> L'énergie révolutionnaire du Mouvement de Libération provient de deux sources : la pauvreté économique des femmes dans le pays le plus riche du monde (comme pour les Noirs), et leur misère psychique et affective même dans les conditions les plus privilégiées de ce pays (comme pour les étudiants et les jeunes).[3]

L'objectif global de la présente étude est de montrer qu'il existe au Québec un début de conscientisation face à la situation des femmes dans l'Eglise. Dans un premier temps, j'indiquerai les événements et témoignages qui permettent de juger s'il y a présentement une ouverture progressive à la participation des femmes dans l'Eglise au Québec. Dans un second temps, j'analyserai et critiquerai les éléments importants des différents types d'intervention. Dans un troisième temps et plus brièvement, je tenterai de situer les efforts québécois par rapport à l'ensemble de l'entreprise féministe telle qu'elle se présente sur le plan international, plus particulièrement aux Etats-Unis.

1. DOSSIER RAPIDE SUR LES FEMMES ET LA RELIGION AU QUÉBEC OU SE PASSE-T-IL QUELQUE CHOSE POUR LES FEMMES DANS L'EGLISE AU QUÉBEC?

A la fin de janvier 1977, nous parvenait la Déclaration romaine sur la question de l'admission des femmes au sacerdoce ministériel. Les réactions publiques dans les mass-media au Québec ont été plutôt clairsemées,[4] il n'etait évidemment pas question de manifestation extérieure comme l'ont fait nos soeurs des Etats-Unis. J'ai essayé

de dresser un dossier nous permettant de découvrir les
éléments qui contribuent au Québec à la promotion des
femmes dans le domaine religieux et ecclésial. Tout ce
qui a été recueilli n'a pas toujours une saveur féministe, mais concerne au moins les femmes.

1.1. Quelques événements

- 16 février 1967 : Création de la Commission royale
  d'enquête sur la situation de la femme au Canada˜

- mars 1968 : Congrès des religieuses à Montréal;

- 28 septembre 1970 : Rapport sur la situation de la
  femme au Canada, appelé Rapport Bird, du nom de la
  présidente Florence Bird;

- 1971 : Déclaration de l'épiscopat canadien à l'Assemblée
  tenue à Edmonton, du 19 au 24 septembre - étude sur
  l'accession éventuelle des femmes aux ministères;

- 10 mars 1972 : Formation par l'épiscopat canadien d'un
  comité d'étude sur le rôle de la femme dans l'Eglise;

- 8 juillet 1973 : La loi créant le Conseil du Statut de
  la Femme a été adoptée en troisième lecture;

- 16 novembre 1973 : Première rencontre du comité d'étude
  sur le rôle de la femme dans l'Eglise;

- 25 janvier 1975 : Inauguration de l'année internationale
  de la Femme par le Mouvement des Femmes chrétiennes.
  Thème : "La femme chrétienne, agent de changement dans
  l'Eglise."[5]

1.2 Présence des femmes au niveau paroissial, diocésain
et provincial

Dans l'Eglise catholique, les femmes peuvent maintenant
exercer de nombreuses fonctions au plan paroissial. Autrefois, elles étaient vouées à être ménagères du curé ou de
fidèles assistantes aux célébrations liturgiques; aujour-
d'hui elles sont élues marguillières, elles assurent différents services liturgiques, tels que la lecture, le chant,
l'animation, le service à l'autel, la distribution de la
communion, elles s'engagent dans toutes sortes de formes
de pastorale, seulement elles ne peuvent devenir ministres
du culte. Des religieuses sont même responsables de paroisse, mais n'ont pas les pouvoirs ministériels; un ex-

emple typique est Soeur Claire Richer qui est depuis août 1975 à la tête de Saint-Michel de Napierville dans le diocèse de St-Jean.[6]

Au niveau diocésain, plusieurs femmes oeuvrent dans les offices; elles sont des conseillères appréciées. Ce sont surtout des religieuses qui sont présentes dans ces services, ce qui a l'inconvénient de mettre en veilleuse l'apport des femmes mariées, question d'économie! (Les religieuses peuvent vivre avec des petits salaires.)[7]

A l'Assemblée des Evêques du Québec (A.E.Q.), deux femmes sont adjointes, l'une au secrétaire général pour l'education, l'autre au secrétaire général pour les affaires sociales; deux autres femmes travaillent à l'Office de Catéchèse du Québec.[8]

Le dossier de l'Archevêché de Montréal, La femme, un agent de changement dans l'Eglise, soulignait que "dans l'ensemble des manifestations de la vie de l'Eglise, les femmes se retrouvent majoritaires à peu près partout...", tant dans l'assistance aux rassemblements dominicaux que dans la participation à divers mouvements. "Toutefois un autre fait demeure : si, au niveau des mouvements, les femmes ont un membership quantitativement plus considérable que celui des hommes, ce membership décroît (ou est limité) au niveau des activités de planification, d'administration ou plus simplement de direction."[9]

Dans l'Eglise anglicane au Québec, on ordonnera à la prêtrise pour la première fois, une femme, Ruth Matthews, à Drummondville, le 5 juin 1977, alors qu'il y a douze femmes d'ordonnées au Canada depuis le 30 novembre 1976.[10] Une autre femme exerce la fonction de diacre à Montréal.[10] Dans l'Eglise Unie du Canada, dès 1964, des femmes ont été ordonnées pasteurs au Québec.[11]

1.3 Des femmes théologiennes

Vers le milieu des années soixante, les Grands Séminaires québécois ont ouvert leurs portes aux femmes qui désiraient étudier la théologie. A Rimouski, c'était en 1966,[12] et depuis la proportion des etudiantes n'a cessé d'être assez forte : en 1976, le module des Sciences religieuses de l'UQAR compte 60 pour cent de femmes aux études à temps plein et à temps partiel. Cependant, au Québec, très peu de femmes poursuivent des études avancées en théologie ou en sciences religieuses. Un tableau de la répartition par sexe des détenteurs d'une maîtrise ou d'un doctorat, en 1970-71, dans les universités québécoises, est assez éclairant.

Tableau 1 :

Université Laval	3 hommes	aucune femme
Université McGill	9 hommes	aucune femme
Université de Montréal	14 hommes	2 femmes
Université de Sherbrooke	9 hommes	3 femmes [13]

Très peu de femmes également enseignent dans les facultés de théologie et les départements de sciences religieuses; on en retrouve une ou deux à chaque endroit.

1.4 Documents et livres

Quelques documents et livres traitent spécialement des relations entre les femmes et le christianisme ou les femmes et l'Eglise.

En 1967, Fernande Saint-Martin écrivait pour le compte du Mouvement laïque de langue française une petite brochure intitulée : La femme et la Société cléricale.[14]

En 1968, paraît le volume contenant toutes les conférences et activités du grand congrès des religieuses à Montréal.[15]

Marc Rondeau publie en 1969 La promotion de la femme dans la pensée de l'Eglise contemporaine.[16]

En 1974, l'AFEAS (Association féminine d'éducation et d'action sociale) donnait le résultat d'une enquête sur La participation de la femme dans la société et dans l'Eglise auprès de cent quarante-trois femmes entre quarante et quarante-cinq ans.

En 1975, le Département de la Recherche de la Conférence Religieuse Canadienne livrait une étude sur Le rôle de la femme dans la société civile et dans l'Eglise.

En janvier 1976, l'Archevêché de Montréal faisait connaître un dossier de travail constitué à la suite d'une enquête menée auprès des femmes du diocèse de Montréal, à l'occasion de l'Année internationale de la Femme, dans

le but de recueillir leurs opinions et leurs aspirations
quant à la situation des femmes dans l'Eglise. Le dossier a pour titre: La femme, un agent de changement dans
l'Eglise; il a été élaboré par une équipe composée de
six femmes et trois hommes.

En avril 1976, le réseau des Politisés chrétiens four-
nissait un texte-outil consacré au Féminisme, socialisme,
christianisme, d'après une entrevue avec une théologienne
américaine, Rosemary Ruether, précédée de quelques commentaires d'un groupe de femmes du réseau des Politisés chrétiens.

1.5 Articles de revues

J'ai relevé les articles portant sur les femmes dans les
revues religieuses les plus connues au Québec. Le dépouillement a été effectué de façon systématique dans les
revues Relations, Maintenant ainsi que dans l'Eglise
Canadienne. Quelques autres articles de revues religieuses ont été également notés. La Semaine religieuse de
Québec a été négligée, vu qu'elle ne contenait que des
entrefilets au sujet des femmes. Il n'y a pas eu de tri
opéré parmi les articles pour déterminer la cote féministe.
La revue Maintenant m'a paru beaucoup plus orienté que
les autres vers une radicalisation du processus de promotion de la femme; de fait, plusieurs femmes ont colla-
boré à la revue, dès ses débuts en 1962, Hélène Pelletier-
Baillargeon en devenait directrice, en 1973.

Tableau II : Les femmes et la religion, dans les revues:

	Relations	Maintenant (à partir de 1962)	L'Eglise Canadienne (à partir de 1968)	Autres revues
1960	3			
1961	-			
1962	-	5		
1963	1	5		
1964	2	6		
1965	4	8		1
1966	-	4		1
1967	2	8		2
1968	5	3	4	
1969	5	-	-	
1970	1	-	-	
1971	3	2	3	
1972	2	2	3	
1973	2	-	2	
1974	1	un numéro entier	3	
1975			4	

1.6 Thèses

Les thèses de maîtrise et de doctorat sont aussi un matériel précieux pour découvrir l'orientation de la pensée.
J'ai réussi à recueillir quelques titres de thèses présentées dans des universités du Québec, à partir de 1960.
Comme on peut en juger par l'Annexe II, les sujets relèvent plus de la spiritualité que de la promotion des femmes.

1.7 Groupements

Les femmes essaient de se donner une voix, d'opérer une
solidarité entre elles. Le Mouvement des Femmes chrétiennes qui compte 60,000 membres au Canada français rassemble
des femmes qui travaillent solidairement à leur promotion
humaine, prennent conscience de leurs responsabilités de
chrétiennes dans la famille, la société et la communauté
de foi. Pendant l'été 1976, naissait un autre groupe qui
vise à concerter d'abord les théologiennes, puis les femmes enseignant la catéchèse et oeuvrant en pastorale, finalement toutes les femmes qui travaillent de façon enga-
gée dans l'Eglise. Cette nouvelle solidarité essaie de
se créer par l'intermédiaire d'un feuillet de liaison appelé L'autre Parole.

Ce dossier permet de découvrir qu'on peut au Québec
indiquer de façon précise des activités qui concernent
particulièrement les femmes par rapport à la religion.
Depuis 1967, on peut noter un intérêt croissant pour ce
secteur de réflexion et de vie.

2. ANALYSE ET ÉVALUATION DU DOSSIER OU QUELS SONT LES TYPES D'INTERVENTION?

Toutes les structures traditionnelles véhiculées
par la religion peuvent constituer un obstacle à
l'évolution de la femme québécoise. C'est que
même si, la femme d'aujourd'hui peut trouver
occasionnellement, un clerc qui puisse la guider
intelligemment dans une oeuvre d'émancipation
qui est un besoin urgent, elle en trouvera véri-
tablement peu qui puissent remettre en question
efficacement toutes les influences néfastes que
véhicule encore le cléricalisme.[17]

Après avoir jeté un coup d'oeil sur l'ensemble du dossier
concernant les femmes et la religion au Québec, je me
propose maintenant d'indiquer les points saillants de ce

dossier et de porter un jugement sur ses forces comme sur ses faiblesses. Trois aspects m'apparaissent importants d'être retenus : la critique d'une société cléricale, la critique sur les femmes elles-mêmes, et le désir de créativité.

2.1 Critique d'une société cléricale

Plusieurs reproches sont adressés à l'Eglise perçue comme une société dirigée par les clercs qui y exercent sans s'en rendre compte un pouvoir dominateur sur les femmes.

2.1.1 Une société aliénante pour les femmes

Fernande Saint-Martin a énoncé bien clairement que le catholicisme au Québec, loin d'aider à la promotion des femmes, les brime dans leur désir d'affirmation personnelle et collective.

> Je pense qu'il faut reconnaître que le catholicisme, tel qu'il s'est incarné au Québec, constitue l'un des facteurs importants de l'aliénation de la femme dans notre société, c'est-à-dire de ce refus de la considérer et de lui permettre d'exister comme une personne autonome capable de définir ses propres buts et d'élaborer les moyens pour y atteindre.[18]

> L'on pourrait, vous le savez, élargir considérablement ce dossier des situations où l'Eglise utilise tout le poids de son prestige à maintenir les femmes dans l'immobilisme et le statusquo, pour le plus grand profit de ceux qui détiennent actuellement les rênes du pouvoir dans le monde, la caste masculine.[19]

Hélène Pelletier-Baillargeon a aussi signalé dans la revue Maintenant que l'Eglise ne s'est aucunement occupée du féminisme, qu'elle craignait plutôt que les femmes abusent de leurs nouveaux droits.

> Mais dans ses écrits officiels, elle (l'Eglise) multipliait toujours les mises en garde, les "mais" et les "pourvu que", comme si elle soupçonnait d'avance la femme de vouloir secrètement abuser de ses nouveaux droits.[20]

Le groupe des femmes du Réseau des Politisés chrétiens fait remarquer comment l'Eglise s'est servie du sexisme pour se concilier les intérêts des capitalistes.

Le sexisme ayant servi les intérêts des capitalistes, il est bien évident que l'Eglise-institution,
liée à la classe dominante, s'est servie de son
discours idéologique pour maintenir et accentuer
cette oppression.[21]

2.1.2 Discordance entre la théorie et la pratique

Si l'Eglise est heureuse d'affirmer à partir de Galates
3,28, l'égalité pour les femmes et les hommes, il s'agit
bel et bien d'une "égalité théorique".[22] Dans le Dossier
de l'Archevêché de Montréal, Anita Caron énonce franche-
ment :

Même si l'Eglise a toujours défendu au plan théorique l'égalité des hommes et des femmes, dans la
pratique ça toujours été des situations d'inégali-
té. La discrimination s'exerce en ce qui concerne
toutes les fonctions importantes au plan de la
pensée, au plan de la parole, au plan de l'administration, au plan du culte.[23]

En novembre 1963, la direction de la revue Maintenant
faisait remarquer que "la femme reste la grande oubliée
du Concile ", et que même aucune femme n'avait fait partie
des Commissions préparatoires.[24] Dans un mémoire présenté par des femmes canadiennes-françaises à l'Assemblée
plénière de l'épiscopat canadien en 1971, des questions
bien pertinentes sont posées :

Lorsqu'il se présente un poste de premier plan
(par exemple la nomination à des postes de direction au niveau national et au niveau diocésain), à compétence égale, une femme a-t-elle
vraiment chance égale? Ou une discrimination
latente est-elle entretenue par des procédures
de nomination qui seraient peut-être à reviser?[25]

Des observations sévères sont également émises en ce qui
concerne les conditions de travail.

Pour que l'Eglise garde sa crédibilité, elle
doit observer les mêmes normes de justice à
l'égard de son propre personnel; nous ne croyons
pas qu'il s'agisse de mauvaise volonté, mais
plutôt d'ignorance des lois du travail, des
conditions syndicales et des réalités économiques; il n'en reste pas moins que les conditions
faites aux femmes dans les organismes ecclésiaux
sont loin d'être une norme à suivre ailleurs.

> On devrait leur donner chances égales en salaires
> et en promotions, par rapport aux hommes, plu-
> tôt que de les reléguer aux sempiternelles tâches
> de secrétaires, quand les compétences sont égales.[26]

En ce qui concerne les ministères, ce sujet sera traité
plus longuement ultérieurement. Notons toutefois les
commentaires du dossier de l'A.F.E.A.S.

> Que les fonctions ecclésiastiques ne soient
> confiées qu'à des hommes, 23 pour cent des
> femmes y voient une discrimination envers celles
> qui auraient pu choisir cette vocation. Le
> Christ a prêché justice et égalité et on n'ob-
> serve pas ce précepte.[27]

Pour ma part, en réaction au document romain qui ne permet
pas l'admission des femmes au sacerdoce ministériel, j'ai
signalé la difficulté qu'avait l'Eglise à reconnaître l'é
galité de nature pour les femmes et les hommes.

> Je souhaite ... que l'Eglise mère reconnaisse
> aux femmes une nature humaine égale à celle des
> hommes (de sexe masculin). Une des plus grandes
> difficultés de la Déclaration, qui me paraît être
> une insulte faite aux femmes, c'est d'affirmer
> qu'il n'y aurait pas de "ressemblance naturelle"
> entre le Christ et son ministre dans la célébra-
> tion de l'Eucharistie, "si le rôle du Christ
> n'était pas alors tenu par un homme: on verrait
> difficilement dans le ministre l'image du Christ."[28]

2.1.3 Une société fixée sur la maternité

Dans l'Eglise, la femme est définie de façon bien spécifique comme mère. Les Papes n'ont cessé de réaffirmer
la doctrine traditionnelle que la place de la femme est
au foyer comme soutien du mari et éducatrice des enfants.[29]
Le document de la CRC rapporte le texte de Yvonne Pellé-
Douël : "On a surtout pris l'habitude de définir la femme
à partir de sa maternité, réelle ou possible. Cela paraît
une grave déformation; c'est comme si l'on définissait
l'homme par sa paternité, réelle ou possible. Devant
les refus de l'accès au presbytérat pour les femmes,
Lucie Leboeuf souligne que cette attitude de l'Eglise
hiérarchique a valeur de symbole : "symbole d'une culture qui accepte bien la mère, mais pas la femme; symbole
de la situation diminuée de la femme".[31]

L'Eglise a cantonné les femmes dans la fonction maternelle, tout en valorisant l'image du Père. Fernande
Saint-Martin critique la catéchèse à l'élémentaire qui
a repris avec vigueur le thème du père et qui peut ainsi
contribuer à renforcer l'impact des structures paterna-
listes de la famille sur le jeune enfant et à accentuer
la prééminence du rôle masculin dans la société en général.[32]

Cependant, même si l'Eglise hiérarchique privilégie la
fonction maternelle de la femme, elle ne lui permet pas
de décider ce qui se rapporte à cette responsabilité.
C'est le magistère masculin et célibataire qui se charge de
statuer dans des domaines aussi spécifiques que la planification familiale, l'avortement, etc. Le dossier de
l'Archêvé de Montréal avait dans son enquête la question
suivante : "A votre avis, si des femmes occupaient des
postes de décision dans l'Eglise, est-ce qu'on aurait,
concernant la limitation des naissances, les mêmes positions qu'auparavant?" 36.5 pour cent des femmes inter-
viewées ont répondu oui, 54.5 pour cent non et 8.9 pour
cent n'ont pas fourni de réponse.[33]

2.2 Critique au sujet des femmes

L'enquête entreprise à Montréal sur la femme, comme agent
de changement dans l'Eglise, a donné des résultats surpre-
nants. Les compilateurs notent :

> Le jugement que les femmes portent sur l'Eglise
> est un jugement très critique, mais beaucoup
> moins agressif que nous l'avions prévu ou suppo-
> sé. Nous avions en effet émis l'hypothèse que,
> la fièvre de l'année de la femme aidant, la plu-
> part des femmes auraient été plutôt agressives
> face à une institution dans laquelle certaines
> portes (v.g. le ministère sacerdotal) leur sont
> fermées au départ.[34]

Nous verrons, en effet, que la conscientisation des femmes
à leur situation est assez faible et que la participation
active des femmes dans l'Eglise est plutôt restreinte.

2.2.1 Conscientisation assez faible

Les femmes qui ont participé au sondage organisé par l'Ar-
chevêté de Montréal ont été d'accord majoritairement
pour admettre le caractère discriminatoire ou "injuste"
de la société actuelle à l'égard de la femme. Cependant,

peu de femmes ont suffisamment "ressenti" cette
discrimination pour être en mesure de donner un
exemple personnel. Ou bien la sensibilisation
à la situation de la femme n'a pas encore atteint
le niveau des "tripes" ou bien encore les femmes
se sont assez bien accommodées de leur sort.[35]

Le même dossier révèle des contradictions assez étonnan-
tes. D'une part, 75.21 pour cent des femmes sont d'accord
que "la situation de la femme dans notre milieu n'est pas
si dramatique qu'on le dit", alors que 59.07 pour cent des
femmes affirment plus loin qu'"en général les femmes sont
exploitées".[36] De plus, 49.5 pour cent des femmes interrogées pensent que le pape et les évêques sont "suffisamment renseignés" sur la situation de la femme; 72.8 pour
cent d'entre elles déclarent que les prêtres sont "assez
compréhensifs" vis-à-vis d'elles.[37] D'autre part, 51.28
pour cent avouent que "les prêtres confient rarement des
responsabilités aux femmes".[38] Il faudrait se demander
ce que les femmes entendent par "suffisamment renseignés"
et "assez compréhensifs"; leur agrée-t-il de recevoir des
paroles d'encouragement, quelques approbations superfi-
cielles sans jamais accéder à des responsabilités?

Les images et stéréotypes des femmes face à elles-mêmes
ont très peu évolué au Québec. On n'y décèle pas dans
l'enquête de rejet massif des affirmations exprimant des
représentations "traditionnelles" de la femme : soumis-
sion au mari, idéal restreint à l'éducation des enfants,
etc. Appelées à indiquer les domaines où il y a discrimination ou injustice, 40.34 pour cent des femmes pensent
qu'il n'y a aucune discrimination dans le domaine de la
religion, lequel arrive en seconde place au palmarès de la
non-discrimination, juste après le domaine des loisirs
qui remporte la première place avec 41.49 pour cent.[39]
Par contre, 65.12 pour cent des femmes sont complètement
ou plutôt d'accord pour reconnaître que "les femmes ne
sont pas considérées à l'égal des hommes dans l'Eglise".[40]

Faire un effort pour éduquer, créer de nouvelles
images. C'est une grosse conversion à faire parce
qu'il faut partir de bien loin. On se dit trop
facilement : on est bienveillant à l'égard des
femmes, on les invite sur nos comités..., on les
consulte de temps en temps, mais c'est une conversion en profondeur qu'il faut faire, et cela
autant chez les femmes que chez les hommes.(Anita
Caron)[41]

Les compilateurs de l'enquête soulignent que le principal facteur d'inertie, c'est que les revendications des femmes sont fortes au niveau général, mais qu'elles deviennent faibles et plus adoucies au niveau local et que bien des accommodements sont acceptés.[42] Les associations féminines confessionnelles n'aident pas les femmes à être plus "radicales", car les membres tendent à être en accord avec les positions des autorités religieuses.[43]

Une autre difficulté que rencontrent les femmes dans l'amélioration de leur participation dans la société et dans l'Eglise c'est "le manque de consensus sur le point de chute de leurs revendications".[44] Les suggestions demeurent vagues et n'entraînent pas une forte concertation. Les Québécoises ne semblent pas encore décidées de lutter pour obtenir leurs droits. Les solidarités demeurent difficiles à établir; elles exigent une étape de conscientisation qui est à peine commencée. L'expérience entreprise par le feuillet L'autre Parole, visant à regrouper d'abord les théologiennes montre que seulement quelques femmes acceptent ce genre d'initiative, que d'autres paniquent devant la possibilité de la contestation d'une société masculine.

> Au lieu de blâmer celles qui ont le courage de s'exprimer, même s'il leur arrive de défendre l'erreur, nous devons condamner la majorité qui se terre au fond des cuisines croyant, par un prudent mutisme, se protéger des catastrophes collectives possibles.[45]

2.2.2 Participation restreinte des femmes

Si la sensibilisation des femmes à leur situation inférieure dans l'Eglise s'avère plutôt faible, il n'est pas surprenant que leur participation à la vie de l'Eglise se révèle restreinte. Le dossier de l'Archevêché de Montréal fournit les statistiques suivantes : dans 149 paroisses sur un total de 894 marguilliers, 124 sont des femmes (13.8 pour cent). Dans les conseils de pastorale de 34 paroisses, hommes et femmes sont presque en nombre égal, soit 232 hommes, 224 femmes. Par contre dans les exécutifs, on retrouve 47 hommes, 35 femmes dont 20 d'entre elles occupent la fonction de secrétaire. Les femmes semblent "prédestinées" à être d'éternelles secrétaires! Les compilateurs fournissent une raison :

> On dira aussi que si les femmes sont confinées aux postes de "secrétaire" dans l'exécutif d'un conseil

de pastorale, c'est qu'elles sont souvent les premières à élire un homme au poste de président ou d'animateur principal.[46]

Le Comité d'étude sur le rôle de la femme dans l'Eglise, créé en 1972 par la Conférence Catholique Canadienne se proposait d'étudier la question suivante : "Comment encourager les femmes à accepter des responsabilités au sein des conseils paroissiaux,diocésains ou autres?"[47] La première partie du présent travail a cependant fait voir que la présence des femmes s'intensifie aux niveaux paroissial, diocésain.

2.3 Désir de créativité

Après avoir indiqué la critique que les femmes font de la société cléricale ainsi que d'elles-mêmes, je montrerai quelques lignes d'émergence de créativité chez les femmes.

2.3.1 Humanisation

Je crois que s'il y avait plus de femmes dans les postes-clés de l'Eglise (institution ecclésiale) peut-être tiendrait-on plus compte des personnes. On essaierait davantage d'humaniser non seulement les structures mais peut-être la façon de réfléchir sur les problèmes. On mettrait davantage l'accent sur les solutions concrètes... (Hélène Campeau)[48]

On reconnaît facilement que les femmes sont plus sensibles à certaines réalités de la vie, parce qu'elles donnent la vie et s'occupent plus que les hommes de l'éducation des enfants. Les femmes développent aussi beaucoup d'intériorité, d'attention aux personnes; elles sont très conscientes des limites de la logique, des "beaux principes" et donnent plus de place à l'expérientiel. Marc Rondeau soulève la question suivante :

Si une présence féminine est requise pour animer le foyer et pour humaniser la société civile, ne le serait-elle pas dans la société ecclésiale? Une Eglise trop masculine n'a-t-elle pas à craindre un juridisme autoritaire? La femme n'aurait-elle rien à apporter à la pensée théologique, à l'organisation pastorale ou diocésaine? Les institutions ecclésiastiques, dicastères romains et autres, seraient-elles les seules à pouvoir se priver du potentiel de chaleur et de rayonnement féminins?[49]

Les femmes de l'A.F.E.A.S. soulignent à juste titre qu'"il faudrait que tous, autorité civile et religieuse, prêtres et laïcs réfléchissent ensemble afin que la société et l'Eglise mettent à profit toutes les aptitudes, tous les talents détenus par les femmes qui représentent plus de la moitié du genre humain.[50] Le dossier de l' Archevêché de Montréal propose que l'Eglise pourrait demander davantage la collaboration des femmes plus particulièrement sur les questions de l'éducation de la foi des jeunes, la planification des naissances.[51] Fernande Saint-Martin indique une urgence :

> Sans doute le catholicisme devra sous peu permettre à la femme de choisir librement, elle-même, la forme et les conditions dans lesquelles elle entend réaliser sa fonction maternelle. Il sera encore plus urgent qu'il lui reconnaisse ensuite la liberté et le droit de choisir sous quelle forme elle entend réaliser une maternité encore plus vaste, où prenant délibérément en main les problèmes des enfants qu'elle fait naître, la femme accèdera sur le plan philosophique, scientifique, artistique et technique, à une oeuvre de civilisation tout à fait conforme à son "souci" profond de la vie et du bonheur de l'humanité.[52]

2.3.2 Responsabilité

Les femmes ont une responsabilité face à la société civile, à l'Eglise, qu'elles n'ont pas encore assumée. Madeleine Sauvé montre que la source de cette responsabilité provient de son état d'égalité, tel qu'il est proclamé dans Genèse 1,27 : "Homme et femme, il les créa".[53]. Le document de la Conférence Religieuse Canadienne note judicieusement que "la responsabilité du retournement des esprits et la réforme des structures sociales et ecclésiales (...) repose d'abord sur la femme elle-même."[54]

2.3.3 Élaboration d'une nouvelle théologie

Les femmes conscientes de la discrimination à leur égard découvrent la nécessité d'élaborer une nouvelle anthropologie qui viendra conséquemment modifier la théologie traditionnelle.[55] L'anthropologie d'Augustin et de Thomas d' Aquin apparaît définitivement androcentrique;[56] elle a contaminé une bonne partie de leur théologie, laquelle a contribué à supporter un régime nettement masculinisant. La Déclaration sur la question de l'admission des femmes au sacerdoce en est un exemple typique.

C'est à des femmes qu'il incombera sans doute un
jour d'élaborer une nouvelle anthropologie chrétienne de leur sexe et de renouveler pour leur
temps une théologie réaliste de la femme, théologie essentielle pour faire vivre en vraies filles
de l'Eglise celles qui, depuis près d'un siècle,
ont dû choisir sans elle d'être à la fois fidèles
à leur métier et fidèles à leur amour. A ces
chrétiennes du XXe siècle, il ne faudrait pas se
contenter d'entrebâiller les portes.[57]

Quelques théologiennes du Québec se sentent poussées à
se lancer dans cette oeuvre de construction; elles ont
commencé à ouvrir un réseau de communication et à tisser
des liens de solidarité parmi les femmes directement intéressées par l'entreprise. Dans le premier numéro de
L'Autre Parole, le regroupement a énoncé ainsi ses deux
objectifs principaux : "Au niveau de la recherche, reprendre le discours théologique en tenant compte de la femme, et sur le plan de l'action, entreprendre des démar-
ches pour une participation entière de la femme dans
l'Eglise."[58]

2.3.4 Les nouveaux ministères

La question du sacerdoce ministériel demeure pour les
femmes une question épineuse et symptomatique de la mentalité qui prévaut dans la hiérarchie ecclésiastique.
L'étude de Margaret E. MacLellan pour la Commission sur
le statut de la femme au Canada est révélatrice à cet
égard.

L'émancipation des femmes dans de nombreuses professions n'a pas eu de parallèle dans le domaine
de la religion. Mais les opinions de certaines
églises envers les femmes semblent changer progressivement. (...) Les statistiques relatives aux
trois principales professions libérales montrent
qu'en 1961 le Canada était encore, en grande partie,
un pays dominé par les hommes. Cette année-là, les
chiffres du recensement montrèrent que 7 pour cent
des médecins et des chirurgiens étaient des femmes,
et qu'il n'y avait que 3 pour cent de femmes parmi
les avocats. Chez les ministres du culte, 1 pour
cent seulement était des femmes.[59]

Au Québec, plusieurs femmes souhaiteraient pouvoir accéder au sacerdoce ministériel. Voici quelques énoncés
significatifs :

> Pour ne pas encourager l'immobilisme de nos
> sociétés, il faudrait que l'Eglise accepte sur
> un pied d'égalité, les représentants des deux
> sexes aux fonctions les plus sacrées, du sacer-
> doce à l'épiscopat et jusqu'à la papauté.
> (Fernande Saint-Martin)[60]

En 1971, un groupe de femmes canadiennes-françaises avait
demandé aux évêques :

> Que soit rendu possible pour la femme l'accès
> à des ministères (incluant le diaconat et le
> sacerdoce), qui peuvent s'exprimer) 1) dans des
> vocations personnelles 2) et à partir des be-
> soins des communautés diocésaines particulières.[61]

l'enquête de l'A.F.E.A.S. révèle ce qui suit :

> "Croyez-vous que le sacrement de l'Ordre pourrait
> être conféré à des femmes?" A cette question,
> 44 pour cent des femmes répondent affirmativement,
> 39 pour cent de façon négative, 8 pour cent sont
> indécises, et 7 pour cent n'ont pas d'opinion.[62]

Le dossier de l'Archevêché de Montréal dévoile dans sa
compilation les points suivants : 53.2 pour cent des
femmes interrogées donnent actuellement comme raison
pour expliquer le non-accès des femmes au sacerdoce que
"c'est une tradition dans l'Eglise"; 46.4 pour cent des
femmes pensent que les femmes devraient pouvoir devenir
prêtre.[63]

Toutefois, au Québec, les femmes ne militent pas farou-
chement pour accéder au sacerdoce ministériel.

> Se battre pour accéder au sacerdoce, c'est s'atta-
> quer à un symbole plutôt qu'au coeur de la réalité.
> Se battre pour des jobs, se battre pour avoir le
> droit d'imiter les hommes, n'est-ce pas s'acheminer
> vers une pseudo-libération? Les femmes doivent au
> contraire tâcher de relever avec les hommes de bonne
> volonté les défis majeurs posés aujourd'hui par une
> nécessaire révolution sociale, politique et cultu-
> relle : logement, santé, école, services sociaux,
> chômage, rôle aliénant du travail, inflation galo-
> pante, démembrement de la famille, etc.[64]

J'ai moi-même déjà écrit que je ne milite pas actuellement en faveur de l'admission des femmes au sacerdoce

ministériel.[65]

Le Dossier de l'Archevêché de Montréal montre que bien d'autres formes de participation s'avèrent plus urgentes et plus pertinentes au Québec. Il est recommandé

que les évêques de l'Inter-Montréal soient invités à étudier avec la collaboration des laïcs, hommes et femmes, l'opportunité et les modalités éventuel-les de "ministères non-ordonnés", ouverts tant aux femmes qu'aux hommes, et qui seraient institués formellement pour des tâches pastorales et mission-naires.[66]

Le Cardinal George B. Flahiff posait d'ailleurs la ques-tion suivante en 1971 :

En même temps qu'apparaissent de nouveaux minis-tères, pour répondre à de nouveaux besoins de la société en évolution, sous l'action de l'Esprit-Saint, pouvons-nous déjà prévoir quels seraient les nouveaux ministères qui seraient plus adaptés à la femme, à sa nature, à ses dons et à sa pré-paration dans le monde de ce temps, dont Gaudium et Spes parlent éloquemment?[67]

Les Québécoises souhaitent plutôt créer de nouveaux minis-tères que de s'insérer dans ceux qui existent déjà. El-les observent que le clergé masculin a de la difficulté à fonctionner dans son propre statut; elles ne veulent donc pas porter "les vieilles soutanes que les hommes ne veu-lent plus porter."[68]

Les interventions des Québécoises font à la fois preuve d'un esprit critique et créateur. Plusieurs d'entre elles critiquent une Eglise qui leur apparaît une société clé-ricale aliénante pour les femmes, peu cohérente dans la pratique avec des affirmations théoriques d'égalité des sexes et prônant trop exclusivement la maternité pour les femmes. Un petit nombre d'entre elles trouvent que les femmes sont passives, peu sensibilisées à leur situation d'infériorité dans l'Eglise et qu'elles s'engagent encore très peu dans les fonctions décisionnelles dans l'Eglise. Finalement, plusieurs femmes démontrent un désir de créa-tivité, allant de l'humanisation des structures à l'é-mergence de nouveaux ministères.

3. LES QUÉBÉCOISES SONT-ELLES SUR LA CARTE FÉMINISTE INTERNATIONALE?

Chose certaine, l'épopée du féminisme contemporain s'est déroulée sans l'Eglise. Né dans les
pays anglo-saxons et protestants, c'est dans les
pays latins et catholiques qu'il a rencontré et
rencontre encore les plus solides résistances.
L'Eglise officielle n'a pas été plus présente à
ses luttes qu'elle n'a été l'instigatrice de
celles qui réclamaient l'égalité raciale et la
fin de l'esclavage ou la promotion ouvrière.[69]

Dans cette partie, je voudrais situer les féministes
québécoises à l'intérieur du mouvement de promotion de
la femme qui existe dans l'Eglise à l'échelle internationale. Le tableau d'ensemble sera forcément bref et
partiel, vu que je n'ai pas entrepris une étude systématique de l'impact des mouvements féministes sur la
religion à travers le monde. La revue Concilium[70] a
présenté quelques bilans sur le sujet dont je me servi-
rai.

3.1 Un groupe international

Plusieurs groupes existent dans différents pays dans le
but de promouvoir une meilleure collaboration hommes-
femmes dans l'Eglise. Constatant leurs objectifs communs,
ils se sont regroupés en 1970 et ont fondé un secrétariat
international à Bruxelles, désigné sous le nom de "Femmes
et Hommes dans l'Eglise". Ce regroupement possède un bulletin périodique bi-mensuel portant son nom; il organise
aussi un congrès annuel. Ce groupe international vise à
"faire connaître plus largement ce qui se cherche et se
fait en tant que collaboration femme-homme à tous les
niveaux de l'Eglise, et de susciter une action commune en
faveur de cette coopération qui ne peut se réaliser qu'à
travers une plus authentique reconnaissance des femmes
dans l'Eglise.[71] Marie-Thérèse van Lunen-Chenu joue un
rôle très actif dans ce groupe et ne craint pas de porter
ouvertement un jugement sur l'attitude de l'Eglise vis-
à-vis le féminisme.[72]

L'Autre Parole a établi des contacts avec le groupe
"Femmes et Hommes dans l'Eglise"; des Québécois ont é-
galement participé à son Congrès en 1976 à Bruxelles.

3.2 En Amérique Latine[73]

Les femmes, en Amérique Latine, émergent de quatre siècles
de société patriarcale. Deux organismes ont été particulièrement inspirateurs et animateurs de la promotion
féminine sur ce continent, ce sont : la Confédération

Latino-Américaine des Religieux (la CLAR) et celui de la
Coordination d'Initiatives pour le Développement Humain
de l'Amérique Latine (La CIDAL). Les femmes sont présentes à différents niveaux dans l'Eglise, dans les associations religieuses traditionnelles, dans les mouvements
bibliques et de catéchèse, dans les mouvements spécialisés
d'évangélisation, dans les mouvements familiaux, dans les
mouvements ouvriers, dans les paroisses sans prêtre. Quelques   femmes participent aux responsabilités diocésaines
et font partie de Communautés ecclésiales de base. Il ne
semble pas y exister de mouvement organisé qui travaille
de façon exclusive pour la promotion de la femme dans
l'Eglise.

3.3 Aux Etats-Unis[74]

Les Etats-Unis m'apparaissent être le pays où les dynamis-
mes de concertation et de solidarité pour la promotion de
la femme sont les plus actualisés. La présence de nombreuses Eglises protestantes plus ouvertes à l'exercice
des ministères par les femmes a créé tout un climat favo-
rable au militantisme des femmes dans les Eglises.

Quelques groupes spécifiquement consacrés aux problèmes
féminins ont été fondés au cours des quelques dernières
années : le Joint Committee of Organizations Concerned
with the Status of Women in the Church; Worthwhile Human
Encounter Now; Christian Feminists. Il existait déjà depuis 1911, l'Alliance internationale Sainte-Jeanne. Il
faut aussi noter que des organisations nationales de religieuses telles que le National Assembly of Women Religious, la National Coalition of American Nuns, la Leadership Conference of Women Religious, sont très vigilantes
et prennent des positions publiques sur des sujets féminins.

Des théologiennes catholiques et protestantes se livrent
à une véritable critique de la théologie traditionnelle
et tentent de poser les bases d'une théologie plus "res-
pectueuse" des femmes. Les plus connues sont : Mary
Daly,[75] Rosemary Ruether,[76] Letty Russell.[77] Quelques-
unes de leurs oeuvres sont traduites en français et ac-
cessibles aux Québécoises. Le groupe des femmes du réseau des Politisés chrétiens est en communication avec
Rosemary Ruether.

3.4 En Ontario

La province voisine du Québec, l'Ontario, possède des

caractéristiques qui lui permettent de s'ouvrir plus largement à la voix féministe dans l'Eglise : elle est plus
immédiatement en contact avec la littérature américaine,
les Eglises protestantes rassemblent une plus large partie
de la population. De fait, il existe le Movement for
Christian Feminism, regroupant des femmes affiliées à différentes églises chrétiennes. De plus, Mary Schaefer édi-
te une circulaire destinée aux femmes intéressées à l'ordination.

Ce tableau international très rapide démontre que les
forces féministes sont à l'oeuvre plus particulièrement
aux Etats-Unis, en Europe, en Ontario, beaucoup moins en
Amérique Latine. Je ne possède aucun renseignement sur
l'attitude des femmes par rapport à la religion en Asie
et en Afrique. Les Québécoises commencent à découvrir
ce qui se fait à l'extérieur. Des réseaux de communication s'établissent et permettent des échanges fructueux.

CONCLUSION

Et l'on ne s'étonne plus, maintenant, de remarquer
que par des préoccupations essentielles, la Québécoise ne se distingue plus des autres Canadiennes ni des femmes des autres pays occidentaux.
Son indifférence collective a fait place à une
prise de conscience presque générale, et sa fidèle obéissance aux directives religieuses a cédé
le pas à une responsabilité plus avertie dans de
nombreux domaines.[78]

Les trois moments de cette étude sur le féminisme et la
religion au Québec à partir de 1960 me permettent de présenter six observations finales.

1. Les Québécoises connaissent, elles aussi, leur Révolution tranquille. Constatant l'emprise progressive du
mouvement féministe à travers le monde, elles commencent
à réagir. Le militantisme du milieu américain, l'ouverture des Eglises protestantes provoquent les Québécoises
à revendiquer une plus grande participation au plan religieux. Les forces extérieures finiront par leur faire
prendre conscience que l'époque du matriarcat est révolue
et qu'il faut opter pour une égalité sans réticence dans
l'Eglise comme dans la société.

2. Les Québécoises croient plus en la force de la vie
que dans les écrits et la prise de parole. Peu de fem-

mes tentent de défendre leurs idées par la plume ou par des conférences.[79] D'une part, les femmes à travers le monde n'ont pas de tradition de ce côté-là; d'autre part, elles savent expérientiellement que la vie finira bien par triompher des obstacles. Toutefois, des dossiers, des articles de revues sont publiés plus fréquemment sur les femmes et par les femmes au sujet de la religion.

3. Le ton des interventions des Québécoises est plutôt conciliant, montrant peu d'agressivité. Elles n'osent pas afficher leurs divergences avec l'autorité hiérarchique masculine, ni bousculer un clergé perçu comme "assez compréhensif."

4. La concertation des femmes en vue d'une amélioration de leur participation dans l'Eglise est faible et lente à créer. Les femmes qui prennent des initiatives en ce sens doivent être persévérantes.

5. Devant les portes qui s'ouvrent progressivement devant elles, les Québécoises s'engagent de plus en plus aux divers niveaux de la pastorale paroissiale, diocésaine et dans les organismes nationaux. Elles sont aussi attirées par l'étude, l'enseignement et la recherche dans le domaine théologique.

6. Les femmes au Québec s'engagent dans une tâche surtout positive. Elles veulent plutôt créer que contester. Elles ne désirent pas majoritairement l'accession au ministère sacerdotal tel qu'il existe actuellement; elles essaient de découvrir de nouveaux ministères qui répondront à leurs aspirations et à leurs capacités.

FÉMINISME ET RELIGION AU QUÉBEC DEPUIS 1960

NOTES

1. Mgr Louis-Adolphe Paquet, "Le féminisme", Etudes et appréciations. Nouveaux Mélanges canadiens. Québec, Imprimerie franciscaine missionnaire, 1919, p.3.

2. Statistiques de 1971.

3. Juliet Mitchell, L'âge de femme. Paris, Editions des Femmes, 1974, p.21.

4. J'ai personnellement écrit un article, "Dieu est encore au masculin dans l'Eglise catholique," publié dans Le Devoir, 18 février 1977, p.4

5. L'Eglise Canadienne, vol.8, n°3 (mars 1975), p.86.

6. Conférence religieuse canadienne, Le rôle de la femme dans la société civile et dans l'Eglise, Ottawa, CRC, 1975, pp.113-114.

7. Cf. Fabien Leboeuf, "Avons-nous encore besoin des religieux?" Communauté chrétienne, vol.15, n°87 (mai-juin 1976), pp.220-226.

8. Annuaire de l'Eglise du Québec, 1977.

9. Archevêché de Montréal, La femme, un agent de changement dans l'Eglise, janvier 1976, p.36.

10. Informations obtenues par l'intermédiaire d'une correspondance avec Ruth Matthews, en charge de la paroisse anglicane de Saint-Georges à Drummondville.

11. Hélène Pelletier-Baillargeon, "Femme-prêtre à Montréal", Maintenant 31-32 (juillet-août 1964), pp.229-230.

12. La revue diocésaine, Le Centre Saint-Germain novembre 1966, p.205, indique que le Grand Séminaire de Rimouski accueille 43 séminaristes, 53 religieuses, 7 laïques.

13. Thèses canadiennes, Ottawa, Bibliothèque nationale du Canada, 1974.

14. Fernande Saint-Martin, La femme et la société cléricale, Montréal, Mouvement laïque de langue française, 1967.

15. XXX, La religieuse dans la Cité, Montréal, Fides, 1968.

16. Marc Rondeau, La promotion de la femme dans la pensée de l'Eglise contemporaine, Montréal, Fides, 1969.

17. Fernande Saint-Martin, op. cit., p.15.

18. Ibid., p.6.
19. Ibid., p.11.

20. Hélène Pelletier-Baillargeon, "Un concile pour le deuxième sexe?", Maintenant, no53 (mai 1966), p.149.

21. Interview avec Rosemary Ruether, Féminisme, socialisme, christianisme, Montréal, Le Réseau des Politisés chrétiens, avril 1976, p.11.

22. Fernande Saint-Martin, op. cit., pp.7-8.

23. Dossier de l'Archevêché de Montréal, p.67.

24. "Vivent les diaconesses!", Maintenant 23 (novembre 1963), p.360.

25. "La femme dans l'Eglise et dans la société", L'Eglise Canadienne, juin-juillet 1971, p.184.

26. Ibid., p.185.

27. A.F.E.A.S., Participation de la femme dans la société et dans l'Eglise. Montréal, Secrétariat général de l'A.F.E.A.S., avril 1974, p.8.

28. Monique Dumais, loc. cit.

29. Marc Rondeau, op. cit., pp.264-265.

30. Yvonne Pellé-Douël, "Etre femme dans la vie contemplative", Vie consacrée, 42e année, no3 (mai-juin 1970), p.136, cité dans le Dossier de la CRC, p.45.

31. Lucie Leboeuf, "Dans l'Eglise catholique, la femme n'est bonne qu'à faire le ménage!", Plein-jour, juin-juillet-août 1975, p.8.

32. Fernande Saint-Martin, op. cit., p.9.

33. Dossier de l'Archevêché de Montréal, p.60.

34. Ibid., p.76.
35. Ibid., p.75.
36. Ibid., p.50.
37. Ibid., pp.60-61.
38. Ibid., p.58.
39. Ibid., p.52.
40. Ibid., p.58.
41. Ibid., p.73.
42. Ibid., p.61.
43. Ibid., p.65.
44. Ibid., p.75.

45. Suzette D. Cardinal, "La côte d'Adam", Maintenant 3 (mars 1962) p.109.

46. Dossier de l'Archevêché de Montréal, p.38.

47. "Un comité d'étude sur le rôle de la femme dans l'Eglise", L'Eglise Canadienne, novembre 1972, p.274.

48. Dossier de l'Archevêché de Montréal, p.69.

49. Marc Rondeau, op. cit., p.271.

50. A.F.E.A.S., op. cit., p.2

51. Dossier de l'Archevêché de Montréal, p.71.

52. Fernande Saint-Martin, op. cit., pp.15-16.

53. Madeleine Sauvé, s.j.n.m., La femme dans la Bible, cité dans le Dossier de la CRC, p.34.

54. Dossier de la CRC, p.111.

55. J'ai élaboré plus longuement sur le sujet dans une communication à la Société Canadienne de Théologie, Montréal, octobre 1976, "Les femmes théologiennes dans l'Eglise", qui sera publié dans Studies in Religion/Sciences religieuses.

56. Cf. Kari Elisabeth Börresen, "Fondements anthropologiques de la relation entre l'homme et la femme dans la théologie classique", Concilium 111 (1976), pp.27-39.

57. Hélène Pelletier-Baillargeon, op. cit., p.149.

58. L'autre Parole, n°1 (septembre 1976), p.2.

59. Margaret E. MacLellan, Histoire des droits de la femme au Canada. Etudes préparées pour la Commission royale d'enquête sur la situation de la femme au Canada, n°8, Montréal, août 1968, pp.11-12.

60. Fernande Saint-Martin, op. cit., p.8.

61. "La femme dans l'Eglise et dans la société", L'Eglise Canadienne, juin-juillet 1972, p.185.

62. A.F.E.A.S., op. cit., p.9.

63. Le Dossier de l'Archevêché de Montréal, pp.62-63.

64. Lucie Leboeuf, op. cit., p.9.

65. Monique Dumais, loc. cit.

66. Dossier de l'Archevêché de Montréal, p.84.

67. Cardinal George B. Flahiff, "Sur les ministères féminins dans l'Eglise", L'Eglise Canadienne, novembre 1971, p.286.

68. Marie Laurier, "Les femmes réclament place dans le "clergé laic" mais non les soutanes mises de côté", Le Devoir, 31 janvier 1976.

69. Hélène Pelletier-Baillargeon, loc. cit.

70. Concilium 111 (janvier 1976), "Les femmes dans l'E- glise:, particulièrement pp.105-152.

71. Page-couverture du bulletin Femmes et Hommes dans l'Eglise.

72. Marie-Thérèse van Lunen-Chenu, "La libération des femmes, chance et exigence de libération pour l'Egli- se", Idéologies de libération et message du salut. Public. CERDIC, 1973; "Le féminisme chrétien : phé- nomène inéluctable", Naissance de la femme, La Revue Nouvelle (janvier 1974); "La Commission pontificale de la femme", Etudes (juin 1975), pp.879-891. "Le féminisme et l'Eglise", Concilium 111 (1976), pp.131- 143.

73. Cf. Marina Lessa, "La femme dans les mouvements de l'Eglise en Amérique Latine", Concilium 111 (1976), pp.125-129.

74. Cf. Mary Luke Tobin, "L'Eglise catholique et le mou-
    vement des femmes aux Etats-Unis", Concilium 111
    (1976), pp.145-152.

75. Mary Daly, The Church and the Second Sex. New-York,
    Harper and Row, 1968; Beyond God the Father. Boston,
    Beacon Press, 1973.

76. Rosemary Ruether, Liberation Theology. New-York,
    Paulist Press, 1972; Religion and Sexism: Images of
    Women in the Jewish and Christian Traditions. New-
    York, Simon and Schuster, 1974; New Woman, New Earth.
    New-York, The Seabury Press, 1975; en collaboration
    avec Eugene C. Bianchi, From Machismo to Mutuality.
    New-York, Paulist Press, 1976; "Les femmes et le sa-
    cerdoce. Perspective historique et sociale", Conci-
    lium 111 (1976), pp.41-50.

77. Letty Russell, Human Liberation in a Feminist Pers-
    pective. Philadelphia, The Westminster Press, 1974;
    ed. The Liberating Word. Philadelphia, The Westmins-
    ter Press, 1976.

78. Micheline D.-Johnson, Histoire de la condition de la
    femme dans la Province de Québec, Etudes préparées
    pour la Commission royale d'enquête sur la situation
    de la femme au Canada, n°8, Montréal, août 1968, p.41.

79. Elisabeth Hone-Bellemare, "Se taire ou s'exprimer",
    Maintenant, n°140 (novembre 1974), p.7.

FÉMINISME ET RELIGION AU QUÉBEC DEPUIS 1960

ANNEXE I : Les femmes et la religion dans quelques revues
          religieuses, à partir de 1960

L'Eglise canadienne, vol. 1 (1968)

- "Paul VI : message à l'Afrique", nol (janvier 1968),p.30
- "Résolution du Congrès des laïcs", nol (janvier 1968,p.34
- "Les religieuses et le féminisme", no7 (juillet 1968)
  (Mémoire de l'A.R.E.Q.), p.244
- Episcopat canadien. "Le rôle de la femme dans la liturgie",
  noll (déc. 1968), pp.377-378.

L'Eglise canadienne, vol. 2 (1969)

Aucun article

L'Eglise canadienne, vol. 3 (1970)

Aucun article

L'Eglise canadienne, vol. 4 (1971)

- "Déclarations de l'épiscopat canadien à l'Assemblée tenue
  à Edmonton du 19 au 24 sept. 1971", no8 (oct.1971)
  pp.247,248,269.

- "La femme dans l'Eglise et dans la société" mémoire des
  femmes canadiennes-françaises reçues en atelier de travail à l'Assemblée plénière de l'épiscopat canadien,
  no6 (juin-juillet 1971), pp.184-186.

- "Sur les ministères féminins dans l'Eglise" Intervention
  du cardinal George B. Flahiff, no9 (nov. 1971) pp.184-186.

L'Eglise canadienne, vol. 5 (1972)

- "Les femmes dans la liturgie" no9 (nov.1972) pp.269-270.

- "Préparation pour un ministère auprès des femmes (extrait
  du Rapport du Conseil des Laïcs au Synode), no2 (fév.1972)
  pp.61-62.

-"Un comité d'étude sur le rôle de la femme dans l'Eglise"
  (C.C.C.), no9 (nov. 1972) pp.273-274.

L'Eglise canadienne, vol. 6 (1973)

- Léo Foster, "Les femmes séparées et divorcées", nol
  (janvier 1973) pp.15-16.

177

FÉMINISME ET RELIGION AU QUÉBEC DEPUIS 1960

- André Chalifoux, "Femmes et liturgie", n°4 (avril 1973) pp.121-122.

L'Eglise canadienne, vol. 7 (1974)

- "Première rencontre du Comité sur le rôle de la femme", n°1 (janv.1974) pp.26-27.

- "Grossesse-Secours", n°7 (sept.1974) pp.230-231.

- "L'année internationale de la femme en 1975", n°8 (oct. 1974) p.243.

L'Eglise canadienne, vol. 8 (1975)

- "Inauguration de l'année internationale de la femme par le Mouvement des femmes chrétiennes (25 janvier), n°3 (mars 1975) p.86.

- Mgr Robert Lebel, "Paradis ou garçonnière internationale de la femme", n°6 (juin-juillet 1975), p.171.

- "Symposium du Front Commun pour le respect de la vie : "La dignité de la femme dans la liberté", n°6 (juin-juillet 1975), p.179.

- Colette Cousineau, "La religieuse en pastorale paroissiale", n°7 (août-sept. 1975) pp.211-214.

Maintenant (1962)

- Claire Vaillancourt et Lucille Latendresse, "Une expérience de laïques missionnaires en Inde", 2 (février 1962) p.59.

- Suzette D. Cardinal, "La côte d'Adam", 3 (mars 1962) p.109.

- Soeur Sainte Marie Eleuthère, c.n.d., "Futures bachelières qu'attendent-elles?",9 (sept. 1962) pp.285-286.

- Rita Cadieux, "En marge d'une conférence sur l'univers de la femme", 10 (octobre 1962) pp.332-333.

- Ambroise Lafortune, "Les femmes parlent... encore!",11 (nov. 1962) p.396.

Maintenant (1963)

- Madeleine Doyon, "Réformer les Instituts familiaux?",13 (janv. 1963) pp.14-15.

178

FÉMINISME ET RELIGION AU QUÉBEC DEPUIS 1960

- Solange Chaput-Rolland, "La voix des femmes... écrit",13 (janvier 1963) p.18.

- Suzette D. Cardinal, "Vive la théologie!",16 (avril 1963) pp.114-116.

- Solange Chalvin "La femme et la nouvelle religieuse", 18 (juin 1963) pp.190-191.

- La Direction, "Vivent les diaconesses!",23 (novembre 1963) p.360.

Maintenant (164)

- Hélène Pelletier-Baillargeon, "Femmes du monde ou femmes mondaines?",25 (janvier 1964) pp.12-13.

- Bernard Mailhot "Des mythes aux mystères de la femme", 27 (mars 1964) pp.88-90.

- Thérèse Forget-Casgrain, "Des miettes!",28 (avril 1964) pp.127-128.

- Hélène Pelletier-Baillargeon, "Du Bill 16 à la sainte règle",28 (avril 1964) pp.128-129.

- Bérengère Gaudet, "Le Bill 16 et la communauté",30 (juin 1964) pp.210-211.

- Hélène Pelletier-Baillargeon, "Femmes prêtres à Montréal", 31-32 (juillet-août 1964) pp.229-230.

Maintenant (1965)

- Hélène Pelletier-Baillargeon, "Portrait-robot d'une "bonne soeur",40 (avril 1965) pp.128-130.

- Mère Pauline Maillé, "Femme ou soeur?",40 (avril 1965) pp.130-131.

- Sr Ste-Mechtilde, "Soeurs socialisantes!",40 (avril 1965) pp.132-133.

- Sr Louise de Jésus, "Soeurs" nouvelle vague",40 (avril 1965) pp.134-135.

- Alice Parizeau, "La femme : pupille ou paria?",41 (mai 1965) pp.158-160.

- Marie-Andrée Bertrand, "Ménagères ou députés?",41 (mai 1965) pp.160-162.

FÉMINISME ET RELIGION AU QUÉBEC DEPUIS 1960

- Jocelyne Laforce, Francine Séguin, "Etudiante'65", 41
  (mai 1965) pp.170-171.

- Jacques Lamoureux, "Une femme mariée", n°42 (juin 1965)
  pp.214-215.

Maintenant (1966)

- Hélène Pelletier-Baillargeon, "Un concile pour le deuxième sexe?", n°53 (mai 1966) pp.145-149.

- Soeur M.-Thérèse-de-la-Croix, "La femme dans la Bible",
  n°53 (mai 1966) pp.151-153.

- Benoît Lacroix, "Eve la divine!", n°53 (mai 1966) p.180.

- Pierre Saucier, "Les bonnes soeurs ont-elles un avenir?,
  n°54 (juin 1966) pp.200-202.

Maintenant (1967)

- Solange Chalvin, "Le mur du sexe", n°61 (janvier 1967)
  pp.10-11.

- Hélène Pelletier-Baillargeon, "Rosemary à la Curie",
  n°62 (février 1967) p.40.

- H.P.-Baillargeon, "Les bonnes soeurs de Claire Martin",
  n°62 (février 1967) pp.64-65.

- Colette Moreux, "Le dieu de la québécoise", n°62 (février 1967), pp. 66-68.

- H.P.-Baillargeon, "Marie", n°65 (mai 1967) pp.145-148.

- Pierrette Pothier, "Femmes au travail", n°65 (mai 1967)
  pp.167-168.

- Marie-André Bertrand, Réjane Rancourt, "La femme : sujet
  difficile!" n°65 (mai 1967) pp.169-175.

Maintenant (1968)

- Renée Rowan, "Sous le voile : la femme", n°76 (15 avril-
  15 mai 1968) pp.105-106.

- Solange Chalvin, "Les femmes pauvres criant au secours",
  n°77 (15 mai-15 juin 1968) pp.135-136.

FÉMINISME ET RELIGION AU QUÉBEC DEPUIS 1960

- Thérèse-F. Casgrain, "Aux armes citoyennes!", n°78
(juin-juillet 1968) pp.185-188.

Maintenant (1969)

Aucun article

Maintenant (1970)

Aucun article

Maintenant (1971)

- Renée Rowan, "Des femmes déçues par un rapport peureux",
n°102 (janvier 1971) p.6.

- Hélène P.-Baillargeon, Propos de Simone et Michel
Chartrand recueillis par... "Les Chartrand : Trente ans
du Québec", n°109 (oct. 1971) pp.260-284.

Maintenant (1972)

- Francine Chabot-Ferland, "La sexualité féminine... une
dépendance?"n°117 (juin-juillet 1972) pp.28-32.

- Jacques Grand'Maison, "La femme peut réconcilier le privé
et le public", n°118 (août-septembre 1972) pp.8-11.

Maintenant (1973)

Aucun article

Maintenant (1974)

- Numéro consacré à Femmes du Québec, 140 (nov.1974).

Relations (1960)

- Joseph d'Anjou, s.j., "Justice pour Eve", XXe année,
n°231 (mars 1960) pp.72-74.

- _____ "Eve refuserait-elle l'égalité?", XXe
année n°235 (juillet 1960) pp.172-174.

- _____ "Pour la promotion culturelle de la
femme", XXe année, n°239 (nov.1960) p.300.

FÉMINISME ET RELIGION AU QUÉBEC DEPUIS 1960

<u>Relations</u> (1961)

Aucun article

<u>Relations</u> (1962)

Aucun article

<u>Relations</u> (1963)

- Joseph d'Anjou, s.j., "Voix de femme, voix sans écho",
  n°274 (oct.1963) pp.300-301.

<u>Relations</u> (1964)

- Marcel Marcotte, s.j., "La vocation éternelle de la femme",
  n°284 (août 1964) pp.230-232.

- Joseph d'Anjou, s.j., "Absence et présence de la femme",
  n°288 (déc. 1964) p.364.

<u>Relations</u> (1965)

- Albert Bélanger, "La capacité juridique de la femme
  mariée : le Bill 16", n°292 (avril 1965) pp.112-113.

- _____, "La capacité juridique de la femme
  mariée : le Bill 16", n°293 (mai 1965) pp.146-147.

- _____, "La capacité juridique de la femme
  mariée : le Bill 16", n°294 (juin 1965) pp.173-175.

- Michèle Stanton-Jean, "Liberté, égalité...fémininité",
  n°297 (sept. 1965) pp.262-263.

<u>Relations</u> (1966)

Aucun article

<u>Relations (1967)</u>

- Claire Campbell, "Ma vie de femme", n°318 (juillet-
  août 1967) pp.206-207.

- _____, "l'évolution de la femme", n°320
  (oct.1967) pp.267-268.

<u>Relations</u> (1968)

- Claire Campbell, "L'avilissement de la femme", n°323
  (janvier 1968) pp.14-16.

FÉMINISME ET RELIGION AU QUÉBEC DEPUIS 1960

- Lisette Morin, "Sur les femmes-femmes et leur déborde-
  ment" (correspondance) no324 (février 1968) pp.52-53.

- Marie-Thérèse Huberdeau, Félix-H. Trudeau, "Femmes-femmes",
  "femmes ordinaires", femmes journalistes et femmes, tout
  simplement (correspondance), no325 (mars 1968) p.85.

- Claire Campbell, "Pour une femme, aimer, c'est se culti-
  ver", no327 (mai 1968) pp.145-147.

- _____, "Impressions d'une mère de famille sur
  Humanae Vitae",no330 (sept. 1968) pp.252-253.

- _____, "La femme doit humaniser la société",
  no336 (mars 1969) pp.80-83.

- _____, "La femme "moderne", no338 (mai 1969)
  pp.146-149.

- _____, "La femme "ultra moderne", I no339
  (juin 1969) pp.173-175.

- _____, "La femme "ultra moderne", II no340
  (juillet-août 1969) pp.203-205.

- _____, "La femme "dans les limbes", no341
  (sept. 1969) pp.234-237.

Relations (1970)

- Claire Campbell, "Le rapport de la Commission royale
  d,enquete sur le statut de la femme au Canada", no 347
  (mars 1970) p.86.

Relations (1971)

- Marcel Marcotte, "Etre femme aujourd'hui", no357 (février 1971) pp.47-50.

- _____, "La femme devant l'avortement", no358
  (mars 1971) pp.81-85.

- Claire Campbell, "Une clé... pour la compréhension du
  Rapport", no358 (mars 1971) p.85.

Relations 1972)

- Julien Harvey, "La réforme des ministères et la femme
  dans l'Eglise", no376 (novembre 1972) pp.304-305.

FÉMINISME ET RELIGION AU QUÉBEC DEPUIS 1960

- Marcel Marcotte, "Nos ventres sont à nous!" avortement sur demande et féminisme de choc", n°376 (novembre 1972) pp.299-303.

Relations (1973)

- Ginette Deslongchamps, "Le rôle de la femme dans les téléromans", n°384 (juillet-août 1973) pp.203-205.

- Julien Harvey, "La femme dans l'Eglise : une commission", n°386 (octobre 1973) p.262.

Relations (1974)

- Irénée Desrochers, "Barbara Ward à la Bourse de Montréal", n°393 (mai 1974) pp.131-134.

Relations (1975)

- Georges-Henri D'Auteuil, "Théâtre pour l'Année de la Femme", n°406 (juillet-août 1975) pp.220-221.

Relations (1976)

- Georges-Henri D'Auteuil, "Visages de femmes", n°44 (avril 1976) pp.124-125.

- Gabrielle Poulin, "Romans québécois de 1975. Des femmes racontent et se racontent", n°414 (avril 1976) pp.125-127.

- _____, "Roman québécois féminins des années 70", n°421 (décembre 1976) pp.347-350.

Autres revues

- Communauté chrétienne, vol.4, n°22 (juillet-août 1965), numéro consacré aux religieux.

- Jean Francoeur, "Les communautés religieuses dans la nouvelle société québécoise", Communauté chrétienne, vol. 5, n°28 (juillet-août 1966) pp.327-330.

- P.-E. Charland, "La condition féminine", Prêtres et laïcs, vol. XVII (novembre 1967) pp.468-469.

- Anne-Marie Pelzer, "Dieu a besoin des femmes", Prêtres et laïcs, vol. XVII (décembre 1967) pp.503-518.

- Dossier : La femme dans la vie ouvrière : Prêtres et laïcs, vol. XXIII (janvier 1973) p.2-60.

FÉMINISME ET RELIGION AU QUÉBEC DEPUIS 1960

ANNEXE II : Thèses de maîtrise et de doctorat présentées
dans des universités québécoises, concernant
les femmes et la religion à partir de 1960*

- Beaudet, Gisèle, s.g.m., La dévotion au Père éternel
chez Mère d'Youville, M.A., Montréal, 1961.

- Marie-de-Saint-Jules, b.p.a. Soeur (Marie-Anne Granger),
Théologie de la dévotion au coeur de Marie, selon saint
Jean Eudes. M.A., Montréal, 1961.

- Marie-Thérèse-de-la-Croix, s.n.j.m., Soeur (Madeleine
Sauvé), La femme dans la Bible - sa destinée. Ph.D.,
Montréal, 1962.

- Sainte-Madeleine-des-Oliviers, c.n.d., Soeur (Madeleine
Laroche), Analyse de l'attente de religieuses enseignan-
tes vis-à-vis les divers rôles du prêtre. M.A., Montréal,
1962.

- De Koninck, Charles, La mort glorieuse de Marie. Ph.D.,
Laval, 1963.

- Joly, Savio-Alcide, s.c. Frère, La dévotion au Sacré-
Coeur chez Sainte Marguerite-Marie. M.A., Montréal, 1963.

- Marie-des-Anges, soeur, L'ambivalence des facteurs af-
fectifs dans le sentiment religieux des pré-adolescentes.
L. Psy., Sherbrooke, 1963.

- Marie-Colette-de-Jésus, s.s.a. Soeur (Colette Dubé),
Liturgie - morale; projet de catéchèse pour adolescen-
tes. M.A., Montréal, 1964.

- Mignault, Alice (Soeur Saint-Jean-Baptiste, a.s.v.),
La consécration à Dieu de la religieuse enseignante.
Ph.D., Montréal, 1964.

- Saint-Jean-du-Divin-Coeur, Soeur, Le sens de Dieu chez
la fillette d'âge préscolaire, en milieu urbain. L. Péd.,
Sherbrooke, 1965.

- Bibeau, Hector, La pensée mariale de Saint-Vallier,
introduction historique. D.E.S., Laval, 1966.

---

* Thèses canadiennes: Ottawa, Bibliothèque Nationale du
Canada, 1960-1971.

FÉMINISME ET RELIGION AU QUÉBEC DEPUIS 1960

- Martin, Georges-Marcel, La dévotion à Saint-Joseph chez les religieuses hospitalières de l'Hôtel-Dieu de Québec, 1668-1760. D.E.S., Laval, 1968.

- Sénécal, Huguette, Marguerite Bourgeoys; une chrétienne éducatrice. M.A., Montréal, 1967.

- Boulé, Maurice, La notion du mal dans l'oeuvre de Simone Weil, M.A., Montréal, 1969.

- Desmarteaux, Denise, Etude comparative de trois groupes restreints de religieuses du diocèse de Montréal. M.A., Montréal, 1971.

RELIGION, MORALITY AND LAW

ROGER C. HUTCHINSON's paper was first prepared for the
Church Council on Justice and Corrections/Le Conseil des
Eglises pour la Justice et la Criminologie, as acknowledged in the introduction, in 1976. He teaches courses
on Religion in Canadian Society and Religious Ethics
at Victoria College, Toronto, and has written on the
Social Gospel in Canada and Canadian population policy.

RÉSUMÉ

La relation entre la loi et la religion peut être décrite
en quatre points de vue différents, qui sont en même
temps quatre périodes historiques.

Le premier point de vue représente l'extrême de la
tradition chrétienne classique qui identifie la loi et
l'enseignement chrétien. La moralité se base sur la loi
divine biblique. La religion, ainsi justifie une approche dure et répressive à la punition suivant un système
de mérites justes.

Le deuxième point représente l'autre extrême. La religion et la moralité sont des choses privées, détachées
de la diagnose et du traitement béhaviouristes des con-
trevenants. Cependant, ce détour vers la réhabilitation
a produit un dénouement de frustration et l'effet pré-
ventif n'a pas réussi.

Le troisième point examine de nouveau la fonction de
la loi. Le but est la paix, la liberté, la dignité
dans une communauté coopérative. La loi, alors, est
un moyen humaniste de répondre aux actes qui vont contre
ces valeurs. La religion, néanmoins, reste une affaire
privée, même si elle redevient nécessaire.

Le quatrième est un point de vue "transformationniste" :
on accepte la réalité du pluralisme religieux et on cherche en plus à créer une solidarité entre les individus.
La loi devient ici un moyen de réconciliation pour l'outrage moral et juste contre des actes illégaux et erronés.
Mais, au coeur de ce quatrième point est la religion qui
saisit la réalité ultime et qui se rend compte alors que
les situations sont plutôt plus importantes que des principes.

ROGER HUTCHINSON

Religion, Morality and Law in Modern Society

Introduction

One of the purposes of the Church Council on Justice and
Corrections is to promote discussions about the operation and reform of our criminal justice system between
church people and law reformers. This aim is often
frustrated, not only by different assumptions about the
role of religion, but also by each group's lack of
clear understanding of what the other thinks about the
role of religion in relation to morality and law. From
the point of view of church people, law reformers often
appear to underestimate the importance of religion.
Many law reformers, on the otherhand, suspect that
church people simply take it for granted that the
Judaeo-Christian tradition is the authoritative source
of moral norms for all Canadians. In this paper I hope
to clarify the context within which discussions about
religion, morality and law are taking place. I will
identify four stances which co-exist at the present
time but which also represent stages through which we
have passed. My own view of the role of religion in
modern society will be developed in connection with
the fourth stance.

The first two positions represent the two extremes
of too much authority claimed for a particular religious tradition, and too little appreciation shown for
any religious or moral influence on public policy.
These stances closely correspond to Patrick Kerans'
"Classical Natural Law' and "behavioural science"
models.[1] The work of the Law Reform Commission of
Canada provides an example of a third stance which exhibits renewed concern with the moral functions of the
criminal justice system. The fourth stance, represented by the Church Council's response to the Law Reform
Commission is characterized by a shift in focus to the
role of the churches in relation to the criminal justice system, and to renewed concern with the "religious" foundations of the Commission's "public
morality." While in connection with the fourth stance,
I will defend a "transformationist"[2] style of church
involvement and a modified, "contextual" natural law
foundation for our public morality,[3] my main purpose
in the paper will be to facilitate conversations between law reformers and church people, and among church
people who have different views about religion,

morality and law.

1. Law and Morality Grounded in Christian Teachings

There are both historical and philosophical reasons
for believing that the morality underlying Canada's
public institutions is, and ought to continue to be,
grounded in Christian teachings. Between the 1750s and
the 1850s it was the intention of the British Government to make the Church of England "the Church as by law
established."[4] Although the Church of England lost its
status as the legally established church by the mid-
nineteenth century, it was generally assumed at least
for the next one hundred years that Canada was a
Christian society with Anglo-Saxon Protestant and French
Catholic spheres of influence.[5] This self-understanding
was given impassioned confirmation during the 1930s and
1940s when Canada went to war to protect Christian
civilization.[6] The "Christendom" mentality was kept
alive in the 1950s during the "cold war" against god-
less communism, but secularization and pluralism in
the 1960s and 1970s have, in my view, produced a new
social reality which seems to require different symbols
and basic images.

There is, however, an impressive philosophical and
theological tradition underlying the widespread public
conviction that our current sense of crisis and despair
is the result of abandoning an "objective", absolute,
Christian morality, in favour of "subjective", relative,
secular values. The answer, according to public demand
and the Classical-Christian Natural Law tradition, is
to return to a morality based on God's Law as it has
been interpreted by the church.

Not everyone who takes it for granted that Canada is
a Christian society shares this natural law position,[7]
but it represents the commonly held understanding of
what it would mean to reassert the importance of the
role of religion in relation to morality and law.   An
interesting illustration of this stance was provided
by the Rev. E.L.H. Taylor in an article written in
1958 called "A Secular Revolution in Christian Disguise."[8] It was then his view that:

Fundamentally the present movement for abolition of
capital punishment symbolizes an attempt on the part
of scientific humanists and utilitarian pragmatists

to change the essential structure and conception of
Canadian Law and Justice. It marks the climax of the
rationalist and so-called 'progressive' attempt to
place the laws of this realm upon a purely secular
humanist basis.[9]

Taylor traced the emergence of the "Western theory of
Law and Justice" from "Classical Philosophy and Early
Christianity" through Justinian's <u>Corpus Juris Civilis</u>,
the American Constitution, the Code Napoleon and the
Austrian Civil Code. He then asked how this Natural Law
tradition relates to capital punishment.

Did this mighty body of law admit the right of the
State to administer retributive justice in the case
of murder most foul? It did. For two thousand years
our Western ancestors have believed that it is just
for society to demand the supreme penalty of the law.
The murderer must be killed, not simply to deter
others but to restore the just order which he has
made unstable. Having broken the law of God and
human society he deserves to give his life in exchange. Justice herself requires no less. To promote the true ends of justice, however, retribution
was taken out of the hands of the next of kin and
administered in a Court of Justice, so that such just
retribution would be carried out in strictest detach-
ment in favour of society. The wrong doer would thus
receive his just due in the form of a just penalty,
that is a penalty corresponding to the injury. Thus
the primary concept of justice in punishment was seen
to be equivalence, the balance of guilt or injury
with atonement or punishment. That is the meaning of
the falsely decried terms "retribution" and "atonement". The murderer was executed because it was
thought he deserved no less.[10]

Taylor's interpretation of the natural law tradition
shows how religion can be used to justify a harsh and
repressive approach to the punishment of criminals.
Some aspects of his position are shared, however, by
reformers such as Karl Menninger and the Law Reform
Commission of Canada. They agree that all crimes should
not be treated as symptoms of a behaviour disorder.
Some acts are not merely illegal, that is, against
society's rules, or signs of sickness. They are morally
wrong and must be dealt with accordingly. Taylor complained that:

190

Today our Canadian lawyers would seem to have become
sold on the theory that it is the main task of the law
to make saints out of crooks rather than to give them
their just deserts... Apparently justice is no longer
considered an adequate criterion and yardstick for
the punishment of crime in Canada. Henceforth the
special psychological foibles and philosophical **pre**-
judices of whichever legal clique gains control of
Parliament will in future decide matters of criminal
justice in this country. In other words the administration of justice in Canada will become something
purely subjective rather than objective in character.[11]

Taylor wondered where the 'progressives' were going to
draw the line. He concluded that: "Two conceptions of
Canadian Law cannot exist within the bosom of a single
state. Either the new relativistic, pragmatic, positi-
vistic, utilitarian conception must triumph or the old
and well tried Western idea of Natural Law and Justice.
That surely is the basic issue underlying the present
debate in Canada upon the question of abolition of
capital punishment."[12]

If Taylor's position reflects too much moral certainty, and too much confidence that Canada's laws should
be grounded once again in Christian teachings, the reaction to the natural law tradition went too far in the
other direction. In the next section, David Chandler's
recent study of capital punishment in Canada will be
used to illustrate the perspective which advocates the
separation of religion and morality from law.[13]

2. Separation of Religion and Morality from Law

Chandler cites with approval Harold Lasswell's suggestion that "moral indignation will give way to calculated
expediency as a basis of support for public order as
diversity and disciplined calculation flourish in modern
society."[14] This projected victory of instrumental,
rational, technological control over expressive, emotional, ideological reactions, would mark the final
stage in the reduction of religion and morality to
purely private, "subjective" matters. An important
question for church people and law reformers is whether
the assumption that this victory is a good thing can be
challenged in a way that neither flies in the face of
Chandler's empirical findings nor merely reverts to
Taylor's dogmatic natural law position. Before I

191

consider this question, however, it will be useful to
recall how the emergence of positive law and then of
behavioural science techniques gradually rendered religious and moral notions irrelevant in the labelling,
diagnosis and treatment of offenders.

As Taylor pointed out under the impetus of the Enlightenment and "the new science devoted to historical legal
research" a new conception of law emerged during the
first quarter of the nineteenth century in Germany.

> From that time onwards all discussion of Justice as
> the source and essence of Law abruptly disappeared
> from the continent. Why? The answer is that these
> 'positive' lawyers as they were pleased to call them-
> selves managed to drive a fatal wedge between criminal
> justice and Natural Law, between the legal systems of
> the various states and Christian morality... The thin
> edge of this wedge to detach the idea of justice en-
> tirely from its theological and religious context was
> the theory that because human laws vary so much from
> place to place and time to time, they must all be
> considered purely relative... Instead of having a
> timelessly valid justice for all men, there now arose
> a view of Law as the mere product of historical
> growth.[15]

Even within the legal framework of positive law,
however, notions such as justice, freedom of the will,
accountability of each individual, etc., continued to
have relevance. The further shift from a legal framework to a cultural mood in which the scientific
language of the various experts in the explanation,
prediction and control of human behaviour became dominant made these moral notions completely irrelevant.
Karl Menninger's description of the communication
breakdown between lawyers and psychiatrists illustrates
the co-existence of different paradigms of human
behaviour.

> Lawyers are concerned with placing or rebutting blame
> for specific acts of deviant, prohibited behavior;
> psychiatrists are interested in correcting total
> patterns of behavior. Instead of seeking for the
> blame or the exculpation of an accused, doctors seek
> the etiology, the explanation, the underlying motives,
> and contributing facts in the commission of certain
> undesirable acts. Lawyers and psychiatrists speak
> two different languages in regard to professional

192

matters, and hence their common English tongue is of
little help in meaningful communication with one
another...

For example, the word justice, which is so dear to
lawyers, is one which the doctor qua scientist simply
does not use or understand. No one thinks of justice
as applying to the phenomena of physics. There is no
"justice" in chemical reactions, in illness, or in
behavioral disorder.[16]

In his later book he provides a concise summary of
the manner in which both the terms and the personnel of
religious and legal establishments lost their authority
and function.

Much behavior that would be classed a priori as sinful had long since passed into the control of law.
What was considered criminal and so treated was understandably sinful. And now, increasingly, some crime
was being viewed as symptomatic. Sins had become
crimes and now crimes were becoming illnesses; in
other words whereas the police and judges had taken
over from the clergy, the doctors and psychologists
were now taking over from the police and judges.[17]

He is concerned about the fact that the erosion of
the language of morality has left us unable to respond
adequately to the reality of sin, as moral wrong and
not merely as crime or symptom, or to the need for expiation and atonement, and not merely for restraint
and rehabilitation. Before I pursue this line of
thought, however, I must return to Chandler's findings
which prompt him to welcome the "progress" from moral
outrage to rational control as responses to wrongdoing, and from "expressive" to "instrumental" images
of the legal process.

Chandler uses Canadian data to test the hypothesis
first proposed by Emile Durkheim that ethnically and/
or religiously homogeneous societies deal more repres-
sively with deviants than more heterogeneous societies.
According to this view, homogeneous (i.e. primitive)
societies are bound together by common ethnic or religious sentiments (mechanical solidarity), and are,
therefore, seriously threatened by deviation from social
norms. Offenders are treated severely to reaffirm the
shared values and to maintain the social bond. In
complex, religiously and ethnically diverse (i.e.
modern) societies, on the other hand, the recognition

of the need for public order is based on economic interdependence and a pragmatic, rational approach to the
resolution of differences (organic solidarity). His
aim is to see whether the relationship between the homogeneity of their constituencies and the way Members of
Parliament voted in the capital punishment debates of
1966 and 1973 supports his hypothesis.

In order to appreciate his conclusions, and the implications they have for the role of religion in
relation to law, it is necessary to understand some of
the distinctions and assumptions underlying this hypothesis about the link between homogeneity and repressive
law. His key distinction is between "expressive" and
"instrumental" images of the legal system. The former
emphasizes "the symbolic, emotional, non-rational...
features of social life," and sees the punishment of
offenders primarily in relation to the dramatization
of society's core values. The "instrumentalist" image
views law as "a fully and exclusively rational control
system" designed to deter future antisocial or harmful
acts. The criminal law system would thus "be modelled
on the laws and administrative procedures used to
govern a system of roads and highways in a country.
The apparent, although not explicit, goal of the system
is to provide sufficient legal intervention so that
people and goods can be moved from place to place with
maximum efficiency and personal discretion."[18]

In any particular society the law will undoubtedly be
viewed both "as an instrumental control system," and
"as an expressive drama which ritually displays the
ideals of the culture."[19] Societies will, however,
come to be characterized by one orientation or the
other. For Chandler, the "pure" types of each orientation are economic and religious behaviour:

Economic activity is supposed to be characterized by
the most rational, planned, pragmatic considerations.
Quantitative measurement of output and efficiency
checks are normal. There is relatively little that
is sacred about it except the institution itself. (My
emphasis.)
On the other hand, religion is largely an expressive
activity. The activities involved in collective
ritual observance or individual prayer are regulated
by traditional rules or individual innovation. There
is no tangible output from the institution and an
aversion to any quantified interpretation of it.

194

Religious activity is largely an expression by people of their feelings and a dramatization of their ideas.[20]

Built into Chandler's approach is the assumption that societies not only appear to be evolving from expressive to instrumental orientations, but that they ought to be. He admits that punishment can be used to dramatize society's core values without this necessarily representing a regression to primitive vengeance. He makes it quite clear, however, that as societies modernize, and adopt rationality and practicality as their central values, such "morality plays" would no longer be necessary. The language he uses to depict the different rationales for legal punishment carries definite overtones of approval and disapproval which reveal the normative character of his underlying perspective. "One is an indignant, moralistic, vindictive, retributive justification which usually leads to harsh punishment. The other is utilitarian, pragmatic, therapeutic in its rationale."[21]

In view of these basic assumptions, it is perhaps not surprising that his findings about the role of religion in relation to law confirm his hypothesis that religion is a repressive force. In 1966 in constituencies with over 70% of the population professing affiliation with a particular religion 67.6% of the MPs voted to retain capital punishment while 30.1% voted to abolish it. In more religiously mixed constituencies 39.5% were retentionists and 55% were abolitionists. Similarly, MPs from ethnically homogeneous constituencies voted 66.1% to 29.1% in favour of retention, while their colleagues from more ethnically mixed areas voted 54.3% to 42.8% for abolition.[22]

These findings supported his hypothesis that religious concentration is one factor contributing to an "expressive" orientation to law which would "encourage the availability of the death penalty since... law should express the strongest evaluation on human life."[23] The broader implication of this finding is that religious concentration fosters an orientation toward deviance which is "punitive, repressive and retributive. It is an orientation which emphasizes the evaluative and symbolic rather than the practical or utilitarian reasons for legal punishment. This orientation seems to have consistent pattern with other attitudes such as ethnocentrism and dogmatism."[24] Thus, for Chandler, empirical research supports the high-level generalization embedded in much sociological literature that religion is a regressive force which hampers the evolution of society towards more rational, humane, practical procedures for dealing with deviance.[25]

I will return to Chandler's findings in the final section of the paper when I attempt to defend religiously motivated moral outrage as an appropriate response for some offenses. In this section my main purpose has been to show how he illustrates a perspective which encourages the separation of religion and morality from law.

3. Renewed Interest in the Moral Functions of Law

There is a growing sense of crisis and despair at all levels of the criminal justice system. The system is not working. The shift in emphasis from punishment to rehabilitation has produced frustration both for the opponents and the defenders of this trend. Part of the problem seems to be that our present system combines punishment and rehabilitation in a mutually defeating, rather than complementary, fashion. "Incarceration for treatment" continues to punish the offender without mediating to him the expiation that was traditionally thought to flow from the recognition that a moral wrong had been committed and that the debt had been paid. Also, the fact and conditions of confinement counteract the efforts of rehabilitators to correct the defects that caused the crime. Since the offender is neither reconciled with the community, nor cured by the treatment, he will undoubtedly continue to commit anti-social acts. Thus, not only are the goals of retribution and rehabilitation thwarted, but the new overriding aim of deterrence is not achieved.[26]

This sense of crisis has led in some quarters, such as the Law Reform Commission of Canada, to renewed interest in the basic assumptions and moral judgments underlying the whole multi-faceted process by which acts become crimes and offenders are dealt with as criminals. Given the uncertainty about which techniques will be effective, it is timely to return to the question of which theories and practices would be most just and fair. As Menninger suggested, the recovery of notions such as sin, forgiveness, expiation and atonement might better equip us to deal with realities which now seem intractible than our so-called "neutral",

scientific techniques.[27] The Law Reform Commission does
not go that far, but it opens the door for conversations
about the dimension of human existence with which these
terms deal.

The Law Reform Commission recognizes that the criminal
law has "instrumental" and "expressive" functions, but
they reverse Chandler's emphasis. For the Commission,
the main aim of criminal law is not to control the
future, but to respond appropriately to wrongful acts;
"to register our social disapproval, to publicly denounce them and to re-affirm the values violated by
them. Criminal law is not geared only to the future;
it also serves to throw light on the present - by underlining crucial social values."[28]

The values which both are, and in the Law Reform
Commission's view ought to be, fostered are peace,
freedom, justice, human dignity, and any other pre-
requisites for a stable, co-operative community in
which individuals can find fulfillment. Acts which
threaten these values ought to be denounced, not because
they offend God or violate someone's personal ideals,
but because man's nature as a social being requires it.

Suppose a murder is committed in our midst: we must
respond as human beings and as social creatures.
First, "no man is an island" and every person's death
diminishes all other persons: to do nothing and ignore this fact is to be less than human. Second,
murder tramples on our society's basic values about
human life: to do nothing is tantamount to condoning
it and saying murder is all right. To be fully human
and to hold certain values means responding when they
are violated. Such violation requires public condemnation, and this is preeminently the job of criminal
law.[29]

This reaffirmation of the wrongness of some acts does
not, however, lead the Commissioners and their staff
back in any straight-forward sense to the Classical
Natural Law position described above. On the contrary,
they strictly limit the role of criminal law and urge
restraint in its use. They insist that the notion of
retribution "is too complex morally and philosophically
to provide a justification for the criminal law. Besides, making sin reap its own reward is no fit enterprise for mere mortal men and women. Like Blackstone
we prefer to leave this to 'the Supreme Being'."[30]

On the other hand, the role of criminal law cannot be reduced to protection from harm in any simple and direct way.

Much as we might like to think that it protects society through deterrence and rehabilitation, the efficacy of both these methods is problematical. Besides, desirable as it may be, mere protection from harm is not what we want of criminal law. After all, mere non-commission of crimes will not wholly satisfy. To satisfy, the non-commission must result from the view that crimes should not be committed. In short, we want a society where people think they ought not to be criminals.[31]

The criminal law is "fundamentally a moral system", therefore, not primarily through its authority to punish wrong-doers but insofar as it participates in the broader task of "producing a society fit to live in."[32] This emphasis on "the moral educative role of criminal law" shifts our attention from the authority by which acts are declared immoral to the means by which persons and institutions become moral. The society to be created "is less one where people are too frightened to commit crimes than one where people have too much respect for one another to commit them. Fostering this kind of personal respect is a major aim of parents, teachers, churches, and all other socializing agents."[33]

The Commission's stress on the "expressive", symbolic, evaluative function of criminal law, and its recognition of the importance of other socializing agents, reflects both a renewed interest in the relation between morality and law, and a positive attitude toward the role of religious organizations. Its practical proposals for the diversion of cases from the courts to community groups, and the reintegration of offenders into the community, also presuppose the existence of organizations such as church groups which are bound together by intensely enough held altruistic values to motivate and enable them to assume such responsibilities. In their public statements, nevertheless, the Commissioners and their staff do not appear to move beyond the view that religion is a private matter, and that common sense and rationality provide sufficient grounds for affirming and acting in accordance with humanistic values.[34]

In the final section of the paper I will use the

Church Council's response to the Law Reform Commission
to illustrate a fourth stance which sifts our attention
to the public functions of religion in relation to
morality and law.

4. Religious Foundations of a Humanistic Public Morality

There are two main levels at which the Church Council's
response to the Law Reform Commission will be used to
illustrate this fourth stance regarding the role of religion in a modern, religiously diverse society. At one
level attention is focussed on how the churches relate
as organized groups to the rest of society. I will
suggest that the most fruitful response is to become
more self-conscious about what it means to be a "denomination" rather than a "church" or a "sect."[35]

A second level involves examining the way Christian
symbols and doctrines are used in the papers prepared
for the Council to probe dimensions of reality which
appear to be neglected by humanists and "secular"
reformers. My main aim will be to show that a move
away from the "church-type" natural law position of
the first stance does not necessarily involve a "sectarian" withdrawal from public responsibility, or the
privatization of religion which characterized the
second stance. The transformationist stance of denominations which accept the reality of religious pluralism and which look for allies in the task of creating
a just and humane society will be defended as a more
promising possibility.

a. Communities of Faith in a Dialogue Society

Empirical studies of the social thought and practices
of the Canadian churches are badly needed. It is my
impression, however, that most of them would identify
with the following statement from the 1934 report of
the United Church's Commission on Christianizing the
Social Order.

8. ...To do its work effectively the Church must at
   every stage of the world's life discover the mind
   of the Spirit and interpret that mind in relation
   to human need. It is a living body speaking with a
   living voice in the circumstances and conditions of

each age.

9. In the process of time under the guidance of the
   Holy Spirit the Christian Church unfolded the
   standards and principles of Jesus, and
   applied them to the social order. The motives
   which influenced the Church in the development of
   this social consciousness were complex, and the
   pathways along which the development took place
   were many; yet the result was clear - the Christian
   Church became concerned with the redemption of
   society. While it recognized that no perfect
   society could exist as long as men were sinful, it
   sought to purge society of its grosser evils, and
   so to regulate its practice that Christian people
   who desired to maintain the standards of Jesus
   might have the opportunity of developing a Christian civilization, and that all might have an
   environment helpful to Christian living...

11. ... The aim of the United Church is to help to
    interpenetrate our civilization with the Spirit of
    Christ, and to transform those agencies and insti-
    tutions of society which are foreign to that
    spirit, to the end that Christian people may have
    the fullest opportunity for realizing the fullness
    of the Christian life and that others may come to
    the same.[36]

The transformationist stance of a denomination is
characterized by the tension between embracing and resisting pluralism or religious diversity. Pluralism
is affirmed insofar as it is not thought necessary, or
consistent with our own desire to maintain continuity
with our own roots and traditions, to convert Jews,
Muslims, Marxists or Humanists to disciples of Jesus
in order to create a society which would more nearly
conform to our Christian values. Our Christian aims
for society can, for the most part, be translated into
publicly shared humanistic language. I say for the
most part because it is yet to be shown whether humanistic language is doing justice to the dimensions of
reality Christians encounter through symbols such as
sin and redemption.

To the extent that denominations recognize different
communities of faith they are willing partners in what
Charles Taylor has called "the dialogue society."

This society would start from the fact of pluralism,
from the fact that we are of many different faiths,
beliefs, and moralities; but it would also start from
the fact that we are all less than satisfied and dogmatic in our possession of the truth; that we are all
therefore in some sense searchers; and that the fact
of pluralism has entered into the very content of our
varied beliefs so that we are already in dialogue
within ourselves with the ideas of others.37

There are limits, however, to the pluralism affirmed
in this image of "the dialogue society." Just as
pluralism itself is one of the conditions for the dialogue, so is the recognition that caring for one
another is one of the most basic aspects of human existence. Therefore, contrary to some uses of the word
dialogue, all content and moral passion are not depo-
sited at the door as a condition for participating.
On the contrary, the image of interpersonal communication conveys a picture of centred-selves who are both
free and self-determining and related to one another.
To deny either the dignity of individuals or our solidarity with one another in community is to deny our
humanity.

This ancient biblical insight has once again become
popular, especially through the influence of the existential phenomenology underlying the works of persons
such as Rollo May and Gibson Winter. They both place
at the centre of their positions Martin Heidegger's
claim that care is "the basic constitutive phenomenon
of human existence." As May says, "It is thus ontolo-
gical in that it constitutes man as man."38

Winter uses the basic image of inter-personal communication to derive social norms for relationships among
groups as well as in face-to-face settings.39 I am
extending Taylor's notion of "the dialogue society" in
a similar fashion to picture the dialogical relationship
among communities of faith. At one level, therefore, I
am referring to interfaith dialogue about foundational
questions. At a more practical level I am thinking
about the political processes by which a religiously
diverse society decides which wrongs from the standpoint
of a particular religious group ought also to be treated
as violations of public morality, and which moral wrongs
ought to be dealt with as crimes.

As Christians face this common project of creating a

201

society in which love and care are embodied as our highest values it is pointless to keep insisting that we
discovered these values first. Instead, our unique
contribution is to recover the relevance of the Christian symbols, stories and special occasions through
which values such as love and care take on truth and
meaning. The crucial issue is not so much who professes
these values but where they get the power to shape our
responses to social questions such as the nature of our
criminal justice system.

It should be emphasized that the transformationist
stance I am defending rejects the Stance II assumption
that particular religious traditions should not try to
influence legislation, and that there are no "objective"
standards in relation to which our system of justice
and corrections ought to be transformed. Much of the
debate about abortion laws provides a good example of
the polarization around Stance I and Stance II positions
which needs to be transcended.[40]

It is not sufficient simply to proclaim the intention
to be involved in the transformation of society. We
must also explore the obstacles which confront socially
concerned Christians who are trying to make their
churches more responsive to the human suffering in their
midst. To what extent are the members of congregations,
parishes or church-sponsored organizations bound together
by intensely enough held values to take responsibility
for an inmate on temporary leave? As I suggested above,
the Commission's proposed community-based programs for
diverting cases from the courts and reintegrating
offenders into the community presupposes the existence
of such groups. There are probably many congregations
like the one described in Bill Klassen's paper[41] which
have a sufficiently strong core of dedicated, depend-
able members to undertake such tasks. In many local
churches, however, there is an internal pastoral problem
which threatens to overwhelm this traditional capacity
for witness and service. According to John Shea:

> This problem, which is often more felt than defined,
> goes by many names. It has been called "the identity
> crisis", "the inbreak of secularism", "the irrele-
> vance of religion", or simply "lack of faith". But
> perhaps the most accurate diagnosis of this uneasi-
> ness at the heart of Church life is that for many
> people religious language has become meaningless. The
> Christian symbols which once articulated the Church's

faith and directed and motivated its activities have
lost their power. They no longer positively energize
the style of Church life because they no longer en-
thral and persuade with their overwhelming grasp of
the real. This is not just the perennial problem of
the interplay of faith and doubt. To use temporarily
the distinction . . . between meaning and truth, the
pastoral problem concerns more the meaning of the
Christian symbols than their truth. In other words
the churchman does not easily and immediately understand how the religious language he uses fits into
the world he experiences.[42]

In order to appreciate the link between this gap
between religious language and experience, on the one
hand, and effective community involvement, on the other,
it is important to understand the sense in which these
churches no longer perform the basic religious function
for their members. That is, the symbols, doctrines and
practices no longer evoke the conviction that one's
values are rooted in reality. This, according to Clifford Geertz, and I agree, is the main function of
sacred symbols. The central feature of the religious
perspective, in this view, "is the conviction that the
values one holds are grounded in the inherent structure
of reality, that between the way one ought to live and
the way things really are there is an unbreakable inner
connection."[43] (My emphasis.)

This way of looking at religion brings into sharp
focus the function of religious language for those who
live within its influence. "What sacred symbols do for
those to whom they are sacred is to formulate an image
of the world's construction and a program for human
conduct that are mere reflexes of one another." That
is, religious symbols link "the collective notions a
people has of how reality is at base put together,"
i.e., their world view, and "their general style of life,
the way they do things and like to see things done,"
i.e., their ethos, "in such a way that they mutually
confirm one another."[44]

Such symbols render the world view believable and the
ethos justifiable, and they do it by invoking each in
support of the other. The world view is believable
because the ethos, which grows out of it, is felt to
be authoritative; the ethos is justifiable because
the world view, upon which it rests, is held to be
true. Seen from outside the religious perspective,

this sort of hanging a picture from a nail driven into
its frame appears as a kind of slight of hand. Seen
from inside, it appears as a simple fact.[45]

Thus it is no longer experienced as a simple fact,
even by many church people, that man is created in the
image of God, fallen and redeemed through the saving
act of Christ. Furthermore, it is quite likely that
the humanistic values of many church people are no
longer nurtured by and anchored in their religious convictions. On the other hand, there appears to be an
implicit religious grounding for the position of the
Commissioners and their staff insofar as they treat it
as a simple fact that man is a social being, and therefore ought to create institutions which will foster
mutual respect and human well-being.

One can now appreciate more fully what it means to
be a denomination or community of faith in a dialogue
society. There is a great diversity in the ways persons
who take for granted the "fact" of man's obligation to
his fellow man symbolize and experience the truth and
rightness of this conviction. Our notion of interfaith
dialogue must be extended to include both discussions
among Christians, Jews, Muslims, secular humanists,
etc., and the clarification of different ways of being
grasped by one's faith within a particular congregation
or denomination. In addition to identifying the symbols which bring about the belief that one's humanistic
values are rooted in reality, it is important to identify the settings in which these symbols do their work.
For as Geertz reminds us:

> The revelatory encounter with such symbols does not
> take place in the everyday, commonsensical world, but
> in contexts which are, necessarily, somewhat detached
> from it. What religious men have to work with in
> everyday life is not the immediate perception of the
> really real, or what they take to be such, but the
> memory of such a perception.[46]

b. Christian Symbols and "the Struggle for the Real"

Geertz' view of the religious perspective helps us to
clarify three distinguishable but closely related aims
of the papers prepared for the Church Council. First,
they contribute to the descriptive, interpretive task
of discerning the symbols and basic images which fuse

ethos and worldview in the "secular" settings of the criminal justice system. Their second and primary aim is to explore the role of Christian symbols such as sin and reconciliation in linking our beliefs about how offenders ought to be treated to a deeper grasp of the reality with which we are dealing. A third aim is to provide resources for study groups in which persons will have the opportunity to relate Christian symbols to the reform of our system of justice and corrections. These study groups might, then, become the settings in which these symbols regain their power to evoke in at least some of the participants the conviction that their Christian beliefs and values are rooted in reality.

I want now to return to my opening claim that communication between church people and law reformers, and among church people, might break down because they misinterpret one another's understanding of the role of religion. The nature of these misunderstandings, and the manner in which the Church Council is responding to them, can now be drawn into sharper focus.

In their papers prepared for the Church Council, Klassen, Neufeld and Kerans endorse the Commission's shift in emphasis from "incarceration for treatment" to community-based programs of diversion and reintegration.43a They attempt to recover the notions of personal and corporate responsibility, but reject the growing demand for a return from "rehabilitationism" to sterner forms of punishment. There appear to be two main themes underlying the demand for the humane treatment of offenders. There is, in the first place, the recognition that the person who becomes an offender is and must be included in rather than excluded from the community. The line between guilt and innocence becomes blurred with the realization that we are all sinners, that "we" are responsible for the unjust social conditions which prompt "them" to commit crimes, and that even those who commit the most outrageous crimes still participate in God's promised redemption. The second theme, which is closely related to the first, is that while punishment can perhaps be justified as a last resort reconciliation should be our basic aim.

My interest is not in repeating or criticizing the position developed in the other papers, which I share, but in anticipating and correcting two of the possible misinterpretations of this stance.

On the one hand, advocates of a Stance I position who want sterner punishment could equate our plea for the humane treatment of offenders with a Stance II subordination of moral outrage to reliance on a practical orientation and behavioural science methods for controlling behaviour. To these critics we would reaffirm our conviction that one of the legitimate roles of religion, even in a modern society, is to motivate moral outrage and to legitimate the use of criminal law to denounce acts which are not merely illegal but wrong.

On the other hand, persons who are responsible for making the present system work, or for translating proposals for improving the system into practical reforms, might find our emphases on the sinfulness of all of us, and on the greater need for reconciliation than punishment, "utopian" or "idealistic". This might confirm their impression that the role of religion is to show compassion for suffering regardless of the circumstances, and to dream about how society and criminal law might work or ought to work without worrying about the gap between dream and reality. Our answer to these critics is that it is in fact the role of religion to institutionalize compassion or care and to criticize existing institutions and practices from the standpoint of a vision of a better society. The crucial point, however, is whether the "ideal" against which present arrangements are measured is simply a product of our wishful thinking. As I suggested above, the heart of the religious perspective is that one's values are rooted in reality. Our intention, therefore, is to encourage a more adequate grasp of reality not to escape from it. This professed intention to deal with aspects of reality that tend to be neglected by "secular" reformers can be illustrated with a further consideration of the role of religion in motivating and justifying moral outrage at offences against the moral order.

c. Religiously Legitimated Outrage at Offences Against the Moral Order

I am suggesting that the response of the Church Council on Justice and Corrections to the Law Reform Commission of Canada reflects an understanding of the role of religion in relation to morality and law that retains the strength and avoids the weaknesses of the Stance I classical Christian natural law position, and the Stance II scepticism about the use of religion to sanction the punishment of offenders. This discussion of the way I would justify religious legitimations of the use of the criminal justice system to express moral outrage at certain offences is intended to clarify that claim.

My first point will be that at the present time we use unnecessarily harsh forms of punishment to punish the wrong offenders for the wrong offences. Or, to reverse the order, I will suggest that in performing the role of motivating moral outrage it is important to ask which offences should evoke our moral outrage, which offenders should feel the full force of our disapproval, and what means are appropriate for denouncing these sins against the moral order.

(i)   Which Offences?

The criminal justice system performs its symbolic, "expressive" role in two closely related but distinguishable ways. On the one hand, this refers to the use of the stigma of conviction, the solemnity of a public trial and the pain, humility or inconvenience of imprisonment to denounce acts which are both illegal and wrong. It is in relation to this general role that the Law Reform Commission says, "When acts occur that seriously transgress essential values, like the sanctity of life, society must speak out and reaffirm those values. This is the true role of criminal law."[47] Subsidiary aims are the deterrence of further crimes and the rehabilitation of offenders. The Commission thus distinguishes between "real" crimes which violate fundamental values and imply "fault", and regulatory offences such as parking violations which imply negligence but not immoral conduct. (Unless of course a society treats as immoral the breaking of its rules. That is, going through a stop sign may not be morally wrong, but breaking the rule which prohibits that act might be.)

Within this general sense in which the criminal justice system performs a symbolic, "expressive" function, some "real" crimes are of course more serious than others. Shop lifting is not as serious as armed robbery, and armed robbery is a less serious crime than murder. As we move along this spectrum from less harmful to more harmful offences we find ourselves suddenly making a quantum leap into a different order of

207

response to particular acts. Think of two cases in
which persons are mugged in the park. One dies while
the other survives. Although the attackers commit
similar acts of violence, with similar motives, degrees
of sanity, etc., on the basis of the results of their
acts the amount of horror they evoke in us has traditionally justified quite different forms of punishment.
This was most dramatically true while murderers were
still executed. Murder and treason were placed in a
class by themselves. As Taylor, whose position was
used to illustrate Stance I, argued, "the murderer must
be killed, not simply to deter others but to restore
the just order which he has made unstable."[48] The
murderer thus not merely commits the most harmful type
of act, but symbolizes the most extreme form of disrespect for the value of life.

Abolitionists have, quite rightly in my view, argued
that executing the murderer simply compounds this disrespect for life. However, by basing their case
against capital punishment primarily on the evidence
that it is not an effective deterrent they underestimate the importance of the symbolic role of this
"supreme penalty of the law" (Taylor). For example,
in a paper prepared for a Canadian Council of Churches
task force on capital punishment, Professor Thomas
Dailey rejects not only the death penalty as a form of
punishment, but the whole idea that retribution is a
legitimate aim of criminal law. He cites with approval
Karl Menninger's claim that executing a murderer is the
act of a "primitive people wreaking vengeance on a
ritual victim."[49]

I agree that our treatment of murderers is at the
present time a form of "scape goating." Not, however,
because only primitive peoples engage in such rituals,
but because we now allow our response to the wrong
offenders of the wrong offences to carry the symbolic
weight of expressing where we want to draw the line as
a society. Our negative image of "scape goating" can
perhaps be transformed into a positive image of
"rituals of cleanliness," if we select other offences
by other offenders to carry the symbolic weight of
dramatizing the values which are at the centre of our
moral concern.[50] This search for violations which more
appropriately symbolize threats to our well-being as
persons and as a community becomes even more urgent when
we consider the ineffectiveness and unfairness of our
present practices.

A major factor underlying the reaction against the punishment demanded by retributive justice is that the distribution not only of the death penalty but of imprisonment has been appalling. As the Law Reform Commission states, "one of the most disturbing criticisms about sentencing and dispositions is that they tend to fall heaviest on the young, the poor, the powerless and the unskilled."[51] Since many Indians and Métis find themselves in the last three categories, and all of them are in a society deeply permeated with racial prejudice, they make up a disproportionate percentage of offenders.[52] This is not only unfair, but it undermines the ability of the criminal justice system to perform its symbolic function. As Patrick Kerans argues in his paper, most of the persons we now punish in order to express our moral outrage are already stigmatized by the poverty and lack of education, which are "their fault," and by racial factors which are not.[53] He then develops the important argument that distributive justice is prior to retributive justice, and that the injustice and ineffectiveness of punishment point to the more basic need for reconciliation.

Patrick Kerans has thus provided the main answer to church people who worry that our demand for the more humane treatment of offenders simply reflects moral uncertainty and a "cool" rational approach to the "problem" of crime. Our most impassioned demand should be for reconciliation, and our acceptance of the need for punishment should come as a reluctant conclusion after all alternatives have been explored. If left at that point, however, this answer would still beg the question of whether Christians ought ever to justify imprisonment, not merely as a tragic but necessary method for restraining dangerous offenders, but as a form of punishment for immoral acts. That is, should Christians deny the legitimacy of retributive justice all together?

In order to locate the type of action which evokes my own moral outrage, and which prompts me to feel that retribution can be legitimate, it is necessary to follow Patrick Kerans' shift in attention from the individualistic way of thinking that has characterized both our legal and religious traditions to a more communal or social way of understanding ourselves. When we examine the structure of our society it becomes clear that the acts which now shape our lives, and which nurture or undermine our well-being as persons and communities, are

the corporate acts of large organizations. Business
corporations and government bureaucracies are good
examplesof immense concentrations of power combined
with a tragic lack of public accountability. This is
the direction in which I think we should look to find
the most serious violations of our core values. But,
even if these violations are discovered, can we devise
sanctions for corporate irresponsibility - or for the
irresponsibility of corporations - that would be fair,
effective and emotionally satisfying? Can our outrage
at corporate acts be focussed as sharply and as satis-
fyingly as when we "directly experience" the link
between the violent act of an individual, the moral
outrage that act evokes in us, and the punishment such
as death or life in prison which seems to fit the
crime?

First, what type of harmful activity constitutes a
serious enough violation of our core values to evoke in
us the desire to condemn the act and punish the offender? While I was in the early stages of thinking about
this paper, I happened to read Elliot Leyton's book,
Dying Hard: The Ravages of Industrial Carnage.[54] The
personal stories in this book of the Newfoundland miners
who are dying of lung cancer and silicosis moved me to
feel that the mine owners and their collaborators ought
to be brought before a Nuremburg-style tribunal to
answer for their crimes against humanity. Dean Ham's
Report of the Royal Commission on the Health and Safety
of Workers in Mines has reinforced this conviction.[55]
The manner in which hazardous working conditions have
been deliberately perpetuated is a serious violation of
our professed concern for human dignity and deserves to
be denounced as immoral behaviour.

Even persons who share my outrage at unsafe working
conditions, however, might ask whether it would be fair
or feasible to treat as criminals the owners, managers,
politicians, doctors, Compensation Board officials, etc.
for whom unsafe working conditions are an unfortunate
but inevitable side effect of an industrial way of life.
Are they not simply "doing their jobs," or playing their
expected roles in our industrial system which has always
subordinated the health and safety of workers to profits
and productivity. These questions raise the issue of
the kind of society we have and the kind of society we
ought to be working toward. It is around this issue
that the work of the Church Council intersects with
discussions of other inter-church projects, such as

210

GATT-fly, ICPOP, Project North, the Task Force on the
Churches and Corporate Responsibility and Ten Days for
Development, are having about a "New International
Economic Order."

(ii) Which Offenders?

Even a new economic order, however, would have to
deal with the question of ethical accountability in our
corporate roles. The first step is to recognize this
as a serious moral issue. Rollo May is one widely
respected writer who thinks that it is. In connection
with his call for "a new ethic of intention," which "is
based on the assumption that each man is responsible
for the effects of his own actions," he claims:

> The ultimate evil in our day... is inherent in situa-
> tions in which the person is prevented from taking...
> responsibility - as in that involving our hypothetical
> national guardsman (at the Kent State killings), or
> the members of battalions in Vietnam who were ordered
> to shoot innocent noncombatants. The triumph of good
> over evil is shown in individuals like the American
> soldier who landed a helicopter at Mylai and turned
> his gun on Lieutenant Calley to shoot him if Calley
> continued the massacre.[56] (My emphasis.)

His "ethic of intention" should not be confused with
an ethic of "good intentions" or "sincerity."

> The future lies with the man or woman who... uses the
> tension between individuality and solidarity as the
> source of his ethical creativity. So far we have been
> taught to do one or the other. We have learned to
> accept responsibility for our convictions; but that is
> not enough. We have learned to accept responsibility
> for the sincerity of our actions; but that too is not
> enough. These are both individualistic... one can be
> entirely sincere and firm in one's convictions - and
> entirely wrong. We must accept responsibility for
> whether we are right or wrong.[57]

Whereas May stresses the ethical accountability of
persons within their corporate roles, a second step would
be to hold corporations themselves criminally responsible
for "real" crimes. That is, a corporation and not
merely the individuals who work for it could be tried,
convicted and punished for violating society's core

211

values. The Law Reform Commission dealt with this possibility in its working paper, Criminal Responsibility
for Group Action. Two attitudes toward corporations
were recognized:

> There are those who regard the corporation as merely
> symbolic of a process of interaction among people,
> and who would see corporate responsibility as a way
> of making a definite moral statement about the con-
> duct of these people. Others would view the corpo-
> ration as a personality separate from those involved
> in its processes, and, by these, a criminal law that
> convicts little people but not large corporations may
> be perceived not only as unfair but also as ambivalent
> towards the values our criminal law is used to support.
> For many people, then, corporate criminal responsibi-
> lity may work towards the reinforcement of important
> social values reflected in our "real" criminal law.[58]

In order to see more clearly why unsafe working conditions in a mine should be treated as a "real" crime, it
is important to recall how that term is used by the
Commission.

> "Real" crimes... should be primarily concerned with
> fundamental values in our society. By emphasizing
> and reinforcing values considered to be at the basis
> of our social system, "real" criminal law promotes a
> society in which they are respected and are demons-
> trated in behaviour. It responds to social conduct
> that exhibits disrespect for values and is inextri-
> cably bound up with the notion of "fault." Inten-
> tional conduct that injures people, deprives them of
> their property, restricts their freedom or subjects
> them to offensive interferences are examples of con-
> duct that violates values regarded as so important
> to our society or to warrant the designation "crimi-
> nal" and the stigmatization that is associated with
> the use of the criminal justice system.[59]

On the basis of this definition, the Commission then
states that it might be appropriate in some cases to
change what are now regulatory offences into "real"
crimes. This would dramatize the extent to which these
offences involve the violation of fundamental values,
and not simply negligence in relation to regulations.
"Selling bad meat might be an example of a regulatory
offence where evidence shows a higher degree of fault
than negligence."[60] Similarly, I am arguing, operating

a mine in a way that unnecessarily threatens the health
and safety of workers should be treated as an offence
that is more like murder, rape and theft, i.e. a "real"
crime, than like disobeying a traffic signal, i.e. a
regulatory offence. I am making the further claim that
using criminal law to denounce this type of violation
would symbolize our respect for human dignity and well-
being more adequately than our present prosecution of
the individual who performs isolated acts of violence.
This would not detract from the seriousness of individual acts of murder, rape or theft. It would place
them in their proper perspective in relation to the
violence we presently leave unpunished.

(iii) What Means?

I have now indicated the offenders whose offences
should be at the centre of our moral and legal concerns.
It will seem incredible, however, to treat the operation
of an unsafe mine as seriously as the act of murder or
rape apart from a further consideration of the means
appropriate for punishing our most serious offences.
Since I presuppose the abolition of capital punishment
I do not envisage hanging mine owners or bringing them
before a firing squad. This, in my view, would be "the
act of primitive people wreaking vengeance on a sacrificial victim."[61] I am suggesting that by shifting the
focus of our moral outrage from individual offenders
who are already stigmatized to corporations and their
executives who, conscious of their public image, would
be stigmatized by a public trial and a criminal conviction, the death penalty and punitive sentences would be
less necessary. Using criminal law to stigmatize those
who have caused the greatest harm and who have something
to lose would help to regain respect for the law and
accomplish the symbolic "expressive" aim of underlining
society's core values.

There is a further argument against capital punishment, however, which must now be used to qualify the
sense in which it is legitimate to encourage moral outrage as a response to violations of society's values.
I implied above that there could be a "directly
experienced" link between murder as the ultimate crime
and the death penalty as its appropriate punishment.
This suggestion must now be modified.

The references above to Clifford Geertz' description

213

of the religious perspective introduced the idea that
the connection between our experience of the really real
and our judgments in the everyday world is an <u>indirect</u>
one. The belief that the death penalty is an appropriate response to the ultimate outrage against the
moral order is, therefore, an <u>interpretation</u> of what
follows from one's experience of the real. It is not a
direct apprehension of God's will or of the natural
order. This insistence that the connection between
religious experience and moral judgments is indirect
does not necessarily, however, leave one in the desert
of moral scepticism or without the ability to care
passionately. It points rather toward a different
understanding of how religious beliefs themselves are
appropriated in the light of "modern" criticism of all
beliefs.[62]

The persons who find their position more or less
adequately described by this fourth stance are products
of and participants in the modern age. In Paul
Ricoeur's terms, we have lost our "primitive naïvete,"
but we do not wish to remain uprooted from our
religious traditions and unable to reintegrate our
thoughts and actions with our deepest passions. As
John Shea, who was cited above, points out, Ricoeur.

> posits a movement in man's relationship to his
> religious symbols from a primitive to a second nai-
> vete. For pre-modern man, Ricoeur holds, there
> existed an immediacy of belief, a flushtight rela-
> tionship to religious symbols, a primitive naivete.
> But modern man, precisely because he is modern, is
> a critical creature. He is informed by... (many)
> ...disciplines... (which)...form the cultural matrix
> out of which he thinks and acts. Consequently he
> does not have an immediate and undifferentiated
> rapport with the symbols of faith. They do not spon-
> taneously disclose for him the sacred and lead him
> to the experience of God. For modern man primitive
> naivete has been irrevocably lost.[63]

Ricoeur's analysis of religious belief applies also
to the link between religious beliefs and moral judgments. A crucial aspect of the dialectical stance I
have been illustrating in this section is the conviction
that we must not settle for moral arrogance, on the one
hand, and moral uncertainty or indifference, on the
other, as the only options.[64] The recovery of the capacity to care enough to feel moral outrage is closely

related to Ricoeur's claim that modern man can inhabit his religious symbols in a second naivete. According to Shea's summary:

> This second naivete is not achieved by the creation and maintenance of (a faith isolated from the world) but precisely in and through criticism. To recover his inherited symbols modern man must place himself in the hermeneutical circle. Bluntly stated this circle is "We must understand in order to believe, but we must believe in order to understand." Through critical interpretation religious symbols will regain their power and become transparent to the sacred. Modern man must not remain detached but believe in the symbols and live with them. He wagers that in his commitment to the symbols he will have "a better understanding of man and of the bond between the being of man and the being of all beings." If modern man had to understand in order to believe, he must now believe in order to fully understand.[65]

(iv) A Modified, Contextual, Natural Law Theological Stance

It should now be more evident why I call Stance IV a modified, contextual natural law position. It represents continuity with the older Christian natural law tradition insofar as it insists that our values are rooted in reality, and that our deepest encounter with this reality comes through our participation in the Christian tradition. It is modified because our knowledge of what is ultimately real and important is thought to be more partial, limited and related to our historical context than was the case for the older natural law tradition. It is contextual, not just in the sense that principles have always have been applied in concrete cases, but in the more thorough-going sense that how we define the situation is perhaps even more important than the principle we think applies. Thus it is necessary to become more fully aware of the extent to which our ethical and theological judgments are pre-determined by the language we use to describe a situation. Therefore, although we do not wish to reduce behaviour to its social causes, we cannot return to the certainty with which the "classical-legal" model assigned to individuals the responsibility for particular acts without taking into account

215

the social circumstances which produced that response.

This concern with the social setting in which action takes place can be extended to the cultural context. This can be illustrated by re-examining David Chandler's findings about the connection between religious homogeneity and repressive attitudes towards deviants.[66] It seems plausible that communities bound together by the taken for granted validity of their religious views (primitive naivete) would simply equate their attitude towards capital punishment, etc., with God's will. Modern criticism combined with ethnic and religious pluralism undermine this certainty, and, in Chandler's view, ought to lead to a more practical orientation to the problem of crime. I have argued, on the other hand, that the movement away from primitive naivete need not lead to the arrested development of a detached, critical stance as a total orientation to life. It is possible to move on to a second naivete in which one brings to consciousness the myths and symbols which shape one's reactions in the everyday world, and which set the parameters within which one is detached and rational. The use of criminal law to express moral outrage can once again be justified without returning to an untroubled belief in the connection between religious experience and moral judgments.

(v) The Innovative Function of Religion

Chandler used his findings as support for his Durkheimian view that the primary function of religion is to integrate around non-rational sentiments societies in which a particular religion is dominant. He thus concludes that as societies become more pluralistic, persons will become more rational and religion will become obsolete. I am proposing, on the other hand, that it is primitive naivete in relation to traditional religious symbol systems which is becoming less common in modern, religiously diverse societies. The role of religion as a legitimator of social change, which was emphasized by Max Weber, will continue to be important even in modern society.[67] Particular religious groups will continue to provide fellowship and a meaningful interpretation of the world as Andrew Greeley has stressed in his work.[68]

It is hoped that sociologists will help us to discern how the religious function of fusing ethos and world

216

view is performed in modern society either in traditionally religious or secular settings. This will require,
however, a better understanding than Chandler reflects,
not only of the nature of religion, but, as Geertz has
argued, the way we operate in our common sense, everyday lives. The religious perspective is not to be seen
as an alternative to common sense and rationality, but
as one of the perspectives on the everyday world which
places our routine tasks and our most intensely felt
joys and sorrows in the context of our glimpse of the
really real.

Conclusion

My aim has been to clarify the context within which
religion, morality and law are interacting with one
another in modern society. As part of this aim I defended the view that a transformationist, modified, contextual natural law position is a fruitful way for
Christians to reappropriate the resources of our religious tradition.

Since, as I have argued, the central task of religious
symbols is to evoke the conviction that our values are
rooted in reality, it is my hope that church people will
ask whether the faith we profess is real, and that law
reformers will reflect upon the symbols, basic images
and rituals through which their convictions are sustained
that life is worthwhile and that the values they affirm
are not merely the products of their wishful thinking.

The reforms of our system of justice and corrections
advocated by the Law Reform Commission and endorsed by
the Church Council on Justice and Corrections are
integral parts of the broader task of creating a society
fit to live in. Their success will depend upon the
renewal of our communities and a renewed sense of our
responsibility for one another as persons. There will
be a diversity of settings in which this personal and
community renewal will take place, but I am suggesting
that in our modern society a common feature will be
the quest for a "second naivete". This will entail a
plunge beyond reflecting on our dilemma to "living in"
the community of faith in which our deepest insights
and highest hopes are nurtured. As Shea says:

A risk must be taken. A man must live within a con-
stellation of symbols and allow them to interpret and

217

guide his life. This is what the surrender of faith
means. The truth of a symbol, its adequacy to experience, can only be known from within...A man who
lives within the symbol of God experiences the world
as gracious. Despite his fears and anxieties, despite
the possibility of tragedy, he finds a source and a
power that enables him to act beyond himself, to celebrate and to sacrifice. His centre is within yet
beyond himself in the transcendent otherness of his
experience and this centre "will hold".[69]

FOOTNOTES

1. Patrick Kerans, "Punishment vs Reconciliation:
    Retributive Justice & Social Justice in the Light
    of Social Ethics." Prepared for the Church Council
    on Justice and Corrections, Ottawa, 1976.

2. H. Richard Niebuhr, Christ and Culture, New York:
    Harper and Brothers Publishers, 1951, Chapter 6,
    "Christ the Transformer of Culture."

3. See Gibson Winter, Elements for a Social Ethic,
    New York: The Macmillan Company, 1966. His work
    has been the dominant influence on my approach to
    social ethics.

4. J.L.H. Henderson, "The Abominable Incubus: The
    Church as by Law Established," Journal of the Cana-
    dian Church Historical Society, XI, 3 (September,
    1969), 58-66.

5. E.R. Norman, The Conscience of the State in North
    America, Cambridge: Cambridge University Press,
    1968.

6. See the excellent study by Tom Sinclair-Faulkner,
    "'For Christian Civilization': The Churches and
    Canada's War Effort, 1939-1942," Ph.D. Thesis, The
    Divinity School, University of Chicago, 1975.

7. For an evangelical view that Canada is a Christian
    society see Leslie Tarr, This Dominion, His Domi-
    nion: The Story of Evangelical Baptist Endeavour
    in Canada, Toronto: The Fellowship of Evangelical

Baptist Churches in Canada, 1965. N.K. Clifford
discusses the decline of the image "His Dominion"
in the larger denominations in his article, "His
Dominion: a vision in crisis," Studies in Religion,
2, 4 (Spring, 1973), 315-326.

8. Canadian Bar Journal, 1 (1958), 41-46.

9. Taylor, p. 41. NOTE: E.L.H. Taylor has modified
                    the views reported above. See his
10. Taylor, p. 43. The Christian Philosophy of Law,
                    Politics and the State (Craig Press:
11. Taylor, p. 45. Nutley, New Jersey, 1966) and The
                    New Legality (Craig Press, 1967).

12. Taylor, p. 46.

13. Chandler (Carleton Library) Toronto, 1976.

14. Chandler, p. xxi.

15. Taylor, p. 44.

16. Menninger (The Viking Press), p. 96.

17. Whatever Became of Sin?, New York: Hawthorne Books,
    Inc., 1973, p. 45.

18. Chandler, p. xxii.

19. Chandler, p. 11.

20. Chandler, p. 4.

21. Chandler, p. 53.

22. Chandler, p. 164. It falls outside of my interest
    in this paper to do a thorough critique of Chan-
    dler's approach to the analysis of religious
    influence. His findings should, however, be
    compared to Andrew Greeley's who takes a different
    approach. See the latter's The Denominational
    Society: A Sociological Approach to Religion in
    America (Glenview, Illinois: Scott-Foresman and
    Company, 1972: "Religious people are more punitive
    toward criminals...than the nonreligious....However
    ...the relationship between church attendance and
    religiousness on the one hand and bigotry on the

other is curvilinear -- that is to say, the least
prejudiced respondents are the most devout and the
least devout: the most prejudiced are those with
middle levels of religious devotion," p. 207.
Religion is an ambiguous phenomenon, and it is
necessary to distinguish among degrees of involvement and types of religion.

23. Chandler, p. 193.

24. Chandler, p. 67.

25. For a good discussion of the creative role of
religion see Gregory Baum, Religion and Alienation:
A Theological Reading of Sociology, New York and
Toronto: Paulist Press, 1975, esp. Ch. VIII,
"Creative Religion: Max Weber's Perspective."

26. Paul L. Weiler, "The Reform of Punishment," in
Studies in Sentencing, Ottawa: Law Reform Commission of Canada, 1975, pp. 93-205.

27. Whatever Became of Sin?

28. Law Reform Commission of Canada, Report: Our Criminal Law, Ottawa, 1976, p. 3. Hereafter cited as
LRC, Report.

29. LRC, Report, p. 5.

30. LRC, Report, p. 16.

31. LRC, Report, p. 16.

32. LRC, Report, p. 5.

33. LRC, Report, p. 5.

34. Based on comments scattered through working papers
and reports.

35. For a discussion of these terms see Greeley's book
cited above, S.D. Clark's Church and Sect in Canada,
Toronto: University of Toronto Press, 1948, and W.
E. Mann's Sect, Cult and Church in Alberta, Toronto:
University of Toronto Press, 1955. See also note
68 below.

36. Adopted for study by the 1934 General Council of

the United Church of Canada and reprinted as a pamphlet. Record of Proceedings, 6th General Council, Kingston, Ontario, September 1934, pp. 237-8.

37. Charles Taylor, The Pattern of Politics, Toronto and Montreal: McClelland & Stewart, 1970, p. 124. This also means of course that we are in dialogue within our denominations. Our "communities of faith" will not necessarily coincide with our denominational identities.

38. Love and Will, New York: W.W. Norton & Company Inc., 1969, p. 290. Winter's Elements for a Social Ethic was cited above.

39. See also my doctoral thesis on a Canadian Group which developed a similar position: "The Fellowship for a Christian Social Order, 1934-45: A Social Ethical Analysis of a Christian Socialist Movement," Toronto School of Theology, 1975.

40. Alphonse de Valk, Morality and Law in Canadian Politics: The Abortion Controversy, Montreal: Palm Publishers, 1949.

41. William Klassen, Release to Those in Prison, Kitchener: Herald Press, 1977. Prepared for the Church Council on Justice and Corrections.

42. John Shea, "A Second Naivete, A Pastoral Approach," in Andrew Greeley and Gregory Baum, eds., The Persistence of Religion in Modern Society, New York: Seabury, Concilium Series, Vol. 81, 1975, p. 107.

43. Islam Observed: Religious Developments in Morocco and Indonesia, Chicago: University of Chicago Press, 1968, p. 97. Chapter 4 is called "The Struggle for the Real."

44. Geertz, p. 97.

45. Geertz, p. 97.

46. Geertz, p. 110.

46[a] The papers by Kerans and Klassen have been cited above. Thomas R. Neufeld's paper is called, "Guilt and Humanness: The Significance of Guilt for the Humanization and the Judicial-Correctional System."

47. LRC, Report, p. 16.

48. E.L.H. Taylor, "A Secular Revolution in Christian Disguise," p. 43.

49. "Theology and the Death Penalty," Bulletin, Deacon Internship Program, St. Augustine's Seminary, Scarborough, Ontario, 1975.

50. Mary Douglas, Purity and Danger and Natural Symbols, New York: Random House.

51. LRC, The Principles of Sentencing and Dispositions, Working Paper 3, Ottawa, 1974.

52. LRC, The Native Offender and the Law, Ottawa, 1974.

53. Kerans, pp. 33ff.

54. Toronto, 1975.

55. "Governments, companies accused of risking miners health and lives," The Globe and Mail, Toronto, August 24, 1976, p. 1.

56. Rollo May, Power and Innocence, New York: W.W. Norton & Company Inc., 1972, p. 253.

57. May, p. 254.

58. Ottawa, 1976, p. 33. Hereafter cited as LRC, Criminal Responsibility.

59. LRC, Criminal Responsibility, p. 11.

60. LRC, Criminal Responsibility, p. 11.

61. Menninger cited above by Thomas Dailey.

62. I share Greeley's scepticism about much of what has been written about "modern" man's inability to believe, etc. The speed with which public images of the religious life of a society can change could be seen in the U.S. shortly after it became evident that Carter's evangelical conversion was not going to harm him as a presidential candidate. Commentators then said, of course he would win because two thirds of the American people were evangelical Protestants! It might be more useful to think

about co-existing differences within the churches than to become too captivated by the evolutionary assumption underlying notions such as modern, pre-modern or post-modern.

63. Shea, p. 108.

64. See Rollo May, <u>Power and Innocence</u>, p. 239. "The fact that good and evil are present in all of us prohibits anyone from moral arrogance. No one can insist on his own moral supremacy. It is out of this sense of restraint that the possibility of forgiveness arises."

65. Shea, p. 108.

66. Chandler, whose position was used to illustrate the second stance, stresses the integrative role of religion and treats it as an "ascribed" characteristic like ethnicity rather than as an "achieved" trait like education, p. 196.

67. See the reference to Baum's <u>Religion and Alienation</u> in note 24 above.

68. Andrew Greeley, <u>The Denominational Society</u>, pp. 2 and 3. "By the denominational society we intend to describe a religious form found only in Canada, the United States, Holland, and Switzerland -- that is to say, a relationship between religion and society which is characterized neither by an established church nor protesting sect....

American denominations emerged as quasi-<u>Gemeinschaft</u> (i.e. community) groups...because at the same time in history the religious pluralism in the United States made a distinction between membership in a society and membership in a church possible and the industrial revolutions made quasi-<u>Gemeinschaft</u> groups such as the American denominations necessary."

69. Shea, p. 116. cf Yeat's, <u>The Second Coming</u>, "Things fall apart; the centre cannot hold".

PUNISHMENT VS RECONCILIATION IN CANADA

PATRICK KERANS teaches at the Maritime School of Social
Work, Dalhousie University, and is the author of Sinful
Social Structures (1974). His paper is a modified version of one prepared for the Church Council on Justice
and Corrections/Le Conseil des Eglises pour la Justice
et la Criminologie in 1976.

RÉSUMÉ

L'idéal chrétien de la réconciliation se réalise bien
dans la vie privée; mais, se réalise-t-elle dans la vie
politique et juridique au Canada?

Etant donné que la liberté de l'individu dépend dia-
lectiquement de sa communauté, la réconciliation frater-
nelle devient une obligation, et une responsabilité de
la communauté. Cependant, les images classiques et sci-
entifiques du criminel qui sont à la base de notre système légal nous empêchent de réaliser notre idéal. Au
contraire, le système protège la société au prix des
membres qui sont déjà défavorisés : les jeunes, les
moins instruits, les pauvres et les indigènes. Vouloir
réaliser la réconciliation est, donc, vouloir comprendre
et vouloir corriger les défauts d'un tel système.

Un correctif est le concept de la "diversion" où la
communauté s'occupe elle-même de la rétribution judiciaire. Grâce au concept, chaque individu peut prendre
conscience de ses propres faiblesses : les criminels
ainsi que tous les autres membres de la communauté. La
"diversion" nous permet donc de prendre un premier pas
vers la réconciliation. Ce pas est donc essentiel.
Sans prendre les moyens, l'idéal chrétien restera
toujours en conflit avec le système judiciaire et politique du Canada.

PATRICK KERANS

Punishment vs Reconciliation: Retributive Justice and Social Justice in the Light of Social Ethics

Introduction

The Law Reform Commission has observed that "Justice... provides an opportunity...to emphasize the need for reconciliation between the offender, society and the victim." (#3, p. 4) They thereby seem to accept reconciliation as an ideal goal of the criminal justice process. In theory if not in practice this ideal has been central to Christian social thinking. Kindness, forgiveness and reconciliation are at the heart of the Judaeo-Christian vision of man. William Klassen asks, "Can the church ever be the place where offender and victim meet? Can society ever be such a place?" (p. 10) After a discussion of the biblical vision of man's sin and God's forgiveness, he answers:

> The offender is viewed as sharing the sinful state of the Christian but just as the Christian has received the grace of victory over sin, so too for the offender full forgiveness is available no matter how serious the crime. The offender finds acceptance in a society which is made up of offenders as well.
> (p. 13a)

This paper starts from this same vision. My point, however, will be to explore if this ideal of reconciliation is applicable only to our private lives; and if not, how it could be translated into political or even judicial terms.

Political Theology: The Problem of institutionalizing Christian ideals

There is an immediate difficulty in transposing the ideal of reconciliation into public, institutional terms. Traditionally, one of the goals of punishment is the protection of the core values of the community. It has been a political tradition since at least Aristotle that the state as the "perfect community" has the obligation to guarantee the fundamental values (e.g., peace, order, individual rights) necessary for human development, freedom and fulfilment. This seems to imply that while individual dignity and growth usually converge with societal interests, there are

226

nonetheless instances when the state needs to coerce
(i.e., punish) some who, for whatever reason, might decide to disturb the basic social order at others'
expense.

There is a dialectic relationship between individual
freedom and dignity on the one hand, and community order
on the other. While individual freedom is reliant upon
community order, still at least at times the need to
guarantee community order seems to demand the coercion
of an individual.

I wish to explore this dialectic, and to explore it
in a particular way, namely by paying close attention
to the relation between various analytic models of
society and certain basic images of man. Perhaps this
is not necessarily a theological method, the sole
property of theology. But largely for historical
reasons, theologians are the ones who have noticed the
importance of basic images in relation to analysis.
Most people using analysis assume that they are dealing
with reality and that their analytic models, imperfect
as they are, approximate adequate explanations of
reality. But this is possible only because they share
assumptions (i.e., basic images) about the nature of
the reality they analyze. Theologians, plying their
trade in a secular society and confronted especially in
the universities by a rationalist consensus which denies that their theological methods deal with reality,
have found it important to notice that all analysis
finds its root in myth, in basic images.

What I mean by basic image needs further explanation.

...images are not the innocent, purely objective
things they seems to be. The most casual image contains the whole of man. Images are not snapshots of
reality. They are what we have made of reality
Everything in us pours into the simplest image. They
are ourselves. (Lynch 1970, p. 25).

People throughout their lives grapple with situations
and try to cope. This involves more than physical and
economic coping: humans are called to make sense out
of their lives, to forge a biography, an identity.
This task is a constructive, imaginative task. The
imagination, then, is not simply or even primarily an
aesthetic faculty. It is the human person taking on
her full stature as a conscious, responsible fashioner

of history, focussing all her powers, all her past experience, all her vision of the future on to the
situation at hand, grappling with it, trying to make
sense out of it, trying to shape it.[1]

Basic images are intensely personal; they constitute
the heart of an individual's personal ethical stance.
But each person does not make up new ones. People share
images more profoundly than they are often consciously
aware of. For example, those who still feel an explicit
link with the church and its heritage will be consciously willing to understand the ultimate meaning of situations in the light of basic images contained in the
biblical tradition. To the extent that western culture
has been influenced by that biblical tradition, many
who consider themselves non-believers are nonetheless
deeply influenced at a preconscious, imaginative level
in their reading of situations. For example, someone
unjustly charged is, in some cultures, considered the
butt of a cosmic joke; in our culture, his situation
is characterized by a basic image, an archetype rooted
in the story of Jesus' trial. His situation is quite
spontaneously a cause for outrage: he is seen as
"martyr."[2]

Because basic images are profoundly sharable, and
because they give rise to human behaviour, they are
crucial to an understanding of society and politics.
They "define the geography and topography of everyone's
political world." (Edelman 1975, p. 21)

Language can be at once analytical and evocative.
It is theoretical and explanatory when the speaker, in
order to set forth the complexities of our modern
society, forges an analytic model which details the
functional and structural relationships between various
parts of a system. But even theoretical language
includes assumptions about how human beings interre-
late, how life should be lived: basic images are
evoked, and it is largely on the strength and accept-
ability of the images that a politician gains the day,
not on the elegance of his theoretical model.

While much of this paper will deal with theoretical
models seeking to explain the function of sentencing
(or more generally, the criminal justice process)
within the larger societal system, its thrust is to
examine these theoretical models in the light of the
basic images evoked. The ethical-theological question

is: which basic image is more consonant with the
biblical tradition? More precisely, if one basic
image is more consonant with the biblical tradition,
ought adherents to that tradition pursue the practical
implications of the appropriate model?

There is a classical legal model of fault and of
punishment as just retribution. An image evoked is
the goddess blindfolded, holding the scales: nobody
is to receive special favour or mercy. The image of
humans connoted is that of the free person, responsible
for his every action. (LRC #2, p. 19) (Note, the
letters LRC here and elsewhere in this paper refer to
the Law Reform Commission of Canada, or its publications.)

There is, by contrast, a scientific vision of humans,
which tends to concentrate on human behaviour as
patterned and predictable, and which tends to dwell less
on (and in some cases to deny) the relevance of human
freedom. Based on this image there is a model termed
by its critics the "disease" model, which understands
crime as something to be cured, and the sentencing
process as primarily rehabilitative, sending people
into therapeutic programs. Early forms of this vision
dwelt on psychological factors as criminogenic, while
later versions have used the broader idea of social
causation of crime and point to treating societal ills.

It will be the task of the next section to sketch
out a third image of the human, which contains in dialectic tension elements of these two. Later I shall
explore a model of the criminal justice process which
seems more consonant with this third vision of man.

Reconciliation: Responsibility as gift

I begin with the assumption that kindness, forgiveness and reconciliation are values which are at the
apex of the image Christians have of the human. As
William Klassen has pointed out, the person of Jesus
is the central image Christians have of the human.

Reconciliation is not a glib waving away of an
offense and its damage. Many have, for instance, found
the churches' use of the word lately to be mindless and
spineless. Churchmen have at times magnanimously

proclaimed reconciliation in our society without first
clearly identifying longstanding injustices and working
concertedly to eradicate them. In their speech, "reconciliation" tells us nothing of the biblical ideal.

I should like to explore the notion of reconciliation
as it applies to two individuals and then see if this
tells us anything about society.

Reconciliation implies an earlier disruption in a
relation. To forgive another implies that a person has
suffered at the other's hands. Forgiveness does not
mean the denial of the suffering by either party. On
what basis, then, can there be reconciliation?

Obviously the offender must show regret. But even
so, why should the offended forgive? There needs to
be a mutual reconstruction of the offense. The act
remains an inextinguishable part of the past; the
original hurt cannot be talked away. But the two
people concerned can, mutually, transform the meaning
of the act as part of the texture of their two biographies and as part of their joint history. The regret
of the offender transforms the meaning of the offense
within the biography of the offender because the
offender now transforms his self-image such that the
offense, which fitted his earlier pattern, now jars.
It has become an act which he now rejects.

In a parallel way, the offended person must contribute to the transformation of the meaning of the act.
One basis of this transformation comes to us from the
Judaeo-Christian tradition. The offended person,
instead of dwelling on her hurt, sees herself as a
fellow offender, as actually having or as capable of
having hurt others. She recognizes that her continued
inclusion in the community depends upon the forgiveness of others. If, by some slight chance, she has no
need of forgiveness, she at least needs to recognize
that her blamelessness depends upon the preventive
help of others.

Only the recognition of her own responsible use of
freedom being a gift of others in the community will
allow her to see that what she has in common with the
offender is more important than what she holds against
him.

What is crucial to a relationship characterized by

230

reconciliation is the experience that personal worth is
not simply a product of personal responsibility, but is
the gift of the other person. I am perhaps worthy of
another's esteem; but her esteem is also a gift which
bestows worth on me.

This basis of reconciliation - worth as gift, responsibility as gift, freedom as gift - comes to us, as I
mentioned, from the Judaeo-Christian tradition. It
might be argued that there are, historically, many
traditions based on deeply divided interpretations of
the biblical literature. It could be further argued
that history is against my claim; that people have often
interpreted their Christianity narrowly and vindictive-
ly; that at least in their public lives people have
rarely been motivated by their Christian faith to reconciliation.

In reply, those of us who are not fundamentalists
begin by saying that not every word in Scripture has
equal importance. There are cardinal events, key
symbols, privileged themes. The children of Israel
were delivered from the slavery of Egypt, were brought
into a covenant with Jahwe, and thereby became a
nation. These events are dwelt upon, retold and erec-
ted into symbols which inform Israel's understanding
of its history as nation and as people. God's loving
faithfulness to his promise (the Hebrew word hesed)
which was embodied in the exodus and expressed in the
covenant, gives continuity, coherence and meaning to
Israel.

The cardinal events of the New Testament, the birth,
death and resurrection of Jesus, become for Christians
the symbols which deepen and make more personal the
themes sketched above. The deeds and words of Jesus,
as well as the reflections of Paul and John, bring
this out. God's love engulfs man's sin; man lives
under the sign of forgiveness. (Cf. Ro. 5; 1 Jo. 3)
If life conquers death, if love is stronger than evil,
if community can survive selfishness and divisiveness,
this is not man's doing but God's.

Not only is the coherence of history dependent upon
God's promise, but the authenticity and identity of
each person also depends on that promise. Human worth,
human responsibility, human freedom - each is God's
gift. If there have been periods when Christians have
not turned to this affirmation to inform their public

life, it is because they were relying more on various philosophical systems, not because this affirmation is somehow peripheral to the Judaeo-Christian tradition.

One implication of the symbol-event "incarnation" is that we can expect important human experience to tell us something of God's relation to humanity. Paul, for example, tells us that the love of man and woman bespeaks Christ's love for the Church. (Eph. 5) Similarly the various gospel scenes depict Christ forgiving sins; these scenes are clearly meant to signify that God's loving faithfulness to his original promise entails his willingness to forgive people's sins.

Human experience and biblical literature dovetail, each reinforcing the other. Continued community is possible only if we forgive each other; and since authentic personal identity can only emerge in community, personal worth and responsibility is gift: gift of the community and gift of God. Is this affirmation in any sense transferable to our public lives?

This sense of "worth as gift" is available to any of us from childhood when our parents' affirmation was called forth more by our need than by our achievements. However, its import for our understanding of society is closed to most by the individualism which dominates our political imaginations. Individualism builds on the basic image that adults deal with each other in a market situation with self-interested calculation. It assumes that these adults were never children, were never in trouble, have never experienced affirmation as gift, have no sense of mutuality nor of interdependence.

Emerging from an analysis of reconciliation is a fundamental characteristic of the biblical image of the human: a complex vision of the person as free and responsible, whose freedom is a gift of the community. At the end of the first section, I outlined the basic image of the human which grounded two approaches to sentencing: the classical vision of man as sovereignly free and responsible; the scientific vision of patterned, predictable human behaviour, socially caused. The image which emerges from the experience of reconciliation contains in a dialectical tension the fundamental elements of the other two.

Once it is established that other persons, in

face-to-face relationships, call forth by their affirmation the responsible freedom of a person, then that statement can be widened to encompass other relationships which are not face-to-face. These relationships are not immediate; they are mediated by various institutions, whether legal, economic or social. For instance, I am related to a worker on an automobile assembly line when I buy a car both through the economic institution of the car market and through the legal institution of consumer protection laws. The relation will always be anonymous, but it could be quite real to me if his carelessness results in a breakdown or accident. I am also related to decision makers in the engineering department of the automobile firm which plans obsolescence. Not all public, anonymous relationships are unhappy; but we tend to notice them when they go sour. These relations, when functioning well, are the elements which structure our social world, a world we usually take for granted.

Because these relationships are anonymous, it is usually more instructive to focus on the public, institutional structure of the relationship rather than on the fact that there are other people who are related to me. It has meaning then, to say that, when certain institutions function as they ought, people are helped to grow towards free responsibility and that their freedom is a "gift of the community."

Correlatively, if the institutions do not serve an individual or a group well, then it makes sense to say that if one of them behaves reactively and destructively, then his behaviour is ascribable both to his exercise of freedom and to the social structures. There is meaning, I would contend, for a notion of mediated social causation. People ill served by societal institutions have fewer if any growth options open to them. Even more important, their imaginations are constricted such that they cannot recognize even those limited options which might be said to be open to them. Thus many people, while free and indeed exercising freedom, find themselves in situations where the only options really open to them are destructive options, destructive either to themselves or to others. This, to me, is the root of poverty - or, more precisely, of social injustice.

If I am correct, then an adequate response to most delinquent behaviour will have to deal not only with

233

the behaviour but with the societal context of that
behaviour. Crucial to the notion of reconciliation as
elaborated here is the necessity of both the offender
and the offended changing and moving towards each other.
Perhaps when we move the vision of reconciliation into
a public scene, the full force of "forgiveness" will
become weaker. Perhaps all that can be expected is
that the victim of crime will be willing to live within
the same community (however broadly defined) as the
criminal.[4] But what will have to be kept of the notion
of reconciliation is the sense that societal responsibility towards the delinquent might well have been
neglected, that if delinquency is to be adequately dealt
with, society itself will have to change.

There is in contemporary criminological literature a
growing sense of this need to examine society as well
as the delinquent.[5] It is still, in Taylor, Walton
and Youngs' phrase, more of a perspective than a consistent theory. (p. 159) Much of this literature
operates on an assumption (which I find unacceptable)
of social causation to the neglect of personal responsibility. The question, to be dealt with in terms of
the socio-economic system itself, of who brands deviants in whose interests, must be answered. (p. 166)
While this paper does little to satisfy the demand, I
agree with Taylor, Walton and Young when they call for
a truly social theory, informed

Not by a static conception of pathological and/or
anomic individuals colliding with a simple and taken-
for-granted set of institutional orders, but rather
by a conception of the complex interaction between
developments in institutional and social structures
and the consciousness of men living within such
structures. (p. 226-7)

This is the sort of theoretical model most congruent
with the basic image of the human evoked by taking
seriously the implications of the ideal of reconciliation.

I would like to begin my pursuit of the public
possibility of reconciliation by examining, in the
simplest and most experiential terms, the interaction
of society and deviancy.

PUNISHMENT VS RECONCILIATION IN CANADA

The Process of Criminalization: The necessity of punishment

If we are to focus on the dynamic interaction between community and crime, then we will have to begin with the rather obvious repressive reaction Canadians have to crime. MP's mail ran, for instance, about nine-to-one in favour of capital punishment during the last parliamentary debate on the subject.

One of the disabilities of rationalism is that it tends to make us deny the importance of the emotional, of the symbolic in human experience. We are often cautioned when discussing criminal justice or punishment in public, to be dispassionate despite the emotional explosiveness of the topic. At a recent forum on capital punishment the chairman so counselled us. It struck me at the time that he was quite unintentionally ruling out all real arguments for retention. Indeed, he was ruling out all real arguments. For example, that night I heard two people say important things about capital punishment. One said she was for capital punishment because in her neighborhood people would not conform to anti-litter bylaws. The other, a school principal in a poor district, said capital punishment was wrong because children came to her school with nothing for lunch but mustard sandwiches.

Nonsense? Profound sense. Each perceived crime as an undifferentiated continuum: littering and murdering do indeed have a common characteristic. They disrupt social order. They tend to produce chaos. The one woman was frightened by the impending threat and wanted us to strike out effectively. Each of us will react with fear and anger to that form of disorderly behaviour which strikes us as dangerously, actively chaotic. On the other hand, the other woman at the meeting saw the same thrust towards chaos as a chain reaction, starting not with reprehensible behaviour, but with the deprivation of children.

What is at stake here, in theoretical terms, are the benefits of social order and the need for the values of these benefits to be internalized by all. As we have developed rational means to grasp the interdependence of society, we have been able to render it at once more complex and more efficiently provident of benefits. But while there have been enormous benefits

235

derived, the intricacy of men's interdependence in modern society has demanded of us a stern discipline.

Why do people accept the discipline? Freud spoke of repression; sociologists speak of internalization. It seems to be a matter of people accepting certain core values and along with them the price they exact. There are artists at the edge of our culture who scoff at our inhibitions. Most of us, however, when we read or see something like "Zorba the Greek" though we might perhaps feel a twinge of envy, see him to be a creature of another world. In our world there are paramount values: high health standards, high nutritional standards, good schools, opportunity for travel, comfortable homes, opportunities for sports, for reading, for music. We have schooled ourselves to think of human fulfilment and human happiness as comprising these benefits. We have difficulty noticing the cost, in terms of work, discipline, foregone leisure and pleasure.

Indeed, we develop not just a tolerance for the discipline, but we erect it into a positive virtue - maturity, responsibility. Most of us most of the time doubtless think of criminal behaviour as not simply unfair to others, but as a free ride, something we were given as children, but now unworthy of us. Our self-respect as adults is largely framed in terms of steadiness, of self-reliance, of work habits, of responsibility.

Yet what are we to make of the interesting statistic, that when asked anonymously, 91% of a large random sample of North American males admitted to criminal behaviour at some time in their lives? (Becker 1975, p. 166) It would seem that internalization works for the most part, but that each of us, when confronted with the opportunity to cut a small corner, to take a short free ride, find the temptation almost impossible to resist.

Surrounding most people - at least the "good" people - are a series of networks (kin, neighbours, friends, work mates) which fulfill a double role. These networks help individuals solve problems, deal with crises. They hold out, in other words, the promise of societal benefits, but only on condition that the rules upheld by the networks are complied with. Thus there is an extremely effective shoring up of

236

internalized values by the informal networks which surround most of us.

But, shored up as they are by their informal networks, and reinforced as they are by the effective promise of societal benefits, the majority of Canadians still express fear. If the statistic cited means anything at all, then almost everyone has engaged in criminal behaviour. Perhaps many are able to rationalize their occasional lapse; many fear their own potential for further criminality. If one dwells on the negative connotations of the Freudian term, repression, then it is understandable that people would have unnamable fears about a "Zorba" mentality which has been rejected.

Reinforcing these fears, based on the repressed tendencies in the "good" people themselves, are those fears which are aroused by that segment of the population branded criminal. Without quite knowing why, people insist that if the state as the "perfect community" should give them any absolute guarantees, it should guarantee the suppression of these chaotic forces which (from without and within) threaten to engulf peaceful order and the worked-for-benefits. The scope of possible human behaviour is too wide; it becomes frightening. People insist that some possibilities be absolutely excluded.

Kai Erikson sums up this perspective on the necessity of branding certain acts as criminal and punishing the criminal:

> deviance cannot be simply seen as behaviour which disrupts stability in society, but may itself be, in controlled quantities, an important condition for preserving stability. (1964, p. 15)

It misses the point to brand this insistence on punishment as vengeance and to connote that it is somehow reprehensible. The more accurate characterization of this motive for punsihment is denunciation. Through the drama of declaring certain actions criminal and of singling out individuals who have committed those actions, the community engages in a very serious morality play through which it reminds each member of the dire consequences of chaotic behaviour and assures each that protection will continue to be afforded against those consequences.

> Morality and immorality meet at the public scaffold,
> and it is during this meeting that community declares
> where the line between them should be drawn. (Frik-
> son 1964, p. 14)

The Law Reform Commission has repeatedly affirmed this
notion: "...one of the purposes of the criminal law is
the protection of certain core values in society..."
(LRC #3, p. 33; LRC #11, p. 9) Recently the Appellate
Division of the Supreme Court of Alberta cited this
passage approvingly in affirming, at least in principle,
the fittingness of a prison sentence for a "flagitious
offence," even when rehabilitation of the offender was
out of the question.[6]

In summary, human beings, faced with the awful responsibility of managing the human project of history,
find it necessary to exclude some possibilities lest
the lurking forces of chaos become unmanageable. We
need the loose edges of our symbolic universe nailed
down.

But even if there is a human need to punish someone
in order that community life be kept stable, who is to
be punished? How can the punishment be morally justified? There is a utilitarian answer which says
that the good of the greatest number is paramount and
that the good of an individual can be sacrificed to it.
If, from the perspective of the biblical tradition, we
wish to insist on the inextinguishable rights of all
individuals, how can the question be answered?

In Canada today people accept without question that
the community at large is justified in protecting itself as it is, without significant change, and in coercing (i.e., punishing) deviants in order to remain as
it is. Two theoretic models are used to explain, to
channel and to legitimize this self-protective reaction
to crime. These two models are the retributive and the
rehabilitative models.

My intention now is to examine briefly these two
models. I shall argue that the retributive model
assumes personal freedom and responsibility; but that
its notion of freedom precinds from any social or historical context and is thereby inadequate. The

238

rehabilitative model emerged historically as a corrective, to modify and mollify the stern, abstract notion of freedom and responsibility of the retributive model; but since it was rooted in the assumptions of science, it has an inadequate notion of personal responsibility. I shall then return to the sense of freedom-within-community which emerged from the notion of reconciliation and in light of it, lay out the lines of a model of the criminal justice process.

Retribution: The legal quest to distribute punishment justly

The retributionist elevates the question of punishment from a technical problem to an ethical dilemma. He will admit that there are deeply imbedded historical and psychological sources of the impulse to punish. He insists, however, that these do not justify punishing another human being. Given that the community has the need to brand some of its members criminal for its own peaceful continuity, there is still the ethical question of distribution: whom are we to punish? (Weiler 1974, p. 138) This question can be put very rigorously. If the one singled out for punishment is punished justly, then not to punish him would be unjust. The canon of justice as established by Aristotle is such that laxity is as much an offense against it as severity. (Aristotle 1911, p. 109)

What are the conditions necessary for punishment to be just? In communities where the notion of "natural law" has obtained, there was little difficulty answering this question. Natural law theory rests on two basic assertions. The first is that human law, if just, is a reflection and derivation of cosmic order; and that this cosmic order is open to discovery by "right reason." The second assertion is that man is by nature "sociable," that is, he is dependent upon right relations within his community in order to develop his human potential, this development being his fundamental obligation to his "nature." Each person is obliged to obey just laws in order to fulfill his natural obligation to develop humanly. The state is likewise obliged to compel compliance not simply out of deference to the individuals' sociality, but because the state's laws are the mirror of the cosmic order. Not to remedy a breach of the cosmic order is a further continuing breach of that order.

239

The legal doctrine of "mens rea" is firmly rooted in the natural law tradition. A person's obligation to the cosmic order and indeed to one's own entelechy is not magical. It is mediated by the exercise of "right reason." Breaches of the cosmic order which provoke state sanction can only be those which are done knowingly and freely. It becomes therefore necessary, in order that punishment be just, that an offence be proved to have been culpable.

However, the natural law approach implies a notion of freedom which is individualistic and prescinds entirely from any social and historical context. Moral responsibility depends upon the exercise of "right reason." Right reason, in turn, discovers a universal cosmic order. This order is open to anyone of good will, no matter what his social or historical circumstances. With respect to their ability to perceive what is right, the judge, the rich man and the poor man are all equal. Herein lies the basis of the image of justice blindfolded, with neither respect nor mercy for individuals or special circumstances.

Any consensus concerning natural law has long been abandoned. Instead various "social contract" theories have sought to enlist the everyday experience of ordinary people and to build on that a case for the reasonableness of social order. But even with the shift from natural law to social contract, legal philosophers hardly break stride in their insistence upon the equal responsibility of all to comply. The social contract, being an abstraction, is imagined to have been entered into by all men. Cesare Beccaria, writing in the 18th century, is cited to say "Laws are the conditions, under which men, naturally independent, united themselves in society." (Taylor 1973, p. 1) Commenting on this doctrine, Taylor, Walton and Young remark that

> The individual is responsible for his actions and is equal, no matter what his rank, in the eyes of the law. Mitigating circumstances or excuses are therefore inadmissible. (p. 2)

They note that this view is above all a theory of social control; it is a philosophical argument to back up political authority.

Paul Weiler, arguing within the parsimonious framework

of social contract, has sought to demonstrate the possibility of just retribution. His general argument for
punishment is carefully stated:

> It is in nearly everyone's interest that nearly
> everyone comply with some such set of standards but
> in concrete situations, this may require a substantial
> sacrifice of one's private interests. There is al-
> ways a temptation to be a free rider on the sacri-
> fices that others make, especially if one can keep
> his own default secret. (Weiler 1974, p. 126)

In order to ward off this temptation some coercion is
necessary. The question then becomes, who shall be a
proper candidate for this coercion, so salutary for
"nearly everybody?" Surely "he who has deliberately
sought to advance his own interests, but only by using
another as a means to his end." (p. 142) All members
of the community start out equally immune from the
exemplary coercion essential to criminal justice.

> But the offender was given the opportunity to avoid
> that harm, and yet he took the risk in order to ob-
> tain an extra advantage at the expense of someone
> else. Can he complain of an arbitrary denial of his
> rights when society now decides to use him as the
> means to the protection of the ends of others? Surely
> not! By his own choice he has singled himself out as
> the proper candidate for the distribution of punish-
> ment. (p. 142)

While the metaphysical superstructure of the natural
law has been abandoned, the logical structure of the
argument is the same. Instead of a cosmic order to be
protected, the state now is obliged to protect the
interests of "nearly everybody."

Similarly, Weiler's argument hinges on "mens rea."
Legitimate interests are to be protected by various
forms of sanction. Weiler is careful to single out one
of these, punishment, inflicted appropriately on the
one who "by his own choice" has sought an unfair advantage.

Having so defined punishment, Weiler again must ask
how it can be justified. He says clearly that the
criminal's choice to take advantage of the law-abiding
forebearance of others is the only basis for justly

punishing him. (p. 160) Consistently, Weiler argues
that criminals are predominantly "normal" individuals
who, "as other citizens, are responsible for their
actions." (p. 163-64) But his notion of freedom and
responsibility is individualistic, with an inadequate
notion of community context.

I have suggested that, while Weiler has abandoned
the metaphysical superstructure of the natural law
argument, the logical structure of his argument is the
same. He must therefore argue for an absolutely equal
responsibility before the law. But will this hold?
On the natural law view, equality depended upon the
openness of everyone's right reason to a universal
cosmic order. Within the parameters of a social contract model, which Weiler has turned to, equality will
depend upon the openness of everyone to perceiving the
benefits which accrue to "very nearly everybody" when
"very nearly everybody" complies with the law. If it
could be empirically established that those who are
punished (i.e., by and large, those who are imprisoned)
are the very ones in our society who are the "very few"
not included among the "very nearly everybody" who will
benefit from compliance, then there would be no reason
to conclude that they are culpable. When they read
their social situation accurately, they can only conclude that the societal benefits which come with compliance will be withheld from them. Their criminal
behaviour might well be free; but not necessarily
culpable.

Let me put this another way. In order to legitimate
punishment, the judge, the law and the majority assume
that the accused is "like me," that his use of intelligence and freedom have given rise to the same moral
demands in a given situation that would bind me in a
like situation. I am arguing that this cannot be
assumed, but needs to be demonstrated empirically. I
shall argue that empirical evidence makes it likely
that the opposite is the case.

Before I present this empirical evidence, I shall
break off to examine another reaction to the difficulty
just posed. People long ago noticed that the assumption that the criminal is "like me" was questionable.
Their conclusion was that the criminal is not "like
me," that he is pathological, unfree. Latterly, as
the notion of social causation has been invoked, the

criminal is again seen as not "like me," but as deprived, lacking life skills which are essential to the exercise of responsible freedom.

Rehabilitation: The scientific quest to reduce crime

Reduction of crime is, I would suggest, the goal most Canadians would automatically assume to be the main purpose of the criminal process. When, as Solicitor-General, Warren Allmand argued for reforms exclusively on this narrow base, I would suspect that he felt this was the one goal most Canadians accepted as valid.

While "reduction of crime" can be understood to allude to educational or ethical processes, its usage in contemporary public discussion bespeaks a "scientific" approach to the problem.

There are two strategies to reduce crime, deterrence and rehabilitation. Deterrence, the attempt to reduce the further incidence of crime in the general population by dealing appropriately with a criminal, is usually interpreted in strictly statistical terms. By contrast, rehabilitation seems to have been understood in ethical terms.

The Enlightenment invented prisons....Opponents of the indiscriminate death penalty, or torture, or mutilation, or public humiliation, had to answer the question what will you do with criminals? The answer: break men's ties with a criminal society, return them to reflective solitude, and let the affections, twisted under the pressures of a corrupt society, spring back to their natural shape. Put in a cell that suggested the pre-social state, they would emerge new Emiles, ready to sign the social contract and make a better world. (Wills 1975, p. 3)

This ethical understanding is no longer current. Rehabilitation is now understood within a scientific framework. It is assumed that human behaviour is patterned, predictable, controllable. Rehabilitation is primarily a behavioural term: there are no subsequent incidences of criminality. (LRC #3, p. 4) To make such a prediction is possible only with a scientific theory enabling diagnosis and treatment. The assumption, then, is that crime is "primarily the result of personality defect or disorder within the

offender." Thus "'treatment' has replaced penal discipline in our rhetoric." (Outerbridge 1974, p. 10) This
understanding of crime has been dubbed by its critics
the "disease model" of crime.

While the invocation of scientific method in dealing
with criminals has led to a sense of certainty, that
certainty is, unfortunately, false. The approach has
not worked.

> ...there is evidence to suggest that efforts to deal
> with offenders as sick persons is likely to further
> their criminality rather than reduce it. (Hogarth
> 1974, p. 61)

Rehabilitation has been unworkable because of the
contradiction involved in overlaying the perspective of
treatment on an essentially punitive system, thus
making it much more likely to be unjust. At its
limit, a scientific understanding of crime, with the
prognosis and prevention of crime as its goal, would
discard personal freedom as irrelevant to the model.
If the prevention of future criminality is really the
goal, it even becomes irrelevant to ask whether a
person has already perpetrated a crime. "It seems
illogical to act to prevent the second offense
and not the first." (Weiler 1974, p. 188)

Prevention of crime would, if we took this scientific
view to its limit, be identified with the thorough
application of police technique; and these methods
would entail a totalitarianism rejected by most. Thus
what tends to happen is that the language of the scientific approach (with its goal of rehabilitation and
its methods of treatment) is overlaid on the institutional reality of punishment.

Institutions which might be justified if understood
strictly as instruments of punishment - and regulated
as such - are now understood also to be treatment
centers. But because people there are incarcerated
against their will, because they are then subjected to
a rigorous and pervasive discipline, there is little
reason to believe that the "treatment" will be effective. William Outerbridge, chairman of the National
Parole Board, has made this point effectively.

By being placed in a situation that attacks the very

244

basis of his identity as an adult - a situation of
enforced dependency on the non-negotiable authority
of others - the offender is left with only three
possible avenues of redress: 1) he can accept the
new definition of himself as dependent and behave
accordingly; 2) he can try to find ways of manipula-
ting those with power; or 3) he can give vent to his
sense of rage and strike out in violence. (p. 11)

Outerbridge is insisting that we come to terms with the
inmate as a human person who must in one way or another
grapple with the issue of his personal integrity. He
is insisting, in other words, that the enforced relationship between the inmate and authorities becomes an
ethical issue for both the inmate and for us, in whose
name the authorities act.

The injustice which stems from overlaying the rehabilitative model on punitive measures becomes even
starker when we consider the enforced relationship
among inmates.

Prisons teach crime, instill it, inure men to it,
trap men in it as a way of life. How could they do
otherwise? The criminal is sequestered with other
criminals, in conditions exacerbating the lowest
drives of lonely and stranded men, men deprived of
loved ones, of dignifying work, of pacifying ameni-
ties....his own safety depends upon joining the
criminal element against others. And what respect
can he learn for the law when his overseers condone
such acts and inflict further ones?" (Wills 1975,
p. 8)

Those who have experienced our penal system as inmates are also in a position to make these same observations, these same judgements. If destructive
behaviour results, issuing from anger, we need not
tag it either as socially caused or as pathological.
It can be construed as free action for which the agent
is responsible. But this, in turn, does not mean that
a punitive response by the community is adequate. It
is possible that the community could itself recognize
within the social context of the criminal behaviour
its own failed responsibilities and move toward meeting those responsibilities.

If the vision I am trying to build in this paper,

namely of "freedom as gift of the community," is valid,
then the community's failed responsibilities are crucial
to an adequate understanding of crime and how to deal
with it. But on this point, the rehabilitative model
fails utterly. The social theory behind the rehabilitative model, which purports to legitimate coercing
inmates into treatment, supposes a beneficent, humanizing social norm. It assumes that the individual use
of intelligence is simply instrumental, simply a means
to cope with life's problems such that society's norms
are attained. There is no critical questioning of
those norms. (Taylor 1973, p. 89 - 89 p. 104 - 105)
For this reason, there is, within the parameters of the
model, no possibility of the community (through public
or private agency) recognizing structural failures of
its own and moving to meet the needs of the criminal.
In this sense, the rehabilitative model excludes the
possibility of institutionalizing reconciliation.

The Social Reality of Punishment: The need for reconciliation

I have raised the theoretical possibility that,
within a view of crime as free human action, there is
room for a notion of mediated social causation, or a
contextualism. Edwin Schur has spoken of the "enormity" of social conditions such that for some the
criminal choice is "almost rationale." (Schur 1969,
p. 64)

Ironically, the conception of the nature of individual wrongdoing central to at least some religious
thought - with its characteristic emphasis on man's
freedom of moral choice and personal blameworthiness
for the commission of 'immoral' acts - may sometimes
be used to buttress the views of those who refuse to
recognize that some men are more free than others,
and who are unwilling to admit the power of social
forces in shaping patterns of crime. (Schur 1969, p.
85)

In this section, I wish to raise the empirical question of the need in Canada for reconciliation, for the
community moving to recognize its responsibilities to
all its members.[7]

In Weiler's terms, I propose to ask who are the "very

nearly everybody" who benefit from compliance with the
law, and who it is who make the qualifier "very nearly"
necessary. If there is in Canada an identifiable group
who are not among those who make decisions on the basis
of their hope to reap normal societal benefits for
compliance with law, but rather on the basis of their
despair of ever enjoying their normal share, then their
exercise of rational freedom will be on different terms
than that of normal people. If that same group can be
identified as largely those who are punished through
the criminal justice system, then it might be said that
while Weiler has built a sound theoretical case for
the possibility of just retribution, the conditions set
forth in his argument are not met in Canada.

There are several ways to try to discover if such a
group exists in Canada: I could undertake a structural
analysis of the Canadian society and economy; I could
examine the Criminal Code for bias; I could ask about
those "inflictions of serious harm on another and
innocent person," such as industrial pollution or lack
of safety in mines, which are not in the Code. I shall
content myself with focussing on the application of the
Criminal Code, for as John Hogarth has said:

Since we are all 'criminals' as far as our habitual
and routine activity is concerned, it becomes necessary to create a 'second code' which determines how
the 'game' of law enforcement will be played. This
second code consists of all the hidden rules which
determine the exercise of discretion in the enforcement of law.

...Thus, we can seem to eat our cake and have it too.
We can on the one hand believe in the power of the
state to deal with perceived threats in our environment through the uniform application of law, and on
the other hand see to it in its daily application
that it does not interfere with or jeopardize important interests. (1974, p. 50-51)

An American criminologist has said much the same
thing even more starkly:

The morality which is enforced against the poorer
people to preserve a system which benefits the
wealthy is never equally applied against the wealthy
to protect the interests of the poor.[8]

247

The research papers published by the LRC and carried
out within a framework conceived by Hogarth have studied the screening activities of the police. While
they have noted the important influence of various
institutional concerns of the police, they also note
that screening reflects rather accurately the prevailing norms of the community.(Stace 1975, p. 107) No
policeman wants to "stick his neck out."

So there is a funneling of crime. Not all the times
a policeman is called in will be officially reported;
not all the reported occurrences will result in a formal
charge; not all charges will come to court; not all
court cases lead to conviction; not all convicted are
punished; not all those punished are imprisoned. In
their study of the Toronto Police Force, the research
team of the LRC concluded that "of the total number of
occurrences reported to the police as criminal events...
a mere 2.4% were appropriated by the correction systems." (Becker 1975, p. 165; p. 25) If, in the context
of whose interests are being protected against whom,
we are to examine application of the criminal code,
then we must ask against whom is the worst punishment
invoked, namely imprisonment. Those of us who are
middle-aged, middle of the road, fairly well established
are, to put it mildly, underrepresented...if 91% of us
have engaged in criminal behaviour.

Those going to prison are young. For those entering
prison from 1971 through 1973, only 10% were entering
for the first time over 25 years old.[9]

Do those entering prison come from poverty? There
is no clear, convincing answer to that. There are,
however, indications. One of the clearest is the level
of education attained by those entering prison. Most
studies of poverty point to a high statistical correla-
tion between low education attainment and poverty.
Most accounts see an interaction between the two:
poverty is not only caused by lack of education and con-
sequent lack of marketable skills; but poverty leads
(through poorer health, a variety of "learning disabilities," lack of money, less parental guidance, etc.)
to limited educational horizons in lower class youth.

Table 1 compares the educational levels of the males
entering Canadian prisons in 1971 with the educational
levels of the Canadian male population not full time in

TABLE 1

Number of males attaining level of school as % of
total population: Canadian males not attending school
full time and males entering Canadian prisons* 1971

	Prison	Cumul-ative	Canada	Cumul-ative
Illiterate	0.8	0.8	3.4	3.4
Kindergarten	--	0.8	0.7	4.1
Grade 1	0.3	1.1	0.7	4.8
2	0.6	1.7	1.0	5.8
3	1.1	2.8	2.0	7.8
4	2.9	5.7	3.2	11.0
5	4.4	10.1	4.0	15.0
6	7.7	17.8	5.3	20.3
7	11.6	29.4	7.2	27.5
8	20.6	50.0	14.3	41.8
9	16.7	66.7	9.9	51.7
10	17.7	84.4	11.5	63.2
11	7.2	91.6	9.2	72.4
12	5.7	97.3	12.4	84.8
13	0.6	97.9	3.8	88.6
University				
1 year			2.0	90.6
2 years			1.6	92.2
3 years	1.9		1.5	93.7
4 years			2.5	96.2
5 years			1.5	97.7
6+ years			2.3	

Source: Correctional Institution Statistics, #85-207,
1971, Table 12.
Advance Bulletin 1971 Census, #92-764, Table 1.

*Not counting 289 who did not declare educational
attainment.

249

school in 1971. The figures show that those sent to
prison in that year were significantly less educated
than the general population. Those entering prison had
had an average (mean) of 7.75 years of school (not including kindergarten). The Canadian average for males
was almost exactly Grade 9 (8.99 years not counting
kindergarten). The chances are less than one in a
thousand that this difference of 1¼ years is random;
that is, prisons draw from a special, less-than-average
educated population.

The cumulative totals bring out the differences perhaps more starkly. There we find that fully one-half
of the men entering prison have had no high school,
while only 41.8% of all Canadian men have had no high
school. This means that there are proportionately one-
quarter more men entering prison without any high
school than there are in the general population.

It might be noted that those with less than Grade 5,
by contrast, are underrepresented in prison. While it
is difficult to estimate exactly, there is no doubt
that a sizeable proportion of those in the general
population with so little schooling fall under the
general rubric of retardation. Our society tends to
institutionalize such people elsewhere than in prison.
These considerations point to the fact that our
figures probably underestimate how seriously those
without any high school are overrepresented in prison.

Chart 1 is meant to show how bunched the prison population is with respect to schooling. Fully 40% of the
men entering prison had between Grade 6 and Grade 8;
75% had between Grade 6 and Grade 10.

On the other hand, those entering prison with more
than high school - some university - were less than 2%,
while over 11% of all Canadian males have had some
university.

Lack of education, it is generally assumed, leads to
lack of job opportunities. Of the males entering
prison from 1971 through 1973, 69.3% had been unemployed.[10] Not even Newfoundland can match those figures.

The Law Reform Commission summarizes that

...one of the most disturbing criticisms about sentencing and dispositions is that they tend to fall

CHART I

Educational Attainment of Males Entering
Canadian Prisons And of all Canadian Males
Not Full Time in School

1971

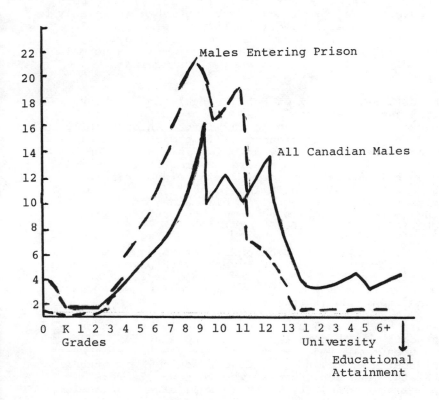

Source: Table 1

251

heaviest on the young, the poor, the powerless and the unskilled. (#3, p. 7-8)

It might be that some will wish to conclude that the drifters end up in jail where they belong. But this conclusion can only be drawn from the data if one's basic image of human freedom is individualistic; if one's basic image of our society is that each member receives basically the same opportunities for development and for responsible choice, then those conclusions will naturally follow. But another reading is possible: that our society affords some people much more scope for development than others; that those who are punished economically for having (typically) been born into poverty are more likely to be punished judicially as well. On this view, criminality is simply the formal, culminating label branding a person already labeled from childhood. It is a label which a normal middle-of-the-road Canadian will almost certainly escape.

The National Council of Welfare published a study in 1975 entitled "Poor Kids". One of the questions they raise is whether the social forces which a child raised in poverty experiences will lead to criminality. Earlier, I defined poverty as being in a situation where the only options open are destructive. The Welfare Council seems to agree. "Being a poor kid is either being helpless or being tough." (p. 29) To be helpless is to be personally debilitated; to be tough, as they mean it here, is to come into conflict with the law.

They also discuss discretionary screening, noting that courts prefer to place juveniles on probation than to institutionalize them. They cite Ontario as an example where in 1973 only 25% of juveniles were institutionalized. But which 25%?

Almost half...were placed under Section 8...which authorizes such placements where no statutory offence has been committed. What then was the basis on which the courts exercised this discretion? If it wasn't what they had done, was it who they were? This appalling possibility may very well have been the case, because a study of training schools in Ontario has found an incredible 92% of those committed... were from low-income or working-class families. (p. 32)11

These statistics are understandable. The obvious place
to spend a probationary period is in a family which is
relatively stable and coping. If that is lacking - as
it so often is among the poor - what other choice does
the court have? But it is, then, little wonder that so
few of the prison population arrive there for the first
time after the age of 25.

Perhaps one of the most startling statistics about
our prison population is its racial composition. Race
is, as viewed here, among the handiest ways of labeling
people deviant everyday. The racial group singled out
for special treatment in Canada are the native Indians
and Métis.

A disproportionate number of Native persons in Canada
are being convicted of offences and sent to jail. In
British Columbia the proportion of admissions of Native offenders to provincial institutions in recent
years has ranged from 14% to 21%; in Alberta, from 23% to
34%; in Saskatchewan from 50% to 60%; and in Manitoba,
from 40% to 50%; even though the Native population is
approximately 5% in British Columbia and Alberta, and
12½% in Saskatchewan and Manitoba. The proportion of
Native offenders in the Saskatchewan Penitentiary is
approximately 30%. (Schmeiser 1974, p. 81)

This study goes on to say that the Natives are jailed
for less serious offences than the whites; the offences
are usually related to alcohol.

Perhaps at this point my argument is worth summariz-
ing. From the ideal of reconciliation we derived a
basic image of human freedom wherein personal responsibility is seen dialectically as a gift of the community.
Opposed to this vision is the abstract, individualistic
image of freedom contained in the doctrine of "mens
rea" essential to the classical legal model.

The communitarian image of responsibility led me to
ask, in Weiler's terms, who it is who are punished in
order that "very nearly everybody" might continue to
regard compliance with the law as a reasonable alternative, with adequate and proportionate societal rewards.
For if the responsible exercise of freedom is to be
legitimately equated with compliance to law, the community ought to have proffered the individual at least
that affirmation of his worth which comes with the

perceptible promise of societal rewards for compliance.
An examination of the prison population leads to the
probable conclusion that it is largely drawn from the
young, shabby, ill educated, often alcoholic, unemployed
or unemployable already stigmatized poor. Criminality
can be viewed as a culminating stigma almost always
labeling those already stigmatized as deviant. Criminality, on this view, only serves to reinforce the
rather generally held opinion that the other labels
were also "their fault."

The freedom implied in "mens rea" assumes the basic
image of a recipient of societal benefits such as education, life and social skills, physical and social
mobility, familial stability, who when given the chance
wants even more, at the unknowing expense of the rest of
us who (at least on this occasion) are law-abiding.
Perhaps the picture so sketchily painted above will
begin to undercut this doctrine of "mens rea" of the
individual who, quite independent of his past, makes
clear, rational choices in each situation whether he
will play according to the rules.

To many, the rules are not clear. And if they are
clear, they hold no promise of societal benefit. There
is a strong likelihood that those presently in our
jails were never among the "nearly everybody" who benefit when nearly everybody complies to the rules. (Mac-
Pherson 1962, p. 98) If they acted freely and ration-
ally, then it was probably not with a freedom we have
experienced, nor according to the rules of our rationality. (Wright 1973, p. 4 - 18)

The quest to distribute punishment justly, is laud-
able; but it would be my contention that it is a never-
ending quest. Retributive justice cannot be fully
satisfied unless we work towards meeting the demands
of distributive justice. Put another way, the classical legal model, with its canon of justice, cannot by
itself justify punishment. The quest for justice leads
to the need for reconciliation.

Diversion: Institutionalizing reconciliation

The statement that retributive justice depends
finally on distributive justice is often taken to mean
that the victim of crime, if he has enjoyed a better
socio-economic status than the criminal, ought to take

254

responsibility for the crime because he has been party
to a prior and wider crime. I think the matter is more
complex than this. If a person - in this case our
hypothetical criminal - is truly a victim of social
injustice, then, as I have already repeated, by definition the various options open to him will all be more
or less destructive and alienating. If from among his
options he chooses theft, that choice is no less destructive because the perpetrator feels constrained by
his circumstances. Even if a crime is an expression
of anger against an unjust system, it is not fair that
one person should be selected to repay the debt, so to
speak. Thus, even if the victim might in a quieter
time be willing to discuss the injustices of the system,
he will not usually be willing to admit that the theft
was, for some historical and complex reason, his fault.

But as it is, our society is far from that course of
action. The criminal justice process has been so set
up that there is no possibility of raising the question
whether society itself should be changed in ways which
would reduce crime. (Wright 1973, p. 160 no. 10) It
might be that within the ranks of those who make the
process work questions about social justice are raised.
But to the extent that the institutions involved in
criminal justice are public and educational; to the
extent that they provide a window for the community
onto crime, the criminal and how the community could
respond to these problems; to the extent that these
institutions are in the broadest sense political, they
tend to bury the dynamic labeling process in which (I
would contend) they are engaged and thereby bury the
political possibility of reconciliation.

Both the police and the courts contribute. They do
it largely by contributing to - or at least not questioning publicly - the dominant stereotype of the
criminal as the "dangerous lurking stranger." Since
the formulation of and reaction to criminality is a
political decision, that decision needs public support.
The basis of that support comes from the diffusion of
emotionally charged and rather well defined stereotypes of criminals, which I would call "basic images."
(Quinney 1970, p. 26, 283)

These stereotypes "exclude us from any real understanding of the situation." (Mohr 1975, p. 61)

The East York study (of diversion) found a marked
attitudinal differential between victims and non-
victims. Although conventional wisdom might suggest
that those having personal experience as victims of
criminal activity would be more inclined to a rigid
attitude to crime, this proved not to be the case.
In fact, victims were generally less harsh in their
judgment of the criminal process, more sympathetic
to offenders and generally less impressed with the
concept of retribution as a rationale for criminal
punishment." (Hogarth 1975, p. 9)

Experience will not support the stereotype. If the
East York research is generalizable, then the typical
criminal is "a neighborhood child or some similarly
manageable, essentially harmless individual." (Hogarth
1975, p. 10)

The empirical research reported in Studies on Diversion can be seen as largely backing up that statement.
They view the criminal law and its enforcement as part
of a total social defense system, designed to help
people cope with trouble. Informal networks of relatives, neighbours, friends and people at work are
people's first line of defense. Usually these networks, especially those of the poor, who even together
find it hard to cope, need some more formal and
professional support at times. The police, highly
visible and available round the clock, are one of the
support systems people turn to help them manage conflict. In fact, it is said that the police, by their
availability, take on the responsibilities which
should properly be handled by many other agencies.
(Hogarth 1975, p. 10-14)

The study suggests, more concretely, that people who
are experiencing a crisis in their relationship, who
are trying to renegotiate or terminate the relationship, turn to the police as part of their strategy.
The police, with their own institutional concerns and
their own "rules of the game" often impose their
particular set of definitions on the situation. If
the police isolate some event which has happened in the
course of people's sorting out their relationship (e.g.
a punch in the eye, a broken window, a car taken for a
joy ride), call the event a crime, ask only those
questions about the event which are deemed relevant in
a court of law, then they have distorted the meaning

of that event.12 This distortion precludes a satisfactory resolution of the original conflict, that is, it
precludes reconciliation. It also contributes to the
frightening stereotype of the criminal. Does this
happen often? The research team typed criminal offenses
along a continuum depending on whether they occurred
between "strangers," "commercial acquaintances," "other
friends and relatives," "neighbours" or "family." They
found that only 15.1% of offences against the person
occurred against strangers. Fifty-seven percent of
crimes against property were committed against strangers.
Slightly less than half of these two categories (46.8%)
were committed against total strangers. (Becker 1975, p.
175 - 191)

These statistics are significant for our question.
We have seen that those who enter prison are young,
ill-educated, unemployed for the most part - in short,
they are poor. We have seen that the juvenile courts
tend, in their discretionary use of sentencing, to
institutionalize the poorer juveniles. Now we find
that the police have very wide discretionary powers
when deciding to charge or not; and that these decisions
are often made within the context of crisis management
when informal networks have proven ineffective. It is
not to condemn the police to conclude that given what
they are asked to do, and given the limited methods at
their disposal, they will tend to lay charges against
those who are ill equipped to cope with crisis. (LeBlanc
1975, p. 104)

The picture can be seen from two sides. On the one
hand, the original problems which led to the invocation
of the law are distorted and badly handled by the law.
Because of this aspect of the picture, reconciliation
between "victim" and "offender," often crucial to both
of them, is precluded because the law insists on dealing with their problem not for their best interests,
but in accord with its own institutional interest.
This is Hogarth's point, and it is well taken.

But the mis-typification of so many criminal events
also leads to the disporportionate suffering of the
poor at the hands of the law. Crucial to my argument
is this: what stands between the suffering of the
poor and the general public are the stereotypes which
preclude public understanding of what really is happening. These stereotypes set up a vicious circle. The

257

frightening image of the dangerous lurking stranger leads people to call for police protection. This insistence that the problem be dealt with by specialized professionals means that the public have no other access to the events than through the stereotypes.

It is true that criminal behaviour tends to degrade and depersonalize the victim. But our societal reaction to what gets typified as criminal behaviour is such that the criminal is also thoroughly degraded and depersonalized. It is true that he is haled in to court to answer, hence is, in one abstract sense, treated as responsible. But he is stripped of his history, even of the immediate history which led to the event. He becomes for the rest of us one more addition to the stereotype, one more reassurance that "our kind" will receive the protection we demand and that our universe will be nailed down along its frayed edges.

We have developed a society which, to diffuse the moral outrage inherent in its inequality, labels the victims lawless, dangerous. In actual fact, police practice so protects the well-to-do that the criminal activity of the poor is channeled against other poor. But that does not affect the stereotype. We demand that the barbaric edge of our society - namely its structural inequalities - be softened. To do this we hire police to keep the poor in line and to select, largely from among them, those who will be labeled criminal. Little wonder that the ultimate punishment is sequestration in prison, since the process is from its origins one of exclusion.

Hogarth has indicated some ill effects of the professionalization of the criminal justice process. (1974, p. 49 - 53) To his list, I should like to add that professionalization contributes to the continued strength of the stereotype. If the community, through private and volunteer organizations, were to be more actively and responsibly involved in the tensions and crises that so often generate what gets labeled criminal, the stereotypes would have to yield to a richer experience.

Diversion is essentially a deprofessionalization of the management of crisis such that criminalization is often averted. As the LRC says,

Only where community organizations, institutions, families, or individuals deal with trouble privately, is there truly diversion 'from' the criminal justice process. (LRC #7, p. 4)

In what sense is this an institutionalization of the ideal reconciliation? It will mean that smaller units of society, which usually contain or comprise the informal trouble-shooting networks, will have to recognize their responsibilities and inadequacies. We began by suggesting that reconciliation implies that not only the offender must show change, but that the victim must come to a new understanding of the offense, of the offender, of himself and of the relation between himself and the offender. At every level of diversion, persons, as part of neighborhoods, would need to face their own short-comings as a community when the labeling process is invoked.

If diversion implies deprofessionalization, then it also implies strengthening the urban neighbourhood. (LRC #7, p. 5-14) The rational models of modern tech-nical civilization, grasped and implemented by profess-ionals, have fostered a rapid urbanization of Canada along with other western countries. But the basic image of the self-reliant husbandman or small artisan remains the ethical ideal. It is, then, little wonder that our cities have become "citadels of loneliness" where isolated people and isolated nuclear families cannot cope with stress and trouble. Into this social scene, the neighbourhood network of several hundred families would be a crucial addition.

Informal diversion has always been available to the more affluent and influential. Criminalization is largely a problem of the poor. Thus the urban neigh-bourhoods most in need of diversion programs are those whose human resources are strained by the problems of survival, whose abilities to manage crises are somewhat threadbare. Yet, precisely because "trouble with the law" is so acute a problem, poor people see diversion as an opportunity to organize from among their own num-bers the creative human resources to deal with trouble. When given a chance, diversion programs work. (Ortego 1977)

Conclusion

I should like to summarize my argument, and to assess
the practicability of some conclusions.

The biblical tradition holds reconciliation up as an
ideal. I have tried to show that this ideal, when
examined, implies persons who are free, responsible,
but whose freedom is, dialectically, a gift of the
community. Correlatively, deviancy must be understood
as - at least possibly - the result of a free choice
for which a person is held responsible; but at the same
time this choice can be the response to a societal process of exclusion, of deprivation, of labeling. Thus,
not all deviant behaviour is to be understood as the
punishable rejection of humanizing social norms.

It is possible to embody reconciliation in public
institutions? Yes, but only if we begin to work our
collective way past the individualistic image of human
freedom which now stunts our political imaginations.
This individualistic image can inform either a classical
legal retributive model of punishment or a scientific
model of rehabilitative correction. Neither of these
legitimating models of society's reaction to crime will
allow room for a criticism of the social structures in
the context of which a person chooses delinquency.
Neither has room to institutionalize reconciliation.

There may be, as I have suggested, an emerging theoretical theory of deviance which might find room for
the ideal of reconciliation; what likelihood, though,
is there of this ideal being incorporated into Canadian
public institutions? I should like to pursue this
question by reflecting on the implications of the two
dialectic poles of our vision of freedom-as-gift-of-
community as it emerges from the experience of reconciliation.

Criminal behaviour must, from this point of view, be
seen as - at least possibly - a free choice. To keep,
within our scheme of social reality, a place for the
freedom of the criminal is to keep a place for evil.
This means one cannot fudge the notion of criminality
by ascribing it always to pathology or deprivation. In
this light, diversion programs need further scrutiny:
can there be a process wherein the guilt of a person is
proclaimed and then there is a process of reconciliation?
Most diversion programs are geared for juveniles where

260

the question of real culpability is not yet pertinent;
the more important question at that point in a person's
life is whether the community can more effectively foster responsibility.

But while the question of human evil is difficult to
face, we can at least say that if criminality were seen
by the community under the rubric of human freedom, our
penitentiary system would certainly change. If, as we
have seen, the criminal is understood to be a free
adult, then our present system cannot be expected to
bring about changes in him.

At his trial, we insist, in finding the criminal
guilty, that he is "like us," that he has acted with
the same kind of freedom that we experience, that in a
like situation we would freely have chosen another
course. But in punishing him, we tend to treat him as
"not like us," as some kind of depraved animal-like
creature who will respond to sequestration and rigid
regulation. The question, in light of our punishment
of him, becomes: do we really see the criminal as "like
us," or do we see him as a caricature of our worst fears
of what we would do if not disciplined? Are we willing
to face the potential evil in ourselves and thus be able
to recognize the evil in the criminal and then be reconciled to him?

To assess the likelihood of this happening, we need
to examine what it is which impels us to brand the
criminal, what is it in criminal behaviour which we
spot to be potentially chaotic, especially when done by
those who, in our society, become branded as criminals.
This leads us to the other dialectic pole: to freedom
as communitarian gift, to crime as socially generated.

For crime to be understood as both free human choice
and socially generated, a social theory is needed which
can show society to be that which structures interpersonal communication. Even in our private lives this is
true (most obviously by language) even when it is not
so noticeable. But the structured societal mediation
of less personal relationships usually fills the horizon. More concretely, criminals and respectable citizens view each other through distortive stereotypes.
They are strangers to each other; they are utterly un-
familiar with the topography of the others' view of
themselves; they also have no reality check for their

own view of the others.

The straights see the criminals as dangerous, as ready to violate person, privacy and property rightfully owned. Their reaction is to want them neutralized, locked up - if not punished. They understand them as alien, as "not like us," whose values are inimical to stable social order; they think of them as "animals" who must be contained.

The criminal on the other hand often sees the straights as people who have been successful in their theft, who are "no better than I am" but who got away with it. He often harbors resentment at his treatment, especially the poverty of childhood and feels those "rich bitches" deserve to be ripped off.

Both stereotypes contain a small grain of truth; both are predominantly distortive. My view is that social reality, for better or worse, is fixed by such stereotypes which structure the public relationships among people. Political processes are methods to decide whose stereotype will effectively determine public situations. "Power," in other words, is the "ability to enforce one's claims....the powerful have the Procrustean ability to mould morality." (Gouldner 1970, p. 297)

To delineate the source of power in our society today; to determine why it is that the powerful define and enforce the kind of morality they do today - these questions are well beyond the scope of this paper. But they serve to raise the ethical question concerning the responsible use of power we have raised with respect to the criminal justice process: are those who are convicted and punished by prison in Canada today legitimately and justly punished? It further raises the practical question whether those with the power to determine these matters would be willing to see the processes and outcomes changed. Or, more concretely, what circumstances will have to be brought about in order that they would entertain real changes?

Who are those with power? In this case, they are not simply those who hatch plots in corporate boardrooms. They are ordinary, average Canadians who, for instance, write to their M.P.'s about capital punishment. What is the source of our power and what is it we wish protected? I have tried to answer these questions only indirectly, since they entail a full scale analysis of

Canadian society. But I have suggested, and brought forward some data to support the suggestion, that the majority of Canadians are on balance the beneficiaries of the economic inequalities both within Canada and in the world. The overwhelming majority of those imprisoned in Canada are not on balance beneficiaries of that same set of economic inequalities. Crucial to legitimating those inequalities is the vision dubbed by C.B. MacPherson as "possessive individualism." This vision also informs our notion of crime. We have found a way to legitimate our system of retributive justice without having to open up the question of distributive justice. Seen from this point of view, there is little likelihood of any change; little likelihood of reconciliation informing our public life.

Is it likely that Canadian society will institutionalize reconciliation as the goal of our criminal justice system? My pessimism is based not on a jaundiced assessment of the good will of Canadians, but on the inability of possessive individualism to encompass reconciliation as a goal. It is a statement not of individual ethics, but of social ethics.

If, however, our political heritage is at odds with the Judaeo-Christian ideal of reconciliation, this does not mean there is no hope. It only means that those who profess the validity of the Judaeo-Christian tradition have yet another reason to feel a tension between their being believers and their being Canadians. Once that tension is faced squarely, once the Churches begin to explicate the social, political and economic implications of their tradition, then people might understand that a call for reconciliation in criminal justice is not simply quixotic, but contains the seeds of fuller human development - indeed of liberation - for those who feel they benefit from our systematic individualism, but who, in the last analysis pay a terrible price for the benefits our society proffers.

1. I am sketching here (and throughout this essay) the
   beginning of a phenomenological view of man as both
   ethical and social. Alfred Schutz' works are basic
   to this perspective. A work which focussed on the
   implications of this philosophical perspective for
   the problem of institutionalization is P. Berger
   and T. Luckmann, The Social Construction of Reality
   (1966). A rather one-sided articulation of the
   implications for criminology is Richard Quinney,
   The Social Reality of Crime (1970). The same vein
   is mined for its social ethical implications in
   Gibson Winter, Elements for a Social Ethic (1968).
   Many scholars are now pursuing the political and
   social implications of a critical phenomenology,
   especially in the pages of journals such as Cultural
   Hermeneutics, Politics and Society and Telos.

2. It has often been contended that this popular use
   of religious tradition distorts the true, deep
   meaning of the tradition. But confer Robert Bellah,
   "Civil Religion in America" Beyond Belief, New
   York, Harper & Row, 1970, pp. 168-189 and his more
   recent Broken Covenant, Seabury, 1975.

3. Sam Keen, a theologian, turns to Erik Erikson, a
   leading psychiatrist writing in Identity and the
   Life Cycle to bring out the convergence of experience and biblical literature:

   "Each of us is redeemed from shallow and hostile
   life only by the sacrificial love and civility
   we have graciously received."

   Cf. Keen, To a Dancing God. New York, Harper and
   Row, 1970, p. 101.

4. This is itself important and recognized by the law
   outside the criminal field. The value of people
   getting along together is prized more highly than
   a pure ideal justice. For instance, the practice
   is to get people to settle out of court in civil
   matters. In criminal matters, however, society
   will never "settle"; it is always right and righteous. The next section will be pursuing why this
   is so.

5. Some of the names associated with this approach

are Howard Becker, Edwin Lemert, Kai Erikson and
Edwin Schur. Richard Quinney and others who define
crime in terms of basic conflict within society
would, from the perspective of this paper, fit under
this rubric.

6. R.vs. Wood. Appeal no. 10188 Supreme Court of
    Alberta 1975, p. 9.

7. For a fuller articulation of this argument, cf.
    Kerans (1977).

8. Joseph P. Fitzpatrick, S.J., "The Role of Religion
    in Programs for the Prevention and Correction of
    Crime and Delinquency." cited in Schur, Our Criminal
    Society, p. 85.

9. Of 12,704 males entering Canadian prisons, 1971-
    1973, only 1319 entered for the first time after
    they were 25 years of age. Cf. Table 11, Correc-
    tional Institution Statistics. #85-207. Ottawa,

10. Ibid. Table 31. Of 12,704 males entering prisons,
     1971-1973, 8,804 had been unemployed prior to in-
     carceration.

11. Cf. also Reynolds (1975), pp. 142-143.

12. Cf. Hogarth (1975), pp. 16-17 and Hogarth (1974),
     p. 53-55. Hogarth's 1974 essay gives the theoreti-
     cal framework for the empirical research reported
     in Studies on Diversion.

BIBLIOGRAPHY

Of works referred to in this Chapter

Aristotle (1947), The Nichomachean Ethics, London: J.M.
Dent and Sons Ltd., #547 of Everyman Library.

Becker, Calvin (1975a), "Discretionary Clearances and
Observations On Police Screening Practices", Studies
In Diversion, Ottawa: Information Canada, p. 147-172.

Becker, Calvin (1975b), "Statistical Follow-up of Cri-
minal Occurrences In Toronto Patrol Area 5411:   An
Examination of the Relationships Between Victims and
Offenders", Studies In Diversion, Ottawa: Information
Canada, p. 173-208.

Bellah, Robert N. (1970), Beyond Belief, New York:
Harper & Row.

Berger, Peter & Thomas Luckmann (1966), The Social
Construction of Reality, New York: Doubleday.

Dauvillier, Jean (1970), Les Temps Apostoliques, Premier
Siecle, Volume II of Histoire du Droit et des Institutions de L'Eglise en Occident, Paris: Sirey.

Edelman, Murray (1975), "Language Myths and Rhetoric",
Society, Vol. 12, No. 5.

Ericson, Richard V., "Turning the Inside Out: On Limiting the Use of Imprisonment", Toronto: John Howard
Society, Community Education Series, Vol. 1, No. 3.

Erikson, Kai T. (1964), "Notes on the Sociology of Deviance", Howard S. Becker (ed.), The Other Side, New
York: Free Press.

Glinfort, E.K. (1975), "Formal Criminal Justice Diversion", Draft, Mimeo.

Gouldner, Alvin W. (1970), The Coming Crisis of Western
Sociology, New York: Avon.

Hogarth, John (1974), "Alternatives to the Adversary
System", Studies In Sentencing, Ottawa: Information
Canada, p. 35-90.

Hogarth, John (1975), "A Synopsis", Studies In

Diversion, Ottawa: Information Canada, p. 5-28.

Kerans, Patrick (1974), Sinful Social Structures, New
York: Paulist.

Kerans, Patrick (1977), "Distributive and Retributive
Justice in Canada", Dalhousie Law Review 4.

Klassen, William (1977), Release to Those in Prison,
Kitchener: Herald Press.

LRC #2 (1974), The Meaning of Guilt: Strict Liability.
Working Paper #2, Ottawa: Information Canada.

LRC #3 (1974), The Principles of Sentencing and Dispositions. Working Paper #3, Ottawa: Information
Canada.

LRC #7 (1974), Diversion. Working Paper #7, Ottawa:
Information Canada.

LRC #11 (1974), Imprisonment and Release. Working
Paper #11, Ottawa: Information Canada.

Law Reform Commission (1974), Studies On Sentencing,
Ottawa: Information Canada.

Law Reform Commission (1975), Studies In Diversion,
Ottawa: Information Canada.

LeBlanc, Marc (1975), "Upper Class Verses Working Class
Delinquency", Robert Silverman (ed.), Crime In Canadian Society.

Lutheran Church In America (1972), "In Pursuit of Justice and Dignity: Society, the Offender, and Systems
of Correction", New York: L.C.A.

Lynch, William S.J. (1970), Christ and Prometheus,
Notre Dame: University of Notre Dame Press.

MacPherson, C.B. (1962), The Political Theory of
Possessive Individualism: Hobbes To Locke, Oxford:
Oxford University Press.

Menninger, Karl (1968), The Crime of Punishment, New

York: Viking.

Miller, Frank P. (1970), "The Reintegration of the Offender Into the Community (Some Hopes and Fears)", Canadian Journal of Corrections, Vol. 12, No. 4.

Mohr, J.W. (1975), "Facts, Figures, Perceptions and Myths - Ways of Describing and Understanding Crime", Robert Silverman (ed.), Crime In Canadian Society.

National Welfare Council (1975), "Poor Kids", Ottawa, Mimeo.

Ortego, W. James (1977), "The Halifax North End Project", Dalhousie Law Review 3.

Outerbridge, William R. (1974), "Public Perceptions and Penal Reality: Some Issues of Prison and Parole", Toronto, Mimeo.

Quinney, R. (1970), The Social Reality of Crime, Boston: Little & Brown.

Rasmussen, David R. (1973), "Between Autonomy and Sociality", Cultural Hermeneutics, Vol. 1, No. 1, p. 3-45.

Reynolds, D.D.G. (1975), "The Use of Diversionary Dispositions For Juvenile Offenders", Studies In Diversion, Ottawa: Information Canada, p. 127-145.

Stace, Anne (1975), "Criminal Justice and Social Justice: Management of Conflict and Social Disorder by the Metropolitan Toronto Police Force", Studies In Diversion, Ottawa: Information Canada, p. 93-126.

Schmeiser, Douglas A. (1974), The Native Offender and the Law. Law Reform Commission, Ottawa: Information Canada.

Schur, Edwin M. (1969), Our Criminal Society, Englewood Cliffs, California: Prentice Hall.

Schur, Edwin M. (1975), "Labeling Deviant Behavior", Robert Silverman (ed.), Crime In Canadian Society, Toronto: Butterworth, p. 243-259.

Silverman, Robert & James J. Teevar Jr. (ed.) (1975), Crime in Canadian Society, Toronto: Butterworth.

Statistics Canada (1975), Advance Bulletin 1971 Census, #92-764, Ottawa: Information Canada.

Statistics Canada, Correctional Institution Statistics, #85-207, Ottawa: Information Canada, Annual.

Stone, Julius (1968), Human Law and Human Justice, Stanford: Stanford University Press.

Tappan, Paul W. (1961), "Pre-Classical Penology", G. Mueller (ed.), Essays in Criminal Science, London: Street and Maxwell.

Taylor, Ian, Paul Walton, & John Young (1973), The New Criminology: For A Social Theory of Deviance, London: Routledge & Kegan Paul.

Weiler, Paul (1974), "The Reform of Punishment", Studies On Sentencing, Ottawa: Information Canada, p. 91-205.

Wills, Garry (1975), "The Human Sewer", New York Review of Books, April 3, p. 3-8.

Winter, Gibson (1968), Elements for a Social Ethic, New York: MacMillan.

Wright, Erik Olin (1973), The Politics of Punishment, New York: Harper & Row.

TWO WISE MEN FROM THE WEST

WILLIAM KLASSEN is Professor and Head of the Department
of Religion in the University of Manitoba. Among other
works,he has published <u>The Forgiving Community</u> (1966).
An earlier version of his paper was given as a public
lecture at McMaster University in 1976.

RÉSUMÉ

Le problème immense de l'identité nationale est complexe
au Canada à cause de la mosaïque religieuse de notre
pays. Cependant, l'étude académique des religions nous
aide à modérer la passion et l'enthousiasme religieux
par la connaissance. Dans cette optique deux sages de
l'ouest du Canada illuminent certains aspects importants
de l'identité canadienne. Ces deux sages sont Louis Riel
et J.S. Woodsworth.

Louis Riel, un métis de Winnipeg, avait une carrière
bizarre qui réunissait la religion et la politique. Pour
Riel, l'identité nationale et l'assertion individuelle
étaient des points clefs afin d'atteindre la liberté,
l'autonomie et la vitalité d'un pays. Sa mission était
celle de la libération de l'ouest et jusqu'à sa mort
tragique, sa source d'inspiration était la foi : il se
voyait comme l'instrument de la Volonté Divine. De la
même façon, Woodsworth se nourrissait de la foi qu'il
envisageait comme la force créatrice de sa carrière
politique. Un pacifiste jusqu'au coeur, sa préoccupation était toujours les pauvres et les opprimés.

Ces deux exemples indiquent que dans l'histoire de
l'ouest du Canada, la religion et la politique se mêlai-
ent profondément. Cette tradition nous laisse aujourd'
hui deux questions : celle du rôle de la violence dans
la politique du pays et celle de l'autonomie canadienne :
à qui appartiennent les ressources nationales? Quelques
fois, les échecs de certains individus nous enseignent
plus que les réussites des autres.

WILLIAM KLASSEN

Two Wise Men from the West: Canadian Identity and Religion

All study is done in a particular context. It is our
privilege to study religion within the Canadian context.
The Symons' Report, To Know Ourselves, has stated: "If
we are to know ourselves, we must be familiar with the
nature and background of the Canadian religious experience."[2] That experience has many dimensions for a
country made up of many various groups.

   The sheer vastness of the land makes it difficult for
us to learn to know each other. Recently a national
Sunday supplement made an effort to educate us about
religion as a force in Canadian life and published an
article entitled "Missionaries in a New Wilderness".[3]
Of the fifty-one "missionaries" there are eleven United
Church, fifteen Roman Catholics and eight Anglicans.
Thus considerably over one half are from what we may
call the "Main-line" churches. Of the fifty-one nine
are from the West and the group does not include one
Mennonite or one from the Ukrainian Christian community!
We may be allowed to conclude that the list reflects
more about where the authors lived and their personal
acquaintance than it does of their knowledge of the
relative strengths of various religious traditions in
this country. The immensity of the problem to learn to
know ourselves therefore must not be minimised. Neither
should the possibility of doing so and the rewards which
come from such a knowledge. Throughout the years we
have made particular efforts to preserve the ethnic
mosaic. There is no doubt that a vital constituent part
of this ethnic mosaic is religion. Therefore it is more
difficult to study religion in a Canadian context than
it is in a more monolithic society or in a society where
the melting pot has been the paradigm rather than the
mosaic.

   Nevertheless it could be argued that it is also more
exciting. It is more interesting to study e.g. Hellenistic religions in this context because there are many
points of view that are brought to bear on the approach
to these religions. Eastern and western religions take
on a different dimension when studied by persons of
various religious traditions.

   There must then never be an assumption that the study
of religion in Canada is in any way insulated from the
study of religion elsewhere in the world. Nor should it

272

mean that because we relate the study of religion to
the quest for Canadian identity, we are less able to
converse with religionists in other parts of the world.
If, however, we do our job well, then the problem of
Canadian identity will continue to be more and more
complex. We have seen in recent months and years what
conflict can erupt when forces that derive their inspiration from religion receive political power - witness
Lebanon and Ireland. So far we have not shared their
experience, even in Riel's time, and the vitality and
strength of this country can be maintained as a force
for sanity and order if we are informed and educated
in the academic study of religion.

Here is the vital role of the academic study of
religion. For the prejudices, the passion and the zeal
which so often permeate religious movements and provide
the dynamics for their existence, are through the
academic study of religion tempered with knowledge. In
this way the study of religion can relate to the matter
of Canadian identity.

To quote the Symons report more fully:

Because religion has played such a basic and pervasive
role throughout Canadian history, it constitutes inescapably an integral and vital part of Canadian studies.
Universities and their supporters must recognize this
fact and provide adequately for teaching and research
about the very significant role played by religion in
past and present Canadian society. In doing so they
need not fear a conflict between the study of religion
in this historical and geographical community, and the
study of religion in its wider and universal context.
The two studies will illuminate and support one another.
There is no reason that they cannot proceed together
in a creative academic partnership.[4]

The present writer claims no detailed expertise in
Canadian history or Canadian culture. Like many Canadians I grew up in a situation where I was relatively
sheltered from my fellow Canadians not only across the
land, but even in my own province. We were not taught
world religions, Buddhism or Hinduism or even Judaism
except as a foil to make Christianity look more attractive. We were taught virtually nothing in High School
about the rich cultural heritage of the Ukrainians who
lived in our community. We knew next to nothing about
their religious heritage, the strength of their church,

273

the depth of their religious devotion. Likewise with
the French Catholics who lived in our province. All we
knew was that they clung to Ukrainian or to French as
we clung to German. We were not introduced to the rich
history of Roman Catholicism, were not taught about the
Mass and its meaning, we were not told why French was
so important to them. The vast Anglican and United
Churches remained unknown except by name.

It was only by accident that a few of us had the rich
privilege of spending a year or two after high school in
a permit teaching situation in communities far different
from the ones that we knew so well. Here we saw for the
first time another tile in the richness of our Canadian
mosaic. Here we became familiar with the Icelandic
community in our province, the Scottish settlers who
came with the Hudson's Bay Company and whose progenitors
now fish the waters in the province. Above all, we met,
for the first time, that strange and exciting group of
people known as Métis who were neither Indian nor white
who lived on the borderline of an existence which for
them still is strange and undefinable. Having met them
we could not shake them loose. Long before Harold
Cardinal wrote and Dan George spoke and before Emma
LaRoque tried to Defeather the Indian,[5] the Métis had
become imbedded in our consciousness in a way that we
have never been able to shake off.

What we shared with the Métis is a profound respect
for the land. Deriving as we did our sustenance from
the land, we were of necessity very close to it. Those
fields we planted, the rows of sugar beets we hoed
and thinned, the sheaves of wheat and oats that we
stooked; all made it impossible for us to remove ourselves from the land. The land had laid its hold upon
us - it was our land. We did not worship it any more
than the Indian did, but we knew that if the land
failed us we could not survive.

When we say that Canadian religion has its roots in
the land, nothing is being said that cannot be said
about primitive Greek religion nor of the Hebrew faith.
The Hebrews especially expressed the strong conviction
that the land belongs to Yahweh and therefore it could
not be sold outright (Leviticus 25:23). It did not
belong to the Canaanite, it did not belong to the
Israelite who conquered it, it did not belong to anyone
who laid his claim upon it. Ultimately and finally
the land belonged to Yahweh and he parcels it out. With

274

monotonous repetition the Israelite is reminded that
Yahweh "gave" him the land. When he does not remain in
covenant with Yahweh he is exiled and the land is taken
from him. The institution of the Jubilee year no matter
how partially it was practised reminded the Israelite
that periodically the land reverts back to its original
owner. The land question haunts us today as well.[6]
What happens to our national identity when our land is
sold to the Americans, Germans and Italians as happens
daily without any governmental restriction in Manitoba
today? How vital is our land and its resources to us?

In order to illuminate what is important and integral
to Canadian identity and the place of religion in it, we
shall look briefly at two wise men from the West, Louis
Riel and J.S. Woodsworth. In particular we shall concern ourselves with their love of liberty for all who
live in this land and their willingness, or unwilling-
ness, to resort to violence in defence of that liberty.

1. Louis Riel

Louis Riel was born in St. Boniface and for him the
Red River Settlement was always home.[7] Of Métis paren-
tage he is today increasingly being recognized as the
founder of Manitoba and slowly gaining national recognition as well. The fact that he is of mixed ancestry
may not have been the decisive factor denying him this
honour. Rather we are reluctant to enshrine someone
as founder of the province of Manitoba who had resisted
the government of Canada and who in effect established
his own state in Manitoba. Solid, conservative citizens
that we are today, you surely could not expect us to
acknowledge as our founder a man about whose sanity
doubts had been raised when he was tried and executed
for treason. There are, to be sure, people among us who
accept as their leader a Jew of the first century whose
relatives also considered him insane, who was also tried
for insurrection and executed for that crime - but there
are accounts to the effect that God raised him from the
dead and in any case he has in the meantime become respectable. Besides he stayed out of politics! Or so,
some believe.

But back to our first wise man from the West. His
statue stands just south of the parliament buildings in
Winnipeg, his back turned to the Assiniboine River and
his contorted face peers in the direction of the halls

where our laws are now enacted and enforced. It took a
city-wide fight to get him turned around for he was at
first placed with his back to parliament and his face
towards the south. It became clear in this discussion
that we had our trouble with Louis Riel. Should we
install him at all around our parliament buildings along
with Queen Victoria and other great figures from the
past? This man whose strange career stood as a reminder
to us that great men whose vision is blocked will sometimes resort to violent behaviour?   With the recent
publication of his dairy,[8] it becomes more and more
clear that there was a strange union of religion and
politics, Canadian nationalism and devout Roman Catholicism, political aspiration and indeed messianism all
intertwined in the mind of this brilliant but thwarted
man.

Yet who can deny the impact of this man, not only
upon Manitoba history, but upon Canadian history? He
was born of a settled Métis family in 1844. He himself
received a good education and spent some years in a
seminary in Montréal which he left in order to marry
in 1866. He left Montréal without wife, career or
money when the marriage was not permitted by her parents
and spent two idle years in the United States. By age
24 he returned to the West and became increasingly
involved in the dream of self-government for what later
became the province of Manitoba.

It was important to Louis Riel that the people who
lived here should have a say in what happened to their
land. It was he who stood firmly against the sale by
the Hudson's Bay Company of its enormous territories
to the new Dominion of Canada just four years before he
returned. He felt that the people themselves should
now decide who would rule them and what happened to
their land. When a surveying team came from Canada to
the farm of André Nault he protested. Since the sur-
veyors did not speak French, André sought Riel's help
who came unarmed with a number of men and simply stood
on the surveyor's chain. They had no authority to
survey their land as the Métis saw it, and they should
not be allowed to do so.

It is perhaps no surprise that we were never told that
15 years after our grandfathers came from the Ukraine
to settle in southern Manitoba Louis Riel was executed
by the Canadian government in part because of the consequences of his beliefs that the land on which he and

276

his people lived in southern Manitoba somehow belonged
to them. This was no part of our religious history.
It is not that the facts were deliberately hidden.   It
was simply that somehow they did not fit into our
existence. They were not part of our story until very
recently.

The main concern of Riel and his committee was that
they be consulted. John A. Macdonald had made his own
position quite clear when he wrote "These impulsive
half-breeds have got spoilt by this émeure (riot), and
must be kept down by a strong hand until they are
swamped by the influx of settlers...."[9] In the nego-
tiations and confrontations which took place between
the Prime Minister and the Provincial Government of
Manitoba during the winter of 1969-70 major concessions
were made. Sir John had to negotiate with "this upstart youth". Fearful of American intervention Sir
John granted them nearly everything they demanded:
guarantees for the French language and the Catholic
religion, recognising the aboriginal rights of the
half-breeds, and the entry of Red River into Confederation, not as a colony but as a Province. It was a
great success from the standpoint of the Métis but even
though they elected Riel three times to be their representative in Parliament, he was never allowed to take
his seat.[10] This fact alone should remind us that the
appearance of parliamentary democracy is not of itself
a guarantee of liberty.

Riel as head of the provisional government of the
Northwest and as spokesman for that government expressed
his concern about the relationships to Canada in the
following way:

> ...it has always seemed strange to the people of
> Assiniboia to hear themselves spoken of in official
> and other documents in Canada as a rebellious and
> misguided population, because we did not want to sub-
> mit to the arbitrary procedures of the Canadian
> government.[11]

As a result of growing confrontation culminating in
the famous case of the young Orangeman, Tom Scott,
Louis Riel allowed his supporters to execute Scott.
There is evidence which suggests that prior to this
time Riel was committed to a strategy of moderation.
At least in the case of C.H. Boulton, who had also been
condemned, he tried to exercise clemency. By March 1870,

277

however, he was no longer in a position of strength. The
Métis had followed him by choice and it is assumed that
Riel felt that an act of capital punishment would
strengthen his leadership role, both among his own people
as well as the outside world. But the execution of Thomas Scott changed everything and marked the beginning of
the end of Riel's career. It was a fatal mistake.

There are a number of issues central to the life of
Riel which are significant and important to us today.
First, there is the great stress which appears in Riel
on the autonomy, freedom and vitality of the land. We
may indeed sing of the "true north, strong and free",
but it was Riel who wrote in his diary the following
words, "The Spirit of God made me see a crate full of
merchandise. On the bottom were written the words,
'The heart of the North'. Oh my God! For the love of
Jesus, Mary, St. John the Baptist, grant me the grace
to conquer the North and to master all within it. Give
me the heart of the North."[12] He saw his mission as
one of rescuing this heart from enslavement by the East.
The motif appears elsewhere as well.

Only he who has grown up on the Prairies can understand the beauty that Riel saw in the wide spaces, the
unlimited view, the land stretching out before us without end or without boundary.

The strength of the North had a meaning for Riel which
it may not have for us today. Nevertheless anyone living
in Canada now cannot underestimate the concern that he
raised. We may enjoy bananas and oranges from the south,
but it is northern oil and gas which help to keep us
alive. Our survival depends on a careful husbanding of
the strength of the North.

For Riel self-determination and national identity
were critically important. National identity derived
its strength from the North and sustained its freedom
by refusing dependence upon the South. Riel had received
a letter from G.W. Gibbons, late Colonel of the U.S.A.
from the American Annexation League written on April 4,
1870 which read as follows: "My Dear Sir, Recognizing
your right in governing the Red River Community - I
tender you my services in upholding the same - in any
attempt made by Great Britain to the contrary. My
assistance of Men, arms, etc., will also be given you.
By all means make a firm and decisive stand. I should
be pleased to hear from you."[13]

278

But Riel stood firm for independence from the Americans. The Americans were better friends of the Métis than were the Canadians. Nevertheless they would act without any help from the Americans. Only the native peoples of the United States should be free to join them at any time.[14]

Later in his diary Riel reports that he dreamed that he was in a carriage with Michael Dumos, one of his associates. Michael was leaving for the United States. They went together for a certain distance and spoke about the United States and after Michael had left Riel wrote in his diary as follows:

> An area around me was clear and open; all the rest of the ground swarmed with snakes. There were more snakes than I could count. Oh, it is a dangerous step to ask the Americans for help. Beware of adventurers from the United States. For I assure you they are to be feared. They have neither morals, nor faith, nor heart. They are dirty dogs, foul jackals, ravishing wolves, raging tigers.
> O my God! Save me from the misfortune of getting involved with the United States. Let the United States protect us indirectly, spontaneously through an act of Your Holy Providence, but not through any commitment or agreement on our part."[15]

It is surely fascinating that a hundred years ago the founder of Manitoba saw that for people to have self-determination they must be represented in the group that makes decisions for them and they must not lean too heavily on their neighbour to the South.

This led him inevitably to regionalism as against confederation. Riel saw the importance of regional units, particularly of clear ethnic identity, in order to remain separate from the larger federalism. He placed his finger on an issue which has yet to be resolved. But as a consequence of resorting to violence he died by violence and did not live to establish the regional autonomy for which he fought.

2. J.S. Woodsworth[16]

The second wise man from the West is James Shaver Woodsworth, founder of the C.C.F. party which later became the N.D.P. As a memorial to this great leader

279

a shining new office building (which he would surely
detest!) in Winnipeg has just been completed.

Woodsworth was born in 1874 of Methodist preacher
parents in Ontario at about the time of the Riel rebellion. His parents moved to Manitoba when J.S. was
young and although he lived for a time in British
Columbia, his base of operations was always Winnipeg.
He was first elected in Winnipeg North to sit in Parliament in 1921 and served for over twenty years. It
sounds strangely modern to read how his first protests
in the House were lodged against the extravagant expen-
ditures of the police to trail "socialists" like
himself and to read of his protests that American spies
were being used in Canada! For him most clearly
religion led not to the nourishment of private piety
but to a concern of the "larger whole in which he
sought to lose himself." The creative zeal which
impelled him forward is well expressed in the scrapbook
clipping, From My Religion:

Haul out; cast off, shake out every sail;
Steer for the deep waters only.
For we are bound where mariner hath not yet dared to
  go,
And we will risk the ship, ourselves and all.
Oh daring joy--but safe!
Are they not all the seas of God?
Oh farther, farther, sail!17

For twenty-one years Woodsworth remained active in
politics. To a much greater degree than a later
politician in the United States, Adlai Stevenson, Woodsworth exercised a more creative influence on Canadian
legislation than many who actually lead a government.

Trained in theology, he also had read widely in social
theory and left the church, not primarily because of
doctrinal differences, but because the church was being
used as a recruiting station for the army.18

Like many prophets Woodsworth was noted for the
strength he brought to his dissent. Logical and clear
in his arguments, driven by a concern for the oppressed
and the poor he fought Canada's increasing dependence
upon the United States in the economic sphere and for a
policy towards Germany which would avoid a bitter back-
lash from the defeat of the World War I. His advocacy
of social welfare legislation was novel for his time

280

even though today it is taken for granted. He was a
great champion of the weak and the poor and worked for
legislation for the older people. To him more than
anyone we owe our unemployment insurance, our medicare
and our old age pensions.

He was a strong man who obtained and maintained the
respect of his Francophone colleagues as well as those
of all parties and leaders even though the party he led
had little impact in Québec.

Woodsworth's greatest hour came in the House of
Commons on the debate concerning the declaration of war.
Although he was a pacifist there was nothing obscuran-
tist about his approach and he knew how fully intertwined were questions of economics and war. Prior to
the debate on the War Declaration he had been a constant
irritation to the Liberal government on the decisions
that were being made which could not help but lead to
that declaration. In the tradition of Gandhi and
Martin Luther King after him, he spoke thus in the
House:

> Well, I left the ministry of the church during the
> last war because of my ideas on war. Today I do not
> belong to any church organization. I am afraid that
> my creed is pretty vague. But even in this assembly
> I venture to say that I still believe in some of the
> principles underlying the teachings of Jesus, and the
> other great world teachers throughout the centuries
> ....War is an absolute negation of anything Christian.
> The Prime Minister, as a great many do, trotted out
> the 'mad dog' idea; and that in the last analysis
> there must be a resort to force. It requires a great
> deal of courage to trust to moral force. But there
> was a time when people thought that there were other
> and higher types of force than brute force. Yes, if
> I may use the very quotation the Prime Minister used
> today, in spite of tyrants, tyrants as bad as even
> Hitler is today, in spite of war-makers--and every
> nation has them--as Lowell reminds us:

> 'Truth forever on the scaffold, Wrong forever
>   on the throne,
> Yet that scaffold sways the future, and,
>   behind the dim unknown,
> Standeth God within the shadow, keeping watch
>   about his own....'

281

It requires a great deal of courage to carry out our
convictions; to have peace requires both courage and
sacrifice....Yes, I have boys of my own and I hope
they are not cowards, but if any one of those boys,
not from cowardice but really through belief, is
willing to take his stand on this matter and, if
necessary, to face a concentration camp or a firing
squad, I shall be more proud of that boy than if he
enlisted for the war.[19]

While we may question his wisdom and disagree with his
actions his courage must elicit admiration. As Kenneth
McNaught puts it:

It would be easy to say Woodsworth had been 'nobly
wrong'; that his fallacy was proven by the strong
voice of the majority. But one question must remain
to plague us. Did that majority have then, and does
it have now, a better answer than Woodsworth's to the
tragic facts of the twentieth century: the increasing
resort to mass war with its accompaniment of chronic-
ally debased human values, the growing militarization
of democracy, and the mounting pressures on the individual to conform to majority ideologies?
    Hitler and all he stood for were consumed, perhaps,
in the Berlin funeral pyre of 1945. But there was
another funeral pyre in that year. It started with
two blinding flashes and was presided over by two
pillars of flaming cloud. The forces of right had
given their answer to the forces of evil. But what
actually was consumed in the fireclouds over Hiro-
shima and Nagasaki?
    In 1939 that future was unknown. To Woodsworth, it
nevertheless was certain. A Vancouver paper, report-
ing his speech, phrased what many felt: 'True to the
principles he has so consistently advocated, this
kindly, courageous man nailed his colours to the mast
and sailed off on the lonely route where conscience
is the only compass.'[20]

The history of dissent is a noble one reaching back
at least to Euripides and Socrates in the Greek world.
In Canadian history no dissenter is as worthy of note
as is J.S. Woodsworth. Although Woodsworth's dissent
led him to break with the church it is crystal clear
that his dissent sprang from religious roots and was
fed by them till the end. In the search of Canadian
heroes none can overlook this statesman.

TWO WISE MEN FROM THE WEST

Conclusion

Finally, I wish to make reference to the contribution
that the example of these men has made to the religious
discussion. Riel, Woodsworth, and other great leaders
of the West have indissolubly joined religion and politics. Eastern politicians may seem more sophisticated
than Louis Riel or Woodsworth or Premier Manning or
W.A.C. Bennett. Nevertheless, it is a striking aspect
of Canadian western history that religious values and
political action are very closely joined together.

With respect to Woodsworth and Riel, there are two
major unresolved problems:

(1) the place of violence in the political sphere. It
is a part of the quest for Canadian identity.

The Canadian ego, if one may be allowed to use that
term, has had its developmental problems. We have not
had a war in which to establish our machismo. We have
not engaged in any great battles with the Indians so
that we could possess this land. In other words our
history cannot point to a war of independence or a
major civil war to mirror our identity. Our leaders
seem to have that strange quality of wanting Canada to
be recognized as a nation in its own right, but reluctant to fight for it. This trait appears to run from
Louis Riel to Pierre Trudeau. (The contrast between
Trudeau's appeals for love in 1976 and his use of force
during the Quebec crisis of October 1970 is striking.)
The crisis of identity is seen in our Armed Forces -
what do we do with men killed in the Sinai or Cyprus as
part of a Peace-keeping Force? Are they heroes or victims of national vanity?

Can we recruit persons into an Army which builds its
reputation on cleaning up oil-spills and aid in disaster
relief rather than bringing them about? In this area
religion and Canadian identity crossed over most distinctly in both Riel and J.S. Woodsworth.

It is hard to find a source which so strikingly jux-
taposes these two traits as does the diary of Riel.
Riel had no love for war. He is not engaged in a battle
in order to prove that he is a man; in fact Louis Riel
is engaged in a holy war. His diary indicates that the
real battle is fought by God and not by him or his
soldiers. On the one side is the conviction:

283

My ideas are right; they are well-balanced. They are
level and clear; there is no mourning in my thoughts.
My ideas are like the sights on my rifle. My rifle
is upright. It is the invisible presence of God which
holds my rifle straight and ready.[21]

Alongside of this there are repeated prayers that God
may be gracious to his enemies. He prays not only for
himself, that he may find it in his heart to be chari-
table to those who are enemies, but also that God will
"let the bullet graze him (the enemy), but spare his
life".[22] Towards the end of his diary when his capture
is coming close he prays "Oh my God, find a way, to be
good to our enemies, while still giving us Your successes,
Your victories and Your triumphs forever and ever."[23]
Riel clearly sees himself as a Holy Warrior. The victory
must come from God.

We are able to see in a way which Riel could not the
dangers of the Holy War motif. The Israelites already
had their troubles with it. For the War of Jahweh,
which He fights with his angels so easily becomes our
war which we fight with our muskets. Riel tried to
shore up his sagging political situation and to demonstrate his muscle by allowing the execution of Thomas
Scott. He learned this from the white men whose
"justice" he was trying to emulate by introducing
capital punishment. The tragic flaw in Riel's character
was this inconsistency; of relying on Jahweh the Warrior
but also eventually, as time dragged on, being drawn
into battle which flatly contradicted the teaching of
the Jesus upon whose name he so frequently called. Our
criticism of Riel must be tempered by the fact that it
was our forefathers who taught him that inconsistency.
The tragedy is that he learned it. Driven from the land
and uprooted from his people this fugitive came to a sad
end when he took up arms against Canada. Nevertheless
that end is a blot on the record of Canadian justice.
If today Riel's people seek to make him their hero, far
be it from us, the descendants of the white settlers,
to sit in judgment on them.

With respect to violence, Woodsworth was more consistent. The reason for this is perhaps that he was never
tested by power - he never ruled. More important is
that Woodsworth, although he also had his emotional
stresses and breakdowns, never lost his place. The way
opened up for him repeatedly so that he could creatively
express the throbbing energy within him. And yet, he

too, had his flaw which was the position he took on restrictions on immigration and the basis on which they rested. Riel was a victim to the ideology of the conquest of the "holy" land. For Woodsworth there are strands of racism in his immigration philosophy. Not only did the Ukrainian joy of life as expressed at weddings and other occasions cause him to wonder whether Ukrainians really belong here but the question of Orientals coming to Canada in large numbers distressed him. While we recognize as strongly as he did that thought must be given to immigration policies, we also affirm that racism and immigration policies are not compatible.[24]

(2) The second question is one which began this essay, "To whom does the land belong?" While that question was faced by Riel at one level, namely who owns it, it was faced by Woodsworth at another related level, namely to whom do the resources of the land belong and who can be allowed to live here? I suggest that these problems are still very much with us. They surface on the questions of foreign ownership and also in such questions as to what proportion of our gross national product should go to the development of the resources and strength of other countries in the so-called developing world. Woodsworth's critique of the exploitation of this country by the major corporations was ignored by the majority, just as Diefenbaker's efforts later seemingly ended in failure.[25]

It has been said that in great men both their virtues and their flaws are great. Certainly this is true of J.S. Woodsworth and Louis Riel. Perhaps their failures are however more instructive than most men's successes. What cannot be denied is that their lives were shaped by religious values. To some extent both of them drew from the faith of Israel with its high commitment to the land and to the poor. Both also had difficulty with the Biblical teaching on exclusiveness and the theocracy of God. Riel was more the religious zealot and yielded to the temptation of becoming God's instrument of vengeance or justice just like the Zealots of the first century did and as did the Münsterites of the 16th century. Nevertheless theirs was a faith which acted, daring to make mistakes as we judge them today. This combination of wisdom and action, insight and deed may well be an aspect of our total Canadian tradition that we can build on even when we build structures differently than they did. National pride is often considered out of fashion these days. Canada however could well do with a pride which is built upon the courage of men like Riel and Woodsworth. We can well pride ourselves that we are still noted throughout the world for being suppliers of food rather than of armaments.[26] Like Woodsworth and Riel, we can also be caught up not in the past and an analysis of its mistakes but with a buoyant hope for the future.

FOOTNOTES

1. Delivered at McMaster University on December 1, 1976 under the sponsorship of the Department of Religion. I wish to thank Professor Eugene Combs and other members of the department who made my stay with them a stimulating learning experience.

2. To Know Ourselves, ed. T.H.B. Symons (AUCC, 1975), p. 108.

3. Kenneth and Barbara Bagnell, "Missionaries in a New Wilderness, A Who's Who of Common Prayer", in The Canadian (n.d. sometime in 1976) pp. 4-8.

4. Symons, op. cit., p. 110.

5. Emma LaRoque, Defeathering the Indian, The Book Society of Canada, Agincourt, Ontario, 1975.

6. Attention should be called in particular to the way in which the Kiowa Indian, N. Scott Momoday, professor of Comparative Literature at Stanford University has written about the land in his various works. My rootedness in the land is also expressed in the piece, "Roots in Manitoba Mud", in Harvest, Anthology of Mennonite Writing in Canada, 1874-1974; pp. 7-14 published by D.W. Friesen and Sons, Altona, Manitoba in 1974. In part I am also indebted to Waldemar Janzen's important article, "Geography of Faith: A Christian perspective on the Meaning of Places", Studies in Religion 3 (1973) pp. 166-182. I would only question whether the subtitle should not read: "A Biblical perspective..."

7. The standard work on Riel is George Stanley, Louis
    Riel (Toronto, 1963) and Hartwell Bowsfield, Louis
    Riel: The Rebel and the Hero (Toronto, 1971).

8. Thomas Flanagan has published the diaries in the
    most reliable form to date: The Diaries of Louis
    Riel, ed. Thomas Flanagan (Edmonton: Hurtig Pub-
    lishers, 1976). Prof. Flanagan is writing a bio-
    graphy of Riel from a religious perspective and has
    already written several articles in learned journals
    on that topic (see his work cited). Without claim-
    ing to provide a complete picture of Riel, I am
    basing myself primarily on the diaries for they pro-
    vide us with an insight into the inner workings of
    Riel. That they will confirm some in the suspicion
    that Riel was mentally unbalanced, I do not for a
    moment evade. It is the lot of creative geniuses
    or people who see issues before their time to be
    considered mad. Did Jesus of Nazareth himself not
    have to contend with this accusation from his
    mother and his brothers and sisters? (See Mark 3:
    21). Others claimed he was demon-possessed (Mark
    3:22; John 8:48, 52). The insights which Riel had
    are not destroyed just because a psychiatrist puts
    a label on him.

9. H. Bowsfield, editor, Issues in Canadian History -
    Louis Riel (Toronto, 1969), p. 34.

10. Flanagan, op. cit., p. 10.

11. Bowsfield, op. cit., p. 36.

12. Flanagan, op. cit., p. 58.

13. The Nor'Wester, 1970, p. 22.

14. The Nor'Wester, loc. cit., p. 56.

15. Flanagan, op. cit., April 29, 1885, pp. 77 ff.

16. I am following here the standard biography of Woods-
    worth by Kenneth McNaught, A Prophet in Politics
    (University of Toronto Press, 1959).

17. McNaught, op. cit., p. 159.

18. I am following here Richard Allen, The Social
    Passion (Toronto, 1971) pp. 49-51, who states that

although Woodsworth's decision to leave the church "stemmed more from his gnawing sense of unorthodoxy than from the extent of 'commercialism', the precipitating factor was his pacifist belief in the face of total church commitment to the war" (p. 50). I am indebted to my colleague, Mac Watts for helpful insights in the discussion of this matter.

19. McNaught, op. cit., p. 311.

20. McNaught, op. cit., p. 312.

21. Flanagan, op. cit., p. 60.

22. Flanagan, op. cit., p. 63.

23. Flanagan, op. cit., p. 85. He stands in the tradition of Socrates and Jesus. All vengeance he leaves to God (Flanagan, op. cit., p. 70) and the victories are God's (Flanagan, op. cit., p. 54) and prays that God's goodness may be done towards the enemies. Even on those rare occasions (Flanagan, op. cit., 48-49) in which he speaks of his enemies in other terms, such as praying that his foes one fine morning may scatter in fear before my hands, ...or expresses the wish that they may grovel in the dust and that he may stamp out their life as reptiles in the dust, his thoughts seem to move along the lines of the Psalms of Imprecation of the Old Testament. The Christian approach of loving one's enemies seems to triumph (see Flanagan, op. cit., pp. 52, 61, 63, 66, 85, 94, 103, 132).

24. On this subject see the article by Keith Clifford, Chapter Two in this volume.

25. See especially the work of that pioneer and doyen of Canadian scholars of religion George Grant, Lament for a Nation, The Defeat of Canadian Nationalism (McClelland and Stewart, 1965 - reprinted as a Carleton Library Reprint, 1970).

26. See E. Regehr, Making a Killing - Canada's Arms Industry (McClelland and Stewart, 1975).

RELIGION AS STORY: NORMAN BETHUNE

C. PETER SLATER is Associate Professor and Chairman of
the Department of Religion in Carleton University and
Chairperson of the Philosophy of Religion and Theology
Section of the American Academy of Religion. His paper
is a revised and expanded part of a more extensive work
entitled <u>Continuity and Change in Religion</u>.

RÉSUMÉ

Des études religieuses envisagent la religion en tant
que force ou puissance qui transforme l'individu. C'est
un processus, alors, de libération qui mène jusqu'à la
liberté finale, définitive. Un tel processus s'étend à
tous les domaines de la vie : la politique, la psychologie, la consommation, même le féminisme.

Cette puissance tire son origine d'histoires de personnages centraux de chaque religion : Jesus, Mahomet, le
Bouddha, ainsi que leurs apôtres à travers les siècles.
Dans l'histoire de Mao Tso-Tong, le récit de Norman
Béthune fonctionne comme un exemple à la fois paraboli-
que et mythique. Touché par la pauvreté des québécois,
il envisageait un système d'assurance médicale telle
qu'on a aujourd'hui, mais qui, à son époque, l'identi-
fiait avec les communistes ou les anarchistes. Il a
donc été renvoyé de son poste à Montréal et a été muté
en Espagne et ensuite en Chine. Luttant avec les pay-
sans, il est devenu un personnage symbolique du mouvement chinois, et leur inspire, à nos jours, une nouvelle
vision et un grand espoir.

L'interprétation de l'histoire de Bethune nous révèle
nos propres idées préconçues. Quelques fois le héros
obscurcit l'être humain; d'autres fois, l'être humain
obscurcit le héros libérateur. Un récit de transformation dépend donc du contexte dans lequel on le raconte.
La responsabilité reste avec l'individu - canadien ou/et
chinois - de dégager les symboles de ce récit, symboles
de la libération qui est le vrai objectif de toutes les
religions.

289

PETER SLATER

Religion As Story: The Biography of Norman Bethune

Especially in the study of religions less creeded than
Christianity scholars have long insisted on the importance in religion of sacred stories. These typically
have been paradigmatic narratives setting forth a
people's sense of time and place in relation to the
forces considered creative and destructive of life. In
the first section of this paper I give reasons for
continuing to work with the concept of paradigmatic
stories while no longer tying it to any archaic dichotomy between things "sacred" and "profane." In the
second section I give the main points of the Bethune
story as these are being presented to us by current
biographers. In the third and final sections I go
into some ways in which this story may be said to have
religious significance.

I

    I begin with some observations concerning our under-
standing of religion. When I was in graduate school
and during my early teaching years the fashion in theology was to stress the contrast between revelation and
ordinary human experiences and to emphasize the givenness of a theologian's starting-point. Accordingly the
intellectual challenge and excitement was mostly in the
study of biblical theology, reflections on the record
of God's revelation through the history of Israel and
so on. At the same time the fashion in religious studies was to branch out into the exploration of other
religious traditions than our own. For these our data
came not only from textual critics, linguists and historians of religion but also from anthropologists and
sociologists. Here the problem came to be partly one
of defining the distinctive contributions and approach
of religious studies as such. And the solution seemed
to lie again in emphasis on the givenness or irreduci-
bility of distinctively religious phenomena. The method
in religious studies was to be the "phenomenological"
method, however loosely defined. To be plausible this
solution had to be able to draw on some aspect of our
culture which seemed indeed to be distinctively "religious." For many that aspect was the experience of
the holy or the idea of the sacred. Thus both theology
and religious studies started with a unique datum for
reflection and no introductory course in religion was

290

complete without its appropriate text from Rudolf Otto, Mircea Eliade or someone similar expounding the awesome experiences of our ancestors.

But fashions change. In our present humanistic climate of opinion appeals to revelation tend to sound like special pleading for one particular kind of religious experience. Religious experiences generally tend to be treated as symptomatic of other currents in human history, not as material to be taken on its own terms.[1] What if anything is distinctive about "religion" has once again become problematic.

We can, of course, reject fashion as a guide to the direction of religious studies and deny that there is a problem about distinctively religious experiences. We have grounds for doing so. The classical texts of all the traditions and the rituals of so-called primitive peoples do as a matter of fact exhibit something like the celebration of the sacred so widely documented by Eliade. They do on occasion record the sense of numinous dread and fascination with transcendent power specified by Otto.[2] But a price must be paid for concentration on such data. In much contemporary experience the classical sense of "the Holy" seems marginal and the sacred structures of the traditions sound like bad news rather than good. Even if we emphasize instead an existential sense of wonder and define the secular city as our "sacred" centre, with presidents and premiers among its reigning high priests, we generally fail to evoke the spirit of worship or joyous celebration which we associate with true religion. Besides, theologically speaking, such an emphasis misplaces the real centre of religious motivation at its best. For I believe this central motivation is not dread of fearsome power as such or a thirst for cosmic order at any price. In Christianity it is faith and hope and love. In Buddhism it is wisdom and compassion. In Hindu traditions it is sexual desire and social duty, personal success and final liberation. In Judaism it is justice, in Islam peace. Thus if our concern is with what is distinctively religious and not merely cultural we should be looking at such springs of inspiration as these and not primarily at stories of the esoteric experiences of our less literate forefathers.

When we look into the history of developed religions for their vital sources of inspiration we find more often than not an ideal of actual living personified in

291

a figure such as Jesus or Gautama, Moses or Muhammad, Confucius or Nichiren. What inspires is not the organizational power of institutionalized religion in which birth, death and marriage receive some sort of social sanction but a vision of personal freedom and corporate destiny expressed in the life or teaching of dominant persons. Their experiences circumscribe our evaluations of everyday affairs. Their traditions carry us towards new possibilities of existence suggested by their images of Nirvana or the Kingdom of God. Their characters and their dreams give life-enhancing power to lesser minds. And what is religiously relevant about this power - whether it be said to come from God, Brahman or the Buddha Nature - is not so much its numinous aura as its liberating effect on the lives of others. It is the liberating power felt by Israel during the Exodus, the Church at Pentecost, Islam during the Hegira, Vaishnavas during recitation of their mantras, Taoists in contemplation of Nature and so on.

The combination of vision and power, for instance of heaven and God in the life and teaching of Jesus and Paul, defines religion not by reference to some transcendent object but by a transcending process whereby those who adopt a religious way of life are brought from fear to love, sickness to health, delusion to enlightenment, misery to bliss. Accordingly, the major world religions are movements of liberation in which what we consider ultimately good, if not in this life then in the next, if not for ourselves then for our heirs. Religions are more or less successful realizations of ultimate freedom by people in transition, whether they see themselves as slaves in Egypt or slaves to lust, as producers alienated from their share of corporate wellbeing or egos out of touch with the well-springs of personal joy.[3]

If ultimate freedom is the end in view, whether understood nationalistically or existentially, psychologically or supernaturally, then religion as the process of realizing this freedom does not belong in just one compartment of life. We cannot classify it along with education, sports, politics and medicine, in the manner of our weekly magazines and encyclopedias. Rather it permeates all these "departments" of life and sets limits on all our neat divisions, including those of churches, monasteries and officially religious groups. Religious questions concerning final priorities, basic principles, ultimate visions and degrees of realization must be asked

of all phenomena and all methods of studying them.
Moreover the study of religion cannot then be restricted
to analyses of other-worldly ambitions from the past or
to mystical visions articulated in wholly medieval
terms. The study of religion must include not only
conventional and traditional ways of transcendence which
are popularly called religious but also those movements
of liberation which inspire our contemporaries, often
outside the churches. Encounter groups, psychotherapy,
feminism, consumerism, scientistic behaviourism, the
various brands of Marxism abroad in the world, all have
religious or quasi-religious significance for some at
least of those who embrace them as "the" way for themselves and possibly all mankind. Whether such movements
eventually become tributaries to the main streams of
the major traditions or new traditions on their own they
belong to the data of religious studies. For finally
what we are studying is, again, not some sacred object
or feeling confined to one side of life but the liberating spirit and joy in fulfillment expressed in the best
of the great traditions and promised in the best of the
new.

What constitutes ultimate freedom is variously conceived in different times and situations. In my view
it is ultimate when its realization extends to the
limits of human experience in a given culture. More
simply, it is ultimate when its realization comes in
the face of death, whether the death in question be that
of the body, of body and soul, of a whole people or a
whole world. Ultimate freedom is that freedom which is
known by those figures in a society who go through the
"boundary situations" of their times in ways which inspire others to imitate them. This applies whether
the boundaries contemplated are between man and nature,
man and society, in-groups and out-groups, nature and
supernature or sanity and insanity. Ultimate freedom
is the greatest possible realization of power for good
in the experience of those who are by nature bound to
disintegrate and liable to evil.

A specific conception of liberation and historical
tradition in religion is shaped by what may be called
the "master story" of some central inspirational
figure. The Buddha, the Prophet, the Christ, the Sage,
are what others would become. They are masters of
their ways, portrayed as realizing in themselves what
other would become. They are masters of their ways,
portrayed as realizing in themselves what others have

only hoped for. Consequently while there are many in
the history of religions who have sought followers these
few have attracted and held them. Theirs have been the
new religious movements which have shaped our culture.
Typically they have challenged the authenticity of conventional attempts to alleviate or escape from evil.
They have suffered with the sufferers and through their
suffering found ultimate freedom for themselves and
others. They have led the Exodus, the Long March, the
entry into the New Promised Land or the inward journey
of contemplatives and in so doing have convinced others
that their ends can be attained. They are talismans of
success, symbolic bridges by which we cross in imagination from death to life and back again. Among such
figures in modern history are Abraham Lincoln, Mahatma
Gandhi and Mao Tse-tung. Theirs are master stories for
countless Americans, Indians and Chinese who may still
be shaped by more conventional religious myths but whose
focus now is on the politics of personal dignity and
common prosperity in the modern world. These too have
a place in any comprehensive study of religions.[4]

In time however the central figures of religious
movements become "immortals" embedded in mythological
traditions. Their stories become so permeated with
fabulous elaborations and their achievements so idealized that they cease to exist on the level of everyday
encounters with evil. Consequently, their inspirational
effect has to be mediated by that of other lives,
touched by theirs but closer to our own. Thus popular
religious imagination soon comes to dwell on a host of
secondary figures whose stories are related to those of
the central figures in a variety of ways. Even where
the original vision is lost in mythology, as in India,
its power is communicated through stories of the Saivite
saints and so forth. As forerunners and followers such
secondary figures furnish the contexts in which the
master stories receive their religious significance.
Students who would understand the ultimate symbolic
references of religious traditions must therefore look
into the whole collection of their stories, both
sacred and popular. Just as personal faith may be
interpreted in terms of the stories which we tell
ourselves of who we are and where we are going so
popular religious thought may be explored through the
images used in religious biographies and hagiographies.
Accordingly scholars are examining afresh the classical
sources for religious studies in conjunction with the
songs, rituals, arts and crafts of the peoples whose

lives are shaped by such paradigms of faith and devotion.[5]
And they are discerning new expressions of faith in those
stories of our times which have the same inspirational
effect on us. One such story in the developing tradition
of Maoism in China is that of Norman Bethune.

When we speak of religiously significant stories we
need to keep in mind a distinction between what may be
called the surface narrative and its "deep" meanings in
the formation of religious traditions. The surface
narrative sets forth the main points of interest in
usual story form. In the lives of "saints" this form
is that of a biography, whether or not the saint's
origins are considered divine or human or the final
scene is set on earth or in heaven. The standpoint of
the story-teller in biography is that of a more or less
impartial observer. The story is told in the third
person and the life of the central character is considered to be over, finished, complete. By contrast an
autobiographical account would be relatively open-
ended and the narrative of events would be in terms of
existential choices still alive in the mind of the
narrator.[6] In the formation of a religious tradition
what happens in effect is that a matter-of-fact biographical narrative is transposed into a symbolic key
which underlines its existential import in the lives
of believers. One person's biography becomes part of
another's autobiography. This transposition is
typically either mythic or parabolic, in senses brought
out below, or a combination of these.[7] Thus the flat
narrative of Bethune's life story may become a paradigmatic element in the thinking of contemporary Canadians
and Chinese. To appreciate how this may be so we must
first review the outlines of his biography.

II

The "surface" story of Bethune's life is of interest
to most of us because he was a Canadian. In itself it
makes interesting reading because he lived through
some of the major conflicts of the first half of the
twentieth century and was one of the very first Canadians to come into contact with the leaders of modern
China. Like so many of his generation he had to gain
recognition elsewhere before being taken seriously at
home. He is not yet a symbolic figure for us, at least
not a symbol of good.[8] But the narrative of his life
is one of transition from ordinary worldly ambition to
universal, revolutionary passion which has possibilities
from a religious point of view. Even on the surface his

295

is a story on the grand scale.

Bethune's experience is true to that of many of us in
that it begins with confusion in his own mind concerning
his national identity. As a student and young professional he was not sure, for instance, whether to pro-
nounce his name "Bay'-tune" like his ancestors from
northern France or "Beetun" as in parts of the British
Isles.[9] (He settled for "Beth-une.") He expected to
find medical fortune, if not fame, working in Detroit
rather than in some small Ontario town like Stratford.
World War I cemented his ties with Britain by drawing
him into the armed forces and it was there later that
he went for graduate work. But he might easily have
become an American citizen as jobs became available
across the border. By birth and natural affiliation
he was an Upper Canada WASP, the medical son of a
minister and grandson of a doctor, a member of one of
the respectable professions in which he could expect to
enhance his social position and personal finances. But
it was not until he abandoned that position to head a
medical unit in Spain during the Civil War of the
thirties that he came to affirm his own identity as a
Canadian. Again like many of us he was most avowedly
Canadian when he was abroad.[10]

Although Bethune was born into Ontario's Protestant
establishment he was never fully of it. His grandfather
had been sufficiently secure to challenge a Toronto
college's demand for religious affiliation as a qualifi-
cation for admission to its medical school. But his
father was forever on the move from one parish to
another and young Norman never spent more than a year
or two at any one school. He lacked funds to further
his education and had to drop out of university for a
time. He worked as a temporary instructor for what was
called Frontier College, a project to educate immigrants
working in lumber, mining and railroad camps in northern
Ontario. From this and various summer jobs he retained
the common touch which modified his otherwise seemingly
unquenchable superiority complex. In fact he was
always a boundary figure, obviously talented and ambitious and never likely to be lost in a crowd, determined
to excel over his medical peers yet unwilling to treat
his patients, whether in Detroit or elsewhere, as just
so many "cases" thrown up by the slums of the inner
city. His was an experience typical of revolutionaries
and reformers who have the qualifications but not the
means to be members of the "top 600." Depending on

events they combine a sense of personal worth with alienation from the leaders of society which provokes them
to join movements for radical social change. But it was
some time before such a sense of alienation set the tone
for Bethune's life.

What first redirected Bethune's career was a long
period of convalescence from tuberculosis coinciding
with the breakup of his marriage, from 1925 through
1926. There is some doubt about how serious his physical condition really was but he himself referred to it
as his first "dying."[11] It marked the end of his conventional climb to successful practice and forced him
to re-examine his goals. Tuberculosis then loomed as
cancer and heart disease do today, a frequently certain
and slow killer striking at all classes in society. His
immediate need was to survive. The prescribed treatment
was rest. But he could never follow that. When he came
across a new surgical procedure which would allow his
lung time to recover he insisted on having it tried on
himself. Once cured he decided to become a thoracic
surgeon in order to bring to others the same hope of
speedy recovery. Here was a dramatic personal challenge
which brought him into the ranks of the pioneers in his
profession. "There was a religious aspect to his commitment," Roderick Stewart comments.[12] But its inspiration was human, not divine, and the cause was science,
not religion.

From a sanatorium in upstate New York Bethune went to
train under the leading Canadian in the field, Edward
Archibald, at the Royal Victoria Hospital in Montréal.
There Bethune soon established an international reputation especially for his invention of ever improved
surgical instruments. But his impatience with his
chief and mentor made him increasingly unpopular with
the English medical fraternity. Always outspoken he
liked to shock conservative audiences. "He was angriest
with people who shared his conclusions and lacked his
courage to act on them."[13] He would not accept the
weight of tradition which made others hesitate to
operate on doubtful cases and slow to improve on prevailing conditions of medical care. His own view of
life was of an adventure in which each does what he can
to promote the common good. He might not be sure of
the results but his intuition was of an evolving process in which progress is assured.[14] He was contemp-
tuous of those who valued their rules and regulations
more than their patients. With no personal ties of his

own he had no sympathy with those who worried about
professional security and family solidarity. In the
face of much hostility he was forced to leave and was
fortunate to obtain what seemed a dead-end position as
"Chef dans le Service de Chirurgie Pulmonaire et de
Bronchoscopie" at Sacré Coeur Hospital on the outskirts
of the city. One condition of his new appointment,
incidentally, was that he train some Québecois to
succeed him. His role was to communicate his knowledge
to those in the community who lacked it and then to
depart. It was a role which he would play again in
China.

   At last Bethune was head of his own unit. But in
that position he soon discovered that he could not cure
his patients' medical problems without changing their
economic conditions. Too many Québecois could not
afford a doctor until it was too late. Then they lacked
the means to purchase the healthful diets which he
recommended. With a friend from the Y.M.C.A. he
decided to open a free clinic in the suburb of Verdun.
Increasingly he spoke out against governmental indifference to the plight of the poor. During an International
Physiological Congress in Leningrad he observed socialized medicine at first hand and came back convinced that
it alone was truly in the interests of the patients.
Soon he was converted from being a conventional anti-
communist to being a fellow-traveller if not a party
member. Those were the depression years when war
threatened in Europe. Because of his speeches and
connections with radical clergymen and union leaders
Vincent Massey, as Canadian High Commissioner in London,
would later refuse to guarantee to the French Government that Bethune was a bona fide physician engaged in
humanitarian work. This would mean that he had to pay
duty on the medical supplies and equipment which he
took with him when he decided to go to Spain.[15] To
those in authority Bethune seemed a politically suspect
troublemaker. But in Montreal he did more than make
angry speeches against capitalistic medicine and "jungle
individualism." As chairman of "the Montreal Group for
the Security of the People's Health" he spent months
drawing up plans for government-sponsored medical care.[16]
Sadly what we expect today from our governments as only
fitting, indeed the right to health of every citizen,
was in those days vociferously attacked by all major
political parties and medical societies on ideological
grounds. Fear of Russian communism and anarchism was
so great that otherwise intelligent men turned deaf

ears to proposals which now seem eminently humane and
practical.

In the face of governmental indifference to his proposals and rejection by his fellow doctors Bethune
began to accept the view that change would come about
only following worldwide political revolution. As well
as a doctor he was a fairly accomplished amateur artist
and among his artistic friends the front line of the
struggle at that time was perceived to be in Spain.
There the legally elected government was engaged in
civil war with Franco's fascists. Bethune welcomed an
opportunity to organize a Canadian medical unit to go
to the aid of the Loyalists in Madrid. In The Watch
That Ends The Night Hugh MacLennan portrays his Bethune
character, Jerome Martell, as allowing himself to be
used by the communists on this occasion. But in real
life Bethune realized early that the struggle was
political as well as economic and social. He chafed at
the need to be evasive concerning his allegiances,
condemned either way by public spokesmen for concealing
or revealing his party membership.[17] But his major
concern then as always was to bring relief as swiftly
as possible to those who most needed it. Thus in
Spain he became highly critical of factional squabbles
among left-wing bureaucrats, referring at one point to
those with whom he was supposed to co-operate as
"anarchist bastards that we will have to put up against
the wall and shoot."[18] At the time he was physically
exhausted from organizing the first ever mobile blood
donor clinics to those wounded in battle. He was infu-
riated by unnecessary delays which cost lives. His
Canadian sponsors decided to recall him for a lecture
tour to rouse support for the Loyalist cause at home.
The tour was a great success. But already Bethune felt
that the cause in Spain was lost and that the new front
line was in China.

China's war with Japan was never as fashionable a
liberal cause as the Spanish Civil War. There were no
Hemingways there to dramatize its sacrifices. An ad
hoc group called the China Aid Council in New York
scraped together resources to start Bethune and a
Canadian nurse-interpreter, Jean Ewen, on their way.
The Canadian-American Mobile Medical Unit, as they
called themselves, sailed from Vancouver for Hong Kong
on January 8, 1938.[19] Bethune was convinced that he
would not return. Once in China he expected to be
behind the enemy lines, cut off from all contact with

his friends and sponsors. But he was not prepared for
the primitive state of medicine in the Communist Eighth
Route Army. This was part of a supposedly united front
with Chiang Kai-shek's forces against the Japanese.
Bethune was put in charge of a hospital consisting of
fifty caves in a hillside where he found the wounded
still lying in their soiled uniforms. Until he realized
that the orderlies were completely untrained he was
furious at their apparent indifference to the risk of
infection and welfare of the patients.

In the biographies Bethune's anger and seeming assumption that he alone had the best interests of the patients at heart are recurring themes. To anyone who
has seen doctors after a series of eighteen and twenty-
hour working shifts such reactions seem typical and understandable. What the Chinese appreciated immediately was
his insistence on sharing their quarters, eating their
food, receiving only their rates of pay and working
longer hours than any of his assistants. Once he had
learned how to work with them he was happier than at
any other time in his life.

During the ensuing months Bethune transposed his
Spanish experience of guerilla medicine to the Chinese
context. He made good on his promise to Mao to cut
the death rate among military and civilian casualties
by seventy-five per cent. The very qualities which had
made him an "impossible" colleague in Montréal now made
him one of the very few Europeans who was of real help
to the People's Army. He was unwilling to stand on
ceremony and eager to improvise. He re-established a
hospital only to see it destroyed by the Japanese.
He wrote a handbook on medicine in time of war. He
laid the groundwork for training peasants as nurses and
orderlies. He contrived new medical instruments from
quite primitive tools. When his supply of drugs ran
out he continued to operate under extremely adverse
conditions. Consequently it was probably only a matter
of time before he suffered some fatal injury. In the
end he died of septicemia brought on by an untended
scratch received while operating on the wounded. He
had been in China little over a year.[20] He died at
peace with himself, knowing that his name would live on
among the heroes of the revolution.

III

Given that Bethune's efforts were certainly not enough

300

to change the course of the war it is hard for westerners
to appreciate why the Chinese Communists have so idolised
him. But precisely because he was a foreigner he became
a major symbolic figure in the story of the liberation
movement on mainland China. We may not regard that movement as religious. But the figure of Chairman Mao has
served as a religious symbol for millions of Chinese.
In his quest for permanent cultural revolution he and
his more visionary followers sought to transcend the
limitations of ordinary life. Their use of uniforms,
slogans, parades, operas and sagas of popular heroes
cannot be considered only on the level of political cause
and effect. The spirit which permeates their movements
defies such reductionism. Of course until Mao's successors have been in power beyond the next generation we can
only speak of a developing tradition and speculate concerning what turn his movement will take in his absence.
But in the telling of the stories of people like Bethune
we see the symbolic patterns of their inspiration and
have our best clues to the ideals which they would
actualize for their successors.

His biographers tend to portray Bethune as a restless
genius who could never have made the compromises
necessary to achieve success in civilian life. Even
if true this would be irrelevant to an evaluation of
his critiques of the social order which presented
medicine as a profitable career for the affluent (medical specialization did not come cheaply) rather than as
a practical vocation for the compassionate (the two are
not mutually exclusive as the example of Wilder Penfield
shows). What Mao appreciated in him was his combination
of idealistic dedication and technical knowledge. Indeed considering what an arch materialist Mao is popularly supposed to have been it is striking how often
the word 'spirit' appears in his memorial notice of
Bethune's death. To leaders who had been betrayed by
the Russian Communists (Stalin had sided with Chiang)
and had little current contact with America and Europe
Bethune came as a vital sign of international recognition and tangible support. He not only believed in the
rightness of their cause but also brought to bear on
their problems all his skill as a renowed surgeon. He
was living proof that one could be a doctor and a revolutionary, a nationalist and an internationalist, whose
concern to combat suffering outweighed all other considerations.

One typically Chinese form of consciousness-raising is

to placard joys and grievances on wall posters and standards borne in processions. Accordingly when Bethune's
model hospital was officially opened he was presented
with banners celebrating him as teacher, fellow-fighter,
adviser, doctor, friend, example and comrade. We might
think these just tokens of reverence for official dig-
nitaries blended with more or less stereotyped communist
categories. But they were honouring a man who had
turned his own salary into a Tobacco Fund for the wounded, who after performing eight or ten major operations
a day lectured in the late afternoons on every aspect
of basic medical care, who donated his own blood for a
transfusion in the middle of an operation when others
hesitated, who gave yet another litre of blood soon
afterwards to initiate the first Volunteer Blood Donor
Group in China and who had to be reprimanded by his
commanding officer for not getting enough food and
rest.21 Despite the barriers of language and short
acquaintance Bethune knew that he was appreciated and
gave joyfully in return all that he could.

In religious terms Bethune was a karma yogi, one who
realizes transcendence through the discipline of social
action and so liberates himself and others. In his
instance the transcendence was "horizontal" rather than
"vertical," moving towards a new order for mankind in
the future in which good would eradicate evil, humanity
would triumph over its alienated condition. In Marxist
terms his work was a "praxis," a realization in the
present of that combination of thought and action which
is meaningful because it brings in this new future. He
died confident that the cause to which he had given his
life would succeed. He had achieved Lifton's third
"mode of immortality" through his deeds and influence
upon leaders of the Chinese revolution.22 In psychosocial terms he was a charismatic figure who lived
constantly on the edge of death himself while symbolis-
ing new hope of life for others around him.

To the Chinese doctors, nurses and medical assistants
Bethune had preached a gospel of good technique. They
should emulate the Japanese in expropriating western
technology while not using it merely for the aggrandise-
ment of the few. How well he caught the spirit of
Chinese philosophy may be judged from part of his response to the presentation of the banners. To those
assembled for the occasion he declared:

    Our organization is not like a good house - settled,

static and still. It is like a globe - round, fluid,
moving and dynamic. It is held together like a drop
of water, by the cohesion and co-operation of its
individual parts. So, when I think of leadership, I
think, principally, of the "little" leader of small
units, and not so much of the big leaders of great
units. This development of the "little" leaders is
the absolute necessity for the revolutionary reorganization of human society into autonomously acting,
socially conscious individuals. When that has been
accomplished, leaders (like the State itself) will
gradually disappear. So, even though you need leaders
now, and will for a long time to come, you must learn
not to depend upon (I mean not to get into the habit
of leaning heavily on) your leaders. Be a leader
yourself, for <u>every leader starts by first leading
himself</u>.

The Scalpel, the Sword p. 221 (his italics)

On the "big" leaders Bethune urged continued self-
criticism and diligence in the service of their patients.
His ideology was clearly communistic but in and through
his rhetoric echoed centuries of Taoist wisdom, the
tradition of China's alienated and dispossessed.

The legend of Bethune's presence had spread throughout
the army. Isolated villagers were told that he might
visit them. Returning soldiers said that he never rested, never abandoned a wounded man or left a patient
until everything possible had been done for him. His
anger was like thunder but his first words to each patient were "My son..." His passage through each village
had become a state procession and units had petitioned
headquarters to have Bethune sent to them.

In theory all doctors put their patients first, just
as teachers are supposed to put their students first.
But in practice western professionals tend to arrange
institutions and training programs primarily to suit
their own interests and convenience. Bethune was revolutionary in that he changed the pattern of his medical
practice to realize his own maxim: "Doctors, go to the
wounded. Don't wait for the wounded to come to you."23
He devised a way of packing all the equipment needed
for a hundred operations, five hundred dressings and
five hundred prescriptions on the backs of two mules.
Included were instruments, an operating table, splints,
anaesthetics and much more. Until his supplies were
exhausted he had the makings of a mini-hospital which

could be moved back and forth through enemy lines. Thus
as the tempo of fighting increased he was still able to
serve the casualties quickly and efficiently.

The link between such seemingly small details and
grandiose conceptions of their importance is well illustrated by a letter addressed to Bethune by his staff, as
he left one base camp for another. It reads in part:

> we should also show our most thankfulness to you for
> you having given our patients a special fund...with
> your own salary....This great kindness shows your
> great consideration for our patients instead of your-
> self. Not only the patients lying on the k'angs
> would wish to thank you, but also the staff members
> would like to show their respect to you. You are
> really one of the saviors of world peace and an inter-
> nationalist fighting for the peace and democracy of
> the world.

The Scalpel, the Sword p. 238

At that time the Allies had not entered the war against
the Axis, the Spanish Loyalists had finally been defeated and the Chinese Nationalists were in collusion
with the Japanese in an attempt to encircle and destroy
the main Communist army. To those who regarded their
movement as the world's last hope for peace and justice
whatever they did to bring closer the day of victory
had immediate practical significance. It also had
universal eschatological implications. Just because
Bethune joined the fight before it was fashionable and
came as a Canadian when most Canadians cared little or
nothing for the fate of the Chinese the symbolic impact
of his presence and his example was immense. From the
Chinese Communist point of view he was the right man at
the right time in the right place.

Social theorists are beginning to suggest that charismatic leadership is not just the expression of some
unique potency given at birth. It results from creative
interaction between a leader and a group which appre-
ciates and supports what he represents. For example,
Jesus' impact on his followers cannot be exhaustively
accounted for by asserting that he was divinely conceived or that his disciples' lives were miraculously
taken over by the Holy Spirit, as if some substance
which had been missing on the human scene was suddenly
supplied from heaven.[24] Rather the encounter between

304

this teacher and those men from Galilee has to be seen
against the wider background of forces at work in
Palestine at the time and the receptivity of the disciples for what Jesus represented. Similarly the fact
that Bethune was let go in disgrace from the Royal
Victoria Hospital and rather hurriedly recalled by his
Canadian sponsors from the Spanish Civil War, but exalted as a great surgeon and humanitarian by Mao Tse-
tung and his followers, tells us much about the differing values and judgments prevalent in North America and
Northern China during the late nineteen-thirties.

In effect Bethune has become part of the foundational
myth of modern China. In the present context 'myth' is
understood to mean an overarching story which sets the
patterns of a people's sense of worth and place. It
oversimplifies sequences of events and glosses over
personal idiosyncrasies to portray ideal characters performing ideal acts. The significance of the action
extends to the boundaries of "real" time and space.
In the telling of the Bethune story this significance
is both creative and redemptive. It is part of the
story of the creation of a new humanitarian state out
of chaotic, inhumane conditions. And it is part of the
story of the transformation of modern technology in the
service of those who most needed it but previously
could not benefit from it. Bethune's own development
exemplified what Maslow and others refer to as "self-
actualization," moving beyond the meeting of basic needs
to a kind of "peak experience" which knows perfect
freedom.[25] But for Bethune this transcendent freedom
from ego-concern came in his realization of freedom for
others and was only meaningful as it contributed to
their liberation. From the mythological point of view
an element of fictitious simplicity is permissible in
the telling of this story since what is of major interest is its symbolic significance rather than its
historical accuracy. At the same time, however, what
makes Bethune such a powerful symbol is the fact that
his was a real life and a real death in a real world
war.

IV

We might react against the Chinese version of Bethune's biography by seeing his virtual canonization as
nothing but a cynical exercise in propaganda aimed at
gullible persons. We might so define the parameters of

World War II that his phase of it would not even belong
in the story of the "real" war. We might dwell on centres of action far from the mountains where he died.
In order to perpetuate an image of ourselves as doers
of good and supporters of democracy we might discount
his genuine achievements and identify ourselves with
the views of our first Canadian Governor-General. We
might agree with Hazen Sise's father, the president of
Northern Electric, who thought that his son was un-
warrantedly interfering in other people's affairs by
going with Bethune to Spain.[26] But in doing so we
would be living out our own myth, our own simplified
vision of life's purpose, by retelling a story of
glorious Allies destroying Nazi tyranny in the 1940s.
Bethune would not be an exemplary image of creation and
redemption for us because, according to our myth, he
worked for the forces of chaos against the sacred values
of private enterprise. Even if our myth of Canadian
origins and aspirations were Marxist rather than
bourgeois-liberal we might regard the Bethune story as
peripheral. In Léandre Bergeron's rendering of the
"real" story of les habitants, for instance, Mussolini
and Salazar are mentioned, but not Franco or Bethune.[27]

The point of a religious story, however, need not be
mythological. It need not depend upon reading cosmic
meaning into particular symbolic acts. The tradition
of realistic narrative in the interpretation of biblical doctrines may incline us in this direction.[28] We
may tie significance particularly to plot and regard the
Bethune story as meaningful only if it lends itself to
interpretation in terms of creation, redemption and
final judgment, i.e., the outlines of the biblical master story. But Zen traditions, for example, remind us
that what is liberating may be more a quality of insight and realization of character than a particular
pattern of praxis.[29] What is religiously significant
about a particular story may be its parabolic effect
rather than its mythical message.

Recent work on the nature of parables suggests among
other things that their impact is due to the reversal
of values and expectations which they induce in believers.[30] Thus if the attitudes inculcated by current
mythology include a high regard for doctors and a low
regard for revolutionaries, the appearance of a revolutionary doctor as the hero of a story may upset any
unthinking acceptance of the status quo. Such a story
would be a parable rather than a myth. So far from

mediating the values of society in mythological fashion
the Bethune story as parable would challenge Canadians
to reevaluate themselves and the values of those who
rejected or belittled his humanitarian work.   Similarly
at a time when the search is on for stories expressing
our identity as Canadians a hero whose actions take him
beyond the border between Ontario and Quebec may serve
to undermine excessive preoccupation with only regional
histories.   The prevailing national myth may allow for
well-meant liberal activities by Canadians working in
the "Third World."   But here is a story where the reci-
pients of medical aid are "the enemy."   Thus its soterio-
logical significance may stem not from its inclusion in
some cosmological myth but from its challenge to the
world-views of comfortably situated Canadians.   Similarly the full Bethune story, including his critique of
Spanish bureaucracies, might provoke some soul-searching
among the Chinese.   What would then be soteriologically
significant would not be any particular moral or message
brought to mind by official biographies.   It would be
rather the parabolic effect of his story on particular
quests for ultimate freedom.

Besides myths and parables there are other kinds of
story in religion.   As well as myths of birth and
resurrection in the New Testament, for instance, there
are healing stories.   These are an intermediate type.
They are mythological in ascribing the source of healing power to agencies transcending surface patterns of
cause and effect.   But they are parabolic in that those
whom Jesus heals and the occasions on which he heals
constitute a challenge to orthodox custom and teaching.
His therapeutic mission was more important to Jesus
than Pharisaic dogmas and Levitical rules.   Likewise
the one consistent image of Bethune is that of his un-
dogmatic concern for the welfare of his patients.   In
order to serve them he could on occasion join forces
with missionaries and rebuke revolutionaries.   In this
he shows a firmer grasp of Christian priorities than
some of his critics at home.

Theological discussions of parables, especially among
Protestants, tend to depict existential confrontations
in individualistic terms.   Their focus is on critical
choices rather than corporate involvement.31   Bethune's
story has its authentic moments of personal anxiety and
self-acceptance.   But it also reveals the cumulative
impact of many small decisions in seemingly unrelated
corners of the world.   It emphasizes the therapeutic

need for scientific research and political planning as
well as for authentic innovators who scorn tradition.
More than most his story drives home to us the extent
to which our reading of events is shaped by our pre-
conceptions and prejudices. Often we do not even notice
the surface story until we have demythologized our
perceptions of ancestors and enemies. Then as we re-
invest it with symbolic significance we tend to direct
energy and attention to debates over meaning at the
expense of action. We prize dogma over therapy and
mistake preferences for values. In order to determine
what is truly necessary we need critical theoretical
principles and not just stories. One positive outcome
of recent Marxist-Christian dialogues is the realization
on both sides that praxis takes precedence over the
passion for purity in matters of opinion.[32]

Religious traditions are carried by a full array of
myths, parables, hymns, prayers and other oral and
written forms. One story does not make a tradition and
the significance of any given story shifts according to
the contexts in which we take it. The meaning of the
Bethune story for us depends upon our general conceptions of men and affairs. At the same time religious
symbols are rich in imaginative possibilities precisely
because their meaning is not exhausted by one version
of one story.[33] Our appraisal of people like Bethune
depends upon our prior understanding of ourselves. But
as we ask how we see him we also come to see ourselves
in a fresh light. Looking through the surface story to
the deeper meanings of his dedication and sacrifice we
reach new levels of insight concerning our times and
places. In this process symbols are the "elevators"
which move us from one level to the next. They evoke
in us a sense of liberating vision and transforming
power.

As a symbol Bethune takes us from existential questions concerning personal identity in the face of death,
through ideological questions concerning political
values, to ultimate questions concerning ways of liberation and the power of the future. We do not have
available in English all the materials on his year in
China. But already in excerpts from his diaries we
meet not only a man of action but also one who raised
questions concerning the final causes of war and the
apathy of many in power towards poverty and suffering.
His was a dream of mankind at peace with justice for
all. As we see the churches' impotence through his

eyes we cannot help but question Christian complacency in the recounting of Christian history and Christian promises for the future. At the same time his story affords no room for complacency among Marxists either. Had he lived through the simplicities of the war against Japan to join in the complexities of nation-building under Mao he might well have seemed less saintly to his admirers than he does now. We do not usually see symbolic power in the lives of our near contemporaries unless they have been martyrs to a cause, as in the case of Bonhoeffer and Bethune. And then the aura of hero worship often obscures the humanity and fallibility of the hero.

A symbol as such is neither good nor bad. It may have moral power and cosmic significance. But such power and potential for meaning can be abused. In religious thinking the critical principle concerning ways of salvation is the principle of ultimate freedom.[34] To determine what this means and consider what genuine means for realizing it are at work in our lives is a task for theoreticians and theologians. But stories such as the story of Bethune provide a touchstone against which their ideas must be tested. What is distinctive of our times religiously speaking is our recognition of the fact that there is no single master story embracing all our myths and parables. This has always been so but now we more readily accept our differences. Thus we may welcome the fact that Chinese communists have embraced Bethune as a symbol of their move from under their ancestors' shadows while we add his name to the list of our own rather meagre collection of "ancestors."[35] As our horizons of expectation overlap more and more the symbol of Bethune may serve both to liberate the Chinese from their traditional xenophobia and us from our mindless anti-communism. It is this liberating power which gives his story religious significance and will continue to do so as long as we resist the temptation to confine it to only one level of experience. The symbol of his life and death can be part of that liberating process which we have declared to be the true objective of all religions.

As myth, parable or something in between the story of Norman Bethune can enrich our own story of Canadian ways of life. His biography can become part of our autobiography.

FOOTNOTES

1. Lucy Bregman has brought this out particularly well with regard to Freudian discussions of the case of Daniel Paul Schreber, forthcoming in the Journal of Religion and Mental Health, paper for the American Academy of Religion, October 1976. See also the discussion in Paul Ricoeur, Freud and Philosophy, tr. Denis Savage, Yale University Press, New Haven 1970.

2. As Robert Lawson Slater points out Otto himself was equally alive to mystical traditions and religions of grace. See "Religious Diversity and Movements of Religious Life and Thought" in the Murti Fest-schrift, ed. Harold Coward, Dharma Press, Berkeley 1977.

3. For definitions and relevant analysis here see Peter C. Hodgson, New Birth of Freedom, Fortress, Philadelphia, 1976 (re freedom) and Frederick J. Streng, "Studying Religion: Possibilities and Limitations of Different Definitions" Journal of the American Academy of Religion, Vol. XL, No. 2, June 1972, p. 219-237.

4. See e.g. Ninian Smart, Mao, Fontana pb., 1974.

5. See the essays and bibliographical data in James Wiggins ed., Religion As Story, Harper Forum pb., New York, 1975, in John S. Dunne, The City of the Gods, Macmillan, New York, 1965 and his subsequent works and Wesley A. Kort, Narrative Elements and Religious Meaning, Fortress, Philadelphia, 1975.

6. On this contrast see John S. Dunne, A Search for God In Time And Memory, Macmillan pb., New York, 1970, p. 17.

7. The categories need to be further defined and the analysis differentiated from that of the structuralists. See Paul Ricoeur, Semeia 4, 1975, "Biblical Hermeneutics."

8. Letters to editors of Canadian newspapers from 1937 to 1976 are predominantly denunciations of the attention paid to Bethune. In what follows I draw primarily on Roderick Stewart, Bethune, Paperjacks,

Don Mills, 1975, for factual data and on Ted Allan
and Sydney Gordon, The Scalpel, the Sword: The
Story of Doctor Norman Bethune, Revised Edition,
McClelland and Stewart, Toronto, 1971, for the
Chinese period. Rod Langley's play Bethune, Talon
Books, Vancouver, 1975 and a one-hour CBC Documentary on Bethune have also been consulted, as well
as material in the national archives. At the time
of writing another documentary and a movie on
Bethune are being produced, the latter mainly dependent on Gordon's material.

9. Stewart, op. cit., p. 7.

10. See the quote in Stewart p. 105 and the Toronto
Star Weekly for February 20, 1937, concerning the
unit in Spain (copy in the Hazen Sise file, Public
Archives of Canada). Note also the two quotes
from Robert McClure in Stewart p. 122 and 134.

11. On November 8, 1926, Bethune wrote from Gravenhurst
to his friend Dr. Edward Kupka: "Well, I am a new
pig but a restless one at times -- too much the
product of my generation to conceive my situation
as tragic -- there has been no tragedy since the
war -- I am forced to regard the situation, if not
with grimness, then at least with a shrug of the
shoulders for an entirely farcical and futile
figure in it. Unable to fall back on the merciful
but mysterious ways of a Hidden Purpose in life,
and having entirely abandoned the anthropological
idea of God, there is but little comfort in the
conception of a Vital Force, one is reduced to the
consolation of similar sufferers....
                                    "....I will get
well, of course, but the interval is wearying...I
am going to take up French...I feel I should read
something 'serious' 'Something worthwhile'— but I
have no heart for didactic -- fiction is as true as
solemn treatises on life and on most fact, too."

                    p. 2 (Public Archives)

The "first dying" remark comes from Allan & Gordon,
p. 9.

12. Stewart, p. 31.

13. Stewart, p. 40f.

14. Stewart, p. 54f.

15. Stewart, p. 95-96.

16. See the seven-page memorandum on "Medical Care For the People of Montreal and The Province of Quebec" circulated to all candidates seeking election in Montréal on August 10, 1936 (Public Archives) with a covering letter from Bethune. The rhetoric is Marxist but the proposals are for a variety of plans, including compulsory health insurance and a common front of professionals to meet the needs of the 346,490 estimated to be on relief in the Province of Québec.

17. The Watch That Ends The Night, Signet pb. New York, 1959, Part 6, Ch. 1, p. 230. Cf. Stewart, p. 109, concerning his speaking tour.

18. Stewart, p. 106, cf. also p. 113.

19. Stewart, p. 119.

20. Stewart, p. 159.

21. Allan & Gordon, p. 217f.

22. See Robert Jay Lifton, Boundaries, Vintage pb. New York, 1970, p. 22 and Revolutionary Immortality: Mao Tse-tung and the Chinese Cultural Revolution, Weidenfeld & Nicolson, London, 1969.

23. Allan & Gordon, p. 225.

24. See John G. Gager, Kingdom and Community: The Social World of Early Christianity, Prentice-Hall pb. Englewood Cliffs, N.J., 1975, p. 28f. citing Peter Worsley and others.

25. Abraham Maslow, Toward a Psychology of Being, 2nd. ed., Insight pb. Van Nostrand Reinhold, New York, 1968. For criticism see Lucy Bregman, "Maslow as Theorist of Religion: Reflections on His Popularity and Plausibility," Soundings, LIX, No. 2, Summer 1976, p. 139-163.

26. See the letter from J.A. Noonan to Paul Sise, December 4, 1936, and Paul Sise's letter to Sir Campbell Stuart, February 8, 1937, Sise file, Public Archives, Ottawa.

27. Petit Manuel d'Histoire du Québec, Editions Québec-
    oises, n.d., p. 194-95.

28. See the discussion of Hans Frei and Tolkien by John
    Zuck, "Tales of Wonder: Biblical Narrative, Myth
    and Fairy Stories," Journal of the American Academy
    of Religion, XLIX, No. 2, June, 1976, p. 299-308,
    and of Barr by Hugh Jones, "The Concept of Story
    and Theological Discourse," Scottish Journal of
    Theology, Vol. 29, 1976, p. 415-433.

29. Concerning character see James Wm. McClendon Jr.,
    Biography as Theology, Abingdon, Nashville, 1974,
    Ch. 1.

30. See John Dominic Crossan, Dark Interval: Towards
    A Theology of Story, Argus, Niles, Ill. 1975,
    p. 66f.

31. See Sallie TeSelle, Speaking in Parables, Fortress,
    Philadelphia, 1975 and the critique of Bultmann by
    Dorothee Soelle, Political Theology, tr. John
    Shelley, Fortress, Philadelphia, 1974. TeSelle
    is already criticising her own earlier perspective
    in this regard.

32. See the review in Thomas Dean, Post-Theistic Think-
    ing; The Marxist-Christian Dialogue in Radical Per-
    spective, Temple University Press, Philadelphia,
    1975.

33. Concerning symbols in this context see Gregory Baum,
    Religion and Alienation: A Theological Reading of
    Sociology, Paulist, New York, 1975, Ch. XI.

34. Readers familiar only with western traditions are
    inclined sometimes to dismiss references to ulti-
    mate freedom in this connection as rather recent
    and dubious conceptual imports. In fact the allu-
    sion is as much to Hindu and Chinese as to western
    principles. On the former see e.g., Raimundo
    Panikkar, "Philosophy and revolution: the text, the
    context and the texture," Philosophy East and West,
    Vol. 23, No. 3, 1973, p. 315-322.

35. On the deadening effect of tradition in China see
    Francis L.K. Hsu, Under the Ancestors' Shadow,
    Doubleday, New York, 1967.

RELIGION AS STORY: NORMAN BETHUNE

Note: the following item from the Globe and Mail, Toronto, June 21, 1977, illustrates the continuing impact of the Bethune story in China today:

CHINA REBUILDS HOUSE IN HONOR OF BETHUNE
Tokyo (AP) - The house were Canadian doctor
Norman Bethune lived while treating Chinese Communist soldiers in the late nineteen thirties has
been rebuilt "to perpetuate his memory and learn
from his internationalist and Communist spirit,"
China's official Hsinhua news agency reported yes-
terday.

The Lingchiu County party committee in north
China's Shansi province also has repaired an operating room in the special surgical hospital in
Yangchinchuang used by Dr. Bethune between Nov.
25, 1937, and Feb. 10, 1939, Hsinhua said.

"Working day and night to save wounded soldiers,
he also found the time to treat local people," the
agency said. "His sense of responsibility in his
work and warm-heartedness toward all comrades and
the people made a profound impression on the people
of Yangchinchuang."

A VOYAGE INTO SELFHOOD

WILLIAM C. JAMES did his doctoral work in Religion and
Literature at the University of Chicago and is Assistant Professor of Religion at Queen's University. He has written
on W.H. Auden and Margaret Atwood and first presented
his paper on Hugh MacLennan at the CSSR/SCER meetings
in Edmonton (1975).

RÉSUMÉ

Le roman de Hugh MacLennan est un portrait de l'homme
moderne qui se met en quête de l'identité, dont le foyer
est le moi plutôt que la société. Cette quête a lieu
quand on se rend compte du vide qui reste lorsque Dieu
est absent; c'est l'écroulement de la société, de l'ancien ordre de la vie après la Première Guerre Mondiale.
On essaie de remplir ce vide par l'amour, la peinture,
même la lutte qui a eut lieu en Espagne durant cette
époque. Car tout homme a besoin d'appartenir à quelque
chose plus grand que lui-même. Ainsi un paradoxe se
développe bientôt : chaque personne est un membre de
l'humanité tout comme les autres, mais chaque personne
a besoin en même temps d'être un individu, un 'moi' authentique et unique.

Grâce aux images religieuses du roman, la quête devient
une découverte de la foi religieuse. Par exemple, le
thème du voyage devient un pèlerinage spirituel. La mer
est le symbole de la mort et de la nouvelle vie. Le navire est une métaphore de la société. A la fin du voyage, on se rend compte que la vraie lumière vient du de-
dans. Chaque personne reste toujours une île solitaire,
mais elle est une île d'un grand archipel. Ce qui reste
à comprendre maintenant c'est la solidarité humaine.
Quelle ordonnance faut-il pour la société en général?

WILLIAM C. JAMES

A Voyage Into Selfhood: Hugh MacLennan's The Watch that Ends the Night

Erich Heller, the eminent critic of German literature,
has remarked that the story of poetry from the Renais-
sance to the present day might be entitled "The Discovery and Colonization of Inwardness." And W.H. Auden,
describing the latter stages of this exploration, declares that the characteristic hero of modern literature
is not the doer of extraordinary deeds, "but the man or
woman in any walk of life who, despite all the impersonal pressures of modern society, manages to acquire
and preserve a face of his own."[1] It was primarily
upon this problem of the acquisition and preservation
of selfhood that the Canadian author, Hugh MacLennan,
was bestowing his attention in his novel of 1959, The
Watch that Ends the Night. Notwithstanding his reputation as a social novelist whose writings depict (to
use George Woodcock's phrase) "a nation's odyssey,"
MacLennan in his recent fiction has increasingly concerned himself with the inner life of the individual in
society and not with the cultural progress of our
nation as a whole. Thus, Paul Goetsch, introducing
a recent collection of essays which document the major
trends in MacLennan criticism, states that MacLennan
"is now more concerned with private than social solutions to the question of how life can be affirmed in
the face of modern scepticism, materialism, violence
and chaos."[2] While undecided whether or not he is
"essentially a religious novelist" (the opinion of Alec
Lucas), Goetsch suggests that it might be rewarding to
investigate this deepening interest in personal and
psychological problems in a number of ways, among them
"to examine the religious imagery he uses in The Watch
that Ends the Night."[3] This present paper might be
seen as furthering such a line of investigation.

In 1969 MacLennan, ever-conscious of the reception
and interpretation of his work, wrote that what he had
been trying to say in The Watch that Ends the Night
"was that the decade of the 1950's was the visible
proof of my generation's moral and intellectual bankruptcy."[4] In one aspect, then, his novel was an indictment of the "fake revolutionaries" of the Thirties who
were convinced that "the combination of politics and
technology is just what the Doctor of History ordered."
But, says MacLennan, "the papier-maché intellectual
armour I had picked up in the Thirties contained more

built-in obsolescence than any shiny new model you see
advertised on the TV screen."[5] It was this obsolescence
that became apparent to MacLennan only in the Fifties,
so he records that during the last few months of his
writing The Watch he was like a snake shedding this
intellectual skin of the Depression generation.

But the novel had a positive aspect too:

In The Watch that Ends the Night my intuitions were
forcing me to utter something socially blasphemous in
those years. They were asserting that God had not
been outmoded by the Christian Church, Bertrand
Russell, the social scientists and modern education.[6]

To put the case as bluntly as possible, The Watch that
Ends the Night is about the recovery or discovery of a
religious faith in the lives of its three main characters. Each of the three is struggling to find, within
himself, a fundamentally religious basis for coping
with the Depression of the Thirties, the tumult of the
Second World War, and the prosperity of the post-war
Fifties.

The Odysseus myth, the love triangle, and the flashback technique are skillfully blended and brought to
focus upon this perennial problem as it is experienced
in its modern context. The Odyssey undergoes a Christian metamorphosis as Jerome Martell (the returned
wanderer) comes home. True to the Homeric archetype,
he returns only to renew his wanderings once more, but
this Odysseus does not put to flight the suitors of
Penelope ("Penelope" in this case being Catherine,
Jerome's wife). Instead Jerome is the means whereby
Catherine's miraculous recovery from an embolism takes
place. To George Stewart (the narrator and the man
Catherine had married during Jerome's absence) he imparts the spiritual wisdom he has acquired during his
journeys. Speaking of the Odyssey, David Grene has
remarked that the domesticity and realism of the world
to which Odysseus returns stands in marked contrast to
the heroic and marvellous world of the Wanderings from
which he has come.[7] Similarly, the reader of The Watch
finds himself less engaged by the exploits of the almost superhuman Jerome than he is by George's effort
to put together the meaning of his life when confronted
by the fact that his wife's rheumatic heart will certainly result in an early death for her.

317

For George, Jerome, and Catherine (each born at about the turn of the century) there is a brief period during which conventional Christianity seems to be adequate. But then the experience of the Great War (for Jerome) and of the Depression (for George) overwhelm the childhood creeds and the old, inherited forms of religion prove to be no longer adequate in this new age. Catherine, too, finds her faith eroded in the trying interim between the wars. She expresses her sense of the vacuum which remains when God is discovered to be absent: "We're not like the man who built his house on the sand. We're like the man who tore down all the walls of his house in November and then had to face the winter naked."[8] So it is that MacLennan sees the major problem of life in the Thirties to be the collapse of the old order and the seeming withdrawal of God from the scene of life. Under these conditions George finds himself left with no resources to draw upon:

This is what happens, I thought, when the leaders close their doors and the walls of custom collapse. This is what happens when people try to play a game making the rules as they go along. I saw Catherine, Jerome, myself and everyone I knew like lost shadows moving perilously over a crust covering a void (p. 283).

Or as Jerome puts it: "A man must belong to something larger than himself. He must surrender to it. God was so convenient for that purpose when people could believe in Him. He was so safe and so remote" (pp. 270-71).

The politics of the Thirties George refers to as the "neo-religious faith." It was, he says, a time when men made gods of political systems, and when people caught politics as they had previously caught religion. But from his narrative vantage point in the year 1951 George has discovered that in the intervening two decades politics has ceased to be fundamental at all. A process of individualization has resulted in such an insularity that although John Donne's famous words may have been true in the Thirties, each man in the Fifties finds himself alone. George Stewart and his contemporaries are bound together by their anger during the Thirties, by their fear during the Forties - when "the whole world went over a frontier" - and by nothing at all during the Fifties:

In the bleak years we at least were not alone. In
these prosperous years we were. The gods, false or
true, had vanished. The bell which only a few years
ago had tolled for all, now tolled for each family in
its prosperous solitude (p. 323).

This collective experience of a generation has its
parallels in the inner life of each member of the central trio of The Watch. Each of the three acknowledges
the truth that a man must belong to something larger
than himself, as Jerome put it. For a time there is an
attempt to find that "something larger" in each other,
in a triangular relationship in which a love relationship is operative between George and Jerome, the latter
becoming George's "spiritual father," as well as between
each of them and Catherine. Finally, Jerome, as fatherless in reality as George is emotionally, pushed outside
the triangle in his search for something greater. Declaring the need of mankind at large to be of greater
import, he leaves his home and family to assist in the
Spanish cause against Fascism. His departure has the
effect of teaching Catherine that "human love isn't
sufficient," so she learns how to paint, declaring that
if only she could paint it would not matter how she
felt about anything. George, disillusioned in Jerome
for what he sees as an abdication of his responsibilities as husband and father, turns to Catherine and
makes her, as he says, "my rock and salvation." When,
two years later, news of Jerome's supposed death leaves
George free to marry Catherine, he feels that at last
all of his dreams have been realized. Only when Jerome
returns ten years later and Catherine suffers the near-
fatal attack does George have this ground of his security shaken. The unresolved problems of the Thirties
come rushing back in upon him.

MacLennan tells us that between 1951 and 1959 he
wrote more than three million words before he produced
his finished manuscript of 140,000 words. Not that
this fact is significant in itself, but what he was
actually doing, he says, was "learning how to shape a
new bottle for a new kind of wine." MacLennan relates
that in 1951 he was struck with the realization that
the modern novel had failed to keep pace with our
changing attitudes. Governed by dramatic requirements,
the novel had tried to render human destiny, as found
in the interplay between characters, into external
actions. The educated public, however, informed by
modern psychology, had realized that "the basic conflict

was within the individual." Thus, MacLennan made a
significant resolution:

> ...somehow I was going to write a book which would
> not depend upon character-in-action, but on spirit-
> in-action. The conflict here, the essential one,
> was between the human spirit of Everyman and Every-
> man's human condition.[9]

The Fifties, then, emerge in MacLennan's scheme as that
decade in which there is, in a sense, nothing really
significant to be done externally, in relation to one's
environment. The interpersonal relationships of the
characters become less important than what is going on
within each of them. Each character finds himself
bound to his mortality by a merciless fate (the human
condition of Everyman), this fate being opposed by the
Life-force within him (the human spirit of Everyman).

The problem of theodicy in its classical form of reconciling God's benevolence with his omnipotence is now
redefined as George Stewart searches for immortality in
the midst of mortality, for the manner in which "all
loving is a loving of life in the midst of death."
George discovers what Amos Wilder has put so well, that
"death is a catalyst of transcendence." Character-in-
action, therefore, becomes spirit-in-action most
clearly when Catherine almost dies and George states:
"Now in her final phase what I used to think of as her
character ceased to matter in Catherine; her character
almost disappeared into her spirit" (p. 323). The
essential Catherine now seemed to George to be "like
the container of a life-force resisting extinction."

MacLennan seems deliberately to have been vague concerning the nature of this "life-force" and it is
difficult to determine precisely what he might mean by
it. Elsewhere he calls it "spirit" and sometimes
"soul." But at the very least the problem of individual
identity is clearly involved. It seems that when
character as such ceases to be of importance, when the
person becomes merely a container of the life-force,
then at this point the individual becomes Everyman.
And yet, as MacLennan points out, "All of us is Everyman and this is intolerable unless each of us can also
be I." When what a man is normally pleased to be able
to call his "character" is minimized then a crisis of
identity occurs as character becomes so overwhelmed and
even obliterated that only the spirit remains. When

this happens a kind of death results, but out of this
death may be resurrected a new self and an appropriate
consciousness of what it means to be an individual.
The isolation of the self in the Fifties, then, pre-
cedes the removal of the very last prop - the personality mistakenly believed to be the real self. When
this prop is removed in its turn there must follow
either a rebirth and the emergence of a new selfhood,
or an annihilation in which the individual is submerged:
the individual must be Everyman, but he must also be an
"I." The rebirth occurs when the life-force unites itself with the Divine to assert itself against the fate
which threatens it. Only then does a man discover
immortality in the midst of mortality such that he can
accept both death and life. The idea that the individual must come to recognize himself both as self and
as Everyman is most clearly expressed by Jerome:

> Each of us is everybody, really. What scares us is
> just that. We want so much to be ourselves, but the
> time comes when we find we're everybody, and every-
> body is afraid. That's when you must die within
> yourself (p. 366).

MacLennan does not really succeed in resolving this
Everyman-self paradox, at least not in such a way that
we can readily reduce it to the logic of discursive
prose. In fact, he sees it as simply one of a number
of paired opposites that no writer can ever satisfac-
torily express. To see an effective resolution he says
we have to turn to music:

> One musical idea uttered in the minor in a certain
> tempo is surrender, despair and suicide. The same
> idea restated in the major with horns and woods be-
> comes an exultant call to life. This, which is dark-
> ness, also is light. This, which is no, also is yes.
> This, which is hatred, also is love. This, which is
> fear, also is courage. This, which is defeat, also
> is victory (p. 344).

In the first instance, then, the Life-force is that
which creates. Looked at again, it becomes that which
has destroyed the very self which it had created.
Again, and it brings together these two contradictions
in an act of re-creation which produces a harmony of
opposites.

Although the nature of man's essential conflict as
something inner becomes clear only towards the end of

the book, it is illuminating to pick up this clue from
the final chapters and to reread the entire novel in
the light of it. Thus, the quest of the Thirties is
the quest of character-in-action in which difficulties
are resolved externally: Jerome goes to Spain;
Catherine takes up painting; George marries Catherine.
Although maturity of character may result from such
action, the inner spiritual conflict is left unresolved,
and the terror of the Everyman seeking a self left
unmitigated. The quest of spirit-in-action is rendered
by MacLennan by means of the archetypal symbol of the
voyage, though I suspect that he is unaware of how well
his imagination resolved for him those contradictions
which his narrator could not harmonize in rational terms
alone.

For most readers the most memorable episode in The
Watch that Ends the Night is that beautifully rendered
and evocative description of the ten-year-old Jerome
fleeing from his mother's murderer in his tiny canoe
down the New Brunswick river. In fact, Dorothy Farmiloe
claims, with forgivable excess, that "Jerome's trip in
the canoe is a Canadian counterpoint to Huck Finn's
flight down the Mississippi on the raft and ought to
occupy the same place in Canadian literature that Huck's
holds in American."[10] She maintains that Jerome's
childhood experience is "a mythologized version of the
early years of this country" and that his canoe trip is
reminiscent of the voyageurs, seen elsewhere by Mac-
Lennan as the true makers of Canada. I agree rather
with Douglas Spettigue's view that this is a "personal
canoe" (not a national one) in the rising sea of the
subconscious or of fate. The quest is universal, not
because Jerome is symbolic of our nation, but because
he is Everyman seeking an identity.[11] The significance
of the voyage as portraying the spiritual pilgrimage
is a theme continuous throughout the entire novel.

The novel's initial flashback shows George just returned from a summer-long canoe trip through a part of
the Great Lakes. But what might have been his initiation into manhood fails to bring him out of his
adolescence, for upon his return an overbearing aunt
badgers his father into making George take another year
of prep school instead of going to McGill with Catherine.
Although Catherine urges George to assert himself -
"Grow up and go" she tells him - he cannot. Nor can he
consummate the love he feels for her in the sexual act
to which she invites him. Catherine has been given a

sailboat that same summer, and she asks George to be
her "crew," to come along and hold the jib sheet for her.
And, indeed, George seems to continue in this role,
metaphorically speaking, for some years, rather than
becoming "captain" of his own vessel.

Jerome, meanwhile, grew up, not on the outskirts of
civilized Montreal, but in a lumber camp in the New
Brunswick bush. His mother, whom later he could barely
remember, was the camp cook, but of his father - "his
unknown begetter" - he had no memory whatever. Two men
particularly were significant in his early childhood,
an old English sailor and the French-Canadian who
fashioned a miniature birch-bark canoe for him. The
sailor tried to make Jerome promise that "when he grew
up he would take to the sea," while the French-Canadian
provides the craft whereby Jerome makes his escape once
he is orphaned. Thus prepared, Jerome is launched on
his career as a seafaring adventurer. But at this
stage, not even knowing his last name, Jerome has no
identity of his own and is Everyman. Striking differences emerge when Jerome's canoe trip is compared with
that of George: George is seventeen, Jerome is ten;
George paddles with a group, Jerome is alone; George's
trip is for pleasure, Jerome is fleeing for his life;
George paddles from one lake into another, whereas
Jerome paddles down a river to the sea. Furthermore,
if the sea is recognized as that primitive, destructive
force which threatens life and society, then George,
who lives well inland, and whose trip takes place even
further inland, is well removed from that threat.
Jerome, of course, grows up in the wilds only a few
miles from the sea.

When the Martells adopt the runaway Jerome and take
him to Halifax, they too help prepare him for the sea.
Giles Martell tells Jerome about Halifax: "There are
big ships and small ships and we'll teach you how to
sail - a real boat and not one of those Indian canoes
you saw on your river" (p. 211). And, sure enough,
during his years in Halifax Jerome has his own sailboat.
Moreover, twice during his youth he hired on to a
schooner and went out with the fishing fleets to the
Grand Banks.

During one of his summer holidays in the early Thirties George sailed to the West Indies on board a fruit
ship. Later he was to discover that Jerome, at about
the same time, had rented a sixty-foot ketch for a

323

month's cruising in the Caribbean "and if his money had not run out he would have taken the craft through the Panama Canal" (p. 156). Once again George's voyage is overshadowed by that of Jerome. George comes to be a kind of protégé of Jerome, duplicating in miniature those actions which Jerome performs on the grand scale. His emasculating dependence upon Catherine keeps him from achieving that creative separation which Jerome was thrust into in his childhood. Jerome becomes master of his own fate and captain of his soul in a way that George does not: whereas George crews or signs on as a hand on someone else's craft, Jerome becomes captain of his own vessel.

One further pair of voyages assumes a large significance in the development of George and Jerome. In 1939 Jerome departed for Spain for the second time, thus beginning an absence which was to last until 1951. During this period of twelve years he was to escape from Spain into France, only to be imprisoned at Auschwitz, from which he went on to become a doctor in a Siberian town. Finally, he made his way to China and thence to Hong Kong. And at last he returned to Montreal by way of Vancouver. Thus Jerome becomes an Odysseus who circumnavigates the globe on a journey which has its beginning and ending in Montréal.

At about the same time - during the summer of 1938 - George took a job leading a tour to Russia. His observations of the situation in Russia and Europe that fateful summer led to a series of radio broadcasts. Thus, the summer tour became the stepping-stone to George's first significant employment as a political commentator. In a later (and typically introspective) glance at this trip, George was to pinpoint it as the event which at last launched him into maturity after a thirty-five year childhood. But for Jerome, who is already mature and professionally successful, his odyssey is a spiritual pilgrimage. When Jerome returns from the death camps, having learned from a rabbi how to lose his life to himself in order to learn to live as well as to die, he imparts this spiritual secret to George, his protégé.

In the midst of all these other voyages, it is Jerome's flight by canoe down the New Brunswick river which becomes the central governing image of the novel. MacLennan uses it to point up the Everyman-self paradox, and to contrast external action in relation to the social

milieu with the inner spiritual pilgrimage. The story
is told by Jerome to George in Part Five of the novel.
Then, in Parts Six and Seven, the picture of Jerome
paddling down the river by night flashes into George's
consciousness in the course of his narration. Indeed,
the image links together these last two parts of the
novel as the action shifts from the Thirties back to
the Fifties once again. Six times in less than one
hundred pages the vision recurs as George remembers
Jerome's story.12 At first, it seems to mean no more
to George than Jerome's quest for identity, as the
little canoe moves out onto the ocean and the storm
rises. Then, in the Fifties, George realizes that
Jerome is Everyman:

> Then a man discovers in dismay that what he believed
> to be his identity is no more than a tiny canoe at the
> mercy of an ocean. Sharkfilled, plankton-filled, re-
> fractor of light, terrible and mysterious, for years
> this ocean has seemed to slumber beneath the tiny
> identity it received from the dark river.
> Now the ocean rises and the things within it become
> visible. Little man, what now? The ocean rises, all
> frames disappear from around the pictures, there is
> no form, no sense, nothing but chaos in the darkness
> of the ocean storm. Little man, what now? (p. 345).

Jerome, fatherless and now motherless, has emerged
from the birth canal of the river apparently to assume
a new identity with his adoptive parents, the Martells.
But in reality he has emerged from the river only to
find himself upon the sea, which is the universal mother
and source of all life. In the cataclysm of the Thirties Jerome's identity is threatened once more as the
sea seeks to engulf him. As the frames disappear from
around the pictures and the forms dissolve, Jerome (and
the entire generation of which he is symbolic) experience "a reintegration into the formlessness of pre-
existence."13 As the darkness descends once more the
sea reverts to its primeval state as primordial undifferentiated flux. There is always the possibility
of storms, of rocks, of hurricanes, and of the ever-
present Leviathan (the monster of the deep) lurking
just below the surface. So then, the sea is experienced
as threat, the threat to identity of final extinction,
and yet it also retains potential as promise for regeneration and new life.

As W.H. Auden has made plain in his book The Enchafèd

Flood, the city is the symbolic opposite of the sea - it is the state of order as opposed to the state of disorder. As a child Jerome had dreamed of a white city on a hill overlooking the sea: "I used to dream that if I worked hard all my life, and tried hard all my life, maybe some day I'd be allowed within its gates" (p. 245). It was when Jerome envisaged this city being besieged by the Fascists that he determined to go to Spain. And so, as Auden points out, when society is in peril then the ship becomes a metaphor for society: when Jerome sees his white city on the hill endangered then he takes to the sea. Spain during the Revolution becomes like Jerome's tiny canoe at the mercy of the ocean. Jerome's initial motivation for making the voyage arises out of his determination to do something about his imperilled society. Here he exemplifies character-in-action, struggling against a hostile environment.

But there is another - more individualized - aspect of the symbolization than the use of the ship as a metaphor for society. The voyage itself becomes a symbol. As Auden says: "The Christian conception of time as a divine creation, to be accepted, and not, as in Platonic and Stoic philosophy, ignored, made the journey or pilgrimage a natural symbol for the spiritual life."[14] MacLennan uses the image of the sea to fuse together these two ideas of the ship as a metaphor for society in peril and of the sea voyage for the spiritual pilgrimage. These two aspects of the symbolism are analogous, of course, to the distinction between the Everyman and the self made earlier, and likewise brought into harmony on Jerome's voyage. When Jerome sets out it is because society is in danger and his character demands some external action on his part to allay this danger. But the symbol becomes individualized and focussed upon this lone figure once more in his tiny canoe trying to find his true identity while at the mercy of the boundless ocean. In this focus is seen the struggle of spirit-in-action. What serves to bring together and to unify these two ideas is precisely the Christian conception of time that Auden speaks of.

An adherence to what Eliade denominates as "the myth of the eternal return" would suggest, in relation to the symbolism of water, an endless cyclical repetition of reintegration with the formless, followed by regeneration. But as soon as form is achieved once more, as soon as separation from water occurs (every voyage has an end after all), then "every 'form' loses its

potentiality, falls under the law of time and of life;
it is limited, enters history, shares in the universal
law of change, decays."[15] Jerome, though involved in
the historical events of his time returns; yes, and may
be seen therefore to have escaped from subordination to
temporality to a kind of timelessness. But George,
meanwhile, is only too aware that for himself, and
especially for Catherine, time is linear. For Catherine
must live her life under the sword of Damocles and her
third embolism upon Jerome's return signals to her -
and to George - that the sword cannot forever remain in
suspension.

The title of MacLennan's novel is, of course, to be
found in a line of Isaac Watts' paraphrase of the Nine-
tieth Psalm:

A thousand ages in thy sight
  Are like an evening gone,
Short as the watch that ends the night
  Before the rising sun.

The entire psalm, referred to several times in the
course of the book, is the meditation of a wise man on
the brevity of life, for the psalmist is aware that the
human animal possesses a privileged item of information,
namely, that he is going to die. Throughout the psalm
a pessimistic view of life seems to hold sway as the
writer compares man to grass that is fresh and new in
the morning but which then withers and dies when evening
comes. Yet towards the end of the psalm the writer
indicates what lesson is to be derived from this sense
of life's transitory nature: "So teach us to number our
days / that we may get a heart of wisdom" (Ps. 90:12).

Against this background the novel's title is found to
be significant at several levels within the story.
First, on the level of the obvious, "the watch that ends
the night" is the afternoon that Jerome spends watching
over Catherine's unconscious form. At supper time
George goes to the hospital expecting to hear that
Catherine has died, but the nurse tells him instead,
"Last night I had no hope, but now I do." A miraculous
change has occurred and Jerome tells George that he
felt death leave the room. Second, "the watch" may be
seen as the long period during which George waits for
some change to occur in his wife. When the story begins it is early February and on the night of Jerome's
return the temperature reaches twenty degrees below zero.

But when Catherine's sudden change takes place the
weather changes too. As George leaves the hospital the
weather is warmer and he can hear the rivulets from the
melting snow. Thus the long, cold night of winter ends
and, as the taxi driver tells George, you can "smell
the spring in the air." At the most significant level,
however, Jerome's absence from 1939 to 1951 is a twelve-
year watch during which time is suspended. Time is
suspended during this period not only because Jerome is
away and has not yet re-entered history, so to speak,
but because it seemed to George that the years which
followed the outbreak of the War up until the start of
the Fifties did not really take place in time at all.
It is only after the decade of the Fifties has begun
that life seems to pick up where it left off after the
Depression. This is the topic of a conversation George
has with a friend in Ottawa the day after Jerome returns. It is the friend who begins:

> "Do you ever have the feeling that time stopped in
> 1939?"
> "Often."
> "We were alive before then, weren't we?" And his
> voice was wistful.
> "I suppose we were."
> "And since then we've had our careers. Successful
> careers!" And he gave a contemptuous laugh (p. 100).

When George married Catherine in 1941 they embarked
upon a period of happiness which lasted for ten years
and during which they both managed to shut out from
their minds the thought that the sword still hung over
Catherine. And, as George remarks, "Happiness annihi-
lates time." But Jerome's return starts the clock
ticking once again and all of the still unresolved problems from the Thirties return with him. Therefore,
the night of "the watch that ends the night" here is
the Depression and the prelude to the Second World War.
This "dark night of the soul" is not ended for George
until Jerome returns from his twelve-year watch in 1951.

Now it is at this point that George comes to an awareness of the nature of the divinely appointed time span
in a significant realization:

> ...it is of no importance that God appears indifferent
> to justice as men understand it. He gave life. He
> gave it. Life for a year, a month, a day or an hour
> is still a gift. The warmth of the sun or the caress

328

of the air, the sight of a flower or a cloud on the
wind, the possibility even for one day more to see
things grow - the human bondage is also the human
liberty (p. 344).

This realization, then, is George's realization of his
createdness which Nathan Scott states comes to the
person who lives in the presence of death: "the very
contingency of his existence, as it is disclosed in the
awareness that he must die, tells him that the origin
and meaning of his life are not wholly immanent within
himself: he did not create himself: life itself is
received, it is a gift."[16] When George Stewart understands time as kairos and not as mere chronicity he
understands as well that life is dependent upon God's
grace. He is no longer troubled with his original
problem, that of theodicy; he no longer wonders why
Catherine should have been condemned to such a short
life "among hundreds of thousands of others who went
free."

Jerome's journey, then, assumes a transitional function between the Thirties when external action mattered
most and the Fifties when the essential conflict was
seen to be within the individual. What begins as a
voyage in which the ship symbolizes society in peril
becomes a voyage which is a spiritual pilgrimage.
Jerome's return signifies the victory of the solitary
regenerated self over that sea of collective humanity
which threatens to submerge it. And what seems to
enable this self to face death squarely is a true
apprehension of the nature of time, viewed now from a
new perspective. For George and Catherine learn to
live under the sword of Damocles that hangs over
Catherine's head: "What if the ocean of time overwhelmed her? It overwhelms us all" (p. 373).

In the end this ocean is transformed in George's
mind, though not as in the eschatological vision of
the Book of Revelation in which there is "no more sea."
The sea, nonetheless, is no longer a sea of darkness
and chaos, but a sea of light. MacLennan expresses
this transformation of the dark watery chaos when he
places together two verses from Genesis:

...And the earth was without form, and void; and
darkness was on the face of the deep.
...And the Spirit of God moved upon the face of the
waters. And God said: let there be light: and
there was light (p. 321).

The sea is transformed for George when the divine act of creation is repeated in his own life and consciousness. The birth of the "new man" is a symbolic reenactment of the birth of the world (Eliade). The light which empties the ocean of its terror also transforms the imperilled city, so that George looking down upon Montréal from a hospital window sees it as a sea of light. George comprehends this light, then, as ordering the cosmos and as ordering his immediate surroundings. He also beholds it in the faces of Jerome and Catherine. But he achieves that long sought after spiritual maturity only when he discovers that same light to be within himself as well. Catherine's face displays what George can only describe as "the joy of the Lord" and, he says, "I knew its light would remain with me."

MacLennan views his first four novels as essentially optimistic. But once he discarded the intellectual skin of the Thirties, he says that the result was that his last two novels, The Watch that Ends the Night and The Return of the Sphinx, have been tragic. The significance of this remark is difficult to grasp, for the aesthetic shaping force which contains that tragic vision (to use Murray Krieger's phraseology) ameliorates the tragedy, making it a vehicle for affirmation. Perhaps MacLennan's understanding of The Watch as tragic becomes clear when one is reminded that it was originally entitled Requiem: "Requiem for one I loved who had died [that is, his wife, Dorothy, who shared Catherine's illness as well as her passion for painting], but also more: requiem for the idealists of the Thirties who had meant so well, tried so hard and gone so wrong."[17]

The tragedy seems to reside mainly in the chaos which MacLennan observes in the social scene at large. But in the midst of this chaos he sees a possibility for the individual to find some manner of transcendence: "It . . . fills me with awe and wonder to know that . . . the species to which I belong is stubbornly, blindly determined to remain human."[18] George Stewart's conclusion seems to be his author's too: "Here, I found at last, is the nature of the final human struggle. Within, not without. Without there is nothing to be done. But within" (p. 343).

What is lacking in MacLennan's account of things is an appropriate understanding of the solidarity of the individual man with his fellows. Perhaps he termed his novel "tragic" because he found himself finally unable to offer a prescription for society at large. MacLennan has rejected as adequate for our age John Donne's concept of man as a piece of the continent. As another critic has perceived, "For MacLennan, man remains an island forever, but an island in position, as it were, as a part of an archipelago; the experience of the one is the experience of all, and each part functions both as an entirety for all and as an entirety in itself."[19] Whether or not the recognition by the self of its identity as Everyman is thought ultimately to be a satisfactory solution, it is the only indication MacLennan offers as to how he sees the individual as bound up in community with his fellow man.

FOOTNOTES

1. The Dyer's Hand and Other Essays (New York: Random House, Vintage Books, 1968), p. 84.

2. "Introduction," in Hugh MacLennan, ed. Paul Goetsch (Toronto: McGraw-Hill Ryerson, 1973), p. 7.

3. Ibid., p. 8.

4. "Reflections on Two Decades," Canadian Literature, no. 41 (Summer 1969), p. 31.

5. Ibid., p. 33.

6. Ibid., p. 32.

7. See "The Odyssey: An Approach," Midway 9, no. 4 (Spring 1969), 47-68.

8. Hugh MacLennan, The Watch that Ends the Night (Toronto: Macmillan, Laurentian Library, 1975), p. 266. Hereafter, all references to this edition are cited parenthetically in the text.

9. "The Story of a Novel," Canadian Literature, no. 3 (Winter 1960), p. 39.

10. "Hugh MacLennan and the Canadian Myth," as reprinted in Goetsch, p. 149.

11. "Beauty and the Beast," as reprinted in Goetsch, pp. 157-61: see esp. p. 159.

12. The relevant passages occur on pp. 271-72, 289, 315, 329, 343, and 367.

13. See Mircea Eliade, "The Waters and Water Symbolism," Chapter V of Patterns in Comparative Religion (Cleveland and New York: Meridian Books, 1963), pp. 188-215. The phrase quoted appears on p. 188.

14. The Enchafed Flood or the Romantic Iconography of the Sea (New York: Random House, Vintage Books, 1967), p. 8n. Throughout these paragraphs I have made extensive use of Auden's and Eliade's treatments of the symbolism of the sea. Also of interest in this connection is Paul Tillich's short piece on the symbolism of water in James Luther Adams, Paul Tillich's Philosophy of Culture, Science, and Religion (New York: Harper & Row, 1965), pp. 62-64. And cf. Northrop Frye, Anatomy of Criticism (New York: Atheneum, 1967), Chapter III, passim.

15. Eliade, p. 212.

16. "Mimesis and Time in Modern Literature," in The Broken Center: Studies in the Theological Horizon of Modern Literature (New Haven and London: Yale University Press, 1966), p. 26.

17. MacLennan, "Reflections on Two Decades," p. 31.

18. Ibid., p. 39.

19. William H. New, "The Apprenticeship of Discovery," Canadian Literature, no. 29 (Summer 1966), pp. 32-33.

LA DIMENSION RELIGIEUSE DANS L'OEUVRE D'EMILE NELLIGAN

YVON DESROSIERS : a publié des articles sur la poésie
et le théâtre au Québec et donne des cours de la
phénoménologie de la religion québécoise à l'Université
du Québec à Montréal. Diplômes supérieurs (Louvain et
l'Angelicum à Rome).

RÉSUMÉ

Although the usual religious themes are absent from a
work of literature, the essential characteristics of the
religious experience may be present. Defining religion
as experiencing somewhere at the limits of the human
condition an awareness of the beyond, an analysis of
the religious dimension in literature asks the question
whether or not a literary piece opens up to this beyond.
Such an opening up is possible because of the symbolic
capacity of the human mind which allows man to transform
the profane into the sacred. A stone, the sky, earth,
a king, history all become potential bearers of the
divine. In thus analysing implicit and potential religious experiences, religious studies takes on not only
the role of evaluation and explanation but also that of
prophecy and liberation.

Emile Nelligan is one of the first poets to introduce
subjectivity into the otherwise more historical and moral
poetry of early Québec literature. In his poetic universe, an angelic world - that of innocence, childhood,
peace - is juxtaposed to the hideous adult world - that
of deception, disgust, and despair. Nelligan's quest is
for salvation - even from himself whom he sees as a play-
thing tossed between the two conflicting worlds. In his
exile from both childhood and adulthood, poetry is his
only relief. His poems become then the vehicle for a
latent but very religious dimension. Further studies
will examine this theme of salvation in traditional
Québec poetry and how this search has taken on a "political" dimension as well in many of Québec's contemporary
poets.

LA DIMENSION RELIGIEUSE DANS L'OEUVRE D'EMILE NELLIGAN

Nous nous proposons, à titre d'exercice, d'analyser une
oeuvre importante de la littérature québécoise, celle
du poète Emile Nelligan, pour en montrer ce qu'on pourrait appeler la dimension religieuse.[1]

RELIGION ET DIMENSION RELIGIEUSE

Notre hypothèse est la suivante : les caractéristiques
essentielles du fait religieux, telles que décrites par
la phénoménologie des religions[2] peuvent être présentes
dans toutes les productions humaines et en particulier
dans la littérature, même si les thèmes religieux habi-
tuellement utilisés (v.g., Dieu, la foi, le péché, le
prêtre, etc...) par la critique littéraire[3] paraissent
absents.

La définition de la religion qui nous fournira les
catégories fondamentales utilisées dans notre analyse
est celle qui voit la religion comme l'expérience des
limites de la condition humaine, avec le pressentiment
d'un au-delà de ces limites (van der Leeuw); il y a
expérience religieuse chaque fois qu'une situation-
limite (le sens de la vie, la naissance, la mort, le
temps, la liberté, la communication humaine, la solitude...) est vécue avec le goût et le sentiment d'un au-
delà de la limite.

Essentiellement, la question que nous nous poserons
est la suivante : l'univers tel qu'il apparaît dans
l'oeuvre analysée est-il expérimenté comme un monde clos
ou comme un monde ouvert, avec présence (même peu expli-
citée) d'un autre monde, d'une altérité radicale (un
"tout autre", qui est le sacré)?

De façon plus détaillée, les catégories dont nous
chercherons la présence (ou l'absence) découlent de la
définition proposée. L'expérience religieuse se présente comme une initiation toujours renouvelée, elle opère
dans l'existence une mutation radicale, une conversion,
qui peut s'exprimer dans les termes dialectiques de chaos et de cosmos (passage d'un ordre de choses ancien
devenu désordre à un nouvel ordre) ou encore de mort
et de résurrection. Ce changement se fait dans le cadre
d'un lieu et d'un temps sacrés, lors d'une fête dans
laquelle les interdits (sacré "négatif") sont trans-

gressés et un nouveau sacré est établi.

On entrevoit comment l'expérience religieuse n'est pas une expérience à part des autres expériences humaines : elle a lieu lorsqu'une expérience quelconque, éthique, esthétique, scientifique, politique ou autre, est portée à la limite, lorsqu'elle est radicalisée; elle n'est jamais faite "à l'état pur", elle est toujours enracinée. L'extra-mondain est pressenti dans l'intra-mondain : la pierre, le ciel, la terre, le roi, la cité, l'histoire ou l'homme-Jésus deviennent porteur du divin, hiérophanie; le sacré est toujours dans le profane.

C'est le symbole, et plus précisément le fonctionnement symbolique de la conscience humaine, qui permet cette transmutation du profane en sacré, qui opère l'éclatement des limites de la condition humaine. L'arrangement dynamique d'un ensemble de symboles constitue un récit sacré, le mythe, qui est aussi geste sacré, le rite, et qui fait entrer et vivre dans le temps primordial, ou essentiel, permettant d'échapper au temps banal ou ordinaire. Le mythe met en scène des personnages surnaturels, surhumains, il raconte un drame, une chute et un salut, et il est la clé explicative de l'ordre actuel du monde. On devine l'importance du symbole dans cette analyse "religiologique" de l'oeuvre littéraire qui est aussi construction, ou reconstruction symbolique du monde.

CRITIQUE DE L'HYPOTHÈSE

Notre hypothèse d'une dimension religieuse de toute production humaine peut être soumise à une triple critique ou à une triple interprétation. On pourrait suggérer que les structures, modèles, valeurs, idées, thèmes, que nous proposons comme spécifiques de l'expérience religieuse sont les mêmes que ceux de toute expérience humaine et qu'il faut trouver une définition plus restrictive du fait religieux.

On pourrait en deuxième lieu proposer qu'une dimension en effet de toute expérience a un caractère "religieux" qui serait implicite seulement et que l'analyse ferait ressortir. L'homme religieux serait celui qui actualise cette dimension et reporte sur un Tout-Autre "véritable" l'expérience religieuse potentielle présente ou contenue en tout aspect de la vie humaine.

LA DIMENSION RELIGIEUSE DANS L'OEUVRE D'EMILE NELLIGAN

On pourrait enfin proposer l'explication "sécularisation" : des structures ou des valeurs qui autrefois cons-
tituaient l'expérience religieuse, ont été évacuées de
leur contenu religieux et véhiculent désormais un contenu sans référence sinon historique au religieux, ou au
couple profane-sacré.

Nous pensons que le choix entre ces trois possibilités
(ou d'autres) constitue le problème central des sciences
religieuses, à savoir celui de définir la nature du fait
religieux. Ce choix dépend sans doute de ce que l'on
pense du symbole[4] : si on conçoit celui-ci comme toujours
ouvert et pouvant évoquer même une réalité infinie, ou
illimitée, ou "divine", selon le fonctionnement de chaque esprit, on acceptera qu'un même symbole puisse mettre
en présence d'une réalité constituant l'objet d'une expérience religieuse. Il est assez évident que nous favo-
risons la seconde interprétation. Nous espérons montrer,
dans les pages qui suivent, l'existence d'une telle dimension religieuse et aussi l'intérêt, pour les sciences
religieuses, de dévoiler cette dimension : d'une part on
élargit ainsi la connaissance générale de l'être humain
et d'autre part, en découvrant des formes latentes, im-
plicites et comme inachevées d'expérience religieuse, on
laisse aussi entrevoir la sorte d'expérience religieuse
qui devient possible (ou impossible) pour une personne
ou une collectivité, suite à l'actualisation de cette
dimension religieuse implicite. On ne fait ici que reprendre l'idée bien connue que le sacré se déplace con-
tinuellement dans l'histoire des civilisations et que les
religions institutionnelles ne s'adaptent pas toujours,
sauf bien sûr dans le cas de prophètes ou de réformateurs,
à ces déplacements des hiérophanies. En montrant ainsi
une expérience religieuse implicite et potentielle, les
sciences religieuses jouent un rôle non seulement critique ou explicatif, mais aussi prophétique et libérateur.

RELIGION ET LITTÉRATURE

Signaler la présence (ou l'absence) d'une dimension religieuse dans une oeuvre littéraire ne veut en rien ré-
duire la littérature au fait religieux. La lecture religiologique se veut une explication additionnelle, à côté,
par exemple, d'une lecture freudienne ou marxiste.

La religion transfigure la "réalité ordinaire" en quelque chose de tout autre, elle donne valeur absolue à ce

qui était vécu comme limité. Parallèlement, on peut suggérer que la littérature transforme aussi la même "réalité ordinaire" en une autre qu'on peut décrire comme plus vraie, plus belle, plus riche, plus humaine ou idéale. En un sens, on pourrait prétendre que le poète, le romancier ou le dramaturge, ne transfigure pas la réalité, mais qu'il la dévoile, ce qui serait vrai d'ailleurs aussi pour l'homme religieux.

C'est la parole qui opère cette transfiguration ou ce dévoilement. L'auteur a pressenti ou vécu une autre réalité et il ne peut s'empêcher de communiquer aux autres cet univers dont il se sent désormais participant. La parole et l'écriture ne sont sans doute pas seulement outil de cette communication, mais aussi moyen de faire, d'achever la récréation poétique, ou romanesque, ou théâtrale. Le littérateur exprime et fait par la parole cet autre monde idéal.

Bien sûr, l'expérience religieuse aussi tend à se dire, à s'exprimer. L'homme religieux emploie la parole et parfois même devient poète, ce qui amène à chercher comment mieux dire la différence entre religion et littérature.

Il serait tentant de suggérer, en première approximation, que la distinction établie plus haut entre réalité autre et réalité tout autre ressemble à une différence d'intensité ; on retrouverait entre les deux le passage à la limite caractérisant la religion, celle-ci étant au-delà de toute expérience possible... Pourtant le poète - et aussi bien tout artiste - évoque un indicible, un au-delà de l'expérience...

Il faut sans doute proposer autre chose. Si on peut dire que l'homme religieux vise un "tout autre" existant réellement, ne peut-on affirmer que l'auteur littéraire vise des idéalités, des modèles exemplaires n'existant pas dans la réalité? Pour le romancier et le dramaturge, la réponse semble devoir être affirmative : l'un et l'autre se situent dans un monde imaginaire, ils créent des personnages et des situations irréels, schématisant et poussant à l'extrême des éléments de réalité; par contre le poète semble vouloir créer la réalité en la disant. A ce plan du "réalisme", le poète semble plus près de l'homme religieux que le romancier ou le dramaturge, mais il faudrait pouvoir mieux dire ce qui les distingue... Cette introduction méthodologique un peu

LA DIMENSION RELIGIEUSE DANS L'OEUVRE D'EMILE NELLIGAN

longue nous semblait nécessaire avant de procéder à l'interprétation que nous allons faire de l'oeuvre d'un poète non contemporain, il est vrai, mais sans doute d'une actualité plus grande que celle de bien des vivants.

LA DIMENSION RELIGIEUSE DANS L'OEUVRE DE NELLIGAN

Emile Nelligan[5] occupe une place particulière dans la poésie québécoise, certains critiques le considèrent même comme notre plus grand poète[6]; en tout cas, il est le premier à avoir introduit la subjectivité dans une poésie jusque là plus historique que littéraire et surtout davantage moralisatrice et religieuse. Il est le premier à avoir créé une imagerie strictement personnelle, même si diverses influences ont été bien démontrées dans son oeuvre[7]. Par ailleurs un critique voit dans son oeuvre un miroir parfait de notre psychisme collectif dans certains de ses traits fondamentaux : le mythe de la mère canadienne-française omniprésente (et du père absent)[8] et le problème de notre aliénation politique[9].

Les poèmes de Nelligan ont été suffisamment analysés[10] pour nous dispenser de toute critique proprement littéraire et nous permettre d'entrer directement dans la problématique qui nous concerne. Nous résumerons l'oeuvre en recueillant et en décrivant les thèmes exploités pour faire, dans un second temps, l'interprétation religiologique.

Il n'est pas nécessaire, pour notre propos, de faire une longue analyse de tous les poèmes (plus de cent-soixante, pour un total de près de trois mille vers) : il y a dans l'ensemble de l'oeuvre, malgré la diversité des sujets, une unité de climat et une convergence de thèmes telles qu'il suffit de s'arrêter un instant sur les plus connus des poèmes du recueil édité par Dantin, sans craindre de faire une présentation faussée de l'oeuvre.

LES THÈMES

Dans les trois poèmes de la première section (L'Âme du poète), Nelligan analyse sa "pensée", son "âme" et son "coeur", de façon générale; on peut dire que le reste de l'oeuvre développera, en référence à des objets concrets

338

ou des aspects particuliers, le climat et les thèmes
essentiels présentés ici.

Le premier poème (Clair de lune intellectuel) laisse
sentir le clair-obscur dans lequel baigne l'esprit du
poète, dont le regard perçoit moins le monde présent et
davantage un monde rêvé :

"Ma pensée est couleur de lumières lointaines
...
Ma pensée est couleur de lunes d'or lointaines."

Cette pensée est aux prises avec la matière et la laideur,
qu'elle semble considérer comme identiques, et les quelques bons moments de la vie qu'"elle a vécu(s) dans les
soirs doux, dans les odeurs" l'amènent à entrevoir et
désirer un autre monde :

"Au pays angélique où montent ses ardeurs,
Et, loin de la matière et des brutes laideurs,
Elle rêve l'essor aux célestes Athènes"

Le second poème (Mon âme) permet d'identifier ce "pays
angélique" comme un monde qui perpétuerait celui de
l'enfance, de la pureté, de la prière, avec le présence de
sa mère pleurant, rêvant et priant la Vierge céleste.
Ce pays est à l'opposé du monde "flétri" et "pervers"
de l'adulte qu'est devenu le poète, dont l'âme voudrait
demeurer pure et "pareille à de la mousseline, Que manie
une soeur novice... Ou comme un luth empli des musiques
du vent..." :

"Mon âme a la candeur d'une chose étoilée,
D'une neige de février...
Ah! retournons au seuil de l'Enfance en allée
Viens t'en prier...
Ma chère, joins tes doigts et pleure et rêve et prie,
...
Ah! la fatalité d'être une âme candide
En ce monde menteur, flétri, blasé, pervers,
D'avoir une âme ainsi qu'une neige aux hivers
Que jamais ne souilla la volupté sordide.
...
D'avoir une âme douce et mystiquement tendre"...

Le Vaisseau d'or mérite d'être cité en entier car il
est sans doute le poème le plus connu et comme le résumé
de la vie de Nelligan. On est ici en présence d'un récit

de chute radicale de l'azur, le "pays angélique" cherché,
"aux profondeurs du Gouffre", qui sont le Dégoût de soi,
dû sans doute aux chutes dans la volupté sordide mention-
née dans le poème précédent, la Haine de soi et la Névrose-
Rêve dans laquelle le coeur du poète sombre ou se laisse
aller au seuil de ses vingt ans :

"Ce fut un grand Vaisseau taillé dans l'or massif:
Ses mâts touchaient l'azur, sur des mers inconnues;
La Cyprine d'amour, cheveux épars, chairs nues,
S'étalait à sa proue, au soleil excessif.

Mais il vint une nuit frapper le grand écueil
Dans l'Océan trompeur où chantait la Sirène,
Et le naufrage horrible inclina sa carène
Aux profondeurs du Gouffre, immuable cercueil.

Ce fut un Vaisseau d'Or, dont les flancs diaphanes
Révélaient des trésors que les marins profanes,
Dégoût, Haine et Névrose, entre eux ont disputés.

Que reste-t-il de lui dans la tempête brève?
Qu'est devenu mon coeur, navire déserté?
Hélas! Il a sombré dans l'abîme du Rêve!"

La seconde section (Le Jardin de l'Enfance) exprime les
sentiments de nostalgie et de regrets du poète au souve-
nir de l'enfance ("La fuite de l'Enfance au vaisseau des
Vingts ans"; "Ah! de franchir si tôt le portail des vingt
ans!"). Le Clavier d'antan fait revivre les moments de
bonheur et d'innocence vécus par le poète auprès de sa
mère, qui était une musicienne d'une sensibilité exquise
et qui a été sa muse, "perdue" lorsqu'il est devenu adolescent et adulte :

"Clavier vibrant de remembrance
J'évoque un peu des jours anciens
Et l'Eden d'or de mon enfance.
...
Vous êtes morte tristement
Ma muse des choses dorées
Et c'est de vous qu'est mon tourment"

Ayant perdu la "vierge espérance" et les "rêves musici-
ens", le poète adulte regrette que sa naissance n'ait
aussi été sa mort, identifiant ainsi l'une et l'autre :

"Quand je n'étais qu'au seuil de ce monde mauvais

> Berceau, que n'as-tu fait pour moi tes draps funèbres
> ...
> Ah! que n'a-t-on tiré mon linceul de tes langes
> ...
> Alors que se penchait sur ma vie, en tremblant,
> Ma mère souriante avec l'essaim des anges!"
> (Devant mon berceau)

La perte de l'Enfance et celle de la mère identifiée à
la poésie et à la musique s'entremêlent dans plusieurs
poèmes (Ma mère, Devant deux portraits de ma mère, Le
Talisman, ...) :

> "Elle a les yeux de ma vague chimère
> Ô toute poésie, ô toute extase, ô Mère,
> ...
> A l'autel de ses pieds je l'honore en pleurant
> Je suis toujours petit pour elle, quoique grand,"
> (Le Berceau de la Muse)

La troisième section (Amours d'élite) montre les désirs
idéalistes du poète, son besoin d'amitié et d'amour purement spirituels :

> "Parfois j'ai le désir d'une soeur bonne et tendre
> D'une soeur angélique...
> ...
> D'une soeur d'amitié dans le règne de l'Art..."
> (Rêve d'artiste)

Cette soeur maternelle prend aussi la forme d'une figure
céleste, objet d'un Amour immaculé :

> "Je sais en une église un vitrail merveilleux
> où quelque artiste illustre, inspiré des archanges,
> A peint d'une façon mystique, en robes à franges,
> Le front nimbé d'un astre, une sainte aux yeux bleus.
> ...
> Telle sur le vitrail de mon coeur je t'ai peinte
> Ma romanesque aimée, ô pâle et blonde sainte".

Dans la section suivante, faite de poèmes d'intérieur
(Les pieds sur les chenêts), le poète dit son "coeur
cristallisé de givre", dans un monde ressenti comme un
soir d'hiver :

> "Ah! comme la neige a neigé!
> Ma vie est un jardin de givre.

341

Ah! comme la neige a neigé!
Qu'est-ce que le spasme de vivre
A la douleur que j'ai, que j'ai!"

Les thèmes du froid de l'hiver et de la vie amènent celui
de la mort souhaitée comme un hiver définitif venant
cueillir le poète abandonné à la musique :

"Loin des vitres! clairs yeux dont je bois les
                                  liqueurs
...
Tels des guerriers pleurant les ruines de Thèbes
Ma mie, ainsi toujours courtisons nos rancoeurs
...
Laissons le bon Trépas nous conduire aux Erèbes
...
Tu nous visiteras comme un spectre de givre
Nous ne serons pas vieux, mais déjà las de vivre
Mort! que ne nous prends-tu par telle après-midi
Languides au divan bercés par sa guitare."
                                    (Hiver sentimental)

La section consacrée à la nature (Virgiliennes) semble
être la seule où le poète contient davantage sa tristesse
pour décrire les paysages environnants; néanmoins la mélancolie reparaît, suscitée en particulier par l'automne :

"Comme la lande est riche aux heures empourprées
Quand les cadrans du ciel ont sonné les vesprées
...
Quelle mélancolie! Octobre, octobre en voie!
                                  (Automne)

Ma sérénade d'octobre enfle une
Funéraire voix à la lune
                Au clair de lune
On dirait que chaque arbre divorce
Avec sa feuille et son écorce
                Sa vieille écorce
Ah! vois sur la pente des années
Choir mes illusions fanées
                Toutes fanées"
                              (Tarentelle d'octobre)

Une section (Petite chapelle) est consacrée aux sentiments de ferveur mystique du poète qui entremêle et identifie musique, beauté, prière, tristesse et fuite du monde

342

présent au profit du passé :

> "Nous étions là deux enfants tristes
> Buvant la paix du sanctuaire
> ...
> Nos voix en extase à cette heure
> Montaient en rogations blanches
> Comme un angélus des dimanches
> Dans le lointain qui prie et pleure."
> (Chapelle dans les bois)

> "La belle Sainte au fond des cieux
> Mène l'orchestre archangélique
> Loin du monde diabolique
> Puissé-je, un soir mystérieux,
> Ouïr, dans les divins milieux,
> Ton clavecin mélancolique"
> (Sainte Cécile)

Deux sections (Eaux-fortes funéraires et Vêpres tragiques) évoquent le thème de la mort et la hantise du cercueil : le désir de la mort est suscité par le regret des
choses perdues (l'enfance) et aussi par l'horreur du péché (d'une vie d'adulte) :

> "Rêvant de choses disparues
> Que vous disent les vieilles rues?
> ...
> De plus d'une âme de vieillard
> Nous sommes l'image...
> En eux ayant les noires urnes
> De leurs ans impurs,
> S'en vont les Remords taciturnes."
> (Les vieilles rues)

> "Et mon amour meurtri comme une chair qui saigne
> Repose sa blessure et calme ses névroses
> Et voici que les lys, la tulipe et les roses
> Pleurent les souvenirs où mon âme se baigne"
> (Soirs d'automne)

Une section (Pastels et Porcelaines) consacrée à des
objets d'intérieur se révèle d'allure plus impersonnelle
et descriptive, mettant au départ les sentiments du poète en retrait, sans cependant les empêcher de poindre
au terme de la description, comme provoqués par celle-ci :

> "C'est un vase d'Egypte à riche ciselure

Où sont peints des sphinx bleus et des lions ambrés,
De profil on y voit, souple, les reins cambrés,
Une immobile Isis tordant sa chevelure.
...
Mon âme est un potiche où pleurent, dédorés,
De vieux espoirs mal peints sur sa fausse moulure;
Aussi j'en souffre en moi comme d'une brûlure,
Mais le trépas bientôt les aura tous sabrés...

Car ma vie est un vase à pauvre ciselure.
(<u>Potiche</u>)

La dernière section (<u>Tristia</u>) est carrément tragique :
le poète se laisse aller à la déception suite au bonheur
perdu de l'enfance, au désespoir d'une âme sensible incapable de supporter les malheurs de la vie, et aussi à
la démence dans laquelle il va sombrer bientôt :

"Ainsi la vie est un grand lac qui dort,
Plein sous le masque froid des ondes déployées
De blonds rêves déçus, d'illusions noyées
Où l'Espoir vainement mire ses astres d'or".
(<u>Le Lac</u>)

"Ainsi mourut l'artiste étrange
Dont le coeur d'idéal fut plein
Qui fit de son enfant un ange
Avant d'en faire un orphelin."
(<u>L'ultimo Angelo del Corregio</u>)

"Veux-tu mourir, dis-moi? Tu souffres et je souffre
Et nos coeurs sont profonds et vides comme un gouffre."
(<u>Tristesse blanche</u>)

... je sens des bras funèbres
M'asservir au Réel, dont le fumeux flambeau
Embrase au fond des Nuits mes bizarres Ténèbres."
(<u>Ténèbres</u>)

Le dernier poème du recueil <u>La Romance du Vin</u>, qui fit
connaître à Nelligan l'ivresse de la gloire, lors d'une
séance publique de l'Ecole Littéraire, montre les derniers
efforts du poète pour surmonter son malheur :

"Tout se mêle en un vif éclat de gaieté verte.
Ô le beau soir de mai! Tous les oiseaux en choeur
Ainsi que les espoirs naguère à mon coeur
Modulent leur prélude à ma croisée ouverte.

...
Je suis gai! je suis gai! Vive le vin et l'Art!...
J'ai le rêve aussi de faire des vers célèbres,
...
Serait-ce que je suis enfin heureux de vivre;
Enfin mon coeur est-il guéri d'avoir aimé?
...
Je suis gai, si gai, dans mon rire sonore,
Oh! si gai, que j'ai peur d'éclater en sanglots!"

L'INTERPRÉTATION RELIGIOLOGIQUE

Avant de décrire la dimension religieuse présente dans
la poésie de Nelligan, mentionnons, pour faire un tableau
plus complet, les thèmes explicitement religieux qu'on
peut relever. Ce qui domine est la présence constante
d'un univers céleste, royaume d'innocence et de pureté,
lieu de félicité spirituelle et esthétique : la musique
de Sainte Cécile et des choeurs angéliques constitue un
des objets du désir du poète. La prière que fait à la
Vierge Marie la mère du poète en faveur de celui-ci, représente le seul élément de pratique présent dans les
poèmes. Soulignons surtout une absence totale de Dieu
comme figure toute-puissante. Le Christ intervient une
fois pour faire connaître ses sentiments intimes, en réponse à une demande du poète :

"Quel fut ce grand soupir de tristesse infinie
Qui s'exhala de Toi lorsque, l'oeuvre finie,
Tu t'apprêtais à regagner le But?

Me dévoileras-tu cet intime mystère?
-Ce fut de ne pouvoir, jeune homme, le fiel bu,
Serrer contre mon coeur mes bourreaux sur la Terre!"
                    (La Réponse du Crucifix)

Il faut encore mentionner la présence de quelques
personnages religieux (carmélites, moines) accordés
d'ailleurs aux sentiments du poète.

"Parmi l'ombre du cloître elles vont solennelles,
...
Une des leurs retourne aux landes éternelles
Trouver enfin l'oubli du monde et des scandales;..."
                    (Les Carmélites)

Rappelons aussi le thème de la culpabilité causée par

le péché de volupté : ce thème, à la vérité d'ordre moral,
baigne dans une atmosphère religieuse : les "fautes" du
poète font pleurer sa mère qui cherche consolation dans
la prière à la Vierge, prière qui veut obtenir le salut
du fils pécheur et lui éviter la damnation de l'enfer.

Notons enfin l'abondance des images utilisant les objets
du culte pour l'expression de sentiments :

> "Sur l'autel de ton coeur (puisque la mort m'appelle)
> Enfant, je veillerai, m'a-t-elle dit, toujours.
> Que ceci chasse au loin les funestes amours,
> Comme un lampion d'or, gardien d'une chapelle."
> <u>(Le Talisman)</u>

Au-delà de ces thèmes, notre analyse religiologique propose de voir dans l'ensemble de l'oeuvre un récit mythique
de chute mettant en scène des personnages surhumains ou
surnaturels avec la recherche d'un salut.

De "l'Eden d'or de l'enfance", le poète passe au monde
sordide et pervers de l'adulte, il se fait "asservir au
Réel". L'Enfance, l'Innocence, la Musique constituent
les forces bénéfiques animant cet Eden auquel la Mère-
Muse-Poésie l'a initié. Ce temps sacré de l'Enfance a été
vécu comme une fête continue, avec comme célébration principale les jeux de l'enfance et surtout la musique jouée
par la mère.

Ce monde ordonné, parfait comme un cosmos, a fait place
au chaos par la venue des forces clairement nommées :
Dégoût, Haine et Névrose et aussi Volupté, Remords, Vide,
etc...

Nous pensons qu'on peut qualifier ces personnages de
puissances maléfiques surnaturelles ou surhumaines, car
dans toute l'oeuvre elles se présentent comme dominant le
poète qui en est comme le jouet; il est au centre du conflit entre les deux sortes de puissances et il est mené
par elles, succombant aux secondes, plus puissantes. Le
monde est vécu par le poète comme le lieu du conflit entre
ces forces. La situation-limite vécue par l'auteur comme au-dessus de ses forces est celle du passage raté de
l'enfance à l'âge adulte. Le poète a été chassé du Paradis par le temps, qui a fait de lui un adulte. Il vivra
désormais comme un exilé :

> "Quelqu'un pleure dans le silence

> Morne des nuits d'avril;
> Quelqu'un pleure la somnolence
> Longue de son exil.
> Quelqu'un pleure sa douleur
> Et c'est mon coeur."
> <u>(Berceuse)</u>

Si on cherche le salut, le rite de passage à l'état
adulte qui eut permis au poète de vivre en attendant les
"célestes Athènes", il semble qu'il faut le voir dans la
poésie. Celle-ci a été le seul "lieu vivable" pour
Nelligan qui a voulu s'y consacrer en entier dès l'âge
de seize ans.

On peut savoir ce qu'a été la poésie pour Nelligan en
relisant quelques lignes de <u>La Romance du Vin</u>. "Cette
pièce   justement célèbre, est à la fois une réponse in-
directe à une critique malveillante ... et une sorte
d'art poétique que Nelligan écrivit moins de trois mois
avant sa maladie"[11].

> "Je suis gai! je suis gai! Vive le vin et l'Art!...
> J'ai le rêve de faire aussi des vers célèbres,
> Des vers qui gémiront les musiques funèbres
> Des vents d'automne au loin passant dans le brouillard.
>
> C'est le règne du rire amer et de la rage
> De se savoir poète et l'objet du mépris
> ...
>
> Femmes! je bois à vous qui riez du chemin
> Où l'Idéal m'appelle en ouvrant ses bras roses;
> Je bois à vous surtout, hommes aux fronts moroses
> Qui dédaignez ma vie et repoussez ma main.

Les mêmes sentiments se retrouvent dans un poème auto-
biographique :

> "Laissez-le vivre sans lui faire de mal!
> Laissez-le s'en aller; c'est un rêveur qui passe;
> C'est une âme angélique ouverte sur l'espace.
> Qui porte en elle un ciel de printemps auroral.
>
> C'est une poésie aussi triste que pure
> Qui s'élève de lui dans un tourbillon d'or.
> L'étoile la comprend, l'étoile qui s'endort.
> Dans sa blancheur céleste aux frissons de guipure.

LA DIMENSION RELIGIEUSE DANS L'OEUVRE D'EMILE NELLIGAN

> Il ne veut rien savoir; il aime sans amour,
> Ne le regardez pas! que nul ne s'en occupe!
> Dites même qu'il est de son propre sort dupe!
> Riez de lui! ... Qu'importe! il faut mourir un jour...
>
> Alors, dans le pays où le bon Dieu demeure,
> On vous fera connaître, avec reproche amer,
> Ce qu'il fut de candeur sous ce front simple et fier
> Et de tristesse dans ce grand oeil gris qui pleure!"
>   (Un poète)

La poésie a été pour Nelligan le salut, ce qui lui a permis de passer de ce monde affectivement et moralement inacceptable pour lui à un monde idéal de musique et de poésie où le poète serait reconnu et où ceux qui l'ont refusé seraient blâmés. On comprend à quel point Nelligan, après avoir réalisé en moins de trois ans l'essentiel de son oeuvre a pu souhaiter la mort. La poésie, tout en débouchant sur le Rêve-"Névrose" et amenant Nelligan à l'état de "malade mental", avait donné à sa vie le seul sens qu'il ait sans doute désiré : "murmurer des musiques aux Anges" :

> "J'ai la douceur, j'ai la tristesse et je suis seul
> Et le monde est pour moi comme quelque linceul
> Immense d'où soudain par des causes étranges
>
> J'aurai surgi mal mort dans un vertige fou
> Pour murmurer des musiques aux Anges
> Pour après m'en aller puis mourir dans mon trou".
>   (Prélude triste)

CONCLUSION

Nous savons peu de chose des croyances religieuses intimes de Nelligan. Tout porte à croire qu'il acceptait la foi chrétienne de son milieu et son oeuvre semble témoigner en ce sens. Mais l'analyse que nous avons faite montre bien, espérons-nous, qu'il y a loin entre cette religion "officielle" ou sociologique et la dimension religieuse véhiculée de façon latente dans son expérience poétique et dévoilée par l'analyse religiologique.

On entrevoit sûrement que pareille recherche de salut et/ou de fuite dans le monde culturel de la poésie et de la musique a été celle d'une grande partie des poètes et des élites québécoises traditionnelles. Il faudrait

348

voir, dans une recherche ultérieure, comment plusieurs
poètes contemporains cherchent plutôt ce salut dans une
poésie à dimension politique poussée dans le sens de la
quête d'un "pays" (extérieur et/ou intérieur) propre au
"peuple" québécois.

LA DIMENSION RELIGIEUSE DANS L'OEUVRE D'EMILE NELLIGAN

NOTES

1. On peut voir un autre exemple de cette démarche dans : Notes pour une lecture religiologique du théâtre populaire québécois, SR II, 1972, pp.131-137.

2. La Religion dans son essence et ses manifestations, G. van der Leeuw, Payot, Paris, et Histoire des Religions, M. Eliade, Payot, Paris.

3. Cf. par exemple : Religion et société québécoise, Gilles Marcotte, dans Littérature et société québécoise, Presses de l'Université Laval.

4. Le symbole, G. Durand, P.U.F., Paris.

5. On trouvera biographie et bibliographie dans : Emile Nelligan, texte établi et annoté par Luc Lacourcière, Fides, Montréal, Paris, 1952, 329 p.

6. Cf., par exemple, l'écrivain américain Edmund Wilson : "... he seems to me the only first-rate Canadian poet ...", cité dans : Emile Nelligan, Poèmes choisis, p.7, Fides, et d'autres critiques, id., pp.18-25.

7. Nelligan, "souvent symboliste par sa conception des entités poétiques, est presque toujours parnassien par leur expression", Louis Dantin, Emile Nelligan et son oeuvre, p.XXV.

8. "On a souvent répété que Nelligan était passé comme un splendide et solitaire météore dans notre poésie; que son oeuvre ne reflétait en rien les choses ni le milieu canadien-français... Il est faux de prétendre que ... (Nelligan) n'exprime ni notre milieu, ni notre société... Le drame de notre psychisme collectif, il l'a vécu dans son propre coeur, au plus intime et au plus douloureux de sa conscience. C'est là une des raisons qui expliquent sa grandeur de poète et sa tragédie d'homme." Gérard Bessette, Une littérature en ébullition, éd. du Jour, Montréal, 1968, pp.61-62.

9. "Convient-il maintenant... d'aller plus loin et de se demander si l'adolescent Nelligan, du fait qu'il avait un père anglophone (représentant pour lui l'autorité, la domination) et une mère francophone (représentant la tendresse et l'art) se soit trouvé à représenter exemplairement lui-même la situation politique et lin-

guistique de notre petit peuple adolescent et à lui servir, sur le plan psychique puis littéraire, "d'écho sonore" ou de caisse de résonnance?" _Ibid._, p.85.

10. Voir l'analyse formelle de Gérard Bessette : _Les images en poésie canadienne-française_, Beauchemin, Montréal, 1972, pp.219-272, et du même auteur, une lecture freudienne dans : _Une littérature en ébullition_, pp.25-85.

11. Luc Lacourcière, _op. cit._, p.307.

LES BRUITS DE LA MER

MICHEL-M. CAMPBELL : ancien rédacteur des Sciences
Religieuses/Studies in Religion et donne des cours
sur la religiologie, la méthodologie et la praxéologie
pastorale (Section d'études pastorale), Faculté de
Théologie de l'Université de Montréal.

RÉSUMÉ

The credibility of a professor in religious sciences
rests often on his study of distant places and times -
possibly to the detriment of material closer at hand.
For example, this paper analyses a popular Québec song,
"Tous les palmiers" by the musical group, Beau Dommage.
Its thematic contents and its existential psychology
raise significant questions for current religious studies.

"Tous les palmiers" sings of a man in his twenties
returning from an idyllic distant land to the harsh
realities of his Montréal home. Like the other songs
by Beau Dommage, it uses the language of the streets
to evoke the every-day despair of solitude and yet fear
of facing life squarely on as it presents itself to us.
A far cry from the love songs and nationalistic poetry
of the Gilles Vigneault style, "Tous les palmiers"
reveals in its anti-hero, the anguish of a modern culture wrestling within itself.

Such struggles within the every-day are not without
parallel in the Bible, as seen for example in the stories
of Caïn or Abraham. Jesus, Himself, maintains a very
down-to-earth openness to the real yet not extraordinary
problems of his fellowmen. The omnipotent God of the
Christians reveals Himself, then, in the powerlessness
of man and the Christian saints attain their grandeur
by reaching deep into all the sufferings of humanity.
In their search among distant places and times, are
religious specialists not running the risk of the Beau
Dommage anti-hero: fleeing from a full confrontation
with reality in the name of an abstract supernaturalism,
or of a methodological purity, or of a literary culture?

353

MICHEL-M. CAMPBELL

LES BRUITS DE LA MER:
essais d'herméneutique religieuse d'un mythe de
l'original dans la chanson populaire québécoise

1. EN GUISE D'INTRODUCTION :

La crédibilité du professeur de sciences religieuses
s'appuie souvent sur un long voyage littéraire loin de
son temps et de son espace immédiats. Nouveau chaman,
il cherche dans l'ailleurs de l'histoire ou de l'anthropologie l'origine qui fondera la production de son discours. Les atterrissages de retour s'avèrent souvent
plus ou moins réussis. Ulysse oublie Ithaque ou s'y
réintègre mal. A trop chercher l'origine, il oublie sa
propre originalité.

La présente contribution se veut un essai d'herméneutique religieuse d'une chanson populaire du Québec actuel:
"Tous les palmiers" du groupe Beau dommage.[1] Oeuvre
banale qui n'aura sans doute pas la durée des grands
mythes. Oeuvre originale qui traduit l'inédit de notre
situation présente et qui, par sa fonction de traduction,
reprend l'archaïque fonction chamanique de l'écriture de
sens.

Dans un premier temps, nous relirons le texte écrit[2]
de cette chanson. Nous en multiplierons ensuite les
analyses psychanalytiques pour en arriver à quelques
interprétations religiologiques et théologiques. Dans
un troisième temps, nous essaierons d'expliciter et de
situer notre méthode et d'en saisir certaines implications. En fait, il s'agit d'exorciser le banal, et
d'exorciser l'exorciste.

2. LE TEXTE : TOUS LES PALMIERS[3]

1. Tous les palmiers, tous les bananiers. 2. Vont
pousser pareil quand j'serai parti. 3. J'm'en vas chez
nous, c'est l'été. 4. Chez nous y'ont sorti les chaises
sur la galerie. 5. Chu tanné d'entendre le bruit des
vagues. 6. Moé j'm'en vas chez nous, 7. J'ai l'goût
d'entendre 8. Crier "Manon viens souper" 9. Attends
pas qu'maman a s'choqué 10. Pis qu'a descende, 11.
Manon, viens souper 12. Si tu viens pas tout-suite
13. Ben la, tu pourras t'en passer. 14. Attends pas
qu'maman a soit tannée 15. Pis qu'a descende". 16.
Adieu, Adieu pays des oranges, 17. J'm'en va aider mon

354

frère qui déménage. 18. Avec l'été qui r'commence,
19. Chez nous y'ont dû sortir 20. Les bicycles du
garage. 21. M'a arriver en ville jeudi midi, 22. M'a
prendre le métro jusqu'à Beaubien. 23. En faisant semblant de rien, 24. M'a arrêter au coin d'la rue. 25.
Pour appeler ma blonde. 26. Ca va sonner 1 coup, 2
coups, 3 coups, 4 coups, 27. Pis là, a va répondre.
28. Là m'a dire :"Comment ça va ma blonde, 29. Ben
oui, chur'venu"· 30. Tous les palmiers, tous les bananiers 31. Vont pousser pareil quand j'serai parti.
32. Vous pourrez m'écrire ici 33. 7760 St-Vallier,
Montréal. 34. 7760 St-Vallier, Montréal. 35. 7760 St-
Vallier, Montréal. 36. 7760 ...

3. LE LEXIQUE : Enumération sériée des éléments sémantiques du texte (par ordre alphabétique).

actions :

de la blonde : répond au téléphone (v.27);

du jeune homme : arrive en ville (v.21); décide de
partir (v.4,6); entend le bruit des
vagues (v.5); fait ses adieux (v.16);
invite à lui écrire (v.32-33); parle
à sa blonde (v.28-29); prend le métro
(v.22); (est) tanné (v.5); va aider
son frère (v.17);

du frère : déménage (v.17);

de la maman : crie (v.8); menace de s'choquer, de
s'tanner, de descendre, de priver
Manon de souper (v.9-14);

de Manon : est menacée (2 fois) des colères et
poursuites de sa mère (v.8-9, 14-15);
de se passer de souper (v.12);

des palmiers et bananiers :
poussent (v.2,31);

de "Vous" : peuvent écrire (v.33);

divers : les 4 coups du téléphone (v.26); la réflexion :
"en faisant semblant de rien" (v.23);

LES BRUITS DE LA MER

<u>éléments de culture</u> : chaises, galerie (v.4); bicycles,
garage (v.20); métro (v.22);

<u>éléments de nature</u> : palmiers, bananiers (v.1, 30);
oranges (v.16); bruit des vagues (v.5);

<u>lieux</u> : Beaubien (v.22); chez nous (v.4, 19); coin d'la
rue (v.24); pays des oranges (v.16); 7760 St-Vallier,
Montréal (4 fois) (v.33, 36);

<u>personnages</u> : <u>la blonde</u> (v.25, 28); <u>le frère</u> (v.17); <u>le
jeune homme</u> qui parle (v.2, 5-7; 21-29, 31-32);
<u>Manon</u> et <u>la maman</u> (v.8-15); <u>Vous</u> : d'autres,
indéterminés, qu'il invite à <u>lui</u> écrire (v.32);

<u>temps</u> : chez nous, c'est l'été (v.3); jeudi midi (v.21).

4. PREMIÈRES LECTURES : DE PSYCHANALYSE EXISTENTIELLE

Au premier abord, l'histoire semble banale. Un jeune
montréalais, désabusé du "Pays des oranges" (la Floride,
la Californie, les Iles?), décide au début de l'été de
rentrer chez lui retrouver les siens. Selon cette lecture, le reste des éléments sémantiques du texte n'est que
remplissage et fioritures. La chanson n'a alors d'autre
sens que sa trame sonore.

Un regard averti de la psychanalyse, <u>i.e. sensible au
non-dit du texte</u>, permet cependant d'articuler une histoire
qui rende compte d'un plus grand nombre d'éléments sémantiques. Dans la description de son retour (v.21-29), le
jeune s'avère prosaïque. Il va arriver à midi, prendre le
métro, s'arrêter au coin de la rue pour appeler sa blonde.
Il ne mentionne même pas le prénom de celle-ci, alors qu'on
connaît (v.8) celui de Manon (sa soeur?). Jusqu'ici
rien de bien excitant.

Sinon, justement que ce prosaïsme fait partie de la
volonté même du jeune homme. C'est "<u>en faisant semblant
de rien</u>" (v.23) qu'il va appeler "sa <u>blonde</u>". Que signifie, donc, cet "<u>en faisant semblant de rien</u>"? Qu'est-ce
qu'il veut faire paraître comme "n'étant rien"? Qu'est-ce
qu'il nie d'original, d'inédit? Son retour qu'il n'a pas
annoncé et qu'il banalise? Son voyage lui-même? L'échec
et l'ennui qu'on y décèle : "chu tanné d'entendre le bruit
des vagues" (v.5); "tous les palmiers, tous les bananiers
vont pousser pareil quand j'serai parti" (v.1-2, 30-31)?

356

De toute façon, ce téléphone "en faisant semblant de rien" prend de l'importance au niveau du récit que le jeune homme en fait. Un premier élément significatif : l'angoisse, l'attente de la réponse. Dans son récit, sa blonde ne répond pas tout de suite. Il compte les coups : "un coup, deux coups, trois coups, quatre coups" (v.26). C'est long chez nous d'attendre quatre coups. On a vite raccroché au troisième. D'ailleurs, deuxième élément significatif, on remarque que s'il est quelqu'un dont il tait le discours, c'est bien "sa blonde". Alors qu'il avait "le goût d'entendre" (v.7) les cris, interminables et répétés, de la maman qu'il cite à profusion (v.8-15), il ne laisse pas la parole à sa blonde. Dans l'évocation de l'appel téléphonique, il ne manifeste d'ailleurs aucune émotion : pas plus celles de sa blonde que les siennes propres.

En réalité, "en faisant semblant de rien", il fait semblant qu'il n'est jamais parti, qu'il n'a jamais quitté sa blonde, ni les siens, ni Montréal. Il tait la rupture de son départ de Montréal et subséquemment il tait son voyage et son retour.

L'analyse des figures féminines de la chanson suggère la raison du refus du jeune homme de manifester sa blonde au niveau même de son récit. Il y a deux autres femmes dans ce récit : Manon, la victime qui supporte en silence les imprécations maternelles, et la maman qui crie et menace (v.8-15). Ce discours de la mère a quelque chose d'obsessif et d'oppressif. Elle menace de poursuivre Manon, puis de la priver de nourriture (de la sevrer). Aussitôt elle se ravise et reprend ses menaces de colère et de poursuite. Les verbes expriment un climat chargé : "Viens" (2 fois), "viens tout de suite", "attends pas" (2 fois), "qu'a s'choque", "qu'a s'tanne", "t'en passer". Il faut absolument que Manon vienne manger. Elle est coupable de ne pas manger. Il y a là une stratégie de culpabilisation avec, en arrière-fond, au risque de caricaturer, un scénario de viol oral par le sein maternel.

Cette relecture, qui rend compte de plusieurs éléments sémantiques, corse la dramatique du récit. Le jeune homme est parti, il a fui la mère violeuse, la soeur victime et sa blonde. Cette dernière peut bien être pour lui, à la fois à l'image culpabilisante de la victime Manon (en fait, en partant il a laissé tomber sa blonde) et, en même temps, à l'image agressive, culpabilisante et menaçante de la maman (durant ce téléphone sa blonde pourrait le

357

culpabiliser et le menacer). Il avait fui les cris et
les violences ou les silences culpabilisants de la fem-
me/mère/soeur. Maintenant qu'il revient et téléphone
à sa blonde (téléphoner : parler de loin), ce téléphone
est parasité par sa peur de retrouver en sa blonde la
même violence.

5. LECTURE RELIGIOLOGIQUE

Il reste que nous n'avons pas encore rendu compte de la
fonction sémantique du "pays des oranges". La dramati-
sation que nous avons fait ressortir jusqu'ici se limite
à celle d'un récit de rapports interpersonnels. Un regard religiologique, i.e. attentif à déceler dans un
texte ou dans un événement des homologies avec le com-
portement religieux, nous permet d'accomplir cette tâche.

Le récit se déroule fondamentalement dans deux espaces
opposés : le Québec, que beaucoup de Québécois quittent
ou rêvent de quitter durant le dur hiver, et le "pays
des oranges". Ce pays, pour les Québécois en général et
dans le texte même de la chanson, apparaît comme un lieu
mythique : terre chaude et fertile, terre de vacances.
Le voyage du jeune homme est une espèce de passage dans
un lieu paradisiaque où l'on échappe au froid, au travail.
Montréal, au contraire, est peuplé de gens qui ont besoin
d'aide : le frère qui déménage (v.17), Manon (v.8-15),
la blonde (?). De gens qui sont plus ou moins menaçants :
la maman (v.8-15), la blonde (?). Le pays des oranges
se caractérise par des éléments naturels (palmiers, bananiers, oranges, vagues) qui suivent leur cours sans
besoin d'intervention du sujet : tout ça va pousser quand
il sera parti (v.1-2, 30-31). La seule activité humaine, en ce lieu, ce sont les lettres possibles d'un "vous"
indéterminé (v.32).

La psychanalyse qui, pour l'analyse des mythes, s'est
souvent adjointe à l'histoire des religions, nous permet
d'ailleurs d'expliciter cette opposition symétrique entre
Montréal et le "pays des oranges". Là-bas, il n'y a
plus de cri, plus de menace, plus d'oppression (v.8-15).
Il n'y a que le battement des vagues et les fruits en
abondance. Ce lieu mythique a les caractéristiques du
sein maternel. Lieu anhistorique, confortable, de vie
végétative. Lieu marqué par l'indéterminé et lieu ry-
thmé par le battement du coeur maternel. Cette opposition symétrique apparaît d'ailleurs dans le texte lui-
même quand le jeune homme oppose, en deux versets consé-

cutifs, le bruit des vagues (v.5), on pourrait dire les
"bruits de la mer" aux cris de la maman (v.9), aux "bruits
de la mère".

Dans ce double espace, le jeune homme accomplit un double passage, en fait, un aller-retour. Il a été trauma-
tisé par la violence des cris de la maman (et de sa blonde?)
et par cette autre violence muette, mais qui n'en est pas
moins culpabilisante, de la victime, Manon (et de sa blonde?).

Il a fui l'image de la mauvaise/mère (ou femme) dans
un lieu qui a les caractéristiques du sein maternel/figu-
re de la bonne mère (ou femme). Il s'agit d'un retour à
l'origine. En ce sens, son voyage réel est aussi un "trip",
pour employer les termes de la contre-culture, un temps
fort. Dans le langage mystique traditionnel, si l'on accepte de prendre le terme en son sens technique sans poser
de jugement de valeur, on parlerait d'une retraite ou
d'une extase, i.e. sortie du monde de la réalié empirique
vers un ailleurs mythique (au sens fort du terme).

Maintenant, il vit l'épectase, i.e. un retour de l'espace mythique au réel concret. Il n'a rien à faire au
pays des oranges. Il se souvient de "chez lui". Il se
lasse de ce lieu sans histoire (au double sens du terme)
de végétaux et de personnages indéterminés. Il se rappelle sa ville où l'été recommence malgré tout, mais aussi
les bicyclettes sorties du garage (mouvement), le métro,
le téléphone, les chaises sur la galerie (repos), et la
maman qui crie après Manon.

Monde culture (vs nature), monde social (vs indéterminé)
où il trouve un sens (il pourra aider son frère alors que
les bananiers pousseront sans lui). Monde où il peut
s'identifier (avoir une adresse) pour communiquer avec les
autres. "Vous pourrez m'écrire ici", dit-il et il répète
son adresse charnellement, par quatre fois, comme en opposition à l'angoisse des quatre coups de téléphone :"7760
St-Vallier, Montréal". (v.34-36).

S'il faut juger de la qualité de ce voyage mythique, ce
récit est celui d'une conversion plus ou moins réussie au
réel. Le départ vers l'Ailleurs était nécessaire (à cause
du trauma), mais l'Ailleurs s'est avéré un non-lieu, un
lieu où il n'y a rien à faire même pas "semblant de rien"
et le jeune homme s'en détourne et revient à sa réalité.
Notons que ce voyage mythique a pu avoir un effet théra-
peutique. Celui-ci reste cependant limité. Le jeune

359

homme revient presque masochistement au dialogue/mono-
logue de la femme/mère/victime : "j'ai le goût d'entendre crier" (v.7). En même temps, il a peur d'écouter sa
blonde. Il lui faut faire semblant de ne plus entendre
les cris érotisés (il en a "le goût" v.7) de la mère qui
parasitent le dialogue avec l'autre femme, sa blonde.

6. UN CONTEXTE : L'OEUVRE DE BEAU DOMMAGE

La volonté de s'en tenir à la dynamique interne du texte,
de rendre compte de l'ensemble de ses semens, l'identification des référents analytiques utilisés jusqu'ici,
ne s'avèreront pas aux yeux de plusieurs des critères
satisfaisants pour justifier la présente interprétation.
Une autre manière de la valider : resituer le texte dans
l'ensemble de l'oeuvre phonographique de Beau Dommage[4].
Ce qui permettra de vérifier la permanence et le développement de la structure dégagée plus haut à travers la
plupart de leurs chansons. En effet, les chansons de
Beau Dommage racontent à peu près toutes 'histoire d'un
jeune homme dans la vingtaine qui termine sa période
d'initiation amoureuse. Le profil existentiel des personnages féminins et masculins, la plupart du temps perçus
du point de vue du jeune homme, s'y avèrent cohérents.

La femme y apparaît toujours lointaine, victime et/ou
agressive. Un être difficile que l'homme s'avère incapable de retenir. Un incident au Bois-Des-Filions, oeuvre majeure (un côté du disque), est la longue complain-
te d'un jeune homme qui n'a pas su empêcher sa blonde
de se noyer. A un moment donné, d'ailleurs, celle-ci mêle
sa voix à la sienne pour évoquer l'image de sa mère; elle
chante : "L'eau c'est la vie, disait ma mère, quand
j'voulais pas aller m'baigner".[5]

Amène pas ta gang est la longue récrimination d'une
jeune femme déçue de se retrouver avec un amant qui
l'évite en traînant ses amis derrière lui. "Des fois,
dit-elle, je me demande si t'as peur de rester seul avec
moi". C'est elle qui multiplie les sollicitations sexu-
elles, avec l'insistance même de la maman de Tous les
palmiers. Dans un monologue de 15 versets, elle se dit
"tannée" (3 fois), elle intime à son amant de laisser
ses amis (3 fois) et elle lui répète par trois fois de
"venir" dans la chambre avec elle. En fait, elle utilise l'impératif "viens", cinq fois[6].

Les héros de Beau Dommage n'ont pas la sexualité facile. Agressive sexuellement la femme surgit liée à l'image de la mort. Que l'on pense à Ginette, "la fille perdue", avec "ses seins et ses souliers à talons hauts" (image sadique des talons hauts associée à celle des seins). Le jeune homme qui la rencontre pour la première fois se souvient : "J'étais v'nu faire mes devoirs ... A m'a d'mandé : "Sais-tu danser?" J'ai dit : Non. Est allée mettre un record. J'avais signé mon arrêt de mort"[7].

Un autre relate : "Ma première blonde j'l'ai rencontrée dans un hangar. On jouait à guerre. Etait espionne. Moi, j'étas mort". Et il continue : "Quand j't'ais jeune, j'ai eu d'la peine, j'ai ben braillé, j'ai cru mourir quand ma Mireille a m'a laissé. A m'avait dit qu'un jour, peut-être a m'appelerait quand ses parents seraient partis pour le chalet". Ce téléphone où la jeune fille devait prendre l'initiative de la première rencontre sexuelle, contraste avec le silence de la blonde de Tous les palmiers. D'ailleurs quand il relate son initiation sexuelle, ce qui, quand il repense "à la fille" lui semble le plus beau jour de toute sa vie - il le fait en employant des termes sordides ou presque tragiques : "Pis't' arriver. Y fallait bien qu'un jour ça vienne. Un soir de pluie au coin Beaubien pis d'la neuvième"[8]. Qu'on pense, encore à ce serrurier "ben tranquille" "d'la rue d'Iberville qui "est occupé à oublier" (à faire semblant de rien), mardi passé, ce jour-là, il a fait une troisième clé d'une femme de St-Lambert qu'il a suivie, le soir, jusqu'à sa maison où il est entré (pour la séduire? la violer? la tuer?). Il en mourra au grand dépit de son ange gardien[9].

En fait, le héros est seul, sans protecteur. Il n'a d'ailleurs pas de modèle d'identification sexuelle. Le père est absent de ces chansons, sinon pour se déguiser en Père Noël[10]. Le jeune homme en est réduit à rêver de géants. Mais "Y'a pas d'géants qui est assez grand pour les rêveurs"[11]. La seule figure paternelle évoquée, le seul modèle auquel le jeune homme s'identifie est celui du "Géant Beaupré", ce squelette qui rapetisse dans une vitrine de l'Université de Montréal[12].

Les jeunes gens de Beau Dommage se retrouvent souvent seuls, abandonnés de leur femme (dans 9 chansons sur 18)[13]. Ebahis, ils se demandent "où est passée la noce". Ils sont ou "trop g'lés" (drogués) ou "trop chauds" (ivres) et "il y en a deux, trois qui sont trop beaux (homosexuels?)[14].

La femme est partie. On la recherche sous d'autres formes. La solitude est souvent vécue au moment de boire (café ou bière), i.e. dans un temps oral[15]. L'homme est fatigué, fatigué même de cette fuite dans l'image du sein maternel.

L'éros s'éteint. Dans Heureusement qu'il y a la nuit, le jeune homme avoue : "Ca fait longtemps que j'ai pas pris une vraie brosse. J'aime p'u la bière. Le vin est cher. Mais ça c'est des excuses. La vraie raison, c'pas la boisson, c'est pas l'buveur, c'est l'fun qui s'use"[16]. Dans A toutes les fois, une jeune fille décrit l'état pitoyable d'un jeune homme qui a perdu la face devant une femme plus forte que lui; elle dit : "Tu trouves que c'est don rendu plat, icitte. De toute façon y a pu grand'chose qui t'excite"[17].

En fait, la mère est toujours là qui s'interpose, au niveau du fantasme, entre le jeune homme et sa blonde. Ce terme archaïque (blonde vs amie, fiancée, femme) a d'ailleurs quelque chose de réductif. Dans Motel "Mon Repos", le jeune homme, presqu'étonné de sa relation amoureuse, confie à sa "blonde" "T'as l'même prénom que ma mère ça fait drôle d'y penser[18]. Ailleurs, désabusé, il dira "Mais qu'est-ce qu'un gars peut faire, quand y'a plus l'goût de boire sa bière? Quand y'est tanné de jouer à mère avec la fille de son voisin[19]. "Fatigué de la vie, seul dans son lit" (sans femme), il retrouve son corps d'enfant à la fin d'Heureusement il y a la nuit: "O.K. la nuit. Chus prêt pour le sommeil. La ville dort déjà mieux, pis moé, j'vais faire pareil. J'm'en vas rêver à poings fermés"[20].

Et pourtant, parfois, comme par miracle, l'amour, la rencontre est possible. Dans Motel, "Mon Repos" le jeune homme est tout étonné. Il y a dans la chambre "une T.V. en couleur". "C'est d'valeur (il) n'a pas le goût d'la regarder. (Lui) qui rêvait d'essayer ça ...". Il est capable de renoncer à l'écran de rêve et de parler à son amie[21]. Dans J'ai oublié le jour, la chanson la plus gaie de Beau Dommage, la jeune fille n'en revient pas ... Ils ont réussi, ils ont "ri ensemble des autres fous qui font l'amour comme on apprend dans les livres dans les vues" mais surtout elle peut dire au jeune homme : "T'étais pas là pour me consoler. T'étais pas là pour me rassurer mais m'écouter comme j'en avais besoin".[22]

Toujours la même structure. La fatique devant l'agression de la vie (figurée par la mère), la difficulté, la peur du face à face, le désespoir de la solitude, la tentation de régresser à l'origine et comme en creux, parfois la possibilité d'écouter.

7. UN DEUXIEME CONTEXTE : LA CHANSON QUÉBÉCOISE RÉCENTE

Ces lectures de Tous les palmiers se limitent tout au plus à l'histoire banale et individuelle d'un jeune montréalais. Malgré l'espace mythique interne au texte, elles restent limitées au récit individuel. L'analyse interne du texte lui-même ne révèle pas de héros, de modèle exemplaire[23]. Le jeune homme reste un garçon de la rue St-Vallier sans plus de prétention. Pourtant, ce récit n'est pas qu'un récit individuel : la confidence à un copain, par exemple. Il est chanté, dansé[24], dans ce que McLuhan appellerait le village électrique du Québec et de la Francophonie et, de ce fait, son personnage central devient modèle exemplaire. La radio comme la discothèque nous le propose et nous pouvons nous interroger sur le (ou les) sens d'une telle proposition.

En fait, Tous les palmiers pourrait servir de manifeste à la chanson québécoise récente et particulièrement de manifeste du groupe Beau Dommage. Les premiers grands chansonniers québécois comme Leclerc et Vigneault proposaient en français international l'image d'un pays idéalisé dans une espèce de naturalisme sublime indéterminé ou épique. Le P'tit Bonheur[25] par exemple, n'a pas de pays. Il peut habiter les grands espaces universalisants de la chanson de l'Expo 67[26]. Le pays de Vigneault reste l'hiver paternel de son Natashquan originel[27]. Beau Dommage, comme beaucoup de chansonniers actuels, se place dans l'univers urbain, parle la langue de la rue et chante le quotidien concret.

Son héros, n'a pas les dimensions épiques d'un Jean du Sud[28] et "sa maison n'est pas la plaine"[29]. C'est un anti-héros qui ne se ressource pas aux grands espaces, mais rêve de quelque chose comme la Floride (lieu plus ou moins aliénant d'après les jeunes québécois). C'est un fils qui ne parle pas de son père (vs les héros du pays de Vigneault) dont le frère n'a pas de lieu fixe (v.17) et qui a du mal à se dégager de la gangue de la mauvaise ou de la bonne mère, pour accéder au dialogue avec sa femme. On est loin de l'idéalisme des chansons d'amour ou de la poésie nationaliste.

Cette chanson-manifeste dénonce, dans son contenu comme dans son écriture, les récits d'origine, en ce qu'elle en marque le caractère onirique et oedipien. En même temps, elle pose le problème du fondement, de l'origine. Ou plutôt elle le renverse. C'est le quotidien, la rue, la petite histoire de chacun, le banal, ce qui n'a pas été fait par les dieux ou les géants, qui devient le fondement, l'origine ou plutôt l'origin(al). Le lieu de l'histoire n'est plus un "il est une fois" ou un Ailleurs, quoiqu'on pourra toujours lire les histoires de ("Vous pourrez m'écrire ici" v.32). L'histoire n'est plus d'hier, elle est à vivre. Elle est d'ici, de ce midi (v.21), même hantée par les bruits de la mèr(e).

Modèle, personnage mythique, l'anti-héros de Beau Dommage manifeste l'angoisse d'une culture qui a mal à s'identifier et qui, malgré tout, prend à tous les niveaux le risque de se dire, dans sa langue, sa propre langue, sa langue maternelle, la langue de la rue. Beau Dommage refuse de faire semblant de rien, de faire du personnage de ses chansons, un personnage du temps des géants (d'origine). Il le regarde (et l'aime?) tel qu'il est dans son originalité avec toutes ses tendances aliénantes.

8. PISTES D'INTERPRÉTATION THÉOLOGIQUE

En fait, les jeunes québécois se récitent ou dansent cette histoire comme ces récits mythiques que l'homme religieux traditionnel reprend sans cesse pour participer à leur réalité. Récit mythique d'un monde sécularisé qui, pour particularisé qu'il soit dans son écriture (cette chanson a une adresse précise), n'en reste pas moins porteur d'intentionalités que partagent d'autres registres de discours mythiques du Québec ou d'ailleurs.

Le mouvement de Beau Dommage ou de son héros est celui-là même de toute une littérature québécoise actuelle. [30] Il se retrouve dans la ligne des "nouveaux pouvoirs"[30], de tous ces mouvements populaires où le peuple et le "populaire" revendiquent le droit au discours et refusent de laisser le monopole du discours et de l'interprétation à ceux qui ont les moyens de voyager dans l'espace et dans le temps. En ce sens, il rejoint entre autres les intentions et la politique de la révolution culturelle chinoise qui dénoncent le mandarinat et prétend établir un contrôle entre la production du discours intellectuel et la parole des masses[31]. Elle rejoint même, qui l'eût cru, les revendications de certains étudiants de théologie qui veulent, comme ils disent, faire descendre la théologie dans la rue[32].

Le rapprochement peut paraître incongru à première vue. Pourtant un rapide rappel de quelques temps importants de la tradition judéo-chrétienne "de lettres qu'on a reçues ici" laissent entrevoir que la dramatique fondamentale de Beau Dommage et de son héros de Tous les Palmiers trouve plus d'un écho structurel dans le mystère révélé au travers de l'histoire des fils d'Abraham.

Une réaction commune devant la dure et froide réalité du quotidien est de se projeter aux "bons vieux temps", sinon aux lendemains fleuris (ciel ou grand soir) : temps d'harmonie, de plénitude. La culture occidentale a d'ailleurs souvent justifié son anti-féminisme en blâmant la femme, Eve/mère, d'avoir privé l'homme du Paradis Terrestre. Or, il est des interprétations de la Genèse qui proposent une autre lecture de cet événement.

Certaine tradition juive, reprise par une psychanalyse consciente de la fécondité de la mythologie d'Israel voit dans la sortie du Paradis une étape de maturation, le moment de la prise de responsabilité, de la possibilité de l'histoire[33]. Dans cette perspective, Adam et Eve renoncent au lieu originel, milieu sur-protégé à l'image d'une mère-nature, d'un père super-ego. Ils se retrouvent nus (Gn.3,7) incomplets, différents, mais c'est à ce même moment qu'ils entreprennent vraiment de réaliser leur mission de "nommer" les choses de la création; ils s'habillent, travaillent, enfantent dans la douleur (Gn. 3,19). Le drame commence alors, difficile.

Caïn assume mal sa différence d'avec l'autre, son frère [34]. Il essaie de le nier en le tuant, comme il essaie d'échapper à Dieu (Gn.4,8-16), à l'Autre. Il refuse d'être le gardien de son frère (il veut faire semblant de rien). Mais l'aventure est lancée. L'homme a renoncé à l'origine, il se trouve désormais voué à son histoire, à son originalité. C'est à lui de découvrir le sens du dialogue fraternel, du dialogue avec l'autre.

Certes, plus d'une tradition se plaindra de cette rupture comme Israël regrettera les oignons d'Egypte (Nb. 11,6). L'histoire des fils d'Abraham est constante tentative pour retrouver une figure d'origine qui libérerait l'homme (le castrerait) de son destin historique. Mais le Dieu d'Abraham n'est pas Chronos qui mange ses enfants. Il initie au dialogue.

L'histoire individuelle d'Abraham illustre d'ailleurs fort bien cette pédagogie divine. Celle d'un Dieu qui refuse d'être l'Autre, de résorber en lui la création et qui initie l'homme à se décentrer de l'originel, à se dépolariser de l'Autre pour apprendre à vivre avec les autres, l'altérité.

Le premier signe de l'alliance, c'est la circoncision (Gn.17,10-14). Ici, il s'agit moins de sacrifier un vivant que de distinguer, de caractériser (de donner "une adresse") une personnalité. En effet, les psychanalystes s'accordent à voir, dans la symbolique de l'ablation du prépuce et de l'apparition du gland dégagé, un graphisme corporel qui permet d'affirmer la distinction des organes mâles et femelles. (A la limite, refermées, les lèvres du prépuce rappellent la morphologie des lèvres vaginales). L'alliance est donc passage du monde de l'indéterminé où tout ressemble à tout (comme au Paradis où Adam et Eve ne réalisent pas leur nudité, leurs sexes différents), à un monde où l'on se découvre autre devant l'autre.

Abram, le stérile, l'impuissant[35], a quitté Ur en Chaldée (Gn.11,31) pour s'abandonner à un Autre qui s'affirmait comme Puissance capable de lui promettre une descendance nombreuse comme les grains de sable de la mer (Gn.22,17). Dur voyage, où la confiance est difficile : Abraham comme Sara ne croient guère à leurs possibilités de fécondité. Quand les mystérieux visiteurs leur réaffirment cette promesse, Abraham et Sara s'esclaffent. Sara derrière une tenture (Gn.18,10-15), Abraham en se cachant le visage contre terre (Gn.17,17). Au fond, ils ne croient pas un mot de ces étrangers. Ils font semblant de rien. Les autres peuvent toujours parler, Abraham et Sara n'écoutent pas. Ils n'entendent que la dure voix de l'Autre, de la nature (figure maternelle) qui les a voulus stériles.

Abraham tient bon malgré tout et Sara lui donne enfin un fils. Il est fécond, mais sa puissance reste contingente. Au fond c'est l'Autre, son Dieu qui est fécond, qui est le tout-puissant. Lorsque Celui-ci exige le sacrifice d'Isaac (Gn.22,1-2), Abraham, déchiré, accepte de tuer son fils (de le castrer et de se castrer). Il renonce à son histoire. L'Histoire, c'est l'Autre, le Tout-puissant qui peut se la permettre. Pour Abraham, il n'y a alors qu'une voix, celle de Yahvé et cette seule voix qu'il entend, empêche un dialogue véritable avec l'autre, avec son fils. Quand, montant au sacrifice, Isaac

lui demande quelle en sera la victime, Abraham "fait semblant de rien", répond de façon évasive (Gn.22,7-8) alors
qu'il sait très bien que c'est Isaac la victime désignée.
On sait le reste. Yahvé refuse de s'identifier aux dieux
anthropophages, d'accaparer, comme Chronos, l'Histoire.
Par son refus du sacrifice du fils d'Abraham, il enseigne
à ce dernier à se respecter, à être un fils de Dieu et,
comme tel, à pouvoir se dresser devant Dieu lui-même.

Abraham était presque préparé à comprendre cette leçon
(à avoir "l'insight"). En effet, il s'est déjà montré
capable de se dresser devant son Dieu, une première fois.
Yahvé lui a confié son intention de raser Sodome et Go-
morrhe (Gn.18,16-21). Notons qu'il y avait là un drame
d'altérité, de rapport de puissance. Le crime des Sodomites : ils refusaient de respecter l'autre, l'étranger,
celui qui est dépourvu et devant lequel on peut s'affirmer outrageusement comme puissance. Ce que la tradition
a d'ailleurs illustré en prêtant aux Sodomites des com-
portements de viols, homosexuels[36], ce qui entraînait la
double image d'un viol et d'une castration aux plans psy-
chologique et social. Abraham parvient mal à accepter
qu'un Dieu proposeur de vie puisse vouloir nier l'histoire d'autres hommes. Il se lève alors devant ce Dieu dans
un admirable marchandage (Gn.18,22-33). Dieu ne peut
plus manifester sa puissance indistinctement, comme une
force de la nature comme l'Autre : Yahvé doit tenir compte de cette justice même qu'il a enseignée à Abraham et
celui-ci exige une espèce de procès où l'on vérifiera
concrètement si le courroux est justifié.

En Jésus, on retrouve la même dialectique pédagogique
du refus de la puissance originelle pour assumer l'originalité humaine. Il est Kénose, puissance qui se manifeste en se vidant de sa puissance (Ph.2,6-11). Dans l'Incarnation, il renonce à la puissance originelle, au sein
du Père. Il résiste au Malin qui lui propose de changer
la roche en pain ("le pays des oranges") (Lc.4,3-4); il
se scandalise de Pierre, celui-là même pourtant sur lequel il a fondé son Eglise (Mt.16-18), quand il veut le
garder de la mort (Mc.8,31-33); enfin, au cours de son
procès, tout en s'affirmant "fils de Dieu" et capable de
commander aux anges (Mt.26,53), il accepte le triste sort
du délinquant. Sa prédication est révolte contre les
puissants qui se réfugient dans une loi, historique,
abstraite, originelle et refusent de regarder les gens
dans leurs situations concrètes. Il permet aux apôtres
de violer le jour du sabbat (temps rituel de l'origine)
et lui-même guérit un malade ce jour-là (Mc.2,23-27).

Il dénonce les gens fixés sur le Temple (lieu originel)
qui ne reconnaissent pas ce blessé au bord de la route;
alors, que le Samaritain, un étranger, lui, saura le reconnaître (Lc.10,24-37). Jésus renonce à la toute puissance de son père, comme il renonce psychologiquement à
sa mère, voire à Jérusalem. Il parle avec la Samaritaine,
une femme et une étrangère (double altérité). Avec elle,
il ne pose pas les problèmes de la conformité à l'origine
(Sur quelle montagne est le vrai Dieu?). Il lui parle de
quelque chose de concret, de banal : de sa soif à lui, de
sa soif à elle. Il lui parle de sa situation existentielle concrète. Ce qui le frappe, ce n'est pas son adultère
(désobéissance à la loi) mais plutôt sa solitude : en vérité, avec tous ces hommes qu'elle a connus (indéterminés),
elle n'a pas encore connu un homme, un autre (Jn.4,1-26).

Jésus renverse complètement le jeu onirique de l'origine, lieu de puissance, et son critère de valeur devient
l'attitude d'ouverture devant l'autre, l'homme impuissant.
Si Chronos s'identifie à l'Histoire et vit par le fait
même sa fonction d'origine, Jésus s'identifie à l'homme
qui manque son histoire : celui qui a faim et soif, celui
qui est nu (comme Adam), celui qu'on emprisonne en se disant qu'il n'y a rien d'autre à faire avec lui (comme
Caïn, en faisant semblant de rien) (Mt.25,35-36 et 42-43).
Il s'y identifie dans sa promesse du jugement à venir
(Mt.25,31-46) et dans sa propre histoire concrète.

Sa mort ignominieuse, mais sans doute banale à l'époque,
laisse ses fidèles devant le tombeau vide, traumatisés,
abandonnés du même abandon qu'il a crié sur la croix.
Plutôt non, les disciples d'Emmaüs n'expriment pas le désespoir cru du Christ en croix. Ils sont déçus (Lc.24,17-
24), ils croyaient avoir atteint l'origine, ils se sont
trompés. Ils n'attendent et ils n'entendent plus rien
de l'Autre. Ils font semblant de rien. Mais le germe
est semé. D'abord ils ne reconnaissent rien de particulier dans cet inconnu, cet autre qu'ils rencontrent (Lc.
24,16). Cependant, ils sont capables de l'accueillir
(au contraire des Sodomites); et de partager leur pain
avec lui (Lc.24,29-30). C'est dans ce partage d'humains
qui ont renoncé à la puissance de l'Autre (Kénose), mais
qui s'avèrent capables de relation à l'autre (Henosis),
qu'ils reconnaissent le sens de leur aventure avec l'Autre.

Le Dieu des chrétiens, Dieu Tout-puissant, s'annonce
dans l'impuissance. Sa parole se transmet au cours des
âges dans des traditions concrètes, d'écrits et de té-

moignages datés. Ce Dieu ne se manifeste jamais en plénitude, mais se dit en images confuses comme celles des mi-
roirs de cuivre de l'époque romaine (I Cor.13,12). Dramatique originale de l'homme, vie des Eglises et des peuples. Celle d'une conscience, blessée de sa relation à
l'autre qui rêve, mélancolique, d'un Autre, d'un centre
fondateur, d'un nombril du monde - que ce soit Moscou,
New York, Jérusalem, Rome ou Pékin - qui la ralierait à
l'origine. Celle, malgré tout, d'une conscience capable
parfois en des gens comme Gandhi, Thérèse de Lisieux,
Simone de Beauvoir, les personnages de Dostoievski, d'é-
chapper à la névrose, de ne plus faire semblant de rien
et de rencontrer l'autre. De reconnaître dans le banal,
l'inédit, l'original, dans l'autre la réalité de l'Autre.

9. INTÉGRATION HERMÉNEUTIQUE

Le texte de Tous les palmiers est, somme toute, un texte
banal qui ne passera pas à l'Histoire. L'histoire qu'il
raconte est tout aussi banale. En un certain sens, son
réalisme plat, comme l'idéologie réaliste qui sous-tend
la chanson, risque de castrer l'auditeur de toute pulsion
d'espérance ou de désir de révolution et, en ce sens, de
confirmer les thèses de Marcuse sur les tendances contre-
révolutionnaires de certaines formes d'art actuelles[37].
La partition musicale, absente de notre analyse, pourrait
peut-être lui redonner cette dimension. Elle échappe à
notre analyse. De toute façon, quand on regarde le monde
des discothèques, on peut douter de son impact révolutionnaire.

Nous avons, pour notre part, choisi de lui donner une
autre dimension musicale, pour paraphraser certaine description du structuralisme par Lévi-Strauss[38]. La recherche des harmonies internes, des homologies de structures du texte lui-même (parag.3 à 5) comme de ses con-
textes immédiats et culturel (parag.6 et 7),leur mise
en relation avec les homologies de structures d'une autre tradition (parag.8), permettent en effet de sortir
de l'impasse de la réduction au/et par le banal.

La lecture psychanalytique a révélé au-delà de l'incident une dramatique existentielle aussi grave que répan-
due. Celle d'un sujet hanté de souvenirs traumatisants
(image maternelle) qui a mal à vivre l'altérité (en l'oc-
currence la relation du couple). Le jeune homme de Tous
les palmiers ne veut plus entendre parler de femme et il

reste pourtant fasciné par la mer(e)[39]. Drame psychanalytique qui a la dimension d'une expérience mystique manquée:
l'extase (le rêve de l'origine) reste artificielle et ne
permet pas la relation à l'autre, l'Henosis.

Paradoxalement, ce drame tragique et, à la limite
désespérant, s'inscrit dans une démarche d'un groupe qui dénonce objectivement le rêve et le mythe d'origine en
s'opposant au style épique de la première vague de chansonniers québécois[40] mais qui risque tout aussi objectivement de proposer, par un réalisme aplatissant, de créer
un contre-rêve tout aussi réductif. L'obsession de la
mère castratrice de l'impuissance du mâle n'est pas plus
stimulante et féconde que la mégalomanie des contes de
fée ou des récits de Géants[41]. Danser sa frustration
dans l'univers clos et indéterminé de la discothèque peut
être une manière de faire semblant de rien[42].

Par ailleurs, la mise en perspective des harmoniques de
Beau Dommage avec la tradition judéo-chrétienne[43] permet
de dépasser ce paradoxe. Franchir l'interdit culturel
qui isole comme des en-soi coexistants une chanson éphé-
mère et une tradition religieuse bien établie, susciter
un inter-dire entre l'un et l'autre, ouvre une possibilité de fécondité.

Les deux ensembles de texte(s) confrontés dans leurs
structures s'éclairent mutuellement. Lus à la lumière
du drame qui structure Tous les palmiers, les récits des
mythes ou des mystères judéo-chrétiennes manifestent une
concrétude anthropologique qu'on ne leur prête guère
d'habitude. Adam, Abraham, Jésus, comme tant de saints
ou de personnages de la tradition, ne sont plus seulement des géants qui parlent uniquement d'un Ailleurs et
qui ignorent l'humaine condition. Ils parlent d'humanité. Leur mémoire ainsi perçue n'est plus seulement
d'hier; elle les rend contemporains.

En ce sens, l'herméneutique s'avère pour l'homme sécularisé une manière de réactualiser le mythe[44]. Les héros
les géants de la tradition judéo-chrétienne perdront
sans doute quelques pouces (phallus-fantasmatique) sous
l'oeil de la psychanalyse, mais comme tant d'autres, ils
risqueront aussi d'y retrouver leur sexualité et leur
concrétude. Il ne s'agit pas, ici, de se laisser aller
à une vulgarisation rapide et démagogique. Il s'agit de
respect de la vérité historique. Les textes judéo-chré-
tiens ont sans doute des épaisseurs que ne sauraient
épuiser l'historicisme des méthodes exégétiques courantes.

LES BRUITS DE LA MER

Une tradition, comme la tradition judéo-chrétienne,
dont l'originalité est de s'être écrite à travers
l'histoire concrète d'un peuple et de certains individus
s'est nécessairement écrite à travers une foule de registres anthropologiques. La relation de l'homme à Dieu ne
s'y définit-elle pas, dans nos plus belles pages, à travers l'incessante reprise de la poursuite du couple (Can-
tique des Cantiques)? Une des grandes pointes de cette
révélation n'est-elle pas celle du mystère de l'Incarnation d'un Dieu qui identifie l'aventure humaine aux dimensions de son amour?

L'homme religieux, le spécialiste des sciences religieuses (qu'il soit d'un département de théologie ou de
sciences humaines), l'institution ecclésiale, n'échappent
pas à la dramatique de Tous les palmiers. Chacun risque
de prendre les faux-fuyants du jeune homme de la chanson,
de faire semblant de rien, de fuir la confrontation avec
la réalité dans l'abstraction d'un surnaturalisme, d'une
pureté méthodologique ou d'un attachement à la culture
littéraire. Par le fait même, d'échapper à l'intuition
critique de Beau Dommage et des mouvements analogues.

Ceux-ci proposent aux sciences religieuses une série
de problématiques pertinentes. Qu'on se contente d'énu-
mérer celles que suggère Beau Dommage par sa chanson.
Relation du problème du sens au vécu et au langage quotidien; articulation particulière de cette problématique
autour de la relation du couple avec, en arrière-fond,
la permanence des figures parentales (père/mère/soeur);
enfin, en prospective, à la fois une dramatique sociale
des coordonnées de la conscience aliénante (nature vs
culture)[45] et, enfin, exigence d'une anthropologie réaliste qui débouche sur l'histoire.

En même temps, la confrontation du texte de Tous les
palmiers et de son premier contexte à la tradition judéo-
chrétienne ouvre des perspectives au monde de Beau Dommage. Elle confirme en quelque sorte son pessimisme,
son réalisme tout en débouchant sur une prospective qu'il
soupçonnait à peine.

Les rapprochements réalisés avec la tradition judéo-
chrétienne corroborent, en effet, la dramatique de fuite
de Tous les palmiers. L'homme judéo-chrétien, que ce
soit Adam, Caïn, Abram, Jésus ou Pierre, est en constante tension entre la réalité de l'autre ou soi-même et
l'image onirique d'une figure d'autorité violeuse. Sa
relation à autrui est marquée de la tentation de céder

à un Sujet-tout-puissant qui exige, par la menace ou par
la promesse de gratification, que l'homme se déleste de
son histoire, comme c'est le cas du garçon de Tous les
palmiers.

En Jésus, par ailleurs, se retrouve un réalisme, un sens
de la concrétude qui rejoint l'intuition d'écriture de
Beau Dommage. L'origine, l'ailleurs, se trouvent dénoncés
comme "pour soi". Le Dieu qu'il annonce n'est ni super-
ego, ni réponse à la pulsion (à l'id). Ni loi, ni rêve.
Il ne se nourrit pas de sacrifices. Il n'offre pas de
royaume magique; c'est, au contraire, l'Esprit du mal qui
se situe dans cette prospective. Son écriture est réaliste. A la loi fort abstraite des pharisiens, au rêve
des zélotes, il oppose un empirisme existentiel fort concret; le poids de la loi, la faim, la soif des gens.

Si le Christ réaffirme constamment la volonté du père,
ce n'est pas pour échapper à la condition humaine bien
au contraire. Cette volonté n'écrase pas le sujet, non
plus qu'elle ne le nie, en le faisant échapper à la mort
ou à la difficulté de vivre. Les miraculés, comme Lazare,
sont morts. La volonté du Père est celle d'une recon-
version de l'homme à la possibilité de sa réalité. Elle
renvoie l'homme à lui-même et à son prochain, cet autre
qui est différent, éloigné, dans lequel je ne me retrouve
pas et qui, en même temps, m'est proche et m'aime.

C'est ici que la tradition judéo-chrétienne fait éclater
la dramatique de Beau Dommage. Jusqu'ici, il y avait con-
cordance dans la perception de l'échec, de la tentation
d'aliénation, dans la nécessité du réalisme. Alors que
la rencontre est possible chez Beau Dommage sans trop de
justification (J'ai oublié le jour surgit comme par hasard
dans leur monde), les textes chrétiens en proposent une
phénoménologie plus articulée mais non nécessairement
contradictoire.

C'est, entre autres, dans l'assomption de sa propre
impuissance (Kénose) que l'homme pourra reconnaître celle
de l'autre et atteindre à l'altérité (Henosis). Dans
l'assomption de sa condition humaine, voire du sens (ou
des sens) concret de sa sexualité que l'homme ou la femme
découvrent leurs possibilités. La femme adultère est
reconnue comme telle avant de s'entendre dire qu'elle
peut aller et ne plus pécher (Jn. 8,1-11). La Samaritaine
se découvre sans homme véritable au même moment où elle
identifie les dimensions de sa soif (Jn. 4,1-25). Jésus
lui-même, dans sa mort qui n'a rien de celle du héros

mythique, pousse à bout cette dialectique de Kénose-
Henosis. Il va jusqu'au bout de la souffrance humaine,
de la sympathie et c'est cette assomption lucide du
drame de l'homme victime d'une loi onirique qui est se-
mence de rencontres avec l'autre comme le montre l'épisode d'Emmaüs (lc 24,13-35).

Il ne s'agit pas ici, de vouloir corriger en aucune
façon l'écriture de Beau Dommage. D'ailleurs en Jésus, le
critère d'évaluation n'est guère critère d'orthodoxie d'
écriture mais bien plutôt de praxis. Si le texte évangélique ne parle pas matériellement de problème, de couple,
de dramatique psychanalitique ou sociale, de problème d'
écriture, il n'en reste pas moins que, pour ceux qui dansent sa musique, les intentionnalités sont là, objectives :

.   L'histoire n'est pas que d'un tout Autre, de
    l'Université ou du Religieux mais de l'humain
    qui sans le savoir apprend à donner à celui
    qui a faim, qui a soif, qui est nu ou exclu.

.   De celui qui accepte d'apprendre dans les di-
    mensions de son histoire à aimer et à s'aimer.

.   De celui qui résiste pour les autres comme
    pour lui-même aux bruits qui le réduisent à
    être éternellement un enfant qui refuse d'
    être violé.

APPENDICE

Ce texte a une adresse : la Faculté de théologie de
l'Université de Montréal où depuis quelques années une minorité de professeurs s'efforcent d'expliciter, dans un
contexte interdisciplinaire [47], les axes méthodologiques
de sciences religieuses qui soient à la fois projets universitaires et projets d'acculturation.

Ces efforts d'explication méthodologique s'articulent
autour de trois pôles principaux :

1) La religiologie, un modèle intégrateur des sciences
   humaines de la religion qui respecte la spécificité
   du phénomène religieux aussi bien comme phénomène
   original que comme réalité historique dont les
   structures permanentes dans la culture sécularisée
   au-delà des lieux religieux traditionnels

2) <u>Le geste théologique</u>, un cadre épistémologique opérationnel qui tente de rendre à l'étude des grands lieux de la tradition chrétienne sa fonction d'intelligence des écritures culturelles actuelles

3) <u>La praxéologie pastorale</u>, un cadre épistémologique opérationnel qui situe de façon expérimentale et expérientielle, au niveau universitaire, l'apprentissage d'intervention chrétienne acculturée

LES BRUITS DE LA MER

NOTES

1. Tous les palmiers, paroles et musique : R. Léger;
    titre de l'album : Beau Dommage; Capitol-Emi du
    Canada, 1974, face A, n⁰ 1 (3 min.20 sec.). Le
    texte est ici reproduit avec la permission des
    Editions Bonté Divine, Montréal.

2. Il va sans dire qu'une interprétation exhaustive
    exigerait une analyse musicale. Nous nous limite-
    rons ici à l'analyse des paroles, ce qui est habi-
    tuel en histoire des religions.

3. La numérotation des versets est nôtre. Les réfé-
    rences au texte de la chanson seront incluses dans
    le texte même de l'article avec l'indication (v...).

4. Même si les chansons de Beau Dommage sont écrites
    par différents auteurs, nous les considérons comme
    un tout. Dans le monde McLuhannien, l'auditeur
    accorde moins d'importance à l'auteur qu'au groupe
    qui présente globalement une vision du monde à
    travers diverses chansons. En plus de leur premier
    album intitulé Beau Dommage, le groupe en a publié
    deux autres : Où est passée la noce, Capitol-Emi du
    Canada, 1976 et Un nouveau jour arrive en ville,
    1977 chez Capitol-Emi du Canada. Notre analyse,
    élaborée avant la parution du troisième album, a
    porté sur les deux premiers, qui, au dire même de
    Beau Dommage, constitue une première époque dans
    leur évolution comme le titre l'indique d'ailleurs.

5. Un incident à Bois-des-Filions, paroles P. Huet,
    musique P. Bertrand, R. Léger, M. Rivard, in Où
    est passée la noce, face B (20 min.30 sec.).

6. Amène pas ta gang, paroles et musique R. Léger,
    ibidem face A (3 min.13 sec.). (On notera la
    dimension fortement sexuelle de la répétition de
    l'ordre : "Viens").

7. Ginette, P. Huet et M. Rivard, ibidem face A, n⁰3
    (2 min.35 sec.).

8. Montréal, P. Huet et R. Léger in Beau Dommage, face
    A, n⁰ 6 (4 min.44 sec.). Il est à noter qu'il y a
    un double rapprochement sémantique significatif
    entre Montréal et Tous les palmiers. On peut se

demander si le silence imposé à la blonde de
Tous les palmiers n'est pas la contre-partie du
silence de Ginette qui n'a jamais téléphoné pour
inviter le jeune homme à venir coucher chez elle.
De toute façon, le téléphone "en faisant semblant
de rien" à lieu au coin de la rue fatidique où
le jeune homme a eu sa première relation sexuelle.

9. Un ange gardien, P. Huet, M. Rivard, ibidem face B,
    n°4 (2 min.56 sec.).

10. 23 décembre, P.Huet, M. Rivard, ibidem face B,n°6.

11. Heureusement qu'il y a la nuit, paroles P. Huet;
    musique M. Rivard in Où est passée la noce, face A,
    (5 min.45 sec.).

12. Le Géant Beaupré, P. Huet, M. Rivard in Beau Domma-
    ge, face B, n° 2 (4 min.02 sec.).

13. In Beau Dommage : "A toutes les fois"; "La complain-
    te du phoque en Alaska"; "Ginette"; "Un ange gardien";
    "Montréal". In "Où est passée la noce" :- "Les blues
    d'la métropole" : "Assis dans la cuisine"; "Heureu-
    sement qu'il y a la nuit"; "Un incident à Bois-des-
    Filions".

14. Le blues d'la métropole, paroles P. Huet; musique
    M. Rivard in Où est passée la noce, face A, (4 min.
    13 sec.).

15. exemples : Assis dans la cuisine, paroles et musique
    P. Bertrand in Où est passée la noce, face A et
    Le blues d'la métropole, op. cit.

16. Le blues d'la métropole, op. cit.

17. A toutes les fois, R. Léger, in Beau Dommage, op.cit.,
    face A,n° 2 (4 min.17 sec.).

18. Motel, "Mon Repos", paroles et musique M. Rivard in
    Où est passée la noce, face A, (3 min.35 sec.).

19. Le blues d'la métropole, op. cit.

20. Heureusement qu'il y a la nuit, op. cit.

21. Motel, "Mon Repos", op. cit.

376

22. J'ai oublié le jour, paroles et musique R. Léger in Où est passée la noce, face A, (3 min.05 sec.).

23. La modélisation exemplaire étant un des critères de distinction entre la fantaisie et le mythe. "Par son propre mode d'être, le mythe ne peut pas être particulier, privé, personnel". Eliade M. Mythes, rêves et mystères. Idée/Gallimard, no 271, Paris 1957, p. 14.

24. Il est important de noter que les chansons se rapprochent du mythe en ce qu'elles sont des récits sans cesse répétés (comme la prière) et même des récits qui impliquent une participation corporelle qui les rapprochent encore plus de l'évocation rituelle du mythe.

25. Le Petit Bonheur, chanson de Leclerc, Poètes d'Aujourd'Hui; Félix Leclerc, Luc Bermont, Félix Leclerc, Seghers, Paris 1964.

    Il est à noter que la chanteuse française Dalida a récemment repris cette chanson se contentant de changer 2 mots, ce qui marque bien le caractère universel de la langue du premier Leclerc (   ). Il serait impossible de faire la même chose avec une chanson de Beau Dommage.

26. Un jour, un jour, S. Venne, Select, Montréal 1967. Dans le blues d'la métropole Beau Dommage évoque l'idéalisme de l'Expo 67 qu'il demeure en quelque sorte en peignant une princesse maintenant désabusée. Le rêve de l'Expo n'aurait rien produit.

27. Brigit et G. Vigneault : Natasquan, le voyage immobile, Stanké-l'ARC, Montréal 1976.

28. Jean du Sud, G. Vigneault, in Les gens de mon pays, Nouvelle édition de l'ARC, Montréal 1974.

29. Mon pays, Vigneault, in Mon pays, Columbia, Montréal 1967.

30. Vers un nouveau pouvoir, Jacques Grand'Maison, Editions H.M.H.., Montréal 1967.

31. Par exemple : "Les mathématiciens chinois qui ont fait leur autocritique lors de la Révolution cul-

turelle ne se sont pas accusés d'avoir produit des
théorèmes faux mais d'avoir pratiqué dans leur
"tour d'ivoire" une science d'académiciens cherchant
seulement le prestige personnel. Aussi n'ont-ils
pas modifié leurs théorèmes bourgeois par des théorèmes "prolétariens", mais modifié le rapport aux
masses qui étaient impliquées dans la pratique".
in Jacques Rancière. La leçon d'Althusser; idée/
Gallimard, Paris 1974, n° 294, p. 255.

32. "La théologie entre le semaire et la rue" mémoire
de la délégation des étudiants de la Faculté de
théologie au premier regroupement des étudiants
québécois en théologie. Québec, 23-25 janvier 76.
Publié dans Relations,février 1976, vol. XXXVI,
n° 412, p.46-50.

33. A propos de la chute connue "possibility of revolution:" "With Adam's "fall" human history began.
The original preindividualist (indéterminé) harmony
between man and nature and between man and woman
is replaced by conflict and struggle"... "(Man's
desire) is to give up reason, self-awareness, choice,
responsibility (de "faire semblant de rien") and to
return to the womb to Mother Earth (à l'origine)...
But he cannot go back... Lord God... placed a che-
rubin... to guard the way to the tree of life (axis
mundi)... Man creates himself in the historical process which began with his first act of freedom -the
freedom to disobey - to say no". In Fromm, Erich
You shall be as gods, Holt, Rheinhart and Winston,
New York, 1966 p.87-88. A propos du rôle de nommer
les choses, Amada Levy Valencin, interprète la première nomination des animaux par Adam seul, sans
Eve comme "asymétrique" et "narcissique". Il lui
faudra Eve, "Ezer Keneguedo", qu'elle traduise, "en
raccourci", comme "Aide comme sa contre-partie ou
comme face à face". Sinon Adam risque le solipcisme
in Eliane Amado Levy Valencin, Les voies et les
pièges de la psychanalyse (1971) p.10 et 11 et le
grand désarroi aux racines de l'énigme homosexuelle
(1973) p.83, tous deux publiés aux éditions universitaires, Paris.

34. S'inspirant de la tradition du Zohar, Amado Levy
Valencin lit la naissance de Caïn et d'Abel comme
un acte manqué. Dans cette perspective il n'y a
pas encore de couple véritable entre Adam et Eve
(pas d'altérité). Elle traduit le "Kanite Lyah êt

Hachem" (Gen.N.1) par "J'ai acheté" un fils de
l'Eternel (de l'origine). Il n'est pas clair dans la
pensée d'Eve si c'est Adam qui la fecondée, elle
reste mégalomaniaque. C'est à l'Eternel qu'elle a
pris ses fils. Ceux-ci ne sont "pas viables," marqué qu'ils sont du désir aliéné de leurs parents"
in Eliane Amado Levy-Valencin, Le grand désarroi
aux racines de l'enigme homosexuelle, op. cit. p. 84-85.

35. On pourra s'étonner de voir Abram qualifié d'impuissant. La lecture machisme de l'Orient comme de
l'Occident rejette rapidement la stérilité du couple
sur Sara. Le fait qu'Abram engrosse Agar (G.N.16)
ne devrait pas suffire à sauver sa virilité. La
psychanalyse a parlé du complexe "madonne - prostituée"
qui empêche l'homme de fonctionner avec une femme
qu'il considère comme son égale. Quoiqu'il en soit
de la psychologie d'Abram, vis-à-vis de la femme, il
n'en reste pas moins qu'objectivement il visait
l'approche de l'homme qui n'est pas capable d'avoir
d'enfant. Notons enfin que le prof. : O. Genest
nous faisait remarquer que selon certaines traditions on considérait la naissance d'Isaac comme
miraculeuse. C'est Dieu lui-même qui aurait alors
fécondé Sara, laissant Abram à une impuissance objective. Notre interprétation d'Abram et de la
circoncision rejoint, entre autre celle d'Eliane
Amado Levy-Valencin in Voies et pièges de la psychanalyse op. cit. p. 261 et 72 et le grand désarroi aux
racines de l'énigme homosexuelle op. cit. p. 86-87.

36. "It has always been accepted without question that
God declared his judgement upon homosexual practices
once and for all time by the destruction of the cities
of the Plain. But Sodom and Gomorrah, as we have seen
(chapître 1, "Sodom and Gomorrah p. 1-28) actually
have nothing whatever to do with such practices; the
interpretation of the Sodom story generally received
by Western Christendom turns out to be nothing more
than a post-Exilic Jewish reinterpretation devised
and exploited by patriotic rigorists for polemical
purposes." In Derrick Sherwin Bailey, Homosexuality
and the western Christian tradition Longmans, Green
and Co., Londres, 1955, p. 155. L'interprétation homosexuelle de l'histoire, de Sodome malgré son manque de fondement historique n'en reste pas moins un
renforcement symbolique du drame d'altérité que révèle l'épisode biblique. Il reste par ailleurs pa-
radoxal qu'un texte qui professait la nécessité de

l'altérité est servie durant des millénaires à justifier un refus de la différence et concrètement,
entraîne une condamnation a Divino, (à l'origine)
de la minorité homosexuelle.

37. "L'aliénation artistique rend l'oeuvre d'art,
l'univers de l'art, essentiellement irréel. Elle
crée un monde qui n'existe pas, un monde de Schein,
d'apparence, d'illusion. Mais c'est dans cette
transformation de la réalité en illusion, et seulement,
en elle, que se manifeste la vérité subversive de
l'art". "La désublimation radicale qui a lieu au
théâtre, en tant que théâtre, et de la désublimation
organisée, calculée, jouée - elle n'est pas loin de
son contraire"...parlant de la musique de groupe il
continue... "En même temps qu'elle perd son impact
radical, cette musique tend à se massifier: auditeur et coparticipants sont des masses qui affluent
à un spectacle, à une représentation. Certes l'au-
ditoire y participe activement: la musique fait
bouger les corps, les rend "naturels". Mais,
l'excitation - littéralement-électrique revêt souvent
l'aspect de l'hystérie. Le répétition agressive d'un
rythme indéfiniment martelé (dont les variations
n'ouvrent pas une autre dimension de la musique), les
dissonnances abrutissantes... ces gestes, ces corps
secoués et contorsionnés mais sans pour ainsi
dire jamais se toucher - n'est ce pas faire du sur-place?
Cela ne mène nulle part, sinon à entrer dans une
foule qui ne tardera pas à se disperser. Cette
musique est littéralement - imitation, mimesis de
l'agression effective; et c'est en outre un cas de
plus de catharsis qui débarasse - temporairement -
des inhibitions. La libération reste l'affaire de
chacun", Herbert Marcuse, Contre-révolution et
Révolte, Seuil, Paris, 1973, pp. 127, 144 et 145-
146.

38. Par exemple, Lévi-Strauss, Claude, Le cru et le cruit,
Plon, Paris 1964, p. 23.

39. Dans la chanson Tout va bien, un autre garçon implo-
re la femme ("Ayez pitié de l'homme qui a peur. Pre-
nez-lui la main quand il pleure") chantera "Caché
dans les bars où la nuit vient tard. Et où le jour
se perd. A trouver des remèdes pour le mal de mer.
Des lendemains de veille. Aussi vidés et creux que
les fonds de bouteilles". Ce paragraphe, où l'on
Parle du mal de mer, paru après notre analyse des
deux premiers albums et le choix du titre de notre
article corroborent en capsule la dramatique que

nous avions dévoilée. L'homme pitoyable en larmes,
qui demande à la femme de le prendre par la main
(la mer) et qui se bat avec la nuit (autre figure
de mère), déçu de ne rien avoir trouver dans cette
autre mère liquide de la bière. Tout va bien.
Parole et musique: M. Rivard. In Un nouveau jour
arrive en ville, face A. n° 1, op. cit.

40. Dans Seize ans en soixante-seize, les jeunes chantent
"Y'paraît qu'on écrit comme on parle. C'qui voudrait
dire qu'on écrit mal . . . Mais c'est donc pas d'not'
faute. Nos mots sont just'l'écho des vôtres. Nous
on arrive, vous nous d'mandez d'écrire. C'que vous
avez jamais osé dire." Seize ans en soixante-seize.
Paroles: P. Huet; musique: M. Richard, ibidem,
face A, n° 1.

41. En plus des trois évocations de géants dont nous avons
déjà parlé, (l'Ange gardien note; le Géant Beaupré;
les Géants;) il faut noter cette fée des étoiles à
laquelle le jeune garçon de 23 décembre n'ose pas
demander de lui réparer son (baton de Hockey). 23 décembre, P. Huet, M. Rivard in Beau Dommage, op. cit.,
face B, n° 5 (2 min. 14 sec.).

42. "C'est pas l'show qui est important. C'est d'être une
gang pour un moment. On n'a pas de cause, on va
s'battre pour autre chose. On va s'battre pour le
fun . . . On est d'accord pour n'importe qu'elle
révolution à condition qu'elle se danse." Ces paroles
laissent songeur (au sens strict du terme) sur les
possibilités de révolution des jeunes. In Seize ans
en soixante-seize, op. cit.

43. "Hypothèse de travail (pour l'interprète): "tout
auteur écrit dans une langue de moi à peu près incon-
nue: l'ensemble de son oeuvre forme une pierre de
Rosette . . . Interpréter c'est appliquer un sous-ensemble de l'oeuvre sur un autre, un espace sur un
autre espace, une région sur une autre région . . .
Découpez les premiers livres de Tite-Live, appliquez-
les sur des sous-ensemble des textes védiques, des
Eddas, du Zand-Avesta, et vous suivrez la méthode
comparatiste de Dumezil, qui ne traduit pas seulement des langues entre elles, mais des sous-langages
réputés, par hypothèse, indéchiffrables, mais qui
s'expliquent d'un corps, par ladite application. Et
qui s'expliquent par la mise en évidence d'invariants,
d'invariants par rotation, par la translation, par

381

l'application, invariants qui traversent les sous-
régions. J'imagine volontiers, en première approximation, que tout interprète n'est jamais que struc-
turaliste." In Michel Serres, Jouvences sur Jules
Vernes, Paris, éd. de minuit, 1974, p.235-236.

44. "Eliade is under a gross illusion in supposing that
modern man" finds it increasingly difficult to re-
discover the existential dimension of religious man
in the archaic society. Modern man, since the elec-
tromagnetic discoveries of more than a century ago,
is investing himself with all the dimensions of
archaic man plus. "in Marshall McLuhan, Gutenberg
Galaxy: the making of typographic man, University
of Toronto Press, Toronto, 1962, p.69. La société
séculière et son refus de toute topologie métaphy-
sique rendent presqu'impossible à l'homme d'aujourd'
hui, de vivre le mythe sur le même mode dont l'ac-
tualisait le primitif. Une herméneutique structu-
relle, qui abolit la linéanté de l'histoire (syn-
chronisme) peut permettre à l'homme moderne de
retrouver dans le récit mythique des dimensions
possibles de son vécu actuel et ainsi de vivre une
dramatique religieuse acculturée.

45. Notre analyse s'est centrée au niveau de la dramatique interpersonnel des individus de Tous les palmiers et des référents bibliques. Nous ne préten-
dions pas épuiser l'épaisseur sémantique du texte.
La dramatique dégage, retrouve des échos dans les
dimensions sociologiques de ces chansons où l'on
retrouve à des homologies de structure entre la
femme, la ville et les mass-média (télévision,
journaux).

HOCKEY IN CANADA

TOM SINCLAIR-FAULKNER's paper was first presented to the
CSSR/SCER meetings at Laval University in 1976. He is
Assistant Professor of Religion at Dalhousie
University and wrote his doctoral dissertation for the
University of Chicago on Anglo-Saxon Protestant and
French Catholic attitudes to Canada's entry into World
War II.

RÉSUMÉ

Suivant les définitions de Berger et Luckmann, la religion se trouve en dehors des bornes des églises et de
la théologie. Il se peut que même le hockey ait une
signification religieuse pour beaucoup de canadiens.
Au moins, l'étude du hockey en tant que religion sert
comme moyen heuristique et un instrument utile pour ceux
qui veulent considérer la religion en critique.

   Le hockey est un univers symbolique qui sert à créer
un certain concept du moi. Ce concept inclut un caractère mâle et agressif, des réflexes entraînés, apte à
gagner coûte que coûte. Ce cosmos inclut également un
ecclesia qui formule et qui fait appliquer d'une manière
autonome ses propres doctrines disciplinaires, doctrines
qui ordonnent et encouragent une conduite permise seulement à l'intérieur de ce cosmos. Il y a même une
institution qui date depuis 23 ans avec sa propre dynas-
tie, la famille Hewitt, qui embrasse les francophones
et les anglophones du Canada entier. En effet, un bloc
énorme du temps de la famille se passe ainsi autour des
patinoires. Et, c'est une tradition qui s'étend des
plus jeunes jusqu'aux plus âgés, car, le hockey donne
aux mordus une couleur vive à leurs vies monotones, un
peu moins d'aliénation entre des étrangers des bars publiques et un sentiment d'identité canadienne. Peu à
peu le hockey devient alors une vache sacrée au Canada.
Cette analyse, cependant, pose deux questions importantes : celle des relations pouvant être trop naïves entre
les églises et le sport; et, celle des valeurs fondamentales du hockey : perdent-elles leur enjouement?
au nom de quoi?

TOM SINCLAIR-FAULKNER

A Puckish Reflection on Religion in Canada

> ...don't the playoff rites each Spring rouse the
> only genuine religious fervor felt by the majority
> of Canadians?
> What else attracts such passionate devotion,
> adoration, yes, even worship, from so many other-
> wise unexcitable Canadians?...(It's) the nearest
> thing to extant religious fanaticism in the
> country today.[1]

Canadian sports writers may be forgiven a measure of
hyperbole during the Stanley Cup Season, but what if
there was a nugget of truth in what Moritsugu was saying? What if being a hockey fan or player is a way of
being religious?

I have set out to raise this apparently frivolous
question as a serious student of religion for four
reasons. First, I am from time to time swept away by
the experience of being actively engaged in the game
of hockey, primarily as a fan, and I should like to make
sense of that "ecstasy" in a reflective way. I feel
the same teasing urge to probe further that drove Al
Purdy to poetic reflection on the game:

> I've seen the aching glory of a resurrection
> in their eyes
> if they score
> but crucifixion's agony to lose - the game?[2]

Second, I am intrigued by the close ties that exist
between churches and ice hockey in many parts of Canada,
and the explicit claim made by some church leaders that
ice hockey is a suitable means to achieve the ends
sought in Christian education.[3] Third, I find here an
opportunity to make use of the fascinating but generally
unapplied sociological model for religion presented by
Thomas Luckmann in The Invisible Religion (1967).[4] Does
it shed light on the human phenomenon of ice hockey? I
think that it does. I hasten to add that I think it
foolish to regard Luckmann's definition of religion as
comprehensive. It is, in fact, what I would call a
"first-level" definition only, but it is adequate to my
present task.

And finally, I find that raising this apparently

384

frivolous but ultimately serious question about hockey
fans and players is a useful way to introduce college
students to the study of religion. They commonly arrive
in the classroom with the conviction that religion is
what happens in churches and synagogues. I find this
to be an inadequate starting point, and have found that
beginning students become critical of it when invited
to apply Luckmann's model to the ice hockey phenomenon
in Canada.

Luckmann's powerful argument for understanding religion to be what humans do when they are being human[5]
has been criticized by his sometime collaborator Peter
Berger for not permitting distinctions between different
ways of being human. Berger accepts Luckmann's analysis,
but reserves the label "religious" for those modes of
self-transcendence (the human quality par excellence)
which have to do with the "sacred," as understood by
Rudolph Otto and Mircea Eliade.[6] Berger's point is well
taken, but I find it a handicap in dealing with beginning students. Most of them resist the conception of
the sacred which embraces not only a mysterium fascinans,
but also a mysterium tremendum. Not only do they tend
to suppose that religion is done in temples, but they
also tend to feel relief that religion has long since
progressed beyond the day when religious persons encountered the holy and found it to be "awful."

I am happy to report that students who have been jol-
ted out of the first preconception by an invitation to
see hockey play and fandom as a way of being religious
soon develop the same yearning that characterizes Peter
Berger. They grant that the characteristically human
drive for self-transcendence is an essential element in
our understanding of the category "religious," but want
to know how one is to differentiate between one way of
achieving self-transcendence and another. At this point
I find students much more open to consideration of the
"sacred" as it is generally understood by historians of
religion, than they were when they first arrived in the
classroom.

I suggest, then, that Luckmann's model of religion is
a useful heuristic device in the general study of religion, as well as a helpful tool for reflection upon the
experience of Canadian hockey fans and players. Let us
test the latter claim by first outlining the pertinent
aspects of Luckmann's model, and then using it to say
something about how hockey fans and players are religious.

Luckmann's model of religion presupposes the sociology of knowledge described in The Social Construction
of Reality, jointly authored by him and Peter Berger in
1966.[7] "Reality" is understood to be "...a quality
pertaining to phenomena that we recognize as independent
of our own volition."[8] Yet it is, they argue, a "social
construct," the product of a dialectical and historical
process in which human beings both create their reality
and are created by it.[9]

There are many different ways by which this process
occurs, by means of which the person finds objective
and moral meaning in her experience. But there is one
thing which knits it all together - the "symbolic
universe", which is

> conceived of as the matrix of all socially objectiva-
> ted and subjectively real meanings; the entire his-
> toric society and the entire biography of the indivi-
> dual are seen as events taking place within this
> universe.[10]

I like this notion of a "matrix of meaning." It
suggests an organic system which is not important in
itself, but important insofar as it is the structure
within which the person apprehends and acts and develops. The matrix is, like the original Latin, a "womb"
whose significance is revealed in the human life that
grows within it.

As the ultimate bestower of all meanings, the symbolic
universe is the means by which the world or cosmos is
created, and by which the individual achieves a biography.
Day-to-day experience is integrated within it, and marginal situations (of which death is the most terrifying)
are legitimated.[11] Thomas Luckmann returns to this
notion of a "symbolic universe" in The Invisible Religion,[12] noting that it is by means of a socially-
constructed symbolic universe that the individual
organism transcends its biological nature, becoming a
Self with a biography and a conscience. This process
of self-transcendence is, he argues, what makes us
human, yet it is also true that that which transcends
is religious. Therefore at its most basic level to be
human is to be religious.[13]

Two matters are worth remarking in an aside at this
point. The first is that although Luckmann is a socio-
logist, his primary interest in this model of religion

is not society (as it is for Durkheim) but the Self.
The second is that Luckmann is arguing that the one
feature which all religions share in common is the
human drive for self-transcendence. I do not infer
from this that he regards self-transcendence as the only
essential characteristic of any one religion. Luckmann
presents what I take to be a "first-level" definition of
religion without precluding more complex, and hence more
satisfactory, definitions.

Luckmann presses his point by arguing that the world
which takes shape as the person lives out his life
within a symbolic universe reveals an "inner hierarchy
of significance." At the lowest level, one finds the
typifications which are so routine as to pose no problem: for example, grass is green. At the next level
are typifications which do suggest a need for some
reflection: grass requires watering in order to thrive.
At a higher level still appear typifications of a much
more general nature which not only require reflection
but may be problematic: a good farmer cares for his
grass. And finally there are typifications at a super-
ordinated level of interpretation which are massively
problematic, widely applicable, and far from concrete -
the grass belongs to the people, all flesh is grass.[14]
Because Luckmann finds a hierarchy of significance
moving from a concrete, everyday level of reality to a
distinct level of reality in which ultimate significance
is located, he feels justified in speaking not simply of
the creation of a "world" but of the creation of a
"sacred cosmos"[15] - plainly intending to exploit the
understanding that the "sacred" is "something more" or
"something different," beyond the everyday.

Having described the process of becoming human as
"religious," and the world that transcends the everyday
as a "sacred cosmos," Luckmann argues that as a human
society becomes more complex, there tends to develop a
specific institution or institutions whose primary
function is to maintain the sacred cosmos.[16] In the
absence of a label in Luckmann's text, I propose to
call this institution an ecclesia, and note that Luckmann assigns to it four characteristics: it is

> characterized by standardization of the sacred cosmos
> in a well-defined doctrine, differentiation of full-
> time religious roles, transfer of sanctions enforcing
> doctrinal and ritual conformity to special agencies
> and the emergence of organizations of the "ecclesiastic"
> type.[17]

In short, an ecclesia has its own doctrine, its own
priesthood, its own judicial system, and is "ecclesiastic." For the sake of clarity I am inclined to invest
this term with perhaps more meaning than Luckmann does.
Luckmann understands it to refer to the replacement of
informal institutional structures realized in lay people
and charismatic leaders by more formal structures realized in a priesthood - a fourth characteristic which I
believe adds little to the second which he has proposed.
I am inclined to stress a notion implicit in Joachim
Wach's original use of the term "ecclesiastic" and
rooted in the Greek word " ἔκκλητος ": that is,
the notion that the ecclesia is a body of people who
are "called out," set over against the rest of the
world.[18]

   The final touch to this sociological model of religion
is Luckmann's observation that in a modern, highly complex society, the person has available to her not only
one but several symbolic universes, each providing a
sacred cosmos sustained by its own ecclesia. Typically
the person moves from one to the other, donning and
abandoning new roles as required:[19] for example, she
may move from the business world to the academic world
to the sports world to the world of the church. In the
face of such a development the person does not have
available to her one sacred cosmos which convincingly
superordinates all reality. In order to tie together
her experience, she must cobble together her own religion, constructing it from material borrowed from her
encounter as a sort of consumer with the different
sacred cosmoses made available to her by the competing
ecclesiae of her society. Of course she has no need to
do this when she stands within the frame of any given
ecclesia, but what is she to do when she steps outside
that frame? She must construct her own "invisible
religion," and the primary context for this distinctively
modern enterprise is the nuclear family.[20]

   How does Luckmann's model for religion apply to ice
hockey? We may begin by arguing that there is indeed a
symbolic universe which characterizes hockey. That we
may do so is not surprising, given the widely accepted
insights into the nature of games in general already
suggested by those philosophers who have shown that
games characteristically have their own "world," distinct from the rest of human reality.[21]

   At the lowest level, hockey is typified by tangible

things (skates, ice rinks, a puck) and less tangible
but still undisputed qualities. It is incredibly fast
(pucks travel at up to 125 miles per hour, lines must
be changed every two minutes or less) and rule changes
have tended to enhance the game's swiftness. It is
colourful, strenuous, and dangerous. These last qualities have been amplified by the technology of television, but even before the camera's eye was able to
bring the game close to the spectator, there were
features of hockey which served to make the spectator
unusually aware of hockey's peculiar qualities. The
action is continuous and tends to involve two or three
players at a time, not entire teams, thus inviting constant and focussed attention. And the game of hockey
tends to place the spectator physically closer to the
action than does any other popular sport, particularly
in small municipal or school rinks.

Continuing at this first level of the hockey world we
note that, like other games, hockey is characterized by
a competitive spirit, by fun, and by graceful physical
activity. But when one reflects upon other qualities
of the hockey world, one finds that they are problematic in varying degrees.

For example, all games are competitive, but hockey
in Canada has tended to go further than most games -
winning is valued more highly than is the graceful
execution of a play. Players report their frustration
with fans who cheer good offensive plays but ignore
graceful defensive manoeuvres,[22] but the players themselves tend to place scoring ahead of grace of sports-
manship. On one occasion a sportswriter attempted to
cheer a defeated Rocket Richard by quoting the founder
of the modern Olympics, Baron de Coubertin - "It's not
who wins but how you play the game." The Rocket's
glum but considered reply was, "That Frenchman sounds
like a born loser!"[23]

The speed and continuous action of hockey favours
tactics which are really trained reflexes, not thought-
ful responses to situations. Doug Harvey, one of the
great professional players, was generally regarded by
fans as "lazy" precisely because his peculiar style of
play was more reflective than reflexive.[24] But there
are other consequences of speed and continuous action.
Some social scientists have argued convincingly that
aggressive action is drastically increased in situations
which produce anxiety but permit little or no time for

rational consideration before a response is demanded.[25]
The hockey world offers solid evidence in support of
this hypothesis, for it is characterized by an extra-
ordinarily high degree of aggressive behaviour.

Some have suggested that hockey tends to attract
violent, aggressive men, particularly from the ranks of
lower class society where open aggressivity is valued
more than at higher levels of social class. The only
careful empirical study that I have encountered which
deals with this issue suggests that aggressive behaviour
is bred within the hockey world, not introduced from
outside. And indeed players having a higher socio-
economic status tend to be more aggressive and assaultive than do those from the lower end of the socio-
economic order.[26]

An increasingly problematic typification of the
hockey cosmos is its masculinity. Recent changes have
created women's hockey leagues at the Canadian college
level with formal NHL sanctions, but the sport is still
overwhelmingly male. Women make their appearance only
as wives of professional players (during period breaks
on television or on special ceremonial occasions) or as
mothers of adolescent players. Tatum O'Neal may pitch
for the "Bad News Bears," but not even superior playing
ability could qualify Abby Hoffman as a hockey player
in St. Catherines.[27]

Problematic in a different way is the manner in which
hockey sometimes appears to be an individual's sport,
and sometimes a team sport. The person who lives out
his life within this matrix of meaning commonly understands it to be both. Related to the "team" dimension
is the fact that one finds new, unique social bonds
developing within the hockey world which ignore or even
contradict one's customary social patterns.

I find that in practise it is difficult to distinguish between Luckmann's second and third levels of
significance in the world of meaning that defines
hockey, but there is clearly a hierarchy of some sort
here. It is also apparent that there is a cluster of
values which give superordinating meaning to the entire
hockey cosmos. Among these I should note the widespread
conviction that in the hockey cosmos one is Canadian,
one is manly (a quality which goes beyond sheer masculinity), and that one is excellent (by which I mean
something that has more to do with winning than with

the ancient Greek notion of ἀρετή).

To list these qualities is merely to remind the reader of what he already knows about ice hockey in
Canada. But how did these particular features of the
game develop? In some measure they are the results of
the physical features of the game - of its technology
and of its participants. But shaping and sustaining
this particular symbolic universe is an ecclesia, of
which the widely ramifying structure of the National
Hockey League is a central but not exclusive component.

First of all, there is a system of doctrine which
defines the hockey world. Some of it takes the obvious
form of legislated regulations, codified in the NHL.
But these formal rules pertain in effect only to the
first level of hockey's symbolic universe rulebook.
There are many other less formal but nonetheless effective sources of doctrine which are available to fans
and players, and which relate to higher levels of typification. These include popular books about hockey,
the ritual pep talks before and during games, special
team rules laid down by coaches and managers, stories
and anecdotes which circulate among players and fans,
commentary and interviews in the news media.

Consider for example the typification that, as a
competitive sport, hockey places a high premium on
winning. Popular sports writer Trent Frayne once wrote
a book entitled, It's Easy All You Have to Do Is Win,
and introduced it with an account of the Montréal
Canadiens refusing to shake hands with the Detroit Red
Wings when the Wings won the Stanley Cup in 1945.

> The only thing that really matters in professional
> hockey (or amateur, too, if you really think about
> it) - is who won - or else, as someone long ago
> observed, they wouldn't bother keeping score.[28]

Stories like the one about Rocket Richard recounted
above make the rounds, and the principal trophy of
professional hockey is the Stanley Cup - not awarded
for overall excellence, but for most games won in a
challenge match at the end of the season. In the
dressing room of the Toronto Maple Leafs hangs the
motto, "Defeat does not rest lightly on their shoulders."[29] And following the 1976 Stanley Cup series
the warmest thing that the announcers could find to
say about the hapless Philadelphia Flyers defeated

in four games straight was, "It's no shame to lose to a club like this year's Canadiens."

The notion that both the team and the individual are to be prized is reflected in the array of trophies for outstanding achievements by both, and by the custom of naming "three stars" immediately upon the announcement of a team victory. When things are going well, team members being interviewed by the media will single out one or two "spark plugs" who have stimulated a team success, and they in turn will praise a team effort that made their achievement possible. Conversely, a team without a few outstanding individuals is considered dull, while an individual like Greg Neeld who plays to the grandstand instead of with his team is bitterly resented by his mates.[30] The same holds true, I have found, at the level of amateur hockey for boys.

The "team" typification extends beyond the team proper. In any Canadian bar during a televised game, one sees perfect strangers intensely bound together in support of one side - and occasionally willing to assault someone who is cheering too loudly for the other side.[31] Interestingly hockey appears to engage its fans more closely with player action than do other sports where spectator violence is common. In hockey, spectator brawls are most often touched off by player brawls.[32] In any case, solidarity with the team is both a fact and a goal. Friends of Conn Smythe were convinced that he believed that universal support from Toronto fans would in some magical way guarantee a Leaf victory.[33]

The notion that hockey is Canadian is sustained in the television show title, "Hockey Night in Canada" - a 23-year-old institution which today attracts four million viewers to regular NHL games alone, and which remains in the familiar hands of the Hewitt dynasty which began in radio in 1922. It is supported by the government-sponsored Hockey Canada, described as "our game" even by critical writers like Bruce Kidd and Bob Bossin who fear that it is being lost to Canadians, and assumed by the NHL whenever the matter doesnot jeopardize gate receipts.

In fact hockey has often been touted as the Canadian institution, one that bridges the traditional gulf between English and French in this country.[34] This was more true in the past than in the present. During the

30s, for example, French Canadian fans rallied fana-
tically around German Canadian Howie Morenz playing for
an English Canadian-owned team that trained and played
in English only: the Montreal Canadiens.[35] Those
sentiments have altered recently: I watched the Team
Canada games in 1972 with both English Canadian and
French Canadian audiences, and found the former to be
uncritically enthusiastic over Team Canada, while
the latter were enthusiastically critical.

One recalls that at the time the Canadiens were in
practise a unilingual club, while francophone WHA clubs
like the Québec Nordiques were ruled ineligible for Team
Canada. Since then the Canadiens have acquired their
first fluently bilingual coach, Scotty Bowman, who
appears regularly in the francophone media, but I suspect that there is still a basic trend among French
Canadians to see hockey as canadien rather than canadien/
Canadian, let alone Canadian.

The typification that hockey is masculine may be under
fire at the rulebook level, as women press for their
own leagues and, less often, for admission to male
leagues. But at the level of informal doctrine, hockey's
masculinity is massively and solidly sustained. "Hockey,"
Gordie Howe declares flatly, "is a man's game."[36] Top
professional players trade upon their unambiguously
masculine image by endorsing commercial products which
marketing experts feel need to be identified with
masculinity. I have four nephews who are outstanding
amateur hockey players; but my two nieces, who have
tried and enjoyed hockey, must accept that they will
be figure skaters instead.

Finally we may consider a typification which is implicitly tied to masculinity in hockey: violence and
aggressivity, qualities which are virtually equated. I
note in particular that the only NHL trophy which
bears a woman's name is the Lady Byng - for gentlemanly
conduct. Almost synonymous in hockey folklore with
Conn Smythe's name is his adage (borrowed, I think, from
Leo Dandurand who was fond of it in the 20s): "If you
can't beat them outside in the alley, you can't beat
them inside on the ice."[37] One wonders why he bothered
to draw a distinction between alley and ice. Bobby
Hull has certainly found no need to do so.

Hockey is no sport for cowards, aggression pays off,
and not only in games won. The aggressive player not

only makes a big contribution to the spectacle, but he is also less liable to be hurt...[38]

Punch Imlach's autobiography bears the self-explanatory title, Hockey Is a Battle,[39] and Toe Blake once incurred a $2000 fine for assaulting a referee solely in order to give his Canadiens a concrete demonstration of what the coach meant by calling for aggressive play.[40] But this commitment to violent aggressivity is not confined to professional adult levels alone. Many parents urge their offspring to "hit 'em" in the amateur rinks, often to the despair of less sanguinary coaches. Still it would be difficult to outdo the Peewee coach who addressed his young charges thus:

If there is any blood on any sweaters, it's going to be on their sweaters - not ours...
I want you guys to hit these bums so hard, they will be scared to come back in the rink.[41]

Some have charged that there has been a marked increase in assaultive behaviour at hockey matches since World War Two,[42] but I doubt that we can muster anything beyond impressionistic evidence for this claim. Surely the record of the famous Ottawa Silver Seven at the turn of the century, and that of the early years of the NHL, bear comparison with post-war bloodbaths on ice.[43] The only assessment which might lay claim to statistical validity is a recent Toronto medical survey which reports that as of 1973 hockey produces more injuries among young Canadians than do baseball, football, and soccer combined. The doctors are convinced that high-sticking habits (nominally illegal) are a major factor in this increase.[44]

That this strong commitment to violence in hockey is in some way peculiar to the Canadian scene is brought home whenever an international match occurs. Europeans charge Canadians with perverting the sport with excessive and even useless body contact, while Canadians take comfort in the fact that the Russians may be good at passing the puck around but "can't take it in the corners."

We may conclude this survey of hockey doctrine by noting that all of the typifications which comprise the matrix of meaning within which Canadians practise and enjoy hockey are understood to stand in some superordinating way to the entire reality of the player or

fan. The point may be made by spokesman for the
ecclesia like Bob Pulford:

> My story is this: That a Canadian kid who can play
> this game well, these days, is the luckiest kid in
> the world. I mean it. There is no limit to how far
> he can go. The opportunities are tremendous.[45]

One finds it legislated directly into the constitution
of the Metropolitan Toronto Hockey League that the
League aims generally to build "good character and
citizenship."[46] And it is symbolically implied by the
presence of the Hockey Hall of Fame at the geographic
centre of the Canadian National Exhibition in Toronto.
(I leave aside the question whether Toronto is the
symbolic centre of Canada.)

The second characteristic of an ecclesia is differentiation of full-time religious roles. Clearly hockey
has come a long way since the first casual matches at
Kingston in the mid-nineteenth century. Referees and
coaches were made official in the 1880s, and professional hockey made its appearance among Ontario mining
towns at the turn of the century.[47] Today there are
not only two major professional leagues, but a vast
network of professional and amateur leagues, most of
them knit together under the aegis of the NHL and embracing almost half a million Canadian males from six
years to aging adulthood - It is worth stressing that
the direction of this network is firmly in the hands
of full-time professionals, and that almost all of the
published commentary is provided by professional
specialists.

The hockey priesthood is as much given to vestments
as any other. I refer not simply to on-ice uniforms,
but note the widespread use of jackets and blazers off
the ice, each emblazoned with the team's badge and
occasionally with the individual's office. Gordie
Howe's owner reported to his biographer that he refused to consider himself a genuine Red Wing until he
had been issued with his red blazer.[48]

One might quibble that not all coaches and players
are full-time, but surely such an objection falls to
the ground in the face of the fact that even young
amateurs play four to six hours per week in a formal
setting, and wear their identifying clothing everywhere.
The non-participant may see them as empty signs at best

and silly costumes at worst, but those who wear them
invest them with tremendous significance.

The development in hockey of an autonomous disciplinary system provides perhaps the most striking evidence
of the existence here of a genuine ecclesia. Not only
are there formal rules which are enforced by three
officials in every game, but each team at the professional levels is provided with an informal set of en-
forcers commonly referred to as "policemen." These
individuals are charged with the task of intimidating
opposing players, delivering hard checks, and ensuring
that the aggressive stance of their own team is maintained. These men are not expected to produce goals,
but to regulate the standard of aggressiveness which
has come to be associated with Canadian hockey. They
are aided and abetted by their coaches, occasionally
with verbal encouragement, and sometimes with fines
for players who have declined to behave in a satisfac-
torily aggressive fashion. In 1969, for example, owner
Jack Kent Cooke fined each member of the Los Angeles
Kings $100.00 for not disputing a referee's call.[49]

When one considers the full disciplinary system in
hockey (officials, "policemen," coaches) one sees that
it relates effectively and flexibly to every point of
the symbolic universe that makes possible the hockey
world. This disciplinary system is also, so far, completely autonomous from the other organs of justice in
Canadian society. The first court case involving
assault charges in a Canadian NHL game occurred in 1970.
Ted Green of the Boston Bruins was charged because of
his participation in a brawl during a game. The judge
dismissed the case, commenting,

> Given the permissiveness of the game, I find it diffi-
> cult to envisage circumstances whereof a charge of
> common assault ... could easily stand.[50]

During the recent past, several charges of assault
have been laid against hockey players and fans in criminal courts in the United States and Canada. So far,
all have been dismissed on the grounds that the hockey
leagues should discipline their own offenders. An
American magistrate has gratuitously suggested that his
Canadian colleagues follow his lead on this matter and
the leagues appear to agree with his position. When
the team members of the WHA Québec Nordiques demanded
en masse the punishment of a rival team member who had

assaulted one of their own, they made it clear that they
did not want outside law courts to interfere. When the
NHL Board of Governors finally responded to increased
public criticism of hockey violence in 1976, the response was a word of caution to each team at the end of
the Stanley Cup playoffs, coupled with the assurance
that the NHL could deal with any such problems without
outside help.

Finally we consider the awareness of hockey fans and
players that they are members of an "ecclesia," that in
some radical sense they are "called out" of the everyday human world. Some hint of this is given in the
preceding comments on the disciplinary autonomy of
hockey, but still more is provided by the customary
behaviour of players and fans. Men who play hockey behave in ways which would be unthinkable to them outside
of the game: I refer here not only to assaultive behaviour but also to affectionate "touching" practices
such as hugging and butt-slapping, or superstitious
gestures such as wearing the same unlaundered article
of clothing for years on end,51 and tapping the goalie's
pads before play starts. Among spectators the clearest
demonstration of "ecclesiastic" behaviour should scarcely require documentation to Canadians. The most placid,
humane person is transformed into a raging, imprecating
enthusiast simply by placing her in an arena or before
a television set. One might almost say that spectators
become, not merely ecclesiastic ("called out of the
world") but ecstatic ("standing outside oneself"), were
it not for the fact that the furious hockey fan is not
"outside" her proper persona but firmly centred in it.

I do not think that we need to dwell upon the way in
which hockey's symbolic universe serves to integrate
the common, everyday experience of players and fans
during those times when they are players and fans.
Surely it is obvious that participants refer, consciously and otherwise, to symbols, myths, models, customs,
rituals, doctrines, etc., that are manifestly part of
hockey while they live out their roles as players and
fans. But what about the legitimation of crises, of
marginal situations? Here I propose to consider three
paradigmatic crisis situations: a crippling injury,
a death, and a mass riot. In each case they were
legitimated within the hockey world under the direction
of the hockey ecclesia.

On 12 December, 1934, during a Leaf game at Boston,

one of the Bruin's toughest players, Eddie Shore, became
enraged at what he felt were unfair calls by the referee,
and delivered a hard check which threw Leaf player Ace
Bailey high into the air. Bailey was knocked out, and
was feared to be dying, but he recovered consciousness
briefly in the dressing room where his first words were,
"Put me back in the game! They need me!" Bailey underwent a series of dangerous operations in the days that
followed, while other players and sports commentators
reported his precarious condition to fans everywhere
hour by hour. Two months later it was apparent that
Bailey would live, but never skate again, and the Leafs
honoured him by holding an Ace Bailey benefit night, the
feature of which was a match between the Leafs and an
All-Star team which included Eddie Shore on its roster.

Fifteen thousand fans attended and, as the two teams
lined up in silence at the blue line, Bailey shuffled
slowly out to the face-off circle. As he reached it,
Eddie Shore broke from his place and skated to join him;
the two men shook hands and clapped each other's shoulders, and the crowd broke into wild cheers. Shore, who
personally collected more than 900 stitches during his
career, played his usual rough game that night.[52]

The NHL did not find it necessary to deal with death
on the ice until 1967. Bill Masterson, a 29-year-old
center for the Minnesota North Stars, was given a clean
check, but suffered a fatal concussion in falling to
the ice. Masterson was not a remarkably distinguished
player, but the accident shocked the League. Responding to the crisis sportswriters combined to establish
the Bill Masterson Memorial Award for the player who
most fitted the description of "unsung hero." They
argued (and still do) that his death was not in vain
but served as an object lesson in favour of protective
headgear in hockey play.[53]

Brawls are a regular feature of hockey matches, but
mass riots are rare. The worst occurred on St. Patrick's
Day in 1955 after NHL President Clarence Campbell had
awarded a season suspension to Rocket Richard for striking linesman Cliff Thompson during a game. When Campbell appeared late at the Montréal Forum to view the
next game, he found the Canadiens losing 2 - 0 and the
fans in a murderous mood. Several fans assaulted the
League President, and for a few moments it appeared that
his life was literally in danger. Happily a police tear
gas bomb diverted the crowd from a rush at Campbell, and

the Forum emptied its fans out on to St. Catherine
Street. The police failed completely in their efforts
to prevent the mob from destroying store fronts and
attacking bystanders, and the disturbance did not
finally come to an end until Richard personally broad-
cast his request that the violence cease. In return he
promised his following that the Canadiens would win the
Stanley Cup next year.

On the day following the riot one unrepentant sportswriter described the man who had launched the first
assault on Campbell as "the real star" of the game.
And the Canadiens who played to make good Richard's
promise during the 1955-56 season were (deservedly)
voted the greatest team of all time by a poll of sportswriters in 1969.[54]

The evidence satisfies me that hockey may be understood in Luckmann's terms as a religion. There is a
hockey world defined by a particular symbolic universe
sustained by an ecclesia, and those who live within
that world order their lives according to its meanings
and standards. There remains the question, What
happens when the individual steps outside the hockey
world and seeks to construct his own "invisible
religion"? Does he avail himself of any of the meanings made available by hockey?

We should not be surprised to find it so. If Luckmann is correct that the invisible religion is constructed primarily within the framework of the nuclear
family, it is worth noting that enormous blocks of
family time are hockey time. Not only do adolescent
boys spend hours in formal play and practice, but their
parents often spend equal amounts of time driving them
to and from rinks and watching their games. The televised hockey game is, in some families, the only
occasion for all members and generations of the family
to gather for the pursuit of common enterprise.
Hockey's matrix of meaning is certainly readily
available to individuals anxious to cobble together
their own invisible religion at home.

Let me suggest eight things which hockey makes available to Canadians engaged in constructing a private
Self, five of which are attributed to sport in general
by psychiatrist Arnold Beisser in his book, The Madness
in Sports: Psychosocial Observations,[55] but which are
present in exemplary fashion in hockey.

399

First of all, it makes available a space and time in which certain actions may be performed which, though stimulated by our culture, are regarded as illegitimate. Men may embrace each other or indulge in what Al Purdy calls "butt-slapping camaraderie," and all people may indulge in loud, aggressive behaviour. Second, it provides biographical continuity. How many other experiences can one enjoy at every stage of one's life? Third, it offers situations in which one may deal with problem situations which are susceptible of fairly clear and therefore satisfying resolution. This is particularly important for the adolescent who is socialized into generally accepted patterns of co-operation and competition, victory and defeat, in the hockey rink, but it is also significant for the adult who may seek without success situations from which she may derive the satisfaction of resolving a problematic issue.

Fourth, we may note that in modern Canadian society the formerly clear line differentiating work from play is being destroyed. Work is increasingly dissociated from its product; play is increasingly organized and disciplined. Canadians who actively play in organized hockey are integrated into a transitional institution where the work/play boundary effectively disappears. And fifth, in a society in which the gender distinctions of masculine and feminine are disappearing, hockey provides unambiguous models of masculinity (and feminity).[56]

I should add at least three other items to the list of ethical and biographical materials provided to Canadians by the hockey world. First, it offers colour and effervescence to many whose lives are otherwise unenlivened. There is ample testimony in wartime accounts of the morale-boosting qualities of hockey to justify this claim. Second, hockey may serve as a counter to the alienation that many individuals experience in urbanized settings. One is a little less lonely in Toronto if one may cheer the Leafs. Related to this is the spill-over from hockey that not only reconciles one to one's spatial location but even builds a measure of positive pride in it. Parry Sound is a place to be valued in part because it is Bobby Orr's home town, and the town honours itself when it observes Bobby Orr Day.

And finally, hockey is indeed a "Canadian specific,"[57] the source of a sense that I as a Canadian am better than Americans, though not so wealthy, and better than Europeans, though not so cultured.

HOCKEY IN CANADA

There is considerable evidence here to support the
view that when one becomes a hockey fan or player, one
is doing more than "merely" taking up a game or an
entertainment. There is a sense in which one is justified in speaking of hockey as a religion - that is,
when one enters the hockey world, there is a tendency
to treat its symbolic universe as ultimately meaningful
so long as one is within that world. One may even
borrow ethical and biographical material from it in
order to construct one's own invisible religion. If
this is indeed true, then the current debates over the
recovery of hockey as a Canadian sport, and/or the
moderation of violence in hockey, appear to be of
greater significance than they do when hockey is regarded as a mere game. One wonders, for example, if the
Attorney-General of Ontario is aware that he is leading
an attack on what may literally be a sacred cow. Or,
for that matter, we may wonder at the naïveté of
churches which assume that hockey is an innocent tool
which may be safely integrated into their Christian
education programmes as just one more facet in their
effort to provide suitable nurture for adolescents.

My own preference as a fan is for hockey to be a
true game, not a religious activity radically autonomous from the rest of reality where ultimate answers to
crises are provided by a hockey ecclesia. The first-
level analysis offered here suggests that hockey is
more than a game in Canada: it functions as a religion
for many, and does so at the expense of its own play-
fulness.

FOOTNOTES

1. Frank Moritsugu, Toronto Daily Star, 17 April, 1965.

2. Alfred Purdy, The Cariboo Horses (Toronto: McClel-
    land & Stewart, 1965), p. 60.

3. For example, see the comments by Peter Gordon White
    in The United Church Observer, 15 February, 1969,
    pp. 14-15.

4. Thomas Luckmann, The Invisible Religion. The Problem
    of Religion in Modern Society (N.Y.: Macmillan, 1967).

5. Luckmann, The Invisible Religion, p. 49.

6. Peter L. Berger, The Sacred Canopy. Elements of a
    Sociological Theory of Religion (Garden City, N.Y.:
    Doubleday Anchor Books, 1967), pp. 176-177, 25, 190.

7. Peter L. Berger and Thomas Luckmann, The Social
    Construction of Reality. A Treatise in the Socio-
    logy of Knowledge (Garden City, N.Y.: Doubleday
    Anchor Books, 1966).

8. Ibid., p. 1.

9. Ibid., pp. 61, 89-90, 152-153.

10. Ibid., p. 96.

11. Ibid., pp. 96-104.

12. Luckmann, The Invisible Religion, pp. 43-48.

13. Ibid., pp. 48-49.

14. Ibid., pp. 58-59.

16. Ibid., pp. 62-63.

17. Ibid., p. 66.

18. In his note 28, Luckmann inaccurately refers the
    reader to Joachim Wach, Sociology of Religion
    (Chicago: University of Chicago Press, 1945), esp.
    pp. 4, 5, for an account of the "'ecclesiastic'
    type" of organization. The proper reference is to
    pp. 141-145.

19. Luckmann, The Invisible Religion, pp. 80-85.

20. Ibid., pp. 101-106.

21. See, for example, Johan Huizinga, Homo Ludens - A
    Study of the Play Element in Culture (Boston:
    Beacon Press, 1950); and Paul Weiss, Sport: A
    Philosophic Inquiry (Carbondale, Ill.: Southern
    Illinois University Press, 1969).

22. E.g. Bobby Hull, Hockey Is My Game (Don Mills,
    Ont.: Longmans, Canada, 1967), p. 96.

23. Andy O'Brien, <u>Fire-Wagon Hockey</u> (Chicago: Follett, 1967), p. vi.

24. Frank Selke with Gordon Green, <u>Behind the Cheering</u> (Toronto: McClelland and Stewart, 1962), p. 147.

25. R. Denker, "Sport and aggression," in <u>Sport in the Modern World. Chances and Problems</u>, Ourmo Grupe (ed.) (N.Y.: Springer - Verlag, 1973), p. 382.

26. Michael D. Smith, "Some determinants of assaultive behavior in hockey: A theory and causal model." Paper presented at the Third International Symposium on the Sociology of Sport, Waterloo, Canada (August, 1971).

27. Bruce Kidd and John MacFarlane, <u>The Death of Hockey</u> (Toronto: New Press, 1972), p. 5-6.

28. Trent Frayne, <u>It's Easy All You Have to Do Is Win</u> (Don Mills, Ontario: Longmans Canada Ltd., 1968), Introduction.

29. G.E. Mortimore, <u>What's Happened to Hockey?</u> reprinted from <u>The Globe and Mail</u> (Toronto: 1963), p. 6.

30. Margaret Drury Gane, "Out of His League." <u>Weekend Magazine</u> (28 February 1976), p. 6.

31. Hull, <u>Hockey Is My Game</u>, p. 177.

32. Michael D. Smith, "Precipitants of Crowd Violence in Sport." Paper presented at the First Canadian Congress for the Multi-Disciplinary Study of Sport and Physical Activity. (Montréal: October, 1973), pp. 10-11.

33. Frayne, <u>It's Easy</u>, p. 144.

34. E.g. Lloyd Finley, "Separatism has no chance against Peewees." Toronto <u>Telegram</u> (17 February, 1969).

35. Z. Hollander and H. Bock, <u>The Complete Encyclopedia of Ice Hockey</u> (Englewood Cliffs, N.J.: Prentice-Hall, 1970), p. 152.

36. <u>Ibid.</u>, p. 229.

37. Frayne, <u>It's Easy</u>, p. 143. Hollander and Bock, <u>The Complete Encyclopedia of Ice Hockey</u>, p. 165.

38. Hull, Hockey Is My Game, p. 74.

39. Punch Imlach, Hockey Is a Battle (Toronto: Macmillan Press, 1969).

40. Hull, Hockey Is My Game, p. 166.

41. Quoted by Dick Beddoes, Globe and Mail (18 November, 1970).

42. E.g. Frayne, It's Easy, p. 53.

43. Henry Roxborough, The Stanley Cup Story (Chicago: Follett Publishing Co., 1964), pp. 26-35.

44. Hospital for Sick Children (Toronto) cross-Canada survey, reported in The Catholic Register (8 May, 1976).

45. Toronto Daily Star (2 December, 1970).

46. Quoted by Jim Crear, "Leave the Hockey to the Kids," Maple Leaf Garden Programme (n.d.), p. 48. (Files of the Hockey Hall of Fame, Exhibition Park, Canada).

47. See Nancy Howell and Maxwell L. Howell, Sports and Games in Canadian Life: 1700 to the present. (Toronto: Macmillan, 1969).

48. Jim Vipond, Gordie Howe: Number Nine (Toronto: Ryerson Press, 1968), p. 32.

49. Allen Camelli, Great Moments in Pro Hockey (N.Y.: Bantam Books, 1971), p. 53.

50. Globe and Mail (4 September, 1970).

51. I refer particularly to Punch Imlach's bird-stained and battered fedora, but other examples might be given.

52. Howard Liss, Goal! Stanley Cup Playoffs (New York: Delacorte Press, 1970), p. 72.

    Frank Selke with Gordon Green, Behind the Cheering (Toronto: McClelland and Stewart, 1972), p. 118. Camelli, Great Moments in Pro Hockey, pp. 80-83.

53. Richard Beddoes, Stan Fischler, Ira Gitler. Hockey!

The Story of the World's Fastest Sport (New York: Macmillan, 1969), p. 99.

Camelli, Great Moments in Pro Hockey, pp. 21-23.

Liss, Goal!, p. 178.

54. Hollander and Bock, The Complete Encyclopedia of Ice Hockey, p. 230.

Liss, Goal!, p. 139.

Camelli, Great Moments in Pro Hockey, pp. 70-72, 39.

Beddoes, Fischler, Gitler, Hockey!, pp. 169-172.

55. Arnold R. Beisser, The Madness in Sports. Psychosocial Observations on Sports (New York: Appleton-Century-Crofts, 1967).

56. I personally should like to see more androgynous models made available to us. I see hockey as a decidedly reactionary, and hopefully atavistic, institution on this score.

57. Purdy, "Hockey Players," p. 60.

RESPONSE TO SINCLAIR-FAULKNER

JOHN BADERTSCHER is Assistant Professor of Religious
Studies at the University of Winnipeg, teaching social
ethics and the sociology of religion. He has written
on the abortion debate and urban studies.

RÉSUMÉ

L'analyse de Sinclair-Faulkner n'est qu'un début, mais
un début important vers une meilleure reconnaissance
de l'esprit moderne.

En revenant un peu en arrière, le roman Glengarry
School Days de Ralph Connor nous décrit le jeu du hockey
à l'époque après la Confédération. Le roman fait briller
un aspect important : la logique du rapport entre les
églises et le jeu. Car, pendant cette époque-là, le
hockey était une école de la vie, enseignant et mettant
en pratique la discipline, la morale, la rationalité -
bref tout l'enseignement chrétien.

Cependant, le hockey, comme la religion, a beaucoup
changé et il y a aujourd'hui une vaste différence entre
l'idéal du jeu et les réalités de l'organisation. (De
cette différence viennent les questions posées par
Sinclair-Faukner à la fin de son article.) Cette division nous montre comment l'esprit moderne crée une
nouvelle forme de "religion" sociale sous la tyrannie
de la consommation. Le jeu, par exemple, est maintenant
plus vite, plus compétitif et offre aux jeunes une
"vocation" prestigieuse et opulente, sans distinction
de race, ni de classe sociale. C'est un moyen donc de
participer dans le monde et ainsi un des aspects fasci-
nants de la société technologique. Cependant, le hockey
est aussi une partie de la vaste industrie internationale du divertissement. Les joueurs deviennent des ressources naturelles d'un pays et bientôt les victimes du
cycle vicieux de la production et de la consommation.
C'est donc aux études religieuses de dégager le hockey
en tant que jeu. Ce sera un premier pas vers la découverte d'une vraie religion pour l'homme moderne.

JOHN BADERTSCHER

Response to Sinclair-Faulkner

Tom Sinclair-Faulkner has done us a great service in
pointing out how the study of popular culture - in this
case, the sport of ice hockey - can illumine the ethos
and help us understand the religious situation of Canadians. It will be the purpose of this response to
argue that his line of inquiry can go much further than
the author indicates, and to suggest some of the direc-
tions it can take. First we will inquire into hockey
as a key to religion in Canada's past. Then we will
turn our attention to the present, hoping that the
contrast between past and present will give us some
clue about where we are going.

1

The author already has alerted us to the fact that
hockey is about as old as Confederation, but he has
told us little about its pre-professional, nineteenth
century days. Fortunately, we have at least one document which gives us some historical perspective; and
which reveals an intimate relationship between hockey,
traditional religion, and the ethos of which these are
a part. The document is Glengarry School Days, a novel
by Ralph Connor (the pen name of the Reverend C.W.
Gordon, then minister of St. Stephen's Presbyterian
Church in Winnipeg).[1] This novel, which was an outstanding commercial success in Canada, Great Britain
and the U.S.A., is set in rural Ontario at about the
time of Confederation. We may assume from its popularity that this novel did a fair job of reproducing that
setting, as it was remembered by those who had then
been children. We may also assume that the way the
struggles and adventures of childhood were selectively
remembered tells us something about the present values
of its author and readers. Thus the novel gives us
insight into both hockey and religion in the first
half-century of Confederation, providing us with a
complement to Tom Sinclair-Faulkner's discussion of the
present and more recent past.

Glengarry School Days is not just about hockey. It
is about growing up; and its main characters are Hughie
Murray, the minister's son; Thomas Finch, his friend;
and John Craven, a supercilious, slightly wicked young
"city slicker" who comes eventually to be teacher at

the one-room school. Moral and social issues in micro-
cosm appear throughout the story. For example, Hughie
is caught up in deception and theft due to his dealings
with "Foxy" Ross, an incarnation of the spirit of deca-
dent commercialism, who dominates the school during the
tenure of female teachers; and Thomas finds himself the
focal point of a civic and family crisis because of his
impulsive leadership of a rebellion against a male
school teacher who turns out to be a tyrant and a bully.
But the climax of the story ("The Final Round" is the
title of the chapter) comes in a shinny match. The
opponents are "the Front", the young men of a nearby
and slightly more urbanized school district. Craven
has undertaken to be the player-coach of a group including the now teen-aged Hughie and Thomas, and he has
introduced some sophistication into their style of play.
At the same time as Craven has been teaching and coach-
ing, however, he has himself become a changed man, for
he has fallen under the influence of the minister's
wife. With her purity of spirit and mature beauty, she
has brought out the best in the young teacher. She has,
in fact, entrusted to him the development of the character of her son and the other young men, all of whom are
dear to her.

Hughie is the team captain, by virtue of his combination of intelligence and fierceness. But this fierceness is tied to a volcanic temper, his chief moral
failing. The game is an occasion for Hughie to master
his temper, for "the responsibility of his position and
the magnitude of the issues at stake helped him to a
self-control quite remarkable in him."[2] This particular
game is an especially severe challenge, for the opponents are reputed to be not only skillful and well-
organized, but larger and willing to fight.

Just before the game, Hughie confesses to his mother
his concern about the opponents' propensity to fight.
The following dialogue ensues:

        The mother smiled a little.
        "What a pity! But why should they fight?
        Fighting is not Shinny."
        "No, that's what the master says. And
        he's right enough, too, but it's awful hard
        when a fellow doesn't play fair, when he trips
        you up or clubs you on the shins when you're
        not near the ball. You feel like hitting him
        back."

"Yes, but that's the very time to show self-
control."
"I know. And that's what the master says."
"Of course it is," went on his mother. "That's
what the game is for, to teach the boys to command
their tempers. You remember 'he that ruleth his
spirit is better than he that taketh a city.'"[3]

The opponents establish their claim to mastery with
two quick goals produced by speed, good passing, and
aggressive checking. But this attack relies largely
on the skill of one player, and the checking lesson is
quickly learned by Hughie and his mates. Hughie
begins to "shadow" the star of the opposition, Dan Munro.
This strategy frees Craven, "the master," and results
in a goal by him. That goal:

...had revealed to Hughie two important facts: the
first, that he was faster than Dan in a straight
race; and the second, that it would be advisable to
feed the master, for it was clearly apparent that
there was not his equal upon the ice in dodging.[4]

The opponents also make some adjustments, however, and
by the intermission between periods (each an hour long!)
have resumed their two goal lead. During this break
two important things happen. Hughie's parents depart
to make a pastoral call, but not before his mother expresses her confidence to Hughie that he will prevail.
Also:

...the team from the Front had been having something
of a jollification in their quarters. They were sure
of victory, and in spite of their captain's remons-
trances had already begun to pass round the bottle in
the way of celebration.[5]

The second period begins with a furious attack by
"the Front." But our heroes have prepared their defen-
ses, and before too long Craven gets a breakaway goal
to close the gap to one. Meanwhile, a member of the
opposition - one Jimmie Ben McEwen, reputed to be a
better fighter than a hockey player - has begun an
attempt to intimidate Hughie with rough play, including
tripping and slashing. An appeal to the official only
increases the fury of the attack, but Hughie is not
daunted. Soon the tying goal is scored while Hughie
is screening the goalie.

410

As the game draws to a close, the opposition is tiring and playing for a tie. At a face-off, a verbal exchange ignites the tempers of Hughie and Jimmie Ben, but their teammates restrain them. The opposition launches one last desperation attack, during which the two antagonists exchange fierce checks. Finally, Jimmie Ben breaks Hughie's ankle with a slash.

Hughie refuses to leave the game, and goes into goal, changing places with Thomas Finch. Finch and Craven, outraged at the foul play and inspired by Hughie's courage, proceed to score the winning goal with a virtuoso performance in the closing seconds. Now Craven confronts Jimmie Ben.

> "The game is over," he said, in a low, fierce tone. "You cowardly blackguard, you weren't afraid to hit a boy, now stand up to a man, if you dare."
> Jimmie Ben was no coward. Dropping his club he came eagerly forward, but no sooner had he got well ready than Craven struck him fair in the face, and before he could fall, caught him with a straight, swift blow on the chin, and lifting him clear off his skates, landed him back on his head and shoulders on the ice, where he lay with his toes quivering.[6]

So ends the game, but the best is yet to come. The following summer Craven returns to the big city and reports to his theologian-uncle, a man who had previously despaired for Craven's character and future.

> "How many did you say, Craven, of those Glengarry men of yours?" Professor Grey was catechizing his nephew.
> "Ten of them, sir, besides the minister's son, who is going to take the full university course."
> "And all of them bound for the ministry?"
> "So they say. And judging by the way they take life, and the way, for instance, they play shinny, I have a notion they will see it through."
> "They come of a race that sees things through," answered the professor.[7]

These men are all inspired, Craven explains, by their love for the minister's wife. And John Craven's name is one of those on the list.

What is to be learned from this vivid piece of social
history? Many of the aspects which Tom Sinclair-
Faulkner finds problematic in contemporary hockey were
evidently there from the beginning. The spirit of competition suffuses the narrative, and winning seems
hardly less important a century ago than today. Victory
is still the product of a careful blend of individual
brilliance with teamwork and strategy. The components
of good hockey are all there; skating, passing, checking,
and what Connor calls "dodging." The violence of the
game is hardly diminished: bones are broken, and there
is a fight. Unambiguous models of masculinity and
feminity, to borrow Sinclair-Faulkner's phrase, are
presented. The "hockey mum" is already here in frontier Ontario. While this rustic madonna shows more
restraint and dignity than many of her modern counterparts, she is perhaps more effective at inspiring
confidence and evoking ecstatic performance.

The novel makes clear one area which seems to puzzle
and dismay Tom Sinclair-Faulkner, namely, the logic
of the close connection between hockey and the religious tradition from which the United Church of Canada
springs. That hockey should nurture manliness by
nurturing self-control makes perfectly good sense to
Calvinistic Canadians. Not only do tempers need to be
mastered, but temperance must be practised as well.
An untimely nip may temporarily ward off the cold of
winter, but in the long run it costs you the game.
Further, the moral and physical virtues which are
natural in a rural setting must be supplemented by
education and organization. The challenges of life
call for the clear-headed application of rational techniques. Both morally and mentally, then, hockey is a
school for life in the inner-worldly ascetic mode. Had
Max Weber's North American travels taken him a bit
farther north in the winter, he scarcely could have
failed to notice.[8] Even the theological anthropology
which Weber pointed to as the psychological mainspring
of the Protestant ethic is manifest in this novel. How
is fistic vengeance a preparation for the Christian
ministry? Craven wonders out loud about his fitness
in the novel's closing lines, to which his uncle re-
plies: "Fit, Jack, my boy! none of us are fit."[9] Yet
somehow the experience of grace and love, mediated
through the minister's wife, has mended the fabric of
his life. To repeat, this all makes good sense to a

Calvinist. The United Churchmen quoted by Sinclair-Faulkner are perhaps not so misled.

The article he cites is itself an interesting document. "What's Hockey Doing to Your Boy?" author James A. Taylor asks.[10] Is hockey inculcating a spirit of violence and other unChristian ways? Of course there is a danger of this, the article recognizes. But a certain amount of "muscular testing" is inevitable and important for growing boys. Peter Gordon White, then secretary of the Board of Christian Education of the United Church, remarks: "...what counts is what they learn to do with their feelings at such times."[11] The benefits of hockey go beyond the sport itself, Taylor reports. Hockey teaches: "the unselfishness of teamwork...the discipline of playing the rules, of taking the consequences... acceptance of the disappointment of losing... how to show humility in victory...bench-warming as a stimulus to self improvement...accepting realistically one's own abilities."[12] Hockey is seen as the means to an end of "discovering and developing oneself in relation to others."[13] P.G. White is quoted in conclusion: "Isn't that exactly what Christian education is all about?"[14] One might want to question this view of Christian nurture, but obviously the connection between hockey and one modern version of the Calvinist ethos is not so far-fetched as Tom Sinclair-Faulkner seems to suggest.

Still, he is right in pointing to an incongruity between this idealized vision of the sport and the "organized" hockey which begins with pre-adolescent leagues and culminates in the NHL. Things have changed, both in hockey and in its cultural context. If people like P.G. White are to be faulted, it should not be for their misunderstanding of the nature of hockey per se, but for failing to be aware of the implications of this shift in cultural context. Both hockey and the religion of the churches have been subtly but profoundly transformed, even as they have been preserved, in the movement from a frontier society and its Protestant ethic to a technologized and urbanized society. The greatest value of Tom Sinclair-Faulkner's essay is that it persuades us to look at hockey and its transformation as a key to understanding the ethos of that new social order.

413

Tom Sinclair-Faulkner does us a service not only by calling our attention to hockey, but also by suggesting that Thomas Luckmann's approach, as seen in The Invisible Religion, is a helpful analytical tool.[15] Again, Sinclair-Faulkner perhaps undersells the possibilities of his own discovery. He seems to suggest that Luckmann gives us a sociological model of religion in general, which we can now apply to hockey. He reports that "the final touch" to Luckmann's model is an observation about the presence of multiple symbolic universes in modern society. In fact, Luckmann's subtitle reminds us that his main point is to raise questions about the way this modern society affects the situation of religion and the religious. It seems appropriate here to review the questions he raises and the conclusions he draws, so that we might better respond to Sinclair-Faulkner's suggestion that we utilize Luckmann's approach.

Thomas Luckmann, noting that religion and church are not necessarily identical, and that church-oriented religion appears marginal in modern society, wonders whether a new social form of religion may not be in the making. In order to provide a backdrop against which this question may be pursued, Luckmann launches into a lengthy excursus (chapters three through five) into the anthropological condition and the social forms of religion, and into the modes of individual religiosity correlated with these forms. In this excursus Luckmann brings into play such concepts as "symbolic universe" and "sacred cosmos"; most of Tom Sinclair-Faulkner's references to the book are to this excursus. But the conceptual framework for understanding religion developed in the three chapters is aimed at preparing us to "see" the "invisible religion" of the modern (i.e., industrialized and urbanized) world. This world, the present terminus of an evolutionary process whose roots are in "the Hellenistic world and the Roman Empire"[16] is one in which institutional specialization is the social form of religion. It is this social form which Sinclair-Faulkner wants to term an ecclesia,[17] and understandably so, for it is the social form of religion embodied in our churches, a form which we sometimes wrongly assume to be the only form of religion in a civilized world. While Sinclair-Faulkner seems in places to argue that hockey is an example of institutionally specialized religion, Luckmann wants to raise the possibility that this form of religion is passing away.

There are, he argues, dangers to individual religiosity in institutionally specialized religion. The various aspects of religion (such as doctrine, ritual, and ecclesiology) tend to become psychologically segregated, threatening the plausibility of the "official" religion as a whole. Religion can be understood as a set of particular requirements, and thus can be routinized. Further the world of religious specialists can become divorced from the world of laymen. Returning to his main argument, Thomas Luckmann asserts that as these dangers have become actualized in the modern world, the institutionally specialized religion of the churches has begun to undermine the validity of its own form. It has lost what, in its emergence, it had originally accomplished: "monopoly in the definition of an obligatory sacred cosmos".[18] Religion, he suggests, has become a private affair with a consumer orientation. That is, apparently autonomous individuals put together systems of seemingly ultimate significance by drawing upon or "consuming" symbols which are culturally available. As Tom Sinclair-Faulkner puts it, a person "must cobble together her own religion."

This kind of religion is a far cry from the institutionally specialized form, for these individual constructions tend to be "both syncretistic and vague".[19] Institutions (such as hockey, I would add) attempt to move into this vacuum by providing their own prefabricated ideologies. But these, however, are:

incapable of providing a socially prefabricated and subjectively meaningful system of "ultimate" significance. The reasons for this inability, as we have seen, are connected with the social-psychological consequences of institutional segmentation and specialization - with the very processes, in fact, that gave rise to isolated institutional "ideologies."[20]

As we can readily see by observing one institution which has borne a disproportionate share of the burden of this modern search for ultimate meaning - namely, marriage - the systems of significance which we construct and consume these days "are relatively flexible as well as unstable."[21]

Thomas Luckmann examines some "modern religious themes", including autonomy, mobility, familism and sexuality. About this last theme he observes that:

to the extent that sexuality is "freed" from external
social control, it becomes capable of assuming a
crucial function in the "autonomous" individual's
quest for self-expression and self-realization.[22]

This sounds very much like some things Tom Sinclair-
Faulkner has said about hockey. Perhaps, then, we can
turn to modern sports, and hockey in particular, as a
modern religious theme, rather than as an ecclesia.
What can we learn from it about the modern world?

4

As we have already remarked, hockey has changed. Some
of the more traditional aspects have been subtly transformed by magnification. Today's hockey is perhaps
faster and even more highly competitive, and certainly
more elaborately equipped. Indoor rinks, ice-making
machinery, and a full range of uniform and protective
gear for even the youngest players are to be found even
in Canada's small towns. Numerically, and perhaps
psychologically, the involvement of "fans" has increased
due to the media of mass communication. Hockey has
become a major spectator sport, and not in Canada alone.
Bobby Orr is known from Siberia to San Diego. This
aspect of modern hockey suggests, in turn, one reason
for the passion of Canadian youth for playing organized
hockey, and the vigorous encouragement of their parents
for this participation. Hockey has become a potential
vocation, and a glamorous one. Not only is there the
possibility of "making it" financially, but in the process the young man may become idolized, even as he now
idolizes. And the way to success through hockey appears
to be open without regard to ethnic background or social
class, unlike most other modes of "meaningful" participation in technological society. Here, as in few other
places, the myth of individual ability and hard work as
the road to success still seems plausible.

We can see that all these characteristics of modern
hockey are shared by other spectator sports. Football,
soccer, basketball and baseball exist in the same sort
of relationship to technological society. They are a
means to participation in the modern world and its
benefits. For the fans, they are a source of excitement in a world that is often dull and routine. They
permit a sense of participation in a common cause; a
participation which seems less and less possible through

politics, religion or work. For the player, they offer
a locus of hope (however unrealistic) for success - that
is, wealth and public recognition - in this generation,
and an arena of respite from the compulsions and limitations of a highly structured world. This is given
through a sport which is technologically complex,
highly organized, and thoroughly "covered" by the mass
media. In all these respects hockey is simply one
manifestation of spectator sports, itself one of the
most fascinating aspects of technological society.[23]
It would be a mistake for us to underestimate the importance of hockey and football in the Canadian ethos.
The religious character of participation by fan and
player, to which Tom Sinclair-Faulkner has called our
attention, tells us that we may with some confidence
utilize an analysis of hockey to gain insight into the
very heart of that technological ethos.

With that in mind, let us examine the current fate of
this legacy of the Canadian frontier and its religion.
First, we must note that hockey has become international.
Players from countries such as the Soviet Union,
Czechoslovakia, and Sweden must be ranked among the
world's finest. Teams of Canadian professionals are
unable to dominate international tournaments. A large
majority of professional teams are now located in the
United States, and the sport is growing there at a far
more rapid rate than in Canada. Technological society
is an international phenomenon, and hockey reflects
that fact. For Canadians to see hockey as a clue to
national identity is to indulge in nostalgia.

The centre of gravity of the NHL, recognized by
Canadians as the highest of hockey worlds, has shifted
south of the border. Professional hockey is, after all,
part of the "entertainment industry." It is a manifestation of that primary institutional form of technological society, the corporation. Professional hockey is
American for the same reason that the automobile industry is - because the USA is the heartland of technological society. Most of the players may have been born
in Canada, but they are bought and sold mainly by
Americans. One might say that hockey players are a
natural resource. Many of them are grown in Canada,
but most are exported to the USA for final production
and consumption.

Our imagery here points again to the intimate

connection of hockey with the technological ethos. If
there is an anthropological metaphor to which we all
subscribe more or less without question, it is that of
the "consumer." We think of ourselves as consumers. A
number of social philosophers have discussed the implications of this way of seeing human life, perhaps none
with the analytical power of the late Hannah Arendt.[24]
She has argued that the characteristic activity of
modern civilization is neither thinking, nor acting
politically, nor fabricating; but it is the unending
and finally meaningless cycle of production and consumption. It is clear that hockey is very much caught up in
just this cyclical process. The fan is a consumer of
hockey, and there must be more consumption for hockey
to be successful. There must be more teams, in both
major and minor leagues. Arenas must be larger, and
media coverage must be greater. What is consumed is,
finally, the player. As the resource has greater demand
placed upon it, the price of the most highly developed
form shoots up dramatically. At the same time, it
becomes desirable to extend exploration and resource
development activities. Organized hockey is extended
to earlier ages and more remote communities. Governments and voluntary associations are called upon to
provide the support systems and infrastructures for
this development. The imaginative reader can easily
extend this description.

Hockey, in this context, has become more than training for life. Tom Sinclair-Faulkner has noted: "Canadians who actively play in organized hockey are integrated into a transitional institution where the work/
play boundary effectively disappears." The significance
of this observation should now be clearer. Hockey has
been integrated into the all-encompassing ethos of
technological society, an ethos which has an immanent
rather than a transcendent focus. Students of the Canadian ethos would do well to pursue empirical studies of
lives which are consumed by hockey. For example, what
are the physical, psychological and spiritual consequences for the lives of young people who are discovered
at an early age to have extraordinary hockey ability?
An informing thesis of such a study might be a much
stronger one than Thomas Luckmann permits himself. We
might attempt to show that technological society is not
only a new form of religion, but an idolatrous one as
well; and, as in the case of all idolatries, it demands
human sacrifice. We could look to these biographical
studies for evidence of human lives being thus consumed.

418

To invoke the judgment of idolatry, however, presupposes true religion as a criterion. For most of us Canadians, that is not a simple matter. Those of us who share the heritage of the Reformation, for example, find it problematic to disentangle our religion from the culture to which it helped give birth. More particularly, we can see that our theologies and religious institutions have been caught up in the same transformative process as hockey. The close connection between hockey and one religious tradition at the beginning of this period of transformation has been noted above. Tom Sinclair-Faulkner hopes that hockey can be a true game; that is, he hopes that it can be extricated from technological society *qua* religion. I would harbour a similar hope for Canada's traditional religions. For if these hopes are fulfilled, both true sport and true religion may help us, each in their own way, to gain some vantage point from which the continuing critique of our modern ethos may be conducted more effectively.

FOOTNOTES

1. Ralph Connor, *Glengarry School Days* (Toronto: the Westminster Co., 1902). Citations are from the New Canadian Library reprint edition, with an introduction by S. Ross Beharriell (Toronto: McClelland and Stewart, 1975).

2. *Ibid.*, 297.

3. *Ibid.*, 300.

4. *Ibid.*, 307.

5. *Ibid.*, 315.

6. *Ibid.*, 329-30.

7. *Ibid.*, 333.

8. Max Weber, *The Protestant Ethic and the Spirit of Capitalism*, Translated by Talcott Parsons, with a Foreword by R.H. Tawney (New York: Charles Scribner's Sons, 1958). Cf. p. 182 and the footnote on p. 283.

9. Connor, Glengarry School Days, 339.

10. The United Church Observer, 15 February 1969.

11. Ibid., 14.

12. Ibid., 15.

13. Ibid.

14. Ibid.

15. Thomas Luckmann, The Invisible Religion. The Problem of Religion in Modern Society (New York: Macmillan, 1967).

16. Ibid., 94.

17. Cf. his citation of Luckmann (Ibid., p. 66) for the characteristics of this social form.

18. Ibid., 94.

19. Ibid., 99.

20. Ibid., 101.

21. Ibid., 106.

22. Ibid., 111-12.

23. Cf. Jacques Ellul, The Technological Society. Translated by John Wilkinson, with an Introduction by Robert K. Merton (New York: Vintage Books, 1964). Cf. pp. 375-84.

24. Hannah Arendt, The Human Condition (Chicago: The University of Chicago Press, 1958).

ARCHITECTURE RELIGIEUSE

NORMAN PAGÉ: Cet article est tiré de deux conférences données à l'Association de la Galerie Nationale d'Ottawa en février 1977. L'auteur est directeur du Départment de Sciences religieuses de l'Université d'Ottawa. Sa recherche porte sur la religion et l'art.

RÉSUMÉ

Modern religious architecture has reached an impasse in North America and Europe alike. Until the 18th Century Roman and Gothic architecture were the dominating influence in any religious structure. From the 18th to the 20th Century, a period of transformation permeated in which mannerism won the day. This tended to create impressionistic structures, often very gracious but often without life or inward feeling.

With the advent of the present century, modern building materials, techniques and new liturgy gave birth to two streams in modern architecture, not unlike the Cluny-Clairvaux controversy of the 12th Centruy. On the one hand, there is a move towards the grandiose, as for example St. Mary's of San Francisco. On the other hand, there is a move towards the austere, rustic simplicity of Matisse's chapel in Vence, France. While inward feeling is evoked in both, attention is drawn largely to the artistic ability of the architect. More recently, however, socio-economic dictates have given rise to a more functional architecture, to a shift in emphasis from the building to the community within. Churches are built as community centres, offering theatre, bingo or receptions to the community during the week and converting efficiently to sanctuaries for Sunday or for special services. While financially more self-supporting, these centres tend to destroy any atmosphere of inward contemplation or union with the transcendent and become another hub of activity in the busy city. In this respect, the new Zen temple of Tokyo has much to teach religious architects in Europe and North America today. Marked by airy simplicity, the temple offers above all a refuge of silence and a sacred space to the city's population.

NORMAN PAGÉ

LA QUADRATURE DU CERCLE EN ARCHITECTURE RELIGIEUSE

L'architecture religieuse, en Amérique du Nord comme en
Europe, semble bien être entrée dans une impasse. Au
grand dam tant des architectes que de plusieurs ministres
du culte, protestants comme catholiques.

Depuis plus de deux décades, la construction d'églises
selon une tradition vieille de seize siècles est à son
point mort. Pourront sans doute surgir encore çà et là,
pour quelque temps, certaines excroissances parasitaires,
mais l'élan créateur ambiant, qui a mu des collectivités
entières pendant des siècles ou suscité chez des archi-
tectes-créateurs comme Le Corbusier des hauts-lieux à
la gloire d'une certaine quête de l'homme, n'est plus.

L'HÉRITAGE SÉCULAIRE

Faut-il le rappeler, toute l'histoire de l'architecture
religieuse occidentale depuis les premières basiliques
romaines (Saint-Jean de Latran, Saint-Paul-hors-les-Murs,
Sainte-Marie-Majeure...) elles-mêmes érigées selon les
plans propres aux édifices de culte païen (atrium, nef,
abside, arcades sur colonnes, arc triomphal) a été axée
sur la monumentalité. Le courant majeur apporté par la
transformation de l'antique Byzance en Constantinople,
sans remettre en cause les données architecturales de
base, ouvrait aux jeux de formes multiples : églises
voûtées sur plan carré (Sainte-Sophie de Constantinople),
sur plan circulaire (Saint-Georges de Salonique), sur
plan octogonal (San Vital de Ravenne, Chapelle palatine
d'Aix-la-Chapelle) ou sur plan en croix (Saint-Marc de
Venise, Saint-Front de Périgueux).

Même l'art roman, celui du Périgord en particulier,
ne sera, somme toute, qu'une variante de cette tradition :
la forme du plan sera modifiée en croix, les nefs seront
prolongées, la voûte en berceau se substituera à la cou-
verture en charpente et les murs se consolideront par les
contreforts. Paray-Le-Monial porte encore sur le carré
du transept une coupole, mais, dans l'ensemble, les
églises romanes, celles du clergé régulier comme du
clergé séculier, sont pourvues de tours carrées ou
octogonales à la façade ou de tours lanternes à l'inter-
section de la nef et du transept. L'école romane de
Normandie, avec son clocher en pyramide quadrangulaire

(Caen, Jumièges) essaimera jusqu'en Angleterre (Norwich, Durham).

Dans la deuxième moitié du XIIe siècle, l'esprit communal et l'émulation aidant, les architectes laïcs s'allient aux moines maîtres-d'oeuvre et donnent à l'art sacré une des formes d'expression les plus hardies, les plus nobles et les plus solennelles qu'il ait pu atteindre; l'effort des poussées est localisé : les voûtes s'élèvent, les murs s'ouvrent à la lumière, parfois même sur toute leur hauteur (Sainte-Chapelle de Paris), les arcs-boutants s'isolent dans l'espace, contrebutent les voûtes superposées (Reims) ou se réunissent par des arcatures (Chartres). Proportions et dimensions évoluent : les façades des cathédrales se divisent en zones horizontales (portails-galeries-tours) et en zones verticales (tour-rose-tour) selon les nefs (latérale-centrale-latérale); les portails se couvrent de sculptures et s'ornent de gâbles, les flèches s'élancent et se garnissent de clochetons et de pinacles; à l'intérieur, les jubés, qui n'avaient été prévus dans aucun plan, s'ajoutent (XIIIe siècle) et les chapelles latérales se multiplient entre les contreforts en accord avec l'essor que prend le culte des saints (XIVe siècle). Si donc le plan de ces églises ou cathédrales gothiques est demeuré substantiellement le même : forme de croix latine, transepts plus ou moins réduits selon le nombre de nefs (de trois à cinq), chapelles rayonnantes, déambulatoires, parvis, le mode de construction cependant a radicalement changé : la voûte articulée (ogives croisées et appuyées sur piles) s'est substituée à la voûte compacte et cette nouvelle technique, souple au point d'ailleurs de s'adapter à tous les plans, qu'il s'agisse d'architecture religieuse, civile ou militaire, dominera, à l'exclusion de toute autre, du XIIe siècle jusqu'au XVIIIe siècle; elle est et est restée la technique de la pierre, car les matériaux non plus n'ont pas changé : ils sont seulement mieux choisis, mieux oeuvrés et soumis à des systèmes de décoration plus affinés selon les époques et les régions : décoration lancéolée (Saint-Denis, Notre-Dame de Paris, Chartres, Amiens, Reims), rayonnante (Beauvais, Tours, Evreux) ou flamboyante (Saint-Jacques de Lisieux, La Trinité de Vendôme, Brou) : ce dernier style ayant été vraisemblablement importé d'Angleterre au cours de la guerre de Cent ans et rendu populaire en France et dans les Pays-Bas à l'heure ou là il tombait en désuétude.

423

ARCHITECTURE RELIGIEUSE

Les périodes qui suivent cet âge d'or de l'architecture religieuse en Europe, quelle qu'en soit leur qualité intrinsèque, restent des périodes de transformation et d'adaptation secondaires, au sens le plus strict. L'influence de l'Italie est indéniable. Les traités d'architecture de Serlio, Seberti et surtout de Palladio et Vignole seront utilisés même au Canada français au XVIIIe siècle. Mais, en France, la ferveur mystique n'est plus du tout la même et l'organisation des travaux de construction non plus. Les campagnes d'Italie ont multiplié de les échanges, favorisé les influences les plus diverses et provoqué des exigences nouvelles de toutes sortes (ce n'est que sous François 1er que le mot architecte devient d'un emploi courant). Réfractaire pour sa part à l'esprit gothique, l'Italie, avec Brunelleschi, avait vraiment marqué cet autre tournant en substituant à la conception médiévale de l'espace, un schéma idéal, unifié, mathématique de l'étendue; les structures sont définies par un calcul abstrait, et non d'abord en fonction des matériaux, et les formes sont empruntées à l'Antiquité. L'art du grandiose, du colossal et souvent du théâtral l'emporte pour verser rapidement dans l'académisme éclectique. Bramante et Michel-Ange n'y échappent pas (Saint-Pierre de Rome), Vignole non plus (Gesu). Bernini jubile. En France, Saint-Eustache de Paris combine la structure gothique et le décor antique. En Belgique, le Palais des Princes-Evêques de Liège mélange les éléments romains aux formes ogivales. Un peu partout en Europe, le maniérisme l'emporte aisément sur le classicisme, le goût du faste et de l'apparat sur la rigueur et la pureté des formes. C'est l'ère de la décoration spectaculaire. La cathédrale a cédé le pas au palais. L'église Sainte-Geneviève de Paris, caractérisée par son idéal de grâce nouvelle, sa virtuosité technique et ses allures antico-renaissantes, devient à juste titre le Panthéon : plan de Bramante, voûtes romanes contrebutées, façade à la Paestum. Même les vaisseaux d'époque sont plaqués de façades baroques (Saint-Sulpice, Saint-Roch) quand ils ne sont pas jetés bas et reconstruits dans le nouvel esprit (Cluny, Chaalis). Il faut bien le reconnaître, toute l'architecture religieuse, du XVIIIe siècle jusqu'au début du XXe siècle, n'est qu'une longue chaîne de poncifs et de pastiches académiques maniérés, somptueux pour certains, grandioses pour d'autres, mais tous hors d'échelle. Structures impressionnantes, souvent gracieuses, mais sans âme.

ARCHITECTURE RELIGIEUSE

LE RAPPORT FORME-FONCTION

Le sursaut régénérateur en esprit provient au XXe siècle
de la découverte et de la mise en oeuvre de matériaux
nouveaux : fer,acier, béton armé, aluminium, verre, et
d'une esthétique nouvelle surgie du conflit exacerbé entre
Art et Technique. Il ne faut pas se leurrer, le rapport
forme-fonction en architecture religieuse, mis à la page
récemment dans les Congrès internationaux d'Art sacré,
n'est pas né d'abord des impératifs économiques des communautés chrétiennes d'entre-guerre, encore moins des
documents conciliaires de Vatican II; il relève avant
tout des remises en questions soulevées par les nombreux
théoriciens de l'architecture dite moderne : Gropius et
l'équipe du Bauhaus en Allemagne, Mies van der Rohe et
F.L. Wright aux Etats-Unis, Nervi en Italie, Le Corbusier
en France. Le fonctionnalisme structurel qui caractérise l'architecture contemporaine est tout à la fois
retour au rêve des maîtres-d'oeuvre du Moyen Age (méca-
nique empirique et illusoire), art social (adaptation
rationelle à l'usage prévu et au paysage ambiant) et
esthétique articulée (styles et techniques adaptés aux
matériaux, schéma constructif sensible). Si F.L. Wright
s'est vite détaché des ossatures métalliques indigentes
et des faciles emboîtements de volumes au nom d'une sorte
d'anti-rationalisme, c'est surtout Le Corbusier qui prou-
vera de façon magistrale de quelle capacité de renouvellement l'architecture était porteuse en créant, par delà
ses "cités radieuses", le chef-d'oeuvre de l'architecture contemporaine et le lieu sacré par excellence du
XXe siècle : l'église Notre-Dame-du-Haut de Ronchamp :
"ce jeu savant, correct et magnifique des volumes assem-
blés sous la lumière"[1].

Ce Ronchamp, malgré les soubresauts critiques inévita-
bles provoqués à l'époque (1952-55) par l'audace et
l'inédit de ses formes, surgit au milieu de notre siècle
comme le "haut lieu" de l'architecture religieuse contemporaine. Par delà la monumentalité de ses formes
de béton, le lyrisme de ses longues courbes asymétriques,
la "mathématique sensible" de ses articulations, par
delà la noblesse, la rigueur et la sobriété plastique
de l'ensemble, comme de son accord émouvant avec le
paysage ambiant des Vosges, Ronchamp renoue avec l'esprit de la plus pure tradition en Art sacré : Ronchamp
incarne la magie de l'"espace indicible", pour reprendre
les termes mêmes de son architecte-créateur.

ARCHITECTURE RELIGIEUSE

L'AXE DE L'INTÉRIORITÉ

Si, en effet, les grandes cathédrales sont entrées dans
l'Histoire de l'Art, c'est de première évidence en raison de leur ordonnance architecturale incomparable :
monumentalité des formes, puissance évocatrice des volumes, subtilité des perspectives, exploitation sensible
de la lumière, intégration principalement de la sculpture
et du vitrail comme en raison, dans l'ensemble, de leur
correspondance à certaines fonctions, mais aussi faut-il
le rappeler, en raison d'un axe autre de toute la tradition chrétienne, moins mesurable que l'extériorité mais
tout aussi déterminant : l'axe de l'intériorité.

Viollet-Le-Duc, du plus haut pinacle de Notre-Dame de
Paris restaurée à sa manière, écrivait un jour : "Le
plus pauvre monument français du Moyen Age fait rêver
même un ignorant". Mis à part son côté "despectio plebis",
la réflexion de cet architecte est des plus justes. Le
propre du génie en architecture est bien en effet, par
sa capacité même d'abstraction, de retrouver et de solli-
citer l'homme, d'établir des rapports et des rythmes qui
créent l'impondérable, comme, par l'utilisation de la
lumière et de l'ombre, "d'ouvrir l'âme à des champs de
poésie"[2]. Et c'est ce qu'il me faut doublement souligner
ici : point n'est besoin nécessairement de miser sur le
monumental pour parvenir à cette qualité intérieure de
l'organisation de l'espace dans un volume architectural.
Nous nous sommes attardés jusqu'à ce point aux prototypes
de l'architecture religieuse, mais au même titre, la
tradition chrétienne est riche d'oeuvres dont les formes
architecturales accentuent tout autant, mais de façon
différente, l'intériorité que l'extériorité dans la création d'un espace-monde-intérieur exprimé différemment :
le premier étant celui du lieu de culte cosmique consacré
à "la gloire de Dieu" dans la magnificence, le second :
le lieu privilégié du silence, du dépouillement évangélique, de la contemplation intérieure. Dualité avant
tout d'esprit qui a été source constante de conflit en
art chrétien et constitue encore pour nous aujourd'hui
la quadrature du cercle en architecture religieuse.

La célèbre controverse Cluny-Clairvaux qui atteignit son
point culminant au début du XIIe siècle peut nous servir
aujourd'hui d'exemple et illustrer de façon très adéquate
ce propos. Une tradition architecturale bien particulière, en effet, sous la mouvance de Cluny (1088-1109),
s'est développée et maintenue à travers les siècles :

426

Moissac, Vézelay, La Charité-sur-Loire, Souvigny ou
Sauxillanges en témoignent. L'espace-monde est celui de
la Jérusalem céleste évoquée en un symbolisme savant :
c'est l'Ancien et le Nouveau Testament illustré, l'hymne
de la création en images, création aux mille visages
associée au monde des anges avec au centre la vision du
Rédempteur, c'est l'hommage cosmique au triomphe universel du Christ célébré par tout un peuple en procession.
Le vieux biographe de St-Hugues, bâtisseur de Cluny,
écrit : "Encouragé par l'avertissement divin, Hugues
construisit comme une tente pour la gloire de Dieu, une
basilique si grande et si belle qu'on pourrait difficile-
ment en citer une autre plus vaste et plus admirable.
Celle-ci est d'une telle splendeur, d'une telle gloire
que si, par hypothèse, les habitants du ciel pouvaient
se plaire dans nos demeures humaines, on dirait ici que
c'est le parvis des anges".[3] Et le biographe enthousi-
aste ajoute : "Considérant que les oeuvres corporelles
ne servent pas à grand chose tandis que la piété est
utile à tout, il veillait scrupuleusement à la perfection
du culte divin et n'avait pas son pareil pour la conscience avec laquelle il s'acquittait du devoir de la lou-
ange".[4] Saint Odon, autre abbé de Cluny, thomiste avant
l'heure, pour qui aussi l'humaine nature ne peut s'ache-
miner au spirituel   que par l'intermédiaire du corporel
et du sensible, écrivait à son tour : "Faute d'orner les
autels comme il se doit, les prêtres deviennent responsables de l'irrespect que les laïcs ont trop souvent à
son égard, les êtres charnels jugeant que la sainteté
et la grandeur divine sont absentes là où ils ne voient
pas la somptueuse décoration".[5]

   L'accent sur les riches splendeurs, la beauté sensible,
l'art sous toutes ses formes sera tel dans la grande
église aux sept clochers de Cluny (dont un seul subsiste
depuis 1812) et dans les nombreuses fondations qui en
dépendaient au début du XIIe siècle (815 en France, 109
en Allemagne, 23 en Espagne, 52 en Italie, 43 en Grande-
Bretagne) qu'il provoquera en ce même XIIe siècle l'apparition d'un contre-mouvement : la réforme cistercienne,
servie par un brûlant ascète, Bernard de Clairvaux, ce
moine blanc dont la rigueur des théories en esthétique
n'avait d'égale que l'austérité de sa spiritualité. A
preuve, ce réquisitoire :

     "Sans parler de l'immense élévation de vos ora-
     toires, de leur longueur démesurée, de leur
     largeur excessive, de leur somptueuse décora-

427

tion et de leurs curieuses peintures dont
l'effet est de détourner sur elles l'attention
des fidèles et de diminuer le recueillement...
car je veux bien croire qu'on ne se propose
en tout cela que la gloire de Dieu... à quoi
bon chez les pauvres comme vous, si toutefois
vous êtes de vrais pauvres, tout cet or qui
brille dans vos sanctuaires?.. De qui voulons-
nous exciter la piété par tous ces moyens, je
vous le demande?.. Que se propose-t-on avec
tout cela? Est-ce de faire naître la com-
ponction dans les coeurs? N'est-ce pas plutôt
d'exciter l'admiration de ceux qui le voient?
O vanité des vanités, mais vanité plus in-
sensée que vaine! Les murs de l'église sont
étincelants de richesse et les pauvres sont
dans le dénuement, ses pierres sont couvertes
de dorure et ses enfants sont privés de vêtements... Il est vrai qu'on peut répondre par
ce verset du prophète : "Seigneur, j'ai aimé
les beautés de votre maison et le lieu où
habite votre gloire" (Ps XXV, 8)... Mais que
signifient dans vos cloîtres, là ou les religieux font leur lecture... ces horribles beautés et ces belles horreurs?"[6]

L'influence de Bernard de Clairvaux fut indéniable sur
l'art de son temps. Les fondations érigées dans l'esprit
de la réforme cistercienne, depuis Citeaux et Clairvaux
jusqu'à Altobaca au Portugal, en passant par Fontenay,
La Ferté, Pontigny ou Fontfroide, pour n'en nommer que
quelques-unes des sept cents qu'elle comptait un siècle
après la mort de Saint Bernard, se caractérisent par
une austérité, une pureté et un dépouillement qui
atteignent au sublime. Contrairement aux monastères
clunisiens, elles sont humblement tapies dans les vallées
et les forêts; leur architecture nue, grave, est d'une
beauté calme, presque sauvage; leur intérieur est pure
exaltation de la lumière blanche et du mystère de ses
ombres; l'harmonie de leurs formes est intérieure et
secrète : nombre obscur mais nombre d'or.

Devant Cîteaux, Le Corbusier, l'architecte du béton
brut, s'émeut :

"L'ensemble comme le détail sont un. La pierre
y est amie d'homme, sa netteté assurée par l'arê-
te enferme des plans d'une peau rude; cette ru-

desse dit : pierre et non pas marbre; et pierre
est un mot bien plus beau. L'appareillage des
pierres tient compte du moindre morceau sorti
de la carrière : économie et ingéniosité; son
dessin est partout varié et toujours nouveau...
Les voussoirs des arcs et des voûtes, les em-
brasures et les ébrasures, les dallages, les
piliers posant au sol et les archivoltes... les
toîts et la terre cuite des tuiles (la même
tuile multipliée indéfiniment, mâle et femelle,
un peuple de tuiles)... les fûts des quelques
colonnes... tels sont les mots et les phrases
de l'architecture. Plénitude... la lumière
et l'ombre sont les hauts-parleurs de cette
architecture de vérité, de calme et de force.
Et rien de plus n'y ajouterait. A l'heure du
béton brut, bénie, bienvenue et saluée soit au
cours de route, une telle admirable rencontre".[7]

Cette "admirable rencontre" entre ce célèbre architecte
du XXe siècle et l'humble maître-d'oeuvre du XIIe siècle
n'est pas le fruit du hasard mais, suite à une enjambée
dans le temps, le résultat d'une parenté d'esprit. Les
motivations profondes quand il s'agit d'ériger un espace
de dépaysement, de convertir un extérieur en intérieur
ou de faire entrer en dialogue le visible et l'invisible,
restent toujours les mêmes. L'homme reste un peuple en
attente. A sa portée, quelques matériaux, les plus vrais
qui soient; pour sa fantaisie créatrice : la lumière et
l'ombre, et, au coeur, une certaine foi.

ART ET TECHNIQUE

Toutes ces constructions de prestige, que les historiens
de l'art se plaisent à répartir selon une conception
linéaire à titre de prototypes d'architecture, qu'elles
soient d'esprit clunisien ou cistercien, érigées à la
gloire de Dieu ou à la gloire d'un homme, séduisent les
foules et triomphent d'abord par leur gigantisme.

En Europe comme en Amérique cette architecture monumen-
tale après s'être complaisamment maintenue dans le pla-
giat (pseudo-roman,pseudo-gothique, pseudo-byzantin ou
pseudo-baroque) tout au long du premier quart de ce
siècle change soudainement et de façon radicale. Notre-
Dame du Raincy en France est le premier et le plus célèbre monument représentatif de ce tournant; cette église

construite entre 1922 et 1925 par le nom moin célèbre Auguste
Perret, marque le triomphe des matériaux nouveaux de
l'entre-guerre : le béton et le verre, et des techniques
nouvelles de construction statique; l'église n'est que
structure et vitrail selon cependant le plus traditionnel
dessin mais elle apparaît pourtant si originale que son
influence se répandra dans tous les pays comme une véritable traînée de poudre. Dans les pays riches d'abord,
il va sans dire, comme en Suisse et en Allemagne, aux
Etats-Unis et au Canada, mais même et rapidement jusqu'au
Mexique et au Brésil.   Ces nouvelles églises-monuments
apparaissent à l'architecte-créateur comme le lieu privilégié où peut s'exercer le génie expressionniste lyrique de chacun. D'où, grâce aux possibilités inouïes des
techniques comme des matériaux nouveaux, ces formes architecturales les plus originales et souvent les plus
fantaisistes : volumes géométriques, voûtes elliptiques,
dômes géodésiques, arcs paraboliques, formes modulaires,
voiles de béton. Tous les clichés possibles de la symbolique religieuse sont exploités en proportions démesu-
rées. Il suffit de comparer la cathédrale de Brasilia
en forme de couronne d'épines, ou le Prieuré bénédictin
de Ste-Marie et St-Louis, Crèvecoeur, Missouri, en pé-
tales recourbés et étagés, avec Notre-Dame-du-Haut de
Ronchamp, pour saisir où peut conduire le lyrisme débridé.
Beaucoup d'églises protestantes d'Europe et d'Amérique,
malgré leur décoration intérieure beaucoup plus sobre,
n'ont pas échappé non plus à ces envolées mystiques et
s'inscrivent dans ce même courant.

RONCHAMP ET VENCE

Parmi les nombreux lieux de culte construits au cours du
XXe siècle, l'église de Ronchamp et la chapelle de Vence
retiennent l'attention à divers titres. Ronchamp d'abord
qui fait à la fois figure de chef-d'oeuvre et de hors-
d'oeuvre. Chef-d'oeuvre parce que cette église constitue
au plan architectural la plus admirable réussite technique du XXe siècle tant par l'utilisation savante des matériaux d'époque que par l'exploitation sensible de ses
puissants volumes. Chef-d'oeuvre parce que cette église,
malgré l'aspect révolutionnaire de ses formes, s'inscrit
dans le plus pur esprit des cathédrales : sa monumentalité, son prestige, son lyrisme, le mystère fascinant de
son espace intérieur subjuguent.

   Mais hors-d'oeuvre aussi : Ronchamp est l'oeuvre d'un

homme, génial il est vrai, mais d'un homme et non d'une
communauté d'hommes. Sous cet angle, Ronchamp apparaît
plus comme une "sculpture" à la gloire de son créateur
que comme un lieu de rassemblement. Cette église est
selon sa fonction première un lieu de pélerinage, il est
vrai, mais sa construction est désincarnée, expression
lyrique d'un architecte-créateur inscrit dans la longue
tradition des bâtisseurs de cathédrales. A ce titre, ce
chef-d'oeuvre est un hors-d'oeuvre.

Vence, de même. Cette chapelle, par opposition à
Ronchamp, est de la plus extrême humilité. Tapie au flanc
de la route montante du village, elle ne s'ouvre qu'à
ceux qui la cherchent. Oeuvre de poésie intimiste, cette
chapelle de Dominicaines n'éblouit pas mais illumine celui
qui y pénètre. Lieu de silence, de contemplation intérieure, de prière à voix basse. Matisse, au cours de sa
convalescence en ces lieux avait communié à la vie intérieure des religieuses dominicaines qui l'avaient hébergé
et traduit en ses mots, dans cet espace clos, le lieu
privilégié où elles se retrouvaient face à Dieu. L'espace
intérieur de la chapelle de Vence n'est pas la création
fulgurante d'un architecte visionnaire mais l'expression
toute en nuance du peintre-poète habité par la grâce,
traduisant le sentiment d'une communauté à laquelle il
est intégré, dégagé des servitudes d'un programme comme
d'une tradition architecturale contraignante.

Si Ronchamp est dans la lignée des grandioses cathédrales, la Chapelle de Vence s'inscrit pour sa part dans
une tradition aussi ancienne mais moins célèbre, celle
des lieux de culte propres aux petites communautés qui
sans faste et souvent sans célébrité, jalonnent l'histoire
de la chrétienté. Des maisons de prière des premières
communautés chrétiennes aux ermitages du Père de Foucauld
il n'est que peu de différence, tant au plan des formes
que de l'esprit de ces formes. En effet, hors des constructions de prestige léguées par les civilisations et
les prototypes d'architecture religieuse établis par les
historiens de l'art, il existe un autre type d'architecture qui n'a même pas de nom. A défaut d'étiquette géné-
rique,on l'appelle selon les cas : rurale, rustique,
spontanée, domestique, populaire, indigène ou anonyme.
C'est pourtant dans cette architecture sans lettres de
noblesse que la société se mire quotidiennement. Pietro
Belluschi a défini cette architecture comme un art commun
non produit par quelques intellectuels ou spécialistes
mais par l'activité spontanée et continue de tout un

peuple à l'héritage commun, agissant avec une communauté
d'expérience.

Cet autre type d'architecture semble bien être celui
qui caractérise de plus en plus l'art sacré de la deuxième moitié du XXe siècle. Depuis 1965, au Canada comme
en Europe et même aux Etats-Unis, l'évolution de l'architecture religieuse s'est radicalement transformée.
Des oeuvres monumentales comme la Cathédrale de Nicolet
(Québec), la Basilique du Cap de la Madeleine (Québec);
genre "Wigwam de pierre de taille", ou comme la nouvelle
cathédrale St-Mary's de San Francisco (Calif. E.U.)
érigée de 1965 à 1971, se font de plus en plus rares.
Cette dernière en particulier, dont les plans sont pourtant dus notamment à un des architectes-ingénieurs-conseils
les plus renommés du siècle, Pier-Luigi Nervi, est souvent
citée par plusieurs comme le scandale du siècle. La
"simplicité" de ses lignes ne ravit guère plus que les
ingénieurs à la recherche des tours de force techniques.
Sa magnificence est à l'égal de son coût astronomique et
en scandalise plusieurs. Comme oeuvre architecturale,
elle s'inscrit dans la lignée des autres oeuvres de
Nervi : le Palais du Travail de Turin, le Palais des
Sports de Rome (dont le diamètre du dôme mesure trois
fois celui de la Basilique St-Pierre) et le Hall des
Audiences de St-Pierre de Rome.

S'il faut en croire l'histoire, ces "monuments de
gloire" continueraient à surgir encore aussi nombreux
dans l'esprit même d'une tradition chrétienne séculaire
vouée à la "gloire de Dieu", aux besoins des adeptes
d'une église dite triomphaliste, et à la mégalomanie de
certains bâtisseurs. Mais la chrétienté connaît présentement une telle remise en question dans notre contexte
occidental que même les valeurs les plus enracinées cè-
dent devant les impératifs d'ordre socio-culturel et
économique. Le détachement des formes sacrales traditionnelles en architecture en est la preuve la moins
équivoque. Et ce par nécessité économique d'abord, sans
doute. Le schéma de la paroisse rurale chrétienne née
aux Xe siècle n'a jamais supporté la transplantation en
milieu urbain. Tous les efforts de restructuration paroissiale n'ont jamais conduit qu'à la diffusion de quelques services de type administratif. La baisse actuelle
de la "pratique religieuse" est devenue encore plus
paralysante sous tout le "pouvoir ecclésiastique central"
fonctionnant par inertie. Autre facteur important : tout
l'ample discours conciliaire sur le regroupement commu-

nautaire: l'intégration au pluralisme culturel, les nouveaux styles de présence, l'église-ferment, va à l'encontre de la vision triomphaliste que nous avons connue. Un texte du Cardinal Lercaro, publié en 1968, l'exprimait déjà très explicitement :

> "Une chose est certainement très claire : les structures architecturales de l'église doivent se modifier aussi rapidement que se modifient aujourd'hui les conditions de vie et des maisons des hommes. Nous devons avoir bien présent à la mémoire, même lorsque nous construisons un lieu de culte, le sens de la fragilité extrême de ces structures matérielles et de leurs fonctions mêmes de service vis-à-vis de la vie des hommes : afin que les générations à venir ne se trouvent pas conditionnées par ce que nous considérons aujourd'hui comme des églises d'avant-garde, mais qui pourraient leur apparaître comme des constructions vétustes... nous sentons avec quelles difficultés les merveilleuses églises du passé s'adaptent à notre pratique religieuse, avec quelle tenace viscosité elles s'opposent aux indispensables réformes de l'action liturgique; comme leur art, leur façon d'être constituent un écran pour une rencontre plus simple et plus réelle entre les hommes et le Seigneur. A l'heure même, nos églises les plus modernes seront rapidement considérées ainsi dans un laps de temps beaucoup plus court que par le passé à cause de l'accélération progressive de l'histoire".[8]

Pour mesurer ironiquement l'impact de la parole prophétique du Cardinal Lercaro, il suffit de citer ces extraits des discours de consécration de la "scandaleuse" cathédrale de San Francisco, trois ans plus tard, de la bouche de Mgr. J.T. McJucken, lui-même archevêque de San Francisco :

> "Magnificently expressed in stone and glass... truly an example of a Cathedral for our modern world... truly an expression of his work... a language of spiritual sincerity..."[9]

ou encore :

> "a monument to the Almighty... the rhetoric of our faith, a courageous proclamation... an ex-

> pression of the way modern man wanted to relate
> to his God... a structure which would complement
> the overall beautification of the city and the
> Bay area... a cathedral which will stand for
> centuries as a symbol of Catholic faith... ...
> symbolic and functional, already regarded as
> outstanding in America and virtually world fa-
> mous... In something truly majestic and beau-
> tiful man first glimpses the reflection of the
> infinite source of all good, the Creator".[10]

Inutile de prolonger les citations, cette rhétorique
nous est familière. Et même la preuve biblique qui
suit :

> "When God in the Old Testament commanded the
> building of the Jewish Temple at Jerusalem, He
> gave very definite instruction to the Israelites
> concerning the beauty of ornementation. It was
> God's intention that a place of worship be wor-
> thy of its sublime purpose, an idea that has
> found expression in the temples, churches and
> cathedrals from ancient times through the Middle
> Ages and the Renaissance to the modern era".[11]

LA SITUATION AU CANADA

Pour avoir oeuvré personnellement pendant les 15 dernières années en diverses Commissions diocésaines d'art
sacré, je sais pertinemment que, quand il s'est agi de
refréner les ambitions des curés constructeurs comme
celles des architectes ou d'adapter la forme à la
fonction, ou de justifier la réduction des formes architecturales, l'argument déterminant a rarement été la
"question de principe" mais presque toujours le condi-
tionnement budgétaire de la communauté chrétienne con-
cernée.

Il suffit d'ailleurs de considérer de plus près et de
comparer deux types architecturaux nés depuis 1960 pour
saisir la force dialectique du mouvement contemporain en
architecture religieuse.

D'une part, une architecture dite "fonctionnaliste",
érigée en relation directe avec les restrictions budgétaires propres à nombre de paroisses et justifiée par
une vision hyper-rationaliste des formes et fonctions par

TYPE ARCHITECTURAL

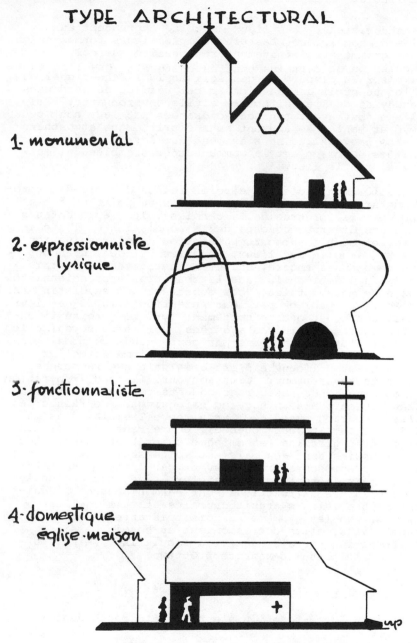

1. monumental

2. expressionniste lyrique

3. fonctionnaliste

4. domestique
église-maison

435

les théoriciens. Ces lieux de culte empruntent aux
volumes géométriques les plus simples leurs formes selon
un programme aussi fortement rationalisé que celui
d'écoles ou de certains centres culturels. Que l'on sup-
prime sur la plupart de ces églises la flèche-signal ou
la longue croix dominatrice et cet édifice se perd dans
l'anonymat de l'architecture civile environnante. Ces
églises sont avant tout caractérisées par leur coût peu
élevé et sont très souvent sans esprit, sans atmosphère
et sans âme. Elles ne s'animent que lorsqu'elles sont
habitées. Ici, c'est la communauté rassemblée qui est
église, non le lieu.

Parallèlement, c'est-à-dire en raison d'abord d'un programme architectural très strict mis au point en table
ronde par les prêtres de la paroisse, les représentants
laïcs des diverses couches de la population et l'architecte, et établi surtout en fonction de l'organisation
très rationnelle des lieux, d'autres églises, beaucoup
plus nombreuses encore, ont été construites sans frais
excessifs additionnels dans la tradition expressionniste.
Sans être monumentales, ces constructions se distinguent
des édifices publics par leur intention symbolique; leur
architecture est encore nettement lyrique : toitures envolées, nefs circulaires ajourées, voiles de béton; elles
attirent l'oeil du passant par cette tendance traditionnelle au lyrisme sculptural, au symbolisme formel et
très souvent à l'oeuvre d'art originale que recherche
l'architecte-créateur. Très souvent, faute d'inspiration
authentique ou de ressources budgétaires suffisantes,
elles versent dans un nouveau baroquisme : certaines des
églises "carton-pâte" de l'architecte Tremblay dans la
région du Lac St-Jean (Québec), comme tant d'autres aux
silhouettes graciles, efféminées ou prétentieuses. Les
plus réussies sont généralement moins séduisantes. Leur
caractère est sobre, rude souvent par l'emploi de matériaux bruts (béton, acier) sans excès géométrique ou lyrique. Formes et fonctions sont harmonisées et l'équilibre entre valeurs architecturales et spirituelles
atteint. Nobles et même parfois puissantes, sans être
monumentales, elles correspondent au besoin persistant
d'affirmation sacrale en milieu sécularisé. Ainsi par
exemple, l'église St-Maurice à Ottawa.

LE NOUVEAU PLAN "LITURGIQUE"

Le rapport forme-fonction n'a pas été ébranlé dans ses

assises uniquement en architecture extérieure; sous
l'impulsion quasi révolutionnaire du renouveau liturgique
imposé par Vatican II et à très court terme, le plan de
base de toute nouvelle construction d'église depuis 1965
a été subitement ouvert aux plus libres interprétations.
En raison de la redécouverte d'une notion théologique
empoussiérée que l'Eglise est d'abord la "communauté
célébrant l'Eucharistie" et que, de plus, les lieux de
rassemblement doivent d'abord favoriser la "participation" des fidèles à la liturgie, curés et architectes
ont pu laisser libre cours à leur imagination, souvent
même à leur fantaisie. D'où l'échantillonnage connu des
églises pleinement circulaires avec autel au centre
(Notre-Dame-de-la-Salette, Montréal) ou légèrement dé-
centré (Saint-Basile, Ottawa), églises semi-circulaires
ou en amphithéâtre avec autel dans le petit axe, églises
ovales avec autel contre le périmètre, églises polygona-
les ou losangées, etc.

La fonction nouvelle des lieux de culte l'emportait de
toute évidence sur la forme traditionnelle du plan cru-
ciforme et se prêtait grâce aux vastes possibilités des
techniques modernes à la création de formes architecturales des plus audacieuses. A ce seul titre, par exemple,
la cathédrale de San Francisco, érigée dans ce nouvel
esprit, rassemble les tours de force : ses dimensions de
base sont 255 pieds par 255 pieds mais 2400 personnes
peuvent y prendre siège dans un rayon de l'autel réduit
à 75 pieds et il y a même place pour 2000 autres personnes debout derrière les sièges. Toute la structure de
la voûte de béton coulé dont la hauteur s'élève à 211
pieds repose sur seulement quatre pylones capables de
supporter un poids de 10 millions de livres chacun. Et
à la grande surprise des visiteurs, ce "monstre sacré"
dont la surface de plancher du lieu de culte est de
45,000 pieds carrés repose sur un rez-de-chaussée de
62,000 pieds carrés de surface réservé à des fins communautaires et sociales (auditorium de 1200 sièges, salles
pluri-fonctionnelles à murs coulissants, librairie, bureaux diocésains, etc...).

Sans atteindre heureusement à ce "gigantisme", la plupart des églises construites ou restaurées depuis Vatican II répondent d'abord à une préoccupation essentiellement liturgique. Le plan d'aménagement intérieur
(orientation du sanctuaire, site de l'autel, de l'ambon,
de la réserve eucharistique, du praesidium, des fonts

437

baptismaux, de l'orgue et même de la sacristie) est déterminé d'abord en fonction d'une "participation active"
à la célébration liturgique : l'action sacrée par excellence. Tout l'espace nef-sanctuaire a même été modifié
à l'encontre de toute la tradition séculaire voulant que
le "saint-des-saints", bien délimité, soit réservé aux
clercs et strictement interdit aux fidèles. Intégré
aujourd'hui dans l'espace-église, le sanctuaire ne se
distingue très souvent de la nef que par le palier qui
le surélève légèrement et par la lumière particulière que
l'on y assure par des agencements savants : puits-de-
lumière, ouvertures latérales dissimulées, mur-vitrail,
etc. plus encore que par des éléments décoratifs traditionnels tels le retable ou le baldaquin dont la fonction
était de mettre en relief l'autel principal. L'accent
mis sur la célébration liturgique a d'ailleurs été si
poussé qu'il a donné lieu dans les églises catholiques
à l'évincement radical de tout ce qui pouvait en décoration distraire du culte de l'Eucharistie. Les statues
de saints, y compris celle du Saint Patron généralement
très en évidence, ont fait marche arrière, progressivement, vers la sacristie. Seule la Vierge a trouvé grâce.
Le document conciliaire sur la liturgie n'était pourtant
pas aussi radical, qu'on en juge :

> "On maintiendra fermement la pratique de propo-
> ser dans les églises des images sacrées à la
> vénération des fidèles; mais elles seront expo-
> sées en nombre restreint et dans une juste dis-
> position, pour ne pas éveiller l'étonnement du
> peuple chrétien et ne pas favoriser une dévotion
> mal réglée".[12]

Dans la plupart des églises d'après Vatican, on est
passé des décors surchargés au dénuement le plus total.
Si certaines y ont gagné en intériorité grâce à l'harmonie des volumes, à la subtilité de la lumière ou plus
simplement encore à la vérité des matériaux, d'autres
sont désespérément vides.

LE CENTRE COMMUNAUTAIRE

Le renouveau liturgique axé sur la "communauté active"
et les contraintes financières de plus en plus gênantes
ont conjointement donné naissance à un lieu de culte
d'un style particulier de plus en plus populaire dénom-
mé Centre communautaire, ou polyvalent, ou plurifonc-

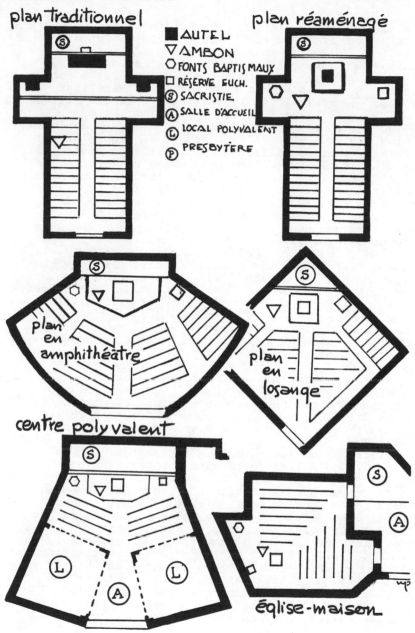

plan traditionnel

plan réaménagé

■ AUTEL
▽ AMBON
○ FONTS BAPTISMAUX
□ RÉSERVE EUCH.
(S) SACRISTIE
(A) SALLE D'ACCUEIL
(L) LOCAL POLYVALENT
(P) PRESBYTÈRE

plan en amphithéâtre

plan en losange

centre polyvalent

église-maison

439

tionnel. Il est de plus en plus évident qu'en milieu
urbain, en banlieue particulièrement, la notion même
de paroisse ne colle plus à la réalité : l'unité géographique est purement arbitraire et n'est même plus
unité de voisinage; l'homme de la banlieue, plus encore
que celui de la ville, est écartelé entre ses lieux de
résidence, de travail, de loisirs et d'intérêts divers.

Quelques animateurs de pastorale, conscients de leur
fonction de "rassembleurs" ont songé, au lieu d'ériger
une église traditionnelle, à créer plutôt un centre où
cette communauté pourrait se rassembler en fonction de
besoins divers : centre polyvalent, répondant aux besoins
culturels mais offrant aussi divers services tout au
cours de la semaine : salle de cinéma, de danse, de
bingos bien sûr, de spectacles et de réceptions aussi,
et même : salon funéraire! L'avantage premier d'un
tel "centre communautaire", tout en assurant géographi-
quement un lieu de culte déterminé est d'être polyvalent
et, comme tel, de pouvoir s'autofinancer. Les diverses
expériences dans ce domaine, au Canada et au Québec en
particulier, ne se sont pas toujours avérées des succès;
il n'est pas toujours facile de transformer une salle de
spectacle en un lieu dit liturgique; les sens sont exi-
geants, aujourd'hui plus qu'autrefois; il ne suffit pas
de tirer un rideau et de rouler un autel au centre de la
place pour qu'aussitôt l'esprit plonge dans "l'espace
sacré"!

Le Centre communautaire St-Camille de Montréal peut
être cité comme prototype, tout en restant sujet à quelques modifications mineures. Cet édifice est réellement
polyvalent : une grande salle avec scène et plancher
étagé, sièges rembourrés, sert principalement comme salle
de spectacle; deux autres salles attenantes, pouvant
aussi servir de salles de réception ou de réunions,
s'ouvrent grâce à des murs coulissants sur la grande salle,
de sorte qu'aux heures d'affluence, pour une messe dominicale comme pour un spectacle, tout l'espace peut
être pleinement exploité. On s'amène à ces salles par
un "labyrinthe" original qui peut autant servir de hall
d'exposition que de lieu d'accueil ou de rencontre. On
pourrait par ailleurs discuter l'aspect "théâtral" du
sanctuaire actuel, l'exiguïté de la chapelle annexe et
la virtuosité de l'installation du tabernacle. Dans
l'ensemble cependant, ce centre répond actuellement à
de nombreux besoins de cette communauté; au plan liturgique, les salles de dimensions variées permettent

d'adapter le choix du lieu au regroupement communautaire,
qu'il s'agisse d'une célébration dominicale, d'un mariage
intime ou de funérailles; la résidence des prêtres est
intégrée à ce complexe; l'architecture de l'ensemble est
sobre, virile, fonctionnelle; elle n'est pas de carton
mais de béton. Financièrement, c'est un succès total.
Les revenus des locations de salles s'ajoutent à ceux
des quêtes et le curé peut orienter l'attention de sa
communauté plus sur le signe de croix que sur le signe
de piastre!

LE CENTRE INTERCONFESSIONNEL

Aux Etats-Unis comme en Suisse et en Allemagne, les conférences sur l'architecture religieuse regroupent plus de
ministres protestants que de prêtres catholiques. Une
conclusion qui fait lentement son chemin dans ces milieux
est celle du centre interconfessionnel : un lieu de culte
regroupant des communautés de confessionnalité différente.

Remarquons que là encore ce sont des raisons économiques, beaucoup plus qu'oecuméniques, qui ont lieu de séduire les uns et les autres. Les problèmes de construction ou de non-construction d'églises sont communs aujourd'hui à la plupart des communautés chrétiennes, protestantes ou catholiques. On apporte aussi comme autre
motif, et à bon droit, la nécessité de témoigner de la
pauvreté évangélique : deux églises ou deux centres
paroissiaux nez-à-nez sur une même rue présentent un
étrange témoignage au "troisième homme"; on invoque également le besoin de plus en plus urgent de regrouper
certaines activités caritatives communes comme, principalement, l'aide aux défavorisés. Au-delà de l'économie
administrative, et malgré les réticences dues à toute
forme de cohabitation et aux problèmes qui en résultent,
de nobles efforts sont tentés actuellement en diverses
villes. Le diocèse de Grenoble en France compte deux de
ces centres à lui seul : le Centre Saint-Marc dans la
ville de Grenoble et le Centre Saint-Esprit dans la station d'hiver de Chamousse.

La ville-champignon de Columbia, Maryland, E.-U., vient
de terminer un modèle imposant dans le genre, à coups de
millions, il va sans dire. Toutes les "religions éta-
blies" de la région avaient d'abord été invitées à pla-
nifier un "Religious Facilities Center". Treize déno-
minations protestantes avaient accepté l'invitation; les

catholiques, après quelques hésitations, étaient venus
se joindre à ce remarquable contingent. L'édifice,
étendu sur huit âcres, compte deux lieux de culte, diverses salles polyvalentes,une chapelle du Saint-Sacrement,
un baptistère muni des dispositifs requis même pour le
baptême par immersion totale, des salles de conférence,
des bureaux réservés à divers pasteurs, des services
communs de personnel et de matériel audio-visuel, etc.
Ce centre interconfessionnel aura coûté plus de six
millions.

Au Canada, même dans les milieux anglophones, mises
à part quelques tentatives d'intérêt très local, la mode
n'est certes pas encore aux centres interconfessionnels.

LA MAISON-ÉGLISE

Si les divers centres communautaires répondent aux cha-
rismes de certains ministres du culte, animateurs et
"rassembleurs", et aux besoins multiples de communautés
disséminées sur de vastes territoires anonymes, si leurs
fonctions se ramènent à l'idée très conciliaire du service et du témoignage et les déterminent comme autant
de lieux de fraternité et de partage, ces centres esca-
motent la plupart du temps un aspect de l'église traditionnelle qu'aucun autre édifice aujourd'hui ne comble,
à savoir : le lieu de recueillement. Dans sa "Théologie
de la ville", J. Comblin écrivait :

> "Il nous faut des maisons d'Eglise, c'est-à-
> dire des ensembles construits qui montrent au
> milieu de la ville, des lieux d'ouverture qui
> soient les signes d'une transcendance; des
> lieux de silence où l'on fabrique le silence,
> où l'on fabrique un recueillement que la ville
> n'offre pas, des lieux de pèlerinage où l'on
> reprend conscience du destin itinérant de
> l'humanité..."[13]

Cette nouvelle ligne de force a été abondamment explici-
tée par Dom F. Debuyst, directeur de la revue "Art d'Eglise" qui en avait d'abord découvert l'esprit dans l'architecture japonaise,en particulier dans le nouveau Centre
Zen situé en plein centre de la palpitante ville de Tokyo :

> "Les rues commerçantes sont toutes proches, bien
> que le voisinage immédiat, planté d'arbustes,

reste calme et discret. L'architecte a pu y
ménager sans trop de servitudes, l'accord
profond de la maison et du jardin qui est
essentiel au climat de la méditation Zen.
Comme dans la maison japonaise classique, on
n'y trouve pas de façade. Un long accès entre deux murs, admirablement dallé, conduit
de la rue au sanctuaire. Lorsque nous essay-
ons d'analyser cette réussite, nous découvrons
par-delà l'extrême perfection du détail, la
délicatesse des proportions et la transparence
des valeurs, une réalité humaine dont la profondeur et la vérité nous confondent... En
plein coeur de la grande ville, le Temple Funi
offre à ses fidèles un lieu humain privilégié
où l'homme peut cheminer progressivement vers
la rencontre de Dieu".[14]

C'est l'asile de silence au milieu de la trépidation
de la ville... une construction simple, aérée, qui laisse
place à la nature, un lieu de recueillement, une vision
de paix, en somme un cadre architectural pur, dépouillé:
un espace sacré.

CONCLUSION

En une décade, la construction d'églises dans les diocè-
ses du Canada est tombée à son point mort, ou presque.

Après une phase florissante (1950-1965) au cours de
laquelle architectes spécialisés et ministres du culte
faisaient front commun pour réinterpréter l'édifice ecclésial en fonction des techniques modernes comme en
raison d'une mentalité chrétienne évoluant hors de la
conception traditionnelle du sacré monumental, l'architecture religieuse avait atteint de toute évidence de
nouveaux schèmes de référence caractérisés par une certaine prééminence formelle, un rapport plus juste entre
forme et fonction, un sens de l'espace intérieur plus pur
axé davantage sur la célébration liturgique communautaire.

Cette architecture dite moderne, établie généralement
sur un programme architectural très analytique a donné
naissance, suite aux impératifs économiques de plus en
plus gênants des communautés chrétiennes, à des édifices
radicalement fonctionnels, aux différenciations extérieures, et même intérieures, des plus réduites. Tout le

mouvement liturgique conciliaire centré sur l'église
comme lieu de célébration et non comme "monument de
façade", accélérait parallèlement ce processus de transformation. Le "Centre communautaire" en est un résultat
original, authentique, des mieux réussis dans nos milieux urbains. Par ailleurs, le mouvement important créé
en France en faveur de la "Maison-église", théorie très
valable en elle-même, n'a eu que peu de suites jusqu'à
présent au Canada, en raison sans doute du grand nombre
de lieux de culte encore disponibles et de la baisse
notable du taux de fréquentation de ces lieux. Dans les
nouveaux développements domiciliaires en banlieue, les
écoles confessionnelles se prêtent à des compromis de
circonstance : auditorium ou gymnases se transforment le
dimanche en lieux de culte comme autant de "dessertes"
d'une paroisse-mère mieux nantie. Plusieurs plans de
projets domiciliaires prévoient l'emplacement d'un "centre interconfessionnel", mais peu d'expériences au Canada, se sont avérées jusqu'à présent déterminantes. Ajou-
tons que ces projets relèvent plus des "concepteurs"
que de ceux appelés à y vivre, la mentalité de l'homme
contemporain étant beaucoup plus à la mobilité qu'à
l'enracinement géographique.

Au cours de la même période cependant, toutes les églises catholiques ont subi une transformation du plan
d'aménagement intérieur en conformité plus ou moins juste
avec les directives du Concile Vatican II. Les sanctuaires de ces églises en particulier ont été l'objet de
transformations souvent radicales et dans un esprit de
dépouillement que d'aucuns déplorent à juste titre. Plusieurs restaurations, en effet, ont été tellement impro-
visées que de nombreuses églises d'un intérêt historique
notoire ont perdu tout leur cachet : un mobilier inesti-
mable (autels, retables, chaires, bancs d'oeuvre) dû au
talent créateur de nos ancêtres-artisans est devenu la
proie de brocanteurs avertis et a été remplacé par un
mobilier liturgique dit moderne mais simpliste. D'autres
églises ont cependant bénéficié de ce remue-ménage et y
ont regagné en simplicité et en rigueur théologique.

Enfin, toutes ces diverses lignées évolutives sont aujourd'hui modifiées en... points de suspension. Deux
mouvements puissants étaient engrenés : la révolution
architecturale contemporaine et la réforme liturgique
de Vatican II. Mais voilà que le terrain de construction
n'est plus le même : les mentalités ont changé. Dans le
contexte chrétien d'autrefois, chacun aurait pu s'atten-

dre à voir surgir de nouveaux hauts-lieux du sacré, du
moins dans l'ordre du signe.   Mais l'architecture pour
être vraie doit être incarnée et les composantes de l'
l'incarnation sont complexes. Nous le réalisons aujourd'
hui.   La phase des styles historicistes semble bien
nettement dépassée, celle des styles hybrides de même.
Par-delà les servitudes économiques que connaissent les
communautés chrétiennes actuelles, de nouvelles priorités
s'établissent : primauté de l'intériorité sur l'extériorité, du provisoire sur le permanent, du fonctionnel sur
l'esthétique.   Proportions et rapports sont modifiés :
le nouveau point d'équilibre qui caractérise l'architecture vraie, religieuse ou non, est encore à atteindre.

ARCHITECTURE RELIGIEUSE

NOTES

1. Hervé, L., Le Corbusier (Carnets), Le Griffon, Neuchatel, 1966, p.14.

2. id., p.26.

3. _____, L'Esprit de Cluny, Zodiaque, 1963, p.71.

4. id., p.72.

5. id., p.84.

6. Cali, F., La plus grande aventure du monde, Citeaux, Arthaud, 1956, p.57.

7. id., Préface par Le Corbusier.

8. Lercaro, G., L'Eglise dans la cité de demain, dans Art Sacré, no 3, 1968, p.4.

9. _____, St-Mary's Cathedral, Custom Book, Hackensack, N.J., 1972, p.5.

10. id., p.18.

11. id., p.23.

12. _____, Vatican II, Les seize documents conciliaires, Fides, Montréal, 1966, p.164.

13. Comblin, J., Théologie de la ville, Ed. Universitaires, Paris, 1968, p.402.

14. Debuyst, F., Vision de Paix dans Art d'Eglise, no 139, 1967, p.33.

RITUALS USED BY SOME CONTEMPORARY MOVEMENTS

FRED BIRD's paper was presented to the CSSR/SCER meetings
at Laval University in 1976 as an interim report on
ongoing research into para-religious movements in Montréal.
He teaches ethics and the sociology of religion at Concordia University and has written on the Horatio Alger
myth and religious ideologies.

RÉSUMÉ

Un rite est une activité partagée, attendue et stylisée
qui mène à une identité avec une réalité ou dimension
qui est la source de l'énergie exprimée par des symboles.
Le but d'un rite est une expérience qui est en même temps
communale et individuelle. Malgré la grande variété des
mouvements spirituels contemporains (Nichiren Shoshu,
Shakti, Sri Chinmoy, etc), les rites de ces nouveaux
groupes partagent beaucoup de parallèles entre eux.

Les rites se distinguent nettement de ceux des religions
traditionnelles par leur manque de rite des cycles de la
vie (mariage, baptême, etc.) et de rite de confession et
d'expiation. Par contre, les rites des nouveaux groupes
comprennent un rite d'initiation, la dévotion des guides
vénérés, l'écoute des témoignages et l'étude d'une pensée
révérée. Ces rites sont tous dirigés par des laïques et
encouragent ainsi une virtuosité religieuse et une participation intensive parmi les membres, l'implication
étant que les plus compétents auront un état de conscience plus purifié. Les rites partagent aussi le même genre
de langage. On évite d'employer sa propre langue afin
de mieux préserver la sainteté des rites par leur langage symbolique. Ce langage devient donc plus iconique
qu'expressif. Par ce langage, les adhérents essaient
consciemment de survaincre les dimensions du temps et de
l'espace, en s'identifiant avec l'énergie des symboles.
L'identité individuelle reçoit par les rites le support
du groupe communal. Ainsi l'individu a une sorte de famille pour son entretien spirituel.

FREDERICK B. BIRD

A Comparative Analysis of the Rituals Used by Some Contemporary "New" Religious and Para-Religious Movements

During the past decade a number of new religious and
para-religious movements have been established in the
Montréal area and elsewhere.[1] The purpose of this
paper is to describe some of the salient, common characteristics of these movements by analyzing the ritual
processes which they practice and/or encourage. Since
ritual practices are integral to all religious movements, including these movements in varying degrees,
then the analysis of such practices has the chance of
yielding information and insights not only about the
beliefs of various religious movements such as these
but also about the differing reasons why persons might
be attracted to one or another religion or para-religion.
This paper hence has two aims: to encourage further
explorations into the sociology and anthropology of
ritual processes and to gain greater insight into the
particular characteristics of some, recently established,
contemporary religious movements.[2]

   The observations of this paper are based on a study
of a number of new religious and para-religious movements in the Montréal area. Some of these movements
are explicitly religious while others are probably best
described as being explicitly secular. All, however,
utilize to some degree ritual practices or techniques
which have been integral to one or more of the great
religious traditions. The groups observed include:
Charismatic Renewal (located in both Catholic and
Anglican parishes), Dharmadatu, Institut de Yoga
Sivananda, Integral Yoga Institute, International
Society for Krishna Consciousness, Nichiren Shoshu
Academy, Sri Chinmoy Followers, Self-Realization Fellowship, Shakti - The Spiritual Science of DNA, Tai Chi
Chu'an, and Transcendental Meditation. (For an over-
view of the saliency of various ritual practices in
these movements, see Tables I, II and III in the appen-
dix to this paper.

   At the outset, it is necessary to define what we mean
by ritual activity. Rituals are part of a class of
stereotyped activities in which persons seek to express
themselves as persons in relation to an already stylized
form of acting. Attention is focused on adherence to
this stylized form rather than consequence of the action,

448

although often certain consequences are felt to result
from such adherence. Rituals are like etiquette in
this sense and in both cases appropriate actions are
identified either by revered customs or charismatic
authorities. Moreover, in both instances, the activities are consciously viewed as being symbolic because
the form of acting is felt to convey to the actor as
well as to others additional, non-verbalized, shared
meanings. However, unlike etiquette, rituals do not
primarily regulate either personal or social relations
even though the structuring and valorizing of certain
kinds of personal and social relations is one of the
primary products of ritual practices. Rather, rituals
are viewed as a way of acting within a revered self-
transcending field of meaning and powers in order to
attune oneself to the reality of these reality-defining
meanings and life-enhancing powers. In most instances,
the focus of persons in rituals is centered on one or
more particularly revered symbols, which represent the
larger fields of meaning and power. By means of the
ritual activities, persons not only identify themselves with this field but also seek to be strengthened
by this field. Many examples could be cited. One does
not seek simply to think about Krishna, for example,
but to be strengthened by and attuned to Krishna. In
lighting the candles for the Sabbath meal, one does not
simply seek to think about this holy day but participates in an age old drama through which one re-affirms
a sense of identity and re-enacts the fundamental
relationship of oneself with the Holy One of Israel.

Rituals are shared expected and stylized activities.
Some are repeated regularly, daily or weekly, as a
part of a standardized occasion, which is set apart
purely for the performance of these activities. Others
may be enacted only once or occasionally, like anniversary celebrations or initiations. In either case,
rituals unlike etiquette, are not performed as a means
to another end or to accompany other activities. Rather participation in the ritual is viewed as being
salutory or efficacious in and of itself. Hence, when
we asked the core members of these groups, why they
participated in the particular stylized activities in
which they did, they almost universally answered that
the experience in and of itself was rewarding. Rituals unlike etiquette are not a standardized way of
acting in given situations; rather they constitute a
situation-defining activity. As Durkheim recognized,
in order to participate in the ritual one must make a

break with everyday awareness or consciousness. This
break may be more or less radical. In several of the
groups we have observed, participants make a deliberate
effort to bracket ordinary ego identity: Such efforts
are made by TMers in meditation, by members of the
Krishna Consciousness group, by participants in Nichiren
Shoshu Academy during their chanting but not during the
latter part of their meetings, by Shakti followers, and
by participants in Subud's Latihans. In most groups
collective songs or chants are used to refocus attention on the central ritualized activities.

By means of the rituals persons seek to orient themselves to fields of meaning and power, or to a field of
power identified by a particular meaning scheme or to
this meaning scheme itself. In all the groups we have
thus far studied, participants seek to tap or to be
open to sources of energy or power identified by a particular meaning system expressed by particular symbols,
identified either with the real inner but often hidden
Self (The Institut de Yoga Sivananda, speaks of the
Christ within) or with presence of a transcendent but
immanently accessible Source (Krishna, The Holy Spirit,
The Gohonzon). In some groups considerable attention
is devoted to instructing adherents so that through the
rituals they may orient themselves to a particular field
of meanings, like, for example, the four Noble Truths.
In general, however, the adherents of these groups seem
to be less concerned to participate in rituals as a way
of defining or redefining their cosmos and/or social
world by means of a meaning scheme. Although the rituals may serve mnemonic functions, most of the ones we
observed did not primarily serve this function. The
focus usually is not on recalling or reaffirming something but on immediately experiencing something.

In so far as any words accompany the ritual acts, the
words do not take the form of talk or conversation.
Rather, the words are structured into highly restricted
linguistic codes or stylized gestures and function not to
convey highly individualized, discrete information to
particular persons but to enhance solidarity either with
others using these codes or within oneself.

One of the first and most noticeable aspects of the
rituals used by these groups is the variety. In Nichiren Shoshu participants chant a Japanese phrase "Mam-
mycho-renge-kyo" as well as Japanese translations of
parts of the second and sixteenth chapters of the Lotus

Sutra but combine this chanting with a testimonial service, using a casual, very this-worldly and almost hip
language. Core members of the Integral Yoga Institute
combine straight hatha yoga with at times intense personal devotion to their leader Swami Satchidananda. In
both the Charismatic Renewal Movement as well as Subud,
participants are encouraged to speak or sing in tongues.
The former also includes a rite for what they refer to
as memory healing. Several groups like Tai Chi Chu'an,
Shakti, and Krishna Consciousness, use stylized dance
movements as a basic part of their rituals. In addition
to Transcendental Meditation, a number of other groups
encourage some form of mantra meditation. On their
retreats TM'ers in a process called "Rounding" combine
several of these ritual-techniques together, including
mantra meditation, breathing exercises, postures, as
well as rapt attention devotion to video-taped messages
from their revered leader Maharishi Mahesh Yogi. The
followers of Sri Chinmoy, who operate a weekly meditation at the United Nations Building in New York, are
encouraged to sit in meditation with half-open eyes
focusing on a picture of this Bengali Swami. The same
group operate a vegetarian restaurant and tell people
if you don't like our way of meditating, then try
another path.

Many of these groups include some kinds of calendric
rituals, which often memorialize a particular important
event in the life of the movement. Followers of Sri
Chinmoy celebrate his birthdate, members of Nichiren
Shoshu celebrate an important date in the life of the
twelfth century monk after which the movement is named.
Members of the Krishna Consciousness Society celebrate
the date on which their fifteenth century founder Cai-
tanya first reached enlightenment. However, in general,
calendric rituals have only marginal significance
assigned to them. Some movements like TM, Tai Chi,
Shakti have developed no central calendric rituals and
seem to place much greater emphasis on individuals
rather than group rites.

Missing from practically all these groups are two
kinds of rituals which have played relatively important
roles in Christianity and Judaism, namely various kinds
of life cycle rites and rituals for confession or atonement. Aside from wedding services, which a number of
movements have developed in response to the interest of
their members in having the association or its leader
celebrate and bless their weddings,[3] these movements

451

have not consciously developed life cycle rites for birth, puberty, and death. The absence of these rites is noteworthy because these rites provide the occasions by which established religious traditions have served to reinforce and act out the fundamental cultural values of their given societies. Moreover, such rites have often in traditional societies served as a means of re-inforcing status differences between members of the society, between adult and children.[4] The rituals which these groups exercise have not been created in response to a felt need by their adherents to define the meaning of life in relation to the events of death, birth and puberty, the way in which almost all major religious traditions, both historical and archaic, sponsor such rituals as a central part of their religious life. Largely, these groups seem concerned about other kinds of events. To the extent that these movements have not created and sponsored these kinds of life cycle rites to that degree they differ from both traditional esta-blished religions and sects.[5]

With one notable exception, almost all these groups lack any kinds of rites for confession, penance, or atonement. To be sure, both NSA, the Charismatic Re-newal Movement, as well as Sri Chinmoy have made the telling and hearing of testimonials a central part of the regular meeting, and testimonials also seem to play some part in Yoga retreats as well as in the Divine Light Mission Satsang sessions. But in all cases these periods for telling experiences do not serve as occa-sions for acknowledging one's shortcomings or mistakes or errors but as times when adherents tell about the wonders worked in their lives since they began chanting, or practising yoga, or attending prayer services. Most of these movements do not contain anything like a recog-nized priesthood which might hear confessions. More importantly, these movements generally place very little emphasis on any kind of established moral code or cove-nant with which adherents identify even while they acknowledge their inability to fulfill these standards perfectly. The absence of these kinds of confessionals is significant because of the central roles which these kinds of rites have played in Christianity and Judaism as a means of reinforcing commitment to specific moral conceptions.

The Charismatic Renewal Movement represents an impor-tant exception to these generalizations for several reasons. One, the members of this movement ordinarily continue to participate in parish activities either of local Catholic Churches or in some instances Protestant Churches. Hence, most participate in the ritual of the eucharist and hence in the prayers of confession which are a part of that ritual. Also, most participate in the life cycle rites which are part of the regular parish rituals. In addition, the Charismatic Renewal Groups which we observed included several rituals which have confessional aspects. These were their own ritual for the eucharist as well as a rite for what is called memory healing. Finally in contrast to the other movements which we have studied, there is a much greater emphasis on and evidence of the participation by family groups rather than by individuals.

It is worth noting at this point that their lack of emphasis on calendric and life cycle rituals renders these movements relatively compatible (or at least not aggressively incompatible) with traditional denominational religious movements, all of which assign much greater value to these kinds of ritual practices. These movements do not attempt to challenge or redefine the given cultural meanings associated with the seasons of the year, the on-going historical processes, or the stages of personal growth. Rather, in varying degrees these movements tacitly devalue these processes and correspondingly like traditional cultic or mystical movements, they seek to foster immediate, self-transcending, self-authenticating experiences.

There are several common features of the ritual-practices of these groups which I would like to analyze. One, almost universally these rituals are led by lay persons. In fact in many groups, like the Nichiren Shoshu Group or Charismatic Renewal, conscious efforts have been made to share and rotate leadership roles. Aside from the particular prophet and his or her special assistants, none of these movements have created a clergy or priesthood with specific responsibility for maintaining the cultic ritual practices. Rather the laity themselves are encouraged to become proficient in the rituals with training and discipline and exercise. In fact, the assumption is clearly made by the Yoga groups, by TM, by NSA, by Tai Chi, and by Shakti that there are various levels of skill in performing these rituals. Hence, special classes are held so that persons can become more expert in performing the rituals and the leaders of these movements are often

viewed as those who have become most proficient. Study
sessions or classes or training programs or retreats
become a major activity for the more active members.
However, the purpose of these classes is not simply to
develop technical skills but rather to acquire what
might best be called charismatic gifts, including the
skills at meditating or chanting or devotion.[6] Thus,
even though these movements are largely lay oriented
and directed, they encourage a form of religious vir-
tuosity among their members.

Two, the involvement of core members in these groups
is intense. To be sure some of these have attracted a
fairly large number of casual participants, especially
the Yoga Groups and even TM. But in other groups such
as Shakti or the followers of Sri Chinmoy, almost all
adherents are intensely involved. There are several
indications of this intensity. Thus, for example, most
core members meet at least twice a week for group meditation or services or participate in periodic retreats
or training camps. Moreover, each of these persons
practises in addition certain rituals, meditation processes, prayers, or postures, daily for a period of
more than a half an hour. Moreover, many adherents
spend extra time practising their meditation techniques
or postures or prayers because it is assumed by many
that one may become more proficient over time and that
as one becomes more proficient one will be able to
realize higher, more purified states of consciousness.

Three, the one rite of passage which practically all
these movements practise and to which they give particular prominence is a kind of initiation rite. The
primary purpose of this rite is not so much to identify
membership as it is to introduce interested persons into
new and higher forms of consciousness, into an awareness
of realities of whose existence they were previously
unconscious. In each group this form of consciousness
is mystical in the broad sense that adherents specifically seek to attune their minds to another more powerful, more Holy reality, variously identified either in
impersonal terms, as the Depths of Consciousness, or
Spirit or Module Code Package or in surprisingly personal terms as Krishna, Jesus, or Nichiren. In this
rite as in other rites practised, adherents seek not
merely to think about this other reality but to act in
such a way that they might experience its power.[7]
However, the ways in which adherents of these movements
describe their relationship to this Other significantly

varies, because some seek a state of dissociated consciousness, while other seek a restful quiet state of
mind, and others a sense of devotion.[8] The initiation
process is then not primarily a public announcement of
changed social status, like Confirmations, Baptismals,
or Bar Mitzvah services, but an often, semi-private
means for imparting knowledge or blessing. In Transcendental Meditation, the initiation takes place
privately between an initiate and the instructor, who
gives to the former a special mantra for meditation.
In Subud, a committee privately passes on the initiate,
allowing her/him to participate in the Latihan.

Although there is a good deal of overlapping in
relation to the rituals practised, there seems to be a
pattern between certain kinds of rituals practised and
the role given to initiation rites. In groups in which
initiation rites mark an entrance into the movement, an
indication of commitment and the acquisition of certain
necessary knowledge, there is a much higher incidence
of collective rituals using songs, testimonials, and
glossalia. On the other hand, in groups without initiation rites or in which there are several initiation
rites which mark higher levels of proficiency, there is
much higher incidence of rituals for focusing or stil-
ling the mind, breathing or posture exercises, chanting
or mantra meditation. Leaving aside TM, the difference
between these two sets of groups roughly corresponds to
Ninian Smart's ideal-type distinction between the
devotee and the yogi. In the former, the primary ritual
activities take place collectively; in the latter, the
primary ritual activities are individual although group
activities and rituals take place in order to facilitate the individual's own development.

Four, many of the adherents of these movements take
part in three ritual activities that have been traditionally associated with pietism: namely, devotion of
a revered leader, the hearing of testimonials, and the
reading and study of revered thought. The prominence
of these ritualized activities seems surprising given
the avowed attempt of several of these movements, like
TM and the Yoga groups, to describe themselves as
purely secular, scientific activities. In the case of
Krishna consciousness and the Charismatic Renewal Movement, the focus of devotion is on a historical person
who is related to as a living presence. Although the
Charismatics are often described as pentecostals, the
majority of their hymns and prayers focus not on the

455

supra-personal Holy Spirit but on the person of Jesus.[9]
The emphasis on personal devotion to a revered leader
is also found among the core members of the Integral
Yoga Institute. While most of the persons who participate in the Integral Yoga's classes identify their
activities as a kind of physical exercise, the core
members who have become leaders of these classes, almost
universally testify to feelings of reverent devotion to
their leader Swami Satchidananda, whom they identify as
their personal guru. Although TM'ers publicly view TM
as a science, their devotion to Maharishi Mahesh Yogi
is enacted and expressed not only by the widely dis-
played photos of their leader, but more importantly
through the attention given to his video-taped messages,
which like traditional homilies or sermons, serve as
the authoritative basis for thinking and meditating.

It is quite evident that there is considerable variety
in these forms of personal devotion. In some instances
the leader-object of devotion is viewed as the incarnation of the Sacred Principle: such is the case, for
example, in Nichiren Shoshu, the Charismatic Renewal,
Krishna Consciousness, the Divine Light Mission and
even Baha'i. In other instances, the leader-object of
devotion is viewed as a specially called exemplary
prophet, like Sri Chinmoy, or Swami Satchidananda, or
Rimpoche, or Bhaktivedanta. In these latter cases the
difference between prophet and mystagogue is fairly
fluid, as Weber observed,[10] so that the focus shifts
from inspired teachings to revered teachings, from a
teacher to a living avatar.

The use of testimonials is fairly wide-spread, even
though the particular style of language and character
of testimonials varies from group to group. The use of
testimonials helps to reinforce the emphasis on developing and expressing specific feelings. Many of the
adherents of these movements are seeking, after all,
to realize a certain kind of mood associated with a
particular kind of consciousness rather than seeking to
acquire a body of knowledge or rather than trying to
exercise a certain kind of will.[11] Casual observations
of two groups indicate that newer members more often
than older members present testimonials,[12] partly perhaps because through the very act of voicing a testimonial, an adherent has the opportunity of gaining a
kind of assurance of his/her own spiritual progression
and partly because the testimonial acts for the new
adherent as a means of re-affirming commitment to the

group and its practices.

Five, in spite of the considerable variety, there are some common features in the language which these groups use as part of their ritualized activities. The basic ritual processes of these groups use relatively restricted linguistic codes that make little or no appeal to cognitive understanding. Adherents variously use mantras, body language, chants, songs, tongue-speaking and even sometimes as in Scientology or Shakti, avant-garde science fiction language, not in order to express and articulate particular cognitive messages[13] but to create a certain kind of consciousness. Unlike the contemporary movements in Catholic Christianity and in traditional Protestantism, these movements seem to seek to avoid the use of vernacular in their most revered ritual processes and instead make use of either foreign or ancient languages (Krishna Consciousness, Nichiren Shoshu, Sri Chinmoy) or glossalia (Charismatic Renewal and Subud) or non-verbal body language (Shakti, Tai Chi Chu'an). There seems to be here almost an intentional attempt to preserve the holiness of these ritual processes by guaranteeing that the symbols used are other than those used in profane everyday discourse. As a consequence many adherents develop a personal attachment to this symbolic language, which is more iconic than expressive. Like the totem that represents the larger sacred reality which it symbolizes, the chants of Nichiren Shoshu, the songs of the Charismatic Renewal, the mantras of TM, seem to manifest as well as express a greater reality.

The various common characteristics of these new religious and para-religious groups thus far described are related to a further common feature, which might best be identified by observing that in participating in these ritual processes adherents consciously seek to step outside of secular time and space. They consciously seek to enter what Victor Turner has described as a liminal existence,[14] an existence in which one's dignity and worth is not gauged by caste or status quo or power or wealth, by acquisitions or achievements. In traditional religious language one identifies oneself not as a role or even as a collection of roles but fundamentally as a soul. The ritual processes, whether chanting or tongue speaking, mantra meditating or singing, enable one to turn away from various pre- and post-liminal attributes, and to find one's meaning and worth in some activity or symbols in relation to which the

457

adherent is an anonymous human being. In these ritual
activities one is not fundamentally identified as a
member of a family (and in this instance the Nichiren
group in Montreal at least differs significantly from
the Sokka Goklai movement in Japan, which has largely
attracted family groups). One of the attractive features of these movements is that in the process of
practising the central ritualized actions of these
groups, adherents gain a sense of self, as one possess-
ing common humanity, not by intellectual analysis or
insight therapy,[15] but by identifying oneself imperson-
ally with symbols of central importance to the rituals.[16]

In this context, finally, it is worth noting the
communal aspect of these ritual processes. The communal
dimension is explicit in the Krishna Consciousness
group. But adherents in all these groups, testify to
the importance of shared common experiences. Thus,
although some groups may ostensibly picture themselves
as helping individuals to meditate or exercise or pray,
the shared experiences in varying degrees become important because it is in relation to these experiences
that many adherents recover or discover the sense of
the reality of their common humanity. Hence, for many
of the individual core members, the group itself becomes a kind of extended, sometimes impersonal but
still supportive family.

RITUALS USED BY SOME CONTEMPORARY MOVEMENTS

FOOTNOTES

1. The research on which this paper is based was made possible by a grant from the Québec Ministry of Education for Team Research. A number of graduate students helped to collect the data consulted in writing this paper; they include: Susan Bernstein, Rich Frankel, Susan Palmer, Steve Paull, Joan Perry, Karina Rosenberg, Elizabeth Sandul, Paul Schwartz, Hugh Shankland, Sam Slutsky, Judith Strutt, and Frances Westley. An earlier version of this paper was presented at the Annual Meeting of the Society for the Scientific Study of Religion, October, 1975.

2. We are in the process of preparing a series of papers on the ritual processes of these new religious and para-religious movements, using this paper as a point of departure. Other papers thus far written and presented at learned society meetings are the following: Frances Westley, "Charismatics Without Charisma" (CSSR, 1976), Frances Westley, "The Cult of Man" (SSR, 1976) (Study of Healing Rituals), Fred Bird, Dennis Lishka, Karina Rosenberg, and Joan Perry, "A Comparative Examination of the Role of Ritual in Three Montréal Buddhist Group" (AAR, 1976), Paul Schwartz, "Testimonial Rituals" (CSSR, 1976).

3. Thus when members of the Integral Yoga held a retreat at their center in Connecticut, a number of couples wanted Swami Satchidananda to bless their weddings, even though Yoga tradition had not developed any special Yogin wedding and even though the ultimate yogin ideal was to become detached from the world and its pleasures.

4. See Turner, Victor, The Ritual Process: Structure and Anti-Structure (Chicago, Aldine Publishers Co., 1969), Chapter 5.

5. There are several interesting exceptions to this generalization: members of the Charismatic Renewal Movement still participate in the regular rites of the Catholic Church; but on this count, it is worth noting that TM, the Yoga Groups, Tai Chi, for example, see themselves as supplementing rather than replacing the religious or non-religious practices of their participants. Also, monastic groups, like

Krishna Consciousness or the Greatheart Buddhist Monastery in Montréal, are in fact sectarian groups which have developed the whole range of religious rituals.

6. See Weber, Religion of China, and "The Typological Position of Confucian Education", pp. 118-128.

7. See Durkheim's, The Elementary Forms of Religious Life, p. 464, London, Macmillan Press, 1935.

8. See paper Frederick Bird and Bill Reimer, "Sociological Analysis of New Religious and Para-Religious Movements in Montreal". To be published in book on Canadian Religion, edited by Stewart Drysdale, Macmillan Press, 1976.

9. The focus is also not on the Word, that is on the second persona of the Trinity, but on Jesus. There is considerable evidence not only in these new religious movements but in the traditional Christian groups that adherents find it easier to relate to the figure of Jesus, even Jesus as Lord, rather than to the transcended figure of God as lordly world ruler. Evidence of this shift in images is found not only in women's reaction to patriarchal figures or the death of God movement, but more importantly in the explicit reference to Jesus or the Spirit of Christ in hymns and devotions.

10. Max Weber, Sociology of Religion, see chapters on Prophet and on Mysticism.

11. The classical statement of such pietism is Johnathon Edwards', A Treatise on Religious Affections, New Haven, Yale University Press, 1959, p. 97.

12. Based on observations of Charismatic Renewal and Nichiren Soshu groups.

13. For a discussion of elaborate and restricted linguistic codes, see Basil Bernstein, Class and Codes.

14. Victor Turner, The Ritual Process, Chapter 3.

15. Herbert Fingarette, The Self in Transformation, Chapters 1 and 2. The rituals emphasized by these groups are generally in contrast to those analyzed by Fingarette.

16. It is worth noting in this context that for some
    TM'ers, their personal mantras are viewed not
    merely as a device for centering the mind but as
    a kind of holy word integrally sacramentally
    related to what is viewed as the Ground of Being
    and Intelligence.

RITUALS USED BY SOME CONTEMPORARY MOVEMENTS

Table One: Rituals Practised By Members of the Following Religious and Para-Religious Movements,
Montreal, 1973-1975

Charismatic Renewal

Primary Activities: Prayer Meetings which include
songs (often repeated), prayers of invocation,
forgiveness, praise, and intercession - sometimes
in tongues; scripture readings; testimonials; kiss
of peace; prayers for healing; communion service.

Additional Activities: Prayers and rituals for
memory healing, healing and deliverance.

Initiation: Baptism of the Holy Spirit, expected
of new participants after initial series of classes.

Dharmadatu

Primary Activities: Meditation services 2 or 3
times-week, which includes chanting in English from
the Sutra "On the Essence of Transcendent Knowledge"; meditation with special emphasis on "mindfulness" or "paying attention"; hearing of tapes by
leader Rimpoche.

Additional Activities: Daily Meditation, which is
the central activity; intensive all day study-
meditation session twice a month and longer courses
at the centers in Vermont, Colorado, etc.; celebration of Rimpoche's birthday.

Initiation: Several steps for more involved participants: Refuge Ceremony at Vermont and Colorado
centers; and Bodhisattva vow for more advanced
participants.

Institut de Yoga Sivananda

Primary Activities: Yoga classes, which include a
pattern of chanting, asanas, pranayanas, and meditation, which are also practised at home. Aim:
greater sense of physical and mental well-being plus
to "give birth to the Christ within you".

462

Additional Activities: Weekend services at special center, Stowe, Vermont.

Initiation: No special activity.

Integral Yoga Institute

Primary Activities: Yoga classes, which involve chanting in Sanskrit, a regular pattern of asanas, beginning with a "salutation to the Sun", pranayanas, relaxation, meditation and chanting.

Additional Activities: Satsang (testimonial, meditation), services once a week; gathering to chant the name of Christ on Christmas; celebration of Swami Satchidananda's birthday; retreats at Yoga Village East in Connecticut, which include: chanting, asanas, pranayanas, nidra yoga (relaxation), Satsang, karma yoga and bhakti yoga.

Initiations: several stages, all for more advanced participants (a) mantra rite - Swamiji gives mantra for individual meditation; (b) pre-sannyas, for those who have renounced alcohol, meat, tobacco and have studied with Swami for 5 to 6 months; (c) sannyas - only a few North Americans.

International Society for Krishna Consciousness

Primary Activities: A well ordered daily schedule which includes chanting the name of the deity, devotion, prasadam (offering of food to deity before sharing in the eating), songs, dance movements, mantra meditation, story telling, work-service, witnessing, study and reading of scriptures.

Additional Activities: Celebrate several calendric rites associated with dates in Krishna's life.

Initiation: Evidence not clear, although must accept certain prohibitions: no meat, no tobacco or alcohol, no sexual relations except in marriage for pro-creation (after special ritual).

RITUALS USED BY SOME CONTEMPORARY MOVEMENTS

Nichiren Shoshu Academy

> Primary Activities: Regular Services, which include
> first chanting the phrase "Nam-Myho-Renge-Kyo" and
> parts of the Lotus Sutra; testimonials; songs, read-
> ing of messages from leaders.

> Additional Activities: Chanting at home before
> one's personal Gohonzon; devotional study of sacred
> writings; Shokabukuing (Japanese for divide and con-
> quer) or witnessing to others (proselytizing). At
> this time one receives a personal Gohonzon. For
> more advanced participants, there are a series of
> classes and exams.

Sri Chinmoy Followers

> Primary Activity: Regular group meditation-
> devotion, which includes silent meditation concen-
> trating on a photo of meditating leader, Swami
> Chinmoy; focus or aim- to bring to fuller realiza-
> tion divinity within persons.

> Additional Activities: Birthday celebrations of
> individual members; celebrations of Sri Chinmoy's
> birthday and the day he arrived in North America;
> special Christmas service at New York center; folk-
> singing of Bengali hymns written by Sri Chinmoy.

> Initiation: Does not mark a distinct stage, rather
> a witness to increased involvement - ceremony con-
> ducted by Swami Chinmoy.

Self Realization Fellowship

> Primary Activity: Prayer Service conducted at home,
> which includes prayers, silent meditation, kriya
> yoga, and a healing ritual, which involves focusing
> on healing powers within and an attempt to disperse
> these powers to others.

> Additional Activities: Regular weekly group medita-
> tions, which include prayers, chanting; (in English)
> individual meditation, readings, affirmations, and
> healing ritual; individual study.

> Initiation: Performed by special monks from center

464

in California, who check on progress of meditators.
A sign of greater advancement.

Shakti

Primary activities: A series of classes, events,
exercises, over time, as part of a long initiation
process, which has no real end, except closer
attachment to group and enlivened consciousness,
i.e. giving birth to the being within. Activities
included exercises of 'mindfulness' or 'paying
attention', dance-movements, a series of encounter-
group exercises including role playing, slowed down
bodily motions, staring at others or trivial ob-
jects, repeating words like 'I', 'You', 'God',
'love' to other, sense-awareness, meditation.

Tai Chi Ch'uan

Primary Activity: Exercise classes, which include
together at the same time bodily motions, meditation on the motions, concentration, martial arts,
and sometimes story telling, massages.

Additional Activities: Practice at home; readings
especially in Tao Te Ching; informal teas after
classes.

Initiations: Ongoing, no special rites.

Transcendental Meditation

Primary Activity: Individual meditation, which is
a form of mantra meditation, twice daily.

Additional Activities: Retreats of various lengths,
which include the practice of rounding-asanas,
pranayanas, mantra meditation, and pranayanas, in
addition to the hearing of video tapes of Maharishi
Mahesh Yogi.

Initiation: Special rite for new participants, at
which time one receives one's mantra, having given
instructors flowers, and gifts.

465

TABLE TWO

Incidence of Particular Ritualized Activities Among
Twelve New Religious and Para-Religious
Movements, Montreal, 1973-1975.

Types of Ritualized Activities	Total Number in in which activity occurs
1. Reading or Study of Revered Thought	9
2. Devotion of Revered Leader (living or dead)	7
3. Initiation Rites	10
a. For New Adherents	6
b. Associated with stages of advancement	4
4. The Hearing/Telling of Testimonials	6
5. Collective Songs	4
6. Speaking in Tongues	2
7. Exercises to Focus or Still the Mind	9
8. Chanting	6
9. Asanas (postures) or Pranayanas (breathing exercises)	6
10. Mantra Meditation	4

N.B. CR - Charismatic Renewal; KC - International So-
ciety for Krishna Consciousness; NS - Nichiren Shoshu
Academy; SC - Followers of Sri Chinmoy; S - Subud; TM -
Transcendental Meditation; D - Dharmadatu; Sh - Shakti;
SR - Self-Realization Fellowshipl IY - Integral Yoga
Institute; IS - Institut de Yoga Sivananda; TC - Tai
Ch'uan

* For those attending retreats or classes for instructors.

** Devotion of leader as living embodiment or personi-
fication of vital or sacred forces.

RITUALS USED BY SOME CONTEMPORARY MOVEMENTS

TABLE TWO

Incidence of Particular Ritualized Activities Among
Twelve New Religious and Para-Religious
Movements, Montreal, 1973-1975

CR	KC	NS	SC	S	TM	D	SH	SR	IY	IS	TC
CR	KC	NS	SC		TM	D	SH	SR			TC
CR	KC	NS	SC**		TM**			SR*	IY**		
CR	KC	NS	SC	S	TM	D	SH	SR	IY		
CR	KC	NS	SC	S	TM						
						D	SH	SR	IY		
CR	KC	NS	SC						IY	IS	
CR	KC	NS	SC								
CR				S							
	KC		SC		TM	D	SH	SR	IY	IS	TC
	KC	NS				D		SR	IY	IS	
					TM*		SH	SR	IY	IS	TC
					TM			SR	IY	IS	

467

TABLE THREE

To What Extent Do Members Practise Any Special
Disciplines, Rituals, or Techniques: Results of
Interviews of Core Members of Five Groups: Per Cent
Practising and Finding Helpful (1975)

Discipline Technique Ritual	Names of Groups		
	Charismatic Renewal	Krishna Consc.	Nichiren Shoshu
Adherance to moral principles	91%(10)	100%(10)	50%(4)
Service to Others	91%(10)	90%(9)	62.5%(5)
Hearing the experiences of others	100%(11)	30%(3)	87.5%(7)
Worship/Ritual	100%(11)	100%(10)	37.5%(3)
Chanting/Singing	100%(11)L	100%(10)	100%(8)
Prayer/Meditation	100%(11)	100%(10)	87.5%(7)
Diet	91%(10)	100%(10)	-
Postures	-	-	62.5%(5)
Breathing Exercises	_	_	12.5%(1)
Concentration of mind on objects or thoughts	9.1%(1)	100%(10)	100%(8)

L - Indicates that subjects assigned low priority to
    this practice

* - Mantra meditation as practised by Transcendental
    Meditation does not involve an active concentrating
    of the mind.

RITUALS USED BY SOME CONTEMPORARY MOVEMENTS

TABLE THREE

To What Extent Do Members Practise Any Special
Disciplines, Rituals, or Techniques: Results of
Intervie s of Core Members of Five Groups: Per Cent
Practising and Finding Helpful (1975)

Yoga Sivananda	Transcendental Meditation	Total
25%(1)	-	64.1%(25)
-	-	61.5%(24)
-	-	53.8%(21)
-	-	61.5%(24)
75%(3)L	-	82.1%(32)
100%(4)	100%(6)	97.4%(38)
75%(3)	-	59.0%(23)
100%(4)	83.3%(5)	36.0%(14)
100%(4)	-	41.0%(16)
100%(4)	*	59.0%(23)

N.B. There are some striking parallels between the
Charismatic Renewal Group and the Krishna Consciousness Group, the Yoga Sivananda and the Transcendental Meditation Groups with regard to the range
of rituals, techniques, and disciplines practised.

A SHAMAN IN TORONTO

JORDAN PAPER is in the Humanities Division of York University and did graduate work in Chinese religions at the University of Chicago. An earlier version of his paper was given at the CSSR/SCER meetings at Laval University in 1976. It was originally meant to accompany a slide presentation illustrating similarities between the present subject's work and early Chinese figures.

RÉSUMÉ

En faisant une distinction entre le primitif et le civilisé (le moderne, le scientifique), les études religieuses négligent parfois certains phénomènes de la vie moderne. Un de ces phénomènes est l'exemple de Della Burford à Toronto.

Quoique ses expériences commencent au début avec la drogue, Della Burford se souvenait clairement des détails de ses visions pendant plusieurs années. Après un certain temps, elle a fait une série de peintures de ses visions en les expliquant par des légendes, et elle les transformait ainsi en mythes. Ces légendes se communiquaient aux autres jeunes gens et peu à peu, une petite communauté s'est formée, unie par les mythes. En même temps, le système scolaire de l'Ontario a reconnu le talent de la jeune femme et l'invita à partager ses expériences créatives avec les écoliers. Le comble de ce partage était la création des masques où chaque écolier pouvait devenir l'animal fantastique qu'il voulait. Pour la plus part d'eux, les masques devenaient un exercice de libération. Tout comme pour les "shamans" d'autrefois, les masques animaient l'esprit des enfants et les enfants se transformaient ainsi.

Par contre, les adultes de la société moderne ont perdu cette créativité libérante et fantastique, le séculaire et le sacré étant devenus tellement divorcés. D'où vient le culte des drogues, de l'alcool, etc., dans notre société consommatrice? On a besoin, donc, de nous occuper plus des aspects éternels de la conscience humaine qui nous donne des moyens pour survivre dans une culture potentiellement destructive. Comprendre ces moyens, c'est mieux comprendre notre culture moderne.

A Shaman in Contemporary Toronto[1]

Introduction

There is a strong tendency in our culture, and hence, in our academic studies, due in part to the predominantly "priestly" characteristic of the Christian synthesis and its relatively sharp differentiation between sacred and secular, to delineate two types of humans and their resultant societies and concepts: primitive (primal, archaic) and civilized (modern, scientific). To the former are relegated the phenomena of shamanism and magic, and to the latter, reason and objectivity, i.e., contemporary values. Such recent phenomena as the growth of Pentecostal Christianity and various movements among youth, e.g., "Hippy," are often viewed as retrogressive, hence undesirable.

Late nineteenth and early twentieth century studies in the history of religion tended to adopt an evolutionary position with, depending on the theorist's values, "ethical monotheism" or post-religious rationalism as the highest stage of religio-cultural development (e.g., from Tylor and Frazer to E.O. James), although a more Biblical "Eden" orientation led to the concept of the primeval high-god (Schmidt). Some contemporary theorists reverse these values, considering the pre-modern period to be of a more religious character, but the distinction is not only maintained but increased. Hence, Eliade distinguishes between "the nonreligious man of modern societies" and "the man of the traditional societies as homo religiosus," and holds that "sacred and profane are two modes of being in the world, two existential situations assumed by man in the course of his history."[2]

Regardless of values, to cast our present culture as post-religious does assume fundamental differences of one sort or another between pre-modern and modern man and, furthermore, implies that the manifestation of religion in our present culture is to be defined by the remnants of pre-modern institutions and concepts (e.g., the surveys of R. Bibby). It is the presupposition of this paper that such distinctions are solely cultural, that there are no important differences in humans since the development of Homo Sapiens, and that while ecological factors determine the form of religion,[3] its

existence is determined by the needs and operations of
the human neural system. Therefore, the position is
taken that religion is a characteristic of all human
cultures and it is further assumed that the maintenance
of these culturally derived distinctions and modes of
defining religion lead to less useful understandings
in the discipline of the history of religions.

For example, the recently completed CN Tower in
Toronto can be discussed as a giant TV antenna or a
tall restaurant, but from the standpoint of religion,
it would be inconsistent to view it as other than an
"axis mundi". Metropolitan Toronto, as certain other
cities past and present, has reached that point in its
development in relation to the surrounding area, central
English-speaking Canada, where its functions include
that of "sacral center." "Civic pride" is a rather
shallow term to explain a structure which would be
grossly extravagant as an antenna or restaurant, but is
reasonable as a concrete (no pun intended) symbol of
Toronto having become, in its own view, the center of
the world and the median point between heaven and earth.
In a contemporary context, the tower functions as the
Altar of Heaven of traditional China, the cathedrals of
medieval Europe, and the U.S. moon shots of the last
decade. It is from this perspective that we shall
discuss the phenomenon of "shamanism."

Shamanism

Although the term "shamanism" has had relatively long
usage in the field of the history of religion, there is
by no means agreement on the precise use of the term.
Mircea Eliade, whose works on shamanism are the most
widely known, has defined the term as a "technique of
ecstasy"[4] "within primitive religion"[5] (or "archaic").[6]
The shaman is one who specializes "in a trance state
during which his soul is believed to leave his body and
ascend to the sky or descend to the underworld."[7]

Åke Hultkrantz, in recent papers, disputes Eliade's
definition in regard to the soul-journey as a specific
attribute of the phenomenon. Hultkrantz has defined
the shaman as "a social functionary who, with the help
of guardian spirits, attains ecstasy in order to create
a rapport with the supernatural world on behalf of his
group members."[8] Ecstasy "interpreted as a state of
trance, a psychogenic hysteroid mode of reaction, ...

473

forms itself according to the dictates of the mind and
... evinces various depths in various situations.   It
thus swings between frenzy and hilarious rapture on one
hand, death-like comatose passivity on the other, and a
mild inspirational light trance in between."[9]   "Ecstasy
is in other words the subject's absorption into an
idea" to the exclusion of outside interference.[10]   The
shaman has a capacity greater than others to induce
trance in himself [or others] .   In other works, Hultkrantz has placed the shaman more properly within hunting society,[11] and has pointed out the distinction
between genuine (or demonstrative) and democratized
shamanism (guardian-spirit quest, puberty-visions),[12]
as well as between general and arctic shamanism.[13]

The social role is designated by Hultkrantz an
essential characteristic; "the shaman's role as a mediator between the social group and the supernatural world
distinguishes him from other visionaries,"[14] and leads
to specific functions as doctor, diviner, hunting magi-
cian, etc.   To this should be added that because in
the cultures where shamanism predominates the ordinary
world includes the "supernatural," the shaman exercising
his/her function of mediator is at the centre of the
community and the community rituals (whether or not
they are "part of the shaman's duties qua shaman"[15]).

Hultkrantz, in noting that shamans are nearly ubi-
quitous in hunting and simple nomadic cultures and of
decreasing importance in increasingly more complex
societies, points out that these cultures are individualistic and the shaman's concerns are more with the
individual than the group.   In more complex and less
individualistic societies, the shaman becomes increasingly peripheral, although "the shift from hunting
culture to other technologically more advanced forms
of culture has changed the shaman's services only to a
slight degree;"[16] Hultkrantz considers spiritualism as
a modern-day survival of shamanism.

A former student of mine came to describe the shaman
rather broadly and neatly as "a man or woman who is
predisposed to religious ecstasy in a culture where
such states are believed to be supreme."   He continues,

He maintains - and they believe - that he has access
to the source realities wherefrom the 'apparent'
world...derives its existence....'Shamanic' peoples
tend to articulate this complex relationship in terms

474

of the metaphor of movement in space: he travels to
where events conspire and returns with knowledge of
their control. It should be borne in mind, however,
that all this is his way of defining what those around
him cannot see. He communicates experience, known
only to him, necessarily through symbols comprehen-
sible to them....In this light, he appears to us in
his most prodigious aspect: he defines consciousness.[17]

The social roles and functions of shamans are diffused
in contemporary Western culture. The shaman as medicine
man has become the physician and psychoanalyst, interesting twentieth-century phenomena, who while redeveloping
the esoteric mystery of healing with ritual garb, paraphernalia and behaviour, do not enter into trance to
remove sickness from the individual, although the patient may. The priest as institutionalized shaman or
mediator between the supernatural and man has in turn
been replaced by the "scientist," complete with awesome
ritual, "theology" and power. The shamanic ritual-
drama, recreating the cosmos and man, bringing the
spectators to an emotional climax, is enacted in contemporary culture, within the Western dualistic tradition, again with or without trance, on the hockey rink
and football field. Nor should we forget the shaman
as war chief in our understanding of the adulation of
sports heroes in these combat situations.

Much closer in role and function, especially in
regard to their capacity to induce trance in others,
are, more obviously, Christian evangelists, and less
so, the more recent phenomena of acid-rock musicians.
Developing from jazz musicians who went into trance,
often drug induced, to create a music which relied
heavily on the drum, the primary trance-inducing instrument of the shaman,[18] the acid-rock musician, using
highly sophisticated audio and visual hallucinatory
effects, goes into a drug-induced trance, bringing his
followers, also drug-stimulated, with him. These
followers, while not the dominant aspect of our culture,
are certainly not a tiny fragment, as seen in the now
classic event of "Woodstock." And the successful maintenance of the shaman's role is as dangerous an activity
as in the past, as seen, for example, in the deaths of
Janis Joplin and Jimi Hendrix.

To consider an individual fully as a shaman rather
than exhibiting aspects of the phenomena, I would

specify a combination of five characteristics: 1) that
ecstatic states be a part of the person's behaviour
pattern; 2) that these states be interpreted by the
person as involving a relationship with guardian or
assisting "spirits" or powers; 3) that the person function socially in a way that relates these "spirits" to
other persons; 4) that the person and his/her ecstatic
state be important to a temporary or permanent community; and 5) that the person exhibit and utilize elements of traditional shamanic garb and symbolism.

In regard to shamanic trance, Hultkrantz delineates
three levels of subliminal experience: 1) light trance
- "a state of incomplete ecstasy, a level of contemplation characterized by only partial suspension of
exterior influences...waking visions"; 2) night dreams
which are clear as compared to ordinary dreams, dreams
in which spirits appear as helpers and informants; and
3) deep trance or excursions into the other world by
the shaman who, with the aid of assisting spirits, is
freed from his body and may appear as if dead. The
latter state exists only in a relevant social context,
the depth of the trance proceeding from the demands
(suggestions) of the group around him.[19] According to
Hultkrantz, "it is rather rare for a person in normal
sleep to have a dream experience of a journey to the
other world. Dream-journeys are not uncommon, but their
goal is for the most part within the frame of the
natural world."[20] I am of the opinion that the third
level of trance may develop in Pentecostal Christianity
and among certain rock musicians, the depth in each
case dependent on the social context. For this paper,
I will describe a person I will term a shaman whose
ecstatic states are of the first and second levels.

I trust it will be understood that I will not be
attempting to make the point that the subject of this
essay is a shaman in the classical mold. Rather, my
point is that we tend to take what I consider a limited
and limiting approach to studying religion in our own
culture. I argue this point both seriously and
"tongue-in-cheek," by attempting to demonstrate that
aspects of the phenomenon of religion in contemporary
culture can be related to primal societies; noting the
similarities and differences presents another tool for
understanding our culture.

A SHAMAN IN TORONTO

The Origin of a Contemporary Shaman

A present resident of Toronto, born and raised in Western Canada, often dreams of journeying with the assistance of a spirit guide to a supernatural realm, a realm inhabited by her friends in fantastic animal form and powerful, friendly assisting spirits. Depicted in tale and paintings, this dream world has become an alternate reality to a small group about her.

The dream first occurred under conditions of partial sensory deprivation.[21] While on a long trip abroad six years previous at the age of twenty-four, our subject was jailed for approximately one month in a northern European country for smoking hashish. Her cell was a solitary one with a window set too high in the wall to allow outward vision, except in an upward direction, where birds could be seen flying. The subject then experienced the beginning of a series of night dreams and light trances which continues to the present (April, 1977), where she travels to another realm called "Dodoland." These dreams and visions, occasionally occurring in the context of smoking cannabis (drugs being a common inducer of trance in shamanistic cultures),[22] were remembered from the start in detailed clarity to the point where the visions would continue in a sequential manner and be painted over an extended period of several years.

In the first dream, the journey to "Dodoland" occurred with the assistance of a spirit-guide, the "Elemental Dodo Fish." In subsequent dreams, a mechanism for the journey evolved, a magic helmet, embodying bird, snake and horns; in essence symbolic of all the major theriomorphic guardian spirits: bird, bull and fish/snake. The helmet, made of feathers, has two "horns" of wings with two further projections which intertwined in snake fashion turn into birds' necks with birds' heads at the ends. Later, she actually constructed a wearable helmet according to the pattern of the dream, as well as a pendant embodying the helmet as her personal emblem. I should like to point out that our subject was not consciously aware of previous use of these symbols, including the concept of "helmet" as opposed to that of "hat," although she certainly would have been subliminally aware of them from her cultural context.

The symbolization here, I believe, is significant.

Although the interpretation is controversial, I hold to
the view that the horned figure of Les Trois Frères and
Le Gabillou are shamans wearing animal skins including
the skull with horns, respectively, of reindeer and
bison.[23] In any case, in a number of later cultures,
the shaman, predominantly a hunting ecology figure,
frequently wears a horned helmet and/or bird feathers,
separately or in combination; the former signifying
the power to control the hunted or herded animal and
of the bull's power in a war setting, and the latter,
the link or journey between earth and the spirit-
realm.[24] Of especial interest is an early Chinese
bronze cup (ca. 12th-11th centuries B.C.) which is
unusual in its combination of decor elements - the usual
animal mask with horns, representing in my view a horned
helmet,[25] with the horns uniquely turning into birds'
necks with the birds' heads at the ends, quite similar
to our subject's helmet, without the intertwine
feature.[26]

Our subject had previously been oriented toward
vivid colours. For example, she had financed foreign
travel by collecting and selling brightly coloured
glass trade beads. The dream-vision was of a brilliant,
multi-coloured realm reached by a spirit-flight from
the ordinary world, inhabited by friendly spirit-guides
and actual friends in extraordinary animal forms. The
connected dream-visions occurred a number of times over
a period of years and were remembered in detail leading
to a series of paintings illustrating the visions now
transformed into myth expressed in the captions attached
to them. Selections from these are as follows:

The Spirit Realm: Journey to Dodoland[27]

1. Bird Helmet - Della put on her Bird Helmet. Outside the window was a Travelling Cloud that she jumped
into to help her sail smoothly on her journey. The
moon seemed to pull her like a magnet over miles and
miles of Pastel Seas.

2. Meeting Neptune - While sailing along on her
Travelling Cloud she met Neptune who was King of all
the Seas. After finding out where she was going he
knowingly said, "If you get in a half-sphere made of
crystal you will zoom faster than the speed of light."
She trusted Neptune's magic hand and got inside a
crystal sphere to be launched by the Dancing Waves to
the Land of Dodo.

3. The Elemental Dodo Fish - When the sphere stopped
she saw the most splendid looking creature. It was the
Elemental Dodo Fish who was part bird, part fish, part
camel and part dragon. He greeted her and said, "I
will be glad to show you around Dodo Land." He told
long tales of how he had been misplaced as a bird on
earth many years ago on the island of Mauritius. This
lasted until he discovered his true nature and purpose
as guide to the land he called Dodo. As they flew
towards the planet he explained, "Since Dodo Land has
twin suns it's day-time all the time in the land.
Around the planet are many rings of brightly coloured
Mineral Bubbles and moon filled Night Bubbles."

4. Cooey - Entrance to Dodo Land required going to the
Pink Sea to find the Cooey and capturing one of the
bright pink hearts that drifted out of its unicorn's
horn. The Cooey was truly a beautiful creature that
was part Nauticulus and part Unicorn. It could hardly
be seen as it was almost the same colour as the sea
it lived in. Della and the Dodo Fish had to stay very
still and listen very closely for the soft loving coo
sound which meant that it was near. Della was able to
capture a heart with the help of the Dodo Fish. She
was surprised to find that it tasted like nectar and
made her want to smile.

5. Marshmallow Mountain - The first place that was
visited in Dodo Land was a Marshmallow Mountain. This
was a volcanic mountain that shot out toasted marsh-
mallows. It was the home of Flutter Flump, a young
elephant, who played and tumbled on the mountain.
Flutter Flump had never left his Marshmallow Mountain
but had always wanted to go to the Ice Cream Caves.

6. Would-be and Could-be - Floating near the Marshmallow Mountain was the Rasberry Jelly Rock. Would-be
and Could-be sat on top of the rock and asked endless
inquisitive questions to Della. They asked Who? What?
Where? and Why?

10. The Dragon Ship - Since the Dodo Fish needed to go
and greet another person to the land, he suggested that
Della visit the Dragon Ship for a few days. A beautiful two-headed Dancing Flamingo waited with Della for
the ship to come. She kicked stars in the air as she
danced around. Leading the ship was Brigadier and
Lady Smagalfoust, who were known by the crew as Dad
and Mom. Della came aboard through the port-hole of

the ship. Once aboard she met The Dancing Bear, Hey
(The Rainbow Dolphin), Bonkers (the Beaver), The Baby
Panda, and the Seeing-Eye Butterfly. She also met The
Wonder Walrus and Folonius the Frog. The Wonder Walrus surprised her by winking three times and turning
into an owl. Folonius the Frog sat on the tail of the
dragon ship and told Della, "I am only serving cumulus
cloud sandwiches aboard the ship until I can get an
electric lilypad." The Silent Owl visited while Della
was aboard and told her of the moon-filled Night Bubbles
where he lived.[28]

11. Into the Night Bubble - Della left the Dragon Ship
riding on the back of the Rainbow Dolphin to The Almost
Invisible Flower Islands. As the Rainbow Dolphin moved
through the sky he left trails of rainbows behind. On
the way to The Almost Invisible Flower Islands they
passed through a Night Bubble. He explained, "Dodo
Land is in daylight all the time, so that when someone
wants night time they go into a Night Bubble. Night
Bubbles are full of Mineral Bubbles to munch on for
those who want to stay awhile."

14. The Island of Eyes - When back on the Dragon Ship
Della told the Dodo Fish that she was anxious to get
back home for a friend's birthday. The Dodo Fish
suggested a visit to the Island of Eyes. He said, "The
Island of Eyes is an island of Water Mountains, many
moons and giant lotus flowers. To sleep for one day in
the center of a giant lotus is enough sleep for a
month." He felt, not only the Island of Eyes would be
a good rest before her journey home, but tells Della,
"The Lotus Dwellers have the secret for your quick
return."

15. The Lotus Pond - Della entered the lotus through
the eye to talk to the Lotus Dwellers who lived in the
center of the giant flowers. They were small blue
people with large ear-wings that would only see on
days that started with rainfall. On the island were
giant Seeing-Eye Butterflies that took them to visit
friends from lotus top to lotus top. A wise old lotus
dweller whispered in Della's ear, "For a quick journey
home, while you sleep and dream in the center of the
lotus, you must repeat to yourself over and over again

> As a worm changes to a butterfly
> Let your spirit fly and fly
> As a worm changes to a butterfly

> Let your spirit fly and fly
> and fly and fly and fly.

The specific mythic components of these visions constitute a unique combination of contemporary and traditional elements. Some of the more obvious ones may be
delineated as follows: The cloud as vehicle motif is a
common symbol of the shamanic spirit-flight or soul-
journey; in China, it is a major motif in aesthetics,
while in contemporary North American culture we find the
device of the tornado in the Oz series. The image of
"Cooey" ejaculating "Valentine" hearts from its symbolic
phallus is an interesting variation of the medieval
European fertility motif of the unicorn which simultaneously represented eroticism and chastity. "Big Rock
Candy Mountain" is reflected by Marshmallow Mountain,
and "Would-be" and "Could-be" are not unlike Tweedledee
and Tweedledum of Alice in Wonderland. The Dragon Ship
motif has a long history; evidence from the prehistoric rock art of a number of cultures indicates
the importance of bowsprit motifs (e.g. in Viking ships
both as original mythological creations and as continuing factors in Western culture.[29]

The Shaman as Social Functionary

Of greater importance for a shamanistic interpretation
is the social aspect. In Toronto, as the visions continued and were communicated via story and painting, Della's
friends found themselves caught up in the vision. They
accepted the myth and their own personal involvement,
identifying themselves with the visionary animals.

All the members of this artist's circle, as is common
for artists in contemporary society, exist on the
fringes of the dominant culture, creating their own
minute, ephemeral ones. Our subject has become the
center of one of these small circles. Her previously
extravagant dress, by culturally normative standards,
became even more bizarre and colorful, her behavior
reinforced by the sub-culture. In other words, in
addition to her entering ecstatic states conceived as a
spirit-journey and the use of shamanic symbols and garb,
her social role became equivalent to the shaman in
small primal societies. Her vision became a cultural
one, reinforcing the cohesive spirit of the group.

The members of this group had been transformed in the
vision into animal spirits, each with a particular attribute. Each accepted the identification and the
specific appellation; e.g., Dancing Bear, Rainbow Dolphin, etc. When they gathered on festive occasions,
they costumed themselves according to these designations.
However, the myth existed without correlative ritual;
the group was accordingly unable to become a community.
Fragmented by the highly diverse modes of attaining
subsistence available in our complex economy, a high
degree of mobility, and the numerous realities presented in the modern cosmopolitan culture of Toronto,
repetitive behavioral patterns and social interactions
(ritual) were unlikely to nor did they develop to
strengthen the centrality provided by the person and
vision of the shaman.

Although the group was inhibited from forming a
community by the cultural dominance of the larger
society, the latter has, in a sense unaware, recognized
the function of the shaman in that she has received
several Ontario Artist in the School Grants. Her task
was to impart her vision to young children, bringing
them into active involvement with this particular
alternative realm to heighten creative tendencies.
In the last to date, our subject spent three weeks in
February, 1977, with grades one to three at the Parliament Oak School in Niagara-on-the-Lake. By the end
of her visit, the three grades, some teachers and the
principal had created masks based on their own dream
visions.

The Mask and Transformative Experience

Shamanic ritual requires ritual paraphernalia (drum,
etc.) and symbolic costumes of which the most important aspect, as previously stated, is the cap or helmet.
Frequently found as well are masks, either separate or
as an integral part of the headgear. The signficance
of the mask lies in its being an aspect of the shaman's
costume.

...we may conclude that the mask plays the same role
as the shaman's costume...the mask manifestly announ-
ces the incarnation of a mythical personage (ancestor,
mythical animal, god). For its part, the costume
transubstantiates the shaman, it transforms him,

before all eyes, into a superhuman being.[30]

But the mask does more than transform the shaman to the
audience, it transforms the donner of the mask's conception of himself; the wearer of the mask becomes the
entity symbolized by the mask. This is why, as shamanic
performance was transmuted into drama, it often maintained the use of the mask.[31]

For example, in an archaic form of drama still performed with its original ritual significance, the Nō of
of Japan, the primary actor, when assuming the role of
deity, demon or female, dons a mask. The mask functions
not to hide the actual human male appearance of the
actor/dancer, for the mask is deliberately smaller than
the actor's face, but to allow the performer to transform himself into the part. The principle of acting in
Nō is that no acting takes place; the performer actually
becomes the role; hence, the necessity of the mask.

The mask aspect of Nō probably derives from the masked
dancers of Bugaku, the classical court dance of Japan
introduced from China in the eighth to tenth centuries.
In turn, the Chinese court dancer's use of the mask may
derive from earlier shamanistic ritual: the exorcists
in the year renewal great exorcism of the Chinese state
ritual of the first century wore animal masks or mask-
helmets,[32] a custom which probably existed in proto-
historic if not prehistoric China.[33]

A particular mask, as a part of myth or ritual, frequently derives from trance experience:

...often only the experiences of the shaman in trance
or dreams are considered strong enough to provide the
mask images or rhythms for the tribal performances.
The winter ceremonies of the Iroquis center upon the
shamanistic False Face Society and are characterized
by performances in which the participants act out the
particularly strong dreams they have had.[34]

It is not that the mask represents the spirit of the
dream state, but as the dance step and song are received
as instructions from the spirit, so too are the essential components of the ceremonial garb. "The mask receives the presence and takes on the functions of the
spirit. The basic relationship is to trance possession
as an actualizer of the spirit."[35] The mask triggers a
trance state of varying depth, an aspect of the trance

being identification with the spirit animating the mask.

Mask, Trance and Children in Ontario

At the Parliament Oak School, our subject appeared as
a magical creature, a fairy figure, to which the young
children responded with interest and affection. She met
with small groups of ten to fifteen children twice a
week for three weeks. In the first meeting, with slide
reproductions of her paintings, she told them her myth
of "Dodoland." The impact of this event on the children
can be seen by the following story written two months
after the visit:

> Once upon a time there was a girl named Della. She
> got this Bird helmet for her 7 Birthday. She flew
> to a land and she met some people like Neptune &
> Dodo fish & the dragon ship, Cooey, fluder flump (sic)
> Woudbe and Couldbe and then she went to the Island of
> eyes to see if he knew the way home. The island
> told about him self and he told her the way home and
> she was just in time for the Birthday.[36]

In the second meeting of the first week, our subject
taught the children to allow themselves to be transformed by sensation using water, the sea and related
images; for example, to "listen" to seashells and become
shells, to feel wind and become wind, to feel water and
then paint with water and water-based paints. During
the second week and early part of the third, she taught
them to make form-fitting masks and to paint them. It
was suggested to the children that they could become
anything they wanted to be, that they could become an
animal of fantasy. The third grade children were also
asked to write down their dreams on which the mask was
based; e.g.:

> I dremt that I was a Leopard! I was chacing, a
> mouse. The next day the same mouse came to the door!,
> The mouses face was a mask! He took the mask, off.
> It was Jasen!   (by Jimmy)

> Once I had dreamed that I was a dancing bunny and my
> dream came true. (by Angie G.)

During the last session, all the children gathered together, wore their masks and acted out their fantasies.
Not surprisingly, the children were highly enthusiastic

at the time they put on the mask; all reported a positive attitude toward the experience. None had required
encouragement to choose the characters portrayed by the
mask or to create them. They seemed to intuitively
apprehend that the wearing of the mask and the resultant
change in identity and behaviour were extraordinary experiences and were in a high state of excitement throughout the last day when the masks were to be worn.

Children are, of course, more prone to accepting fantasy than adults; I would suggest that in certain
respects, their less restricted understanding of reality
is closer to adults living in primal cultures than in
our own. Not only are children receptive to including
"fantasy" in their "reality," but also to accepting
transformation via the mechanism of the mask, although
the participation by some adults in the school indicates
their greater receptivity is but relative. The children on being questioned by myself responded that they
became the dream creature and that they only did so
upon donning the mask. Experienced teachers noticed
personality changes in many of the children on wearing
the mask;[37] that is, the children were indeed transformed by the mask. Hence, our subject again func-
tioned as the shaman in primal culture: by means of
her own trance experience, she stimulated and reinforced the children's awareness of alternate realities
and elicited their undergoing temporary transformative
experience and minor trance (according to the previously stated definition) states.

Implications

Music, art and myth began in a shamanic context, as
inducer of trance, aspect of ritual or depiction of
vision. With the development of civilization, they
assisted priestly religion. Only in the modern world,
with our divorce of secular from sacred, and our identification of the latter with particular institutions
of increasingly minor import in contemporary culture,
do we tend to forget the primary function of music, art,
drama, and myth and lose sight of the manifestations of
religion in our society.

To identify some of these contemporary elements as
shamanic would seem to ignore ecological considerations,
for shamanism originates in hunting cultures, as a
mechanism to enable hunters to gain power in order to

attain and overcome the hunted creature and to enable
the weak human to survive in a world of powerful animals and natural forces, and is also found in conjunction with the related activities of herding and warfare.
In more complex agrarian civilization, with its con-
comitant attributes of sacred kingship and priesthood,
shamanism may continue as a minor tradition exercising
the functions of healing, exorcism and communication
with the spirits of the departed, but in itself no
longer provides the myths and ritual essential to maintaining community. Reality is known through the cycle
of the seasons and is provided by priestly ritual and
the political hierarchy.

In capitalistic industrial culture, agrarian community is destroyed to develop a large alienated population of workers, often numbed by alcohol or drugs, the
ritual inducers of trance in earlier cultures. In
the West, as the imperialistically organized economy
lost its colonies, it was necessary to turn the workers
into consumers and aspects of socialism were combined
with capitalistic ideology to radically improve the
economic situation of the workers. But these rapid
changes (on the total human timescale) further destroyed
community by emphasizing competition over cooperation
and by moving individuals and families about according
to industrial rather than social needs. Dissolution
of community and competitive relationships led to an
increased sense of individualism, returning, in a sense,
full circle to the (differently) individualistic primal
hunting and nomadic groups. Ritual was fragmented and
myth created by scientists, the priests of industrial
culture; reality became bound by material production
and consumption.

In this new world based on the increasingly dehumani-
zing factors of corporation economy, industrialized
production, computerized decision-making and massive
urbanization, the population on the fringes of the
culture increases and alienation within becomes widespread. Survival in this hostile environment requires
power, and, as has been made explicit in the allegories
of Castaneda,[38] the shaman is foremost a warrior, a
manipulator of power. The contemporary "shaman"
through the medium of ecstasy concerns him or herself,
not necessarily deliberately, with those aspects of
consciousness particularly ignored by our dominant
culture, constructs an awareness of alternate realities,
and provides a means for the human spirit to survive in

486

our potentially destructive cultural as well as physical
environment of our own creation.

FOOTNOTES

1. An earlier version of this paper was presented
   before the meeting of the Canadian Society for the
   Study of Religion, Québec, May, 1976.

2. Mircea Eliade (1), The Sacred and the Profane (New
   York: Harper, 1962 ed.), 13-15.

3. Ake Hultkrantz (1), "Types of Religion in the Arctic
   Hunting Cultures, A Religio-Ecological Approach,"
   H. Hoarfner, ed., Hunting and Fishing (Lulea, Swe-
   den: 1965), 265-318.

4. Eliade (2), Shamanism (trans. by W. Trask) (Princeton University Press, 1964 ed.), 4.

5. Ibid., 7.

6. Ibid., from subtitle.

7. Ibid., 5.

8. Hultkrantz (2), "A Definition of Shamanism,"
   Temenos, XI (1973), 34.

9. Ibid., 28.

10. Hultkrantz (3), "Shamanistic Experience and Reli-
    gious Ideology: Levels of Religious Cognition in
    the Lapp Shaman's Trance" (paper delivered before
    the 13th Congress for the History of Religion, Lan-
    caster, 1975), 3.

11. Hultkrantz (4), The North American Orpheus Tradi-
    tion (Stockholm: Statens Museum Etnografisca Mon.
    No. 2, 1957), 236.

12. Ibid., 310.

13. Hultkrantz (5), "Spirit Lodge, A North American
    Shamanistic Seance," C.M. Edson, ed., Studies in

487

Shamanism (Uppsala: Scripto Instituti Donneriani Aboensis, Vol. 1, 1967), 35.

14. Hultkrantz (2), 34.

15. Ibid., 35.

16. Op. cit.

17. Duncan Muirhead, "Shamanism, Music, Hallucinogens, Today" (York University: Seminar Paper for "Origin of Religion," 1975), 2-3.

18. I still recall an experience, twenty years ago, of hearing Gene Krupa begin what was to be a short drum solo and continue for over thirty minutes, obviously in a trance, probably drug stimulated.

19. Hultkrantz (3), 6ff.

20. Hultkrantz (4), 233.

21. Experiments in reduced stimulation, for example, those performed at McGill University, have led to hallucinations, the particular reaction dependent upon the individual subject's personality traits; this phenomenon has been related to the mechanism stimulating shamanistic trance by Nordland. Odd Nordland, "Shamanism as an Experiencing of the Un- real," Studies in Shamanism, 174ff.

22. Since Eliade's seminal studies on shamanism, more recent research has made increasingly clear the importance of hallucinogenic substances in these phenomena. (Several of these studies have been combined in Michael Horner, ed., Hallucinogens and Shamanism.)

23. Weston LaBarre, The Ghost Dance (New York: Delta ed., 1972), 409-411.

24. Eliade (2), 154ff.

25. Jordan Paper, "Shamanistic Decor on Early Chinese Bronzes" (paper delivered before the meeting of the Canadian Society for Asian Studies, Québec, 1976).

26. A transitional chih in the City Art Museum of St. Louis, variously published incl. Max Loehr, Ritual

Vessels of Bronze Age China (New York: The Asia
Society, 1968), p. 45.

27. With kind permission of the author, Della Burford.

28. These figures represent in symbolic form most of
the members of the shaman's "community".

29. Joan and Romas Vastokas, Sacred Art of the Algon-
kians (Peterborough, Ontario: Mansard Press, 1973),
121-129.

30. Eliade (2), 167-68; see also Andreas Lommel, Masken:
Gesichter der Menschheit (Zurich: Atlantis Verlag
AG, 1970).

31. The relationship between shamanism and drama has
been treated in an increasing number of studies,
both historically, as in Ernest T. Kirby's Ur-Drama:
The Origins of the Theatre (New York: New York
University Press, 1975), and theoretically, as in
David Cole's The Theatrical Event (Middletown:
Wesleyan University Press, 1975).

32. Hou Han shu 15/3a-b as quoted in Derk Bodde, Festi-
vals in Classical China (Princeton: Princeton
University Press, 1975), 83.

33. Jordan Paper, "The Meaning of the T'ao-t'ieh" (paper
delivered before the Society for the Study of
Chinese Religion in conjunction with the Association
of Asian Studies, New York, March, 1977).

34. Kirby, 20.

35. Kirby, 21.

36. Kari Lynn Cardife, grade 3, Parliament Oak School.

37. Also teachers noted that the mask had the effect of
reducing inhibition when the children were engaged
in imaginative activities, especially in regard to
performing. The most inhibited child when in public was very comfortable when in the stage area,
even surrounded by an audience, with the mask on.

38. Carlos Casteneda, The Teachings of Don Juan (1968),
A Separate Reality (1971), Journey to Ixtlan (1972),
Tales of Power (1974).

BUDDHIST CHURCHES IN ALBERTA

LESLIE KAWAMURA is Assistant Professor of Religious
Studies at the University of Calgary, specializing in
Buddhism, and is the editor-translator of <u>The Golden
Zephyr: Instructions from a Spiritual Friend</u> (1976) a
commentary by the nineteenth century Tibetan Lama
Mipham on verses by Nagarjuna.

RÉSUMÉ

L'école bouddhiste, <u>Jodo Shin Shu</u>, d'origine japonaise,
était la première école bouddhiste à s'établir au Canada,
suivant l'immigration japonaise à la fin du dix-neuvième
siècle. Un des premiers temples bouddhistes se trouve
à Raymond, Alberta. Avant la deuxième guerre mondiale,
il y avait déjà neuf temples bouddhistes à Vancouver.
Mais à cause de cette guerre, presque tous les pasteurs
bouddhistes étaient expulsés et les communautés
déportées en Alberta. Là, grâce aux efforts du Sénateur
W.A. Buchanan, les communautés se remettaient - au sud
de la province (Picture Butte, Coaldale, Rosemary,
Raymond) et s,étendaient peu à peu jusqu'à Toronto et
Montréal. En 1965, Toronto était choisi comme bureau
principal du Canada et le révérend N. Ishiura était
élu premier évêque national. Sept ans plus tard, James
Burkey est devenu le premier pasteur bouddhiste
caucasien, suivi par la première caucasienne, June King,
pasteur depuis 1976 après James Burkey au temple de
Raymond.

De nos jours, il y a huit communautés bouddhistes
japonaises et une communauté caucasienne au sud de
l'Alberta. A Calgary, il y a aussi une société Karma
Kargyu qui suit les traditions bouddhistes du Tibet.

Le pasteur est chargé de toutes les affaires
religieuses de sa communauté. Le dimanche, un culte
se donne en anglais et en japonais et comprend la
récitation des écritures bouddhistes et un sermon.
Pendant toute l'année, il y a une dizaine de fêtes
spéciales, y compris un piquenique familial.

La communauté de Raymond a joué un rôle important
dans le développement du bouddhisme au Canada. Que
deviendra-t-elle pendant les années qui suivent?

491

LESLIE K. KAWAMURA

Buddhism in Southern Alberta

I. Prologue

In a small town, some twenty miles south-east of Lethbridge, Alberta, stands an old wooden building, almost
dwarfed by a towering, brick structure standing beside
it. If only it were able to speak, the old wooden
building, which now leans a bit with age, would have
many interesting incidents to relate. It was once, like
its neighbour, a Mormon church, but now the townsfolk
know that it is a religious centre quite unlike the one
it housed formerly. The people in the district refer to
it, erroneously, as the "Japanese Church." This is a
story of how Buddhism, which originated in India, was
transferred to this old wooden building and how the
building served as the basis for the development of
Buddhism in Southern Alberta.

II. Buddhism

   Buddhism is an anglicized word referring to a system
of thought founded by a historical personage, Siddhar-
tha Gautama, some 2,500 years ago in India. By comparison with other views, his way was called The Middle
Path.

   The Middle Path is a practice of avoiding extreme
views - that is, it is the practice by which one over-
comes one's attachment to absolutism and by which one
sees properly the interdependent nature of all exist-
ences. One who traverses the Middle Path sees reality
as it actually is without the desire to see it as one
would like it to be. Without this proper view, man's
emotions and actions take over and become the causes
for his frustrations.

   A person who actively engages himself in the avoidance of frustrating situations and in the expansion and
elevation of his outlook in life is called a "Buddha"

- an enlightened being. The term "Buddha" is, therefore, a word describing a person's state of mind and is
not a proper noun "pointing to" a particular person.
Thus, when the Buddhists talk about Shakyamuni Buddha,
they mean the person "Shakyamuni" whose mental state is
enlightened. "Buddhism" is a term which refers to the
system of thought which elucidates a possible method by
which one can become enlightened - i.e., Buddhism explains how one can remove the causes for frustrations.
However, the method by which one can become enlightened
has been interpreted differently by different people.
As a consequence, a variety of Buddhist Schools have
arisen.

In India, two great divisions arose - one advocated
the importance of man's ability to act with decorum, to
be in control of his own behaviour, and to expand his
perspective on life; the other advocated the importance
of abstaining from all worldly concerns. The former one
is called the Mahayana (great vehicle) and the latter
one is called the Hinayana (small vehicle) or more
properly the Theravada. It was the Mahayana form of
Buddhism which, in the main, was transmitted to China
and then to Japan through Korea. In some form or another, most of the Buddhist Schools that developed in
China were transmitted to Japan, but the particular
School of Buddhism which found its way to Canada was
developed in Japan. The Jodo Shin Shu (True Pure Land
School) was founded by Shinran (1173-1262) in the thir-
teenth century, some seven hundred years after the
introduction of Buddhism into Japan.

III. Japanese Buddhism

By the time Buddhism was introduced into Japan, the
Chinese had already made many pilgrimages to India and
had completed a vast number of translations. By the
middle of the T'ang Period, all of the Chinese Buddhist
Schools had been established. With the decline of the
T'ang dynasty, political and economic upheavals took
place, thus forcing many of the Chinese to Korea and to
Japan. It was the migration of these people that
brought Buddhism to the shores of Japan.

The first politically organized period in Japanese
history is known as the Nara Period. This period derives its name from the place at which the Capital was
located. Buddhism of this period can be characterized
as a Period of Introduction wherein the major concern

was to transcribe Chinese Buddhist Texts. Thus, Buddhism was the occupation of the élite class who were familiar with the Chinese language. Buddhist temples were built in the Capital and were centres of great learning and education. Towards the end of the Nara Period, Buddhism was firmly established as a Japanese religion when Prince Regent Shotoku Taishi (574-622) gave it official recognition in his Seventeen Article Constitution.

The shift of the Capital from Nara to Heian (Kyoto) became paramount when Buddhist monks became too actively engaged in the affairs of the Imperial family. A marriage of one of the princesses to a Buddhist monk finalized the need for a move.

Buddhism of the Heian Period can be characterized as "Mountain Temple Buddhism." Unlike the former Nara Period in which temples were built right within the city compound, in the Heian Period, temples were built high in the mountains. Representative of those Mountain Temples were the Tendai School on Mt. Hiei and the Shingon School on Mt. Koya. Those temples were the homes of the ascetics, but out of them grew religious developments more suited to the public. For example, out of the Tendai School grew the Nembutsu (recitation of the Buddha-name) practice.

The Kamakura Period was a period in which more Buddhist schools developed. Some, such as the Zen School which flourished among the Samurai (warrior) class were already known in China, but others, such as the Nichiren School, were founded by a Japanese priest named Nichiren (1222-1282). The Nichiren School gave birth to a quasi-Buddhist School, the Sokagakkai, a religious organization which has exerted its influence in many parts of the North American Continent in recent times.

Although the immigrants to Canada from Japan represented all of the Japanese Buddhist Schools, it was the Nishi Honganji which first established a systematic organization in Canada. The Nishi Honganji is one of two Jodo Shin Shu schools. The other is the Higashi Honganji. The Jodo Shin Shu is an outgrowth of the complete secularization of the Tendai Nembutsu practice. Because the Jodo Shin Shu gained too much political and economic power, the officials at the time divided it into the Nishi and Higashi Honganji. The Nishi Honganji is also known by the name, Honpa Honganji Temple and

494

the Higashi Honganji is also known as the Otani-ha
Honganji.

IV. Buddhism in Canada

The early Japanese immigrants to Canada located themselves along the coastal regions of British Columbia.
Vancouver was the centre of their activities. A few,
however, moved as far inland as Raymond, Alberta.

Unlike the early Chinese immigrants, the Japanese
faced a more favourable condition due to the Anglo-
Japanese Treaty signed in 1902 between the Japanese and
British governments. However, the Japanese were not
without problems, for unlike their counterparts, the
Chinese and other Asian immigrants, they chose to engage
themselves in occupations such as fishing, farming, and
lumbering - industries in which the white Canadians
claimed a monopoly.

Prior to World War II, Vancouver was like a little
Tokyo. In 1941, there were some 23,000 Japanese people
living along the coastal areas of British Columbia. Of
those, 17,255 were either naturalized Canadians or
Canadians by birth, although none of them had voting
privileges. The common language which they spoke was
Japanese, and in many cases, it was not until after the
evacuation that some Canadian born Japanese felt the
need to learn the English language. In many respects
they remained more traditional than their contemporaries
still in Japan.

It was into this atmosphere that the first Buddhist
priests were sent from the Nishi Honganji Temple as
early as 1907. Unlike the situation in Japan which the
priests left, when they arrived in Canada, they found
that they were not the owners of their temples. Instead,
they were paid employees of the congregation to cater to
the needs of those immigrants. Like the Nara Period in
Japan the priests were considered to be next to divine.
The Buddhist temples were centres of learning. However,
in Canada, "learning" did not mean the study of Buddhist
scriptures. The role of the priests changed almost
overnight from that of spiritual leader to that of
instructors in the Japanese language.

With the evacuation of the Japanese in Vancouver in
1942, the people moved eastward to the interior parts
of British Columbia and Southern Alberta. Many of
their priests received deportation orders and returned
to Japan when the Canadian Government provided passage.

495

Six ministers remained.[1] In April of 1946, four of them got together to form the Canada Bukkyo Fukyo Zaidan (An Economic Committee for the propagation of Buddhism in Canada)[2] Shortly after the meeting, two more received deportation orders and left for Japan. This left two ministers in Alberta and one in Slocan City for all Buddhist adherents in Canada. In June of 1946 the Rev. S. Ikuta was sent a deportation order and in July of the same year, the Rev. Y. Kawamura received deportation orders. This meant that the Buddhists who by that time had formed organized bodies throughout Alberta would be without spiritual leadership. Under the direction of Senator W.A. Buchanan, the Editor of the Lethbridge Herald, the Japanese signed a petition against such a move. The two ministers were allowed to remain in Southern Alberta. Otherwise Buddhism in Southern Alberta may have faded out.

After serving as beet labourers in Southern Alberta and as quasi-war prisoners in the interior of British Columbia, the Japanese people were once again free to move about Canada. Many chose to return to familiar areas in British Columbia, while others took the opportunity to find a new life in Eastern Canada. In each centre of substantial Japanese population, the Japanese Buddhists got together to form Buddhist organization under the directive of the Canada Bukkyo Fukyo Zaidan. Steveston, Vancouver, Kelowna, Lethbridge, Picture Butte, Coaldale, Taber, Raymond, Winnipeg, Toronto, and Montréal became centres of Buddhist activities. For the first time after the War, the Buddhists got together to have a National Meeting held at the Raymond Buddhist Church in 1946. The first National headquarters was housed in the Raymond Buddhist Church and from there newsletters were turned out to inform the congregation of the Buddhist activities throughout Canada. The headquarters was to be rotated from temple to temple throughout Canada, which was divided into four ministerial areas, each bearing the title Kyoku (area of ministerial jurisdiction) - British Columbia, Alberta, Manitoba, and the Eastern District made up of Ontario and Québec.

In January of 1965, a ministerial meeting was held in Winnipeg to reorganise the Buddhist Churches of Canada. It was agreed that their headquarters should remain in one place. Toronto was selected. Also, it was resolved that the Buddhist Churches of Canada should have its own Bishop. The Rev. N. Ishiura was elected the first Bishop in the history of Canadian Buddhism and he was followed by Bishop S. Kosaka, a clergyman from Japan.

V. Buddhism in Southern Alberta

Prior to 1929, only a few Japanese families were living in the Raymond area. There were even fewer families living in outlying areas such as Hardiville, Coalhurst, and Fort Macleod. Many of the immigrants came with the intention of staying a few years, making a sum of money, and then returning to Japan. As it turned out, many of them passed away before their dreams were fulfilled and many who survived have yet to return even for a visit. Those were the people who immigrated during the Meiji and Taisho Periods of Japanese history. They brought with them the culture and language of the time and were successful in maintaining them until very recent times. Two examples will elucidate the matter.

Firstly, those people left Japan when it was unheard of for a man and a woman to look at each other longingly, let alone hold hands openly. When the young people wanted to organize dance parties in the churches shortly after the war, they were forbidden to do so. What a disgrace to the Japanese people if the young were to hold a dance and hold each other in their arms in public! Happily, things have changed now, and dance parties are organized by those senior citizens who once forbade such ugly acts.

Secondly, it comes as an amazement that anyone living in Canada as long as the issei (first generation) have, could have done so without knowing the English language. In a sense, they must be credited with conserving a language of their own in a foreign culture as long as they did.

In any event, on July 1, 1929, the Japanese who were living in the Raymond area gathered together for an Obon (Memorial) service.[3] The Rev. G. Taga, a resident minister of the Honpa Buddhist Temple in Vancouver, was invited to conduct the service. On that occasion, Mr. Taga expressed his desire to see a Buddhist organization and a temple established in Raymond. Directed by him, the people in Raymond gathered together to discuss the possibility. Messrs. Yoichi Hironaka and Yoshio Hatanaka were elected to negotiate with the L.D.S. church for the purchase of their old building.[4] The price? Five thousand dollars. When the negotiation for the

purchase of the building was going on, the Japanese
people were not organized as a Buddhist organization.
They were organized under the auspices of the Japanese
Society. The interior of the building required remodelling to suit the needs of the Japanese people. A local
Japanese carpenter[5] directed this project to which many
others donated time and labour. When the remodelling
was completed, the people wanted a resident minister.

Now the people faced a real problem. They had made
their request for a minister and had negotiated for the
purchase of the building. But how were they to finance
it all? The solution - a Hundred Years Plan! Under the
plan, each person would pledge a certain amount of money
which would be paid during a hundred years period. If
the one who made the pledge could not pay it, then his
son or daughter would be responsible. In this way, a
grand sum of seven thousand three hundred and eighty-
seven dollars was raised. One hundred and twenty-four
people made pledges. The names of the donors can be
seen artistically inscribed and framed over the chapel
entrance of the Raymond Buddhist Church.[6]

By the time the pledges had been gathered they had
news of their new priest, the Reverend Shinjo Nagatomi.
He arrived with his family on June 4, 1930 and remained
until 1933. (One of them, Dr. Masatoshi Nagatomi, now
teaches Buddhism at Harvard University.) There followed
a succession of ministers, the most permanent of whom
was the Reverend Yutetsu Kawamura. He was followed for
various terms by three niseis (second generation Japanese), Ensei Nekoda, Takashi Tsuji and his son, Leslie
Kawamura.[7]

In 1972 the Reverend James Burkey, the first caucasian
minister to serve any Buddhist church in Canada, joined
the church in Raymond. And in 1976 the Reverend June
King, the first caucasian woman to serve a Canadian
Buddhist congregation, joined Yutetsu Kawamura, who had
come out of retirement in Hawaii. Thus, presently
(1977), June King and Yutetsu Kawamura are serving the
Raymond congregation.

Due to the continual change in the ministers of the
Raymond Buddhist Church, the organizational structure
of Buddhism in Southern Alberta also underwent changes.

Prior to the evacuation, a small number of Japanese
families had moved from Raymond to farming areas in

498

Rosemary, Brooks, and Rainier. They were families who
were in search of more fertile soil after the depression
of the 1930's deprived them of all that they had ever
owned.

With the evacuation of the Japanese from the coastal
regions in British Columbia, Southern Alberta had a
great influx of Japanese who were hired as farm labourers
in the sugar beet fields. Almost overnight, Japanese
seemed to be everywhere.[8] Only Lethbridge was without
Japanese families, because they were not allowed to live
within the city boundaries. The growth of the Japanese
population meant growth in Buddhist activities. The
Japanese got together to form new Buddhist organizations
in Coaldale, Taber, and Picture Butte. Gradually, the
people were able to accumulate enough money to purchase
buildings for their services.

In Coaldale, for example, one of the supporting organizations was the Society of People from Okinawa. From
very early times, the Okinawa people had lived in Hardiville and Coalhurst. They worked in the coal mines and
after the mines closed, they moved to farming areas
around Coaldale. When the Japanese evacuees came, the
Okinawa people co-operated with them in establishing
the Buddhist church in Coaldale.

In Picture Butte, one-half of an old bowling alley
was purchased. In the other half, grain was stored.
The half which was the minister's residence, a Japanese
co-op store, and the church chapel gave only very cramped
quarters. A few years later, the congregation was able
to purchase the whole building and a grand construction
project was launched. The minister's manse was located
mid-way between the co-op store and the chapel. A long
hallway which interlinked the co-op store with the
chapel cut through the minister's manse. This building
served the people for several years until the house next
door was purchased. Mazes of hallways now linked, in
good Japanese fashion, the co-op store, the manse, and
the chapel. Today, the congregation has purchased
another building adjacent to the manse, and thus, the
Picture Butte Buddhist Church owns three buildings
side by side.

Why did the Picture Butte Buddhist church begin with
a Japanese co-op store? The co-op store was started in
the Raymond Buddhist church as a means of aiding the
financial affairs of the church and of providing the

Japanese people with the kinds of food to which they were accustomed - rice, soya sauce, fermented soya bean, and so on. For example, when Yutetsu Kawamura left Raymond to establish the church in Picture Butte (1942), he had to do so with the understanding that he would have no salary. The Raymond church offered him some commodities from their co-op store on consignment. The profit from the sale of the commodities would be his to live on; the cost would be returned to Raymond.

Thus with the development of the Buddhist churches throughout Southern Alberta, of the ministerial jurisdictions, and of the umbrella organization which coordinated the Buddhist activities throughout Canada, the Alberta Kyoku became actively engaged as the liaison body between the congregation and the National organization until March 8, 1965.

On the evening of March 8th, the Alberta Kyoku had one of its regular meetings. But, due to a disagreement, some of the delegates declared dissolution of the Alberta Kyoku and left. Only those delegates who were interested in continuing their liaison with the Buddhist Churches of Canada remained. A resolution was then passed to the effect that the organization which developed as a result of a steering committee's finding would be the official Alberta representative to the Buddhist Churches of Canada.

The steering committee met on many occasions and finally drew up the constitution of the Honpa Buddhist Church of Alberta, the name that they proposed as the title of the new organization. However, those who did not approve of the new constitution got together and formed another Buddhist organization. Thus Alberta Buddhists were split into two major groups. In the meantime, the Buddhist Churches of Canada passed a resolution, unknown to the Alberta Buddhists, that those who did not favour the new constitution would be the official body with which the Buddhist Churches of Canada would continue its liaison.[9]

The constitution of the Honpa Buddhist Church was ratified by the Raymond Buddhist Church, the Coaldale Buddhist Church, the Rosemary Buddhist Church, and individuals of Buddhist faith living in Lethbridge, Taber, and Picture Butte. Whereas the people in Raymond, Coaldale and Rosemary had their original church building in which to congregate, those who lived in Lethbridge,

500

BUDDHIST CHURCHES IN ALBERTA

Taber, and Picture Butte had to leave their churches to be with the Honpa Buddhist Church of Alberta. As a consequence, those people held their religious services in private homes, libraries, or schools.

Shortly thereafter, a majority of the members left the Coaldale Buddhist Church to join with the groups in Lethbridge, Taber and Picture Butte. Those people then got together and formed the Lethbridge Branch of the Honpa Buddhist Church of Alberta. Within five years, they purchased land and built a new temple in Lethbridge.

The situation of Buddhism in Southern Alberta at the present time is, therefore, as follows:

The Alberta Kyoku - four branches:

1. Picture Butte Buddhist Church,
2. Taber Buddhist Church,
3. Coaldale Buddhist Church, and
4. Lethbridge Bukkyokai Church.

The Honpa Buddhist Church of Alberta - three branches:

1. Raymond Buddhist Church,
2. Rosemary Buddhist Church, and
3. Honpa Buddhist Church of Alberta, Lethbridge Branch.

In Calgary, a Buddhist group was formed shortly after the War. This group, which was known as the Calgary Hoyukai, requested a minister from the Buddhist Churches of Canada in 1972. The Rev. Kyojo Ikuta, who had been studying at the Ryukoku University in Japan under a Canada Council Grant and who had served the Vancouver Buddhist Church formerly was sent to Calgary after his return from Japan to serve the Buddhists in Calgary. At present, the group is still without a church building, but it is working towards building one in the near future.

There were Buddhist activities taking place outside the Japanese communities. As one of the services of the Honpa Buddhist Church of Alberta, the Rev. Leslie Kawamura travelled to Edmonton once a month. There he formed the

Edmonton Dharma Sangha, a group of caucasians interested
in the study of Buddhism. Since its inception, the
Edmonton Dharma Sangha has undergone organizational
changes and is now the Edmonton Buddhist Society. This
group is heterogeneous consisting of people who
follow the Japanese Jodo Shin Shu and Zen, and those
who follow other Buddhist traditions such as the Vaj-
rayana tradition of Tibet.

In Calgary, there is a Zen Buddhist group which has
Edo Roshi, a Zen Buddhist Meditation Teacher, of New
York as its official leader. Also, with the recent
visit of His Holiness, The Gyalwa Karmapa to Canada and
to Calgary, interest in the Kargyu order of Tibetan
Buddhism has grown. The Karma Kargyu Society is headed
by Mrs. Hanne Marstrand of Calgary. This society is in
the process of establishing branches in Lethbridge,
Calgary and Edmonton.

In summary then, the picture of Buddhism in Southern
Alberta is as follows:

1. There is the Alberta Kyoku, which has liaison
    with the Buddhist Churches of Canada (Japanese
    oriented).
2. There is the Honpa Buddhist Church of Alberta,
    which is an independent Buddhist organization
    (Japanese oriented, but extending its activities
    to include the caucasians);
3. There is the Calgary Buddhist Church, which has
    liaison with the Buddhist Churches of Canada.
4. There is the Edmonton Buddhist Society, which
    is affiliated as a Dharma-dhatu with Trung-pa,
    Rin-po-che, in Denver, and with the Honpa Buddhist
    Church of Alberta.
5. There is the beginnings of the Karma Kargyu
    Society in Calgary.

Before concluding this paper, a few words about the
organizational structure of the Raymond Buddhist Church
and the religious ceremonies accompanying that structure
would be of value. The other Buddhist churches with a
predominant Japanese congregation have similar structures
and ceremonies.

First, the organizational structure - The Buddhist
Church is referred to in Japanese as the Bukkyokai.
This term is used to describe the umbrella organization
of a particular church. It consists of representatives

502

from various groups within a church. The Bukkyokai in
Raymond, thus, comprises five groups:

1. The Ho-on-kai (first generation men),
2. The Fujin-kai (first generation women),
3. The YABA (Young Adult Buddhist Association made
   up of young married couples),
4. The Youth Group, and
5. The Sunday School students.

With the exception of the Sunday School students, representatives are sent to the Bukkyokai (central board)
where all the problems related to the church are discussed. In reality, however, the Youth Group is represented by the YABA. Any resolution which has been proposed
by the Bukkyokai is reported back to each of the smaller
groups, discussed, and the poll of the group is reported
back to the central board. The central board then
tallies the votes, and the resolution gets passed or defeated.

The minister of the church is in charge of all religious affairs. He is responsible for all Sunday services and special services held throughout the year.
On Sundays, the congregation comes together for a
family service. The first portion of the service is
oriented to the English speaking people and the latter
portion is oriented to the Japanese speaking people.
Traditionally, a Buddhist sutra was chanted by the
whole congregation in Chinese, but recently, the sutra
has been translated into English, and the young children chant it in English. A sermon is given in both
English and Japanese.

Aside from the regular Sunday Services, there are
special services held throughout the year. They are
as follows:

1. Shu-sho-e - New Years Service, held on January 1st.
2. Nehan-e - Nirvana Day Service, held in February.
3. Nigan-e - Equinox Day Service, held twice yearly
             at the times of the spring and autumn
             equinox.
4. Hanamatsuri - Buddha's Birthday Service, held in
                 April.
5. Fubo-no-hi - Parent's Day Service: to express
                gratitude to one's parents, held in
                May.

6. <u>Gotan-e</u> - Shinran's Birthday Service, held in May.
7. <u>Church Picnic Service</u> - held on picnic site in
   July or August.
8. <u>Obon-e</u> - Memorial Day Service: to express one's
   gratitude for the indebtedness to those
   who have passed the Buddha's teaching on
   to those who are still alive.
9. <u>Ho-on-ko</u> - Memorial Day Service for Shinran, held
   in December.
10. <u>Joya-e</u> - New Year's Eve Service: held at midnight
    on New Year's Eve. The Church gong is
    struck 108 times, symbolizing the 108
    emotions which man possesses.

Before World War II, it was also customary to celebrate
the Emperor's birthday, although the Emperor had no formal
connection with Buddhism. Celebrations take place on
the 10th, 15th, 20th, 50th and 100th year anniversary of
a church. On those occasions, a special guest minister
is invited to deliver the sermon. In some instances,
two or more guest ministers may be invited.

VI. Epilogue

The old building, which now leans a bit with age, still
stands on the Main Street of Raymond. It has played an
influential role in the development of Buddhism in
Southern Alberta and in Canada. Will it withstand
another war? Will it continue to exert the same kind
of influence as it has done in the past? It stands
quietly, smiling at the people who go by. In its book-
case stand books on Buddhism published by the Buddhist
Society of London, England. What will its role be in
the development of Buddhism from the Eastern quarters
instead of the Western quarters as in the past?

FOOTNOTES

1. The six ministers were R. Hirahara, S. Asaka, S. Ikuta, Y. Kawamura, T. Tsuji and H. Matsubayashi. Prior to their evacuation the situation was as follows:

    In Vancouver:

    > Honpa Buddhist Temple - 3 ministers
    > Fairview Buddhist Temple - 1 minister
    > Kitsilano Buddhist Temple - no minister

    In the outlying areas were:

    > Steveston Buddhist Temple - 1 minister
    > New Westminister Buddhist Temple - 1 minister who served North Surrey, Queensborough and Aldergrove
    > Maple Ridge Buddhist Temple - 1 minister who served Port Hammand, Haney, Whonock, Mission City, Ruskin and Pitt Meadows
    > Roystone Buddhist Temple, on Vancouver Island - 1 minister who served Cumberland and Duncan

    Still further out were:

    > The Kelowna Buddhist Temple, served by the Vancouver ministers, and
    > The Raymond Buddhist Temple, which by 1930 had its own minister.

2. Mr. Matsubayashi was interned and then deported and Mr. Tsuji evacuated to Slocan City and subsequently settled in Toronto.

3. In the home of Kyojun Iwasa.

4. In addition to these two and Mr. Iwasa the leaders were Tanesaburo Kosaka, Eita Sonomura, Takejiro Koyata, Kisaboro Sugimoto and Buhachi Nishimura.

5. S. Motoyama.

6. This document was designed and written by Mrs. Toshiko Moriyama.

7. When war broke out Takashi Tsuji was studying in
    Japan and only just returned to Canada before Pearl
    Harbour. Ensei Nekoda was interned in Slocan City
    and joined the Rev. Shinjo Ikuta as minister in
    Raymond on February 4, 1950. Leslie Kawamura served
    from 1962 to 1972, when he left to study under
    Herbert Guenther at the Far Eastern Studies Depart-
    ment, the University of Saskatchewan. Nobuyuki
    Kasagi came from Kagoshima, Japan, to replace him.

8. In Picture Butte, Diamond City, Taber, Coaldale,
    Barnwell and in Raymond the population more than
    doubled.

9. The main consideration seems to have been that those
    against the new constitution would otherwise be
    left without the services of a minister.

THEOLOGICAL PERSPECTIVES ON NATIONALISM

ANTONIO R. GUALTIERI's paper first appeared in the Anglo-Welsh Review 22:49 (1973). He writes on issues arising from the thought of Wilfred Cantwell Smith and teaches religious ethics and world religions at Carleton University.

RÉSUMÉ

Les symboles de la tradition chrétienne, les concepts de l'histoire, de la société et de l'individu nous offrent une norme, un impératif moral vis-à-vis du nationalisme. En général, le nationalisme semble opposé à la foi chrétienne qui au nom de l'amour, embrasse toutes les races, toutes les nations. Cependant, en vue de l'empiétement américaine sur le Canada une compréhension de la justification chrétienne du nationalisme devient décisive. Il est possible que l'abandon de la souveraineté canadienne soit une folie et même un manque de responsabilité morale.

Il s'agit de bien comprendre ce que c'est le nationalisme. Ce n'est pas l'impérialisme. Ce n'est pas non plus quelque chose qui va contre un vrai internationalisme. Pour bien saisir le concept, on nous offre une comparaison entre une théologie des religions et une théorie des relations internationales. Longtemps, on voyait le Christianisme comme l'unique, vraie religion. Aujourd'hui, par contre on a tendance à voir toutes les religions comme une seule. Ce point de vue, cependant, néglige les différences profondes qui enrichissent d'une manière fondamentale l'existence humaine. Entre ces deux opinions extrémistes, Gualtieri nous propose un troisième alternatif : le syncrétisme fonctionnel. Chaque religion fonctionne d'une manière positive à créer un concept valable de l'individu et de la société. Peu à peu, néanmoins, une société globale surgit. Tant qu'elle surgira, chaque religion doit contribuer à la religion éventuelle de cette société future. Sur ces entrefaites, des histoires nationales, comme des religions différentes doivent être respectées. Un vrai internationalisme humain ne se construit qu'à base de différence dans la famille de l'homme.

ANTONIO R. GUALTIERI

Towards a Theological Perspective on Nationalism[1]

Methodological and Contextual Preface

The premise on which I conduct religion study is that
religious traditions are, in a wide sense, symbol systems whose function it is to induce a selfhood in which
transformation is effected from an old self perceived as
broken and awry to a new identity of ultimate integration and well-being. In short, religions, by varying
strategies, seek for their participants a passage from
plight to redemption. Somewhat more specifically, the
religious intention is a personal state in which in one
sense or another, alienation yields to reconciliation,
chaos to meaning, guilt to forgiveness, insecurity to
acceptance, death to life, bondage to freedom.

Implied in this idea of human transformation is the
adoption of new sets of commitments which provide norms
for self and society. In Malinowski's phrase, religions provide "charters for action;" in Geertz's terms
religious symbol systems provide "model's for reality"
(because they are grounded in "models of reality").

The essay which follows is first, and most importantly,
an illustration of how the symbols of a particular tradition - in this case basic conceptions of history,
society and the self in the Christian tradition - provide a norm, a moral imperative, for the question of
nationalism. For the purpose of this essay it is not
necessary to consider the question whether the Christian
doctrines about history, society and man represent
literal facts (i.e., God really was redemptively present
at the Red Sea; the early Christian was factually called
by God to be a member of his missionary people, the
church) or are existential myths.

The present point is that regardless of which interpretation is made, one who accepts these doctrines,
i.e., has faith in them, is committed to adopting certain correlative attitudes and acting in a way appropriate to them.

The second major section of this essay explores the
connection between a theology of religions and a theory
of the proper relations between nations. The thesis
defended there is that a valid Christian theological

508

interpretation of mankind's religious diversity provides a highly illuminating paradigm for understanding mankind's national, cultural diversity.

This essay may be approached in two ways. It is clearly animated by prescriptive and hortatory consideration since it deals with the transformative dimension of religious phenomena as it pertains to social and cultural existence. Accordingly, those who share the basic symbol system of the Christian tradition may be persuaded that this particular application to nations inherently follows from the theological premises and is, therefore, morally normative.

But secondly, this study may also be read in a more neutral way as a description of how a particular religious community - the Christian - perceives, or should perceive, the phenomenon of societies and cultures on the basis of its own tradition's presuppositions. It is widely assumed that the proper duty of the academic study of religion is to attend only to this second, descriptive task and, if one is investigating normative concerns about what is true and what is right, to do so only in an objective, unengaged way.

I regard this as a mistaken truncation of the scholar's vocation and in any case a self-deceived interpretation. For it ignores what in manifold explicit or subtle or disguised forms is done in any case, namely, the promulgation of what is really true about existence (and not merely what so and so says is true about it); what is in fact good, and what is in reality the right course of action appropriate to that good (and not only what an historical catalogue of figures have claimed to be so).

I deem it more intellectually honest and humanly more helpful to bring such normative judgments, hazardous as they are, out into the open where in the dialogical forum of competing interpretations they may win their way, succumb to better views or contribute to a wiser synthesis. Consequently, the confession is readily made at the outset that the proposition that history, community, and the earthly self are more real and valuable than abstract ideas, individualism and angelism corresponds more truly to the way things really are.

But those still offended by the spectacle of openly parti-pris academics, can still, with a slight shift of perspective, see this material as a description of a particular way of relating theological symbols to social problems.

This piece was written out of the background of the sale by The United Church of Canada of which I am a member of the oldest publishing house in Canada, the Ryerson Press, to an American firm. It is my conviction that this sale was undertaken without adequate understanding of the Christian theological justification of nationhood. My article was an attempt to provide such a theological warrant which, I feel, might have prevented the sale of the Press which, while owned by the Church, had a much wider cultural significance since it was perhaps the chief publisher of Canadian poetry and novels as well as one of the main producers of school textbooks. But although this statement is an apologia for the Church's responsibility for defending the right sort of Canadian nationalism, especially in the face of American encroachments, its arguments apply to similar expressions of nationalism that are so marked a feature of contemporary history. I have in mind, for example, the Vietnamese, the Irish, the Jews and Palestinians, the Welsh, and the French Canadian Québecois experiences.

It must be conceded at the outset that to speak of a theology of nationalism must certainly strike many Christians at first glance as a logical contradiction. Given the universalistic understanding of the Christian Church, and further, the Christian imperative to love men across all social, cultural, economic and sexual boundaries, it must seem that nationalism is a regrettable violation of Christian premises and hopes for mankind. I can still clearly recall the difficulty with which I preached thanksgiving sermons where it was customary to draw attention not only to God's beneficence in nature but also to his gracious acts in the national life of the country. This reservation was reinforced by the nationalistic tone of some thanksgiving hymns. These reservations were heightened at Remembrance Day services. Influenced as I was at that time by my excitement in grasping the supranational and supraracial character of the Christian fellowship, it seemed to me that these nationalistic allusions were a regrettable reversion to an Erastian conception of the Church.

Furthermore, there was the strong influence of Toynbee's analysis of modern history as a period of the emergence of divisive pseudo-religions, chief amongst

510

which was nationalism. Toynbee condemned this modern
nationalism as a form of collective pride - 'nosism' as
he called it.

It must, therefore, seem strange to some to invoke
certain insights and presuppositions of the biblical
tradition as a justification for national affirmation.
Yet, in what follows I wish to do precisely that: I
want to suggest that not only is there a form of
nationalism which is permissible for the Christian, but
that its affirmation is, in fact, a moral imperative in
the exercise of the prophetic, ethical function of the
Church. What follows is a brief enumeration of some
biblical assumptions that serve as a warrant for affirming a vibrant and humane nationhood.

1. The Importance and Worth of History

Among the several biblical insights and motifs that
help us understand the meaning and validity of nations
is the centrality of history. The biblical writers
affirm the reality, importance and value of history.
The biblical perspective contrasts with certain oriental
philosophical doctrines which deprecate history as at
best a relatively real process, characterized by
suffering, ignorance and limitation; and which needs to
be transcended in order to find salvation in a non-
historical realm of pure being, consciousness and bliss.

The central biblical authors are seized by the importance of history because of their doctrine of God and
of his salvation. They hold that God is the sovereign
ruler of history and, though transcendent, is yet immanent in the historical process seeking to achieve his
purpose to save mankind. History is viewed as the
arena in which God acts to unfold his purposes, to
reveal himself and to judge and redeem. Though the
stress falls on the history of a particular nation,
Israel, the histories of other nations are also seen as
the result of a dialectic between the divine intention
and human response. The empires of Assyria, Babylon
and Persia serve, though unwittingly, the historical
objectives of the living God known, the biblical witness
maintains, most intimately by Israel.

This assertion of the meaningfulness of history has
certain implications for our understanding of nationalism. Nations are historical realities. They are the

consequences of a people's common historical experience
of exploration, conquest, defence, cultural and institutional innovation and development as they aspire and
struggle to carve out a satisfying life. Nations are
bound by common language, institutions, heroes, vocation and destiny, and by loyalty to certain symbols that
have served through the people's history to interpret
their distinctive experience and human existence
generally.

It follows, therefore, that if history is valuable in
the divine perspective, then the history of nations
shares in this general worth. This is not to claim that
all history is of a piece, equally valuable, equally
redemptive; for history is characterized by contradiction and paradox as well as by divine presence and providence. But, history can no longer be devalued as
irrelevant or meaningless in favour of some abstract
notions of universal human essence or transcendent
Being detached from man's historical nature as a creature both shaping and shaped by history. While it is
true that there is a common humanity because of God's
creation of man in His image, this common humanity is
refracted through particular histories which leave
their impress upon it.

2. The Role of Society in Salvation

The second theological insight that illumines our
understanding of nationalism is entailed in the prior
assertion of the importance of history, for national
communities are historical phenomena and, accordingly,
the redemptive role of history implies the value of
those societies. Now, however, I wish to focus on the
biblical idea of society and its place in the salvation
of man.

The Bible's understanding of God's reconciling relationship to mankind is that it operates primarily
through a collectivity of men, and not simply on an
individualistic level. Here we are faced with the
doctrine of corporate election, that is to say, the
choice and utilization by God of a people to receive
the disclosure of His will and commands, and to be
His instrument in disseminating this knowledge to other
nations, and to future generations. The prophetic
interpreters of Israel's history see it primarily as
a relation between God and His people.

Christian theology subsequently appropriated this idea, and in our own century the theology of God's mighty acts amongst His people has had great prominence. Neo-orthodoxy asserts that in the history of the nation of Israel, and subsequently in the history of Jesus and the primitive apostolic community, is contained the redeeming activity of God. This theology, unfortunately, tends to restrict the holy history idea to the social history contained in the Bible. God's saving historical acts are limited to Israel and Christ both in space and time, and the Church's function is to contemporize this revelatory history through its preaching and cultus.

We have already noted, however, that even within the Old Testament tradition there is the understanding that God works among other collectivities, among other nations, contemporary with Israel, even though it is maintained that God's normative activity is among the covenant nation, Israel.

Now it is necessary to extend the idea of holy history in time. It must be recognized that God continues to work in the history of other nations and cultures, inasmuch as he is the living God who is never absent from His creation and from man, the summit of His creation. Accordingly, all national histories are potentially salvation history in as much as the ever present living God works through men and their institutions in our own time.[2] The spiritually significant question always is whether these are responses to the divine will and serviceable to His saving purposes.

The theology of the Church has usually sought to deal with this problem of the spiritual significance of nations by claiming that the Church supersedes the nation Israel and that thereafter secular national realities have no redemptive significance, this being found only in the new supranational institution of the Church. I should be the first to acknowledge, in principle, the glory of the Church as a community that is not limited by racial or notional or cultural boundaries. In a sense, the Church provides a pledge of that universal fellowship of men where all are bound together by the bonds of mutual respect, help and love.

But it must be noted that the Church does not obliterate certain natural distinctions among men. It is true that in Christ, in the body of the Church, the distinctions of race, economics and sex no longer

indicate spiritual superiority; they are not barriers
to entry into the new comprehensive fellowship. But
neither does the Church require the obliteration of
these differences, as is most obvious in the sexual
instance, but is little less evident in the other
differentiations that naturally emerge among men as
they live out their history in distinctive times and
places and conditions.

The Church at its best has recognized this fact.
When an obligation was felt to evangelize among alien
cultures, its most progressive elements sought to indi-
genize the Christian Gospel so that it would be suited
to the distinctive cultures amongst which it sought to
take root. In our own time the most severe criticism
that has been levelled against the Church's missionary
enterprise is that it has often sought to export not
only the Christian community's insight into God and the
meaning of life, but also a foreign Western culture
which, while supplanting and destroying archaic cultures, was not able in most instances successfully to
replace them. Moreover, to argue that the historical
activity of God is contained entirely in the Church
which supersedes the old Israel is, in fact, to eva-
cuate the greater part of world history of divine
presence and activity. This, of course, has implications for the doctrine of God. It collapses God into
a rather diminutive being whose realm is limited to
the religious one of the Church. Without minimizing
the role of the Church, as perpetuator of a tradition
that points men to the divine ground of their lives
and recapitulates paradigmatic revelatory events in its
cultus, it must, in the interest of fidelity to the
biblical understanding of God, be insisted that He
continues to work in the secular history of nations as
well as in the religious history of the Church.

3. Respect for Culture as Corollary of Love for Persons

My third theological point is in some respects the
most important: it is an implication of the scriptural
mandate to love other persons and proceeds by recognizing the role that history and society play in forming
the self. When we adequately perceive the role of
society and history in shaping the self, we see that
persons do not exist as some de-historicized ideal
essence. Instead, their selfhood - their perception
or reality, their values, their interpretive symbols -

514

is in great measure shaped by the historical tradition
of the society in which they participate.

Taken as a whole, the Biblical tradition, while not
denying the aspect of autonomy, acknowledges that
personality is corporate, rooted ineradicably in the
career of our fathers. In the past, such formative
traditions have usually been religious traditions but
these do not exhaust the multiform participation of
men in history and society. Men also share in, affect,
and are influenced by their national cultures. In the
present period of increasing secularism, that is, of
separation of religious traditions from national cultures, we must recognize the growing part played in the
formation of selfhood by national heritages.[3] These
cultures transmit to their participants a way of understanding themselves and viewing the world. Moreover,
they supply their members with symbols that allow them
to express creatively their selfhood.

It follows, therefore, that to assault a culture is
not simply an attack on an external congeries of institutions or mores or rituals (sacred or secular); it is
also an assualt on the individual persons who have been
nurtured by that tradition and whose understanding of
life has been moulded by it. The attack on a culture
also deprives its participants of the historic and traditional symbols that have been found emotionally and
intellectually fruitful in understanding and relating
to existence. We have seen this often enough, especially in the encounter of dominant while, technological
culture with primitive cultures. Much of our own
native population has been reduced to alcoholism and
indolence and meaninglessness by the destruction of the
culture which shaped their lives and allowed them to
understand their place in the cosmic scheme of things.[4]
George Ernest Wright pointed out how the assaults on
Kikuyu culture by British colonialists resulted in
fragmentation of personality, mental sickness and
alcoholism.

To preserve a viable culture is an act of love for
personality, whose sacred quality is presupposed by
the biblical tradition.

Christian Situation Ethics

In addition to these more strictly theological insights

515

which validate respect for distinctive cultural identities, there are broader ethical justifications for preserving Canadian independence at this time. It should be remembered that Christian moral decisions are not taken in a vacuum by simple reference to an objective, revealed moral code. Rather, they are situational decisions forged out in the encounter of the divine demand for love with the actual circumstances in which the Christian finds himself. When we apply this ethical direction to the present circumstances of Canadian history we see that Canada is threatened by absorption, culturally, economically, and politically by an American power that shows grave evidence of serious moral decline.

One does not have to search too diligently to see that American society suffers from grave malaise. Its culture is becoming increasingly typified by militarism, racism, savagery, materialism, alienation and imperialism. The evidence is in the Chicago police riots, the widespread failure of school integration, the horror of the Vietnam massacres epitomized by My Lai, the frightening size of the Wallace right-wing support, the alienation of large numbers of young people from the affluent goals of their parents, and still largely uncontrolled pollution.[5] Without exaggerating the health and sanity of Canadian society and without ascribing to Canadians superior moral virtue, it should be observed that the unfolding of history has left positive alternatives open to Canadians in ways that seem not presently available to Americans. In this time of United States sickness and travail it is foolish and indeed morally irresponsible to abandon Canadian sovereignty to the United States, not only for our sakes but ultimately for theirs and for the world's. Otherwise, we shall scarcely be in a position to make a distinctive and useful contribution to a global society.

Demonic and Humane Nationalism

One of the objections frequently encountered in attempting to explain the validity of nationalism is the accusation that nationalism can become divisive and destructive. Usually, this charge goes hand in hand with allusions to the National Socialism of Germany in the thirties and forties. On scrutiny, this objection, though useful as a warning, cannot serve to discredit a realistic and humane nationalism. For on Christian theological premises (and, I should imagine, on most humanistic premises) it is clear that evil is usually the perversion of something that is good. This was the point made by Paul Tillich in his formulation of the concept of the demonic: evil is good gone awry. The natural need for enjoyment of food can turn into gluttony, but we do not for that reason recommend the abolition of eating. Sexual expression can turn into rapacious lust, but we do not advocate becoming celibates. Justifiable satisfaction in one's achievement may be transformed into pharisaic pride, but we do not for that reason encourage the abandonment of work. The Church as a loving relationship can be perverted into the Grand Inquisitor, but this does not logically entail the destruction of the Church. One could multiply these obvious examples whose application is clear. Nationalism, then, can become demonic, can be twisted into a vehicle of collective egoism and messianic self-assertion. It is the case historically that nationalism has sometimes become imperialistic and has encroached upon the rights and lives of other national groups. But this cannot be taken as justification for the eradication of nationalism. Rather it is a summons to discover and pursue a true nationalism that, at the same time as it allows the retention of distinctive human histories and heritages, seeks to enter into relations of mutual help and respect with other peoples.

Internationalism and Canadian Nationalism

Again, critics of nationalism usually proceed by setting up a dichotomy between nationalism on the one hand and internationalism on the other. Sometimes the terms are slightly altered to read 'economic interdependence' and 'economic isolationism.' In their understanding, internationalism is a good thing; the word is highly charged with connotations of universal brotherhood, fairness, tolerance and openness. Nationalism, on the other hand, is a pejorative term; it indicates those who are fearful of contacts with others, who are envious and spiteful, who are reactionary and isolationist.

The critics' first error lies in their failure to distinguish between nationalisms. They are parti pri on the subject of nationalism and refuse to acknowledge the reality and necessity of an ethically and theologically justifiable nationalism of the sort outlined above. It should be clear that the kind of nationalism

which is espoused here is not that of a messianic superiority that leads to national imperialism but, rather
and more simply, the retention of a historical heritage
which has shaped the life, perspective and values of a
distinct people.

The second false move of the opponents of nationalism
appears when they proceed to identify their position
with the concept 'internationalism,' the advocates of
the Canadian reality, for example, being construed as
'narrow, petty' nationalists.

To those who argue that the affirmation of distinctive
nationalities is a denial of the humane and necessary
spirit of brotherhood across all divisions of national
particularity, it must be replied that the affirmation
of one's distinctive identity, culture and history is
the precondition of a true internationalism. Even
those who aspire ultimately to a true synthesis of dis-
parate cultures and traditions (including religious
traditions) must concede that this wider fusion is
possible only if separate cultures and traditions are
allowed to retain their integrity until the time comes
when they may be offered as a distinctive contribution
to the coming world culture. Accordingly, it is a
moral demand that our energies in this particular moment be directed to the pursuit of national self-
determination and national excellence as the precondition of a responsible and mutually enriching internationalism.

Perhaps this thesis may be further illustrated by the
analogy of person to person relations. There cannot be
true love between persons unless it springs from autonomous individuals who freely will to offer themselves to
the other, in the attainment of a union that is a new
complementary creation. Similarly, different nations
and cultures must secure their identity before they can
contribute their gifts to a syncretistic global culture
and society.

What we are experiencing in Canada today is not the
recrudescence of an obsolete isolationist and idolatrous Canadian nationalism, but rather resistance to
the extension of a depersonalizing and homogenizing
imperialism from the south.

The issue for Canadians is not a choice between a
wicked and reactionary nationalism on the one hand, and

an open and progressive internationalism on the other.
Rather, in the present undermining of Canadian sovereignty and identity by the United States and its Canadian
collaborators, they face the encroachment of an imperial
nationalism. Canadian nationalists seek the attainment
of a true internationalism, one which presupposes the
continued existence of independent communities of
peoples faithful to their historical traditions, their
cultural heritages, their national heroes and symbols.
Only on the basis of this willingness to allow national
groups to preserve their identity can there be that
mutual fecundation which is the glory of genuine internationalism. It must be seen that the Canadian
nationalists are the true internationalists. They wish
to affirm their national history, culture, and expectations for the future, not out of any chauvinistic
superiority or sense of messianic obligation. Instead,
they seek the preservation of the heritage of their
people in order to understand themselves better and to
relate with other people in a hoped-for and eventual
global sharing of historic experience and insight.

The American continentalists who subvert the efforts
of Canadian nationalists to retain their identity and
sovereignty are - their rhetoric of internationalism
notwithstanding - the agents not of internationalism
but of a depressing cultural, economic, and political
domination of the smaller nations by the stronger.

Theological Reflection of the History of Religions

It may help to understand my views on nationalism if
I explain, at least in part, how I came to them. I
have studied and teach the history of religions.
Besides that, being a member of the Christian Church
and a practising theologian, I concentrated my studies
on what is sometimes called missiology, that is, the
investigation into Christian attitudes and actions
towards men of other religious beliefs.

1. Religious Imperialism

It is possible to discern several main attitudes that
have been held by Church theologians towards other
religious cultures. The first is a view of radical
displacement, or alternatively, religious imperialism.
On this view, Christian faith and tradition is regarded

519

as the only true faith, as the only divinely revealed
message of salvation. All others are in error, either
the result of deliberate falsification, the products of
the devil, or the tragic results of man's projection of
his own mundane being and self-therapy onto a cosmic
scale. Consequently, the holders of this view feel
obligated to engage in a missionary enterprise whose
function is to replace all other religious cultures by
the one true religion, Christianity.

I think it is safe to say that this view is not held
by most of the historic Christian denominations at the
present time. The reasons for the shift in attitude
are many; perhaps they are to be ascribed as much to a
sense of bewilderment and aimlessness resulting from
the failure of this attempt to evangelize the world, as
from any more profound theological motives. In my
judgement, a sound Christian theology that takes into
account the new situation of knowledge of other faiths
provided by the history of religions since the nineteenth century, would invalidate the old Christian
imperialist strategy of the displacing of other faiths
by the Christian.

One can readily see the application of this to my
understanding of national cultures. If it is wrong to
destroy religious cultures by attempting to supplant
them with the Christian tradition, is it not possible
that this provides an analogy of our attitudes towards
national cultures? They, no less than religious cultures, ought to be respected for their distinctiveness
and particular richness and encouraged to exist in the
face of all dominating and eradicating national
imperialisms.

2. Equivalence Theories of Religion

A second view that is held by some theologians of
religions is that all religions are essentially the
same: they all teach the same thing, it is alleged.
In attempts to substantiate this view, comparative
tables of the teaching from the various faiths were
drawn up. Set side by side, one could see the universality of the golden rule: Do unto others as you would
have them do unto you. Observers were encouraged to
believe that beneath the overlay of strange rituals
and language there was a universal essence of religion,
usually understood to be a uniformity of teaching. But

the careful history of religion suggests that this view is, if not absolutely false, superficial. It forces the similarities; it fails to see that the different religious traditions are the products of distinctive insights and forms of expression peculiarly adapted to the cultural, geographic and psychological conditions of their participants. Although in some functional way there are universals in the various religions, they must not be falsified by claiming that they all say the same thing.

Again, the relevance of this to an understanding of nationalism is evident. Peoples are not all the same as some superficial exponents of universality declare. They do have their distinctive heritages, languages, world views, and symbols. Though this is not to deny that a common humanity exists in dialectical tension with this historical particularity, it must be noted that this common humanity does not exist as a pure Platonic form, but is always refracted through the particularities of time and space.

A variant of the equivalence theory of religions seeks to eliminate religious traditions altogether. In the interests of affirming sacred presence, diffused in a general way in all worldhistory or available to the human consciousness regardless of its particular historical placing, this view maintains that the accidental, historical development of religious traditions must be abandoned. Then all human beings - regardless of where or when they live, regardless of the economic, political and cultural pressures that play upon their minds - will be open to the constant radio beams of a non-historical divine reality. Attractive as this may appear to some, it simply does not do justice to the facts. And, the facts are that in spite of the propensity of religious traditions to become demonic, to become ends in themselves, to become the instruments of exploitation of the mighty over the weak and of the authoritarian over the gullible, they nevertheless still function in the lives of many people to mediate that divine presence. Accordingly, religious history and its capacity to transmit the divine must be taken into account.

The implications of this for an understanding of nationalism are also evident. One meets universalists whose wish to achieve world brotherhood prompts them not only to minimize the importance of national

distinctions but also to eradicate them. But this intention, even if it were theoretically justifiable (and
I think it is not inasmuch as it denies the existential,
historical nature of man) would hardly be desirable.
For it would result not in the millenium of harmony but
in the achievement of a drab, uniform, undifferentiated
humanity which could not reciprocally enrich the lives
of its members by the contrast of their distinctive
historical experiences.

One can readily see that an understanding of the
nature and validity of distinctive religious traditions
and cultures sheds considerable light on our understanding of particular national cultures. More than this,
such insight serves to recommend the human and theological legitimacy of struggling to preserve these local-
isms and particularities that enrich the total pattern
of human existence - at least until such time as a true
fusion of cultures becomes possible.

3. Functional Syncretism

My own theological view of religious diversity may be
termed "functional syncretism," by which two meanings
are intended. The first is that the various great religions of the world function, in their particular
cultural and historical contexts, to induce and express
a selfhood in which God is present to their participants.

On this view there is no question of seeking to repu-
diate the revelational quality of faiths other than
one's own; nor is there any cheap attempt to purchase
good will by asserting the identity of their content or
the irrelevance of historical uniqueness. Instead the
various faiths are generally understood as diverse but
valid media for the transcendent in the lives of their
respective adherents, in the particular situations in
which they find themselves.

My position is called syncretistic, secondly, because
it envisages the emergence of a synthetic
religious tradition as men move toward a global society.
The need for a serviceable religious tradition in such
a new world would be met by an open colloquy among men
of diverse faiths with an eye to fusing, under the
divine pressure, various elements from their respective
traditions into a new creation, through which God could
disclose his will and presence to men in their altered

circumstances. Such a syncretistic alternative, admittedly, visionary and contingent on the development in fact of a common world culture that would demand a new, relevant and correlative religion. It serves, however, as a challenge here and now for members of different religious communities to incorporate such elements from other traditions as are useful in generating a spirit-filled selfhood.

These reflections upon religious pluralism provide analogies for understanding the direction to be taken on the debate over nationalism. On the one hand the legitimacy of distinctive national histories has to be respected just as does the redemptive function of religious traditions other than the Christian. On the other hand, isolationism - religious or national - is ethically unacceptable in a world growing ever closer. But just as superficial theories equating religions or dismissing specific histories are ultimately to be rejected in favour of a syncretistic exchange among believers, so is an obsolescent internationalism of universal essences (e.g., political animal, workers, consumer, socialism, world order) to be eschewed. Rather, the aim to be attained is a dialogical internationalism which respects historical particularities and seeks a mutually enriching relation that builds on these distinctions.

FOOTNOTES

1. With the exception of most of the preface and a few minor emendations, the present text is that of the Anglo-Welsh Review in Spring, 1973.

2. Lest this be thought an expedient trotted out to serve the immediate purposes of Canadian nationalism, I shouldpoint out that this line of argument was advanced in a thanksgiving sermon I preached at Vassar College, Poughkeepsie, N.Y., in 1966 entitled, "Is American History Salvation History?" At that time I asked, in a section discussing 'The Analogy of Israelite History with American History': "Is there any salvation history in American History? Is it a locus of the divine activity to reconcile

523

men to him and to one another?"

There was a time when the answer would have been "No", for the simple reason that it was impossible to conceive of any salvation history outside the Biblical history. But suppose now that God's redemptive work is not restricted to the history of Israel and the Church? Suppose...that Christ transcends the Church and is present wherever we discern creative attempts to actualize the new humanity of reconciled brothers? This general thesis that broadens the concept of holy history to include (though dialectically) what has often been characterized as profane or secular history does not, of course, preclude a negative answer in particular cases.

3. Cf., "The new spirit running through Western Europe in the eighteenth century was to change all this. Terrestrial communities were no longer built up around a god, but only within the framework of a state. The world of religious communities began to disappear, to be replaced by the world of nations." Maxime Rodinson, Israel and the Arabs (Middlesex, England, Penguin Books, 1970), p. 9.

4. This judgement was confirmed during a study I undertook in the summer of 1971 on 'Indigenization of Christianity Among the Indians and Eskimo of the Mackenzie'.

5. While the examples I have cited in evidence of the American malaise are obviously dated, I have not bothered to amend the text on the assumption that plus ça change plus c'est la même chose. If I were writing this piece today I would allude by way of illustration to such things as Watergate and the corruption of American political leaders, the American involvement in the overflow of the democratically elected Allende government in Chile, C.I.A. drug experiments on unwilling subjects, the development and deployment of the cruise missile and the neutron bomb.

524

NATIONALISM: PROBLEMS AND PERSPECTIVES

MICHEL DESPLAND's paper is a revised version of a public lecture given at Carleton University in 1973. He is Professor of Religion at Concordia University and author of <u>Kant on History and Religion</u> (1973).

RÉSUMÉ

Le rôle de la religion dans la quête de l'identité canadienne était souligné par un bon nombre d'historiens francophones et anglophones au Canada. Aujourd'hui, on a un point de vue plus tempéré et on souligne par contre l'origine non-religieuse de notre pays, l'influence plutôt modérée de l'église dans l'histoire canadienne. Ce deuxième point de vue nous amène à une crise dans le concept de la tradition nationale et le rôle des églises. D'un côté, la religion est liée avec la rationalité, c'est-à-dire, avec un Dieu qui communique avec l'homme par la conscience, la compréhension. La religion nous appelle donc au sacrifice du moi au nom d'une perfection qui se réalisera au-delà du présent. De l'autre côté, l'identité nationale se construit des goûts et des amours acquis. La politique est l'assertion de soi-même, coûte que coûte, la simulation étant quelques fois essentielle au pouvoir politique. Il y aura toujours donc une brèche entre l'identité nationale et la religion chrétienne, entre la vie de la foi et la vie politique qui la dernière, aujourd'hui, interprète et crée l'identité canadienne.

Confondre ensemble la religion et la politique c'est créer une sorte d'unité primitive qui nécessite la fin de la religion chrétienne et de la politique démocratique. Etre chrétien et vouloir garder une démocratie nous obligent par contre à créer et à reconnaître des liens artificiels entre la religion et la politique. Quoique les deux ne s'engrènent pas, les deux représentent des aspects différents de l'être humain. Chacune a un rôle dans le développement des traditions nationales.

MICHEL DESPLAND

Religion and the Quest for National Identity: Problems and Perspectives

Many today may very well doubt that there are clear links between the religious life of people and their quest for national identity. For one thing some will think of churches when they hear of religious life and will not associate very vital cultural developments with them. And most will think that in any case the quest for national identity is an aspect of human life only tenuously related, if at all, to the aspirations and experiences of religion.

This was not always the case. Not so long ago nearly all thought of Canada as a Christian country and did not doubt that the Christian faith shaped the Canadian identity. Our libraries still contain the works of clerical schools of historiography. Most people are familiar with the work of French-Canadian Abbés like J.P.A. Ferland and Lionel Groulx. Their history books contain strong claims for the positive contributions of the Church in laying the basis and ensuring the survival of the French-Canadian nation. Their patriotic speeches did not hesitate to refer to the high purposes which Divine Providence had for the French-Canadian race. Such clerical views are also found in English Canada, although mainly in an earlier generation. It was the Reverend George M. Grant who contributed with Ocean to Ocean (1873) something of the patriotic fervour that was lacking in the BNA Act.[1] Not so long ago however A.R.M. Lower made a contribution to the theology that was so popular in the good days of NATO by stating in This Most Famous Stream that "take our English-speaking Protestantism and its derivatives from the modern world and the major creative force left is Russian Communism."[2] The Anglophone side thus also had its voices who based the grandeur of Canada on the plan of a providential God who seemed to be most efficient when he did his work through English-speaking Protestants. Interestingly enough, I suspect that each one of these messianic views is currently more accepted in the other part of Canada than in the one for which it was originally composed. Lionel Groulx is not taken very seriously among Québec nationalists any more but many Québécois suspect that the English-speaking majority still believes in its divine mandate to guarantee the safety of the high seas or the airways.

526

Inflated and clerical accounts of the role of the churches, catholic or protestant, in the edification of the nation, are no longer accepted; more sober views prevail. Church historians themselves now emphasize the rather non-religious origins of Canada. "Canada was not founded like New England as an experiment in Government by the godly, nor was it colonised to any great extent by religious enthusiasts. Most of our ancestors were attracted here by such tangible assets as fish, furs, gold or wheat (...). The influence of the Christian churches is a hypothesis of which, apparently, a Canadian historian has felt little need."[3] A whole library of books on religion in America has won an enviable place among U.S.A. historical works. There the most hardened secularist historian will feature the religious origins of the nation. No similar Canadian books have emerged. The Race Question in Canada of André Siegfried (1906) began with a discussion of the role of the churches in the "psychological formation of the two races."[4] Insightful though the book is, and appreciated though it has become, Siegfried has not become the De Tocqueville of Canada and not many think of Canada as a uniquely significant lab where an experiment is being pursued blending religion and life in an original way.[5]

This situation may partly reflect the state of Canadian historiography, where for a long time little attention was given to intellectual history, but it has deeper roots as well. Messianism, religious or secular, has not been a strong strain in Canadian life.[6] As a matter of fact we may even contradict the whole clerical school and affirm that the religious traditions in Canada had a moderating influence upon the development of national feeling. For one thing the churches were at least as prone as the rest of Canada to look abroad for leadership. I even suspect there has been here some mutual reinforcement. French-Canadian Catholics responded to the role of London by exalting the role of Rome. English Protestants nurtured their European ties as if they were afraid of being left without allies in the contest with Romanism. Moreover, the churches cultivated a sense of the higher loyalties. Claude Ryan has stated that religion may help to contain "the ferment of nationalism within reasonable boundaries."[7] While Abbé Groulx was writing his nationalist histories, his contemporary, Father Louis Lachance o.p, writing on Nationalisme et Religion (1936) marshalled all the resources of thomism

to affirm the supremacy of intelligence and of faith
over immediate patriotic feelings. He concluded that
in those states where more than one nationality live in
a single political order, the first moral demands to be
addressed to the State are those of justice rather than
those of nationalism.[8] The pronouncements of the
United Church have done much to chart the way towards
social justice in domestic affairs. They have not
fanned the embers of Canadian nationalism. The Québec
bishops are constantly reproached by the more conservative wing of the nationalist movement for pussy-footing
on the question of national survival.

The great thing about the Canadian identity, wrote
Northrop Frye, is that it is yet uncreated or that we
have failed to achieve it.[10] Frank Underhill referred
to our "habit of carrying on our communal affairs at a
level at which ideas never quite emerged into an articulate life of their own."[11] Many Canadians, like the
Swiss, probably find it safer never to allow their
thoughts about each other to come to full consciousness
and full expression.[12]

While we might agree that the Canadian Churches have
not contributed as much as some thought to nation
building, we should readily allow, as John Webster
Grant points out above, that they have done much for
the shaping of the national character. A certain
version of Christian virtues has gone into the making
of the reticent virtues of Canadians. So we could
rehearse the list of ministers and priests who have
left their mark on our country. Our history is full of
Presbyterian ministers who turn novelists, Baptist
ministers who become army recruiters or socialist premiers, Methodist ministers' sons who become Nobel Peace
Prize winners, economists born in Elgin County who take
calvinist wit to yet drier heights, cardinals who go to
Africa to heal lepers while their brothers go to Ottawa
to become governors-general, not to mention priests
who get involved in building - or rerouting - railways.
One could prolong many of the lines already drawn in
A.R.M. Lower Canadians in the Making.[13]

II

But out topic is today's quest for national identity.
Many Canadians are not content with the prospect of just
letting national feeling burn quietly with its faint

glow, trusting that there is still enough warmth for a
blaze should the need arise. For many the national
identity is being eroded, or has yet to be found, and
they believe deliberate efforts are necessary to seek
it or to provide backbone for a national culture.

A national culture is of course a rich and complex
thing and it will be wise to acknowledge that it contains both conscious and unconscious elements.[14] I
might also add that we cannot grasp the nature of a
national culture unless we have a sense of at least
three of its constituent parts: the national feeling,
the intellectual tradition (with the literary tradition
taking now the lion's share) and the political ethos.
In each of these aspects there are abundant signs of
unease. Rehearsing the symptoms is now a familiar
litany. Children seem to be inadequately exposed to
these traditional influences. The literati are doing
very well right now, thank you, but they thrive on the
sense of being precarious. The political constitution
is under debate and every fresh discussion renews
division. Relationships between the two linguistic
groups are more unsettled than ever. American impact
on Canadian economic life remains excessive. And our
whole cultural life seems increasingly shaped by forces
that are commonly called "international" or "multi-
national" and about which it is wise to repeat that
there is nothing genuinely cosmopolitan. There are
indeed many reasons to believe that a strengthened
sense of nationhood would be a gain.

The problem of our (uncertain) national identity is
compounded by the problem of our (divergent) awareness
of it and response to it. For it must be allowed that
there is in Canada a variety of nationalisms that map
out programmes of action. There is French Canadian
nationalism; it shows all signs of being taken over by
a powerful Québécois political movement and there is
little doubt now about what it wants. English Canadian
nationalism is much more fragmented. Some English
Canadian nationalism thrives upon hatred of all things
French. Others applaud Québec's "liberation." Yet
others are convinced that one serious talk (with the
help of interpreters?) between the "genuine" English
Canadian nationalists and Québécois nationalists would
resolve all differences. Finally, a brand of English-
Canadian nationalism seeks to compromise and maintain
an alliance with those francophones who currently
believe in Canada. (These are mainly by politicians

and élites close to the Liberal Party of CCanada. Richly
endowed with routinised charisma, they are short of the
effervescent variety.) With this complex picture,
activist nationalist programmes often cancel each
other or exacerbate each other.

Canadianism therefore is not easily aroused in a
divided country and is not very helpful when aroused.
We cannot preach ourselves into a healthier future.
Some course has to be found between mere tub-thumping
and confident abandonment to the idea that our peculiar
climate will keep making a nation out of us. Cultural
strengths have to be nurtured and developed. That
means artistic activity, literary activity, educational
activity, but also laborious economic endeavour and
political common sense and savvy. All that means much
spirit and energy, much consensus and cooperation, the
very virtues that are supposed to flow more easily in a
healthy national culture.

III

What links are there between today's quest for
national identity and religion, keeping in mind the
fact that we are in a secular, pluralistic society?
The cultural life of all groups and any religious life,
I submit, have in common a preoccupation with belonging
and with self-realisation in the context of belonging.
National and religious communities both strive to enhance the sense of self and the sense of participation.
Both put forward the claims of "higher" loyalties and
offer to the self the support of an encompassing authority. National rhetoric and religious rhetoric are
very similar. Both play upon memory and hope. ("Héritage et projet" was the subtitle of the Dumont Report
(1971) and the phrase has been applied both to the life
of the church and that of the "nation québécoise.")[15]
Some find it natural to belong to both a national and a
religious community. Others experience a tension. Some
finally believe there is a mutual exclusion. In the
modern context much nationalism is secular or anti-
religious and offers itself as able to deliver a personal fulfilment that religion forever postpones to
another world. (Jacques Grand'Maison also stresses that
in the last two centuries politics have tended to control more and more of life while religion has become an
increasingly private matter.)[16]

530

The student of politics and the student of religion,
if they share a humanistic perspective, will thus have
much in common as they observe men's wrestling with the
tensions of their social life and their quest for meaning. But we have already noticed that our Christian
theological tradition has not maintained an even-handed
scholarly balance in its estimate of the phenomenon of
nationhood and nationalism. It is clear that in the
thirties the theological world perceived nationalism in
largely negative terms. It seemed accepted that lucid
Christians found Action française, Fascism, National-
socialism or Stalin's takeover of the Internationale
morally repugnant. Internationalism (socialist or not),
world federalism, pacifism, were the political beliefs
shared by progressive ecumenical Christians. The tide
has now clearly turned, and the sophisticated find
these earlier generations naive.[17] Many find it axio-
matic that justice for the Third World comes through
national liberation movements. A theological rehabilitation of nationhood has therefore been undertaken and
many have affirmed the Christian's duty to be a nationalist. Sympathies thus vacillate between the
Herodians and the Zealots, the two parties that keep
reappearing in history whenever conflicts occur between
a stronger and a weaker culture. The Herodians transform their identity by the selective assimilation of
characteristics of the stronger culture. The Zealots
reject the new influences. Clearly the Zealots have
now the cote d'amour in many theological circles. I
should add that both parties commonly fail to understand
each other: to the Zealots all Herodians are mercenary
traitors and to the Herodians all Zealots are violent
bandits - either view is emphatically not true.[18]

These recent theological developments which praise
collective self-realisation have tended to obscure the
differences between a national community and a religious
community as Christianly interpreted. I will therefore
suggest three propositions that aim at articulating as
clearly as possible the distinction between these two
communities.

1. Christian theology is firmly committed to a view
that invites the Christian community to interpret itself
as being gathered by the grace of God. In contrast a
national community understands itself as being gathered
by kinship and by common achievement. I realize that,
ever since Montaigne, sociologically inclined people

have believed that one becomes a Christian by pretty
much the same sort of process that makes one a Frenchman
or a German. But I am here involved in a theological
argument that seeks to identify the norm toward which
acts of belonging ought to aspire. And it seems to me
pretty indubitable that for all the talk of reowning
the past and reliving the promises of God, Christians
in their community are invited to trace their call to a
common life all the way to the divine mercy itself.
Christian belonging and national belonging thus have
radically distinct sources. This point is frequently
overlooked in the recent theological literature on
nationalism. (I should add that it is somewhat suspect
to me that most of these treatments rely heavily upon
the Old Testament and its representations of the people
of God.[19] Whenever Christians rely so heavily on the
Old Testament, I fear that they prefer it to the New
and I am confident that what they are doing is as un-
Christian as justifying apartheid by texts from Genesis.
I hasten to add that it is not Jewish either.) Canadians, that is English-speaking ones, have a long tradition of retiring their old flags under the vaults of
their places of worship. They may thus be easily misled on this point. But one should be reminded that
one's Christian and one's national families are not the
same. The roots of membership are different and so is
the extent of each family.

2. The Christian faith is committed to a story and a
body of doctrine growing out of it that tend to call
for the use of reason. In contrast, group feelings are
made up of irrational factors; pride is taken in a set
of stories and images, in a vision of the past and of
the future, and this pride does not extol reason but
often denigrates it. (It is not entirely rational, for
instance, to contend against geographic dispersion and
linguistic division and try and build a nation of 20
million on the northern half of this continent.) Some
may be surprised to see me state that our religion is
committed to rational norms. (By rational norms, I
mean principles transcending the pragmatic rules of
success in history, arrived at by open reasoning and
persuasion before a universal audience.) Have we not
heard countless definitions of religion that make of
it the surge from the depths of something beyond
reason? Do we not see countless new movements, magic,
astrology, drug cults, that testify to the hunger for
the irrational? True, but organised Christian religion
in our country is committed to the extension of rational

532

procedures. The United Church of Canada handles its
finances in an open and rational manner. The authority
of Roman Catholic bishops hides less and less behind the
screen of incense. Our churches are also very rational
on the doctrinal level. The United Church took great
pains to have the results of biblical criticism taught
in Sunday school. The Roman Catholic Church takes
elaborate precautions before officially allowing the
faithful to believe that a miracle has occurred in their
midst. By contrast, E.S.P. groups acknowledge miracles
in a most slap-happy manner.[20] It will take some time
before a satanist with a good record of successful exor-
cisms becomes an Anglican bishop or before a drugged
high priest wears the lace of the Presbyterian modera-
tors. Christian theology remains committed to the proposition that God is good, just and consistent and that
he created the world and all of us with some sensible
purpose in mind. God's ways are indeed mysterious, and
we do not get answers that we can understand to all our
questions. But Job was not allowed to feel that there
was no answer or that the answer was there only for the
very few. That God and man can reason together is not
something the Church is about to exchange for desperate
techniques to manipulate the Divine or for the despair
that gives up trying to communicate among human beings.
"In the beginning was the Word." God speaks and
addresses himself to that part of us which is capable
of understanding through the use of speech. At this
level the commitment to reason in the church is deep
and I think definitive.

National feelings on the other hand are based upon
acquired loves. There is nothing ignoble about them.
There is, however, nothing rational about them either.
Acquired loves cannot be upheld by principle. Furthermore, national feelings never take demands for consistency very seriously. We often hear that Canadian
nationalism is a good progressive thing while Québec
nationalism is a narrow backward thing. These acquired
loves also tend to make disproportionate demands upon
our affection. Conventions graced by tradition have a
way of claiming that they are the natural way of doing
things and that any other way will probably be dis-
ordered and destructive and certainly too costly. Traditions have a way of making us morally blind. There
is much that is good among the familiar loves of Canadians. But our decency can make the indecent familiar
and tolerable. Consider the treatment accorded the
Métis. This example will suffice. Recently Margaret

533

Lawrence made a profound statement on it in The Diviners. And this example indicates something of the attitudes of the majority either to the racial minority or to the linguistic one. There is an irrational need for immediate self-assertion in any national feeling and this need is impatient of any contradiction.[21]

Thus a religion committed to a rational norm will have to keep suspicious of the workings of national feelings, even though love for country takes quick and deep roots in Christian hearts.[22]

The Christian's ultimate commitment is of course not to reason. Deep though it is, this commitment is penultimate. The ultimate commitment is to self-sacrificing love. "He who shall lose his life for My sake, shall gain it." The love of God may entail contempt for self. It is true of course that people are also capable of sacrificing themselves for their nation, but here also cautious distinctions must be be made. Sermons on fallen soldiers are a very difficult genre. To lay down one's life for one's country is a sacrifice that I am not about to belittle but I will stress that the country which presumes to make this demand is often guilty of the greatest perversity. Exploitation of the self-sacrifice of many often expresses crude self-aggrandizement of the few. Christian faith transcends reason into something nobler. National feeling often remains this side of reason, below it, in something more elemental.

So much for the attitude of the theologian in relation to inherited national feelings. What about the Christian attitude toward the quest for national identity? Since I believe I can reason about my vote but am sure I cannot write a novel, I shall primarily focus on that part of the quest which is political rather than artistic. And here my third proposition emerges.[23]

3. Qualitative differences exist between the rationality to which Christian theologians are committed and the rationality which our Western politics have achieved in their democratic forms.

The rationality to which the Christian tradition is committed has come to be closely identified with that of classical Greek metaphysics. Man has a final end. This beatitudo is something toward which all strive and which is ahead of us, somehow, waiting for us. Replacing

the terms of the Aristotelian-Christian synthesis by
those of the Kantian one we can say that there is a
categorically imperative moral law, that brooks no
exception, and has a rational basis rooted in God Himself. This law gives us an absolute, unmixed, uncom-
promised and uncompromising. For one view there is a
human perfection as a goal toward which we can aim in
an orderly manner. For the other the good will is a
goal we can achieve now. In either case, certitude of
being on the right way is possible for man and so is
the overcoming of ambiguity and duplicity. Acknowledging the complexities of life here and now, Christian
theology has come to present this perfection in eschatological terms. We are in via not in patria. God
shall be all in all only in the end. Our affections
now are more mixed, less ordered, less single-minded.
But that ambiguous state is a transitory one. And from
the perfection that is to come issues a call and a norm
that judges severely all the accommodations we make
under pressure that stay short of the perfect transparence and perfect community to which human beings are
destined.

The rationality which Western political life achieves
when rational, that is when democratic, is of a different nature. It has its roots in those aspects of Greek
thought which emphasize that morality is an art, not a
science. The rationality of our political tradition
praises compromise and accommodation. It does not
probe too much into motives but rests content with results. It cultivates the art of harnessing impure
motives. Since Plato, the political problem has been
about the marriage of honest intelligence with the un-
intelligent conventions of a group. Can intelligence
ally itself with the morally sound elements of the
magic found in any society without compromising itself
with the darker side of that magic? With characteristic imprudence, Plato confessed that wile was necessary.
He has been in trouble over it ever since. Idealists
do not want lies and realists do not confess that they
profit from them. Democracy is a considerable achievement because it has diminished the amount of lying in
the operation of social organisms. But it cannot prevent those who handle the public interest from keeping
some of us always in the dark and sometimes all of us
in the dark.[24]

A gap will therefore always remain between political
life which is mixed, pragmatic, devoid of absolute

certainties, and the religious dimension of life in
which the self refuses to accept ruse, manipulation,
ulterior motives and has a grasp of some uncompromising
standards, or is rooted in some ultimate myth the meaning of which is not always open to reconsideration.
The most eloquent spokesman for Christian involvement
in politics, Reinhold Niebuhr, has accordingly commen-
ded a rather dialectical stance toward politics: to
have them as if one does not have them, or to put all
our minds in them but not all our hearts. Christians
will of course participate in the political life of
their city. But their terms of participation are not
exactly those of other participants. A gap exists
between the life of faith and the conscious political
life that today reinterprets, develops, or betrays the
national identity.

IV

The Christian community, we have said, is gathered
by grace while the national community is gathered by
history. One is committed to God-given rational forms
while the other nurtures acquired loves. The church
cultivates the hope for a perfect community, while the
State maintains a community in which perfection consists in a balance of imperfections. To me it follows
that national feelings are a good thing, as far as they
go; that a national literary tradition is a good thing,
as far as that goes; that democracy or national self-
affirmation through the democratic process is a good
thing and so is the religious affirmation of the self
as member of the Christian community. And it also
follows that these four good things are not the same.

This emphasis on distinction gives my essay a polemical thrust. I believe that much of the current
nationalistic literature in Canada (by which I do not
mean essays that examine national problems but essays
that promote nationalistic solutions) and many current
theological appraisals of nationalism err because of
confusions. Consider for instance this definition of
nationalism: "What is nationalism? It is simply the
manifestation of the natural and spontaneous solidarity
that exists among members of a human group sharing a
historical and cultural tradition from which the group
derives its distinctive identity."[25] It is too naive
to think that human beings can possibly experience
such an easy undialectical continuity between their

culture and their natural spontaneity. We ought to know
better and not paper over the chasm between nature and
culture. Beings who have a culture are beings who have
made choices and who keep making choices; their historical solidarity cannot ever be a natural one. Consider
also the argument according to which "the national
dimension of man is unavoidable" and ought to be "frank-
ly accepted" by theologians.[26] This also is too undialectical. Every human reality, I always assumed, had to
be accepted by theologians only juxta modum, and that
even more so in the case of nationhood in the contemporary era, a phenomenon so hard to grasp and define
and thus so fraught with ambiguity. Polemics, of
course, are easily misunderstood. So let me assure
you that mine are directed against nationalism as a
modern political phenomenon (which I will try to charac-
terize more precisely in my next section) and that I do
not aim to depreciate the experience of nationhood. I
am not among those who see a simple alternative between
national and international values. I am among those
who believe that attacks on group solidarity go a long
way toward our crippling as moral creatures. Acquired
loves are part of our concrete dignity; they may give
us moral blind spots but they also kindle our affection
for other human beings. They give us a tradition that
has taught us to see things and care. The quest for a
national identity, the effort to increase our grasp and
control of our national affairs are to me among the
duties of Christians. And since in the eyes of many,
national choices are visceral matters, I should also
perhaps indicate why I am roused to polemics. I am a
new Canadian who keeps strong Swiss attachments. My
maternal language is French and I earn my living in a
Québec anglophone institution. Some raw spot in my
sensitivities is hurt when a powerful anglophone union
insists on imposing the exclusive use of English in
ground to air communications in Québec to the point of
paralyzing air transport and forcing the Federal Government to chip away at the Official Languages Act. And I
am also angered by the double talk of the new Québec
that speaks of welcoming immigrants and schedules ethnic
broadcasts between 2 am and 4 am on Radio Québec. These
kinds of phenomena in the country hurt me and I believe
they hurt all of us.

V

But what then is the case against nationalism?

NATIONALISM: PROBLEMS AND PERSPECTIVES

The overarching problem in Canada today, I think, is one of representation.[27] The quest for national representation is an eminently cultural as well as political phenomenon.[28] Poets who sell their books and politicians who get elected are our "representatives" in the sense that they present to us reasons for action. They state why we should act together as well as what should be done. Poets as they make their statements plumb the depths of our distresses and our aspirations. When elected politicians make their statements they begin to apply the power of the State. That difference is a sizable one. It should not obscure the continuity in the endeavour: both organise groups for the actions historical beings must undertake, one through imagination, the other through the law. Now I fear today that the clash of groups is causing us to find our representatives in men who bring a new hardness to the State. The War Measures Act may well have given us a taste of things to come. Everyone knows that disruptions of public order bring about, inevitably and justifiably, such a hardening. But one should also add that most culture critics today end their discourses with a demand for stronger government policies. (This of course reaches its maximum form in Québec, where the best minds are trying to find a sane, reasonable, legal way of forcing children into schools other than those chosen by their parents.) So it is along a broad front that I see threatening forces that may usher in a national representation that would cause us to sacrifice much of what we have come to associate with our freedoms in our society.

A more specific definition of nationalism is now in order. It is a modern political ideology that causes all our energies to be absorbed in the problem of who shall govern us and lose sight of the other half of the political problem, namely, how far we shall let ourselves be governed. Under the impact of this ideology, "French rule" in Ottawa, or being a minority in Confederation, becomes so automatically repugnant that ordinary political prudence goes out the window. That a normal country should be culturally homogeneous and unilingual becomes such a firm creed that some of the other normalcies we expect from our social and political organisation become sacrificed. Such nationalism brings about such a clouding of political judgment that very real threats to our cultural identity become ignored. Among the threats I would number economic, technological and bureaucratic rationalities; part of

538

the magic of nationalistic ideology is the promise that
the problem will just go away - or be easily solved -
once the "national question" is settled. With that
magic in the air nationalism makes the political process
less rational (in the sense of less reasonable) than it
can ordinarily be, and human freedoms, tolerance for
minorities (all kinds of minorities), suffer.

How then are we to live, torn as we are between the
claims of national feeling, national tradition and
national political affirmation and that enemy which I
will call distorted nationalism and which will give us
a national identity of sorts but may rob it of its
personal dimension?

The student of religion has here perhaps a point to
contribute. Nationalism brings a religious (or should I
say superstitious?) dimension to politics. The vibrancy
of the sacred is again allowed to bring a thrill to
political speeches that in our pluralistic age has
tended to become hackneyed or technical, namely always
dull. Religion and national identity then become
melted in a primaeval identity.

The primaeval identity recreates the situation when
the shaman beats the drum while the chief leads his
people in the dance. I cannot commend such a reintegration of all our religious and social values. The
Christian faith keeps in us the nostalgic dream of the
Garden of Eden and implants in us the hope for the new
Jerusalem. But it will always protest the confusion
between religious and political messianisms. We must
not yield to the arrogant effort to recreate the Garden
of Eden now or seize the Kingdom of God with violence.
For such man-made reintegrations of everything that is
broken never manage to reconcile everything that ought
to be reconciled. Euripides' Bacchae makes a powerful
statement of that. The Bacchanals, ecstatic in the
hills, dance and give the breast to wild animals. Man
and nature are reconciled. Yet there is a jarring note.
The Bacchanals have left their babies hungry in their
villages. One moral obligation has been forfeited on
the way to the orgiastic salvation. Our dreams of fulness - even our less grandiose ones - must be chastened
by reason. A rational theology will temper our religious
enthusiasm with a repetition that God founds the new
Jerusalem in his own time. A rational political life
will also subdue our national emotional aspirations and
will insist that democracy comes first, before

Canadianism, before the German soul, the French mind or the British genius.[29]

Remote though they may appear to be, Euripides' pages seem to me to be entirely topical in the present debate first of all because they offer a classical insight into the psychology of religion and reveal the tension between nature and culture. But they may also give some sense of the savagery which threatens our societies. The distresses of the modern century have given to many an unprecedented cultural hunger for an earthly saviour and the political processes of our advanced societies have already demonstrated the ability of political leaders to claim a cultural mission. Modern nationalism is not concerned with limited worthy objectives such as the preservation of folk dances or the correction of borders. It tends to fight a cultural battle and make promises of cultural fulfilment through political means.[30] The magnitude and nobility of the objectives serve to arouse the necessary exertion in political effort - and excuse the stringency of the means. (Those who claim we live in a post-national state may well be right in that we no longer need fear the old nationalism but they are wrong in that there is today the potential for a newer more totalitarian nationalism.)

It is a mark of the primaeval unity between religion and national identity to be ignorant of any sense of distinction among the four good things we identified earlier. National self-affirmation becomes a single act in which the claims of feelings of a tradition, of democracy and of religious faith all seem to coalesce. But in this coalescing each one of these things ceases to be the good thing it was. Feelings become coloured by hatred rather than affection. Tradition becomes a tool of political control instead of being a possession of the people. Democracy becomes an empty claim exploited by those who manipulate the political system rather than the very substance of the political process. The Christian faith becomes an adjunct tool to the national policy rather than the judge of it.

The drifting toward such primaeval identity can be arrested by insisting on the differences among our four good things.

Each one of the four good things will have a vigorous life of its own only if it is allowed to remain true to its own dynamics. National feelings should not be

540

politically manipulated into expressions of prejudice.
The national tradition should not become the tool of
some who cultivate a peculiar vision of their country.
Democracy should not be allowed to function only if it
brings about the ends dear to a political group. And
Christian faith should not be allowed to become some
kind of extra appendage one finds expedient to add to
something else. So the relationships between the four
good things can only be artificial, by which I mean
that they must be contrived by a special skill. This
means that a constantly lame kind of contact will be
established between very dissimilar things that do not
easily mesh together and yet have to be related because
they have all gone into making the complicated kind of
people that we are.

Artificial links will need to be forged afresh from
time to time. They will prevent the naive and immediate flow between the emotions of religion and those
of nationhood. Two filters will be particularly effective. The first one will insist that that part of the
commitment of the Christian which is commitment to this
city is not just to nation but to justice and democracy
in that nation. The second one will repeat that this
commitment to the city of our father takes second seat
to commitment to the city of God.

It is my hope that this should not be too difficult
for a Canadian to understand. Margaret Atwood, following Northrop Frye, pointed out that Bréboeuf, the archetypal Canadian poem, constantly presents the social
order not as a result of nature but as a product of
art.[31] The ordered society is a result of toil, of a
common effort which opposes nature and does not identify with it. The virtues proper to ordered human
society are courage, dedication, loyalty, love, sacrifice. They are tempered artificial virtues, born of the
experience of compromise among men. They are not the
natural primal virtues of spontaneity, self-affirmation,
enthusiasm and joy. They are the democratic virtues of
dialogue and mutual restraints, not the blood and soil
virtues of individual or group self-realization.[32]
They are the virtues of federalism, not those of a culturally homogeneous state. If you acknowledge the
claims of these artificial virtues, you will see that
the yearning for authenticity is very destructive in
politics. It seeks to realize in political life a kind
of fulness, a kind of absolute purity that the political life cannot achieve.[33]

I realize that most nationalist leaders claim to be
pragmatic and quite capable of compromise on most issues.
It still remains true that a nationalist ideology begins
to legitimize a psychological phenomenon which, I am
convinced, is both powerful and dangerous in our twentieth century context. The reintegration of religious
and social values is just too attractive for many in a
society that experiences deep stresses on account of
its pluralism. Nationalism in a country like Canada
today is a pathological response because it is a simplistic dogmatic answer offered by a section of society
which offers its powerful but sectarian views as a
remedy to the ills of the whole.

To the traditional criticism that sees nationalism as
"collective self-worship" or a tending to err on the
side of ethnocentrism, must now be added one more relevant to the contemporary scene: in nationalism the
planning of the life of a culture becomes the self-
appointed mission of an eloquent, hortatory élite. The
culture ceases to be the property of many. The voluntary and conceptual parts of it are singularly privileged by an "alert" élite that proceeds to lecture the
rest as a prelude to exercising power over them. (How
many intellectuals today denounce the manipulations to
which the masses are submitted only to embark upon
counter-manipulations?)

Theologians therefore would do well to heed the
warning issued by Ramsey Cook who amasses quotations
to argue that "our nation state is more seriously
threatened by appeals to nationalism than by lack of
nationalism." There is also a spiritual insight that
should not be lost on Christians in Kedourie's theory
according to which nationalism develops to replace a
lost sense of belonging. "Such a need is normally
satisfied by the family, the neighborhood, the
religious community."[35] The national tradition too,
I would want to add. But with this collapse of these
institutions, nationalistic leadership attempts to
manipulate our environment to recreate fulness of
identity and cultural wholeness. Such attempts
do not work and the cost of the attempt is very high.
The national traditions are violated by empires. That
is where we become victims. But most nationalists do
violence to the national tradition. That is where we
enter into self-incurred tutelage. The nationalistic
self-affirmation of the national tradition truncates
that very tradition because it reduces it to those
elements that can result from concerted efforts of will
focussing upon formulated objectives. Political life

results from such efforts, but national life must not be
entirely under the sway of political life. The
nationalist who wants, through political mechanism, to
impose the dictates of nationalist doctrine upon all
aspects of national life embarks upon totalitarianism
and no healthy national tradition really wants that.

My arguments so far are based upon political prudence.
I should also perhaps remind the theologian that Jesus
rejected the alternative between Herodians and Zealots.
He was crucified between two Zealots while the Herodians
looked the other way. He was joined to Zealots; he did
not join them. I would expect the theologian to remember - and share - the reasons Jesus had for rejecting
the alternative and the polarisation it entails. I
would also expect the theologian not to share in the
bent of the imagination toward the assurances of
nationalists or internationalist ideologies: his
imagination after all is nurtured by a richer stream.
Our national needs must be perceived fairly. There is
much national effort called for in Canada but the doctrines of nationalism are no help. What is required is
critical work not group ecstasies. Chansonniers can
help elect a Prime Minister. A Prime Minister however
should not behave like a chansonnier.

VI

I may seem too apocalyptic to some in discerning in
the issue of nationalism a contest between totalitarian
forces and what I take democracy to be. I will therefore try to conclude my case in simpler more concrete
terms. The works of Anglophone Canadian nationalists
are full of hand-wringing over moral decay in the U.S.
and feel a great moral opportunity in Canada. Much in
this appears to me to be strangely blind (and I do not
wish to whitewash either Vietnam or Nixon's crimes).
Any statement differentiating one's moral sensibilities
from that of others promptly becomes a dubious statement of moral superiority (and it is very hard to
affirm superiority only piece-meal). But how many
Canadian nationalists are ready to allow that the U.S.
has taken up the challenge for equality for all its
citizens so much more squarely than Canada? For it
seems clear to me that nothing in the anti-black back-
lash in the U.S. achieved the strength and legitimacy
reached by the anti-French attitude in the Summer and
the Fall of 1976. Great strides have been made in the

U.S. toward equality of opportunity for all with a comparable education. The unilingual Francophone is nowhere near equality when compared to the unilingual Anglophone in Canada.[36] We saw the waves of anti-French prejudice roll on and on without a B'nai B'rith or an NAACP raising its voice to recall that one is not supposed to speak of human beings that way.[37] When a strong moral voice arose on that scene it came not from an Anglophone Churchman but from a Montréal Irish politician who wept for the future of his country and confessed that what he saw in it was as ugly as what is ruining Northern Ireland and Lebanon - and less excusable.[38] The Canadian identity wrote Northrop Frye is "expressed in our culture but not attained in our life."[39] The gentle decent spirit of accommodation is not a fact of life.[40] The national sentiments of Anglophone Canadians frequently lose sight of that truth.

Perhaps national sentiments may also be set in perspective by perceiving the partly pathetic nature of the choice they necessarily entail. David Hume rejected his Scottish background and brought to Edinburgh a gentleman from Dublin who had a good English accent and could help Scottish tongues correct their brogue. The union of the Parliaments led him to choose British nationalism: he wrote a history of England and proudly called himself a North Briton (and suggested to the others they might call themselves South Britons). We know that history did not go exactly Hume's way but on the positive side of the ledger we should note that his choice of nationalist sentiment did achieve something: he convinced Gibbon to give up French (the language of history then) and write the Decline and Fall in English. And he also knew enough of what was going on North to Edinburgh to refute the pastoral nonsense of the Tories on the moral health of old-fashioned rural life. Walter Scott later restored Scottish pride: he caused a gun to be returned to Edinburgh castle and launched a mystique about tartans. But he was blind to economic realities. Both men are somewhat pathetic as British or as Scots nationalist and there is something greater in each than what appears in their respective national choices. Contemporary nationalists correct Scott's economic sins but should we not be ready to think that their choice too is not devoid of pathos? Nationhood is an arena in which we never win all.

The problem of national affirmation is perhaps the clearest reminder of the fact that we can together

pursue and achieve some goods, but only by maintaining
an uneasy balance between these goods which frequently
conflict. I will therefore have to return to disjunc-
tions between the four good things. God wants more for
us than having lots of children and raising them in
French, or elaborating a newer Canadianism. Literary
tradition requires more than legislation that protects
native authors. Social justice requires more than the
privilege of being exploited by people who speak your
own language. We need images that protect our group
sanity (slogans that express our yearning and will come
naturally enough). We are whole men and uneasy compromises keep having to be made in history but let the
last word be to the prudent, negative imperatives. In
our innermost selves, everything is related to everything else. But in our public life, we should remember
that religion and politics should not be mixed, that
feeling and politics should not be mixed, and that art
and politics should not be mixed.

FOOTNOTES

1. For further less cheering examples, see N.K. Clifford, "His Dominion: a vision in Crisis", Studies
   in Religion, Vol. II:4, 1973, p. 315-339.(Above Ch. 3.)

2. This Most Famous Stream, Toronto, Ryerson Press,
   1954.

3. J.W. Grant, Introduction to J.S. Moir, editor, The
   Cross in Canada, Toronto, Ryerson Press, 1966.

4. Original edition 1906. First English translation
   1907. Reprinted by McLelland and Stewart, Toronto,
   1966.

5. An important article of J.W. Grant suggested in 1955
   four areas where the Canadian ecclesiastical experience might prove unique; the influence on the
   political tradition, the problem of church and
   state, the attitude to denominations and some
   features in church life. See "Asking Questions of
   the Canadian Past" in Canadian Journal of Theology,
   July 1955, 98ff. The article is reexamined in
   N.K. Clifford, "Religion and the Development of

Canadian Society: An Historiographical Analysis"
in Church History, Vol. 38, 1968, p. 520.

6. Allan Smith gave us an excellent study contrasting
    the U.S. and the Canadian senses of nationhood in
    "Metaphor and Nationality in North America", Cana-
    dian Historical Review, Vol. 51, 1970, p. 247-75.
    See p. 275, "Canadian Nationalism because it has
    no choice, is predicated upon the toleration of
    differences.(...) It cannot be conformist or
    totalitarian; if it is, the state it seeks to serve
    will perish."

7. In P. LeBlanc, and A. Edinborough, eds., One Church
    Two Nations, Don Mills, Longman, 1968, p. 13.

8. Ottawa, Collège dominicain, 1936.

9. L. Bergeron, Petit Manuel d'Histoire du Québec,
    Montréal, Editions Québecoises, 1970.

10. The Modern Century, Toronto, Oxford University
    Press, 1967, p. 123.

11. "Some reflections on the liberal tradition in
    Canada", reprinted in C. Berger ed., Approaches
    in Canadian History, Toronto, University of Toronto
    Press, 1967, p. 32.

12. See the contrast in the two citations P. Desbarats
    put at the head of his The State of Québec, Toronto,
    McLelland and Stewart, 1965. The one who broke from
    the ethos by declaring "I have to say what I think"
    is now the Premier trying to lead Québec to inde-
    pendence.

13. Canadians in the Making. A social history of Cana-
    da. Toronto, Longman, Green and Company, 1958.

14. "Culture can never be wholly conscious - there is
    always more to it than we are conscious of; and it
    cannot be planned because it is also the uncon-
    scious background of all our planning." T.S. Eliot,
    Notes Toward the Definition of Culture (1948),
    London, Faber and Faber, 1967, p. 94. There is
    much more planning going on now, and the nature of
    mass media keep warranting it in the eyes of most.
    We no longer quite shudder at the thought of a
    Minister of Culture, although prudence in Québec

City called it Ministry of Cultural Affairs and an even more subdued expression was found in Ottawa.

15. L'Eglise du Québec, un héritage, un projet. Montréal, Fides, 1971. See the analysis by R. Lapointe, "Chassez le national et il revient au galop", in Studies in Religion, 2:3, 1972, p. 210-225.

16. J. Grandmaison, Nationalisme et Religion, Montréal, Beauchemin, 1970, Vol. II, p. 126.

17. To be fair to that generation, I should say that its greatest representative Reinhold Niebuhr, gave us in The Structure of Nations and Empires, New York, Scribners, 1959, an analysis which still deserves to be read.

18. There are unusually rich ironies in the conflict between the two groups. We know the story of the Zealots thanks to a notorious Herodian, Josephus, who led armies against them and wrote in the imperial language. And, whenever half-successful, Zealots assimilate many of the ways of their adversaries.

19. For a recent illustration of this use of biblical material see Roger Lapointe, "Chassez le national et il revient au galop," Studies in Religion, 2:3, p. 210-255. See also the essay by N. Gualtieri, "A theological perspective on nationalism," above.

20. There is something profoundly ironic in this situation. The Protestant youth who was taught that he did not need to believe that Jonah stayed for 3 days and 3 nights in the belly of the whale is now listening to the revelations of some wise illiterate bathed in the Ganges and is practising birth control according to a rhythm method that is based on astrological data. The Catholic youth who learnt that fish is no longer compulsory on Fridays is now discussing the mystical significance of beans.

21. The fate of Socrates is paradigmatic. In a city that prided itself on freedom of speech he merely asked for such freedom. He never asked Athens anything that went beyond the values Athens professed. But the natural, irrational functioning of groups cannot stand such a rigorous demand for rationality and consistency. Socrates died because no society

really wants to live consistently according to its own beliefs. The irrational spirit of immediate self-assertion quickly becomes an irrational self-assertion that brutalises individuals or minorities, even those that merely ask you to be true to yourself. And that I believe is true even in societies that have a strong commitment to civil rights as ours.

22. To cite but one example, two or three generations after the lions and the catacombs, the early Christians were so fond of their Roman city and its institutions that they felt deep anxiety at their passing. Augustine, however, was very clear on one point: if it ever comes to a choice between the city of our fathers and the city of justice, the Christians' love must be for the city of justice. Civitas est in civibus, non in parietibus.

23. I should add that in a literary tradition, national feelings also come under the power of rational norms of sorts. An analysis I believe would show that here too the rational norm is not the same as that which theologians try to bring to hear upon the religious life of their community.

24. A fine study of this problem by W.J. Barnes is made available along with three commentaries in The Right to Know, to withhold and to lie, New York, The Council on Religion and International Affairs, 1969.

25. Michel Brunet, "The French Canadian Search for a Fatherland" in Nationalism in Canada, p. 47.

26. R. Lapointe, "Chassez le national et il revient au galop", Studies in Religion, 2:3, p. 217-222.

27. I focus on the problem of representation because it is in my opinion the trickiest today. The problem of definition of who constitute the nation is more frequently alluded to in the literature. It is equally serious, but more obvious. The search for appropriate borders for an independent Québec would be I am sure as painful as the search for the "national" borders of Eire or the "safe" borders of Israel. Let no one object that Canadians are more reasonable. As limited a conflict as that over the creation of the new canton of Jura in Switzerland showed that even these solid citizens

could emulate Irish tempers or middle Eastern
volatility.

28. I use the word "representation" in the sense of E.
Voegelin. See the New Science of Politics, Chicago,
The University of Chicago Press, 19 , p. 36-7.
"Political societies, in order to be in form for
action, must have an internal structure that will
enable some of its members - the ruler, the government, the prince, the sovereign, the magistrate,
etc., according to the varying terminology of the
ages - to find habitual obedience for their acts of
command; and these acts must serve the existential
necessities of a society, such as the defense of the
realm and administration of justice - if a medieval
classification of purposes will be allowed. Such
societies with their internal organization for
action, however, do not exist as cosmic fixtures
from eternity but grow in history; this process in
which human beings form themselves into a society
for action shall be called the articulation of
society. As the result of political articulation
we find human beings, the rulers, who can act for
society, men whose acts are not imputed to their
own persons but to society as a whole - with the
consequence that, for instance, the pronunciation
of a general rule regulating an area of human life
will not be understood as an exercise in moral
philosophy but will be experienced by the members
of the society as the declaration of a rule with
obligatory force for themselves. When his acts are
effectively imputed in this manner, a person is the
representative of a society."

29. To be fair I must stress that Lapointe's apology
for nationalism clearly states that the national
dream must be less grandiose than it used to be.

30. It might bear repeating that the political life
alone does not provide a suitable total context
for the human quest for fulfilment or for the
Christian obedience.

31. M. Atwood, Survival, Toronto, Anansi, 1972, p. 93.

32. See the example of mutual accommodation given by J.
W. Grant, "At Least You Knew Where You Stood With
Them. Reflections on religious pluralism in
Canada and the United States", Studies in Religion,

2:4, p. 347.

33. Our Canadian society, in principle, is based on allegiance rather than contract. (The point is made by W.L. Morton, The Canadian Identity, Toronto, The University of Toronto Press, 1965, p. 111. It reappears in A. Smith, op. cit. p. 265 and in J.W. Grant "At Least You Knew Where You Stood With Them: Reflections on religious pluralism in Canada and the United States", p. 345-6.)

Allegiance is an act of affection; it claims no profound rationality. The contract theory tries to see a rational undertaking in public organization. The great merit of the principle of allegiance is that it does not attempt to see the rationality where there is none. The great flaw of contract theories (from Hobbes to Locke to even the great Kant) is that they lure us into believing that the life of the State can be made rational through and through and will provide us with a complete context for our rational self-realization. Such hopes are illusory and mislead us dangerously since they tempt us into ruthless efforts toward a thought-out order in our political life. A society of allegiance accepts the premise that we are united primarily by acquired loves and that this will do for a while.

For a most thorough look at the early nationalist ideas and the various perspectives used to write the history of Canada in English, see the two books by Carl Berger, The Sense of Power. Studies in the Ideas of Canadian Imperialism 1867-1914, Toronto, University of Toronto Press, 1970. And The Writing of Canadian History. Aspects of English Canadian Historical Writings 1900-1970, Oxford University Press, 1976. Professor Berger also gave us a useful anthology on the French-English conflict in Imperialism and Nationalism 1884-1914. A Conflict in Canadian Thought. Toronto, Copp Clark, 1969.

34. "Many are called but none is chosen" in R. Cook, The Maple Leaf For Ever. Essays on Nationalism and Politics in Canada, Toronto, MacMillan, 1971, p. 195-214.

35. Nationalism, p. 101, quoted in R. Cook, p. cit. p. 86.

36. This inescapably is how the problem must be posed.

The social scales are tipped of course very unevenly
simply because of the size of the two linguistic
groups. But a democratic state with two language
groups cannot but be committed to the definition of
rights that would tend to counter that social
inequality.

37. I realize that with the political reality of Québec
    and of Québec ministers in the Federal Cabinet the
    dynamics of equality in Canada have not called for
    organisation along the lines of voluntary organisa-
    tions. The moral vacuum however remained entire.

38. Address by the Hon. Bryce Mackasey to the Scarborough
    East Federal Liberal Association on October 10, 1976.
    One can still hope that the ugliness is not as
    widespread or does not have as deep roots.

39. The Modern Century, p. 123.

40. One could also document much moral blindness in
    francophone nationalism. But I am now writing in
    English. I will add how frequently unilaterally
    anglophone are expressions of - and studies on -
    Canadian nationalism. The Peter Russell collection
    has two French articles out of 22. And the article
    by N.K. Clifford, "Religion and the Development of
    Canadian Society and Historiographical Analysis",
    cites no francophone author and alludes to the exis-
    tence of French Canadians only in so far as one of
    his anglophone sources (R.M. Lower) does. The
    finest analysis I know of what this state of affairs
    spells for the future of Canada has been written by
    Charles Taylor. See his "A Canadian Future?",
    The Pattern of Politics, Toronto/Montreal, McLelland
    and Stewart, 1970.

resources, 407,417-419;
church finances, 15,
124-125,496;exploitation
of workers, 210-212;
Japanese co-operative,
497; land, 274-276;Mar-
chands, 48-49;medicare,
110-112,281,289;Newfound-
land, 97,108-111; prison
inmates, 250-251,256;
social Catholicism, 123-
146.

Education - adult in Antigonish, 123-136;cultural
history and knowledge, 272-
274,276;immigrants at
Frontier College, 296;
labour school in Cape Breton, 139-140;profile of
prison inmates, 248-249;
dans les séminaires, 46;
des theologiennes, 153,
154,163,164;
- and religion - Cana-
dianization of immigrants,
31-32; denominational
principle, 99-102; hockey
as education for life,
384,407,412-414; Shama-
nism and creative art,
483,484;use of schools,
31-32.

Eglise Catholique (see also
Catholicism), 47,48,55,
117,151.

Eliade, M., 82,291,326,330,
385,472,473.

Esprit, pionnier, 56.

Ethics - basic image of
human, 5,232,234,385;
ethical ideal, 258; of
intention, 211; of punishment, 237-238; society's
core values, 226,237-240;

love and care, 207;
- social contrast theory,
238-240;individual vs
solidarity, 209,216;
rationality and emo-
tionality, 192-195,367,490
490;soul-body, 113-114;
of power, 261-262;
- Protestant, 118,142,
143;Catholic, 118;
- in Newfoundland, 103-
114;in Nova Scotia,
116,133.

Ethos (see also Canadian
Character), 127,203,
216,408,412,418.

Evangelicals, 36-37.

Existentielle, psychana-
lyse de chanson popu-
laires, 308,353-382.

Expérience, religieuse/
religious experience in
Canadian Mosaic, 272,
273; paradigm of, 291-
293; 'Numinous' experi-
ence, 291; in poetry of
Nelligan, 333-350.

Faillon, E.M., 43,45,46,
55,56,58-59.

Faith (also foi), 164,
202,317,318,520,526;
and attitudes, 506.

Feminism/me, 289;in Qué-
bec, 149-186;interna-
tionale, 166-168; défi-
nition de, 150; l'iden-
tité de la femme, 156-
160;des images et des
modèles, 158-162,343,
357-259,390,393,412;
types d'intervention,
154-157;sacerdote

ligious Origins, 524-
531;as continuity of
culture, 7-15, 509-514;
religious history, 9-13,
270-272;by missionaries,
13-16;by immigration, 16-
19,21-35;by hockey, 399,
415; by land, 45,57,272-
278;by visions, 276,294-
295;in Newfoundland, 94-
96; by Canadianization,
30-37;
- as homogeneous ideal, 27,
31-34;as heteregeneous, 33,
34-35;as welfare state, 36;
analytic model of, 225;
sociological model, 382-
385;412-413;
- self and participant in
whole, 524-528.

Identité Personnel/Personal
Identity, 5,7,159-163;225,
226, 230-232,245,353,524-
528,305-307,363-365;Self-
Everyman parodox, 317-339;
des femmes, 156-160;self,
320-330,387,399-401;458,
512,513.

Image/s, definition/basic,
227-229,232,254;religieuses/
religious, 7,25-37,159-161,
297,229,240,250-254,294,
339,358-362,390-394,412;in
legal system, 194-195,207

Immigration, response to, 16-
30,24,283-285;oriental, 25-
27,469,489,493,494;Slav,
27-28;Mormon, 29-30.

Independent Labour Party,
138.

Indians/Indiens/Amerindians,
5,13,49,68,89,209,252,
274,281;their literature,
65-74,81-90.

Industrialization, 24,
35-36,119,120,128.

Institute de Yoga Siva-
nanda, 448,459.

Integral Yoga Institute,
448,460.

International Psycholo-
gical Conference, 298.

International Society for
Christian Consciousness,
448.

Internationalism, 515,
527-529;and nationalism,
6,535.

Islam/Mahomet/Muhammad,
287,291,292.

Japanese/Culture, 495-
500.

Jesuits, 13.

Jesus, 51,281,284,289,
292,304,353,454,455.

Jodoshin Shu (True Pure
Land) School, 490.

Justice (see also Capital
Punishment, Morality,
Punishment, Aim and De-
finition of, 191-195;
retributive, 190-192,
207-213,235-238,260,
262;legitimacy as felt
by dispossessed, 208,
215;legitimation of
distributive, 209,262;
reconciliation, 209,
229-253;institutional-
ization and diversion,
254-262.

variety of, 132,432,448;
goals and involvements,
454,457;communal aspects
of, 453,458,leadership,
302,304;mystical elements
in, 454,457;use of rituals,
451-453;initiation rite,
454,455;social,120,121.

Munsterites, 285.

Mysterium Tremendum, 290-292,
385.

Myth/Mythe (see also littérature,religieuse), 43,53-55,
87;structural approach to,
82-84;methods of analysis,
83-88;tradition orale, 68-
69;dangers dans d'inter-
pretation, 81-85,89,90.
- du fondement de Qu/bec, 44-
58;des Iroquois, 44-59;of
the Athabaskans, 69-78;and
parable, 306-7.

NDP, 279.

National Council of Women
Religious, 169.

National Coalition of
American Nuns, 169.

National Culture (see also
National Identity, Iden-
tité Nationale, Nationalism)
importance of history to,
509,510;politics and
assault on, 277,512,513;
ethical morality of, 514;
conscious and unconscious
elements in, 524-533;dicho-
tomy between nature and
culture, 512,513,537-539;
attitude of churches to
other religious cultures,
517-520.

Nationalism (see also Na-
tional Culture, Syncre-
tism, Pluralism, Inter-
nationalism), theology
of, 508-515;definition
of, 534-536;varieties
of, 276,527;case ag inst,
535,536;ethics of, 530;
demonic and humane, 514,
515;and internationalism,
513-518,521;ethical de-
mand, 515,516;functional
syncretism, 520-521;
litterature nationale,
57.

National Socialism, 282,
514.

Natural Order, 100;and
art, 539.

Newfoundland, ethnic homogeneity and distinctive
identity, 95-96;denomina-
tional politics and
education, 97-99;social
posture of churches,
100,106;miners of, 208,
209.

Newfoundland School
Society, 96.

Nichiren/Shoshu and
Academy, 292,447-448,
450,451,453,454,456,
457,461,492.

Niebuhr, H. Richard, 6.

Niebuhr, Reinhold, 534.

Numinous, 291,336.

Novelty, 12, 17.

Odon, Saint, 427.

Other/Altérite, 454.

Otto, R., 291,385.

Pacificism, 281.

Pentecostal Assemblies, 97, 99.

Pietism, 455.

Plato, 519,531,533.

Pluralism, Religious...
emerging, 19,20;heteroge-
neity and, 34,36,37;
transformationist legal
stance and, 200,201,207,
216;and master stories,
309;nationalism and, 520,
521,526;et architecture,
433.

Politics (see also Nationalism, National Culture),
agriculture and urbaniza-
tion, 17,45,47;immigration
threats, 25,31;fishing and
mining, 96-101,123-140;
health and communism, 295-
310;religion and politics
joined, 275-283;religious
and national communities,
531-537.

Politique et Réligion Unis,
271;et violence, 275-283.

Population Data, Buddhist,
492-493;eastern Nova Scotia,
121-124;Newfoundland, 96;
prison inmates, 247-249;
women, 154,155.

Power, fields of meaning and,
450;liberating, 292;respon-
sible use of, 261,262.

Praxis, 302,306,370,371,
373.

Prejudice, 16,27,33,35,
158,207.

Presbyterian, 11,13,26.

Project North, 114,211.

Protestant, 14,17,38,120,
296,307.

Providentialisme, 46.

Punishment (see also
Capital Punishment,
Discipline, Justice,
Law), as retributive
justice, 190-192,204-205,
238-242;as treatment,
203;as protector of core
values, 226,238;as be-
haviour modification,
237;legitimation of,
240;as discipline, 394,
395;profile of inmates,
248,249;police routines
and stereotypes, 250-253.

Puritans, 12.

Québec, Québécois, 43f,
149f,281,298.

Racism, 252,283.

Rationalism, 235,527.

Raymond Buddhist Church,
489,494,498,500,502.

Realité/Reality, 43,120,
203,212,215,227,353,
359,365,369,407,457,
474,489.

Reconciliation - notion

of, 229-231;ideal Chris-
tian, 225,506;responsibi-
lity as a gift, 225,231-
234;institutionalization
of, 246,266;private diversion, 258.

Red River Settlement, 279.

Regina Manifesto, 120,141.

Regionalism, 95,96,279.

Réligion/Religion, definition
of, 1,2,117-119,120,292-
203,334,384-385,471,506;
function of, 216;evolution
of, 269;national, civil
and invisible modern, 45,
51,59,414,415 (see also
hockey);primitive and
scientific, 471-472;and
emancipation/feminism,
149-186;and identity (see
identité, identity);and
language, 203 (see also
language);and law, moral-
ity, 187f.;and literature,
43-92,289-353 (see also
littérature, mythe, story);
and politics, 271,276 (see
also politics);and rationalism, 192-195,523;and
society, 117-122 (see also
movements, socialism).

Religious Experience (see
also experiénce religieuse)
in Canadian mosaic, 272,
273;paradigm of, 291-293;
numinous, 291.

Religious Studies/Sciences
Religieuses, 1-4,290,293,
333,351,373,374.

Richelieu, Cardinal, 49,51.

Ricoeur, Paul, 214,215.

Riel, Louis, 269-286.

Rites and Ritual, 45,54,
59;definition of, 447,
448;and personal iden-
tity, 447;time and
space limits, 447,457;
characteristics of,
447-457; varieties of
450-453;of St. Jean
Baptiste, 45,51,59;and
syncretism, 451-453.

Roman Catholic (see also
Catholic, Eglise
Catholique), 12,13,38,
97,99.

Royal Commission on
Health and Safety of
Workers, 208.

Royal Commission on
Status of Women, 152.

Ruether, Rosemary, 155,
169.

Rural and Industrial Life
Conference, 139.

Russell, Letty, 169.

Russian Communists/ism,
299,524.

Ryan, Claude, 525.

Ryerson, Egerton, 12;and
Ryerson Press, 508.

Sacerdote Ministeriel,
151,165-167,171.

St. Francis Xavier Uni-
versity, 125,126,133,
134,141.

St. Jean Baptiste, 55,59.

Structuralism/isme –
method of analysis, 81-89;
grammar of mythe, 90;
l'espace de la rue et
l'epique nationale,
49f,81f,358-363; la
tradition écrite et la
tradition orale, 68-69.

Subud, 451,457.

Sulpiciens, 46.

Symbol/e, religious and
society, 118,119,488;
use, function and role of,
203,205,214,215,230,309;
rôle de subjectivité, 346,
347; in legal system, 194,
195,207;values rooted in
reality, 203,204;meaning-
less, 202,203;ethos and
world view, 205;examples
of; hero as liberation
or founder, 308,309;of
Shamanism, 483-486;of
spiritual voyage, 324-326,
330; de voyage mystique,
359-360;univers symbolique,
383,386;l'espace-monde,
427.

Syncretism (see also Nationalism), 413,414,516, functional, 520,521.

Tai Chi Chu'an, 448,451,
457,462.

Taoist, 292.

Task Force on Churches and
Corporate Responsibility,
114,211.

Taylor, Charles, 200,201.

Temperance, 14,25,31,44,49,
107.

Tillich, Paul, 55.

Time in Myth, 82,86;
symbolism, 326-330;life
cycle rites, 482.

Tompkins, J.J. (Father),
125,128,132,135.

Transcendence, 302,320,
329-330,385,456,506,
520.

Transcendental Meditation,
448,451,453,454,455,
456,462.

Tsuji, T. (Rev.), 496,503.

Ukranian, 27,28,272,276,
285.

Underhill, Frank, 526.

Université Laval, 57.

United Church of Canada,
(see also Eglise Unie
du Canada), 17,49,99,
153;Home Mission Board,
35.

United Farmers, 135,137,
138.

Urbanisation/Urbanization
(see also Seculariza-
tion), 16,24,35,260.

Values (see also Ethics,
Personal Identity) and
religion, 189-214;core
values and criminal
law, 237-240;love and
care as, 201-229;ob-
jective and absolute,
189-191;subjective and
secular, 199.

 SUPPLEMENTS

1. FOOTNOTES TO A THEOLOGY
The Karl Barth Colloquium of 1972
Edited and with an Introduction by
MARTIN RUMSCHEIDT

1974   149 pp.
ISBN 0-919812-02-3 $3.50 (paper)

2. MARTIN HEIDEGGER'S PHILOSOPHY OF RELIGION
JOHN R. WILLIAMS

1977   198 pp.
ISBN 0-919812-03-1 $4.00 (paper)

3. MYSTICS AND SCHOLARS
The Calgary Conference on Mysticism 1976
Edited by
HAROLD COWARD
and
TERENCE PENELHUM

1977   viii + 118 pp.
ISBN 0-919812-04-X $4.00 (paper)

4. GOD'S INTENTION FOR MAN
Essays in Christian Anthropology
WILLIAM O. FENNELL

1977   vi + 56 pp.
ISBN 0-919812-05-8 $2.50 (paper)

Available from:

WILFRID LAURIER UNIVERSITY PRESS
Wilfrid Laurier University
Waterloo, Ontario, Canada N2L 3C5

EDITIONS

1. LA LANGUE DE YA'UDI

Description et classement de l'ancien parler de Zencirli dans le cadre des langues sémitiques du nord-ouest

PAUL EUGENE DION, O.P.

1974   509 pp.

ISBN 0-919812-01-5 $4.50 (paper)

STUDIES IN RELIGION / SCIENCES RELIGIEUSES
Revue canadienne / A Canadian Journal

Abonnements / Subscriptions

Abonnement personnel: $10.00 (quatre fascicules)
Abonnement pour les institutions: $15.00 (quatre fascicules)
Fascicule isolé : $4.00

Individual subscriptions: $10.00 (four issues)
Institutional subscriptions: $15.00 (four issues)
Individual issues: $4.00

ISSN 0008-4298

Tout chèque doit être fait à l'ordre de Wilfrid Laurier University Press.

Make cheques payable to Wilfrid Laurier University Press

WILFRID LAURIER UNIVERSITY PRESS
Wilfrid Laurier University
Waterloo, Ontario, Canada N2L 3C5